CHILDREN, Adolescents, &the MEDIA

Ch.2

Victor C. Strasburger / Barbara J. Wilson

CHILDREN, Adolescents, & the MEDIA

with contributions by
Jeanne B. Funk • Edward Donnerstein • Bob McCannon
Foreword by Dorothy G. Singer

SAGE Publications
International Educational and Professional Publisher
Thousand Oaks ▪ London ▪ New Delhi

For information:

Sage Publications, Inc.
2455 Teller Road
Thousand Oaks, California 91320
E-mail: order@sagepub.com

Sage Publications Ltd.
6 Bonhill Street
London EC2A 4PU
United Kingdom

Sage Publications India Pvt. Ltd.
M-32 Market
Greater Kailash I
New Delhi 110 048 India

Printed in the United States of America

Library of Congress Cataloging-in-Publication Data

Strasburger, Victor C., 1949-
  Children, adolescents, and the media / Victor C. Strasburger,
Barbara J. Wilson ; with contributions by Jeanne B. Funk, Edward
Donnerstein, Bob McCannon.
      p. cm.
Includes bibliographical references and index.
  ISBN 0-7619-2124-9 (cloth) — ISBN 0-7619-2125-7 (pbk.)
  1. Mass media and children—United States. 2. Mass media and
teenagers—United States. I. Wilson, Barbara J. II. Title.
  HQ784.M3 S78 2002
    302.23′083—dc21   2002000436

This book is printed on acid-free paper.

02 03 04 05 10 9 8 7 6 5 4 3 2 1

Acquisitions Editor:	Jim Brace-Thompson
Editorial Assistant:	Karen Ehrmann
Production Editor:	Sanford Robinson
Copy Editor:	Gillian Dickens
Typesetter:	Rebecca Evans
Indexer:	Molly Hall
Cover Designer:	Michelle Lee

To the late Dr. Michael Rothenberg: pediatrician, child psychiatrist, and teacher extraordinaire, who knew most of this a long time ago. And to my children, Max and Katya, who have taught me a lot about the impact of the media.

—VCS

To my bright and beautiful daughters, Isabel and Grace, who have enlivened my research and teaching in countless ways.

—BJW

Contents

Introduction

In 1974, a 9-year-old girl was attacked by three girls and a boy and raped with a soda bottle. The children later admitted that they got the idea for the rape from a TV movie, *Born Innocent,* which had been aired on NBC. In 1977, a 15-year-old boy was put on trial for the burglary and murder of an elderly woman. The boy claimed that he was merely copying an episode from *Kojak,* one of his favorite TV programs, where a woman had been shot by intruders. The boy had even wanted to shave his head so he could look more like his hero, Kojak.

In 2001, a 13-year-old boy inadvertently killed a much younger girl as he wrestled with her. He was a fan of wrestling programs on television and did not understand that the wrestling acts are carefully staged. In 2001, a young boy who watched *Jackass* on MTV set fire to himself in his backyard after he had started a fire and then fanned the flame with his hands. In the ensuing pain, he put his hands to his chest and ran wildly around the yard, suffering severe burns. He admitted that he was emulating the star of the program who had set fire to himself during one of the shows.

Thirty years have passed between the first two and the latter two incidents, yet television producers still continue to offer viewers much violence whether in dramatic programs or on specialty programs. In fact, 50% of the crimes in reality-based TV programs are murder, but in reality, only 0.2% of the crimes reported by the FBI are murder (Bushman & Huesmann, 2001). Well aware of the problem of violence on television, Victor Strasburger and Barbara Wilson, authors and editors of this excellent book, *Children, Adolescents, and the Media,* present a cogent argument for more reduction of violence on TV and for more vigilance on the part of parents and other caregivers. Not only are TV programs playing a role in instigating violence, but also the authors note that particular video games, music videos, and rock music contribute to the climate of violence and aggression. To counteract such violence, the authors present a chapter on media literacy, offering possible solutions by discussing various curricula that teach young people and adults how to decipher the media messages and how to be more critical of what they watch on television.

Strasburger and Wilson selected particular topics relating to the most pressing issues on television. These chapters should appeal to college audiences and to the general public. Not only is TV violence discussed, but there are also chapters on commercials, sexuality, nutrition, and the Internet. I am impressed by the extent of research the authors bring to this book, but I have some additional comments to add to their fine reviews of the literature.

Video games are of particular interest to young people, and that topic is well covered in this book. We know that the teenage shooters in Paducah, Kentucky, Jonesboro, Arkansas, and Littleton, Colorado, were students who habitually played video games. Games such as *Doom* were favorites of the boys involved in the Columbine High School murders. Although the fact that these boys were addicted to such games is not enough evidence to insist that violent video games are the cause of such behavior, surely they contribute to some degree. Young people between the ages of 8 and 18 spend more than 40 hours per week using some form of media, and among boys ages 8 to 13, the average amount of time spent with console and computer video games is 7.5 hours per week. College students play at least 6 hours per week. Thus, it behooves us to pay attention to a meta-analysis of the research involving video games. One significant finding is that exposure to violent video games is negatively associated with prosocial behavior and positively related to aggressive affect and physiological arousal (Anderson & Bushman, 2001). Playing such games reduces the likelihood of children evidencing empathy or helping others.

Commercials are also affecting young people's lives, as the chapter on this topic asserts. Kuczynski (2001) reported on the popularity of teenage magazines. Not only are the ads on TV influencing purchases for girls, such as the styles of clothes worn by actresses on nighttime situation comedies or by the stars on MTV, but the ads and articles in the magazines themselves also contribute to the teenage consumerism. *Cosmogirl, Teen People, FM,* and *Teen Vogue* are just a few of the magazines that hype makeup and fashions but also talk about relationships and, when daring, even AIDS, as in *Teen People.*

Commercials also affect toy purchases. When war-related toys are advertised on TV, children coax their parents to buy these, and when using such toys, children act out their aggressive scripts on the playground, imitating Power Rangers, Ninja Turtles, or any of the characters who use fists, karate kicks, or laser weapons. In a study of toy gunplay and aggression, for example, Watson and Peng (1992) found that toy gunplay and parental punishment were positively associated with a higher level of real aggression, not pretend aggression.

Unfortunately for children, the 12th Annual Consumer Kids Conference in Florida, May 2000, was designed to help the talented and creative people in advertising learn how to capture the consumer children's market. In response to this, a think tank called "American Values" has issued a statement called "Watch Out for Children: A Mother's Statement to Advertisers." The statement has eight points relating to the protection of children from advertising by educating children about ads and by asking for an increase of parental values and involvement in children's lives (Motherhood Project, 2001).

Commercials affect not only children's desires for the purchase of toys but also their food habits. More Americans are becoming obese, and, indeed, the authors present an excellent chapter with much evidence concerning how the media affect nutrition and our eating habits. TV ads for food and toys are the two largest categories targeted to children. Two thirds of advertising on Saturday morning consist of ads for fats, oils, sweets, and high-sugar cereals. In a recent monograph (Anderson, Huston, Schmnitt, Linebarger, & Wright, 2001), the authors state that one effect of television viewing is the obesity of girls who are heavy viewers of TV. The authors also suggest that it is possible that girls who are obese may feel less popular than others and therefore spend more time at home, using TV as a substitution for social relationships.

The chapter on the Internet is valuable in terms of the electronic boom in our society. Computers are currently in 70% of homes with children, and 20% are in children's bedrooms (Woodard & Gridina, 2000). The Children's Online Privacy Protection Act of 1998 requires parental permission for a commercial Web site to collect personal information from a child under age 13. But there are no laws protecting children from chat rooms or from Web sites that offer pornography or hate information.

Teenagers are becoming "multitaskers," the practice named for the computer term describing a machine's ability to run several programs at once. Many teenagers are able to use their computer, talk on the phone, and listen to the radio at the same time. Hafner (2001) describes one teenager who worked on a class paper, searched the Web for information, checked her e-mail, kept up to eight messenger screens running, engaged in online conversation with friends, and listened to her MP3 player and a CD with songs. Some studies suggest that excessive use of computers has been linked to increased risk of obesity, repetitive-strain injuries, impaired vision, declines in social involvement, and feelings of loneliness and depression. Given the fact of multitasking among many teenagers, the social involvement issue, for this group at least, seems moot.

Children, Adolescents, and the Media offers a chapter listing many recommendations for parents, educators, and television personnel. If followed, we would see some significant changes not only in the content of the media but also in how our youth use and process the electronic sources of information and entertainment. Although the authors touch on many vital issues dealing with the media, there are topics that have been omitted, such as morality, stereotypes, prosocial learning, and the economics of the television industry, to name just a few. For more information on these and other topics, the reader is referred to the *Handbook of Children and the Media* (Singer & Singer, 2001). As both that book and this present volume assert, it is important to stress the fact that the content of television is the issue and not the technology itself. Television can be a powerful teacher if it is used wisely and if parental mediation and guidance are offered to children and to adolescents.

Dorothy G. Singer

References

Anderson, C. A., & Bushman, B. J. (2001). Effects of violent video games on aggressive behavior, aggressive cognition, aggressive affect, physiological arousal and prosocial behavior: A meta-analytic review of scientific literature. *Psychological Science, 12,* 353-359.

Anderson, D. R., Huston, A. C., Schmnitt, K. L., Linebarger, D. L., & Wright, J. C. (2001). *Early childhood television viewing and adolescent behavior.* Boston: Blackwell.

Bushman, B. J., & Huesmann, L. R. (2001). Effects of televised violence on aggression. In D. G. Singer & J. L. Singer (Eds.), *Handbook of children and the media* (pp. 223-254). Thousand Oaks, CA: Sage.

Hafner, K. (2001, April 12). Teenage overload, or digital dexterity? *New York Times,* pp. G1, G5.

Kuczynski, A. (2001, April 2). The age of diminishing innocence. *New York Times,* pp. C1, C6.

Motherhood Project, Institute for American Values. (2001). Watch out for children: A mother's statement to advertisers. (Available from 1841 Broadway, Suite 211, New York, NY 10023)

Singer, D. G., & Singer, J. L. (Eds.). (2001). *Handbook of children and the media.* Thousand Oaks, CA: Sage.

Watson, M. W., & Peng, Y. (1992). The relation between toy gun play and children's aggressive behavior. *Early Education & Development, 3,* 370-389.

Woodard, E. H., & Gridina, N. (2000). *Media in the home 2000: The fifth annual survey of parents and children.* Philadelphia: Annenburg Public Policy Center, University of Pennsylvania.

Preface

American youth spend inordinate amounts of time with the mass media. They laugh with characters who are funny; they viciously attack and destroy evil creatures as they play their favorite video games; they see advertising for candy, makeup, and even liquor; they listen to rap lyrics about sex and violence; and they interact with people all over the world online. Needless to say, it is a very different social world than the one their parents and grandparents faced during childhood.

The purpose of this book is to present an overview of what is known about the impact of mass media on youth in the 21st century. The goal is to provide a comprehensive, research-oriented treatment of how children and adolescents interact with the media. In each chapter, we review the latest findings as well as seminal studies that have helped frame the issues. Because research alone can often be dry and difficult to follow, we have generously sprinkled each chapter with illustrations, examples from the media, policy debates, and real-life instances of media impact. Our intent is to show the relevance of social science research to media-related issues involving youth.

One of the unique features of this book is its developmental focus. In Chapter 1, we begin with a discussion of how children and teens are unique audiences of the media, and we outline developmental differences in how young people process and make sense of media content and form. This developmental framework is used throughout the remainder of the book to help readers appreciate how, for example, a 5-year-old might respond differently to a media message than a 10-year-old or a 15-year-old would. In subsequent chapters, we discuss advertising (Chapter 2), media violence (Chapter 3), sexuality and the media (Chapter 5), drugs and the media (Chapter 6), nutrition (Chapter 7), and rock music and music videos (Chapter 8). In addition, we asked several experts to author particular chapters on the cutting-edge topics of video games (Chapter 4), the Internet (Chapter 9), and media literacy (Chapter 10). Finally, we close with a chapter on solutions to many of the problems that arise when youth confront the media (Chapter 11). Our solutions are broad based and are targeted to the media industry itself as well as to policymakers, health practitioners, parents, and even children.

Two other features make this book unique. First, the book covers the entire developmental period of childhood and adolescence. Other media-related books have been limited to addressing only children or only teens, but to our knowledge this is the first media book of its kind that deals with the entire age span that characterizes youth. Second, the two authors bring very different backgrounds to the issues at hand. Victor C. Strasburger is a Professor of Pediatrics who has spent most of his career looking at the impact of the mass media on children's health. Barbara J. Wilson is a Professor of Communication who conducts research on child development and mass media. Together, we have identified the media topics that are most pressing to parents, health care practitioners, educators, and policymakers today. As coauthors, we bring our rich and diverse experiences in medicine, social science, child development, public policy, and media to those topics. We also both have families, with two children each, which of course gives us firsthand experience with many of the issues we raise.

The approach we have taken is certainly grounded in the media effects tradition. Where appropriate, we have highlighted other perspectives and readings that take a more cultural or critical approach to the study of media and youth. Those perspectives sensitize us to the importance of considering children and teens as active and powerful agents of their media experiences. We agree with the idea that youth cannot be shielded from the media, nor should they be. Clearly, children use the media to learn about their culture as well as about childhood itself. Still, we can do much to help children and teens approach the media as critical consumers, a topic that is touched on throughout the book but covered extensively in the chapter on media literacy. Readers will notice that we have selected the most controversial topics about the media for this book. Our aim is not to be one-sided but instead to target the areas that are most consequential and at the heart of debates in the United States about mass media and public health.

This book is designed to serve as a core text for courses in communication or psychology on children and the media. It could also serve as supplemental reading in courses on child and adolescent development, issues in child development, or issues in the media. The book is most appropriate for an upper-level or advanced undergraduate course or even a beginning graduate seminar in the area. We assume some basic knowledge of research methods in social science, but we also provide background to help readers distinguish and compare different research traditions and methodologies. As a way to engage students, we provide a series of exercises at the end of each chapter. The exercises are meant to stimulate debate and can serve as paper assignments or as small-group discussion activities. To our minds, the exercises illustrate just how complex and engaging the media environment is for today's youth.

ACKNOWLEDGMENTS ●

Dr. Strasburger would like to thank his colleagues in the American Academy of Pediatrics who have supported his interest in the media and his colleagues at the University of New Mexico School of Medicine who have allowed him time to write this book, especially Dr. Robert Katz, Chair of the Department of Pediatrics, and Dr. Paul Roth, Dean of the School of Medicine.

Professor Wilson would like to thank I-Ling (Elaine) Hsieh, a doctoral student in the Department of Speech Communication at the University of Illinois at Urbana-Champaign, for her creative and persistent efforts to track down journal articles, book chapters, and online references for the writing of this book.

Both of us would like to thank our eminent contributors, Professors Donnerstein and Funk, Mr. McCannon, and Dr. Dorothy G. Singer. We would also like to thank all of our reviewers—Tarleton Gillespie, Matthew Lombard, Gary Ferrington, Dorina Miron, and Bella Mody—and our in-house reviewers.

Victor C. Strasburger
Barbara J. Wilson

CHAPTER **1**

CHILDREN AND ADOLESCENTS
Unique Audiences

Sometimes wise and disconcertingly like adults, children are nonetheless children. To the wonder, joy, and vexation of adults, they are different. As they grow older, they become increasingly like us and therefore intelligible to us, but at each age or stage of development there is something for adults to learn more about, to be amused by, and to adjust to.

—Professor Aimee Dorr,
*Television and Children: A Special Medium
for a Special Audience* (1986, p. 12)

Over the past twenty or thirty years, the status of childhood and our assumptions about it have become more and more unstable. The distinctions between children and other categories—"youth" or "adults"—have become ever more difficult to sustain.

—Professor David Buckingham,
author of *After the Death of Childhood: Growing
Up in the Age of Electronic Media* (2000, p. 77)

Young children's life experiences are limited. They have barely emerged from the preverbal fog of infancy. It is disquieting to consider that hour after hour of television watching constitutes a *primary* activity for them.

—Marie Winn,
author of *The Plug-In Drug: Television, Children,
and the Family* (1985, pp. 10-11)

Parents could once easily mold their young children's upbringing by speaking and reading to children only about those things they wished their children to be exposed to, but today's parents must battle with thousands of competing images and ideas over which they have little direct control.

—Professor Joshua Meyrowitz,
author of *No Sense of Place: The Impact of Electronic
Media on Social Behavior* (1985, p. 238)

Because it was one of her favorite movies, Louise decided to rent *E.T.—The Extra-Terrestrial* on videocassette to share with her two children, a 4- and a 10-year-old. The 10-year-old immediately liked the alien character, laughing at the creature's peculiar appearance and eating habits. The 4-year-old, on the other hand, tensed up the first time she saw E.T.'s strangely shaped hand with its two slender, protruding fingers. The young child asked several nervous questions: "What is that?" "Why is he hiding?" "What's wrong with his fingers?" Shortly there-after, the 4-year-old announced that she did not like this "show" and that she wanted to turn the channel. When E.T.'s face was finally revealed on screen, the 4-year-old let out a yelp and buried her face into her blanket. Louise was dismayed at her young child's reaction, wondering how anyone could be frightened by such a benevolent creature.

Although this example involves a fictitious family, the incident is likely to reso-nate with parents who are often perplexed by their children's responses to the media. Indeed, a great many parents have reported that their preschool children were unpredictably frightened by the gentle but strange-looking alien called E.T. (Cantor, 1998b). Likewise, G-rated movies such as *Bambi* and *Beauty and the Beast* have provoked fear in younger children (Hoekstra, Harris, & Helmick, 1999). One study even found that younger children were frightened by Michael Jackson's music video "Thriller," which involves the popular singer transforming into a werewolf (Sparks, 1986).

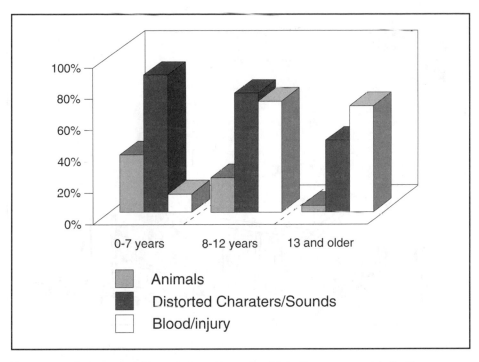

Figure 1.1. Percentage of Respondents Reporting Fright Responses to Media Themes as a Function of Age at Time of Exposure
SOURCE: Adapted from Harrison and Cantor (1999).

These reactions are not unique to a few films or videos. A recent study found strong differences in the types of media themes that frighten people across age (Harrison & Cantor, 1999). The types of stimuli that most often upset children under 7 involve animals or distorted-looking characters such as ghosts and witches (see Figure 1.1). These themes greatly diminish in impact by the time people reach adolescence and adulthood. Instead, portrayals involving blood and physical injury are most likely to trigger negative emotions in older viewers.

From an adult perspective, a young child's fears of monsters and ghosts are difficult to explain. But they signal the importance of considering children's unique orientation to the world in trying to understand how the mass media can affect younger audiences (see Figure 1.2). In this chapter, we will explore how children and adolescents interact with the media, concentrating on the crucial role that human development plays in this process. As background, we will first give an overview of the media environment and media habits of today's youth. Next we will explore several major principles or ideas that can be gleaned from child development research: Children are different from adults, children are different from each other, and adolescents are different from children. We will conclude the chapter with a focused look at specific cognitive skills that emerge during childhood and adolescence that are relevant to making sense of the mass media.

Figure 1.2
SOURCE: Copyright John Branch, *San Antonio Express-News*. Used with permission.

● MEDIA ENVIRONMENT AND HABITS OF TODAY'S YOUTH

A recent headline in the *New York Times* warned that "Studies Detail Solicitation of Children for Sex Online" (Schwartz, 2001). According to research cited in the article, 19% of children ages 10 to 17 who regularly use the Internet have been approached online by a stranger for sex, and 3% of the children characterized the solicitation as aggressive. Such statistics help to stir a sense of panic about the impact of media technologies on youth. But even more traditional forms of media can raise concerns. Reality programs on television feature couples who are tempted sexually in remote locations. Rock stars such as Eminem and Marilyn Manson celebrate hatred, revenge, and death in their music. And video games have become increasingly violent. A popular game called *Doom* features a lone gunman who is rewarded with points as he uses increasingly gory weapons to kill off a variety of monsters.

There is no doubt that today's youth are confronted with a media environment that is very different from the one faced by their grandparents or even their parents (see Figure 1.3). Terms such as *digital television, gangsta rap,* and *World Wide Web* did not even exist 20 or 30 years ago. One of the most profound changes concerns

Figure 1.3
SOURCE: Copyright Sidney Harris. Reprinted with permission.

the sheer proliferation of media outlets and technologies. The advent of cable and satellite television has dramatically increased the number of channels available in most homes today. Digital cable is multiplying this capacity. Many homes in the United States also are equipped with CD players, DVD players, personal computers, modems, and digital cameras. At a very young age, then, children are learning about keypads, joy sticks, mousepads, and remote controls.

As these technologies proliferate, they are changing the nature of more traditional media. The TV screen, which once provided a way to watch broadcast television, is now being used for a much wider range of activities, including online shopping, video-on-demand, and videocassette recording and viewing. Newspapers can still be delivered to the doorstep or they can be received online. In other words, old distinctions between the television screen and the computer screen or between print and broadcast are becoming less meaningful.

And as media technologies converge, so too are the corporations that own them. Announced in January 2000, the merger of America Online, the largest Internet service provider, and Time Warner, the world's biggest entertainment company, is one of many examples of corporate synergy and partnership. Together, these two media giants will own three film studios; CNN, HBO, and the WB networks; several book publishers; three major record companies; the second biggest cable television system; and a host of popular magazines. All of this, plus the merger, means access to 22 million Internet subscribers. The deal represents a powerful integration of content and delivery, meaning that programming can be created, promoted, and delivered by a single corporation.

Such mergers have sparked heated debates in the United States about the dangers of monopolistic growth (Bagdikian, 1998; Noam & Freeman, 1997). Furthermore, media corporations that were once primarily American based now have major stakes in the international market. So our capitalistic, privately owned media system and the cultural messages we produce are being exported worldwide. And as these media industries grow, they are becoming increasingly commercial in nature. For example, advertising is now a regular part of the Internet (see Chapter 2) and is creeping into cable television and even movie theaters.

In the relentless search for new markets, media corporations are increasingly recognizing and targeting youth as a profitable group of consumers (see Chapter 2). Television channels such as WB and the Cartoon Network are designed for young viewers; magazines such as *Seventeen, Cosmo Girl!, Sci-Fi Teen,* and *Teen Voices* are a growing phenomenon; and even Web sites are aimed specifically at children and adolescents.

Finally, digital technology is altering the very nature of media experiences. Images and sounds are more realistic than ever, further blurring the distinction between real world and media events. Children can enter virtual worlds in arcades and even in their bedrooms, traveling to different places, encountering strange creatures, and playing adventurous and often violent games. And these new media are far more interactive, allowing youth to become participants in their quest for information, action, and storytelling.

How are youth of today responding to this modern and complex media environment? A recent national study took an in-depth look at the media habits of American children (Roberts, Foehr, Rideout, & Brodie, 1999). Surveying more than 3,000 children ages 2 to 18, the study documented that youth today are surrounded by media. The average child in the United States lives in a home with three TVs, three tape players, three radios, two VCRs, two CD players, one video game player, and one computer. More telling, the media have penetrated young people's bedrooms. More than half of all children in the United States have a television in their room and nearly 30% have a VCR (see Figure 1.4). As might be expected, these figures go up when just 8- to 18-year-olds are considered. Furthermore, having a TV in the bedroom is more common among African American and Hispanic than Caucasian youth.

In terms of exposure, the average child in the United States spends 5½ hours a day using media (Roberts et al., 1999). Yet, despite all the technologies available, most of this time is spent watching television (see Figure 1.5). The average child watches more than 2½ hours of TV per day; one out of every six children in this

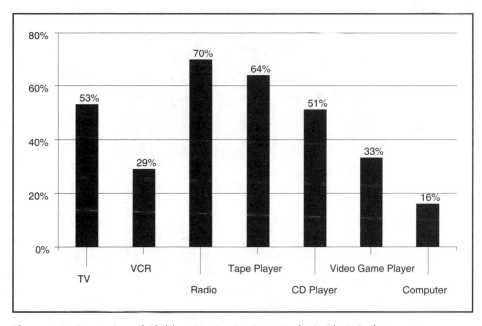

Figure 1.4. Proportion of Children Having Various Media in Their Bedroom
SOURCE: Adapted from Roberts, Foehr, Rideout, and Brodie (1999).

country watches more than 5 hours of TV a day. The study also revealed that parents typically do not exercise much control over their children's media experiences (see Figure 1.6). About half (49%) of the children reported that there are no rules in their home about how much and what they can watch on TV, and children over the age of 7 said they almost never watch TV with their parents. Of course, when parents themselves are queried, many more report supervising their children's media exposure (Woodard & Gridina, 2000).

Although computers are rapidly spreading in American homes, access to this technology continues to be closely tied to income. Only 22% of children in families with annual incomes of less than $20,000 have access to a home computer, compared with 91% of those in families with incomes over $75,000 (Becker, 2000). Even when they have a computer, children in low-income families are less likely to have an Internet connection.

American children are not so different from some of their counterparts abroad. One study of more than 5,000 children living in 23 different countries found that the average 12-year-old spent 3 hours a day watching television (Groebel, 1999), a figure remarkably comparable to that found in the United States. Another recent study of 12 European countries found that televisions and VCRs are in nearly every home, but having such technology in a child's bedroom varies considerably by country (Livingstone, Holden, & Bovill, 1999). For example, more than 60% of children in the United Kingdom have a TV in their bedroom, whereas less than 20% of

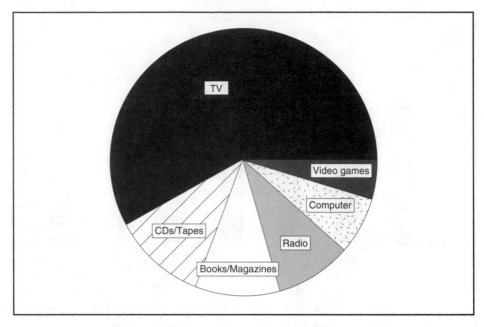

Figure 1.5. Average Time Spent With Different Media Each Day
SOURCE: Adapted from Roberts, Foehr, Rideout, and Brodie (1999).

children in Switzerland do. As in the United States, those children who have technological equipment in their bedrooms also spend more time with the media each day.

To summarize, youth today are confronted with a media environment that is rapidly changing. Technologies are proliferating, merging, and becoming more interactive. And the content featured in these technologies is increasingly graphic, realistic, and commercial in nature. At the same time, media use is at an all-time high. Youth today spend anywhere from one third to one half of their waking hours with some form of mass media. And this media use is becoming more private as children recede to their bedrooms to watch TV or listen to music alone. We will now highlight several developmental principles that underscore the need to consider youth as a special audience in today's media environment.

● CHILDREN ARE DIFFERENT FROM ADULTS

Most adults believe that they personally are not affected much by the mass media. In a well-documented phenomenon called the "third-person effect," people routinely report that others are more strongly influenced by the mass media than they themselves are (Gunther & Thorson, 1992; Perloff, 1993). This difference in per-

Figure 1.6
SOURCE: Reprinted by permission of the Kent-Ravenna, Ohio, *Record-Courier* and Patrick O'Conner, cartoonist.

ceived impact gets larger as the age of the "other" person decreases. In other words, adults perceive that the younger the other person is, the stronger the effect of the media will be (Eveland, Nathanson, Detenber, & McLeod, 1999). Interestingly, even children endorse a kind of third-person effect, claiming that only "little kids" imitate what they see on TV (Buckingham, 2000).

Are children more susceptible to media influence than adults are? At the extremes, there are two radically different positions on this issue (see Buckingham, 2000). One view is that children are naive and vulnerable and thus in need of adult protection. This stance sees the media as inherently problematic and in some cases evil because they feature material that children are simply not yet ready to confront. Buckingham (2000) points out that "media panics" have been with us a long time, especially those concerning the impact of sex and violence on children. Such panics gain steam any time a public crisis occurs such as the massacre at Columbine High School or any time a new and unknown form of media technology is developed (Wartella & Reeves, 1985).

A contrasting view is that children are increasingly sophisticated, mature, and media savvy (Tapscott, 1998). According to this position, efforts to shield youth from media are too protectionist in nature and smack of paternalism. Instead, children should be empowered to take control of their own media experiences, negotiating and learning along the way. Buckingham (2000) argues that this position is widely shared among those who see children as independent consumers who should be able to spend their own money and buy what they want.

These very different perspectives illustrate that notions of childhood are constantly being defined, debated, and renegotiated over the course of history (James, Allison, Jenks, & Prout, 1998). In truth, neither of these extreme positions seems very satisfying. Children are not entirely passive in the face of the mass media, nor are they extremely worldly and discriminating. The reality is probably somewhere in between. Nevertheless, most parents, developmental psychologists, policymakers, and educators would agree that children are not the same as adults.

Several features of childhood support this distinction. First, children bring less real-world knowledge and experience to the media environment (Dorr, 1986). Every aspect of the physical and social world is relatively new to a young child who is busy discovering what people are like, how plants grow, what animals eat, and where one neighborhood is relative to another. As they get older, children explore increasingly abstract concepts and ideas such as the social norms of their culture, what prejudice is, and how life begins. In almost every arena, though, children possess a more limited knowledge base compared with adults.

One implication of this is that children can fail to understand a media message if they lack the background knowledge needed to make sense of the information. As an illustration, in 1996 researchers at the Children's Television Workshop (now called Sesame Workshop) wanted to produce a *Sesame Street* segment about visiting the doctor. Based on preliminary interviews, the researchers discovered that preschoolers mostly associated doctor visits with getting shots and that they had little knowledge of the importance of such vaccinations (Children's Television Workshop, 1996). Had the producers not discovered this, they might have created a script that focused too much on getting shots, inadvertently reinforcing children's negative and limited impressions of the purpose of going to a physician.

As another example, researchers working on the TV program *Ghostwriter* wanted to create a story about a character who experiences peer pressure to use drugs. Prior to production, the researchers discovered that elementary schoolchildren did not understand the differences between marijuana and other illicit drugs and also expressed overly simplistic strategies for how they themselves might resist a drug offer (Williams & Hall, 1994). In other words, the children's background knowledge was quite limited. Taking this into account, the final script was designed to portray the physical effects of marijuana use as accurately as possible and also to model for child viewers some concrete and realistic ways to turn down drugs.

The lack of real-world knowledge also can make children more willing to believe the information they receive in the media. It is difficult to evaluate a story for accuracy or truthfulness in the face of no alternative data. An adult watching a TV advertisement is able to evaluate that message in the context of knowledge about the television industry as well as a vast array of personal experiences purchasing products. A child, on the other hand, rarely has this rich set of knowledge structures on which to rely. As an illustration, Figure 1.7 presents children's per-

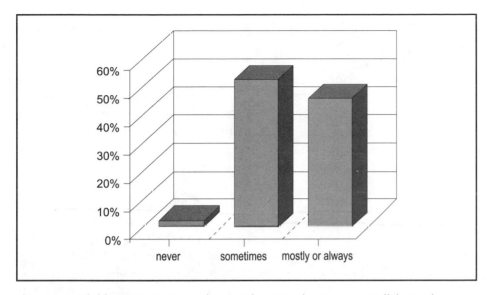

Figure 1.7. Children's Perceptions of How Often TV Advertisements Tell the Truth

ceptions of how truthful advertisements are (Wilson & Weiss, 1995). In a sample of nearly 100 girls ages 4 to 11, a full 45% reported that ads tell the truth "most of the time" or "always." Given this level of trust, a young child seems fairly defenseless when confronted with a slick TV ad that costs thousands of dollars to produce and may yield millions of dollars in sales profit.

A second feature that distinguishes childhood from adulthood is the strong eagerness to learn that marks the early years (Dorr, 1986). Parents experience this with exhaustion sometimes, as their infant daughter puts one more object in her mouth or their preschool son asks for the twentieth time, "What's that?" or "Why?" Such curiosity is a hallmark of childhood and is celebrated by educators. But it means that children are as open to learn from the mass media as from other sources, particularly in situations when firsthand experience is not possible. For example, most American children are not able to visit China, but they can learn about it by reading a book or viewing a TV documentary. A preschooler can even watch *Big Bird in China*, a Sesame Workshop production available on video-cassette. These examples show the educational benefits of the media. But compare them to a situation in which a child first learns of China by visiting a Web site created by a hate group that disparages people of Asian descent.

A third feature that characterizes childhood is a relative lack of experience with the media. Admittedly, these days some children are actually more media savvy than their parents. In fact, children in certain families know how to boot a computer or program the videocassette recorder while their parents fumble with these technologies. But it is still the case that with most media, adults simply have spent more time with the technology. Adults readily appreciate, for example, that the placement of a story in a newspaper signals something about its importance, that public television is a noncommercial channel in contrast to the broadcast networks, and that there are different genres and subgenres of movies. In contrast, children often show an incomplete understanding of production techniques such as flashbacks (Calvert, 1988; Lowe & Durkin, 1999), have difficulty distinguishing nightly news programs from shows such as *Hard Copy* and *Current Affair* (Wilson & Smith, 1995), and do not fully appreciate the commercial nature of most media in the United States (Dorr, 1980). This lack of familiarity with the technical forms and structure of the media makes a child less able to critically evaluate the content presented.

To summarize, children differ from adults in a number of ways that have implications for responding to the mass media. Younger age groups have less experience with the real world and at the same time possess a strong readiness to learn about those things with which they are unfamiliar. They also tend to be less savvy about the nature, the intricacies, and the potential distortions of the mass media. Such naïveté makes a preschooler and even an elementary schooler more likely to believe, learn from, and respond emotionally to media messages than is a more mature and discriminating adult.

● CHILDREN ARE DIFFERENT FROM EACH OTHER

It may be easier to recognize that children are different from adults than it is to appreciate how much children differ from one another. In some ways, the label *children* itself is misleading because it encourages us to think of a fairly homogeneous group of human beings. As the E.T. example at the start of this chapter illustrates, a 4-year-old thinks and responds to the world very differently than a 12-year-old does. But even a group of 4-year-olds will exhibit marked differences in how they respond to the same situation. In fact, sometimes it is difficult to believe that two children are the same age or in the same grade level.

On any elementary school playground, kindergartners can be readily distinguished from sixth graders—they are shorter in height and normally weigh less. Their heads are smaller, they dress differently, and they tend to be more physically active. But even more profound differences exist in their cognitive functioning. Younger children attend to and interpret information in different ways than do their older counterparts. Several influential perspectives on children's development support this idea, including Piaget's (1930, 1950) theory of cognitive development as well more recent models of information processing (Flavell, Miller, & Miller, 1993; Siegler, 1991).

Age is often used as a marker of these differences in cognitive abilities, although there is tremendous variation in how and when children develop. Still, most research reveals major differences between preschoolers and early elementary schoolers (3-7 years of age), on one hand, and older elementary school children (8-12 years of age), on the other, in terms of the strategies that are used to make sense of the world (Flavell et al., 1993). These strategies have important implications for how children respond to mass media, as will be discussed below in the section entitled "Developmental Differences in Processing the Mass Media."

Cognitive development is not the only factor that distinguishes children from each other. Personality differences also set children apart. For instance, some children are withdrawn or inhibited in unfamiliar situations whereas others are not (Kagan, 1997). Children also differ in the degree to which they possess prosocial dispositions toward others (Eisenberg et al., 1999), the degree to which they are capable of regulating their emotions (Murphy, Eisenberg, Fabes, Shepard, & Guthrie, 1999), and the degree to which they enjoy novel or stimulating situations (Zuckerman, 1994).

Research consistently shows sex differences among children too. For example, girls tend to prefer activities that are less vigorous than boys do (Eaton & Enns, 1986), and boys typically are more physically aggressive (Parke & Slaby, 1983). In terms of cognitive skills, girls generally possess stronger verbal abilities, whereas boys do better on visual-spatial tasks (see Halpern, 2000).

The fact is that children, even those who share biological parents and are raised in the same environment, differ on many dimensions (Scarr, 1992). And children themselves recognize these differences early in development. For example, children become aware of their own gender by around age 2 (Witt, 1997). By kindergarten, they begin to recognize gender as a social category that does not change based on hair length, dress, and other superficial qualities (Ruble, Balaban, & Cooper, 1981). At this point in time, children become keenly interested in gender-role information in the culture (Stangor & Ruble, 1989). They actively search for cultural meanings about gender in their homes, on the playground, and in the mass media (O'Bryant & Corder-Bolz, 1978; Thorne, 1993). In other words, the unique characteristics that differentiate children in turn get represented and reinforced in the culture.

All of these unique characteristics make it difficult to come up with a single prototype for what a child is like. Therefore, when we make generalizations about children and the media, we must be careful to take into account the developmental, personality, and gender characteristics of the individuals involved.

ADOLESCENTS ARE DIFFERENT FROM CHILDREN ●

Adolescence is often characterized as a time of challenge and turbulence (Roth & Brooks-Gunn, 2000). Along with bodily changes that can be quite dramatic, teens are faced with increased independence and growing self-discovery. Scholars of adolescent development refer to these changes as developmental transitions or passages between childhood and adulthood (Arnett, 1992a). In other words, the sometimes stormy periods are a necessary and normal part of growing up (Gondoli, 1999).

Unfortunately, parents and even the general public often view the teenage years with some trepidation. A recent national poll revealed that 71% of adults describe today's teenagers negatively, using terms such as *irresponsible* and *wild* (Public Agenda, 1999). Some of this public opinion is likely fueled by the mass media's preoccupation with high-profile cases of troubled teens who become violent. Contrary to public opinion, though, most teens are able to navigate adolescence in a socially responsible way, learning new competencies and new roles on the path to adulthood (Graber, Brooks-Gunn, & Petersen, 1996; Petersen, 1988).

What are some of the developmental hallmarks of adolescence? One of the main challenges a teen faces is identity formation. During the teenage years, boys and girls alike begin to ask questions about who they are and how they differ from their parents (J. D. Brown, 2000). This emerging sense of the self is fragile and malleable as teens "try on" different appearances and behaviors. A recent article in *Newsweek* magazine described the teen years like this: "From who's in which clique to where you sit in the cafeteria, every day can be a struggle to fit in" (Adler, 1999, p. 56).

A second challenge of adolescence is increased independence. Parents naturally feel less need to supervise a 13-year-old who, compared with a 5-year-old, can dress, study, and even go places alone. Teens often have jobs outside the home and by age 16 can typically drive a car, furthering their autonomy. In one study, the percentage of waking hours that teens spent with their families fell from 33% to 14% between the 5th and 12th grade (Larson, Richards, Moneta, Holmbeck, & Duckett, 1996).

Time away from parents can provide teens with opportunities to make independent decisions. It also can allow for experimentation with a variety of behaviors, some of which are not very healthy. A large national study involving adolescents in grades 7 to 12 found strong differences between those teens who regularly ate dinner with a parent and those who did not (Council of Economic Advisors, 2000). In particular, teens who spent less dinner time with parents showed significantly higher rates of smoking, drinking, marijuana use, and getting into serious fights. Other studies also have documented the importance of parent involvement as a buffer against unhealthy behaviors during the teenage years (Resnick et al., 1997).

This point leads us to a third feature of adolescence—risk taking. Today's teens face tough decisions regarding a number of dangerous behaviors such as smoking, drug use, and sexual activity. And there is no doubt that adolescence is a time of experimentation with reckless activities (Arnett, 1992a). For example, recent estimates suggest that every day, more than 3,000 American youth become regular smokers (National Center for Chronic Disease Prevention and Health Promotion, 2000). Furthermore, a national survey revealed that 50% of 9th through 12th graders reported having had sexual intercourse (Youth Risk Behavior Surveillance System, 1999). The same study found that 17% of the teens had carried a weapon during the 30 days preceding the survey, 50% had drunk alcohol, 27% had used marijuana, and 42% of sexually active students had not used a condom.

Some of this risk taking may be a function of what scholars have labeled "adolescent egocentrism" (Elkind, 1967, 1985). In particular, teenagers often seem preoccupied with their own thoughts and appearance and assume others are equally interested in their adolescent experiences. This view of the self as unique and exceptional can in turn lead to a feeling of invulnerability to negative consequences (Greene, Krcmar, Walters, Rubin, & Hale, 2000). In other words, self-focused teens think they are different from everyone else and that tragedies occurring to others "won't happen to me." Indeed, studies show that teens routinely underestimate their own personal chances of getting into a car accident compared with the risks they assume others face (Finn & Bragg, 1986). Similar misjudgments have been found among sexually active young girls who underestimate the likelihood that they themselves might get pregnant (Gerrard, McCann, & Fortini, 1983).

Risk taking also can be viewed as an adolescent's effort to assert independence from parents and to achieve adult status (Jessor, 1992). However, not all teens engage in reckless behaviors, and even the ones who do seldom limit their activities to those legally sanctioned for adults. Arnett (1992b) argues that risk taking must be viewed in the larger context of an adolescent's socialization. Some teens experience *narrow socialization*, which he characterizes as involving strong allegiance to the family and community, clear expectations and responsibilities, unambiguous standards of conduct, and swift sanctions for any deviation from those standards. Other teens are raised in an environment of *broad socialization*, where independence and autonomy are encouraged, standards of conduct are loose or even self-determined, and enforcement of standards is lenient and uneven. Arnett argues that in addition to parents, the schools, the legal system, and even the media contribute to these overarching patterns of socialization. As might be expected, risk taking is more prevalent in cultures in which socialization is broad rather than narrow (see Arnett, 1992b, for review).

A fourth feature of adolescence is the importance of peers. Teens spend a great deal of time with friends and place a high value on these relationships (Berndt, 1996). In her highly controversial book *The Nurture Assumption: Why Children Turn Out the Way They Do,* Harris (1998) argues that parents play a minimal role in their child's development other than to nurture and shape the child's peer group (Harris, 1998). Peer groups certainly do make a difference during adolescence. Studies have documented the role of peers in the initiation of behaviors such as cigarette smoking (Chassin, 1985), drug use (Halebsky, 1987), and sexual intercourse (Whitbeck, Yoder, Hoyt, & Conger, 1999). Engaging in reckless behavior often helps a teen become a member of a peer group, and the group itself can foster a sense of collective rather than individual invincibility (Arnett, 1992a).

But peer influence is not as straightforward and not necessarily as negative as some might assume. Friends actually can be a source of support for teens and also can increase self-esteem (Hartup & Stevens, 1999). Generally, adolescents are more susceptible to *antisocial* peer pressure when they have poorer relationships with their parents (Dishion, 1990) and when they are alienated from community support structures such as schools (Arnett, 1992b; Resnick et al., 1997).

Last but not least, puberty and sexual development are hallmarks of adolescence. Body hair, acne, muscle growth, and weight gain are only a few manifestations of the dramatic physical changes that occur during the teenage years. Puberty typically begins during early adolescence, around age 9 or 10 for girls and roughly 2 years later for boys (Brooks-Gunn & Peterson, 1983), although there are large individual variations. At the same time as their bodies are changing, many teens experience an increased energy level as a function of significant changes in their endocrine system (Petersen & Taylor, 1980). Furthermore, increased hormonal production of androgens and estrogens stimulates the growth of reproductive organs (see Rekers, 1992).

As might be expected, the hormonal and physical changes associated with puberty are accompanied by an increased interest in sexuality. In one study, for example, 11- to 15-year-old girls who were more physically mature showed a higher interest in sexual content in the media (Brown, White, & Nikopoulou, 1993). Thus, most teens can be expected to be intensely curious about the opposite sex and to seek information about sexual norms, attitudes, and practices in their culture. It is no accident, then, that popular teen magazines devote a great deal of space to sexual issues and relationships (Walsh-Childers, 1997).

Whether the teenage years are characterized as tempestuous or transitional, there is no doubt that significant developmental changes occur during this period. Adolescents spend more time alone or with friends and less time with parents. This growing independence comes at the same time that teens are exploring their own identities and their sexuality. The challenge is to provide these young people with enough latitude as well as guidance so that the decisions they make will result in a healthy rather than risky lifestyle.

● DEVELOPMENTAL DIFFERENCES IN PROCESSING THE MASS MEDIA

So far we have focused on broad developmental features that characterize childhood and adolescence and that differentiate these periods from adulthood. Now

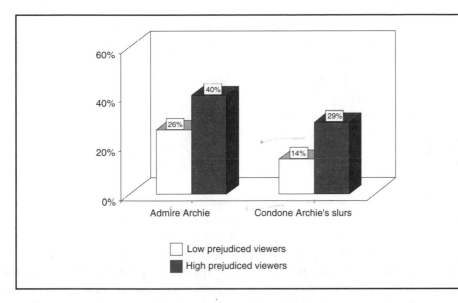

Figure 1.8. Adult Reactions to the TV Show *All in the Family* as a Function of Viewer Prejudice
SOURCE: Adapted from Vidmar and Rokeach (1974).

we will turn our attention more directly to young people's interactions with mass media. Any individual who confronts a mediated message must make sense of and interpret the information that is presented. Like adults, children and adolescents construct stories or readings of media messages that they encounter (Dorr, 1980). Given some of the pronounced differences in experience and maturation described above, we can expect that interpretations of the same content will vary across the life span. That is, a young child is likely to construct a different story from a TV program than is an older child or a teenager.

These different interpretations may seem "incorrect" or incomplete to an adult viewer. But even among mature adult viewers, there are differences in how people make sense of stories. For example, one study looked at people's reactions to a 1970s TV sitcom called *All in the Family,* which featured a bigoted character named Archie Bunker (Vidmar & Rokeach, 1974). The research revealed that interpretations of the program varied widely based on individual attitudes about race. Those viewers who held prejudiced attitudes identified with Archie Bunker and saw nothing wrong with his racial and ethnic slurs (see Figure 1.8). In contrast, viewers who were less prejudiced evaluated Archie in negative ways and perceived the program to be a satire on bigotry.

What cognitive activities are involved when a young person watches a television program, enjoys a movie, or plays a video game? In general, five mental tasks are involved (Calvert, 1999; Collins, 1983). First, the child needs to select important information for processing. When viewing television, for example, a multitude of auditory and visual signals are presented in a particular program or advertisement. Moreover, there are cues in the environment that often compete with the television, such as family members talking in the background or loud music from another room. A viewer must allocate attention to these myriad cues, consciously or unconsciously filtering out what is not essential and instead focusing on what is important in the situation.

Second, the child needs to sequence the major events or actions into some kind of story. Most media messages feature a narrative or story line (Grossberg, Wartella, & Whitney, 1998). Television plots are the easiest example of this, but even an advertisement, a video game, a song, and a radio program convey stories.

Third, the child needs to draw inferences from implicit cues in the message. The mass media do not have the space or the time to explicitly present all aspects of a story. Television programs jump from one location to another, characters in movies have dreams or experience flashbacks, and even in video games characters travel in ways that are not always orderly or linear. A sophisticated consumer recognizes the need to "read between the lines" to fill in the missing information. But a young child may fail to recognize that time has passed between scenes (Smith, Anderson, & Fischer, 1985) or that the events depicted are only part of a dream (Wilson, 1991).

Fourth, to make sense of both explicit and implicit cues in the message, a child must draw on the rich database of information he or she has stored in memory that relates to the media content. For instance, a child who lives in a rural community will have an easier time making sense of a movie about a family that loses a farm to bank foreclosure than will a child who lives in an apartment complex in New York City. The rich set of past experiences and acquired knowledge forms a mental database that helps a child interpret new messages.

Fifth, the child typically will evaluate the message in some way. The simplest evaluation pertains to liking or not liking the message. Children as young as 3 years of age already show preferences for certain types of TV programs, such as those featuring babies and young children (Lemish, 1987). As they grow older, children become increasingly sophisticated and critical of media messages (Potter, 1998). Not only are they capable of evaluating the content, but they also begin to appreciate the forms, economic structure, and institutional constraints that characterize different media (Dorr, 1980). An adolescent, for example, may reject all mainstream American television programming because of its inherent commercialism.

Given this set of tasks, we can expect that children will process media messages in different ways across development. We now describe some of the major shifts in cognitive processing that occur during the transition from early to middle childhood and during the transition from late childhood to adolescence. This is by no means an exhaustive list but instead reflects some of the skills most relevant to interacting with the media (for further reading, see Dorr, 1980; Flavell et al., 1993; Valkenburg & Cantor, 2000).

Two caveats need to be made here. First, most of the changes highlighted below occur gradually rather than abruptly during development (Flavell et al., 1993). Piaget (1950, 1952) argued that younger children's thinking is qualitatively different from that of older children, such that their cognitive systems progress through distinct stages (i.e., sensorimotor, approximately 0-2 years of age; preoperational, 2-7 years; concrete operational, 7-11 years; formal operational, 11 years and older). However, recent research indicates that cognitive performance can be uneven across different types of tasks and that children exhibit varied skill levels even within a particular domain (Siegler, 1991). Thus, it is widely believed that development is far less stagelike or abrupt than Piaget's theory would have us believe.

Second, the ages during which these shifts occur vary markedly across children. For rough approximations, we define young children as those between 2 and 7, older children as those between 8 and 12, and adolescents as those between 13 and 18.

Younger Children Versus Older Children

From Perceptual to Conceptual Processing. Preschoolers pay close attention to how things look and sound. This focus on salient features has been referred to as *perceptual boundedness* (Bruner, 1966). For example, preschoolers frequently group objects together based on shared perceptual features such as color or shape (Bruner, Olver, & Greenfield, 1966; Melkman, Tversky, & Baratz, 1981). In contrast, by age 6 or 7, children begin sorting objects based on conceptual properties such as the functions they share (Tversky, 1985). With regard to television, studies show that younger children pay strong visual attention to perceptually salient features such as animation, sound effects, and lively music (Anderson & Levin, 1976; Calvert & Gersh, 1987; Schmitt, Anderson, & Collins, 1999). On the other hand, older children tend to be more selective in their attention, searching for cues that are meaningful to the plot rather than those that are merely salient (Calvert, Huston, Watkins, & Wright, 1982).

One creative experiment involving television reveals this distinction quite clearly. Hoffner and Cantor (1985) exposed children to a television character who was either attractive or ugly and who acted kind toward others or was cruel (see Figure 1.9). Preschoolers generally rated the ugly character as mean and the attractive character as nice, independent of the character's actual behavior. In other words, their evaluations were strongly affected by the character's physical appearance. Older children's judgments, in contrast, were influenced more by the character's behavior than her looks.

Why are younger children so perceptual in their focus? Tversky (1985) has argued that all children can be swayed by strong perceptual cues in a situation, but that with development children come to suppress immediate, salient responses in

Figure 1.9. Television Characters Used in Hoffner and Cantor's (1985) Experiment on Children's Responses to Appearance Versus Behavior
SOURCE: Reproduced from Hoffner and Cantor (1985). Used with permission.

favor of slower, more thoughtful ones. This shift undoubtedly is fostered by the acquisition of knowledge that is conceptual in nature, such as the idea that motives are an important predictor of behavior.

We can apply this developmental trend to the example at the beginning of this chapter. The preschool child is transfixed by E.T.'s strange physical appearance, reacting with fright when she sees its distorted form. In contrast, the older child is able minimize the character's looks and instead focus on the creature's behavior and motivation.

From Centration to Decentration. As noted above, children and even adults can respond strongly to salient features in a message. But another characteristic of younger children's thinking is that they often focus on a single striking feature to the exclusion of other, less striking features. This tendency has been called *centration* and is illustrated in some of Piaget's classic liquid conservation tasks (see Ginsburg & Opper, 1979). In these tasks, a child is shown two glasses contain-

CENTRATION

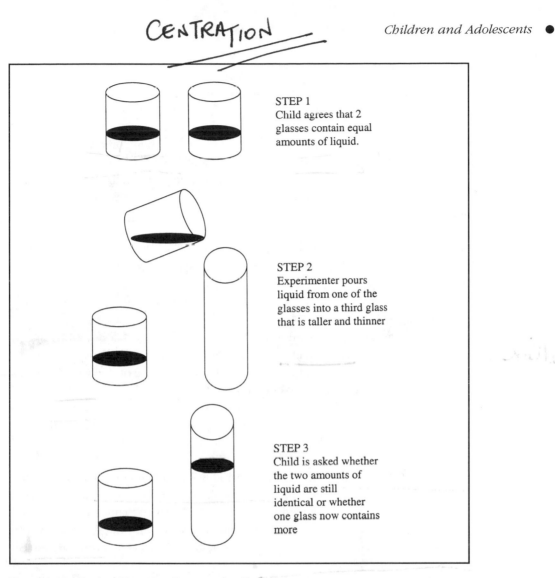

STEP 1
Child agrees that 2
glasses contain equal
amounts of liquid.

STEP 2
Experimenter pours
liquid from one of the
glasses into a third glass
that is taller and thinner

STEP 3
Child is asked whether
the two amounts of
liquid are still
identical or whether
one glass now contains
more

Figure 1.10. Typical Piagetian Conservation Task

ing identical amounts of water. Once the child agrees that the amounts are identical, the experimenter pours the water from one glass into a third glass which is
taller and thinner (see Figure 1.10). The experimenter then asks the child whether
the two amounts of liquid are still identical or whether one glass now contains
more water. The typical preschooler concludes that the taller glass has more liquid
in it. Why? Because the taller glass *looks* like it has more in it. In other words, the
differential height of the liquids captures most of the preschooler's attention.

In contrast, older children are increasingly able to "decenter" their attention and
take into account the full array of perceptual cues. The liquid in one glass is higher
but that glass also has a different shape to it. It is taller and thinner. Also, pouring
the liquid from one container to another does not change the quantity. The

"amount" of the liquid stays the same. By recognizing that the liquid is the same, the older child is able to *conserve* continuous quantities.

The same developmental differences are found with other types of conservation tasks. For example, two rows of six pennies can be laid out next to one another, in a one-to-one correspondence. If one row is then compressed, a younger child is likely to perceive it as containing fewer coins because it is now shorter (Ginsberg & Opper, 1979). In contrast, the older child notes all the perceptual data in the situation and recognizes that the number of pennies is conserved or unchanged despite appearances.

O'Bryan and Boersma (1971) documented these differences further by examining children's eye movements during conservation tasks. They found that younger children who are unable to conserve or master the task correctly tend to fixate on a single dimension, such as the height of the liquid in a glass. Older children who are able to conserve show more varied eye movements, shifting their gaze over many parts of the testing display.

Applying the idea of centration to the media, younger children are likely to respond strongly to a single feature in a television or movie scene, such as a character's red dress or a hero's shiny weapon. The prominence of the cues as well as the child's own interests will help determine what is most salient. Other perceptual cues such as the character's hair color, name, physical size, and even certain overt behaviors may go unnoticed. In some cases, we can expect that this centration will interfere with a young child's comprehension of the story line.

From Perceived Appearance to Reality. Another important cognitive skill during childhood concerns the ability to distinguish fantasy from reality. Much to a parent's amazement, a 3-year-old child may attribute life to an inanimate object such as a rock, have an invisible friend, and want Barney the dinosaur to come over to the house for a play date. All of these tendencies reflect a fuzzy separation between what is real and what is not.

Numerous studies have found strong developmental differences in children's perceived reality of television (see Dorr, 1983; Wright, Huston, Reitz, & Piemyat, 1994). Very young 2- and 3-year-olds show little understanding of the boundary between television and the real world (Jaglom & Gardner, 1981). In fact, at this age, children routinely talk to the television set and wave at the characters (Noble, 1975). For example, in one study, many 3-year-olds reported that a bowl of popcorn shown on TV would spill if the television set were turned upside down (Flavell, Flavell, Green, & Korfmacher, 1990).

By around age 4, the young child begins to appreciate the representational nature of television but still tends to assume that anything that *looks* real is real (Brown, Skeen, & Osborn, 1979). This literal interpretation has been called the "magic window" perspective, reflecting the idea that young children naively assume that television provides a view of the real world (see Figure 1.11). Grad-

Figure 1.11
SOURCE: PEANUTS reprinted by permission of United Feature Syndicate, Inc.

ually, children come to appreciate that some of what is shown on television is not real, although most of this centers first on perceptual cues. For example, 5-year-olds typically judge cartoons as not real because they feature physically impossible events and characters (Wright et al., 1994). In other words, the young child assesses content by looking for striking violations of physical reality (Dorr, 1983). It is important to note, though, that these emerging distinctions are initially quite fragile. Young children may be able to report that an animated character is "not real" yet still become quite frightened of it (Cantor, 1998b).

As children mature, they begin to use multiple criteria for judging reality on television (Hawkins, 1977). Not only do they notice marked perceptual cues but they also take into account the genre of the program, production cues, and even the purpose of the program. Most important, older children begin to judge content based on how similar it is to real life (Brown et al., 1979). Although they recognize that much of television is scripted, older children are likely to judge a scene or a program as realistic if it depicts characters and events that are *possible* in the real world (Dorr, 1983; Hawkins, 1977). In one survey, 28% of second and third graders and 47% of sixth graders spontaneously referred to "possibility" criteria in judging whether a series of characters and events on television were realistic (Dorr, 1983). In contrast, only 17% of kindergartners used this type of criteria. These trends are congruent with research on language comprehension, which suggests that the concept of possibility is not fully understood until around 8 years of age (Hoffner, Cantor, & Badzinski, 1990; Piaget & Inhelder, 1975).

Obviously, a child's personal experiences will place a limit on how sophisticated these reality judgments can be. As an illustration, Weiss and Wilson (1998) found that elementary schoolers rated the TV sitcom *Full House* as very realistic, indicating on average that "most" to "all" real-life families are like the family featured in this program. These perceptions seem a bit naive given that the program is about a widowed father raising his three daughters with live-in help from his brother-in-law and his best friend.

From Concrete to Inferential Thinking. A final cognitive trend during childhood that has implications for mass media is the shift from concrete to inferential thinking. As we have mentioned above, a young child's thinking is very tangible, focusing closely on what can be seen and heard (Bruner, 1966). For a 2- or 3-year-old, this means that attention can be swayed by highly salient cues that might actually be extraneous to the plot (Schmitt et al., 1999). For example, a purple costume might get more attention than the actions of the character who is wearing this garment.

By age 4, children can begin to focus more on information that is central to the plot more so than incidental details (Lorch, Bellack, & Augsbach, 1987). Of course, younger children do best with age-appropriate content, programs that are relatively short in duration, and comprehension tests that assess recognition rather than recall (Campbell, Wright, & Huston, 1987). With development, children become increasingly able to extract events that are central to the story line in a program (Collins, 1983). Yet the information younger children focus on is still likely to be fairly explicit in nature. For example, one study found that 4- and 6-year-olds most often recalled actions after watching televised stories, whereas adults most often recalled information about characters' goals and motives (van den Broek, Lorch, & Thurlow, 1996). Actions typically are concrete and fairly vivid in television programming, making them easy to understand and represent in memory.

As discussed above, however, full comprehension involves apprehending not only explicit content but also implicit information in the unfolding narrative. For instance, in one scene, a protagonist might discover that a "friend" is trying to steal his money. In a later scene, the protagonist might hit the friend. The viewer must deduce that the protagonist's aggression, which in isolation might appear unprovoked, is actually motivated by a desire to protect personal property. In other words, the viewer must link scenes together and draw causal inferences about content that is not explicitly presented. Studies show that older children are better able than their younger counterparts to draw different types of inferences from verbally presented passages (Ackerman, 1988; Thompson & Myers, 1985). The same pattern emerges in the context of television. By roughly age 8 or 9, children show dramatic improvements in their ability to link scenes together and draw connections between characters' motives, behaviors, and consequences (Collins, Berndt, & Hess, 1974; Collins, Wellman, Keniston, & Westby, 1978). This shift from concrete to inferential processing has implications for other forms of mass media as well. A video game and even a Web site require the user to make connections across space and time. dimensions-

To summarize, there are a number of important cognitive shifts that occur between early and middle childhood. A preschooler watching television is likely to focus on the most striking perceptual features in a program. This child may comprehend some of the plot, especially when the program is brief and age appropriate. Yet comprehension will be closely tied to concrete actions and behaviors in the story line. In addition, the preschooler is likely to have difficulty distinguishing reality from fantasy in the portrayals. As this same child enters elementary school, she will begin to focus more on conceptual aspects of the content such as the characters' goals and motives. She will increasingly be able to link scenes together, drawing causal connections in the narrative. And her judgments of reality will become more accurate and discriminating as she compares television content with that which could possibly occur in the real world. Clearly, her overall understanding of a media message is quite advanced compared with what she was capable of as a preschooler. Nevertheless, her skills are continuing to develop even during her later elementary school years. Next we will explore some of the cognitive shifts that occur between late childhood and adolescence.

Older Children Versus Adolescents

From Real to Plausible. As described above, older children use a variety of cues to judge the reality of media content. One of the most important yardsticks for them is whether the characters or events depicted in the media are possible in real life (Morrison, Kelly, & Gardner, 1981). Adolescents become even more discriminating on this dimension, judging content as realistic if it is *probable* or likely to occur in real life (Dorr, 1983; Morrison et al., 1981). In Dorr's (1983) research, almost half of adolescents defined real television events as those that were probable or plausible in real life, whereas probability rationales were seldom used by older children. To illustrate this distinction, a movie featuring an evil stepfather who is trying to poison his stepchildren might be very upsetting to a 9- or 10-year-old because this scenario *could* happen in real life. A teenager, on the other hand, is less likely to be disturbed by such content, reasoning that the vast majority of stepfathers in the world are not murderers. The movement to probabilistic thinking is consistent with studies of language comprehension that indicate that the ability to differentiate probability from possibility crystallizes during early adolescence (Piaget & Inhelder, 1975; Scholz & Waller, 1983).

From Empirical to Hypothetical Reasoning. A related development that occurs between late childhood and early adolescence is the shift from empirical to hypothetical reasoning (Flavell et al., 1993). Adolescents become increasingly able to understand abstract concepts, use formal logic, and think hypothetically (Inhelder & Piaget, 1958). An older child is able to reason conceptually too, but much of this process is based on collecting empirical evidence. A fifth or sixth grader, for example, may watch a person's behavior across several situations and infer from these actions what the person's motives are. In contrast, an adolescent might begin with a theory or hypothetical set of motives for a person and then observe behaviors to see if the theory is correct. In other words, the teenager is capable of more abstract thinking that need not be tied too closely to observable data.

The ability to think hypothetically means that a teenager can anticipate different plot events and predict logical outcomes as a story line unfolds. The teen also is able to critique the logic and causal structure of different media messages. As abstract thought flourishes, the adolescent also may consider the meaning behind the message—who is the source and why is the message constructed this way? How would the message differ if it were designed by someone else with different motives?

Metacognitive Thinking. Metacognition refers to the ability to understand and manipulate one's own thought processes (Metcalfe & Shimamura, 1994). It is called *meta*cognition because it refers to second-order mental activities: A person thinks about his or her own thinking. Adults routinely reflect on their own cognitive processing, especially during situations that highlight the need to do so. For instance, studying for a test or actually taking one requires a person to carefully concentrate on cognitive enterprises such as attention, comprehension, and memory.

Flavell and his colleagues (1993) have distinguished between two types of metacognition: metacognitive *knowledge* and metacognitive *monitoring and self-regulation*. Metacognitive knowledge refers to a person's knowledge and beliefs about the human mind and how it works. For example, most adults realize that short-term memory is of limited capacity (see section below on processing capacity), that it is generally easier to recognize something when you see it than to recall it outright, and that certain tasks are more difficult and demanding of the human mind than are others. But young children do not necessarily possess such metacognitive knowledge. In one study, for example, Lovett and Flavell (1990) presented first graders, third graders, and undergraduates with three tasks: a list of words to be memorized, a list of words to match up with a picture, and a list of words to memorize and match. Unlike the first graders, the third graders and the undergraduates were able to select what type of strategy—rehearsal, word definition, or both—would work best for each task. Yet only the undergraduates understood that the tasks would be more difficult with longer lists and unfamiliar words.

The second type of metacognition involves monitoring and readjusting one's ongoing thinking. Consider the test-taking instance, for example. An adult who is having difficulty with a certain section on a test might decide to jump ahead to an easier part for efficiency's sake and to build confidence before returning to the harder material. Research suggests that this type of self-monitoring is difficult during early childhood (see Flavell et al., 1993). In one study, preschoolers and elementary schoolers were instructed to examine a set of objects until they were sure they could recall them (Flavell, Friedrichs, & Hoyt, 1970). Older children examined them for a period of time, determined they were ready, and typically recalled all the items correctly. In contrast, the preschoolers examined the items, thought they were ready, and generally failed on the recall test. In other words, the preschoolers were not capable of monitoring their memory processes very accurately.

How does metacognitive knowledge and monitoring relate to the media? We can expect that as children approach adolescence, they will be better able to analyze the cognitive demands of different media and even different messages within a particular medium. According to Salomon (1983), some media require more nonautomatic mental elaborations or more AIME (amount of invested mental effort) than do others. In general, television requires less effort and concentration than reading, for example, because the former is highly visual and relies less on language skills (Salomon & Leigh, 1984). Thus, a teenager is more likely than a young child to recognize that a difficult book or a television documentary requires higher concentration than watching MTV. Their awareness of different media will affect the depth of processing they will use, which in turn will enhance comprehension and learning. Interestingly, when children are instructed to pay attention and to learn from TV, their mental effort and performance increase compared with what they do without such instruction (Salomon, 1983).

Also, as children reach the teenage years, they should increasingly be able to monitor their own reactions to the media, slowing down when they do not understand a book passage or reminding themselves it is only a movie when they feel scared. In one illustration of this, preschoolers and 9- to 11-year-olds were given different types of instructions for how to think about a frightening program they were about to watch on television (Cantor & Wilson, 1984). Children were told either to imagine themselves as the protagonist (role-taking set) or to remember that the story and the characters were make-believe (unreality set). The cognitive-set instructions had no appreciable effect on the preschoolers' emotional reactions to the program. In other words, they showed little ability to use the information to alter how they perceived the program. In contrast, older children in the role-taking condition were more frightened by the program, and those in the unreality condi-

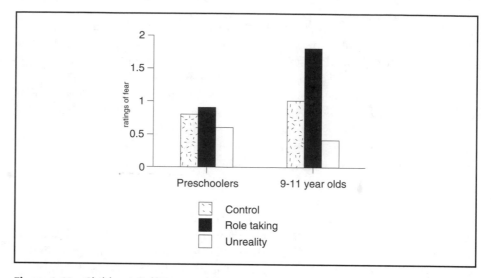

Figure 1.12. Children's Self-Reported Fear Reactions to a Scary Program as a Function of Instructional Set

SOURCE: Adapted from Cantor and Wilson (1984).

tion were less frightened compared with a control group that received no instructions at all (see Figure 1.12). The findings are consistent with the idea that as children develop, they are increasingly able to modify their thought processes while watching television.

Two Overall Developmental Trends

Two other important trends occur continuously throughout childhood and adolescence and are not specific to particular age groups: increasing knowledge about the social, physical, and mediated world in which we live and increasing processing capacity.

Increase in Domain-Specific Knowledge. It may seem obvious to state that children gain increasing amounts of knowledge across different domains as they grow. But the point is still worth making because it has such important implications for interacting with the media. With each new experience, a child stores more and more information in highly organized ways in memory. The resulting knowledge structures, sometimes called mental templates or schemas, are powerful organizers that help children anticipate and assimilate new information (Fiske & Taylor, 1991). Research suggests that children as young as 2 years of age possess well-developed schemas or scripts for familiar events such as getting ready for bed and taking a bath (Nelson, 1986). As evidence of the power of these mental organizers, a young child is likely to protest quite strongly if someone tries to alter these routines.

Young children also develop schemas for stories that include information about the typical structure and components of a narrative (Mandler, 1998). Research suggests that a well-developed story schema can help a child to organize and interpret television programming (Meadowcroft & Reeves, 1989). In addition, children can form schemas about the social and physical world in which they live. In the social realm, for example, children develop templates for emotions that include information about expressive signals, situational causes, and display rules associated with each affect (e.g., Campos & Barret, 1984). These schemas undoubtedly assist a child in making sense of an emotional scene on television. Such schemas, in turn, can be shaped and modified by exposure to the media (see Wilson & Smith, 1998).

Not surprisingly, children develop schemas about the mass media as well (Calvert, 1997). Each form of the media has its own special audiovisual techniques and codes, which at least in the case of television have been referred to as "formal features" (Bickham, Wright, & Huston, 2001; Huston & Wright, 1983). Television and film, for example, use production techniques such as cuts, zooms, fades, and special effects to signal shifts in time and changes in setting. Video games and computers have their own technological conventions. A user of the World Wide Web, for example, needs some understanding of search engines and hypertext. Knowing what to expect from each medium greatly increases a child's sophistication with it (Calvert, 1997; Smith et al., 1985). For this reason, efforts to teach youth to become critical consumers of the media often include instruction about the conventions of different technologies (see Chapter 10).

In addition to developing schemas *about* the media, spending time with certain technologies can actually enhance cognitive thinking (Greenfield, 1984). For example, one study found that practicing a video game improves children's dynamic spatial skills (Subrahmanyam & Greenfield, 1994). There is also evidence that video game playing improves strategies for dividing visual attention, presumably because players must cope with events that occur simultaneously at different places on the screen (Greenfield, deWinstanley, Kilpatrick, & Kaye, 1996). In addition, listening to a song seems to stimulate imagination more so than watching a music video of the same song does (Greenfield et al., 1987). All of these studies suggest a kind of interactive relationship between media exposure and schematic processing and development.

To summarize here, children can call on larger stores of remembered information across a variety of domains as they grow. In addition, they can integrate and combine information in more complex ways, forming more elaborate connections with what they already know (Siegler, 1991). In other words, their schemas become more elaborate and differentiated. Hence, their interpretations of media content will be richer and more complex.

Having a great deal of knowledge and experience in a given area has all kinds of benefits for cognitive processing. Compared to a beginner, the veteran has familiar concepts and ready-made strategies to apply to a problem (Siegler, 1991). Given that the terrain is familiar, the expert expends less cognitive energy and is free to apply mental workspace to high-order activities such as metacognition (Flavell, et al., 1993). Consider for a moment how a 6-year-old might respond to a cigarette advertisement in a magazine compared with how a 16-year-old would process the same message. The 6-year-old presumably has never smoked, has little knowledge of how the lungs work, is unaware of the legal battles ensuing against the tobacco industry, is not cognizant of who paid for the placement of the ad in the magazine, and has little experience with the cost of various products in a grocery store. The teenager certainly has less experience than an adult would have in this domain, but compared with the grade schooler, the adolescent brings a much broader knowledge base from which to draw in interpreting and evaluating such an ad.

Increase in Processing Capacity. Regardless of age or level of development, all humans experience limits in the capacity of their working memory (Case, 1995). In other words, certain situations and tasks are so demanding that they exceed a person's available cognitive resources. One way to demonstrate this has been through reaction-time studies that show that people perform slowly or poorly on secondary tasks when their mental energies are consumed by a primary task (Kail, 1991; Lang, 2000).

Developmental research demonstrates that as children mature, they are able to hold increasing amounts of information in working memory (Cowan, Nugent, Elliott, Ponomarev, & Saults, 1999; Kail, 1990). For example, a 5-year-old typically is able to deal with only four or five bits of information at once (e.g., digits, letters), whereas the average adult can handle seven (Dempster, 1981). There are differing theoretical accounts for this increased processing capacity. Some have argued that the structure or size of one's memory space actually increases with development (Cowan et al., 1999). Others have argued that the size remains fixed but the functional use or efficiency of the space increases (Kail, 1991). As certain tasks become familiar, they are easily categorized into preexisting schemas. This categorization and routinization mean that fewer demands are placed on the cognitive system, and hence space is freed up for other cognitive processing.

Regardless of which view is correct, the implications are the same. Younger children have difficulty considering multiple pieces of information in working memory. In addition, their capacities may be taxed quickly by a single cognitive activity that is somewhat novel and thus cannot be easily schematized. As children mature and gain experience in certain arenas, they can quickly classify new information into preexisting schemas. This schematization allows them to consider and interrelate more bits of information at once and to engage in concurrent cognitive tasks. In other words, they become more efficient information processors.

How does processing capacity affect children's interactions with the media? Research suggests that older children are better able than younger children to consider multiple cues within a scene or across several scenes when interpreting a television portrayal (Collins et al., 1974; Hoffner, Cantor, & Thorson, 1989). Likewise, older children are able to track the main plot of a television story even when there is a subplot interspersed throughout, whereas younger children's comprehension suffers in the face of a distracting subplot (Weiss & Wilson, 1998). Older children also are better equipped to handle fast-paced programming that involves the integration of information across rapid changes in time and place (Wright et al., 1984). As discussed above, older children also are better able to consider their own thought processes while attending to a television program (Cantor & Wilson, 1984).

Any time a media message is complex, lengthy, fast-paced, or delivered in a distracting environment, it is likely to present a cognitive challenge to younger children because of their more limited processing capacities. Extending these ideas to newer technologies, we might also expect that interactive media such as computers will quickly tax the mental resources of a young child because of the need to simultaneously comprehend content and respond cognitively and physically to it. As processing capacity increases throughout childhood and adolescence, these once very difficult types of media interactions will become increasingly routinized.

CONCLUSION ●

The purpose of this chapter has been to underscore the fact that children are very different from adults and from each other when they interact with the media. Children are eager to learn, have less real-world experience, and have less developed cognitive skills, making them ultimately more vulnerable to media messages. The remainder of this book will explore how children and teens respond to different types of media content such as violence and sexual messages as well as to different media technologies such as video games and the Internet. We will continually draw on the concepts and developmental trends presented in this chapter to explain how children deal with the stimulating media world that confronts them. Clearly, there are robust developmental differences in children's attention to and comprehension of media messages. These cognitive processes in turn have implications for emotional responding as well as behavioral reactions to the media.

Exercises

1. Think about your childhood. What is the first experience you remember having with the mass media? How old were you? What medium was involved? What type of content was involved? What was your reaction or response to the experience? Did your parents know about it? Could a child today have a similar experience? Why or why not?

2. For one day, chart the time you spend with the mass media (e.g., television, radio, book, Internet). Note which media you are using and what type of content you are experiencing. Also note when you are using two or more media at once (i.e., reading a book and listening to music). How much of your day did you spend with the media? Is your media use similar to that of the typical American child (see the Roberts et al. [1999] study described in this chapter)? How is it similar and how is it different?

3. Watch an episode of a TV sitcom that is popular with children. Think about the main theme of the program, the sequence of events in the story line, and the nature of the characters. Based on developmental differences in cognitive processing, describe three ways in which a 4-year-old's interpretation of the episode would differ from that of a 10-year-old. How would a 10-year-old's interpretation differ from that of a teenager? What type of viewer do you think the program is targeted toward? Think about the program itself as well as the commercial breaks in addressing this question.

4. Some scholars argue that childhood is disappearing in today's modern society. They maintain that children are dressing more like adults, talking like them, and experiencing adult activities and even adult media content. Can you think of examples to support this thesis? Can you think of examples that challenge it? How is childhood changing in the 21st century? Do you agree that childhood is vanishing? How critical are the media in addressing these issues?

5. When you were a child, did your parents have rules about what you could do with the mass media? Did they have rules when you were a teenager? Did you have a TV set in your bedroom? Do you think parents should exercise control over their children's media experiences? Why or why not?

6. Compare and contrast two rating systems designed to inform parents about media content: (a) the Motion Picture Association of America's ratings for movies (see Web site: www.mpaa.org/movieratings/) and (b) the TV Parental Guidelines for television shows (see www.tvguidelines.org/guidelin.htm). Evaluate the two systems in terms of what we know about child development, as discussed in this chapter. Do the systems seem accurate? Are they likely to be

helpful to parents? How could they be improved? Can you think of a movie or TV show that you think is rated inappropriately?

7. Watch a program targeted to children that airs on public broadcasting (e.g., *Sesame Street, Dragon Tails, Zoboomafoo*). Now compare it with a cartoon that airs Saturday morning on one of the commercial channels. Compare and contrast the two programs in terms of plot, characters, formal features, and degree of realism. Which program seems better suited to the developmental capabilities of a 4- or 5-year-old? Why?

8. Find the lyrics to a song from a genre of music that is popular among young people today (e.g., hip-hop, rap). Now compare the lyrics to those from a Beatles' song of the 1960s or 1970s. What do the songs say about adolescence? How are the songs similar in their representation of adolescent themes such as risk taking, social identity, peer relations, and sexuality? How are they different? Think about the social and political context in which these songs were written in addressing these issues.

CHAPTER **2**

ADVERTISING

Mass-market commodities are woven into the social fabric of children's lives; they are seen on sleepovers, at show-and-tell in school, on the block or in the apartment building, on the T-shirt.

—Ellen Seiter,
author of *Sold Separately: Children & Parents
in Consumer Culture* (1993, p. 8)

Too many companies simply see our children as little cash cows that they can exploit.

—Former First Lady Hillary Clinton,
quoted in the *New York Times* (Nagourney, 2000, p. B5)

Thanks to advertising, children have become convinced that they're inferior if they don't have an endless array of new products.

—Allen D. Kanner, psychologist,
as cited in *Monitor on Psychology* (Clay, 2000, p. 52)

In certain categories kids are perhaps the most fickle of consumers. They can tire very quickly of certain kinds of products and programs. The implication is to constantly "freshen" your product lines and program lineups to cater to this desire for the new.

—Dan S. Acuff,
What Kids Buy and Why (1997, p. 190)

Five-year-old Isabel came home from kindergarten one day and announced to her mother, "I need a Powerpuff Girl, Mom." Her mother was a bit surprised given that, to her knowledge, Isabel had never even seen the popular TV cartoon featuring three female superheroes with oversized heads.

"What's a Powerpuff Girl?" her mother asked.

"Their names are Blossom, Bubbles, and Buttercup," replied Isabel.

"How do you know about them?" her mother continued.

"My friends told me. We play them during recess."

"What do the Powerpuff Girls do?" probed her mother.

"They save people and stuff," Isabel replied.

On the next trip to Walgreens, Isabel spotted a display of small, plush Powerpuff Girl dolls in one of the aisles and shrieked, "Mom, can I have one, PLEEEESE!"

Isabel's mom checked the price, weighed this struggle against all others she might encounter that day, and reluctantly tossed one of the $4.99 dolls into the shopping cart. Along with millions of other parents, she caved in to what has been called the "nag" factor in the world of television advertising. Just to be clear, Isabel's mom is one of the authors of this book. In other words, even researchers who study children and the media can feel the pressure of commercialism. As it turns out, Isabel's mom got away pretty cheaply that day. Anyone searching the Amazon.com Web site can find 59 different toys associated with this successful cartoon, including Powerpuff Girl lunch boxes, key chains, banks, sleeping bags, wristwatches, costumes, inflatable dolls, backpacks, pencil cases, diaries, and even a four-piece dinnerware set (see Figure 2.1).

It is estimated that more than $12 billion a year is now spent on advertising and marketing to children, representing almost double the amount spent just 10 years ago (Lauro, 1999; McNeal, 1999). Marketers are paying more attention to young consumers these days for at least three reasons (McNeal, 1998). First, American children today have a great deal of their own money to spend. Consumers under the age of 12 spent $2.2 billion in 1968; just 30 years later, this amount rose dramatically to $23.4 billion (McNeal, 1999). As seen in Figure 2.2, children's spending power is still climbing. Much of this increase comes from children earning more money for household chores and receiving more money from relatives on holidays (McNeal, 1998). As might be expected, teens spend even more than children—roughly $155 billion in the year 2000 alone (Salamon, 2001).

Second, in addition to spending their own money, young people influence their parents' consumer behaviors. At an early age, children give direction to daily household purchases such as snacks, cereals, toothpaste, and even shampoos. As they get older, teens often voice opinions about what type of car to buy, what new media equipment is needed, and even where to go on vacation (Gunter & Furnham, 1998). And this influence has grown over the years. In the 1960s, children influenced about $5 billion of their parents' purchases. By 1984, that figure

Figure 2.1. Merchandise Related to the TV Cartoon *Powerpuff Girls*

increased to $50 billion, and by 1997, it had tripled to $188 billion (McNeal, 1998). Relaxed parenting styles, increased family incomes, higher divorce rates, and more parents working outside the home are some of the historical changes that may account for children's increased economic influence in the family (see Valkenburg & Cantor, 2001).

Third, marketers recognize that the children of today represent adult consumers of tomorrow. Children develop loyalties to particular brands of products at an early age, and these preferences often persist into adulthood (Moschis & Moore,

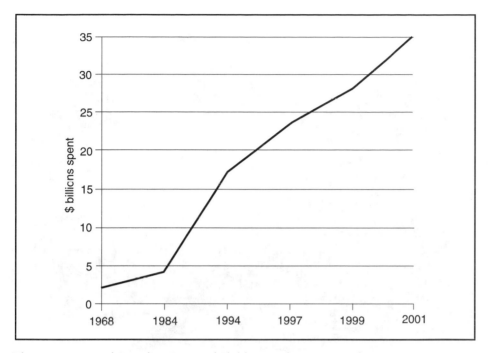

Figure 2.2. Annual Spending Power of Children Under 12 Years of Age
SOURCE: Adapted from McNeal (1998).

1982). Many companies today such as McDonald's and Coca-Cola engage in what is called "cradle-to-grave" marketing in an effort to cultivate consumer allegiance at a very early age (McNeal, 1998).

Marketers have developed sophisticated strategies for targeting young consumers. Magazines such as *Teen Beat* and *Sports Illustrated for Kids* contain glossy full-page ads promoting clothes, shoes, and beauty products. Web sites targeted to children feature all types of advertising, and even schools are marketing products to children. By far, the easiest way to reach young people is through television. Recent estimates suggest that the average American child sees 40,000 television ads per year (Kunkel & Gantz, 1992), although it varies depending on the types of channels watched most often (see Figure 2.3).

In this chapter, we will explore advertising messages targeted to children and teens. First, we will examine how marketing to children has changed over the years, focusing primarily on television advertising. Then we will look at the amount and nature of television advertising targeted to youth. Next we will give an overview of how children cognitively process and make sense of advertising. Then we will examine the persuasive impact of advertising on youth. The chapter will then turn to more recent marketing efforts targeted to children, including toy-based programs, marketing in schools, and online advertising. We will close with a discussion of the regulation of advertising in the United States as well as in other

Figure 2.3
SOURCE: Tribune Media Services, Inc. All rights reserved. Reprinted with permission.

countries and with an overview of efforts to teach advertising literacy. It should be noted that two other chapters in this book deal with advertising as it relates to specific health hazards. Chapter 7 looks at the impact of food advertising on nutrition, and Chapter 6 examines advertising of cigarettes and alcohol. The focus here is primarily on advertising of toys, clothes, and other consumer goods, although food products will be referenced occasionally as well.

● HISTORICAL CHANGES IN ADVERTISING TO CHILDREN

Efforts to advertise products to children date back to the 1930s, the early days of radio. Companies such as General Mills, Kellogg, and Ovaltine routinely pitched food products during child-oriented radio shows such as *Little Orphan Annie* and *Story Time* (Pecora, 1998). Household products such as toothpaste and aspirin also were marketed during children's programming. In these earliest endeavors, children were considered important primarily because they were capable of influencing their parents' consumer behavior.

In the 1950s, children gradually became recognized as consumers in their own right (Pecora, 1998). During this decade, the sheer number of children increased so dramatically that it is now referred to as the baby boomer period. In addition, parents who had lived through the Depression and World War II experienced a new level of economic prosperity that they wanted to share with their offspring (Alexander, Benjamin, Hoerrner, & Roe, 1998). As noted by Kline (1993), "the 1950s' family became preoccupied with possession and consumption and the satisfaction that goods can bring" (p. 67). And of course, the advent of television offered new ways to demonstrate products to captive audiences of parents and children (Pecora, 1998).

The earliest television advertising looked very different than it does today. At first, programmers were more interested in getting people to buy television sets than in attracting advertisers (Adler, 1980). Some programs were offered by the networks themselves with no commercial sponsorship at all. Other programs had a single sponsor that would underwrite the entire cost of the 30-minute or 60-minute time slot. Consequently, there were fewer interruptions, and the sponsors sometimes pitched the company rather than any specific product. As more and more American homes purchased sets, the focus shifted toward attracting this large potential audience to one program or network over others. Programs also became more expensive to produce, thereby increasing the cost of advertising time so that more sponsors were necessary to share the burden.

In one of the only systematic studies of early TV advertising, Alexander and her colleagues (1998) assessed 75 commercials that aired during children's shows in the 1950s. The researchers found that the average length of a commercial was 60 seconds, considerably longer than the 15- and 30-second ads of today. In addition, less overall time was devoted to advertising—only 5 minutes per hour in the 1950s compared with roughly 10 minutes per hour today. Reflecting the fact that ads were directed more at families than specifically at children, household products such as appliances, dog food, and even staples such as peanut butter were commonly pitched. The vast majority of ads were live action rather than animated. And the practice of host selling, using a character from the interrupted program to endorse a product in the commercial segment, was quite common. In fact, 62% of the ads featured some form of host selling, which has since been banned.

In his book *Out of the Garden: Toys, TV, and Children's Culture in the Age of Marketing*, Kline (1993) argues that 1955 was a turning point in television advertising to children. That year marked the debut of the highly successful TV show *The Mickey Mouse Club*. In great numbers, children rushed out to buy Mickey Mouse ears, guitars, and other paraphernalia, demonstrating their own purchase power. Shortly thereafter, the toy industry moved aggressively into television.

In the 1960s, the networks too recognized the revenue potential of targeting children. However, adults continued to be the most profitable consumers to reach.

So those children's programs still airing in the valuable prime-time period were shifted to Saturday morning, when large numbers of children could be reached efficiently and cost-effectively with cartoons. Throughout the 1970s, the networks increased the number of Saturday morning hours devoted to children's programming in response to marketers' increasing interest in young consumers.

The 1980s saw the birth of toy-based programs (Pecora, 1998). Creating spin-off toys based on popular children's shows is a practice that dates back to the early days of radio. Toy-based programs are slightly different, however, because they are *originally* conceived for the sole purpose of promoting new toys. Hence, critics have charged that the shows themselves are actually half-hour commercials. In an unusual twist, toy manufacturers and producers come together at the earliest stage of program development. Shows are created with the consultation and often the financial backing of a toy company. In her book *The Business of Children's Entertainment*, Pecora (1998) argues that in the 1980s,

> the line between sponsorship and program became blurred as producers, looking to spread the risk of program production costs, turned to toy manufacturers, and toy manufacturers, wanting to stabilize a market subject to children's whim and fancy, turned to the media. (p. 34)

The first example of such a partnership occurred in 1983, when Mattel toy company joined together with Filmation production house to create *He-Man and the Masters of the Universe*. In the deregulated era of the 1980s, these mutually beneficial arrangements proliferated. In 1980, there were no toy-based programs; by 1984, there were 40 of them on the air (Wilke, Therrien, Dunkin, & Vamos, 1985). According to Pecora (1998), the success of toy-based shows such as the *Smurfs* means that "neither toy nor story is now considered without thought of its market potential" (p. 61). She goes on to argue that today, "Programming evolves not from the rituals of storytelling but rather the imperative of the marketplace" (p. 59).

In the 1990s, the proliferation of cable and independent channels opened up new avenues for reaching children. Disney now has its own network, and others such as Nickelodeon and Cartoon Network have been tremendously successful in targeting the child audience. And marketers are now segmenting the child audience into different age groups. Teenage consumers are widely recognized for their spending power, as evidenced by the creation of MTV, WB, and other specialized channels devoted to attracting adolescents and young adults. And advertisers are responsible for coining the term *tweens,* referring to 10- to 13-year-olds who are deeply interested in products targeted to older adolescents and who spend a lot of time at shopping malls (Springen, Figueroa, & Joseph-Goteiner, 1999).

Thus, the current media market is far different than in the 1950s when the broadcast networks dominated television and there were only a few other media options. Today, licensed characters such as Arthur and Big Bird routinely cross over from television to other media such as books, home videos, CDs, motion pictures, and even computer software. And numerous media outlets actually specialize in child- and teen-oriented content in an effort to attract affluent young consumers.

CONTENT ANALYSES OF TELEVISION ADVERTISING ●

What do ads that are targeted to children look like? Most of the research has focused on television advertising, in part because children continue to spend so much time with this medium. In one early content analysis, Barcus (1980) looked at advertising during children's shows in 1971 and in later samples of programming from 1975 and 1978. In 1971, roughly 12 minutes of each broadcast hour were devoted to commercials, a marked jump from the 5 minutes documented in the 1950s (Alexander et al., 1998). Given that the typical ad had shrunk to 30 seconds, children on average were exposed to 26 different commercials each hour. The time devoted to advertising dropped in 1975 to roughly 9 minutes per hour (Barcus, 1980). This shift reflects pressure on the industry in the mid-1970s from child advocacy groups and the federal government to reduce advertising to children (see section on regulation below).

What products were being pitched? In the 1978 sample, Barcus (1980) found that most advertisements were for cereal, candy, toys, and fast-food restaurants. In fact, food ads generally accounted for nearly 60% of all commercials targeted to children (cereal, 24%; candy, 21%; fast foods, 12%). Barcus also found that the appeals used in children's ads were mostly psychological rather than rational. Instead of giving price, ingredient, or quality information, ads typically focused on how fun the product is or how good it tastes.

By the 1980s, commercials were shortened even more so that many lasted only 15 seconds (Condry, Bence, & Scheibe, 1988). Although the total time devoted to ads remained somewhat constant, the briefer messages meant that children were exposed to a greater number of ads during any given hour of broadcast television.

In one of the most comprehensive analyses in recent years, Kunkel and Gantz (1992) examined a composite week of child-oriented programming during February and March 1990. Programming was sampled from seven different channels: the three major broadcast networks, two independent stations, and two cable channels (Nickelodeon and USA). The researchers found significantly more advertising on the networks (10:05 minutes/hour) than on independents (9:37 minutes/hour) or cable (6:48 minutes/hour). Consistent with earlier research, the same types of products dominated commercials during children's programming. Roughly 80%

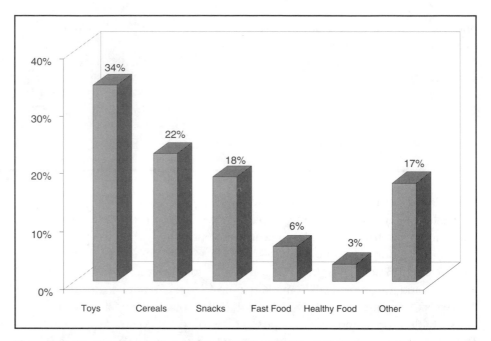

Figure 2.4. Types of Products Advertised During Children's TV Programming
SOURCE: Adapted from Kunkel and Gantz (1992).

of all ads were for toys, cereals, snacks, and fast-food restaurants (see Figure 2.4). Interestingly, only 3% of all ads were for healthy foods. When the researchers compared channel types, they found that toy ads were most prevalent on independent channels, whereas cereals and snacks were most common on the broadcast networks. Cable channels offered the most diverse range of products, with 35% of the ads falling into the "other" category. Kunkel and Gantz (1992) reasoned that toy ads, which have been consistently criticized for deceptive practices, may show up less often on the broadcast networks because of their more rigorous self-regulatory standards.

The researchers also coded the primary persuasive appeal used in each ad. The most prevalent theme was fun/happiness, which accounted for 27% of all ads. Two other common appeals were taste/flavor (19%) and product performance (18%). In contrast, appeals based on price, quality of materials, nutrition, and safety each accounted for less than 1% of the ads.

Therefore, despite the proliferation of channels on television, it seems that advertising to children has not changed much over the years. The same products dominate commercials, and the selling appeals continue to focus more on fun and happiness than on actual information about the product. Research on television ads in the 21st century will ascertain just how deeply ingrained these patterns are.

Content analyses also have looked at other qualities inherent in children's advertising, such as how gender is portrayed. In a recent study of nearly 600 commercials targeted to children, Larson (2001) compared ads that feature only girls or only boys with those that feature both girls and boys in them. She found that girls-only ads were far more likely to feature a domestic setting such as a bedroom or a backyard than were boys-only or mixed-gender ads. Boys-only ads seldom occurred around the house and instead featured settings such as restaurants, video arcades, and baseball diamonds. The types of interactions that occurred also differed across ads. More than 80% of the girls-only ads portrayed cooperation, whereas less than 30% of the boys-only ads did. Consistent with gender stereotypes, nearly 30% of the boys-only ads featured competitive interactions, but none of the girls-only ads did. Finally, there were gender differences across the types of products being pitched. Food commercials were most likely to feature girls and boys together, whereas toy ads typically were single gender in nature. Commercials targeted to boys were frequently for video games or action figures, and those targeted to girls were for Barbie dolls.

Single-gender commercials can convey stereotypes in more subtle ways as well. One study examined the production techniques used in toy ads directed to boys versus girls (Welch, Huston-Stein, Wright, & Plehal, 1979). Toy ads for boys were faster in pace, used more abrupt transitions such as cuts, and had more sound effects and other types of noise. In contrast, toy ads directed at girls used smoother transitions such as fades and dissolves between scenes and had more background music. In a follow-up study (Huston, Greer, Wright, Welch, & Ross, 1984), elementary schoolers readily identified these different production techniques as being associated with a "boy's toy" or a "girl's toy" even when the toy itself was gender neutral (e.g., a mobile).

Commercials for children also have been analyzed for violence. Palmerton and Judas (1994) looked at ads featured during the 21 top-rated children's cartoons in 1993. One third of the ads contained overt displays of physical aggression, most commonly found in toy commercials. Furthermore, ads that were clearly targeted to boys were far more likely to feature violence than were ads targeted to girls. Literally every commercial for action figures in the sample contained violence.

In summary, the typical hour of commercial television for children features anywhere from 9 to 11 minutes of ads for products. Most of these are marketing toys or a food product that is not particularly healthy. The commercials designed for youth do not offer much in the way of "hard" information about products such as what they are made of or how much they cost. Instead, the appeals are largely emotional ones based on fun or good taste. Toy ads in particular are fairly stereotyped in terms of gender. Ads targeted to boys typically sell violent toys that are demonstrated through action, force, and noise. Ads for girls, in contrast, are for dolls that are featured in a quieter, slower, and more domestic environment. The next section addresses how children respond cognitively to these messages.

● CHILDREN'S PROCESSING OF ADVERTISING

In the United States, policies dating back to the Communications Act of 1934 stipulate that advertising must be clearly identifiable to its intended audience (Wilcox & Kunkel, 1996). In other words, commercials should be recognized by the target audience as obvious attempts to persuade. If a viewer is unaware of or incapable of recognizing an ad, then he or she is presumably more vulnerable to its persuasive appeals. Under these circumstances, commercial messages are thought to be inherently unfair and even deceptive. Because of the potential for unfairness, researchers as well as policymakers have focused on how children of different ages make sense of advertising.

Attention to Advertising

One of the first questions to ask is whether children pay any attention to advertising. Certainly many adults use commercial time to engage in other activities or even to turn the channel. Based on in-home observation, one study found that adults pay visual attention to programming 62% of the time and to ads only 33% of the time (Krugman, Cameron, & White, 1995). As it turns out, children's attention depends on the age of the viewer. In one early study, mothers of 5- to 12-year-olds were trained to observe their children's attention to commercials aired during different types of TV programming (Ward, Levinson, & Wackman, 1972). All children exhibited a drop in attention when a commercial was shown, and attention also decreased over the course of several ads shown in a series. However, the youngest children (5-7 years) generally displayed higher levels of attention to both commercials and programs, whereas the 11- and 12-year-olds were most likely to stop looking when an ad came on. These findings suggest that older children, like adults, screen out advertisements. The data also suggest that younger children may not be making clear distinctions between program and nonprogram content, an issue we will turn to in the next section.

Similar age differences have been found in laboratory research. Zuckerman, Ziegler, and Stevenson (1978) videotaped second through fourth graders while they watched a brief program with eight cereal commercials embedded in it. Overall, children paid less attention to the ads than to the program, but once again attention to the commercials decreased with age.

Younger children's greater attention to ads may be due in part to attention-getting techniques such as jingles, animation, and slogans used to pull in the audience. Greer, Potts, Wright, and Huston (1982) found, for example, that preschoolers paid more attention to advertisements that contained high action, frequent scene changes, and numerous cuts than to ads without these production features.

Similarly, Wartella and Ettema (1974) found that compared with kindergarten and second-grade children, preschoolers' level of attention to ads varied more as a function of visual and auditory attributes of the message. Such patterns are consistent with younger children's tendency to focus on and be swayed by perceptually salient cues in the media, as discussed in Chapter 1.

Overall then, preschoolers and early elementary schoolers pay more attention to television advertising than do older children. In part, this may be due to the strong perceptual attributes commonly found in commercials. However, the relatively steady attention patterns during transitions from programming to advertising also suggest that younger children may not be distinguishing these two types of messages very clearly.

Discrimination of Ads From Programming

Discrimination can be tested by showing different types of television content and asking children to identify what they are watching. For example, Palmer and McDowell (1979) stopped a videotape of Saturday morning content at preselected points and asked kindergartners and first graders whether they had just seen "part of the show" or a "commercial." The young elementary schoolers were able to accurately identify commercials only 53% of the time, which is roughly equivalent to chance guessing.

In other studies employing similar techniques, young children's discrimination skills have sometimes been better and often above chance levels (Butter, Popovich, Stackhouse, & Garner, 1981; Levin, Petros, & Petrella, 1982). Nevertheless, age differences are consistently found through the preschool years; 3- and 4-year-olds are less able to make these distinctions than are 5-year-olds (Butter et al., 1981; Levin et al., 1982).

Once children learn to discriminate a TV ad from a program, they often do so on the basis of perceptual features rather than more conceptual properties of the two messages. For instance, when Palmer and McDowell (1979) asked kindergartners and first graders how they knew a particular segment was a commercial, the predominant reason cited was the length of the message ("because commercials are short"). Other studies that have interviewed children about ads versus programs without showing television content support this finding (Blatt, Spencer, & Ward, 1972; Ward, Wackman, & Wartella, 1977).

We should point out that the television industry employs separation devices to help signal to child viewers that a commercial break is occurring. These devices vary considerably in degree, from the simple insertion of several seconds of blank screen between a program and an ad to a more complex audiovisual message indicating that a program "will be right back after these messages." As it turns out, these types of separators do not help young children much. Studies comparing blank screens, audio-only messages, visual-only messages, and audiovisual separators have found little improvement in young children's discrimination abilities with any of these devices (Butter et al., 1981; Palmer & McDowell, 1979; Stutts, Vance, & Hudleson, 1981). One possible reason for the ineffectiveness of such separators is that they may be too brief to be noticed. Another possibility is that they look too much like adjacent programming. In many cases, visuals of the characters or part of the soundtrack from the show are actually featured in the separators. A more effective device may be one that is far more obvious. For example, a child or adult spokesperson who has no affiliation with programming could state, "We are taking a break from the program now in order to show you a commercial."

To summarize, the research shows that a substantial number of preschoolers do not recognize a commercial message as distinctly different from programming. By age 5, most children are capable of making this distinction, although it is typically based on somewhat superficial qualities of the messages such as how long they are. Still, being able to identify and accurately label a commercial does not necessarily mean that a child fully comprehends the nature of advertising, a topic we turn to next.

Comprehension of Advertising

Adult consumers realize that advertisements exist to sell product and services. This realization helps a person to interpret a commercial as a persuasive form of communication. According to D. F. Roberts (1982), an "adult" understanding of advertising entails four ideas: (a) the source has a different perspective (and thus other interests) than that of the receiver, (b) the source intends to persuade, (c) persuasive messages are biased, and (d) biased messages demand different interpretive strategies than do informational messages. Most research dealing with children has focused on the first two ideas, encompassed in studies of how and when young viewers understand the selling intent of ads. Less attention has been given to children's recognition of bias in advertising, relating to the last two ideas. Not reflected in Roberts's list is the notion that other facets of advertising require understanding too, such as disclaimers. This section will consider all three topics: children's comprehension of selling intent, of advertiser bias, and of disclaimers such as "parts sold separately."

Understanding Selling Intent. Recognizing the selling motive that underlies advertising is not a simple task. For one thing, the actual source of a commercial is rarely identified explicitly. A television commercial, for example, might show children playing with a toy or eating a type of cereal and yet the company that manufacturers these products is invisible. It is easy to assume that the "source" of the message is the child, the celebrity, or the animated character who in fact is merely demonstrating a new product that is available.

Research suggests that younger children's views are just this naive. In one early study, Robertson and Rossiter (1974) asked first-, third-, and fifth-grade boys a series of open-ended questions such as, "What is a commercial?" and "What do commercials try to get you to do?" First graders often described commercials as informational messages that "tell you about things." Although older children did this too, they were far more likely to describe advertising as persuasive in nature (i.e., "commercials try to make you buy something"). In fact, the attribution of selling intent increased dramatically with age: Only 53% of the first graders mentioned persuasive intent, whereas 87% of third graders and 99% of fifth graders did so.

A more recent study found a very similar pattern (Wilson & Weiss, 1992). When asked what commercials "want you to do," only 32% of 4- to 6-year-olds mentioned the selling intent of ads. Instead, this youngest age group was far more likely to cite an entertainment (e.g., "they want you to watch them," "make you laugh") or informational ("show you stuff") function for commercials. In contrast, 73% of 7- to 8-year-olds and a full 94% of 9- to 11-year-olds spontaneously mentioned the selling intent of commercials. A host of other studies using similar interviewing techniques support these age trends (Blatt et al., 1972; Ward, Reale, & Levinson, 1972; Ward et al., 1977).

Given variations in development, it is difficult to pinpoint the specific age at which the idea of selling intent is mastered. Nevertheless, most studies suggest that children begin to develop an understanding of the persuasive purpose of advertising around the age of 7 or 8 (for reviews, see Calvert, 1999; John, 1999; Kunkel, 2001; Wartella, 1980).

Some scholars have argued that the reliance on verbal measures can mask younger children's true abilities, which may be hampered by language difficulties (Macklin, 1987; Martin, 1997). To test this notion, Donohue, Henke, and Donohue (1980) devised a nonverbal measure to assess 2- to 6-year-olds' understanding of selling intent. After watching a Froot Loops commercial, children were asked to choose which of two pictures—one of a mother and child picking out a box of cereal at a supermarket and the other of a child watching television—illustrated what the commercial wanted them to do. A full 80% of the young children selected the correct picture, well above chance level with two options. However, as seen in Table 2.1, several efforts to replicate this finding with younger children have been unsuccessful (Macklin, 1985, 1987). For example, Macklin (1985) used a set of four pictures, reasoning that the two used by Donohue et al. were too easy (i.e., only one of the pictures featured cereal, which made it obviously more relevant). When four pictures were shown, 80% of 3- to 5-year-olds could *not* select the correct one.

Theoretically, it makes sense that comprehension of selling intent might be difficult for younger children. Certain cognitive skills seem to be required first, such as the ability to recognize the differing perspectives of the seller and receiver. In support of this idea, one study found that the ability to role take was a strong and significant predictor of elementary schoolers' understanding of the purpose of

TABLE 2.1 Comparison of Preschoolers' Correct Responses Across Studies Using Different Nonverbal Measures of Comprehension of Selling Intent (in percentages)

Nature of Nonverbal Task	Incorrect	Correct
Select from 2 pictures (Donohue, Henke, & Donohue, 1980)	20	80
Select from 4 pictures (Macklin, 1985)	80	20
Select from 10 sketches in a game (Macklin, 1987)	91	9
Enact selling intent in creative play (Macklin, 1987)	87	13

SOURCE: Adapted from Macklin (1985, 1987).

advertising (Faber, Perloff, & Hawkins, 1982). Interestingly, exposure to television did not correlate with comprehension of selling intent, suggesting that viewing numerous television ads is not enough to help a child recognize the purpose of commercials.

In addition to role taking, comprehension of selling intent also seems to depend on the ability to think abstractly about what persuasion is and who the true source of the message is. Supporting this idea, one study found that the ability to identify the source of advertising and the awareness of the symbolic nature of commercials were two skills that helped differentiate children who understood the purpose of ads from those who did not (Robertson & Rossiter, 1974).

To summarize, a large body of research suggests that very young children do not comprehend the purpose of advertising and often view it as informational in nature. The ability to role take as well as the ability to think conceptually have been identified as important precursors to being able to appreciate advertising as a form of persuasion. Given that such skills do not emerge until the later elementary school years (see Chapter 1), it stands to reason that understanding the selling intent of commercials does not occur much before the age of 7 or 8.

As a final issue, we might ask why comprehending the purpose of advertising is so important. Perhaps the naive view of a young child is just that—a naive view, with little or no consequence. Several studies suggest otherwise. Comprehension of selling intent seems to alter a child's reactions to advertising (Robertson & Rossiter, 1974; Ward & Wackman, 1973). For example, Robertson and Rossiter (1974) found that elementary schoolers who understood the persuasive intent of commercials were less likely to trust ads, more likely to dislike them, and less likely to want advertised products. In other words, recognizing the motives behind commercials may help trigger a cognitive defense or shield against such messages. Interestingly, the opposite pattern was found among children who viewed ads as informational—they expressed higher trust and more liking of such messages. The next section will explore skepticism toward advertising more fully.

Recognition of Bias. Appreciating that advertising is inherently one-sided and therefore biased is another facet of sophisticated consumerism (D. F. Roberts, 1982). This realization also is age related in its development. In interview situations, younger children are more likely to report that they believe what commercials say than are older children (Bever, Smith, Bengen, & Johnson, 1975; Robertson & Rossiter, 1974). For instance, Ward and his colleagues (1977) found that 50% of kindergartners said yes when asked, "Do commercials always tell the truth?" Only 12% of third graders and 3% of sixth graders responded affirmatively to this question.

More recently, Wilson and Weiss (1995) asked 4- to 11-year-olds a series of questions about advertising, including how much commercials tell you about a toy and how often commercials tell the truth. As seen in Figure 2.5, strong age trends were found on three different measures, all indicating growing skepticism of advertising across the childhood years. Even while watching television, older children spontaneously express more negative comments and criticisms of ads than do younger children (Ward, Levinson, & Wackman, 1972).

Several factors contribute to younger children's trust in advertising. First, younger children have more difficulty differentiating appearance from reality, as discussed in Chapter 1. They rely heavily on perceptual cues in judging an ad (Ward & Wackman, 1973) and thus are likely to believe that products look and perform the way they are depicted in commercials. Second, younger children have less experience as consumers. One way to learn expeditiously that ads can be deceptive is to experience disappointment over a purchase. By sixth grade, the vast majority of children can describe a product they bought that turned out to be worse than what was depicted in an ad (Ward et al., 1977). As children grow older, they are more likely to cite their own consumer experiences as reasons for not trusting ads (Ward & Wackman, 1973). Third, the failure to understand selling intent makes a young child more trusting. In one study, a full 100% of older, cognitively mature children referred to advertisers' motives when asked to explain why commercials do not always tell the truth (Ward & Wackman, 1973). For example, older children based their assessments of bias on the fact that advertisers "want you to buy their product," and "they want you to think their product is good."

Skepticism toward advertising continues to develop into early adolescence. One longitudinal study found relatively high levels of mistrust in commercial claims as well as advertiser motives in a large sample of middle schoolers (Boush, Friestad, & Rose, 1994). On a 5-point scale, the students' average ratings were all around 4.0, indicating strong agreement with statements such as "Advertisers care more about getting you to buy things than what is good for you," and "TV commer-

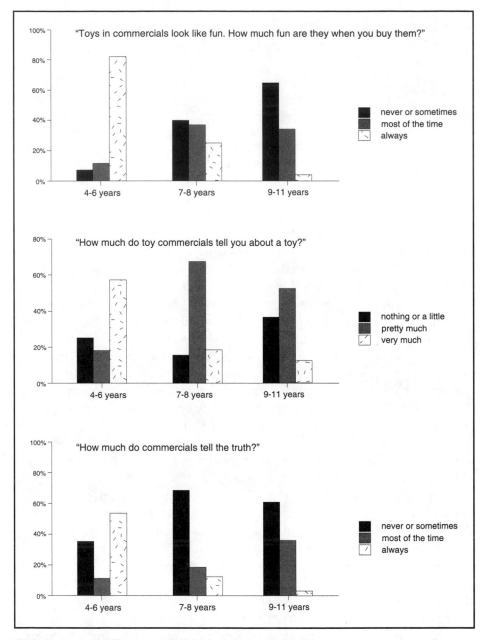

Figure 2.5. Age Differences in Children's Trust in Advertising

cials tell only the good things about a product; they don't tell you the bad things." Yet skepticism did not increase much within a single school year, nor were there any significant differences between 6th and 8th graders in these beliefs.

As a child reaches the teen years, then, factors other than cognitive develop-ment may be important in predicting who is most critical of advertising. One study found that skepticism toward advertising is higher among teens who watch more television, who come from families that stress independent thinking, and who rely on peers for information about products (Mangleburg & Bristol, 1999). In contrast, skepticism is lower among teens who report trying to impress peers with product purchases. This research suggests that once a young person is cognitively capable of recognizing the motives and tactics of advertisers, socializing forces such as par-ents and peers may be needed to make such information salient on a regular basis.

Comprehension of Disclaimers. Disclaimers are warnings or disclosures about a product, intended to prevent possible deception caused by an ad. "Batteries not included," "parts sold separately," and "part of a balanced breakfast" are examples of disclaimers that are quite common in advertising to children. Kunkel and Gantz (1992) found that more than half of the commercials targeted to children contained at least one disclaimer, and 9% featured two or more. Typically, disclaimers are conveyed by an adult voice-over or by inserting the words in small print at the bot-tom of the screen (Muehling & Kolbe, 1999). It is rare for a disclaimer to be pre-sented both auditorily and visually (Kunkel & Gantz, 1992).

Disclosures exist because of consumer pressure to ensure that advertisements give accurate information about products (Barcus, 1980). Yet disclaimers have been criticized as "jargon" because the wording is often fairly obscure (Atkin, 1980). In fact, research indicates that young children do not comprehend disclaim-ers very well. One study found that preschoolers exposed to a disclaimer in a toy ad were no better able to understand the workings of the toy than were those who saw the same ad with no disclaimer (Stern & Resnick, 1978). Another study revealed that kindergarten and first-grade children had little understanding of what a "balanced breakfast" means and were far more likely to remember the Rice Krispies cereal in an ad than the milk, orange juice, or strawberries that accompa-nied it on the table (Palmer & McDowell, 1981). Cognitive as well as language development should help to make these disclaimers more accessible with age. One study found that 85% of 10-year-olds understood "partial assembly required" in a toy ad, whereas only 40% of 5-year-olds did (Liebert, Sprafkin, Liebert, & Rubinstein, 1977).

Yet disclaimers could be designed in a more straightforward way even for youn-ger children. In an innovative experiment, Liebert and her colleagues (1977) exposed kindergartners and second graders to a toy commercial under one of three conditions: no disclaimer at all, a standard disclaimer ("partial assembly required"), or a modified disclaimer that contained simpler wording ("you have to put it together"). Regardless of age, children who heard the simplified disclaimer were significantly more likely to understand that the toy required assembly than were those who heard the standard disclaimer (see Figure 2.6). Interestingly, the

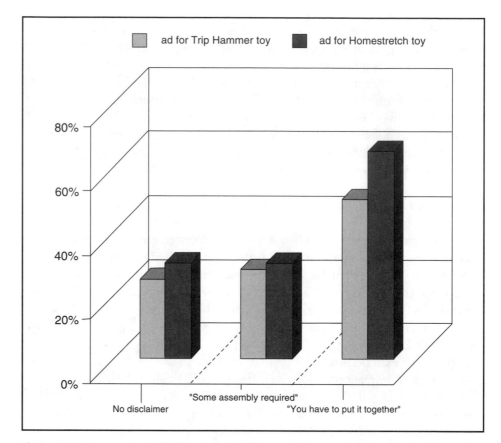

Figure 2.6. Percentage of Children Who Understood That Toy Required Assembly as a Function of Type of Disclaimer in Ad
SOURCE: Adapted from Liebert, Sprafkin, Liebert, and Rubinstein (1977).

standard wording was no more effective in helping children understand that the toy needed assembly than having no disclaimer at all; less than 25% of children in either condition understood this idea.

To recap how children process advertising, most preschoolers have difficulty differentiating a television commercial from programming, and they do not comprehend the standard wording used in disclaimers in advertising. Thus, for this age group in particular, advertising may be unfair given the legal principle that the audience must be capable of recognizing such content. By age 5 or 6, most children have mastered the distinction between an ad and a program, although it is based primarily on perceptual cues such as the length of the messages. As commercials get shorter and as they increasingly resemble adjacent programming, a kindergartner or first grader may have more difficulty making this distinction.

Yet being able to identify an ad still does not mean that a young child comprehends its purpose. Initially, ads are viewed as informational or entertaining in nature, and young children express a high degree of trust in such messages. It is not until 7 or 8 years of age that a child begins to understand the selling intent of such messages. This transition is facilitated by the development of role-taking skills and conceptual thinking. By age 12 or so, most children are able to recognize the source of the message, the advertisers' motives, and typical strategies that are used to persuade. This level of awareness, coupled with a rich base of consumer experience, means that by the teenage years, most youth are fairly critical and skeptical of advertising. But like many adults, they can still be persuaded by commercials, as we will discover next.

PERSUASIVE IMPACT OF ADVERTISING ●

The most direct effect of an advertisement is to convince a consumer to purchase a new product. Advertisers and companies alike believe in the power of advertising to do just that. There is no other way to explain the fact that companies now pay $2.4 million for a 30-second commercial during the Super Bowl. But there are more subtle consequences of advertising too. For example, commercials can influence family interactions. Whenever a child tries to get a parent to buy something or a parent tries to resist that effort, conflict can occur. Researchers have looked at how often this occurs and with what consequence. In addition, extensive exposure to advertising may affect more general attitudes or values that youth hold regarding consumption, money, and even physical appearance. We discuss each of these potential influences in this section.

Desire for Products

Asking whether advertising creates a desire for products may seem like a ridiculous question to some. American children wear T-shirts emblazoned with Pokémon characters, carry lunch boxes decorated with Disney images, wear designer jeans and Nike athletic shoes, and love anything with the word "Gap" on it. Adolescents seem even more conscious of brand names as well as the latest fads in clothing and technology. Where does all this consumer desire come from? When asked, most children report that they bought something because "you see it a lot" or "everybody has one" (Fox, 1996). As noted above, advertising often conveys the idea that a product will bring fun and happiness to a youngster's life. Images of other children playing with a toy or eating at a fast-food restaurant reinforce the notion that everyone else is doing it too.

It is not surprising that children are highly aware of brand names, jingles, and slogans associated with specific commercials and of the celebrities who endorse certain products (Burr & Burr, 1977; Fox, 1996). One study revealed that children between the ages of 8 and 12 could name five brands of beer but only four American presidents (Center for Science in the Public Interest, 1988). Another study found that teens remember brand names and recognize ad content better than adults do (Dubow, 1995).

But does exposure to advertising create desires? A number of surveys show that children who watch a lot of television want more advertised toys and actually consume more advertised foods than do children with lighter TV habits (Atkin, 1976, 1982; Goldberg, 1990; Goldberg, Gorn, & Gibson, 1978; Robertson & Rossiter, 1977; Robertson, Ward, Gatignon, & Klees, 1989). As an example, one recent study asked 250 children in the Netherlands to list their Christmas wishes and then compared them with the commercials that were aired on TV at the time (Buijzen & Valkenburg, 2000). More than half the children requested at least one advertised product. Moreover, heavy exposure to television significantly predicted requests for more advertised products, even after controlling for age and gender of the child.

Among adolescents too, exposure to television has been linked to increased desire for products and brand names (Moschis, 1978; Moschis & Moore, 1979). However, evidence suggests that the strength of this relationship may decrease somewhat with age (Buijzen & Valkenburg, 2000; Robertson & Rossiter, 1977), consistent with children's growing awareness of the purpose of advertising as well as increased skepticism about such messages.

Clearly, correlational evidence reveals that there is a relationship between TV advertising and product desires, but it is difficult to establish causality in such studies. It is possible that youth who are eager to buy toys, games, clothes, and snacks actually seek out television more often to find out about new products, a reverse direction in this relationship. Thus, researchers have turned to experiments to more firmly establish the impact of advertising.

In the typical experiment, children are randomly assigned to either view or not view an advertisement for a particular product. Afterward, children are allowed to select the advertised product from a range of other choices, or they are asked a series of questions about how much they like or want that product compared to others. Experiments generally show that commercials are indeed effective. In one study, preschoolers exposed to a single ad for a toy were more likely than those not exposed to (a) choose the toy over the favorite activity at the school, (b) select the toy even if it meant playing with a "not so nice boy," and (c) choose the toy despite their mother's preference for a different toy (Goldberg & Gorn, 1978). In a study of older children, exposure to a single ad for acne cream caused fourth and fifth graders to worry more about skin blemishes and to want to buy the cream (Atkin, 1976).

Although one ad can increase desire for a product, multiple exposures may be even more influential. Gorn and Goldberg (1977) found that viewing one versus three commercials was equally effective in increasing positive attitudes toward a new toy, but only the three-exposure condition made children try harder to win the toy compared to a control group. Other research supports the idea that a single ad can increase awareness and liking of a product, but multiple exposures to varied commercials is most effective in changing consumer behavior (Gorn & Goldberg, 1980; Resnik & Stern, 1977).

Beyond repetition, there are other ways to enhance the impact of an advertisement. One tactic is to include a premium or prize with the product, as is done in boxes of cereal. In 1975, premiums were offered in nearly 50% of cereal ads targeted to children (Barcus, 1980). This practice is less common today in cereal ads, but fast-food commercials routinely entice children with small toys that come with kids' meals (Kunkel & Gantz, 1992). In 1997, McDonald's had difficulty keeping Teenie Beanie Babies in stock once it began offering them as premiums in kids' Happy Meals. Research suggests that premiums in commercials can significantly increase children's desire for a product (Miller & Busch, 1979) and actually can affect children's requests for cereals in a supermarket (Atkin, 1978).

Another strategy involves the use of a celebrity or a popular character to endorse a product in an ad. Professional athlete Michael Jordan has long been associated with Nike and even has a pair of athletic shoes (Air Jordans) named after him. There are countless other examples. Teen pop star Britney Spears suggestively dances her way through a TV ad for Pepsi and endorses Clairol shampoo in magazines (see Figure 2.7). Tennis sisters Serena and Venus Williams pitch Avon products, and Bart Simpson claims to love Butterfinger candy bars.

Research supports the idea that popular figures can be effective sources of persuasion. One study found that teens perceived celebrities as more trustworthy, competent, and attractive than noncelebrity endorsers featured in nearly identical ads (Atkin & Block, 1983). Furthermore, the celebrities resulted in more favorable evaluations of a product. In a controlled experiment, Ross and her colleagues (1984) exposed 8- to 14-year-old boys to a commercial for a racecar set but systematically varied whether a celebrity endorser was included in the ad. The researchers found that exposure to the celebrity significantly enhanced boys' liking of the racing set and increased their belief that the celebrity was an expert about the toy.

Taken as a whole, the research demonstrates that commercials can have quite powerful effects on children's desires. Even a single ad can change the way a child perceives a toy or a game. Ads also can persuade young viewers to eat foods that are not very nutritional (see Chapter 7) and to try certain drugs such as tobacco (see Chapter 6). As it turns out, even a bland ad can make a product appealing (Resnik & Stern, 1977), but incorporating tactics such as premiums and celebrity endorsers can make a pitch even more effective. Next we will consider effects of advertising that are more indirect and not necessarily intentional on the part of advertisers: increased family conflict and changes in youth values.

Figure 2.7. Sample Celebrity Ads

Parent-Child Conflict

Most advertising agency executives believe that TV commercials do not contribute to family conflict (Culley, Lazer, & Atkin, 1976). Yet research suggests otherwise (see Figure 2.8). One study presented stories to elementary schoolers about a child who sees a TV commercial for an attractive product (Sheikh & Moleski, 1977). When asked if the child in the story would ask a parent to buy the product, nearly 60% of the children responded affirmatively. When asked what would happen if the parent said no, 33% of the children said the child in the story would feel sad, 23% said the child would be angry or hostile, and 16% said the child would persist in requesting the product. Only 23% indicated the child would be accepting of the decision.

Figure 2.8
SOURCE: Tribune Media Services, Inc. All rights reserved. Reprinted with permission.

According to mothers, children's efforts to influence purchasing occur most often for food items, especially cereals, snacks, and candy (Ward & Wackman, 1972). Coincidentally, those same products are among the most heavily advertised to children. Requesting a parent to purchase something does seem to decrease with age (Ward & Wackman, 1972), in part because as children get older, they have more of their own money to make independent decisions. Yet for expensive items, even adolescents can pester parents. In one study of 180 African American teens, 56% reported that they had had disagreements with parents over the purchase of athletic shoes, mostly over price (Lee & Browne, 1995). Interestingly, nearly three fourths of the teens spontaneously cited Michael Jordan as their favorite celebrity in shoe commercials, and almost half of the teens were wearing Nike shoes on the day of the interview.

Several studies have actually observed parents and children as they shop together in an effort to assess conflict more directly. In an early study, Galst and White (1976) observed 41 preschoolers with their mothers in a grocery store. The researchers documented an average of 15 purchase influence attempts (PIAs) by the child in a typical shopping trip, or one every 2 minutes! Most of the PIAs were for cereals and candy, and 45% of them were successful. In other words, the mother acquiesced to nearly half of the children's requests. In another observational study, Atkin (1978) found that open conflict occurred 65% of the time that a parent denied a child's request for a cereal in a supermarket.

One experiment creatively linked PIAs directly to advertising. Stoneman and Brody (1981) randomly assigned preschoolers to view a cartoon that contained six food commercials or no commercials at all. Immediately afterward, mothers were told to take their preschoolers to a nearby grocery store to buy a typical week's worth of groceries, purportedly as part of another study. Posing as clerks in the store, research assistants surreptitiously coded the interactions that occurred. Children who had been exposed to the food commercials engaged in significantly more purchase influence attempts than did children in the control group. Children exposed to the commercials also made more requests for those foods that were featured in the ads. In addition, the mothers' behavior was influenced by the commercials. Mothers of children who had seen the ads engaged in significantly more control strategies during the shopping trip, such as putting the item back on the shelf and telling the child no.

In sum, advertising can produce pressure on parents to buy products, which in turn can cause family conflict when such requests are denied. Research suggests that this type of discord is not just an American phenomenon. One cross-cultural study found that heavy television viewing among children is linked to higher parent-child conflict about purchases in Japan and Great Britain as well as in the United States (Robertson et al., 1989).

Materialism and Value Orientations

Critics worry that in addition to creating demand for certain products, advertising may contribute more generally to materialistic attitudes in our youth. Fox (1996) claims that "when kids are saturated in advertising, their appetites for products are stimulated. At the same time, kids desire the values that have been associated with those products—intangible values that, like sex appeal, are impossible to buy" (p. 20). Others argue that advertising should not be singled out for attack and that youthful consumerism is part of children's participation in a larger culture that has become rooted in commodities (Seiter, 1993).

Disentangling advertising from all the other forces that might foster materialism is difficult, especially because nearly all children are exposed to a world filled with toy stores, fast-food restaurants, movies, peer groups, and even schools, all of which promote consumer goods. One large survey of more than 800 adolescents found that heavy exposure to television was positively correlated with buying products for social acceptance, even after controlling for age, sex, socioeconomic status, and amount of family communication about consumption (Churchill & Moschis, 1979). In this same study, teens who reported watching a lot of TV also

Figure 2.9. Ads Taken From *Teen People* Magazine, June/July 2001

were more likely to associate possessions and money with happiness. Yet these patterns are only suggestive and do not permit firm causal conclusions. Materialistic youth could seek out advertising, advertising might cause materialism, or both. Clearly, longitudinal research is needed to ascertain whether heavy exposure to advertising during early childhood leads to more materialistic attitudes over time, even after controlling for other relevant socialization factors.

Another concern is whether advertising contributes to a preoccupation with physical appearance, especially among female adolescents. Teen magazines, in particular, are rife with ads featuring thin, attractive models (see Figure 2.9). Studies have found that female adolescents and college students do compare their physical attractiveness to models featured in advertising (Martin & Kennedy, 1993; Richins, 1991). Moreover, looking at ads of highly attractive models can temporarily affect self-esteem and even body image (Stice & Shaw, 1994), especially among girls who are encouraged to evaluate themselves (Martin & Gentry, 1997). In one experiment, adolescent girls who were exposed to a heavy dose of commercials emphasizing physical appearance were more likely to believe that being beautiful is an important characteristic and is necessary to attract men than were those in a control group exposed to other types of ads (Tan, 1979). Once again, longitudinal studies are needed to fully assess advertising's long-term contribution to young people's attitudes about beauty and physical attraction.

● PHASES OF CONSUMER BEHAVIOR DURING CHILDHOOD

Valkenburg and Cantor (2001) recently outlined four phases of consumer development in childhood, which provide a nice overview of much of the material covered in this chapter so far. The first phase, which they call "Feeling Wants and Preferences," characterizes infants and toddlers. During this phase, young children show distinct preferences for smells, colors, sounds, and objects, an important component of consumer behavior. Still, at this young age, children are primarily reactive rather than goal directed, so they are not capable of acting like true consumers.

The second phase, "Nagging and Negotiating," captures the preschool years. As we have noted above, preschoolers have difficulty distinguishing ads from programs and do not fully comprehend the intent of commercials. Consequently, Valkenburg and Cantor (2001) argue that marketing efforts have a strong impact on this age group. Because of the idea of centration (see Chapter 1), preschoolers are likely to gravitate toward products that are visually striking. They also want what they see immediately, so this age group is most likely to pester parents and to exhibit noncompliant and emotional behavior when they are denied something.

Phase 3, "Adventure and the First Purchase," characterizes the early elementary school years, between the ages of 5 and 8. Cognitive abilities are in transition here as children gradually consider more conceptual information, become more responsive to verbally presented information, and increase their attention span. But this age group can still be confused about the purpose of ads and can still respond strongly to perceptual cues. Children typically make their first solo purchase during this phase, becoming a bona fide consumer independent of a parent.

Phase 4, "Conformity and Fastidiousness," marks the tween years, from 8 to 12. The ability to critically evaluate information, compare products, and appreciate the selling intent of ads develops during this time. Because of their attention to detail and quality, many children become serious collectors of objects during this period. Tweens show a strong sensitivity to the norms and values of their peers, as well as to what older adolescents are buying and doing. Most tweens regularly visit different types of stores, making independent purchases and influencing house-hold buying practices. Valkenburg and Cantor (2001) argue that consumer skills continue to develop during adolescence, but by late elementary school, all the fundamentals of consumer behavior are in place (i.e., child shows preferences, can evaluate options, and can choose and purchase a product).

MARKETING STRATEGIES IN THE 21ST CENTURY ●

As youths' spending power continues to increase, marketers are constantly experi-menting with new ways to reach these young consumers. In this section, we will examine three techniques that are burgeoning as we enter the 21st century: multi-media toy franchises, marketing in schools, and online marketing.

Multimedia Toy Franchises

The promotion of toys that are based on popular programs is not a new phe-nomenon, as discussed earlier in this chapter. As early as 1969, the cartoon *Hot Wheels* was criticized as nothing more than a 30-minute commercial for Hot Wheels toys (Colby, 1993). Roughly 20 years later, the *Teenage Mutant Ninja Tur-tles* cartoon helped to sell more than $500 million worth of toy merchandise in 1990 alone (Rosenberg, 1992).

Nowadays, toy-based cartoons are quite common and can be even more suc-cessful. Consider the Pokémon craze. The 150 cute pocket-sized monsters origi-nated in Japan as characters in a Nintendo video game. In 1998, U.S. marketers simultaneously launched a TV cartoon series, trading cards, a video game, and toy merchandise. Later came party products, a Warner Brothers motion picture, a CD, children's apparel sold at J. C. Penney, kids' meal premiums at Burger King, and even Pokémon tournament leagues that meet weekly at Toys 'R' Us to play the video game (Annicelli, 1999; Brass, 1999; Jones, 2000). The *Pokémon* cartoon explicitly reinforces the idea that the best way to become cool is to collect as many monsters as possible. Apparently, children are convinced; in the United States alone, the Pokémon franchise was projected to pull in more than $2.8 billion in retail revenues in 2000 (*It's a Pokémon World,* 2000).

Due to their remarkable success, toy-based programs have been criticized as "animated sales catalogs masquerading as entertainment" (Waters & Uehling, 1985, p. 85). Such tactics do seem to thoroughly blur the differences between advertising and programming. Toy-based cartoons feature popular characters, slogans, and sound effects that are also employed in related commercials for the toys. Several studies reveal that the combination of a cartoon and related advertising can be very confusing for young children (Hoy, Young, & Mowen, 1986; Kunkel, 1988). For example, Wilson and Weiss (1992) found that 4- to 6-year-olds were less able to recognize an ad for a Beetlejuice toy or comprehend its selling intent when it was shown with a *Beetlejuice* cartoon than with an unrelated *Popeye* cartoon. Moreover, the confusion occurred regardless of whether the related *Beetlejuice* cartoon was immediately adjacent to the ad or separated from it by 5 minutes of filler material.

Interestingly, the evidence is mixed on whether airing ads together with related programming is a good marketing strategy. Some studies have found that this technique enhances children's desire for a product (Kunkel, 1988; Miller & Busch, 1979), whereas others have not (Hoy et al., 1986; Wilson & Weiss, 1992). Success presumably depends in part on the nature of the product as well as the popularity of the related cartoon.

Thus, as commercials increasingly resemble TV programs and programs spin off into movies, CDs, and computer software, the young child is likely to become even more confused about what advertising actually is. On occasion, even sophisticated consumers may feel bewildered or perhaps overwhelmed by these multimedia marketing endeavors.

Marketing in Schools

Commercialism in schools has soared in recent years, spurring much public debate about the ethics of such practices (Aidman, 1995; Richards, Wartella, Morton, & Thompson, 1998). Corporations are eager to partner with schools as a way to reach young consumers, who spend almost 20% of their time in the classroom. In turn, public schools often feel desperate to augment tight budgets, and corporate support offers one way to do so.

Four types of commercial practices can be found in various degrees across American schools (Consumers Union Education Services, 1995; Wartella & Jennings, 2001). First, marketers often advertise directly to students by placing ads on school billboards, buses, athletic scoreboards, and even in student newspapers and yearbooks. Second, corporations occasionally give away products or coupons to expose children to different brand names. For example, Minute Maid, McDonald's, and Pizza Hut have offered food coupons to students who meet their teachers' reading goals.

Third, corporations frequently sponsor fund-raisers to help schools afford new equipment, uniforms, or class trips. Students themselves become marketers in these efforts, approaching aunts and uncles, neighbors, and even parents' work colleagues. Pitching anything from poinsettia plants to gift wrap to frozen pizzas, students can earn prizes for themselves and money for their school. Fourth, marketers often create educational materials such as workbooks, brochures, and videos on specific curriculum topics. For instance, Kellogg publishes nutrition posters that give health information and also display the corporate logo and several Kellogg cereals. Unfortunately, one study found that nearly 80% of these corporate-sponsored materials contain biased or incomplete information (Consumers Union Education Services, 1995).

A fifth and more controversial form of commercialism in schools is Channel One, a 12-minute daily news program designed for middle and high school students. Introduced in 1990 by Whittle Communications, the program includes 10 minutes of originally produced news for teens and 2 minutes of advertising. Schools sign a 3-year contract that provides them with a satellite dish, two VCRs, television sets for each classroom, and all wiring and maintenance for the equipment. In exchange, a school agrees to have 90% of its students watch the program daily. More than 12,000 American middle and high schools have entered into this contractual arrangement (Smolkin, 1999).

Channel One has been challenged on several fronts (see Figures 2.10 and 2.11). Critics charge that the arrangement cedes control of the curriculum to outside parties, requires students to be a captive audience to ads, and exposes students to messages that run counter to nutritional lessons taught in school (Consumers Union Education Services, 1995). A study by Brand and Greenberg (1994) supports some of these concerns. The researchers found that compared with nonviewers, students exposed to Channel One gave more favorable ratings to products that were advertised during the newscast. Viewers also expressed more materialistic attitudes than nonviewers did. On the positive side, viewers do seem to learn more about news, particularly those events covered in the daily programs (Greenberg & Brand, 1993).

Unlike Channel One, a similar initiative in Canada, called Youth News Network (YNN), has had minimal success. The 12½-minute daily newscast, which includes 2½ minutes of ads, is shown in only about 15 schools across Canada. This corporate initiative, which promises audiovisual and computer equipment in exchange for the newscast, has been banned in every Catholic school in Canada and in 6 of the 13 provinces. A recent report by the Canadian Centre for Policy Alternatives concluded that

> having a corporate presence in the classroom is tantamount to giving such companies school time—and the public money which pays for that time—in which to advertise their products to kids. Our taxes are literally paying for the commercial targeting of

Figure 2.10

our students, and diverting time and money from their education. (Shaker, 2000, p. 19)

Today, more than 8 million American teens watch advertising on television each day in the classroom (Smolkin, 1999). Other students enter contests, receive curriculum materials, and are exposed to hallway ads that promote products. Some believe these arrangements represent innovative ways to support struggling schools (see Richards et al., 1998). Others view this growing trend as a violation of "the integrity of education" (Consumers Union Education Services, 1995). Regardless of which view is taken, such practices are likely to continue as marketers search for creative ways to reach youth.

Online Marketing to Children

Millions of American children go online each week, and there are countless Web sites to attract them (see Chapter 9). In fact, several lists exist to help parents and children identify Web sites designed just for young people. Berit's Best Sites for Children names the 25 most popular sites visited by kids, and among them are ones sponsored by Barbie, Disney, and Life Savers.

As anyone who goes online knows, the Internet is filled with advertising. In fact, Internet ad spending is projected to grow to $33 billion by 2004 (MarketResearch. com, 2001). Many online commercial messages are targeted directly to children. Banners lure children to commercial Web sites to advertise and sell products. And some Web sites for children blend commercialism with content in ways that make them indistinguishable (Center for Media Education, 1996). For example, the Crayola Web site offers the child user a variety of games to play, crafts to make, e-cards to send, and even contests to enter. Of course, it also sells Crayola products.

Unlike other media, the Internet also allows marketers to collect personal information from individuals to be used in promotional efforts, market research, and electronic commerce. And this makes parents worried. According to a national survey, 74% of parents with home Internet connections are concerned their children will give out personal information on the Net (Turow & Nir, 2000). Research suggests parents should be. One study of 166 Web sites designed for children found that nearly 60% requested personal information from the user such as name, e-mail address, and postal address (Cai & Gantz, 2000). Roughly 20% of those sites requesting information asked for a credit card number. Most alarming, two thirds of the sites requesting information failed to disclose that personal data would be sought or that parental permission should be obtained first.

Recognizing these problems, in 1998 Congress passed the Children's Online Privacy Protection Act. To be enforced by the Federal Trade Commission, the law requires that all Web sites targeted to children under 13 must have a prominent link to a privacy policy that clearly identifies how personal information is collected and used. Despite this ruling, some children's Web sites still do not post a privacy policy, and many that have one do not make the link very prominent or the policy itself very accessible or readable for parents (Center for Media Education, 2001; Turow, 2001).

Yet a privacy policy may not be enough to protect families. In a national survey of 10- to 17-year-olds, 31% reported that they had given out personal information to a Web site (Turow & Nir, 2000). Moreover, 45% of the youngsters said they would exchange personal information on the Web for a free gift, and 25% reported never having read a site's privacy policy. As long as marketers are free to collect information about users regardless of age, the Internet will be a relatively easy way to discover and try to influence the consumer preferences of youth.

REGULATION OF ADVERTISING TARGETED TO YOUTH ●

As described above, the Children's Online Privacy Protection Act illustrates that the federal government is indeed willing to set policies to protect young children from marketing. This willingness dates back to the early 1970s, when questions first arose concerning the fairness of advertising to young children. In this section, we give an overview of major efforts by the government as well as by the industry itself to regulate advertising to youth.

Government Regulation

In 1974, the first U.S. policy regarding children and advertising was issued by the Federal Communications Commission (FCC). The FCC, which is responsible for allocating and renewing licenses to broadcasters, explicitly acknowledged younger children's vulnerability to commercial messages and issued two guidelines that year. First, the overall amount of time that could be devoted to ads during children's programming was limited to 9.5 minutes per hour on weekends and 12 minutes per hour on weekdays (FCC, 1974). Second, stations were required to maintain a clear separation between program content and commercial messages during shows targeted to children. Three aspects of this separation principle were outlined: (a) separation devices, known as "bumpers," were mandated to clearly signal the beginning and end of a commercial break during children's shows; (b) host selling was prohibited, meaning that no program characters were allowed to sell products during commercials embedded in or directly adjacent to their show; and (c) program-length commercials, or the promotion of products within the body of a program, were forbidden.

Led by a group called Action for Children's Television (ACT), several public interest groups felt that the 1974 policy did not go far enough in protecting children. Out of frustration, they turned to the Federal Trade Commission (FTC) and pushed for a complete ban of all ads targeted to children too young to recognize commercial intent (FTC, 1978). The FTC considered the petition for several years, proposing rulings, holding hearings, and reviewing evidence. During this time, the broadcasting and advertising industries along with several major corporations lobbied heavily against such a ban (Kunkel & Watkins, 1987). In 1981, the FTC issued a final ruling acknowledging that children under age 7 "do not possess the cognitive ability to evaluate adequately child-oriented television advertising" and that because of this, such content represents a "legitimate cause for public concern" (pp. 2-4). Yet the FTC ultimately decided against a ban, asserting that it would economically threaten the very existence of children's programming.

The Reagan presidency helped turn the 1980s into a decade of deregulation. Responding to this trend, in 1984 the FCC relaxed its policies toward children's advertising in two ways. First, it revoked its earlier restrictions on the amount of advertising permissible during children's shows (FCC, 1984). In doing so, the FCC asserted that marketplace forces should be left alone to determine the appropriate levels of advertising. Critics have pointed out that if very young children are unable to recognize or be critical of ads, it is doubtful whether they as consumers can register complaints over too many commercials (Wilcox & Kunkel, 1996). Second, the FCC rescinded its earlier ban on program-length commercials, asserting

instead that they represented an innovative means of financing children's programming (FCC, 1984). Shortly after, toy-based programming flooded the broadcast schedule (Colby, 1993).

Out of increasing concern about children's television, Congress stepped in and
passed the Children's Television Act in 1990. The law mainly dealt with educational programming, but it also reinstated time limits on advertising to children.
The new limits are still in effect today and apply to broadcasting as well as cable,
permitting no more than 10.5 minutes of advertising per hour on weekends and 12
minutes per hour on weekdays during children's programming. As part of the law,
Congress also ordered the FCC to reconsider its lenient stance on program-length
commercials. One year later, the FCC decided to reinstate its earlier ban on such
content, but in doing so it more narrowly defined a program-length commercial as
"a program associated with a product in which commercials for that product are
aired" (FCC, 1991, p. 2117). Readers may recognize that this new definition is
essentially the same as host selling, a practice that has been prohibited since 1974.
In other words, the FCC's ban imposes nothing new; it continues to allow for toy-
based programs to promote products within the body of the show so long as
related commercials are not aired directly within or adjacent to that show.

Although the FTC and the FCC have openly recognized the vulnerability of
younger children, their policies reflect political compromises that also satisfy the
broadcasters and advertisers involved. In contrast to the United States, other industrialized nations have much stronger laws to protect children from marketing. For
example, Sweden does not allow any television advertising that directly targets
children under the age of 12 (Valkenburg, 2000). In Greece, commercials for toys
are banned until 10 p.m. on television, and in Belgium commercials are not
allowed during children's programming. Countries such as Australia, Canada, and
England forbid any advertising targeted to preschoolers (Kunkel, 2001). Given the
strong political forces that oppose such measures in the United States, a ban of any
type would be difficult to implement here. Yet as recently as 2000, a prestigious
coalition of more than 50 scholars, health professionals, and child advocates sent a
letter to the three presidential candidates urging them to establish policies to dras-
tically reduce the marketing aimed at American children (Center for Media Education, 2000).

Industry Self-Regulation

Public criticism and threats of government action have forced the industries
involved to engage in efforts to self-regulate. As early as 1961, the National Association of Broadcasters (NAB), a trade association representing the industry,
adopted its own code of guidelines that included provisions about advertising to
children. However, the code was completely eliminated for legal reasons in the
early 1980s as part of a federal antitrust case.

Today, the main effort to self-regulate comes from the advertising industry itself. In 1974, the Children's Advertising Review Unit (CARU) was created by the Council of Better Business Bureaus. It is probably no accident that CARU came into being around the same time that the FCC issued its first policy regarding children's advertising. CARU's job is to review advertising and marketing material directed to children in all media. As part of this review process, CARU has established an extensive set of guidelines for advertising targeted to those under 12 years of age. The guidelines offer recommendations on topics such as the presentation of products, disclaimers and disclosures, premiums, and the use of program characters as endorsers (CARU, 2000). Some of the guidelines explicitly recognize developmental considerations, such as children's limited vocabulary and difficulty evaluating the truthfulness of information (CARU, 2000).

CARU actively monitors a certain number of ads each year, but it relies heavily on voluntary compliance by advertisers. One study of more than 10,000 ads directed at children found a high rate of overall adherence to the CARU guidelines (Kunkel & Gantz, 1993). Still, some of the guidelines are rather vague, and none of them question the overall legitimacy of targeting young children with advertisements (Kunkel, 2001). In other words, CARU is still primarily a political effort to ward off more formal regulation, and it is fundamentally supportive of the major manufacturing firms that underwrite this organization.

● TEACHING ADVERTISING LITERACY

Recognizing the difficulty of changing the advertising environment in the United States, some have called for efforts to teach children how to be more critical consumers. As it turns out, even older children who clearly recognize the selling intent of ads do not typically critique commercials spontaneously while viewing them (Brucks, Armstrong, & Goldberg, 1988; Derbaix & Bree, 1997). In other words, their general skepticism toward ads is not always activated when they actually watch TV. One study suggests that a simple cue or reminder can trigger a viewer's cognitive defenses, raising the number of counterarguments that older children produce during exposure to commercials (Brucks et al., 1988).

Other studies have explored more formal training procedures to help children deal with advertising. Roberts, Christenson, Gibson, Mooser, and Goldberg (1980) compared two 15-minute instructional films designed to teach children about commercials: *The Six Billion $$$ Sell*, which focused on tricks and appeals used in ads, and *Seeing Through Commercials*, which focused on how ads are made. Second, third, and fifth graders were randomly assigned to view one of the two films or a control film unrelated to advertising. Results revealed that the treatment films increased children's general skepticism toward advertising as well as their ability to be critical of specific ads. The strongest effects were observed for *The Six Billion $$$ Sell*, the film that detailed specific strategies and showed ad examples. Moreover, the youngest participants learned the most from the films, the same children who initially were far more accepting of advertising.

Christenson (1982) used excerpts from *The Six Billion $$$ Sell* to create a 3-minute public service announcement (PSA) about the nature of advertising. One group of children saw the PSA before watching cartoons embedded with ads, whereas another group simply watched the content without the PSA. The insertion of the PSA increased first and second graders' comprehension of the selling intent of ads, and it enhanced skepticism about ads among this younger age group as well as among fifth and sixth graders. Furthermore, the PSA actually lowered children's taste ratings of two food products advertised during the cartoons.

More traditional instruction also can teach children about advertising. One study found that half-hour training sessions over the course of several days were effective in teaching children as young as 6 how to detect persuasive tricks and strategies in ads (Peterson & Lewis, 1988). In another study, Donohue, Henke, and Meyer (1983) compared two types of instruction: role-playing, which had children assume the role of an advertiser to create a commercial, and traditional, which had children watch TV ads and discuss the purpose and nature of commercials. Compared with a control group, both treatments helped first graders to better discriminate ads from programs and to be more skeptical of commercials. However, only the traditional instruction increased children's understanding of the persuasive intent of advertising.

It would be a mistake to conclude, however, that formal instruction is the only way to help children become discriminating consumers (see Figure 2.11). Most parents report that they talk to their children about commercials, and such discussion can improve younger children's understanding of the nature and purpose of advertising (Ward et al., 1977). Furthermore, teens who talk with their parents about consumption show a higher knowledge of prices (Moore & Stephens, 1975) and more discriminating behavior when making purchases (Moschis & Churchill, 1978). Finally, critically discussing commercials with a parent can reduce children's desire for an advertised product (Prasad, Rao, & Sheikh, 1978). As with other types of media content (see Chapter 11), parental mediation can play an important role in preparing children for their daily encounters with commercial messages.

CONCLUSION ●

Children are literally born to become consumers in the United States. They typically visit their first store at the tender age of 2 months, and by the time they reach 2

Figure 2.11

years, most have made a request for a product (McNeal, 1999). Their bedrooms are filled with Disney characters, designer crib sheets, and BabyGap clothes, and their playrooms are stuffed with all kinds of toys. By the time children reach preschool, they are watching their favorite toy-based cartoons, seeing several hours' worth of TV advertising each week, and making regular trips with a parent to the grocery store, fast-food restaurants, and Toys 'R' Us. All of this exposure comes at a time when children are very naive about commercial messages and trusting of their content.

As children reach the early elementary school years, they gradually learn about the motives behind advertising and the tactics used in commercials. Some of this knowledge helps them to be more skeptical of such messages. Yet keeping these cognitive defenses in mind is not always easy when confronted by a slick and highly entertaining commercial suggesting that everyone else has a particular new toy. Certainly, television is not the only source of these desires. School-aged children may be most vulnerable when commercialism invades their classroom, becoming part of the decor or even the curriculum itself. And spending time online may confuse children even more as marketing becomes intimately intertwined with content.

In the face of all this commercialism, some critics have argued that advertising is inherently unfair to young children and ought to be eliminated from content targeted to this age group. An opposite position holds that children will never learn to be consumers unless they are exposed to commercial messages. A third intermediary position is that parents and educators need to develop ways to help youth become more critical consumers. As children's discretionary income grows and they spend more time surfing the Web, wandering in shopping malls, and watching TV alone in their bedrooms, early training in critical consumer skills seems vitally important.

Exercises

1. Find a magazine advertisement targeted to children. What type of product is being advertised? Does it fit into one of the top four categories of children's ads found on television (see the Kunkel & Gantz, 1992, study above)? What is the main appeal used in this ad to persuade children? Is there any disclaimer offered in the ad? If so, is it likely to be noticed or understood by a child? Is there anything in the ad that might be misleading or confusing for a 5-year-old child? For a 10-year-old child?

2. Find a magazine ad targeted to teens. What type of product is being advertised? Do you see evidence of gender or racial stereotyping in the ad? What is the main appeal used in the ad? Is there anything about the ad that might make teens feel self-conscious about their own physical appearance?

3. Think about your childhood. What is the first toy purchase you remember being disappointed about? How old were you? Did you buy the toy with your own money? Did advertising have anything to do with your disappointment? How did your mother or father respond to your disappointment? Did your parents discuss advertising with you?

4. Go to the Children's Advertising Review Unit (CARU) Web site: www.bbb.org/advertising/caruguid.asp. Examine the guidelines for advertising to children. Find two guidelines that are clearly worded and easy for an advertiser to follow. Now find two guidelines that are vague and difficult to follow. Of the ones listed, which guideline do you think is violated most often in children's advertising?

5. In 2001, Sweden launched a movement to ban television advertising aimed at children in all member states of the European Union. Sweden itself has had

such a ban in place for the past 10 years, yet other countries in Europe are not so supportive of the idea. Do you think such a ban is a good idea in the United States? Why or why not? Instead of an all-out ban, can you think of any other types of regulation of children's advertising that might be easier to enact in the United States?

6. Find two popular Web sites for children, one that is commercial and one that is not (check Berit's Best Sites for Children: www.beritsbest.com). For example, you could compare the Barbie Web site with a site called Maths Year 2000, which is designed to get children interested in math. How much advertising is on each Web site? Are there features of the Web sites that look like content but are actually advertising? Do the sites ask children for personal information? If so, is there a privacy policy? Critique the marketing strategies used in each site, thinking about a 10-year-old user without a parent in the room.

7. The 1994 Disney movie *The Lion King* was enormously successful and spawned numerous tie-in products and services. List as many examples as you can think of that reflect how this movie has been commercialized across different media. Did you spend any money on the movie or its spin-off products? When you were a child, was there any movie you can remember that was similarly successful? What has changed in the past 20 years regarding the promotion of movies and their characters?

8. You are a principal of a large high school in a rural area. Your school band has been invited to perform in Washington, D.C., and your basketball team is ranked highly in the state. But the band desperately needs new uniforms and the basketball team needs new athletic equipment, both of which are not in your budget. You are approached by the head of B & W Marketing, who offers you $100,000 in exchange for placing a select number of advertisements in school hallways. What would you do? What factors should you consider in making your decision?

CHAPTER 3

MEDIA VIOLENCE

True, media violence is not likely to turn an otherwise fine child into a violent criminal. But, just as every cigarette one smokes increases a little bit the likelihood of a lung tumor someday, every violent show one watches increases just a little bit the likelihood of behaving more aggressively in some situation.

—Psychologists Brad J. Bushman and L. Rowell Huesmann
(2001, p. 248)

America's young people are being exposed to increasing amounts of media violence through television, movies, video games, and popular music. . . . One of this year's best-selling music CDs contains a song in which the protagonist lovingly puts his baby to bed and engages in a fight with the child's mother, which ends in him slitting her throat, her screams of fear subsiding in the gurgle of blood.

—Donald E. Cook, M.D.,
President of the American Academy of Pediatrics (2000)

Television is not a schoolhouse for criminal behavior. . . . Viewers turn to this light entertainment for relief, not for instruction. Video action exists, and is resorted to, to get material out of minds rather than to put things into them. . . . Television violence is good for people.

—Jib Fowles,
author of *The Case for Television Violence* (1999, pp. 53, 118)

There are certain milieus, which by their very nature, are violent. If you are to depict those events, then you have to depict violence. If you tell that kind of story without violence, then you are not being honest.

—TV producer Christopher Crowe, quoted in the *Los Angeles Times*
(Braxton, 1991, p. F1)

Violence in America threatens the very fabric of contemporary society. At least 2.5 million people are victims of violent injury each year (U.S. Department of Justice, 1998), and homicide is the second leading cause of death among 15- to 24-year-olds (National Center for Injury Prevention and Control, 2000a, 2000b). Every day, 13 children in this country die as a result of gun violence (Office of the Surgeon General, 2001). Despite a drop in violent crime in the 1990s, the United States still ranks first among industrialized nations in youth homicides (Snyder & Sickmund, 1999). And the recent deluge of shootings in American schools has shocked adults and frightened many children across this country ("Speaking Out," 2000). Responding to these school tragedies, Attorney General John Ashcroft has argued that there is an "ethic of violence" among America's youth ("Ashcroft Blames 'Culture,'" 2001).

As violence permeates our society, government officials, health professionals, educators, and scientists struggle to understand the complex causes of human aggression. To be sure, no single factor propels a person to become violent. Neurological and hormonal abnormalities (Berman, Gladue, & Taylor, 1993; Miles & Carey, 1997), deficiencies in cognitive functioning (Dodge & Frame, 1982), and even parental punishment (Stormshak, Bierman, McMahon, Lengua, & Conduct Problems Prevention Research Group, 2000) have been linked to aggression. So too have social forces such as poverty, drugs, and the availability of guns (Archer, 1994; Guerra, Huesmann, Tolan, VanAcker, & Eron, 1995). Another factor that continually emerges in public debates about violence is the role of the mass media. Public opinion polls indicate that 75% of American adults believe that televised violence contributes to real-world crime and aggression (Lacayo, 1995), and a comparable proportion feels that Hollywood should do more to reduce violence in entertainment programming (Lowry, 1997).

Are the mass media part of the problem, or do they merely reflect the violence that is occurring in society? Is media violence chiefly a form of entertainment that dates back to the ancient Greeks, or is it a cultural tool that serves to legitimate violent means of power and social control? There are many opinions about the topic

Figure 3.1

of media violence, and we cannot possibly resolve all of the issues in a single chapter. Consistent with the approach taken throughout this book, we will focus primarily on social scientific research regarding media violence and youth.

There are literally hundreds of published studies on the impact of media violence. Researchers who have comprehensively reviewed these studies argue quite conclusively that media violence can have antisocial effects (Comstock, 1991a; Strasburger, 1993). In recent years, several professional organizations also have examined the evidence and concurred that TV violence is harmful to children (e.g., American Medical Association, 1996; Centers for Disease Control and Prevention [CDC], 1991). In fact, a 2001 report on youth violence by the Surgeon General states that "research to date justifies sustained efforts to curb the adverse effects of media violence on youths" (*Youth Violence,* 2001).

This chapter will begin by addressing the issue of how much violence exists in American media. Then we turn to the question of whether media violence appeals to young people. Next we will give an overview of the research regarding three potential harmful effects of exposure to media violence: (a) the learning of aggressive attitudes and behaviors, (b) desensitization, and (c) fear. As an important contrast, we will present some of the views of critics who disagree with this research.

We will conclude with brief sections on guns and the media, suicide and the media, a cross-cultural look at violence in Japan, and prosocial effects of media violence on youth.

● HOW VIOLENT ARE AMERICAN MEDIA?

American television and movies provide young people with a relentless diet of violent content. Conservative estimates indicate that the average child or teenager in this country views 1,000 murders, rapes, and aggravated assaults per year on television alone (Rothenberg, 1975). A more recent review by the American Psychological Association puts this figure at 10,000 per year—or approximately 200,000 by the time a child reaches the teenage years (Huston et al., 1992). This statistic may be even higher if a child concentrates his or her viewing to certain channels and types of programming, as we will see below.

In one of the earliest efforts to quantify violence on television, George Gerbner and his colleagues analyzed a week of programming each year from 1967 until the late 1980s (e.g., Gerbner, Gross, Morgan, & Signorielli, 1980b; Gerbner, Gross, Signorielli, Morgan, & Jackson-Beeck, 1979). Looking at the three major broadcast networks, the researchers found a great deal of consistency over time, with roughly 70% of prime-time programs and 90% of children's programs containing some violence (see Signorielli, 1990). The rate of violence was fairly steady too, with 5 violent actions per hour featured in prime time and 20 actions per hour in children's shows (see Figure 3.2).

More recently, the National Television Violence Study assessed violence on broadcast as well as cable television (Smith et al., 1998; Wilson, Kunkel, et al., 1997, 1998). In this large-scale content analysis, researchers randomly selected programming during a 9-month period across 23 channels from 6:00 a.m. to 11:00 p.m., 7 days a week. This method produced a composite week of television consisting of more than 2,500 hours of content each year. For 3 consecutive years (1996-98), the researchers found that a steady 60% of all programs contained some violence. However, violence varied a great deal by channel type. More than 80% of the programs on premium cable channels featured violence, whereas fewer than 20% of the programs on public broadcasting did (see Figure 3.3).

But violence in the media is not all the same. To illustrate, compare a film such as *Schindler's List*, about the brutality of the Holocaust, with a movie such as *The Terminator*, which features a cool-looking and ruthless robot played by Arnold Schwarzenegger. One movie shows the tragic consequences of brutality, whereas the other seems to celebrate or at least condone violence. The National Television Violence Study assessed how often violence is shown in a way that can be educational to viewers. Despite the overall pervasiveness of violence, less than 5% of

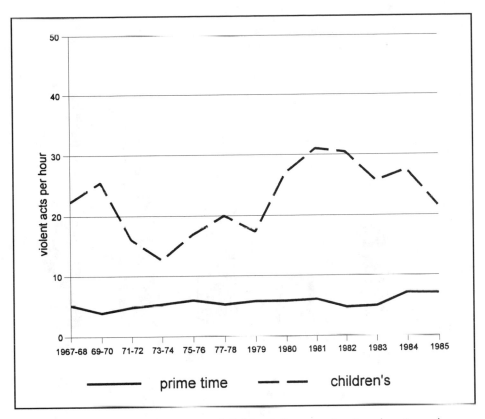

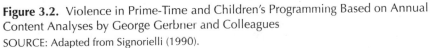

Figure 3.2. Violence in Prime-Time and Children's Programming Based on Annual
Content Analyses by George Gerbner and Colleagues
SOURCE: Adapted from Signorielli (1990).

violent programs featured an anti-violence theme across the 3 years of the study
(Smith et al., 1998).

The researchers also examined contextual features of violence such as who
commits the aggression, whether the violence is rewarded or punished, and
whether it results in negative consequences. The study drew several conclusions
from the findings:

Violence on television is frequently glamorized. Nearly 40% of the violent
incidents were perpetrated by "good" characters who can serve as role
models for viewers. In addition, a full 71% of violent scenes contained no
remorse, criticism, or penalty for violence.

Violence on television is frequently sanitized. Close to half of the violent incidents on television showed no physical harm or pain to the victim. Furthermore, less than 20% of the violent programs portrayed the long-term
negative repercussions of violence for family and friends of the victim.

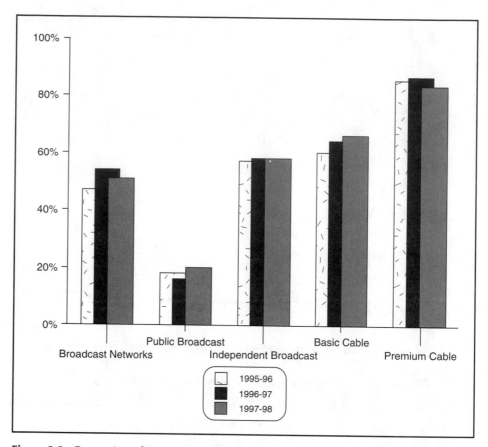

Figure 3.3. Proportion of Programs Containing Violence by Channel Type
SOURCE: Adapted from Smith et al. (1998).

Violence on television is often trivialized. More than half of the violent incidents featured intense forms of aggression that would be deadly if they were to occur in real life. Yet despite such serious aggression, 40% of the violent scenes on television included some type of humor.

As we will see below, all of these contextual features increase the chances that media violence will have a harmful effect on the audience.

Of course, the patterns outlined here characterize all programming taken together, not necessarily the shows that young people spend most of their time viewing. In subsequent analyses of the National Television Violence Study sample, researchers looked specifically at two genres that are popular among youth: programs targeted specifically to children under 12 (Wilson, Smith, et al., in press) and music videos (Smith & Boyson, in press).

In programs targeted to children, nearly all of which are cartoons, violence is far more prevalent. For example, roughly 7 out of 10 children's shows contained

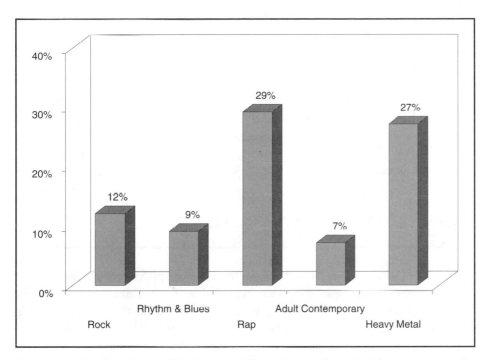

Figure 3.4. The Prevalence of Violence in Different Types of Music Videos
SOURCE: Adapted from Smith and Boyson (in press).

some violence, whereas 6 out of 10 nonchildren's shows did (Wilson, Smith, et al., in press). Furthermore, a typical hour of children's programming contained 14 different violent incidents, or 1 incident every 4 minutes. In contrast, nonchildren's programming featured about 6 violent incidents per hour, or 1 every 12 minutes. The researchers also found that children's programs were substantially more likely than other types of programming to depict unrealistically low levels of harm to victims compared with what would happen in real life. This pattern is particularly problematic for young children under the age of 7 who have difficulty distinguishing reality from fantasy (see below) and may assume such aggression is harmless. Finally, when children's shows were divided into categories, superhero cartoons such as *Exosquad* and *Spiderman* as well as slapstick cartoons such as *Animaniacs* and *Road Runner* were far more saturated with violence than were social-relationship cartoons such as *Care Bears* and *Rugrats* (Wilson, Smith, et al., in press). Magazine-formatted shows such as *Barney, Blue's Clues,* and *Bill Nye the Science Guy* rarely contained any violence at all.

Looking at music videos, which are particularly popular with preteens and teens, the overall prevalence of violence is quite low (Smith & Boyson, in press). In fact, in a typical week of television, only 15% of all videos featured on BET, MTV, and VH-1 contained violence. However, violence varied by music genre. As seen in Figure 3.4, rap and heavy metal videos were more likely to contain violence than other genres were. In fact, nearly one in three rap videos featured physical aggression. Also, the researchers found more violence on BET than on the other two channels, in part because BET features more rap.

The statistics presented here demonstrate what many adults increasingly recognize—there is a great deal of violence on American television. And today, there are far more channels available on which to find it. Furthermore, much of this violence is portrayed in formulaic ways that glamorize, sanitize, and trivialize aggression. Finally, violence is particularly prevalent in many of the very programs that are targeted to younger viewers.

● DOES MEDIA VIOLENCE ATTRACT YOUTH?

Writers and producers often claim that there would be less violence in the media if people would stop being attracted to it. Certainly we can think of many films and television shows that have drawn huge audiences and are brimming with violence. Slasher films are an example of violent content that has been extremely popular among teenagers. And the success of *Mighty Morphin Power Rangers*, the *Powerpuff Girls*, and even *Pokémon* demonstrates that violent programming can be popular with children too.

But does violence ensure that a movie or TV show will be appealing? One way to answer this question is to look at viewership statistics. Hamilton (1998) analyzed Nielsen ratings for more than 2,000 prime-time TV movies airing on the four major broadcast networks between 1987 and 1993. Controlling for factors such as the channel and time the movie aired, the popularity of the program preceding the movie, and the amount of advertising in *TV Guide*, he found that movies about murder or about family crime did in fact have higher household ratings. He also found that films explicitly described in *TV Guide* as "violent" attracted higher viewership as measured by household ratings. Yet despite all the factors Hamilton controlled for, there are still many differences among movies that could account for their varying popularity.

Other researchers have exposed viewers to different programs to determine whether those with violence are rated as more appealing (Diener & Woody, 1981; Greenberg & Gordon, 1972). Even with this methodology, it is difficult to tease out the role that violence plays in enhancing appeal given that programs differ on so many other dimensions. What is needed is a controlled study that varies the level of violence while holding all other program features constant. Berry, Gray, and Donnerstein (1999) did just that. In a series of three experiments, the researchers left a movie intact or cut specific scenes of graphic violence from it. Across all three studies, undergraduates rated the cut versions as less violent than the uncut versions. The presence of violence also influenced enjoyment, but the findings dif-

TABLE 3.1 Top Programs Among Children Ages 2-11: 2000-2001 Broadcast Season

Rank	Program	Channel	Genre
Saturday morning			
1	*Pokémon2*	WB	Cartoon
2	*X-Men*	WB	Cartoon
3	*Disney's Saturday Morning*	ABC	Cartoon
4	*Digimon: Digital Monsters*	FOX	Cartoon
5	*Static Shock*	WB	Cartoon
6	*Jackie Chan Adventures*	WB	Cartoon
7	*Cardcaptors*	WB	Cartoon
8	*Digimon (10:30 a.m.)*	FOX	Cartoon
9	*Digimon (10 a.m.)*	FOX	Cartoon
10	*Digimon (9:30 a.m.)*	FOX	Cartoon
All day parts			
1	*Survivor II*	CBS	Reality/adventure
2	*Wonderful World of Disney*	CBS	Movie
3	*Malcolm in the Middle (8:30 p.m.)*	FOX	Family sitcom
4	*Simpsons*	FOX	Animated family
5	*Pokémon2*	WB	Cartoon
6	*King of the Hill*	FOX	Animated family
7	*Malcolm in the Middle (8 p.m.)*	FOX	Family sitcom
8	*X-Men*	WB	Cartoon
9	*Disney's Saturday Morning*	ABC	Cartoon
10	*Digimon: Digital Monsters*	FOX	Cartoon

NOTE: Rankings are based on national ratings from Nielsen Media Research for the broadcast season from 10/2/2000 to 5/23/2001. Used with permission.

fered by the sex of the student. In contrast to what Hamilton (1998) found, removing violence from a full-length movie actually increased women's enjoyment of the content but had no impact on men's ratings of enjoyment.

The evidence is similarly mixed for children. In one random survey of parents in Madison, Wisconsin, nearly 30% named the *Mighty Morphin Power Rangers* as their elementary schoolers' favorite TV show (Cantor & Nathanson, 1997). Nevertheless, the family situation comedy *Full House* was cited as a favorite more often. A look at Nielsen ratings reveals that violent cartoons such as *Digimon: Digital Monsters* and *X-Men* are quite popular among 2- to 11-year-olds, especially during the Saturday morning time block (see Table 3.1). However, family sitcoms such as *Malcolm in the Middle* and reality shows such as *Survivor II* rank high when all times of the day are considered.

These types of divergent patterns have led several researchers to conclude that violence is not necessarily always attractive (Cantor, 1998a; Goldstein, 1999; Zillmann, 1998). Instead, the appeal of violence seems to depend on several factors, including the nature of the aggression involved. For example, undergraduates who were exposed to a graphic documentary-style film portraying the bludgeoning of a monkey's head or the slaughtering of steer uniformly found the content disgusting, and most chose to turn the television off before the program ended (Haidt, McCauley, & Rozin, 1994). On the other hand, brutal violence against a vicious villain who deserves to be punished can be enjoyable (see Zillmann, 1998).

The appeal of violence not only depends on its form but also on the type of viewer involved. A large body of research documents that there are sex differences in attraction to violence (see Cantor, 1998a). Compared with girls, boys are more likely to enjoy violent cartoons (Cantor & Nathanson, 1997), select violent fairy-tale books (Collins-Standley, Gan, Yu, & Zillmann, 1996), prefer violent video games (Funk, Buchman, & Germann, 2000), and play with violent toys (Servin, Bohlin, & Berlin, 1999). Various theories have been posited for these patterns, some focusing on gender-role socialization and others on biological differences between the sexes (see Oliver, 2000). Nevertheless, greater attraction to media violence among males is not merely a childhood phenomenon—it persists into adolescence and adulthood (Hamilton, 1998; Johnston, 1995).

Certain viewers possess personalities that seem to draw them to media violence as well. Zuckerman (1979) has argued that individuals vary in their need for arousal and that those high on "sensation seeking" will generally seek out novel and stimulating activities. Indeed, studies show that sensation seeking does predict exposure to violent television shows among adolescents and adults (Aluja-Fabregat, 2000; Krcmar & Greene, 1999). Moreover, sensation seeking is positively related to the enjoyment of graphic horror films (Tamborini & Stiff, 1987; Zuckerman & Litle, 1986). High sensation seeking among teens has even been linked to a preference for listening to heavy metal music (Arnett, 1995).

Finally, children who are more aggressive themselves seem to prefer violent television. In one survey, parents who rated their children as aggressive also rated them as more interested in violent cartoons (Cantor & Nathanson, 1997). A similar pattern has been documented among adolescents. In a study of eighth graders, boys who were rated as more aggressive by teachers also watched more violent films (Aluja-Fabregat, 2000). Huesmann and Eron (1986a) have found longitudinal evidence showing that more aggressive children seek out more violent television programs over time. Fenigstein (1979) and others (Cantor & Nathanson, 1997) speculate that aggressive people use violent scenes in the media to understand and justify their own behaviors.

To summarize, there is good deal of evidence supporting the idea that violence sells. But a closer look at the data suggests that it is not that simple. Nonviolent themes in programming can attract large audiences too. However, given that nearly two out of three programs on television contain some violence (Smith et al., 1998), there are simply fewer options available if someone is seeking nonviolent content. Yet it is not enough to think of violence in a unidimensional way as either present or absent. Certain forms of violence seem to be more popular than others. In addition, particular individuals enjoy aggressive portrayals more than others do. To complicate matters further, Cantor (1998a) speculates that there may be a relationship between an individual's personality and the types of violence that are most appealing. For example, highly anxious children may seek out portrayals in which good wins over evil, whereas an aggressive bully may enjoy a good TV battle regardless of the characters involved or the outcome. In other words, more research is needed on the types of violent messages that are most appealing and on the types of youth who seek out this content.

CAN MEDIA VIOLENCE LEAD TO AGGRESSION? ●

Undoubtedly, the single issue that has received most attention with regard to the media is whether violent content can lead to aggressive behavior. No researcher today would argue that the media are the sole or even the most important cause of aggressive behavior in youth. Yet there is strong agreement among social scientists that extensive exposure to media violence can *contribute* to aggressiveness in individuals (see Friedrich-Cofer & Huston, 1986; Huston et al., 1992; Smith & Donnerstein, 1998). This section will begin with an overview of the research evidence that has been brought to bear on this issue. Next we will present three theoretical perspectives that can help explain the relationship between media violence and aggression. The section will conclude with a discussion of who is most at risk for learning aggressive attitudes and behaviors from the media.

Experimental Studies

Some of the earliest evidence linking media violence to aggression comes from laboratory studies of children in controlled settings. In a series of classic experiments, Bandura and his colleagues exposed nursery school children to a filmed model who engaged in violent behaviors, often directed against a plastic, inflatable Bobo doll or punching bag (Bandura, Ross, & Ross, 1961, 1963a, 1963b). Afterward, children were taken to a playroom that contained a number of toys including a Bobo doll, and their own behaviors were observed from behind a one-way mirror. The purpose of such research was to investigate the circumstances under which children would learn and imitate novel aggressive acts they had seen on film. The researchers consistently found that children who were exposed to a violent model were more likely to act aggressively than were children in control groups who had not viewed such violence (Bandura et al., 1961, 1963b). Furthermore, children were more likely to imitate a violent model who had been rewarded with cookies than one who had been punished. In fact, children generally imitated the model so long as no punishment occurred, suggesting that the absence of punishment can serve as a tacit reward or sanction for such behavior (Bandura, 1965).

Bandura and his colleagues also found that children could learn novel aggressive responses as easily from a cartoon-like figure, a "Cat Lady," for example, as from a human adult (Bandura et al., 1963a). This finding clearly implicates Saturday morning TV as an unhealthy reservoir of violence. Subsequent studies using similar procedures revealed other aspects of imitation. For example, children exposed to televised aggressive sequences could reproduce the behaviors they had seen up to 6 to 8 months later (Hicks, 1965). In addition, preschoolers would aggress against a human adult dressed as a clown just as readily as they would a Bobo doll (Hanratty, O'Neal, & Sulzer, 1972; Savitsky, Rogers, Izard, & Liebert, 1971). This finding helped to undercut the criticism that attacking an inflatable is merely play behavior and not akin to real aggression.

Experimental studies have looked at older age groups too. For instance, research shows that adolescents and even adults who are exposed to television violence in laboratory settings will engage in increased aggression (Berkowitz & Geen, 1967; Berkowitz & Rawlings, 1963).

However, the experimental evidence has been criticized on several methodological grounds (Fowles, 1999; Freedman, 1984, 1986). Laboratory studies often (a) employ unrealistic or "play" measures of aggression, (b) are conducted in artificial viewing situations, (c) involve adult experimenters who willingly show violence on TV in a way that may seem to be condoning aggression, and (d) are able to assess only short-term effects of exposure. According to Fowles (1999), "Viewing in the laboratory setting is involuntary, public, choiceless, intense, uncomfortable, and single-minded. . . . Laboratory research has taken the viewing experience and turned it inside out so that the viewer is no longer in charge" (p. 27).

To overcome some of these limitations, researchers have conducted field experiments in nonlaboratory settings with more realistic measures of aggression (Friedrich & Stein, 1973; Josephson, 1987). In one early study, 3- to 5-year-old children were randomly assigned to watch violent or nonviolent TV shows for a period of 11 days at their school (Steuer, Applefield, & Smith, 1971). Children in the violent viewing condition displayed significantly more physical aggression against their peers (e.g., hitting, kicking, throwing objects) during play periods than did children in the nonviolent TV group.

More recently, researchers exposed elementary schoolers to a single episode of the *Mighty Morphin Power Rangers* and then observed verbal and physical aggression in the classroom (Boyatzis, Matillo, & Nesbitt, 1995). Compared with a control group, children and particularly boys who had watched the violent TV program committed significantly more intentional acts of aggression inside the classroom, such as hitting, kicking, shoving, and insulting a peer. In fact, for every aggressive act perpetrated by children in the control group, there were seven aggressive acts committed by children who had seen the *Power Rangers*. Notably, these types of bullying behaviors are no longer seen as part of normal development and have been linked to poor social and emotional adjustment as well as failure in school (Nansel et al., 2001).

With regard to the *Power Rangers*, the Boyatzis et al. (1995) study reveals that the prosocial message delivered at the end of each episode in this program is not nearly as salient to children as the perpetual violence that the superheroes commit. At least one other study has demonstrated that moral lessons on television are relatively ineffective when they are couched in violence (Liss, Reinhardt, & Fredriksen, 1983).

In general, controlled experiments dating back to the 1960s clearly demonstrate that media violence can *cause* short-term increases in aggression in some children. Moreover, this effect has been found with various age groups and in laboratory as well as more naturalistic studies. But such evidence is still limited in that it points only to immediate effects that may not persist much beyond the viewing situation. In addition, most experiments involve small samples of children or teens who may or may not be representative of young people in general.

Correlational Studies

In the 1970s, a number of investigators surveyed large populations of children and teenagers to determine if those who were heavy viewers of TV violence also were more aggressive. As an example, one study surveyed 2,300 junior and senior high school students in Maryland and asked them to list their four favorite programs, which were then analyzed for violent content (McIntyre & Teevan, 1972). Measures of aggression were compiled from a self-reported checklist of activities, using five scales that ranged from aggressive acts (e.g., fighting at school) to serious delinquency (involvement with the law). Results revealed that children whose favorite programs were more violent also were higher in overall aggressive and delinquent behavior.

Other studies used slightly different measures of aggression, including peer ratings (McLeod, Atkin, & Chaffee, 1972a, 1972b) and self-reports of willingness to use violence in hypothetical situations (Dominick & Greenberg, 1972). Across different samples in different regions of the country, the findings were remarkably consistent. Higher exposure to TV violence was positively associated with higher levels of aggressive behavior (Belson, 1978; Dominick & Greenberg, 1972; McLeod et al., 1972a, 1972b; Robinson & Bachman, 1972). Furthermore, the relationship held up even after controlling for factors such as parental education, school achievement, socioeconomic status, and overall amount of television viewing (McLeod et al., 1972a, 1972b; Robinson & Bachman, 1972).

The large and often representative samples in these studies suggest that the causal effects documented in experimental studies can be generalized to the real world. However, the problem with correlational studies is that we cannot be certain about which variable came first. TV violence could be causing an increase in aggression. Alternatively, youth who are already aggressive could be seeking out violent content. To disentangle the direction of causality, longitudinal studies are needed.

Longitudinal Studies

In the past several decades, social scientists have increasingly moved toward longitudinal studies, which involve surveying the same group of individuals at repeated intervals over time. This type of design permits a researcher to test the cumulative effects of exposure to the media. It also provides a test of the "chicken and egg" quandary: Does violence in the media lead to aggression, or do aggressive people seek out such content?

In one of the most impressive longitudinal studies, Leonard Eron, Rowell Huesmann, and their colleagues tested the same sample of children, originally from upstate New York, over a 22-year period (Eron, Huesmann, Lefkowitz, & Walder, 1972; Huesmann, 1986; Huesmann, Eron, Lefkowitz, & Walder, 1984; Lefkowitz, Eron, Walder, & Huesmann, 1972). The researchers measured television viewing habits and aggressive behavior at three different points in time: when the participants were 8, 19, and 30 years of age. As seen in Figure 3.5, the results revealed that among boys, the relationship between viewing TV violence in the third grade and aggressive behavior 10 years later was positive and highly significant. In other words, exposure to TV violence during early childhood was predictive of higher levels of aggression at age 19. This relationship persisted even after controlling for IQ, socioeconomic status (SES), and overall exposure to television. In contrast, aggressive behavior in the third grade was *not* predictive of violent TV consumption at age 19. Thus, the idea that being aggressive can lead a child to watch more TV violence did not receive support. Interestingly, neither of the cross-lagged correlations from Time 1 to Time 2 was significant for girls.

The researchers followed these same individuals up another 10 years later, most of them now age 30 (Huesmann, 1986). In some of the most compelling evidence to date, the data revealed a link between exposure to TV violence at age 8 and self-reported aggression at age 30 among males (Huesmann & Miller, 1994). Moreover, violent TV habits in childhood were a significant predictor of the seriousness of criminal acts performed at age 30 (see Figure 3.6). Once again, this relationship held up even when childhood aggression, IQ, SES, and several parenting variables

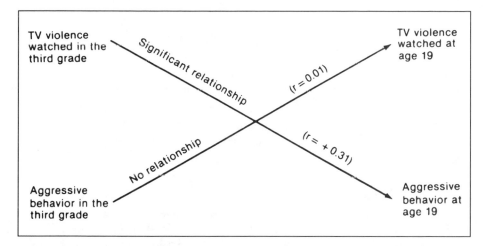

Figure 3.5. TV Violence Watched in Third Grade Correlates With Aggressive Behavior at Age 19

SOURCE: Reproduced from Liebert and Sprafkin (1988). Used with permission.

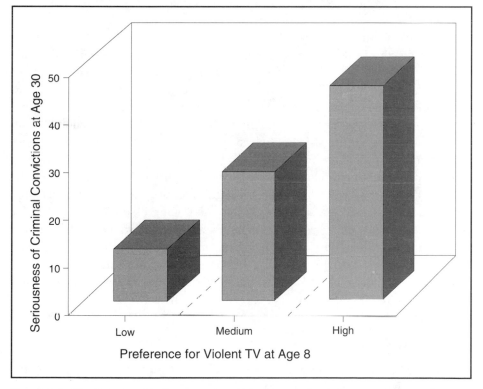

Figure 3.6. The Relationship Between Boys' Viewing of TV Violence at Age 8 and Violent Criminal Behavior 22 Years Later

SOURCE: Adapted from Huesmann (1986).

were controlled. Huesmann (1986) concluded that "early childhood television habits are correlated with adult criminality independent of other likely causal factors" (p. 139).

Using a similar longitudinal approach, these same researchers conducted a 3-year study of more than 1,000 children in five countries: Australia, Finland, Israel, Poland, and the United States (Huesmann & Eron, 1986). Despite very different crime rates and television programming in these nations, early childhood exposure to television violence significantly predicted subsequent aggression in every country except Australia. Furthermore, the relationship was found just as often for girls as for boys in three of the countries, including the United States. Finally, although the relationship between early TV habits and later aggression was always stronger, there was some evidence for the reverse direction: Early aggression led to higher levels of violent viewing. Based on this pattern, Huesmann and his colleagues now argue that pinning down the precise direction of causality between TV violence and aggression is not so crucial because the relationship is probably reciprocal: Early violent viewing stimulates aggression, and behaving aggressively then leads to a heightened interest in violent TV content (Huesmann, Lagerspetz, & Eron, 1984).

With one exception (Milavsky, Kessler, Stipp, & Rubens, 1982), other longitudinal evidence corroborates these findings. For example, in one 5-year study, children who had watched the most television during preschool, particularly action adventure shows, were also the most aggressive at age 9 (Singer, Singer, & Rapaczynski, 1984). Early viewing of violence in the preschool years also predicted more behavioral problems in school. These relationships remained just as strong after the effects of parenting style, IQ, and initial aggressiveness were statistically removed.

To summarize, longitudinal studies provide powerful evidence that television violence can have a cumulative effect on aggression over time. Childhood exposure to such content has even been shown to predict aggression in later years and even serious forms of criminal behavior in adulthood. Some of the earliest research indicated that these effects held true only for boys, but more recent studies have found significant relationships over time for girls too. Finally, the relationship between TV violence and aggressive behavior may be cyclical in nature, such that each reinforces and encourages more of the other.

Meta-Analyses

When researchers conclude that media violence can increase aggressive attitudes and behaviors, they typically look at all the evidence collectively. Lab experiments provide convincing evidence of causal effects, but they may be detecting outcomes that would not occur in everyday life, and they assess short-term effects only. Field experiments increase our confidence that real aggression is involved, correlational studies show that there is a positive relationship between TV violence and aggression in large samples of youth, and longitudinal studies suggest a cumulative effect of TV violence over time, even after controlling for other potential causal variables. In other words, each method has its strengths and weaknesses, but collectively the research shows a consistent pattern.

Another way to detect patterns is to conduct a meta-analysis. A meta-analysis is the statistical analysis of a large collection of results from individual studies. In this case, each study becomes a data point in a new, combined "super-study" (Mullen, 1989). The goal of a meta-analysis is to synthesize findings from a large body of studies but to do so in a statistical rather than a descriptive way (Cooper & Hedges, 1994). Meta-analyses produce numerical estimates of the size of an effect across all studies combined.

Several meta-analyses have been conducted on the research regarding media violence and aggression. In the earliest one, Hearold (1986) looked at 230 studies of the impact of TV on both prosocial and antisocial behavior. Antisocial behavior consisted mostly of physical aggression but also included other outcomes such as theft and rule breaking. Hearold found an average effect size of .30 (similar to a correlation) between violent TV content and the broad category of antisocial behavior. According to scientific conventions, any effect around .10 is considered to be "small," around .3 to be "medium," and around .5 to be "large" in magnitude (Cohen, 1988).

In a much smaller meta-analysis, Wood, Wong, and Chachere (1991) examined only those experiments that actually observed children's aggressive behavior after viewing violence. The goal was to isolate those studies that used the most realistic measures of aggression. Across a total of 23 experiments, the researchers found a significant aggregate effect of media violence on aggression. They concluded that "media violence enhances children's and adolescents' aggression in interactions with strangers, classmates, and friends" (p. 380).

Updating the Hearold (1986) study, Paik and Comstock (1994) analyzed 217 studies of the impact of television violence on antisocial behavior (the researchers did not include studies of prosocial behavior, as Hearold did). Paik and Comstock found that the overall effect size between TV violence and antisocial behavior was .31, surprisingly consistent with that found by Hearold. Another way to interpret this statistic is that roughly 10% of the variance ($.31^2$) in antisocial behavior can be accounted for by exposure to TV violence.

More recently, Bushman and Anderson (2001) limited their meta-analysis to studies looking at aggression as an outcome rather than the broader category of antisocial behavior. Across 212 different samples, the researchers found a positive and significant relationship between media violence and aggression. In addition, the study found that since 1975 the effect sizes in media violence research have increased in magnitude, suggesting that the media are becoming more violent and/or that people are consuming more of this type of content.

Bushman and Anderson (2001) also compared the overall effect of media violence with other types of effects found in scientific research. As it turns out, the link between media violence and aggression is much stronger than several effects that today go unquestioned, such as the link between ingesting calcium and increased bone mass or the link between condom use and decreased risk of contracting HIV. Furthermore, the correlation between media violence and aggression (.31) is only slightly smaller than that between smoking and lung cancer (nearly .40). Obviously, not everyone who smokes will develop lung cancer, but the risk is real and significant. The analogy to media violence is clear; not every child or teen who watches a heavy dose of violent programming will become aggressive, but some young people are certainly at risk to do so.

Why Does Exposure to Violence Encourage Aggression?

Many theories have been offered to account for the relationship between media violence and aggression. Catharsis theory was first proposed by Aristotle, who argued that good drama offers the audience a way to purge their negative feelings of emotion. Extended to media violence, the idea is that exposure to such content can cleanse one's feelings of anger and frustration, resulting in a therapeutic *reduction* of aggression. There is very little empirical support for catharsis theory, as most data suggest an opposite, instigational effect of media violence (see the review above). Yet catharsis theory continues to be cited today, especially by some members of the media industry. Another theory called excitation transfer posits that any type of media content can enhance aggression so long as the material is arousing (Zillmann, 1991). According to excitation transfer theory, an erotic film is more likely to enhance aggression in an angered individual than a violent film is, so long as the erotic material is more arousing (Zillmann, 1971).

In this section, we will review three major perspectives, all of which focus on the content of media portrayals rather than their arousal properties. Each perspective has generated much research and made significant contributions to our understanding of how media violence might facilitate aggression.

Cognitive Priming. Cognitive priming is a perspective developed by Berkowitz and his colleagues to explain short-term reactions to media violence (Berkowitz, 1984; Jo & Berkowitz, 1994). According to the theory, violent stimuli in the media can activate or elicit aggressive thoughts in a viewer. These thoughts can then "prime" other closely related thoughts, feelings, and even motor tendencies stored in memory. For a short time after exposure, then, a person is in a state of activation whereby hostile thoughts and action tendencies are at the forefront of the mind. Research supports the idea that violent media content can "prime" aggressive thoughts in people (Bushman & Geen, 1990). For example, in a study by Berkowitz, Parker, and West (cited in Berkowitz, 1973, pp. 125-126), children who read a war comic book were more likely to select aggressive words when asked to complete a series of sentences than were children who read a neutral comic book.

Several conditions can encourage these aggressive thoughts and feelings to unfold into aggressive behavior. One such condition is the person's emotional state. Berkowitz (1990) has argued that individuals who are experiencing negative affect, particularly anger or frustration, are more likely to be primed to act aggressively by the media because they are in a state of readiness to respond in a fight-or-flight manner. Indeed, angered individuals do seem to be more strongly influenced by media violence (Paik & Comstock, 1994).

Another condition that helps encourage individuals to act out their aggressive thoughts is justification (Jo & Berkowitz, 1994). If media violence is portrayed as morally proper, it can help to reduce a person's inhibitions against aggression for a short time afterward, making it easier to act out such behavior. Justified violence in the media may even help a person rationalize his or her own aggression (Jo & Berkowitz, 1994). There is a great deal of evidence indicating that justified violence can facilitate aggression (Paik & Comstock, 1994).

Finally, cues in the environment that remind people of the media violence they have just seen can trigger aggressive behavior (Jo & Berkowitz, 1994). Such cues help to reactivate and sustain the previously primed aggressive thoughts and tendencies, thereby prolonging the influence of the violent media content. In a classic study that demonstrates such cuing, second- and third-grade boys were exposed to either a violent or a nonviolent TV show (Josephson, 1987). The violent program prominently featured walkie-talkies in the plot. Immediately afterward, the boys were taken to a school gymnasium to play a game of floor hockey. At the start of the game, an adult referee interviewed each boy using a walkie-talkie or a microphone. Results revealed that aggression-prone boys who had viewed the violent program and then saw the real walkie-talkie were more aggressive during the hockey game than were those in any other condition, including boys who had seen the violent show but no real walkie-talkie. According to priming theory, the walkie-talkie served as a cue to reactivate aggressive thoughts and ideas that had been primed by the earlier violent program.

Cognitive priming theory helps to explain how media violence can have short-term effects by triggering already learned aggressive thoughts and behaviors. But where do these aggressive tendencies come from originally? Social learning theory focuses on how the media can help children acquire aggressive attitudes and behaviors in the first place.

Social Learning. Developed by Bandura (1965, 1977), social learning theory posits that children can learn new behaviors in one of two ways: by direct experience through trial and error or by observing and imitating others in their social environment. Bandura (1994) has pointed out that observational learning ultimately is more efficient than trying to discover everything on your own. Children can and do learn from other people in their environment, including parents, siblings, peers, and teachers. Children also can learn from characters and people featured in the mass media.

According to social learning theory, a child observes a model enact a behavior and also witnesses the reinforcements that the model receives. In a sense, the child experiences those reinforcements vicariously. If the model is rewarded, the child too feels reinforced and will imitate or perform the same behavior. If the model is punished, the child is unlikely to perform the behavior, although the actions may still be stored in memory and performed at a later date (Bandura, 1965).

Early experiments supported social learning theory and demonstrated that children could learn just as easily from a filmed model as from a real person (Bandura, 1965; Bandura et al., 1963a, 1963b; Walters & Parke, 1964). In addition to imitation, early research showed that the media could encourage children to act aggressively in ways that differed from the precise behaviors seen in a portrayal. In one study, nursery school children viewed either a violent or a nonviolent cartoon and then were given two toys with which to play (Lovaas, 1961). One toy had a lever that caused a doll to hit another doll over the head with a stick; the other toy consisted of a wooden ball that maneuvered through obstacles inside a cage. Compared with those in the nonviolent condition, children who had seen the violent cartoon used the hitting doll more frequently. Bandura and his colleagues (1963b) called this process "disinhibition," whereby exposure to media violence can weaken a child's normal inhibitions or restraints against behaving aggressively, resulting in acts of violence that are similar but not identical to what was seen in a program.

Today, certain models in the media can have remarkable effects on young people. Consider the thousands of preteen and teen girls who donned chains and skimpy clothes in an effort to emulate Madonna during her Material Girl phase. More recently, the Spice Girls and Britney Spears are captivating youth. As a well-known Hollywood producer once stated,

> I'd be lying if I said that people don't imitate what they see on the screen. I would be a moron to say they don't, because look how dress styles change. We have people who want to look like Julia Roberts and Michelle Pfeiffer and Madonna. Of course we imitate. It would be impossible for me to think they would imitate our dress, our music, our look, but not imitate any of our violence or our other actions. (cited in Auletta, 1993, p. 45)

In the 1980s, Bandura (1986) reformulated his theory because it had been criticized as too behavioristic, focusing mostly on reinforcements and how people act. Now called social cognitive theory, the newer perspective acknowledges that cognitive processes such as attention and retention are involved in observational learning. These mental activities place more emphasis on how children symbolically construe or make sense of a model's behavior. Children selectively pay attention to different features of a model's behavior, they bring forth different experiences to interpret and evaluate the model's actions, and they store different information in memory. These types of cognitive processes can be used to help explain why some children might imitate a model but others do not.

Social learning and social cognitive theory are useful frameworks for understanding how children can learn new behaviors from media violence. But they tend to focus most on short-term learning. The final theory we will discuss takes observational learning a bit further and provides a perspective to account for cumulative or long-term effects of media violence on a child's behavior.

Social Informational Processing Theory. Huesmann (1998) has developed an information-processing model that deals with how aggressive behaviors are both developed and maintained over time. The model focuses on scripts, which are mental routines stored in memory that are used to guide behavior and social problem solving (Abelson, 1976). A script typically includes information about what events are likely to happen, how a person should behave in response to these events, and what the likely outcome of these behaviors will be. For example, young children possess scripts for common activities such as going to the doctor and getting ready for bed.

Scripts can be acquired through personal experience as well as through exposure to mass media. Huesmann (1998) has argued that a child's early learning experiences play a critical role in the development of scripts. According to the theory, a child who is exposed to a great deal of violence, either in real life or through the media, is likely to develop scripts that encourage aggression as a way of dealing with problems (Huesmann, 1986, 1988).

Once scripts are learned, they can be retrieved from memory and tried out in social situations. Some scripts are easier to retrieve than others. Those that are rehearsed by the child, through simple recall, through fantasizing, or even through playacting, will be more accessible in memory. In addition, cues in the environment that are similar to those present when the script was first developed can encourage retrieval of that script (Tulving & Thomson, 1973). Similar to priming, then, a situational cue can prompt an aggressive memory based on a previously seen violent TV show or film.

Regardless of how a script is retrieved, once an aggressive strategy is employed, it can be reinforced and elaborated by new information in a given situation, and eventually the script becomes applicable to a wider set of circumstances (Geen, 1994). According to this perspective, the aggressive child is one who has developed from an early age a network of stable and enduring cognitive scripts that emphasize aggression as a response to social situations. Consistent and repeated exposure to violent messages in the media can contribute to the creation of these scripts and to the retrieval of already learned ones.

Huesmann's theory incorporates ideas from observational learning and from priming but takes a broader view of how the media can contribute to aggression over time. The perspective reminds us that media violence is only one of many environment influences that can foster habitual forms of aggression in some children. Next we turn to the types of media portrayals that are most likely to teach aggressive patterns of behavior and the types of individuals who are most at risk for this learning.

Types of Portrayals That Encourage the Learning of Aggression

As discussed earlier, violence can be portrayed in a variety of ways. For instance, the same act of aggression looks very different when it is perpetrated by a law officer trying to save lives than by a thief trying to steal something. As it turns out, the way in which violence is portrayed may be even more important than the sheer amount of it when trying to assess its likely impact on a viewer. Research has identified seven contextual features of violence that affect the likelihood that a viewer will learn aggressive attitudes and behaviors from a portrayal (see Wilson, Kunkel, et al., 1997).

First, an *attractive perpetrator* increases the risk of learning aggression. In accord with social learning theory, children as well as adults are more likely to attend to, identify with, and learn from attractive role models than unattractive ones (Bandura, 1986, 1994). The most obvious way to make a perpetrator appealing is to make him or her a hero (Liss et al., 1983). But even characters who act in benevolent ways can be attractive to young people (Hoffner & Cantor, 1985). Moreover, characters who are similar to the self can be potent role models. Research suggests that children, for example, are more likely to imitate peer than adult models (Hicks, 1965). Viewers also pay attention to and identify more with same-sex characters than opposite-sex ones (Bandura, 1986; Jose & Brewer, 1984).

Second, the motive or *reason for violence* is important. Consistent with cognitive priming, violent actions that seem justified or morally defensible can facilitate viewer aggression, whereas unjustified violence can actually diminish the risk of learning aggression (Berkowitz & Powers, 1979; Geen, 1981). Third, the *presence of weapons* in a portrayal, particularly conventional ones such as guns and knives, can enhance aggressive responding among viewers (Berkowitz, 1990; Carlson, Marcus-Newhall, & Miller, 1990). Weapons are assumed to function as a violent cue that can prime aggressive thoughts in a viewer (Berkowitz, 1990).

Fourth, violence that seems *realistic* can promote the learning of aggressive attitudes and behaviors among viewers (Atkin, 1983; Feshbach, 1972). From this finding, it is tempting to conclude that cartoon or fantasy violence in the media is relatively harmless. However, research with very young children, to be discussed below, challenges such an assumption.

Fifth, we know from social learning theory that violence that is explicitly *rewarded* or that simply goes *unpunished* increases the risk of imitative aggression, whereas violence that is condemned decreases that risk (Bandura, 1965; Bandura et al., 1961). Sixth, the *consequences* of violence for the victim are an

---

**TABLE 3.2   Risky Versus Educational Depictions of Violence
in the Media**

Media themes that *encourage* the learning of aggression
   "Good guys" or superheroes as perpetrators
   Violence that is celebrated or rewarded
   Violence that goes unpunished
   Violence that is portrayed as defensible
   Violence that results in no serious harm to the victim
   Violence that is made to look funny

Media themes that *discourage* the learning of aggression
   Evil or bad characters as perpetrators
   Violence that is criticized or penalized
   Violence that is portrayed as unfair or morally unjust
   Violence that causes obvious injury and pain to the victim
   Violence that results in anguish and suffering for the victim's loved ones

---

important contextual cue; explicit portrayals of a victim's physical injury and pain actually can decrease or inhibit the learning of aggression among viewers (Baron, 1971a, 1971b; Wotring & Greenberg, 1973). Finally, violence that is portrayed as *humorous* can increase aggression in viewers (Baron, 1978; Berkowitz, 1970). Part of the reason for this effect is that humor can trivialize the seriousness of violence (Gunter & Furnham, 1984). Researchers have speculated that humor also may serve as a positive reinforcement or reward for violence (Berkowitz, 1970).

Taken as a whole, the research clearly suggests that there are risky and not-so-risky ways of portraying violence. If a parent is concerned about a child learning aggressive behaviors from the media, then programs that feature heroes or good characters engaging in justified violence that is not punished and results in minimal consequences should be avoided (see Table 3.2). As it turns out, this formula is very common in cartoons (Wilson et al., 1998). On the other hand, portrayals that feature less attractive perpetrators who are punished in the plot and whose violence results in serious negative consequences can actually teach youth that aggression is not necessarily a good way to solve problems.

Types of Youth Most at Risk

Not only do certain messages pose more risk, but certain young people are more susceptible to violent content. In their meta-analysis, Paik and Comstock (1994) found that viewers of all age groups can be influenced by television violence but that preschoolers show the strongest effect size. This is consistent with

Huesmann's (1998) argument that early childhood learning is critical. It also reflects the fact that younger children are least likely to have developed and internalized strong social norms against aggression. As will be discussed later, younger children also have difficulties in distinguishing reality from fantasy on television (see Chapter 1), making them prone to imitating even the most fantastic presentations.

The heightened vulnerability that characterizes the preschool years means that parents should be especially cautious about mindlessly using television as a baby-sitter for their young children. Indeed, studies indicate that even 1- and 2-year-olds are capable of imitating what they see on television (McCall, Parke, & Kavanaugh, 1977; Meltzoff, 1988). Fortunately, when busy parents need a break, public broadcast channels contain very little violence and feature educational programs such as *Sesame Street* that are truly enriching for children (Fisch & Truglio, 2001).

Research also indicates that at any age, children who perceive television as realistic and who identify strongly with violent characters are most likely to learn from violent content (see Huesmann, 1986; Huesmann, Lagerspetz, & Eron, 1984). In a tragic case recently, a 12-year-old fan of TV wrestling claimed he was simply imitating his favorite heroes when he threw a 6-year-old playmate into a metal staircase, killing her (see box on p. 97). It seems that even some older children can be confused by highly scripted and unrealistic portrayals of violence.

Being in a particular emotional state also can make a child more vulnerable. Numerous studies reveal that viewers who are made to feel angry or frustrated are more likely to behave aggressively after exposure to media violence than are nonangered persons (see Paik & Comstock, 1994). According to priming, angered individuals are in a state of readiness to respond that facilitates aggressive actions (Berkowitz, 1990). It is important to note, however, that a child does not have to be angry to learn aggression from the media (see Hearold, 1986).

Being unpopular with peers and doing poorly in school also place a child at greater risk for learning aggression from media violence (see Huesmann, 1986). Social and academic failures can be frustrating experiences that instigate aggression (Huesmann, 1988). Such experiences can in turn lead to more social withdrawal and more television viewing, making the process a vicious cycle. Finally, children raised in homes characterized by parental rejection and parental punishment show stronger effects of media violence (Huesmann, Eron, Klein, Brice, & Fischer, 1983; Singer & Singer, 1986).

It is important to remember that no single factor will propel a child from nonviolence to violence. Instead, each risk factor increases the chances that a child will internalize and act out the violence that he or she witnesses in the media. Huesmann and Eron (1986b) summarize risk in the following way:

> For most children, aggressiveness seems to be determined mostly by the extent to which their environment reinforces aggression, provides aggressive role models, frustrates and victimizes the child, and instigates aggression. (p. 4)

TELEVISION PRO WRESTLING ON TRIAL

On July 28, 1999, a 12-year-old boy named Lionel Tate beat to death his 6-year-old playmate, Tiffany Eunick. The two were playing in the Florida home that Lionel shared with his mother, who was baby-sitting for the girl. The mother was asleep at the time.

An autopsy showed that Tiffany suffered a fractured skull, lacerated liver, internal hemorrhaging, and more than 30 other injuries. The 170-pound boy allegedly had punched, kicked, and thrown the 48-pound girl around the room. When questioned by authorities, Lionel claimed to have accidentally thrown Tiffany into a metal staircase and a wall while trying to toss her onto a sofa.

During the murder trial, defense attorney Jim Lewis argued that Lionel was an avid fan of pro wrestling who was imitating moves he had seen on TV without realizing the damage that could occur. He claimed that Lionel was too immature to understand that pro wrestlers are not actually hurting one another. "He wanted to emulate them," Attorney Jim Lewis said (Spencer, 2001). "Like Batman and Superman, they were his heroes. He loved to play." Earlier, Lewis had tried unsuccessfully to subpoena professional wrestlers to testify at the trial.

Prosecutor Ken Padowitz argued that television violence was not on trial and that the boy knew he was savagely beating Tiffany.

After only 3 hours of deliberation, a Florida jury found Lionel guilty of first-degree murder. Pointing to the cruelty and callousness of Lionel's acts, Judge Joel T. Lazarus sentenced the boy to life in prison without the possibility of parole. Tate is one of the youngest defendants in the United States to be sentenced to spend the rest of his life in prison.

The sentence is being appealed, and attorneys for Tate have asked the governor of Florida for a shortened sentence. In the meantime, Lionel Tate has been transferred to a juvenile facility until age 21, when he will be moved to a federal prison.

Developmental Differences in Processing Media Violence

Chapter 1 describes several ways in which younger and older children differ in their processing of media messages. At least three of these have important implications for how young people are likely to interpret media violence. First, children differ markedly in their cognitive ability to distinguish reality from fantasy (see Dorr, 1983; Wright et al., 1994). Preschoolers often assume that anything that looks or sounds real *is* real (Brown et al., 1979). Consistent with this tendency, studies show that preschoolers and even young elementary schoolers will readily imitate violent cartoon characters such as the Ninja Turtles and even Bugs Bunny (Bandura et al., 1963a; Friedrich & Stein, 1973; Steuer et al., 1971). Such portrayals are likely to be discounted as fantasy by older, more sophisticated viewers who are far more responsive to portrayals of violence involving events and characters that are possible in the real world (Atkin, 1983; Thomas & Tell, 1974).

The new television rating system takes this developmental consideration into account with its "TVY7" label. Programs rated TVY7 are designed for children 7 years of age and older who have "acquired the developmental skills needed to distinguish between make-believe and reality" (*TV Parental Guidelines,* n.d.).

A second relevant cognitive skill concerns the shift from perceptual to conceptual processing. Younger children pay close attention to perceptually salient features in a program, such as what characters look like and what they do (Gibbons, Anderson, Smith, Field, & Fischer, 1986; Hoffner & Cantor, 1985; van den Broek et al., 1996). Older children and teens, on the other hand, can consider more conceptual or abstract information in a plot (Collins, 1975; van den Broek et al., 1996). In the realm of violence, this means that younger children are most likely to comprehend and learn from those violent behaviors and consequences that are explicitly portrayed on screen in concrete ways. When events are implied or not visually depicted, they will be more difficult for a young child. In support of this idea, Collins et al. (1974) found that younger elementary schoolers evaluated a TV perpetrator mostly in terms of the punishments he received, whereas older elementary schoolers focused more on the character's motives, which are typically depicted in more subtle ways.

A third important skill is the ability to draw inferences. As seen in Chapter 1, younger children are less able than their older counterparts to link scenes together, integrate information, and draw causal conclusions from the plot (Collins, 1983). Therefore, contextual cues that are separated from the violence itself will be more difficult for younger children to appreciate. Collins (1973) demonstrated this in an intriguing study involving 3rd, 6th, and 10th graders. Children viewed a violent scene in which the perpetrator was punished either immediately after engaging in violence or after a 4-minute commercial break. The results revealed that 3rd graders gave more aggressive responses themselves in the separation than in the no-separation condition (see Figure 3.7). In other words, the commercial break interfered with younger children's ability to connect the punishment to the violence—the violence stood alone as a model for behavior. In contrast, older children's responses were unaffected by the separation manipulation, suggesting that they appreciated the punishment even when it occurred at a different point in the story line.

Unfortunately, television supplies numerous instances in which aggressive behavior goes unpunished, at least in the short run; if punishment is delivered, it typically happens toward the end of the plot (Wilson et al., 1998). A child under the age of 7 or 8 is not capable of connecting this delayed consequence back to an earlier transgression. Therefore, if punishment is temporally separated from the act, it will seem to a younger viewer like the perpetrator "got away" with violence.

One last developmental consideration is the age of the perpetrator. As discussed above, people tend to like characters in the media who are most like themselves. It stands to reason, then, that young people will be most attracted to youn-

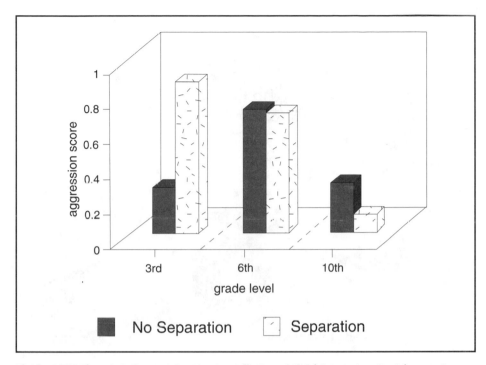

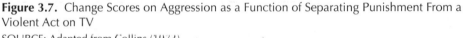

Figure 3.7. Change Scores on Aggression as a Function of Separating Punishment From a Violent Act on TV
SOURCE: Adapted from Collins (1973).

ger characters. Studies support this; children's visual attention to the television screen increases when a child character appears (Schmitt et al., 1999). Moreover, children typically choose characters who are similar in age as their favorites (Cohen, 1999; Hoffner, 1996). Although there are far fewer child and teen perpetrators than adult ones on television (Wilson, Colvin, & Smith, in press), these young aggressors should be particularly salient for a younger viewer. Movies such as *Home Alone* or *Karate Kid* that feature a child engaging in justified violence are likely to be very appealing to children. Likewise, music videos, which often feature teen perpetrators (Wilson, Colvin, & Smith, in press), can be potent messages for preadolescent and adolescent audiences.

CAN MEDIA VIOLENCE DESENSITIZE YOUNG PEOPLE? ●

Concern about children's aggressive behavior has certainly dominated most of the public debates and the research on media violence. But an outcome that may be far more pervasive is desensitization (see Figure 3.8). Desensitization refers to the

Figure 3.8
SOURCE: Copyright Mike Luckovich and Creators Syndicate. Reprinted with permission.

idea that extensive exposure to a stimulus can lead to reduced emotional responsiveness to it. In clinical settings, desensitization techniques have been used to treat people's phobias (Graziano, DeGiovanni, & Garcia, 1979). For example, a person who is frightened of dogs is gradually exposed under nonthreatening circumstances to a variety of these types of animals. Eventually, the person acclimates to dogs and the fear is eliminated. Can repeated exposure to media violence be similarly therapeutic?

We do know that repeated viewing of violent materials can affect a person's arousal responses. For example, one study found that boys who were heavy viewers of television exhibited less physiological arousal during selected scenes from a violent film than did light viewers (Cline, Croft, & Courrier, 1973). Other studies have documented that even within a single program, people's heart rate and skin conductance go down over time during prolonged exposure to violence (Lazarus & Alfert, 1964; Speisman, Lazarus, Davidson, & Mordkoff, 1964). Some critics have speculated that American films and television programs are becoming increasingly graphic and violent because audiences are desensitized to tamer versions of such content (Plagens, Miller, Foote, & Yoffe, 1991).

If repeated exposure to media violence merely resulted in decreased arousal, there might be little cause for concern. In fact, one could argue that a reduction in arousal is even functional given that being in a heightened state of arousal for too long can be taxing to the body (Ursin & Eriksen, 2001). What alarms people is the possibility that desensitization to entertainment violence might in turn affect responses to real-life violence. In their book *High Tech, High Touch: Technology and Our Search for Meaning*, Naisbitt, Naisbitt, and Philips (1999) write,

> In a culture of electronic violence, images that once caused us to empathize with the pain and trauma of another human being excite a momentary adrenaline rush. To be numb to another's pain—to be acculturated to violence—is arguably one of the worst consequences our technological advances have wrought. That indifference transfers from the screen, TV, film, Internet, and electronic games to our everyday lives through seemingly innocuous consumer technologies. (pp. 90-91)

Research suggests that there is some merit to this concern. For example, one study found that both children and adults were less physiologically aroused by a scene of real-life aggression if they had previously watched a violent drama on TV than if they had watched a nonviolent program (Thomas, Horton, Lippincott, & Drabman, 1977). In other words, the fictional portrayal produced an indifference to real-life violence.

Even more troubling, can desensitization affect people's willingness to intervene or take action on behalf of a victim? In one experiment (Thomas & Drabman, 1975), first and third graders were shown either a violent or a nonviolent TV program and then placed in charge of monitoring the behavior of two preschoolers at play. Older children who had seen the violent TV show were significantly slower in seeking help when the preschoolers broke into a fight than were those who had seen the nonviolent show. In fact, more than half the older children in the violent TV condition never left the room even though they had been told to get an adult if trouble erupted. This type of callousness to real violence has been replicated in other media studies involving children (Drabman & Thomas, 1974; Molitor & Hirsch, 1994).

Research suggests that young adults can become callous too. Over a period of 1 or 2 weeks, Linz, Donnerstein, and Penrod (1984, 1988) exposed male undergraduates to five full-length "slasher" films depicting violence against women, such as *Texas Chainsaw Massacre* and *Toolbox Murders*. After each film, emotional reactions, perceptions of violence in the films, and attitudes toward the women in the films were measured. Supporting the idea of desensitization, males perceived less violence in the films and evaluated the films as less degrading to women over the course of the exposure period. At the end of the viewing period, participants were asked to evaluate a videotaped enactment of a legal trial involving a rape victim.

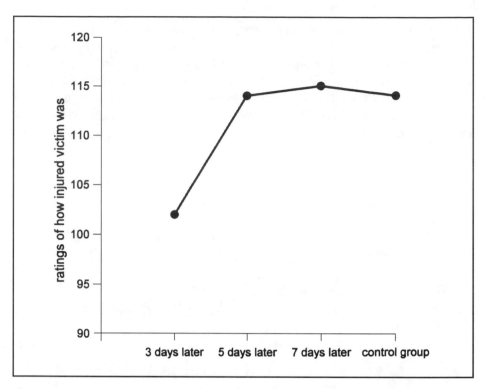

Figure 3.9. Perceptions of Domestic Violence Victim Days After Desensitization to Media Violence
SOURCE: Adapted from Mullin and Linz (1995).

Compared with various control groups, males who had been exposed to a heavy dose of slasher films were less sympathetic toward a rape victim and more inclined to hold her responsible.

One critical question is whether desensitization is a transitory effect or a more permanent state that persists beyond the exposure period. That is, can people become *re*sensitized to real-world violence? Mullin and Linz (1995) tested this idea by varying the amount of time that lapsed between exposure to fictional violence and evaluations of real victims of violence. In this experiment, male college students were exposed to three slasher films over a 6-day period. In a supposedly unrelated context, they were asked either 3, 5, or 7 days later to watch a documentary about domestic abuse. The researchers found that 3 days after exposure, males expressed less sympathy for domestic violence victims and rated their injuries as less severe than did a no-exposure control group (see Figure 3.9). However, 5 and 7 days later, levels of sympathy had rebounded to the baseline level of the control group. In other words, the desensitization effect seemed to diminish after about a 3-day period.

Of course, resensitization requires that a person is no longer exposed to entertainment violence during the "recovery" period. As we have seen, most children watch between 2 and 3 hours of television per day, and many watch a great deal more. Given the pervasiveness of violence in this medium, heavy viewers are presumably exposed to a fairly constant diet of aggressive behaviors. If these same children also play violent video games, listen to violent music, and go to a violent film or two a month, there are ample occasions for desensitization to occur and not much of an opportunity to reestablish sensitivity to aggression.

Because desensitization is construed as an automatic process similar to habituation, it can happen without a person's awareness. Furthermore, unlike aggression, which is easy to see, there are fewer outward manifestations of this type of effect. Thus, large numbers of young people in our society may be gradually becoming desensitized by media violence without us ever knowing. The popularity in recent years of graphically violent serial killer movies such as *Hannibal* and *Scream* suggest to some that we are already experiencing a cultural shift in our tolerance for violence in the media. The danger of course is in the possibility that such an effect will spill over into real life, resulting in a society that is increasingly indifferent to the plight of others.

CAN MEDIA VIOLENCE PRODUCE FEAR? ●

The third potential effect of media violence is to create fear in audiences. Many of us can remember a movie or TV show that frightened us as a child. In one recent study, more than 90% of college students could vividly describe a film or television program that caused intense fear when they were younger (Harrison & Cantor, 1999). *Psycho, Jaws,* and *The Exorcist* were just a few of the more common movies cited. Amazingly, one fourth of these students said they were still bothered today by what they had seen.

These patterns are consistent with research involving children themselves. Surveys indicate that a majority of preschoolers and elementary schoolers have experienced fright reactions to mass media programming, much of which is violent (Cantor & Sparks, 1984; Sparks, 1986; Wilson, Hoffner, & Cantor, 1987). Furthermore, many of these reactions have endured beyond the viewing experience, resulting in nightmares, sleep disturbances, and even acute fears in some cases (see Cantor, 1998a).

The types of images that frighten children change as a function of age or developmental level (for reviews, see Cantor, 1994; Cantor & Wilson, 1988). Preschoolers and younger elementary schoolers respond most to characters and scenes that *look* scary, consistent with the idea of perceptual dependence discussed in Chapter 1. Therefore, younger children are often frightened by programs that feature monsters, gory-looking characters, and witches. *The Wizard of Oz* and even certain Disney films are examples of upsetting content for this age group. In contrast, older elementary school children are less upset by surface features and more concerned about whether a violent portrayal could happen in real life. Again, this is consistent with the gradual understanding of reality-fantasy distinctions. Thus, more realistic programs that involve harm to human beings, especially family members, are often cited as frightening by 8- to 12-year-olds. Interestingly, this age group also is more likely to be scared by TV news stories of violent crime than their younger counterparts are (Cantor & Nathanson, 1996; Smith & Wilson, 2002). Adolescents respond to realistic depictions too, but their abstract thinking skills also allow them to imagine implausible and inconceivable events (see Chapter 1). Therefore, teens are far more susceptible than children to intangible threats in the media such as global conflict, nuclear war, and political attacks (Cantor, Wilson, & Hoffner, 1986).

Gerbner and his colleagues have taken the idea of fear one step further, arguing that extensive exposure to media violence can lead to a greater sense of apprehension, mistrust, and insecurity about the real world (Gerbner & Gross, 1976; Gerbner, Gross, Morgan, & Signorielli, 1994). In other words, violence in the media can cultivate a "mean world syndrome" in viewers (Signorielli, 1990). According to cultivation theory, heavy exposure to television can alter a person's perceptions of social reality in a way that matches the TV world. Given that television features so much violence, heavy viewers should come to see the world as more violent. In numerous studies with samples of all different ages, Gerbner and his colleagues consistently have found that frequent viewers of television perceive the world as a more violent place and perceive themselves as more likely to become a victim of violence than do light viewers (see Signorielli & Morgan, 1990).

Cultivation theory has been rigorously critiqued by other researchers (Hawkins & Pingree, 1981; Hirsch, 1980; Hughes, 1980; Potter, 1993). One of the most widespread concerns is that most of the findings that support the theory are correlational. The cultivation effect does typically hold up even after controlling for demographic variables as well as other factors that could explain the relationship between TV and perceptions of reality (see Morgan & Shanahan, 1996). But even after controlling for "third" variables, it is difficult to determine the direction of causality from correlational data. Does television cause fear, or are frightened people drawn to watching more TV, in part because such content allows them to work out their fears? In support of cultivation theory, experimental evidence shows that repeated exposure to television violence, for as little as 1 week or as much as 6 weeks, under controlled conditions can heighten fear and anxiety in viewers (Bryant, Carveth, & Brown, 1981; Ogles & Hoffner, 1987). However, research also shows that crime-apprehensive people seek out violent drama, especially that which features the restoration of justice (Zillmann & Wakshlag, 1985). As with aggression, then, the relationship between entertainment violence and anxiety may be cyclical in nature.

Another criticism is that the theory is too simplistic because it predicts an effect for anyone who watches a lot of television. In fact, not all of the subgroups in Gerbner's studies show a cultivation effect (Gerbner et al., 1980b), suggesting that intervening variables are at work. Some studies indicate that cultivation is more likely to occur among those who perceive television as realistic (e.g., Potter, 1986). Also, research suggests that personal experience with crime as well as motivation for viewing television (i.e., to learn vs. to escape) may be important mediating factors (Perse, 1990; Weaver & Wakshlag, 1986). In addition, the cognitive abilities of the viewer may make a difference. Preschoolers, for example, lack the ability to distinguish reality and fantasy and the ability to integrate information from a program, so their perceptions may be less influenced by media content (Hawkins & Pingree, 1980). However, a recent study found that by the elementary school years, exposure to news programming on TV is associated with exaggerated perceptions of certain types of crime (Smith & Wilson, 2002).

Finally, the way in which a person makes judgments about social reality may determine how influential television is. In one recent study, college students who were encouraged to think carefully and accurately in answering questions about the incidence of crime in the world were *less* likely to show a cultivation effect than were students encouraged to make rapid judgments or students given no instructions about how to answer the questions (Shrum, 2001). These findings suggest that under most circumstances, people make rather quick and unsystematic judgments about social reality and that for heavy viewers, television can provide salient examples on which to base such heuristic processing.

Despite the criticisms of cultivation theory, there is still a great deal of evidence supporting the idea that media violence can make people feel more anxious about real-world crime (see Potter, 1999). As Schrum (2001) recently stated, "The notion that the viewing of television program content is related to people's perceptions of reality is virtually undisputed in the social sciences" (p. 94). The challenge for the future is to better understand how and when this cultivation effect occurs. Also, research needs to explore the relationship between fear and desensitization, which seem like contradictory outcomes. Perhaps repeated exposure to media violence frightens some and numbs others, depending on the nature of the content that is sought as well as the type of individual who seeks it.

CULTURAL DEBATES ABOUT MEDIA VIOLENCE ●

Despite all the evidence presented here, there are critics who disagree that media violence is harmful. Some of the most vocal opponents are people who work in the industry. To many of them, media violence has become a convenient scapegoat for politicians who refuse to grapple with more deep-seated causes of violence such as gun access and poverty (Schaefer, 1999). Another argument often

Figure 3.10
SOURCE: Copyright Sidney Harris. Reprinted with permission.

made is that good drama requires conflict and conflict means violence (see Figure 3.10). This position is reflected in the quote by TV producer Christopher Crowe at the beginning of the chapter. Others in the industry argue that media violence will disappear if people simply quit watching it and paying for it (Pool, 1991). In other words, in the marketplace of American culture, consumers are ultimately responsible for the violence that surrounds us. Violence does seem to attract audiences, as we discussed above. Yet there are many examples of good storytelling with little or no physical aggression. Cartoon series such as *Doug*, situation comedies such as *Malcolm in the Middle*, and even movies such as *Annie* illustrate this point. One of the problems is that violence is relatively easy and cheap to produce and has a strong international market. Action heroes such as Sylvester Stallone and Arnold Schwarzenegger seem to move easily across cultural, national, and linguistic borders.

There also are scholars who challenge the research. Some are social scientists themselves who critique the validity and reliability of the studies. For example, Freedman (1984) points out the limitations of laboratory studies, field experiments, and correlational research and concludes that the evidence does not yet support a causal relationship between TV violence and aggression. Others argue that focusing on the "effects" of media violence on children is too simplistic and unidimensional, ignoring how young people choose, interpret, and negotiate violent media texts in their lives (Buckingham, 2000). Still others believe that social science research obfuscates larger issues such as how media violence as a cultural institution legitimates power and control in our society (Ball-Rokeach, 2000). A more radical view is represented by Fowles (1999), who believes that media violence is therapeutic for people. At least in the social science arena, though, there is little evidence to support this position.

Obviously, there are many points of view regarding media violence. The debates are heated, and given the stakes involved, there are no easy solutions. Social scientists are just beginning to wrestle with the politics of their work and their data (Bushman & Anderson, 2001). The challenge, it seems, is to stay focused on children in the midst of these political and scholarly disputes.

GUNS AND THE MEDIA ●

Firearms play a leading role in mortality and morbidity among American youth (CDC, 1997). In fact, the death rate due to firearms among U.S. children is nearly 12 times higher than among children in 25 other industrialized countries *combined* (CDC, 1997). Every day in this country, 16 children are killed by firearms (Office of the Surgeon General, 2001). Moreover, gunshot wounds to children have increased 300% in major urban areas since 1986 (Gaensbauer & Wamboldt, 2000). In 1992 alone, more than 23,000 youth were treated in emergency rooms at hospitals for nonfatal gunshot injuries (Annest, Mercy, Gibson, & Ryan, 1995).

There is little doubt that the United States is "the most heavily armed nation on earth" (Davidson, 1993), with approximately 35% of homes with children under 18 years of age having at least one firearm (Schuster, Franke, Bastian, Sor, & Halfon, 2000). Of these, 13% or 1.4 million homes store the firearms unlocked and either loaded or with ammunition nearby. And children seem to know it. In a 1993 national survey, 59% of junior high and high school students reported that they could get a gun if they needed one (LH Research, Inc., 1993). Two out of three of these same students said they could get a gun in 24 hours.

Unfortunately, guns kept at home can be more dangerous to the people who live there than to any criminal intruder (Kellermann et al., 1993; Kellermann, Somes, Rivara, Lee, & Banton, 1998). In one 5-year study of youth brought to a medical trauma center, 75% of the guns used in suicide attempts and unintentional injuries came from the victim's home or the home of a relative or friend (Grossman, Reay, & Baker, 1999). In another study in New Mexico, 25 unintentional firearm deaths and 200 woundings were identified within a 4-year period, mostly involving children playing with loaded guns at home (Martin, Sklar, & McFeeley, 1991).

Large epidemiological studies show that keeping a gun in the home increases the risk of suicide and homicide among adults who reside there (Bailey et al., 1997; Kellermann et al., 1993) and even increases the risk of suicidal tendencies and vio-

Figure 3.11
SOURCE: Copyright John Trever, *Albuquerque Journal*. Reprinted with permission.

lence among teen residents (Resnick et al., 1997). One study found that the odds of a depressed teenager successfully committing suicide increase 75-fold if there is a gun kept at home (Rosenberg, Mercy, & Houk, 1991). Yet 23% of gun-owning parents believe that their child can be trusted with a loaded gun (Farah, Simon, & Kellermann, 1999).

Very recent data graphically demonstrate just how naive children can be about firearms. Jackson, Farah, Kellermann, and Simon (2001) observed more than 60 boys between the ages of 8 and 12 as they played in a room full of toys. The room also contained an unloaded .380 caliber handgun concealed in a drawer. Within 15 minutes of play, the vast majority of boys (75%) discovered the gun. More disturbing, 63% of the boys who found the gun handled it, and 33% actually pulled the trigger. When questioned afterward, almost half of the boys who found the gun thought it was a toy or were not sure whether it was real (see Figure 3.11). Children from gun-owning families behaved no differently than children from non-gun-owning families.

Despite all the risks, many Americans seem to have a longstanding love of guns, and this passion is frequently played out in the movies and on television. A recent study of 50 top-grossing G- and PG-rated nonanimated films revealed that 40% of the movies featured at least one main character carrying a firearm (Pelletier et al.,

Figure 3.12. Images of Guns in the Media

1999). In fact, across the films, a total of 127 persons carried firearms, resulting in a median of 4.5 armed characters per film. Nearly all of these movies were comedies or family films likely to be seen by children.

But such images are not limited to the movies (see Figure 3.12). Young children can readily witness laser guns and a variety of other types of firearms being used in cartoons such as *Men in Black* and even *Bugs Bunny*. Using data from the National Television Violence Study described above, Smith, Boyson, Pieper, and Wilson (2001) found that 26% of all violent incidents in a composite week of television involve the use of a gun. Three types of programming accounted for most of this gun violence: movies (54%), dramatic series (19%), and children's shows (16%). Looking at rate, a child viewer on average will see nearly two gun-related violent incidents every hour that he or she watches TV. That rate goes up if the child selectively watches gun-filled genres such as movies or children's shows.

According to cognitive priming, images of guns in the mass media can trigger aggressive thoughts and ideas in young viewers. In one recent study, just flashing pictures of guns and other weapons on a computer screen served to prime aggressive-related thoughts in college students (Anderson, Benjamin, & Bartholow, 1998). In other words, a gun need not even be fired to incite aggression. In support of this idea, a meta-analysis of 56 experiments found that the mere presence of weapons, either pictorially or in the natural environment, significantly enhanced aggression among angered as well as nonangered adults (Carlson et al., 1990).

Clearly, the portrayal of guns in entertainment media is a public health concern. For many young children, television will be the first place they encounter such weapons. Repeated exposure to images of heroes and other attractive role models using firearms will at the very least help to glorify these deadly devices.

● SUICIDE AND THE MEDIA

The suicide rate among U.S. teens has increased dramatically in the past few decades (CDC, 1994a). Suicide is now the third leading cause of death among adolescents ages 15 to 19 (Guyer et al., 1999). However, many teens consider suicide without attempting it or attempt it without being successful. Suicidal thoughts are alarmingly common among teenagers. In one study, 20% of all high schoolers reported having seriously considered or attempted suicide in the previous 12 months (Youth Risk Behavior Surveillance System, 1999). Given such a high figure, having firearms in the home and making firearms a common feature in the media both seem like dangerous practices.

In addition to glorifying guns, the media may contribute to adolescent suicide by highlighting such behavior in public cases (Phillips, Carstensen, & Paight, 1989). On April 5, 1994, lead singer Kurt Cobain of the popular rock group Nirvana put a shotgun to his head and pulled the trigger. The highly publicized suicide prompted a great deal of public concern about the potential of this event to spark copycat behaviors among anguished teen fans (Jobes, Berman, O'Carroll, Eastgard, & Knickmeyer, 1996). In fact, a number of studies, both in the United States and Europe, have demonstrated a link between media coverage of suicide and subsequent increases in such behavior among teens (Gould & Davidson, 1988; Gould & Shaffer, 1986; Gould, Shaffer, & Kleinman, 1988; Phillips & Carstensen, 1986). In addition, the more TV networks that feature a suicide story in the news, the greater is the increase in suicides thereafter (Phillips & Carstensen, 1986).

One key factor in this phenomenon may be the extent to which a susceptible teen identifies with the publicized suicide victim (Davidson et al., 1989). However, because the studies to date all involve large numbers of young people, it is difficult to know precisely what influenced any particular individual. In addition, although such research typically controls for factors such as time of year and yearly trends in suicide, the data are still only correlational so they are always subject to alternative explanations. And it should be noted that a few studies have found no relationship at all between media coverage and suicide rates (Baron & Reiss, 1985; Davidson, Rosenberg, Mercy, Franklin, & Simmons, 1989; Phillips & Paight, 1987).

Clearly, the causes of suicidal behaviors are complex and multifold (Gould, Fisher, Parides, Flory, & Shaffer, 1996). Yet a great deal of research supports an idea known in the medical field as suicide "contagion" (Gould & Davidson, 1988), whereby exposure to the suicide of one person encourages others to attempt such behavior. The contagion effect appears to be stronger among adolescents than adults (Gould, Wallenstein, Kleinman, O'Carroll, & Mercy, 1990) and is quite consistent with the idea that suicidal tendencies might be learned and/or primed by observing the behavior of others. Given that troubled teens do seem to take notice of public suicides, the CDC together with the American Association of Suicidology have issued guidelines for reporting suicide in the media (see www.suicidology .org/mediaguidelines.htm). They recommend that news stories avoid sensationalizing the act, glorifying the person involved, or providing how-to details. Such suggestions can apply just as easily to entertainment programs that feature suicide in the plot.

JAPAN VERSUS THE UNITED STATES: ● A CROSS-CULTURAL COMPARISON

The only country in the world with nearly as much entertainment violence as the United States is Japan. Yet Japanese society is far less violent than American society. If media violence contributes to real-life aggression, why is Japan not more affected? There are several important differences between the two countries. First, the portrayal of violence is different in Japan. A 1981 study found that compared with American television, programming in Japan more heavily emphasizes the negative consequences of violence in the story line (Iwao, Pool, & Hagiwara,

1981). Interestingly, in Japan, the "bad guys" commit most of the TV violence, with the "good guys" suffering the consequences—a pattern that is exactly opposite to what is found in American programming (Smith et al., 1998). As discussed earlier, featuring unattractive perpetrators and showing victim pain both reduce the risk that a portrayal will encourage aggression in viewers.

Second, children are raised in fairly traditional family structures with strong emphasis on discipline and control. Third, Japan has very strict gun control laws. Individuals are not allowed to own guns, and very few exceptions are allowed. The only type of firearm a citizen may acquire is a shotgun, for hunting purposes only, and only after a lengthy licensing procedure involving classes, a written exam, and medical certification of mental health (Kopel, 1993).

Despite these cultural differences, teen violence in Japan is on the rise. By U.S. standards, the figures are still low. But the number of teens who committed violent crimes doubled in just four years, reaching 2,263 in 1998 (Gaouette, 1998). And a recent rash of knifings by Japanese adolescents has been attributed to a popular TV drama in which a teen star uses a butterfly knife to administer justice (Skelton, 1998). Others have blamed violent video games, an intensive educational system, and a breakdown in traditional values for the escalation in violence (Lies, 2001). Nevertheless, Japan still can be considered a relatively peaceful country relative to the United States.

● CAN MEDIA VIOLENCE HAVE POSITIVE EFFECTS?

Much of this chapter has focused on the negative effects of exposure to media violence. However, violent portrayals can have prosocial effects as well. In June 1998, Court TV commissioned a study to assess whether television violence could help teach young people to be *less* aggressive (Wilson, Linz, et al., 1999). In the study, 513 young adolescents from three different middle schools in California were randomly assigned to receive or not receive an anti-violence curriculum in school. The *Choices and Consequences* curriculum was presented by the regular teachers during normal class time (see www.courttv.com/choices). The 3-week curriculum involved watching videotaped court cases about real teens who had engaged in risky behavior that resulted in someone dying. In one case, for example, a group of teens pushed a young boy off a railroad trestle and he drowned.

Each week, students watched portions of the videotaped trial, discussed them in class, engaged in role-playing activities, and completed homework assignments based on the trial case. Compared with a no-curriculum control group, the intervention significantly reduced middle schoolers' verbal aggression and curbed their physical aggression. The curriculum also increased empathic skills and knowledge of the legal system. In other words, exposure to programming that emphasized the lifelong negative consequences of antisocial behavior had prosocial effects on teens.

Other types of critical viewing curricula have been tested as well. For example, Huesmann et al. (1983) had second and fourth graders write essays about the harmful effects of television violence and the unrealistic nature of particular violent shows. Then children were videotaped while they read their essays, and the footage purportedly was to be used to create a film about the problems of media violence. Compared with a control group that wrote essays about hobbies, the intervention group showed several positive effects. The intervention significantly altered children's attitudes about TV violence, decreased their aggressive behavior, and eliminated the relationship between TV violence and aggressive behavior. Most of these effects were measured 4 months after the intervention, suggesting that a rather simple treatment can produce lasting changes. Such efforts are consistent with larger programs designed to teach media literacy to children (see Chapter 10).

CONCLUSION

Today there is strong consensus among social scientists that exposure to aggressive messages on television and in movies can have harmful effects on youth (Bushman & Huesmann, 2001; Smith & Donnerstein, 1998). The most well-documented effect concerns aggression. Experimental studies, correlational research, longitudinal studies, and meta-analyses of published data all point to the same conclusion: Aggression is a learned behavior that can be acquired, reinforced, and primed by media messages. Young children are particularly vulnerable, as are children who strongly identify with violent characters, who are doing poorly in school, who perceive television as realistic, and who are unpopular with peers. The evidence does not suggest that media violence is the major cause of violence in society, but it is certainly a socially significant one. The media are part of a complex web of cultural and environmental factors that can teach and reinforce aggression as a way of solving problems.

But aggression is not the only possible outcome. Extensive exposure to media violence also can desensitize young people and make them more callous toward real-world violence. And in others, it can lead to exaggerated concern and fear of becoming a victim of violence. None of these outcomes is straightforward and universal. Instead, certain children and teens are more vulnerable depending on cognitive development, the types of media violence they like, and the amount of exposure they have to media violence in relation to other types of messages (see Figure 3.13).

One could advocate that violence should be eliminated from the media given all these potential risks. But violence does seem to turn a profit at least with some

Calvin and Hobbes

Figure 3.13
SOURCE: Used with special permission of Universal Press Syndicate.

audiences, so it is unlikely that in a free-market society it will ever go away. Nor should we necessarily advocate that it do so. Research shows quite clearly that certain portrayals are less harmful than others and that some depictions actually can have educational or prosocial effects on youth. The challenge for parents and educators is to ensure that youth are exposed to these alternative messages that accurately portray the seriousness of violence in society. The challenge to the media industry is to create more of these alternative messages and to ensure that they are just as appealing as those that glorify violence.

Exercises

1. Suppose you were asked to monitor the amount of violence on television. How would you define *violence*? What types of issues need to be considered in crafting your definition? Would you include fantasy violence? Would you include slapstick violence? How might your definition differ if you were a media researcher versus an executive in the television industry? What channels would you include in your study?

2. What is the most violent movie or television program you have ever seen? What made it so violent? Did you enjoy the program? Why or why not? As a parent, would you let your 6-year-old watch this program? Your 10-year-old? Your 15-year-old? Think about cognitive development as well as the nature of the content in addressing these issues.

3. Watch a popular cartoon and an evening crime drama on television. Compare the two in terms of *how* violence is portrayed. Think about contextual features such as the nature of the perpetrators, whether violence is rewarded or punished, and the consequences of violence. According to the research cited in this chapter, which program poses more risk to a young child viewer? Why?

4. In 1999, Mario Padilla and Samuel Ramirez, two teenage cousins, said the movie *Scream* inspired them to kill one of their mothers. That same year, 12-year-old Lionel Tate claimed he was imitating wrestling moves he had seen on TV when he killed his 6-year-old playmate, and two troubled teens who were obsessed with violent video games walked into Columbine High School and started shooting. Media violence is often blamed in these and many other "copycat" behaviors. Should the media be placed on trial? Who or what is responsible for violence in these cases? Should writers and producers be held to any standards regarding the violent material they create?

5. Critics charge that television news is more violent than ever, often relying on the "if it bleeds, it leads" rule of practice. Do you think TV news is too violent? Should news be treated differently than fictional content in the debates about media violence? In addressing this issue, you will need to consider what constitutes news versus entertainment programming. Is there a difference? Where do reality-based programs such as *Cops* fit in?

6. In his provocative book *Channeling Violence: The Economic Market for Violent Television Programming*, James Hamilton (1998) argues that television violence, like pollution, generates negative externalities or costs that are shouldered by others rather than the people who produce this material. Using pollution as an analogy, he goes on to say that restrictions should be devised that place more responsibility on the TV industry while still protecting artistic freedom. For example, a violence tax could be imposed on those responsible for aggressive portrayals. How might such a tax work? Who should pay, and how should the amount be determined? Can you think of other approaches that could be implemented, using the pollution comparison? Would such efforts be constitutional?

7. Think back to your childhood. Can you remember a TV program or movie that really frightened you? How old were you? How long did your fear last? What aspect of the show frightened you? Did you change your behavior in any way as a result of seeing this show? Analyze your reaction in light of what we know about cognitive development and children's fear reactions to media, as discussed in this chapter.

8. In the debates about media violence, much less attention has been paid to desensitization as a harmful outcome than to aggression. Can you think of an occasion during which you felt desensitized to media violence? If our society

gradually becomes desensitized to media violence, what are some of the possible outgrowths of this? Will it affect parenting? Will it affect the legal system? Explore some of the ways desensitization could affect individuals as well as our culture.

9. America is a violent country. Do you believe that the media have been unfairly blamed in public debates about this problem? Think about how you would respond to such questions if you worked in the media industry. Now think about how you would respond if you were a parent of a young child who had seriously injured a friend on the playground while imitating a cartoon superhero.

CHAPTER 4

ELECTRONIC GAMES

Jeanne B. Funk

So, you gotta be like "Ok, I'm gonna have to win this game, or else I'm dead." Boom!
Kabash!

> —Quote from a fourth-grade girl describing her
> experience while playing a violent video game

Playing violent video games increases aggression in males and females, in children
and adults, in experimental and non-experimental settings.

> —Brad Bushman and Craig Anderson,
> University of Iowa psychology professors
> (Anderson & Bushman, 2001, p. 358)

There is not the slightest evidence that playing violent video games causes any long-
term or lasting increase in aggressiveness or violence.

> —Jonathan Freedman,
> University of Toronto psychology professor
> (Freedman, 1984)

• VIDEO GAMES GROW UP: ELECTRONIC GAMES IN THE 21ST CENTURY

Video and computer ("electronic") games are "new media" that have experienced phenomenal success and growth over the past three decades. This chapter will review the history of electronic games and describe current research in the following areas: time commitment, ratings and classification systems, game preference, the impact of violent games, addiction, physical health risks, and potential for positive applications.

Definitions

Electronic games have outgrown platform-based definitions (see Figure 4.1). These games may now be played on dedicated console-type systems, on personal computers, on handheld systems, and via the Internet. The focus of the present chapter will be on games that are played by individuals or in direct contact with another player as the opportunities for anonymous, real-time, real-player interactions make Internet game playing quite different.

The Development of Video Games

The first electronic game was introduced about 30 years ago. In the early 1970s, adult consumers became fascinated with the first arcade version of *Pong,* which was basically a simple visual-motor exercise. Soon home systems and cartridge games became available, and electronic games became popular across all age groups. In the early 1980s, consumers became disenchanted with uninspiring copycat games and sales dropped precipitously. At this point, electronic games were dismissed as just another toy fad.

The industry recovered in the second half of the 1980s when special effects were improved, new game accessories were made available, and games with violent content were promoted. In addition, the industry introduced cross-media marketing, with game characters featured as action figures and in movies. At the same time, children became targeted consumers (see Figure 4.2). Beginning with *Mortal Kombat,* violent games with ever more realistic graphics became an industry staple. The typical goal of violent games is to maim or kill one's opponent, and in many cases, players can choose the level of realism of the battle, including very graphic portrayals of injuries. In recent years, sales of electronic games have exceeded several billion dollars annually worldwide.

Figure 4.1

Time Commitment

Electronic games are now well established as one of the most popular choices in the array of leisure activities available to most children and adolescents. Gender differences in time commitment to game playing are consistently reported, with boys playing more than girls at all ages (Funk & Buchman, 1996a; Roberts, Foehr, et al., 1999; Subrahmanyam, Greenfield, Kraut, & Gross, 2001). Gender differences are critical to understanding the implications of some game-playing habits, so gender-specific information will be selectively highlighted throughout this chapter.

Figure 4.2

Several recent studies have investigated children's time commitment to various media activities. Huston, Wright, Marquis, and Green (1999) studied the media use of low- and moderate-income children beginning at ages 2 and 4 from 1990 through 1993. They interviewed parents yearly, asking them to describe the child's activities in the previous 24-hour period. The authors noted gender differences in time commitment to electronic games as early as age 3, and gender differences increased with age. For example, at age 3, girls rarely played electronic games, whereas boys played 10 minutes on weekends, on average. By age 6, girls played about 15 minutes, and boys typically played 40 minutes.

Another media use study was recently completed by the Kaiser Foundation (Roberts, Foehr, et al., 1999). Two national samples were used, including more than 3,000 children ages 2 through 18. Among 8- to 18-year-olds, 55% of boys and 23% of girls reported playing console-based electronic games on a typical day. International studies also demonstrate the popularity of electronic games. Van Schie and Wiegman (1997) used diaries to examine the game-playing habits of seventh and eighth graders in the Netherlands. For boys, 75% reported playing electronic games in a typical week. The figure for girls was 63%. About 30% of the boys and 9% of the girls reported more than 30 minutes of playing time in a typical day.

Most current research suggests that playing time peaks for many in middle childhood to early adolescence. In surveys of fourth through eighth graders, Buchman and Funk (1996) found that fourth-grade girls reported playing about 4.5 hours in the home in a typical week, whereas eighth-grade girls reported playing only about 2 hours. Fourth-grade boys reported about 7 hours of average weekly home play, whereas eighth grade boys reported less than 4 hours.

Most time use studies identify a small group of players who spend considerable time playing each week. For example, Griffiths and Hunt (1995) reported that about 7% of their sample of 12- to 16-year-old British adolescents played electronic games at least 30 hours each week. Defining "heavy play" as more than 2 hours each day, Roe and Muijs (1998) found that about 9% of their sample of 9- through 13-year-old Flemish children from Belgium fit this description. These authors also reported that frequent players were more likely to prefer fighting games.

In summary, research indicates that for most children under high school age, some time is devoted to playing electronic games. Across all ages, boys play much more than girls. In most cases, playing electronic games occupies only a relatively small percentage of total leisure time. There is a group of children, probably about 5% of players, whose excessive time commitment may interfere with other activities.

Game Ratings

As electronic games became a common leisure choice for children and adolescents, researchers and policymakers, as well as some members of the general public, became concerned about the increasing realism and graphic violence of many popular games. As a result, pressure was placed on the industry to self-regulate by the threat of government-imposed regulation (Funk, Flores, Buchman, & Germann, 1999). Two voluntary systems were developed, one by the Interactive Digital Software Ratings Board, now the Entertainment Software Ratings Board (ESRB), and the other by the Software Publishers Association, whose ratings group was called the Recreational Software Advisory Council or RSAC. The content-based RSAC system is no longer being used to rate games, but a version of the ratings is now available to developers for rating Web sites.

The ESRB was initially sponsored by the console manufacturers, including Nintendo and Sega. Its age-based system has been expanded to cover console games, PC software, and Internet games (Entertainment Software Ratings Board, 2000). The ESRB game classifications are presented in Table 4.1. Each game is rated independently by three trained raters. Raters come from a variety of occupational and ethnic backgrounds and are paid for their work. Because a solely age-

TABLE 4.1 Entertainment Software Ratings Board Ratings Classifications

Recommended Age Group	Content Suitable For
Early childhood	Age 3 and older
Everyone	Age 6 and older
Teen	Age 13 and older
Mature	Age 17 and older
Adults only	Only for adults
Rating pending	Submitted; awaiting final rating

NOTE: From the ESRB's *Guide to Interactive Entertainment* [Online]. Available: www.esrb.com/parent.html.

based system did not seem adequate, content descriptors were added to highlight content in the following areas: violence, sexual themes, and language. Other specific areas such as the use of alcohol and tobacco may be added at the discretion of each individual rater.

Game Classification

Several researchers have developed game classification systems to answer specific research questions. A system based on children's perceptions of game content was developed and revised in the early 1990s (Funk, 1993; Funk & Buchman, 1995) (see Table 4.2). This system has been used in several published studies (e.g., see Funk, Buchman, & Germann, 2000; Funk, Flores, et al., 1999). One study found that the ESRB system as then configured (without content descriptors) did not reflect consumer perceptions of game content for more subtle forms of violence (Funk, Flores, et al., 1999). This finding was replicated in a recent study by Walsh and Gentile (2001) and indicates that more work is needed to make the ratings consistent with consumer perceptions and needs.

Wright et al. (2001) designed a game-coding system for use in their national survey conducted in 1997. Their categories were designed to reflect the types of mental and sensorimotor activities required of the player and include the following: educational/informative, sports, sensorimotor (including action/arcade, fighting/shooting, driving/racing), other vehicular simulations, strategy (including adventure/role-playing, war, strategic simulations, puzzles/games), and unknown (other content, unspecified games, platform only).

It is possible that different game classification systems are needed to examine different research questions. However, to improve comparability of research, it may be reasonable for researchers to develop general classification standards.

TABLE 4.2   Revised Video Game Categories With Descriptions

Category	Description
General entertainment	Story or game with no fighting or destruction
Educational	Learning new information or figuring out new ways to use information
Fantasy violence	Cartoon character must fight or destroy things and avoid being killed or destroyed while trying to reach a goal, rescue someone, or escape from something
Human violence	Human character must fight or destroy things and avoid being killed or destroyed while trying to reach a goal, rescue someone, or escape from something
Nonviolent sports	Sports without fighting or destruction
Sports violence	Sports with fighting or destruction

NOTE: From Funk and Buchman (1995). Adapted with permission.

Game Preference

Early research on electronic games paid little attention to the kinds of games children were playing. When used, systems were dichotomous, and games were either considered violent or nonviolent. The simplistic nature of early games encouraged this commonsense approach to content definition and limited interest in studying the implications of game preference. With the advent of movie-quality images and virtual reality technology, it became necessary to systematically evaluate game content from the participants' perspective. This resulted in the development of game categories from the perspective of children and adolescents (Funk, 1993; Funk & Buchman, 1996b). In addition to providing more specific information about age and gender-specific preferences, these categories are useful in examining the meaning and importance of game preference. Game preference for a group of 900 fourth through eighth graders is presented by age and gender in Table 4.3. Across grade levels, girls tend to prefer cartoon or fantasy violent games, whereas boys prefer more realistic, human violent games. Few boys stated a preference for educational games. Researchers are just beginning to study the importance of this widespread preference for violent games.

The Importance of a Preference for Violent Games

At the same time that electronic games have become more violent and realistic (see Figure 4.3), there has been a dramatic increase in lethal violence involving children and adolescents in the United States. This led to increased concern about the possible impact of exposure to violent media and, in particular, violent

TABLE 4.3 Percentage of Favorite Games in Each Category by Gender and Grade

	Grade 4		Grade 5		Grade 6		Grade 7		Grade 8	
	Girl (n = 289)	Boy (n = 241)	Girl (n = 197)	Boy (n = 187)	Girl (n = 157)	Boy (n = 169)	Girl (n = 126)	Boy (n = 177)	Girl (n = 166)	Boy (n = 183)
General entertainment	14.0	6.3	16.8	5.9	16.0	8.9	33.3	7.3	28.9	14.2
Educational	17.6	2.9	24.4	4.3	8.3	3.6	1.6	0.0	5.4	.5
Fantasy violence	32.7	27.5	30.5	26.2	44.6	24.9	43.7	24.9	44.6	19.1
Human violence	11.5	25.0	10.2	26.2	16.0	26.0	7.1	29.4	7.2	20.8
Nonviolent sports	9.3	17.9	12.7	19.8	10.5	20.1	4.3[a]			
Sports violence	14.7	20.4	5.6	17.6	5.7	16.6		38.4	13.9	45.4

NOTE: n refers to number of games listed.

a. When seventh and eighth graders were surveyed, there was only one sports category.

Figure 4.3

electronic games (Grossman & DeGaetano, 1999; *The Impact of Interactive Violence on Children,* 2000a, 2000b, 2000c). For the majority of players, no significant impairment in psychological functioning has been proven to be caused by electronic game playing. However, some children may have special vulnerability. This group has been labeled "high-risk" players (Funk & Buchman, 1996b; Funk, Buchman, & Germann, 2000). For example, high-risk players could be those vulnerable children in whom even a small increase in the likelihood of aggressive behavior triggers aggression.

Mechanisms

Several theoretical perspectives have been used to understand the possible effects of playing violent electronic games. For example, game playing has the characteristics of a powerful learning environment. Players' experiences of repeated demonstrations of violent behavior, coupled with the contingent reward of "winning" for choosing built-in violent strategies, are integral to playing violent electronic games (Provenzo, 1991). Successful players will consistently choose the preprogrammed violent alternatives and receive cycles of positive reinforcement.

From another perspective, it is possible that the actual structure of experience could be affected by repeated exposure to violent electronic games. Children learn general social rules and specific behaviors from observation, practice, and reinforcement. The development and internalization of behavioral scripts are one component of this process. A behavioral script is a set of situation-specific expectations and behavioral guidelines. A behavioral script helps an individual to predict what will happen in a certain situation and to implement a preprogrammed sequence of behaviors without really thinking about it (Huesmann & Miller, 1994). For example, most adults have driving scripts: find the keys, walk to the car, open the door, get in the car, shut the door, put on the seat belt, turn on the ignition, and so forth. A restaurant script is another common example: walk in the door, be seated, order, eat, pay, leave. Scripts may be triggered by internal or situational cues, causing the individual to behave based on the previously internalized set of guidelines. Although they increase efficiency, scripts are not always entirely accurate and may cause an individual to misinterpret or disregard new information. Perceived experience may even be altered to conform to a script (Guerra, Nucci, & Huesmann, 1994; Huesmann & Miller, 1994). That explains why it can be difficult to get used to a new car: Your driving script must be altered to accommodate differences in the location of the windshield wipers and other controls.

During childhood, scripts are constantly being developed and revised in response to many different types of learning experiences. In theory, a child could develop and internalize scripts for situations that trigger aggression based in part on playing violent video games. If such scripts are derived from unreal violence with no negative consequences, then the child's response to violence in real life will be influenced accordingly: The child will be less sensitive to the true consequences of violent actions, and violence will seem to be a reasonable alternative in many interpersonal situations.

Related media research suggests that there are sensitive periods when exposure to media violence can have a significant impact on the development of a behavioral predisposition to aggression in young children (Eron, Huesmann, Brice, Fischer, & Mermelstein, 1983). However, there is also a cumulative effect of long-term exposure to violent media; therefore, violent media may also affect older children and adolescents. From a biological standpoint, it has long been established that early experience affects neural connections; newer imaging techniques have recently revealed that dramatic anatomical changes in the brain emerge in adolescence (Thompson et al., 2000). The behavioral implications of this information about brain development have not yet been determined, but this finding does raise interesting questions about how vulnerable adolescents may be to negative impact from continued exposure to violent media.

What Happens During Game Playing?

It has been proposed that immersion in electronic games may precipitate an altered state of consciousness (Funk, 2001; Glickson & Avnon, 1997). When positive, this may be an example of the "flow" state described by Csikszentmihalyi and Csikszentmihalyi (1988). *Flow* is a term used to describe the intense feelings of

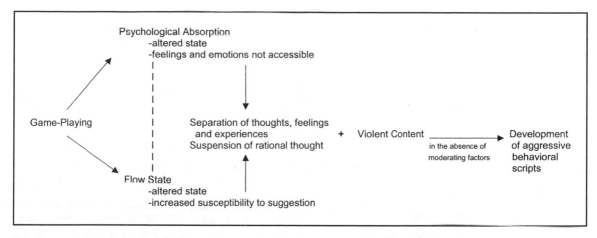

Figure 4.4. A Working Model of How Playing Violent Electronic Games May Affect Behavior

enjoyment that occur when a balance between skill and challenge is attained in an activity that is intrinsically rewarding (Csikszentmihalyi & Csikszentmihalyi, 1988; Moneta & Csikszentmihalyi, 1996, 1999). Being in a flow state may enhance learning (Moneta & Csikszentmihalyi, 1996) and make a person more susceptible to suggestion (Center for Media Education, 1996).

Psychological absorption is a related example of an altered state of consciousness, occurring when one becomes totally immersed in the present experience (Irwin, 1999). Psychological absorption is considered to be a form of "nonpathological dissociation" (Irwin, 1999). Nonpathological dissociation is a commonly experienced state, especially in childhood. These experiences, including daydreaming and fantasizing, peak before adolescence, by about age 9 or 10 (Putnam, 1993). The most common example of this phenomenon for adults is "highway hypnosis," the state in which a driver may travel for some distance and then suddenly become aware that he or she has not been paying attention to the typical demands of driving (Ross, Joshi, & Currie, 1990).

By definition, when an individual becomes psychologically absorbed, the logical integration of thoughts, feelings, and experiences is suspended. Some have suggested that the state of absorption involves a temporary suspension of reality testing (Preston, 1998; Qian, Preston, & House, 1999; Roche & McConkey, 1990; Tellegen & Atkinson, 1974). The capacity for psychological absorption has also been viewed as a stable personality trait that involves a high capacity for imaginative involvement and openness to a variety of experiences (Gilsky, Tataryn, Tobias, Kihlstrom, & McConkey, 1991; Merckelbach, Muris, & Rassin, 1999; Roche & McConkey, 1990).

A working model of the possible relationship between playing violent electronic games, flow, psychological absorption, and the development of aggressive behavioral scripts is presented in Figure 4.4. Game playing may produce either a flow state or psychological absorption. When the associated affect is positive, absorption may be very similar, if not identical, to flow. When the associated affect is negative, absorption is a very different experience. Either way, there is a separation of thoughts, feelings, and experiences and a suspension of rational thought. When game content is violent, aggressive behavioral scripts may develop outside of conscious awareness. This would increase the probability of actual aggressive behavior in real life unless moderating factors such as parental influence are active.

This model can be tested, but as yet, data are limited and tangential. In one study, young adults with high tendencies to become absorbed were more likely to experience an altered state of consciousness during a virtual reality game (Glickson & Avnon, 1997). Interestingly, participants reported that the violent content tended to interfere with their concentration on their own subjective experience. Gupta and Derevensky (1996) concluded that some of the 9- through 14-year-olds in their computer blackjack game study became so caught up in the game that they were unable to rationally judge the probability of success. These findings are intriguing, but much more research, including observational studies, is needed to carefully examine what happens when children play electronic games, particularly violent games.

The Appeal of Violence

One of the most interesting questions about violent electronic games is why they are so popular. The gaming industry asserts that violent games account for only a small percentage of sales and that the ultra-violent games are only bought by adults (see Figure 4.5). However, a recent Federal Trade Commission investigation found that children have been targeted consumers for violent electronic games, as well as for other violent media (Federal Trade Commission, 2000).

The reasons behind the attraction to violent media have long been a subject of professional study and debate (Funk, 2000; Goldstein, 1998). Industry spokesmen often cite catharsis or tension release as a benefit of exposure to many forms of violent media, but this claim has been disproven in a sizable body of research (e.g., see Calvert, 1999; Cantor, 1998a; Zillmann, 1998). Others suggest that ratings actually enhance the appeal of violent media, but there is only mixed support for this "forbidden fruit" explanation (Bushman & Stack, 1996; Cantor, 1998a). For children, it is most likely that violence is appealing to different children for different reasons. Personal history seems to be a key variable, with callous children who have been overexposed to violence looking for continuing arousal, whereas anxious and emotionally reactive children are trying to master anxiety-provoking experiences (Cantor, 1998a).

There has been minimal research directed specifically to understanding the attraction of violent electronic games. Hind (1995) investigated the game prefer-

Figure 4.5

ence of 72 juvenile offenders and 30 nonoffenders, ages 15 to 18. Participants played two computer games, one violent and one nonviolent, and then rated their satisfaction with each game. The juvenile offenders preferred the game that involved simple destruction of objects to the nonviolent game that required planning to achieve success. This finding may provide support for arousal as the explanation of the appeal of violent games, at least in the case of juvenile offenders.

Much more work is needed to understand the appeal of violent electronic games. At this point, personal history of exposure to violence and the ability to become absorbed and achieve a flow state seem to be promising variables for future study.

Research on the Effects of Playing Violent Electronic Games

The effects attributed to exposure to violent electronic games range from no measurable effects (Scott, 1995); to minimal effects (Office of Film and Literature Classification, 1999); to desensitization, including decreased empathy and stronger pro-violent attitudes (Funk, Buchman, Schimming, & Hagan, 1998); to increased feelings of hostility and increased aggression (Anderson & Bushman, 2001; Anderson & Dill, 2000; Dill & Dill, 1998). It must be recognized that most published research does report some type of negative effect. Two organizing principles were used to guide the choice of literature for the following summary. The first principle was to include only the most recent research because today's violent electronic games are very different from the "violent" games of the late 1970s and the 1980s. Electronic games are now much more realistic, with much more graphic violence. For example, it is now possible to personalize the images of game characters, and the technology is available to scan in, for example, a yearbook picture of a peer or teacher onto a potential victim.

The second principle was to separately consider studies of short-term and long-term effects. Short-term effects are the immediate results of a specific game-playing experience, either observable behavioral change or change in some specific aspect of thinking. Short-term effects may be representative of real-life experience, and they may be long lasting and cumulative; however, this is not proven in the laboratory setting. Long-term effects are determined by examining relationships between certain behaviors, personality characteristics or cognitions, and game-playing habits, such as a preference for violent games.

Short-Term Effects

In examining short-term effects, it is also important to distinguish between changes in behavior and changes in cognition or thinking. Neither are guaranteed to generalize outside the game-playing situation, but some believe that research demonstrating cognitive change is less convincing than research that shows specific behavioral change (Office of Film and Literature Classification, 1999).

One recent study examined the immediate behavioral impact of playing a violent or nonviolent electronic game on younger children's behavior (Irwin & Gross, 1995). Sixty second graders played either a martial arts or a motorcycle racing game. Children playing the violent game displayed more aggression toward objects during free play than did children who played the racing game. After playing, these children also often imitated the moves of the game characters. Some pretended to harm an opponent, and some were actually aggressive later in the experiment. This study clearly demonstrates that playing a violent electronic game caused an immediate increase in aggressive behavior in younger children.

Kirsh (1998) used cognitive analogues of aggression as his measure of the effect of playing a violent electronic game. Working with 52 third and fourth graders, Kirsh asked children to react to stories describing common situations after playing a violent or nonviolent game. After playing a violent electronic game, children were more likely to attribute negative intent to the actions of others. Kirsh concluded that playing violent electronic games may lead to the development of a hostile attribution bias, which could lead to aggressive behavior. For example, when a child with a hostile attribution bias is pushed accidentally on the playground, that child is more likely to push back because he will view the accidental push as an intentionally negative action.

Short-Term Effects as Moderated by Stable Characteristics

In studies that focus on short-term effects, it may be critical to consider what characteristics participants bring into the game situation. This has led to a "hybrid" of the short-term laboratory approach and the long-term survey approach. This hybrid takes into account preexisting characteristics that may have an important influence on participants' response to the experiment. For example, in research with third through fifth graders, Funk, Buchman, Myers, and Jenks (2000) studied children's responses to stories about everyday situations after they played either a violent or nonviolent electronic game. Prior to game playing, participants completed standardized measures of empathy and attitudes toward violence and listed and categorized up to three favorite games using standard definitions (Funk & Buchman, 1995). Following game playing, children responded to several questions ("You see a child sitting on the side of the playground crying. What happens next?"). Half the situations would commonly trigger empathic responses, and half would commonly trigger aggressive responses.

There were no differences in empathic or aggressive responses between children who played the violent or nonviolent game. However, children whose favorite game was violent gave more aggressive responses than those whose favorite game was nonviolent. Significant relationships were also identified for preexisting empathy and aggression: Children with more empathy before the experiment had higher empathy scores. Similarly, stronger pro-violence attitudes were associated with higher aggression scores on the aggression vignettes. In this study, preexisting characteristics were a more important determinant of postexperiment behavior than the short-term manipulation. It may not be reasonable to expect that brief periods of game playing will cause measurable change in relatively stable traits such as empathy and attitudes toward violence, even in relatively young children.

Cohn (1995) conducted a similar study with young adolescent boys, and her findings were similar. Sixth- through eighth-grade boys played either a violent or nonviolent video game or a puzzle. Game type did not produce different effects in the areas of aggression, arousal, or desensitization. However, past playing experience with *Mortal Kombat* was associated with the posttreatment measure of aggression (delivering noxious feedback [noise] to an "opponent" during a game of *Battleship*). Cohn found that players with more *Mortal Kombat* experience were significantly more aggressive than those with less *Mortal Kombat* experience.

Scott (1995) had university students play a nonaggressive, a moderately aggressive, or a highly aggressive game. Students also completed questionnaires measuring hostile feelings and personality before and after game playing. Scott found that more game violence was not associated with an increase in hostile feelings. He concluded that individual personality differences are more important determinants of aggressive feelings than exposure to violent electronic games.

Calvert and Tan (1994) compared the effects of playing versus watching versus going through the motions of a violent virtual reality game. Prior to game playing, undergraduates completed a measure of trait hostility. Participants who played the violent game had increased physiological responses and aggressive thoughts compared with observers and simulation participants, independent of their scores on the measure of trait hostility. The authors concluded that the experience of playing a violent virtual reality game has the potential to override even relatively stable personality characteristics such as trait hostility. These results are contrary to those reported by Scott (1995), but these studies are not completely comparable. It may be especially important that the Calvert and Tan study used a more realistic virtual reality game, which may have had a stronger impact on participants than the games used by Scott.

In other studies with undergraduates, Anderson and associates have also demonstrated increases in hostile cognitions and aggressive behavior after playing violent electronic games (Anderson & Dill, 2000; Anderson & Morrow, 1995). In one recent study, 210 undergraduates played either a violent or nonviolent electronic game. Then participants completed a competitive reaction time test in which their goal was to push a button faster than their opponent. The loser of the race received a blast of noise, with the noise level supposedly set by the opponent (but actually controlled by the computer). Aggressive behavior was operationalized as the intensity and duration of the noise blast chosen by the participant. Students who played the violent game delivered longer noise blasts than did those who played the nonviolent game and therefore were considered to be more aggressive.

In summary, results of recent research on the short-term effects of playing a violent electronic game on children and adolescents are mixed. In some cases, short-term negative impact is clearly identified. In other cases, there is a complex relationship between preexisting characteristics and response to the game. Although causal relationships can be studied in the laboratory, this setting cannot take into consideration all the potential mediating and moderating variables that may be active in the real world.

Long-Term Effects

Surveys, including self-report and reports from other observers, are typically used to examine relationships between experience with electronic games and what are presumed to be enduring behavioral characteristics. For example, investigators have tried to link game preference and real-world problem behaviors, including aggression. Wiegman and van Schie's (1998) survey of 278 Dutch seventh and eighth graders did identify a positive relationship between aggressive behavior and a preference for violent electronic games. In other words, a stronger preference for violent games was associated with more self-reported aggression.

Associations between a preference for violent electronic games and adolescents' self-perceptions of various problem behaviors and emotions were examined by Funk et al. (in press). Based on past media research, it was predicted that adolescents with a preference for violent games would report more aggressive emotions and behaviors on the Youth Self-Report (YSR). The YSR is a widely used measure of adolescent psychopathology. Although expected relationships with externalizing behaviors, including aggression, were not found, relationships were found with total number of problem behaviors and with some internalizing behaviors, including anxiety. Across all YSR subscales, children with higher preference for violent games had more clinically significant elevations (indicating more psychopathology) than did those with a low preference. This approach cannot establish a causal relationship between a preference for violent electronic games and psychopathology, but the associations are interesting and need further study.

Anderson and Dill (2000) surveyed 227 undergraduates to examine links between typical time spent playing electronic games, game preference, personal history of aggression and delinquent behavior, perception of the likelihood of being a victim of common crimes, and college grade point average (GPA). Participants also completed scales measuring irritability and anger. Undergraduates whose favorite games were violent were more likely to report aggressive delinquent behavior, trait aggressiveness, and an aggressive personality style. In addition, higher time commitment to game playing was associated with lower GPA.

Because they reflect core attitudes and coping abilities, self-esteem and self-concept have also been examined in relation to game-playing habits. Fling et al. (1992) surveyed 153 sixth through twelfth graders about their time commitment to game playing, their self-esteem, and their aggressive behavior. In addition, teachers rated the children on self-esteem and aggression. The researchers reported a positive correlation between amount of time spent and both self-reports and teacher reports of aggression. No clear relationship was identified with self-esteem.

In studies considering game preference, in each case where a significant relationship was identified, Funk and colleagues found only negative associations between a preference for violent electronic games and several aspects of self-concept in fourth through eighth graders (Funk & Buchman, 1996b; Funk, Buchman, & Germann, 2000). Children with a stronger preference for violent games rated themselves lower in one or more of the following areas: academic competence, behavioral conduct, social acceptance, athletic competence, and self-esteem.

Other studies have examined relationships between game-playing and moral behaviors such as empathy. Barnett et al. (1997) examined game preference, self-esteem, and empathy in a survey of 15- to 19-year-olds. Although no significant relationships were found with self-esteem, adolescents whose favorite game was violent had lower scores on a measure of trait empathy. Sakamoto's (1994) survey of 307 fourth, fifth, and sixth graders in Japan identified a negative correlation between simple frequency of electronic game use and empathy. Funk et al. (1998) surveyed 52 sixth graders to examine associations among preference for violent electronic games, empathy, and attitudes toward violence. All results were generally in the expected directions, although not statistically significant. An interesting trend was noted: Children with a high preference for violent games and high time commitment to playing demonstrated the lowest empathy.

The studies described above suggest that there is developing support for the contention that playing violent electronic games is associated with less prosocial behavior in children, including increased aggression and lower empathy. In a meta-analysis of 35 studies, including both adults and children, Anderson and Bushman (2001) concluded that the body of research now available indicates that playing violent electronic games is likely to increase aggressive behavior, thoughts, and feelings and decrease prosocial behavior.

Addiction

Studies of time commitment continue to identify small groups of very high-frequency players, and serious questions have been raised about the addictive potential of electronic game playing (see Figure 4.6). For example, Phillips, Rolls, Rouse, and Griffiths (1995) reported that about 7% of their sample of 11- to 16-year-olds played 6 or more days each week for more than 1 hour. Because these children reported that they played longer than intended and neglected homework to play, the authors concluded that these children might be "addicted" to playing electronic games. Griffiths and Hunt (1998) surveyed 387 adolescents and identified 20% of them as being "dependent" on electronic game playing. Adolescents who started playing at younger ages were more likely to be classified as being dependent. Fisher (1995) surveyed 460 children ages 11 through 16. She found that regular arcade players were more likely to score positively on an addiction screening measure than infrequent players.

In a hybrid survey/experimental study, Gupta and Derevensky (1996) examined the game-playing and gambling habits of 104 children ages 9 to 14. Children

Figure 4.6

also played a computerized blackjack game. High frequency electronic game players were more likely to have gambling experience. High-frequency players also took more risks on the computerized gambling task and noted that gambling made them feel important. These authors concluded that high-frequency video game players are at increased risk for the development of pathological gambling habits and other addictions.

Kubey (1996) notes that electronic games are fine-tuned to present a surmountable challenge, and this is likely to result in the previously described positive balance between challenge and skill, called flow. A wish or need to remain in this altered state may be one factor that increases the probability that a vulnerable individual could become addicted to electronic game playing. It is beyond the scope of this chapter to address the related issues of online gambling and the controversial topic of Internet addiction. The entire area of addiction to interactive experiences deserves much more research attention.

Health Risks

Since electronic games first became popular, there have been various case reports of minor negative health impact, primarily temporary musculoskeletal injury (see, e.g., Greene & Asher, 1982). There is one report of a possible "syndrome" associated with playing computer games for long periods of time (2-5 hours per day) (Tazawa, Soukalo, Okada, & Takada, 1997). This syndrome consists of headache, abdominal pain, tiredness, poor eating, weight loss, nausea, low-grade fever, chest pain, and sweating of unknown origin. According to the authors, all 19 patients' symptoms completely disappeared within 1 week on discontinuation of game play.

For a small group of players, an increased risk of seizures has been identified. In a larger group, health risks associated with cardiovascular reactivity and sedentary behavior have been proposed.

Seizures

The risk of video or computer game-related seizures in photosensitive individuals, even those without a previous seizure history, is well established (Graf, Chatrian, Glass, & Knauss, 1994; Kasteleijn-Nolst Trenite, 1994; Kasteleijn-Nolst Trenite et al., 1999; Maeda et al., 1990; Millett et al., 1997). For at least the past decade, game cartridges have included warnings against play for those with known seizure disorders. However, approximately 95% of those with established seizures do not have the kind of epilepsy associated with "video game seizures" (Fylan, Harding, Edson, & Webb, 1999; Maeda et al., 1990; Millett, Fish, & Thompson, 1997; Millett, Fish, Thompson, & Johnson, 1999). These seizures seem to be triggered by specific features, including the display flicker of the screen, screen brightness, distance from the screen, and the specific pattern of the images (Badinand-Hubert et al., 1998; Ricci & Vigevano, 1999). Treatment alternatives include avoidance of electronic games and administration of sodium valproate for those whose seizures are persistent (Graf et al., 1994; Maeda et al., 1990).

Cardiovascular Reactivity

Several studies have identified increases in the cardiovascular reactivity of children and adolescents during electronic game play (Ballard & Wiest, 1996; Murphy, Stoney, Alpert, & Walker, 1995; Segal & Dietz, 1991; Wilson, Holmes, Arheart, & Alpert, 1995). This finding is important, as it has been suggested that cardiovascular reactivity may serve as either a marker or mechanism for the development of essential hypertension or coronary disease (Alpert & Wilson, 1992; Murphy et al., 1995). Study results have varied according to gender, ethnicity, and game content.

In a group of 295 third-grade children, game-related differences in cardiovascular reactivity by gender and ethnicity were persistent over a 7-year study period (Murphy et al., 1995). Black children consistently demonstrated greater blood pressure and heart rate reactivity than White children. Across ethnic groups, boys demonstrated greater blood pressure reactivity than girls. Similar ethnic differences were also reported in a study of 341 children reported by Musante, Turner, Treiber, Davis, and Strong (1996).

In a study of 30 male undergraduates, playing either *Mortal Kombat I* or *II* resulted in greater heart rate reactivity than playing billiards. In addition, those who played the more violent version of *Mortal Kombat* had greater cardiovascular reactivity than those who played the less violent version (Ballard & Wiest, 1996). As yet, the clinical significance of increasing cardiovascular reactivity over extended playing periods has yet to be determined, but further research is clearly indicated.

Health Risks Associated With Sedentary Behavior

Like all media, playing electronic games may contribute to a sedentary lifestyle with the accompanying health risks. Using a 24-hour recall method, Myers, Strikmiller, Webber, and Berenson (1996) assessed the activity levels of 995 children ages 9 though 15 in relation to watching television and playing video games. More time was spent in these sedentary activities by girls and by African Americans when compared, respectively, with boys and with European Americans. The authors also reported that physical activity declined with age.

Obesity is a particular risk associated with a sedentary lifestyle. Epstein, Saelens, Myers, and Vito (1997) proposed that for children with obesity, sedentary behaviors must be more reinforcing than physical activity. Therefore, changing the reinforcement contingencies should be an effective way to change children's behavior. To examine this hypothesis, children were brought into the laboratory and given a choice of activities. The sedentary activities were a VCR with current children's movies, a Super Nintendo video game player, books, and drawing materials. The physical activities were a stationary bicycle, a low-impact climber, a Nordic Track Speed Skating Slide, and a Nordic Track Twist'N Ski Junior.

The researchers randomly assigned children to one of four experimental groups. In the reinforcement group, children gained points toward a prize for not engaging in their two highest preference sedentary activities. The punishment group lost points for engaging in their two most preferred sedentary activities. A restriction group simply did not have access to their two favorite sedentary activities, and the control group had no consequences for engaging in high-preference sedentary activities. Each child participated in three sessions. Children were given a free choice of activities in the first session, then told about the contingencies just prior to a second session, then again given a free choice of activities without contingencies in a final session. Activity choices were compared across the three sessions. Children in both the reinforcement and punishment conditions decreased their high-preference sedentary activities and increased physical activity. In addition, expressed preference for sedentary activities decreased for the reinforcement and punishment groups. Children who were only restricted from their favorite activities did not show a significant increase in physical activity. The message from this study is that the best way to decrease high-preference sedentary behaviors (such as playing electronic games) is to reinforce more physically active choices.

Positive Potential

Electronic games have great positive potential in addition to their entertainment value. Many positive applications in education and health care have been developed. There has been considerable success when games are specifically designed to address a specific problem or to teach a certain skill. However, generalizability outside the game-playing situation remains an important research question.

Generalizability

There is continuing debate about whether either motor or cognitive skills practiced and developed during game play will generalize outside the game-playing situation. Lieutenant Colonel David Grossman has been highly vocal in asserting that electronic games are potent teaching environments and that violent games teach antisocial behavior (Grossman & DeGaetano, 1999). Lieutenant Colonel Grossman has stated that practice with certain game controllers develops sharp-shooting skills that can transfer out of the game situation. Although it is possible that skills gained during game playing could transfer to very similar motor activities, there is no direct supporting research at this time. In one well-designed study that compared players and nonplayers, undergraduates were asked to track a moving light stimulus with a stylus (Griffith, Voloschin, Gibb, & Bailey, 1983). Players were better than nonplayers at the task, but there was no relationship with the specifics of game-playing experience, such as time commitment in an average week. This leaves open the question of whether game playing attracts or creates individuals with better coordination.

Some work has been done to examine whether information-processing skills improve as a result of game playing. Yuji (1996) assessed whether use of computer games would affect information-processing skills in 4- to 6-year-olds. Yuji first divided the children into player and nonplayer groups based on their past experience with computer games and then administered a computerized test of discrimination perception. There was no difference between players and nonplayers on the discrimination test, but players had faster reaction times. This led Yuji to conclude that experience with computer games may help to develop information-processing skills. Graziano, Peterson, and Shaw (1999) reported using the *Spatial-Temporal Math* video game to teach fractions and proportional math to a group of 237 second graders. Their results indicated that this method was an effective teaching approach, and its effectiveness was enhanced when piano keyboard training was added. The authors concluded that both the video game and the keyboard training tapped into basic cortical processes involving spatial-temporal reasoning. Dorval and Pepin (1986) examined whether playing a video game would improve scores for undergraduates on a test of spatial visualization. After eight sessions, undergraduates scored significantly higher on the Space Relations Test of the Differential Aptitude Test than a comparison group who did not play the video game.

These three studies provide some research support for a possible transfer of various kinds of skills outside of the specific game-playing situation. This is both an exciting development for positive applications and a sobering one with respect to games that demonstrate antisocial behavior. Much more work is needed to determine the variables affecting the generalizability of skills developed and acquired during game play.

Education

Computer-assisted instruction, including games, has been a classroom option for many years, and a full review of the history and current status of this approach is beyond the scope of the present chapter. Educators are now grappling with a host of issues related to the use of computers, including when they should first be introduced, as well as problems with accessibility. Recent meta-analyses suggest that computer-assisted instruction has a modest advantage over traditional instruction (Fletcher-Flinn, 1995). It is believed that using electronic games as one teaching approach strengthens student engagement in the learning environment (Jones, 1999). There are many innovative approaches, including using game-based training to improve information-processing skills in children with language-learning impairments (Merzenich et al., 1996; Tallal et al., 1996) and using games in after-school programs to support the development of traditional academic skills as well as problem solving and social development (Blanton, Moorman, Hayes, & Warner, 1997).

Health Care

Electronic games have also been used to improve children's health care. Several games have been developed specifically for children with chronic medical conditions. One of the best studied is an educational game called *Packy and Marlon* (Brown et al., 1997). This game was designed to improve self-care skills and medical compliance in children and adolescents with diabetes. Players assume the role of characters who demonstrate good diabetes care practices while working to save a summer camp for children with diabetes from rats and mice who have stolen the supplies. *Packy and Marlon* is now available through Click Health (www.clickhealth.com), along with two additional health-related software products, *Bronkie the Bronchiasaurus* (for asthma self-management) and *Rex Ronan* (for smoking prevention).

In a controlled study using *Packy and Marlon* (Brown et al., 1997), 8- through 16-year-olds were assigned to either a treatment or control group. All participants were given a Super Nintendo game system. The treatment group was given *Packy and Marlon* software, and the control subjects received an entertainment video game. In addition to more communication with parents and improved self-care, the treatment group demonstrated a significant decrease in urgent medical visits.

There are several case reports describing the use of electronic games for rehabilitation. In one recent application, an electronic game was used to improve arm control in a 13-year-old boy with Erb's palsy (Krichevets, Sirotkina, Yevsevicheva, & Zeldin, 1995). The authors concluded that the game format capitalized on the child's motivation to succeed in the game and focused attention away from potential discomfort.

Electronic games have also been used to enhance adolescents' perceived self-efficacy in HIV/AIDS prevention programs (Thomas, Cahill, & Santilli, 1997). Using a time travel adventure game format, information and opportunities for practice discussing prevention practices were provided to high-risk adolescents. Game playing resulted in significant gains in factual information about safe sex practices and in the participants' perceptions of their ability to successfully negotiate and implement such practices with a potential partner.

Virtual Reality

Virtual reality also has many established health applications, particularly in rehabilitation (Riva, 2000; Wilson, Foreman, & Stanton, 1997). Virtual reality technology allows the individual to become immersed in a programmable synthetic or "virtual environment" where real-life physical limitations can be erased. However, there is some concern that virtual environments may actually become too attractive for some individuals, especially children with physical disabilities. This could lead to withdrawal from the real world and avoidance of developmentally appropriate interactions. Another concern is that playing virtual reality games that reward antisocial behavior may promote similar behavior in the real world. These possible effects, as well as factors that may influence outcomes, are important topics for future study.

Virtual reality technology has been used to link children who are hospitalized with serious illnesses. A consortium of technology, medicine, and entertainment professionals and organizations developed Starbright World, a virtual reality intranet. Children use the network to communicate, play games, visit one of several virtual worlds, or research medical questions and procedures. Participants report statistically significant decreases in pain intensity, pain aversiveness, and anxiety (Holden, Bearison, Rode, Kapiloff, & Rosenberg, 2000). Descriptions of several ongoing research projects may be accessed through the Starbright Web page (www.starbright.org). The Starbright World Network is now operative across the country, and membership is open (for information, see the Starbright Web site).

Other Positive Applications

Electronic games have also been used in creative ways to change behavioral precursors, including moral development and impulsivity. For example, Sherer (1998) developed a computerized board game that presented moral dilemmas about family, peer relationships, criminal activities, sex, and drugs. Points were accumulated over a 20-week training period for choosing more prosocial options. Sherer reported that three of six indices of moral development in high school students improved as a result of the training.

Kappes and Thompson (1985) tried to reduce impulsivity in incarcerated juveniles (ages 15-18) by providing either biofeedback or experience with a video game. Impulsivity scores improved for both conditions. Improvement was also noted in negative self-attributions and in internal locus of control. The authors concluded that both experimental conditions provided immediate feedback, which was the most likely explanation for the improvement.

CONCLUSION: WHERE DO WE GO FROM HERE? ●

It is vital that we continue to develop the positive potential of electronic games while remaining aware of possible unintended negative effects when game content is not prosocial. At the present time, the most popular games are usually violent. Given current findings, it is reasonable to be concerned about the impact of violent games on some children and adolescents (Anderson & Bushman, 2001; Funk, in press). Game developers need support and encouragement to put in the additional effort necessary to develop interesting games that do not rely heavily on violent actions. Relationships between playing violent electronic games and negative behaviors and emotions may never be proven to be causal by the strictest standard of "beyond a reasonable doubt," but many believe that we have already reached the still-compelling level of "clear and convincing evidence."

Directions for Public Policy

Several states have proposed that the sale of violent electronic games to minors be banned or at least closely regulated, with harsh punishments for retailers who violate this regulation (Harris, 2000). This does not appear to be a viable option for many reasons, not the least of which are First Amendment considerations. Electronic games are a form of protected speech. There are alternatives, particularly with industry cooperation. Children are attracted to violent games in part because of heavy advertisement in other children's media. In a follow-up report released in April 2001, the Federal Trade Commission noted that the industry has made some progress in restricting the marketing of adult games to minors since this problem was identified in their original report of September 2000 (see the FTC Web site at www.ftc.gov for additional information about both reports). Senator Joseph Lieberman is sponsoring a bill to ban targeted advertising of adult entertainment media to minors. This bill would authorize the Federal Trade Commission to levy fines against companies who give products adult ratings but then market the products to children. More information about this proposed legislation can be found on Senator Lieberman's Web site (lieberman.senate.gov).

High-Risk Players and High-Risk Content

There is much to learn about which environmental, situational, and personality factors place children at increased risk for negative impact as a result of playing violent electronic games. An emerging body of research does suggest that some children are "high-risk" players (Funk, in press). Time commitment may provide one indicator for high-risk status. The work of various investigators hints that girls who play more than their peers may have adjustment issues (Colwell, Grady, & Rhaiti, 1995; Funk & Buchman, 1996a; Roe & Muijs, 1998). Any child, boy or girl, who typically plays more than 2 hours each day and who demonstrates an extreme negative reaction if play is limited should be considered at risk for negative impact simply due to time displacement from other developmentally appropriate activities.

A strong preference for violent games may be another indicator of high-risk status (Funk, Buchman, & Germann, 2000; Funk, Buchman, Myers, & Jenks, 2000; Funk et al., in press; Roe & Muijs, 1998). However, electronic games with violence are popular with many children, and the level at which preference for such games becomes pathological has not yet been established. Irwin and Gross (1995) noted that the children in their study often copied the aggressive behavior of human-like video characters after playing a violent game. The presence or absence of violence against humans may be one way for parents to decide if a particular game is acceptable for their child to play.

Ever-more realistic games are on the horizon, and technology to personalize game images is a troubling development in the field. An Atlanta gaming company, 3Q, has set up booths where, for $25.00, an individual's picture is taken, transformed into a 3-D file, and burned into a CD-ROM. Then the image can be uploaded into certain games, and the person can literally become one of the game characters. This development is troubling because the more realistic the game situation, the more likely that lessons learned will transfer into real life. At the time of this writing, only first-person shooter games support this technology.

Regarding personality features that may increase susceptibility to negative influence, Anderson (1997) reported that people who are more irritable have a lower threshold for aggression. Children with lower frustration tolerance and high general irritability appear to be at above-average risk for at least short-term negative impact, including unpleasant and uncooperative behavior, particularly after a prolonged period of play (Funk, in press). These children's electronic game play should be limited to shorter intervals, no more than 30 to 60 minutes without a significant break.

The bottom-line recommendation is that parents need to be actively involved in children's game playing, at least to adolescence. Then they need to be aware of the adolescent's game choices, particularly if the adolescent has a strong preference for violent electronic games. Parents can counter negative messages by sharing their own ideas about conflict resolution and the use of violence to solve problems. Data suggest, however, that parents are not really aware of what their children are playing. In one recent study, most parents of third to fifth graders were unable to correctly name their child's favorite game (Funk, Hagan, & Schimming, 1999). In 70% of these incorrect matches, the child's favorite game was violent. Parents and children also disagreed on what amount of supervision was typically provided by parents. This suggests that many parents may overestimate their knowledge of their child's game-playing experiences and underestimate their child's exposure to violence in electronic games.

It is recommended that parents observe their children's play at all levels of difficulty or play the games themselves. Content may change dramatically as the player progresses through different levels. Parents should become familiar with how the existing ratings system considers features such as violence and sexual material so they can use these guidelines to help them decide what games are consistent with their value system. If a child resists monitoring, if limiting play is not effective in reducing negative behaviors, or if the child frequently demonstrates and cannot suppress negative actions learned from violent electronic games, then parents should consult with the child's pediatrician or with a mental health professional. In such cases, playing violent electronic games may be either a symptom of a developing problem, or this activity may have a causal or exacerbating role. It really does not matter whether a behavioral problem starts with game playing or is worsened by game playing. Setting aside the contentious issue of causality, there is no credible evidence to suggest that playing violent electronic games will improve adjustment.

Exercises

1. Design a nonviolent electronic game that would be a big seller for 8- to 12-year-old girls. What features in terms of content and playability would be important?

2. What should the government's role be in the marketing of adult games to minors? Should there be monitoring, penalties, or a total "hands-off" approach?

3. Assume that people can become addicted to electronic games. What criteria should be used to determine "addiction"? How do you think this problem could be treated?

4. Could there be any unintended negative effects if a parent limits access to violent electronic games? What might they be?

CHAPTER **5**

SEXUALITY AND
THE MEDIA

American teenagers seem to have inherited the worst of all possible worlds regarding their exposure to messages about sex: Movies, music, radio and TV tell them that sex is romantic, exciting, titillating: premarital sex and cohabitation are visible ways of life among adults they see and hear about. . . . Yet, at the same time, young people get the message good girls should say no. Almost nothing they see or hear about sex informs them about contraception or the importance of avoiding pregnancy.

—Jones et al. (1985, p. 61)

Sexually speaking, playing catch-up is what being a teenager is all about, and movies like *American Pie* are, by now, an essential part of the ritual.

—*Entertainment Weekly* critic Owen Glieberman
(1999, pp. 43-44)

No wonder teenagers are drawn to Britney Spears, a proudly self-identifying virgin who practically pole-dances on prime-time TV then says she's waiting for true love. In one navel-baring, camera-ready package, she personifies teenagers' semiotically schismatic world. Like the Sisquo videos they watch, the shampoo commercials they channel-surf past, the Web sites they check out alone in their rooms, Spears saturates kids with sexuality; then, like their teachers, she tells them to guard their chastity.

—Susan Dominus,
New York Times Magazine (2001, pp. 9-10)

One erect penis on a U.S. screen is more incendiary than a thousand guns.

—*Newsweek* critic David Ansen
(1999, p. 66)

Figure 5.1
SOURCE: Jeff Stahler; reprinted by permission of Newspaper Enterprise Association, Inc.

In the absence of widespread, effective sex education at home or in schools, television and other media have arguably become the leading source of sex education in the United States today. As one noted researcher observes, "Long before many parents begin to discuss sex with their children, answers to such questions as 'When is it OK to have sex?' and 'With whom does one have sexual relations?' are provided by messages delivered on television" (Kunkel, Cope, & Biely, 1999, p. 230) (see Figure 5.1). This is a rather sad commentary, considering that American media are the most sexually suggestive and irresponsible in the world. Although other countries may show more nudity, only American media titillate their viewers with countless jokes and innuendoes about all aspects of human sexuality. Yet although advertisers are using sex to sell virtually everything from hotel rooms to shampoo, the national networks remain reluctant to air advertisements for birth control products (see Figure 5.2).

Unfortunately, the body of research about how children and teenagers learn about sexuality from the media and whether it affects their behavior or not is slim at best (Brown & Steele, 1995; Brown, Steele, & Walsh-Childers, 2002; Donnerstein & Smith, 2001; Greenberg, Brown, & Buerkel-Rothfuss, 1993; Gruber & Grube, 2000; Huston, Wartella, & Donnerstein, 1998; Malamuth & Impett, 2001; Strasburger & Donnerstein, 2000).

Figure 5.2
SOURCE: Jeff Stahler; reprinted by permission of Newspaper Enterprise Association, Inc.

On television each year, American children and teenagers view nearly 14,000 sexual references, innuendoes, and behaviors, few of which (less than 170) involve the use of birth control, self-control, abstinence, or responsibility (Harris & Associates, 1988). The most recent content analysis of television found that 75% of prime-time shows on the major networks contain sexual content, but only 10% of incidents include any mention of the risks or responsibilities of sexual activity or the need for contraception (see Figures 5.3a and 5.3b). This figure rises to 25% for shows depicting or implying intercourse, however (Kunkel et al., 2001). Since the 1997-1998 season, the amount of sexual content has increased from 67%, but there has been no change in the responsible content figure (Kunkel, Cope, Farinola, et al., 1999). Movies and sitcoms contain the most sexual content (Kunkel, 2001) (see Figure 5.3b). In fact, talk about sex or sexual behavior can occur as often as 8 to 10 times per hour of prime-time television (Kunkel, Cope, & Colvin, 1996; Lowry & Shidler, 1993).

Prime-time television is also very popular with teenage viewers, and much of what they see contains appreciable sexual content, according to three separate content analyses. In 19 prime-time shows viewed most often by 9th and 10th grad-

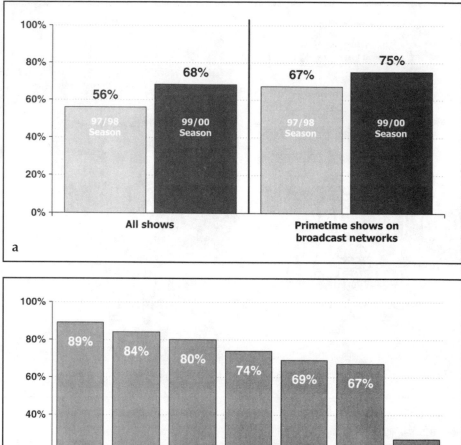

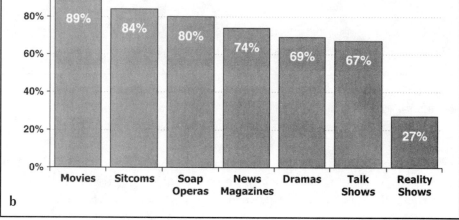

Figure 5.3. Results From the Only Ongoing, Biennial Content Analysis of Sexual Content on TV

SOURCE: Kunkel, Cope-Farrar, Biely, Farinola, and Donnerstein (2001). Reprinted with permission.

NOTE: Not only is there a lot of sexual content on mainstream American television, but most of it does not deal with the risks and responsibilities of sexual activity.

ers, just under 3 sexual references per hour occurred, usually long kisses or unmarried intercourse (Greenberg, Stanley, et al., 1993). In action adventure series, most of the sex involved either unmarried intercourse or prostitution (Greenberg, Stanley, et al., 1993). Ward (1995) found that one fourth of all verbal interactions on prime-time series watched by teens contained sexual content. Most recently, an analysis of the sexual messages in the top 15 shows according to Nielsen ratings of

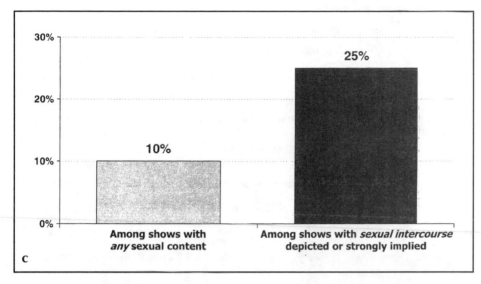

Figure 5.3. Continued. How much responsible sexual content is there on American TV?

TABLE 5.1 Top 10 Shows Viewed by Teenagers (1999-2000)

Males, 12-17 years	Females, 12-17 years
1. *Malcolm in the Middle*	1. *Sabrina the Teenage Witch*
2. *The Simpsons*	2. *Odd Man Out*
3. *WWF Smackdown*	3. *Dawson's Creek*
4. *Titus*	4. *Malcolm in the Middle*
5. *Family Guy*	5. *7th Heaven*
6. *King of the Hill*	6. *Boy Meets World*
7. *Who Wants to Be a Millionaire?*	7. *ER*
8. *The X-Files*	8. *Wonderful World of Disney*
9. *The Drew Carey Show*	9. *Charmed*
10. *That '70s Show*	10. *Who Wants to Be a Millionaire?*

SOURCE: Nielsen Media Research (2001). Used with permission.

---

teenage viewers found that two thirds contain sexual talk or behavior, with intercourse depicted in 7% of the programs (see Tables 5.1-5.3) (Cope-Farrar & Kunkel, 2002).

All of this talk about sex and sexual behavior on television (see Figure 5.4) contrasts dramatically with the fact that in the new millennium, adolescent sexuality and sexual activity—teen pregnancy, AIDS, other sexually transmitted diseases (STDs), and abortion—have all become battlegrounds in the public health and political arenas (R. T. Brown, 2000). With one million teen pregnancies a year, and with

**TABLE 5.2   Sexual Content in Teens' Favorite Primetime Programs
(*N* = 37 programs studied)**

Percentage of programs with any sexual content	82
Average number of scenes per program with sexual content	4.5
Average number of scenes per hour containing sexual content	7.0

SOURCE: Data from Cope-Farrar and Kunkel (2002).

**TABLE 5.3   Themes of Sexual Responsibility in Teens' Favorite
Programs**

Theme	% of All Scenes With Sexual Content
Saying no/waiting/keeping virginity	8.8
Taking "precautions"	2.5
Negative consequences of sex	2.5
Scenes without the above scenes	86.3

SOURCE: Adapted from Cope-Farrar and Kunkel (2002).

**TABLE 5.4   Sexual Behavior Among U.S. High School Students, 1999
(*N* = 16,262) (in percentages)**

Grade	Ever Had Sexual Intercourse		First Sex Before Age 13		Four or More Lifetime Sex Partners		Condom Use at Last Sex	
	Female	Male	Female	Male	Female	Male	Female	Male
9	33	45	6	18	8	16	63	70
10	43	51	5	14	10	21	55	70
11	54	51	5	8	15	19	50	69
12	66	64	2	8	21	21	41	56
Total	48	52	4	12	13	19	51	66

SOURCE: Data from Centers for Disease Control and Prevention (2000c).

the highest rate of STDs occurring among adolescents, the United States leads all Western nations in such statistics (Kaufman et al., 1998; Miller, 2000; Singh & Darroch, 2000). Teen pregnancy costs the nation an estimated $21 billion a year,

Figure 5.4
SOURCE: Copyright Chris Britt and Copley News Service. Used with permission.

although the rate has been decreasing during the 1990s (see Figure 5.5) (Miller, 2000). By age 17, nearly two thirds of males and one half of females have begun having sexual intercourse (see Table 5.4) (Centers for Disease Control and Prevention [CDC], 2000c; Terry & Manlove, 2000). And a sexually active American teenager has a one in four chance of contracting an STD (Kirby, 1997).

So what is shown on American television is largely unrealistic, unhealthy, suggestive sexual behavior, or sexual innuendoes (American Academy of Pediatrics [AAP], 2001c; Malamuth & Impett, 2001). It is sex as a casual pasttime, a romp in the hay, with little or no consequences. What is meant by content that is sexually suggestive? A few examples will suffice:

• In 1993, FOX network launched *Martin,* a sitcom popular with young Blacks. In one episode, Martin and his girlfriend have a contest to see who can go without sex for 2 weeks without giving in. FOX also developed *Living Single,* a sitcom about four women who share an apartment and who frequently deal with the problem of finding men: One of the women is about to go on her first date in 6 months. Her roommate remarks, "I would slide down the bannister at city hall." Another one remarks, "No butt, no date." At some point, the women also discuss going to see a movie but then decide that there is no point in seeing a film in which Denzel Washington "keeps his shirt on." Queen Latifah, a rap artist and the star of

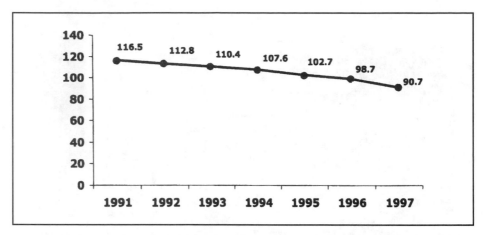

Figure 5.5. Decreasing Teen Pregnancy Rate

SOURCE: Kaiser Family Foundation (2000a). Reprinted with permission.

NOTE: In the 1990s, the teen pregnancy rate steadily decreased as the result of an increase in contraceptive use and a decrease in sexual activity. Pregnancy rate data include live births, induced abortions, and fetal losses. Data are among all females ages 15 to 19.

the show, then suggests, "Let's see the new Wesley Snipes movie. I hear there's much nipple" (Shales, 1993).

• The famous sitcom *Seinfeld* repeated the abstinence plot line later in the 1990s, with a story about who could be "the master of his own domain" by going without masturbating for the longest period of time. *Seinfeld* also had a notorious story involving Jerry confusing a girlfriend's name for a part of the female pelvic anatomy (which later became part of a sexual harassment lawsuit in real life).

• In the late 1990s, a rash of teenage sitcoms appeared on prime-time TV. In *Popular,* a mom confronts her daughter and soon-to-be stepdaughter: "One of you is thinking of Doing It, if not already Doing It." In *That '70s Show,* one dim teenager asks, "Why cuddle when you can Do It?" These, along with several others representing the new generation of shows for teens, have been termed "Happy Days With Hormones" (Tucker, 1999).

• HBO's hit of the 1999-2000 season, *Sex in the City,* features four single women who can never seem to get enough sex or talk enough about it. Various conversations have dealt with oral sex, anal sex, spanking, and other fetishes (Jacobs, 1999). Nudity is not uncommon. Curiously for a show that is so explicit, the risks of casual sex and the need for birth control are rarely mentioned.

By contrast, consider the various messages and information presented in the following synopsis of a 1996 episode of *Malibu Shores* (Kunkel, Cope, & Biely, 1999):

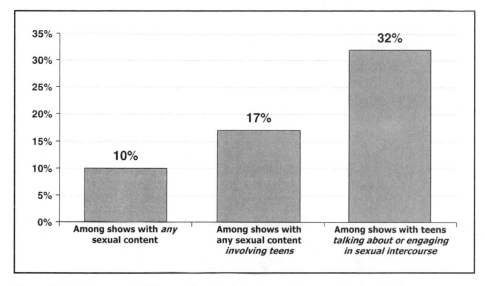

Figure 5.6. Percentage of Shows That Contain Any Reference to Sexual Risks or Responsibilities: Shows With Teens Versus All Other Shows

SOURCE: From Kunkel, Cope-Farrar, Biely, Farinola, and Donnerstein (2001). Reprinted with permission.

NOTE: Programs that depict teen characters in sexual situations are more likely to include references to the risks and responsibilities of sexual intercourse.

> Two teenagers are making out on the couch. Zach wants to have intercourse, but Chloe is not sure. He moves his hand underneath her shirt but she pushes it away, explaining "a month from now I don't want to be taking a pregnancy test." Zach says that he will use "protection" but Chloe says she's afraid that "protection" is not 100% effective. A friend of hers had a recent pregnancy scare. Finally, Zach says, "It's OK. I can wait. As long as it takes. I can wait. I don't want you to do something you're not ready to do. (*Malibu Shores,* NBC, March 30, 1996)

A distinct minority of TV shows in the 1990s have wrestled successfully with sexual responsibility. Beginning with *Beverly Hills 90210,* the character of Donna (played by Tori Spelling) maintained her virginity throughout high school, when everyone else was losing theirs. At the end of the decade, during the 1999-2000 season of *Dawson's Creek,* the two major characters, Dawson and Joey, remained virgins as they approached their senior year in high school (Jacobs & Shaw, 1999). One expert notes that this is the one encouraging sign in all of the recent content analyses of mainstream television—that shows popular with teens may be more willing to address risks and responsibilities of early sex (Kunkel, Cope, & Biely, 1999). However, the actual percentage of such shows still remains surprisingly low: 10% of any shows with sexual content in 2001, but 32% of shows with teens talking about or engaging in sex (see Figure 5.6) (Cope-Farrar & Kunkel, 2002; Kunkel et al., 2001).

TABLE 5.5   Best and Worst Programs for Women, According to NOW (National Organization for Women)

Grading the Networks

NBC   B+

CBS   C+

ABC   C

FOX   D–

Best Shows: Top 10

1. *Family Law* (CBS)
2. *Chicago Hope* (CBS)
3. *Once & Again* (ABC)
4. *ER* (NBC)
5. *Sabrina the Teenage Witch* (ABC, WB)
6. *20/20* (ABC)
7. *Providence* (NBC)
8. *Becker* (CBS)
9. *Touched by an Angel* (CBS)
10. *Friends* (NBC)

Thumbs Down To

1. *Perfect Murder, Perfect Town* (made-for-TV movie about JonBenet Ramsey) (CBS)
1. *Getting Away With Murder* (another Ramsey movie) (FOX)
2. *Who Wants to Marry a Multi-Millionaire* (FOX)
3. *Norm* (ABC)
4. *The Drew Carey Show* (ABC)
5. *Spin City* (ABC)
6. *The World's Wildest Police Videos* (FOX)
7. *Walker, Texas Ranger* (CBS)
8. *Nash Bridges* (CBS)

SOURCE: Adapted from Gorman (2000).

NOTE: Eighty-one shows were analyzed during February 2000 "sweeps" weeks using four criteria: depiction of violence, gender composition and stereotypes, level of sexual exploitation, and social responsibility.

Sex on television is much more than sexual intercourse or sexual intimacy, however. Children and adolescents also can learn a great deal about sex roles: What does it mean to be a man or a woman? What makes someone "cool"? Attractive? Successful? How should one behave around the opposite sex (Signorielli, 1993, 2001; Steele, 1999)? Mainstream television is not kind to adolescent girls, for example (Pipher, 1997). A 1988 report found that teenage girls are stereotyped as obsessed with shopping and boys and incapable of having serious conversations about academic interests or career goals. Their looks seem to be far more important than their brains (Steenland, 1988). Likewise, a new report from the National Organization for Women (NOW) finds great disparities in the quality of programming for adolescent and adult women on the major networks (see Table 5.5) (Gorman, 2000).

● BACKGROUND

In 1976, the NBC Standards and Practices Department (the network censors) refused to let writer Dan Wakefield use the word *responsible* when *James at 15* and

Figure 5.7

his girlfriend were about to have sexual intercourse for the first time and wanted to discuss birth control (Wakefield, 1987). To date, the networks still reject public service announcements (PSAs) and advertisements about contraception, fearing that they would offend some unknown but vocal population in America's hinterland (Quigley, 1987). If an occasional ad for a birth control product does make it to the air, it is because of the noncontraceptive properties of the product (e.g., Ortho Tri-Cyclen is usually advertised as a treatment for acne, not a means of preventing pregnancy)(see Figure 5.7). Public service announcements that mention condoms—for example, ABC's 1994 campaign entitled "America Responds to AIDS"—are largely confined to late-night TV (Painter, 1994).

Sex (the commercial networks seem to be telling us) is good for selling everything from shampoo, office machinery, hotel rooms, and beer to prime-time series and made-for-TV movies (see Figure 5.8), but a product that would prevent the tragedy of teenage pregnancy—the dreaded "c-word"—must never darken America's television screens. Other media have become increasingly sexually explicit

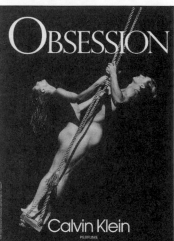

Figure 5.8. Using Sex to Sell

From the classic Maidenform bra ads of the 1950s to modern times, advertisers have always used sex to sell products. But many ads are becoming more graphic.

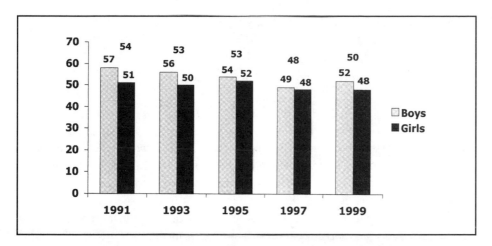

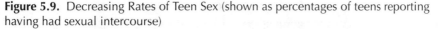

Figure 5.9. Decreasing Rates of Teen Sex (shown as percentages of teens reporting having had sexual intercourse)

SOURCE: Data from Centers for Disease Control and Prevention, Youth Risk Behavior Surveys, 1991-1999. Reprinted from Kaiser Family Foundation (2000a), with permission.

NOTE: Rates of teenage sexual intercourse have been decreasing somewhat during the 1990s.

as well, particularly in the past two decades, without much regard for discussing either contraception or sexually transmitted disease. At the same time, a certain "raunchiness" has crept into mainstream American media, with four-letter words even heard on prime-time television (Rice, 2000). Only AIDS has begun to threaten the conspiracy of silence about the health consequences of sexual activity and to free up the flow of useful and factual information to teenagers, who need it the most.

Why and how has this paradox occurred, and what effect does it have on teenage sexual activity? As with violence, the rate of sexual activity among young people has increased dramatically in the past two decades, although it shows signs of leveling off in the late 1990s (see Figure 5.9) (CDC, 2000c; Strasburger & Brown, 1998). At the same time, the amount of sexual suggestiveness in the media has increased dramatically as well (Donnerstein & Smith, 2001). Although the data are not quite as convincing as with media violence, a handful of studies show that media sex still warrants considerable concern.

TELEVISION AS A SOURCE OF SEXUAL INFORMATION •

In any given society, at any given moment in history, people become sexual the same way they become anything else. Without much reflection, they pick up directions from their social environment. They acquire and assemble meanings, skills, and values from the people around them. Critical choices are often made by going along and drifting. People learn when they are quite young the few things they are expected to be, and continue slowly to accumulate a belief in who they are and ought to be throughout the rest of childhood, adolescence, and adulthood.

—John Gagnon, social science researcher (Roberts, 1983, p. 9)

Content analyses can determine what is being shown on television, but they do not reveal what teenagers actually learn from these portrayals. Apart from its pervasiveness, accessibility, and content, television is an effective sex educator for several other reasons (Brown & Steele, 1995; Haffner & Kelly, 1987; Huston et al., 1998). Alternative sex educators, such as parents, may supply only restricted or biased information (Pearl, Bouthilet, & Lazar, 1982). Parents rarely discuss sexual activity or birth control, making a majority of teenagers dissatisfied with parents' educational attempts (Selverstone, 1992). Sex education programs in school may also have a limited impact on adolescents: Only 10% to 30% of schools offer comprehensive, high-quality programs; gains in knowledge may be small; and many curricula begin after teenagers have already begun having intercourse (Dawson, 1986; Furstenberg, Moore, & Peterson, 1985; Harris & Associates, 1986; Kirby, 1997; Landry, Kaeser, & Richards, 1999; Marsiglio & Mott, 1986; Selverstone, 1992; Zelnik & Kim, 1982). The latest survey of sex education programs around the country found that 35% teach abstinence only, 51% teach abstinence "plus" (meaning that contraception can be mentioned but not emphasized), and only 14% are comprehensive (Landry et al., 1999). Yet the latest nationwide poll of adults shows that 93% support sex education in high schools and 84% support it in middle schools, including contraception information as well as abstinence (Sexuality Information and Education Council of the U.S. [SIECUS], 2000).

Peers, too, may play a limited role in sex education—not that their counsel is infrequently sought but because the information offered may be incomplete, misleading, distorted, and transmitted by means of jokes or boasting (and may, in fact, be influenced by the media as well) (Coles & Stokes, 1985). One author has hypothesized that the media may function as a "super-peer," in terms of pressuring teens into having sex earlier than expected (Strasburger, 1997c). Teenagers already overestimate the number of their peers who are engaging in sexual intercourse (Zabin, Hirsch, Smith, & Hardy, 1984). Several studies document that teens who are avid consumers of media are more likely to overestimate the number of their peers and friends who are sexually active and to feel more pressure from the media to begin having sex than from friends (Brown & Newcomer, 1991; Kaiser Family Foundation, 1996; Kaiser Family Foundation/Children Now, 1999; Roper Starch Worldwise, Inc., 1994; Tucker, 2000). For example, in one survey, teenagers reported that TV was equally or more encouraging about sex than either their best male or female friends (Brown & Newcomer, 1991). In a recent anonymous survey of 1,015 *Seventeen* readers, ages 13 to 19, three fourths believed that most teenagers are having sex, whereas only about half actually are (Tucker, 2000). A survey of 2,100 teenage girls found that only 11-year-olds say that they do not feel pressure

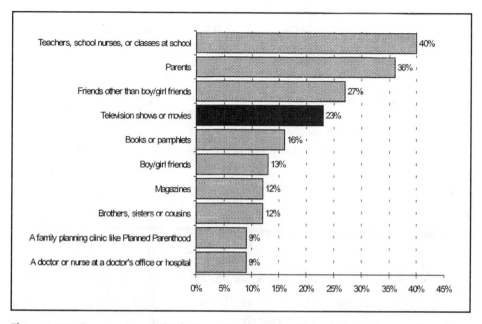

Figure 5.10. Sources From Which Teens Have Learned "A Lot" About Pregnancy and Birth Control

SOURCE: From Kaiser Family Foundation (2000b). Reprinted with permission.

NOTE: Although TV and movies rank fourth in a national survey of 1,510 teens ages 12 to 18 about sources of sex information, when other media are added in (books and magazines), media become the leading source.

from the media to have sex (Haag, 1999). Fans of music videos tend to overestimate the prevalence of sexual behaviors in the real world (Strouse, Goodwin, & Roscoe, 1994). And, finally, in a recent study of 314 students ages 18 to 20, greater exposure to sexual content on TV led to higher expectations of the sexuality activity of one's peers and a more positive attitude toward recreational sex (Ward, Gorvine, & Cytron, 2001; Ward & Rivadeneyra, 1999). Heavy doses of television may accentuate teens' feelings that everyone is "doing it" except them and may be contributing to the steadily decreasing age at first intercourse for both males and females that has been occurring during the past two decades (Braverman & Strasburger, 1993; Strasburger, 1997c).

When teenagers or adults are asked about the influence of television, they acknowledge its role as an important source of sexual information but are equally quick to point out that the media have no influence on *their* behavior. This is the well-known third-person phenomenon (Eveland et al., 1999): Everyone is influenced by media except oneself, and it seems particularly prevalent among teenagers. For teens, the very idea that something as simplistic and ordinary as the media could influence them is insulting; they are far more "sophisticated" than that. Yet in the most recent national survey, media ranked close to first as a source of adolescents' sexual information (see Figure 5.10) (Kaiser Family Foundation, 1996). In

TABLE 5.6   Television and Birth Control (N = 1,250 adults) (in percentages)

	Yes	No
Should characters on TV shows be shown using birth control?	59	34
Is contraception too controversial to be mentioned on TV shows?	32	64
Are you in favor of advertising birth control on TV?	60	37
Would birth control advertising		
encourage teenagers to have sex?	42	52
encourage teens to use contraceptives?	82	14

Adapted from Harris and Associates (1987).

TABLE 5.7   Concerns About Sex: Hollywood Versus the American Public (in percentages)

	Americans	Hollywood
Percentage who feel that TV and movies contribute to these problems:		
Extramarital sex	84	43
Casual sex	83	56
Teens having sex	90	63
Violence against women	94	61
Percentage who are concerned about the following:		
Verbal references to sex	82	38
Nudity or seminudity	83	42
Premarital sex	83	38

SOURCE: *U.S. News & World Report* and UCLA Center for Communication Policy polls, April 15, 1966. For details, see Impoco (1996).

another study, one in five teens said that they learned the most about sex from the media (Brown & Steele, 1995).

Many older studies found media ranked highly as well (Harris & Associates, 1986, 1987; Pearl, Bouthilet, & Lazar, 1982; Sexuality Study Group, 1990; Thornburg, 1981). A 1987 Harris Report, which surveyed 1,250 adults nationwide, found that more than 80% of adults felt that TV was a major influence on teenagers' values and behavior (see Table 5.6) (Harris & Associates, 1987). Again, when one hypoth-

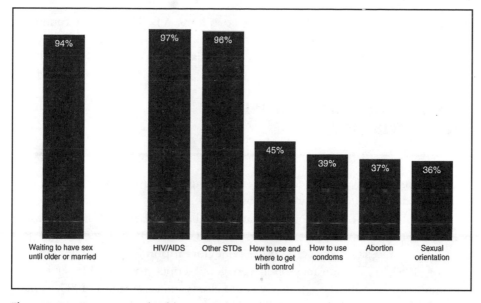

Figure 5.11. Percentage of Public Secondary School Principals Reporting Each Is Included in Their Schools' Sex Education

SOURCE: From the Kaiser Family Foundation (1999b). Reprinted with permission.

NOTE: How "comprehensive" is comprehensive sex education? According to a national survey of 313 secondary school principals (Kaiser Family Foundation, 1999b), 58% of their sex education programs are comprehensive in nature versus 34% abstinence only. But the comprehensiveness varies considerably according to topic.

esizes that friends and even parents may all be greatly influenced themselves by television, the cumulative effects of television may outweigh all other influences. At the same time, there seems to be a dissociation between the concerns of the general public and those in power in Hollywood (see Table 5.7) (Impoco, 1996). If anything, American parents seem more concerned about media sex than about media violence, which is the exact opposite of parents in other Western countries.

Not only are the media important generic sources of information, but particular topics may also be far more intensively discussed in the media than elsewhere (Harris & Associates, 1988). For instance, television may be the "medium of choice" for dissemination of information about AIDS (Goldberg, 1987). Of nearly 2,000 adults surveyed in a 1988 Roper poll, 96% said they had heard a report on AIDS in the past 3 months on TV, and 73% thought that TV was doing an effective job of educating the public (Jones, 1988). Media might also step in when others (i.e., schools) do not provide comprehensive information: A 1996 survey of 719 students and 13 school board members nationwide found that 93% of the students said that schools should teach about birth control and sexually transmitted diseases but that teachers are "scared" to discuss sex in the classroom (*USA Today,* July 3, 1996, p. 7D). A Kaiser study of 313 school principals nationwide found that more than half of students are not being taught how to use condoms in sex education programs (see Figure 5.11) (Kaiser Family Foundation, 1999b). Yet adults increasingly want children educated about condoms. A poll by the CDC found that 86% of adults surveyed supported the airing of information about HIV and AIDS prevention, and 73% favored condoms being discussed on TV (CDC, 1994b).

● WHAT DO CHILDREN AND TEENAGERS LEARN FROM TELEVISION?

Many studies have documented television's ability to transmit information and to shape attitudes (Sutton, Brown, Wilson, & Klein, 2002). Television influences viewers' perception of social behavior and social reality (Bandura, 1977; Hawkins & Pingree, 1982), contributes to cultural norms (Gerbner, 1985; Greenberg, 1982), and conveys messages concerning the behaviors it portrays (Bandura, 1977; E. Roberts, 1982). Television may offer teenagers "scripts" for sexual behavior that they might not be able to observe anywhere else (Gagnon & Simon, 1987; Kunkel, Cope, & Biely, 1999; Silverman-Watkins, 1983). In one experiment, exposing teens to programming with a lot of sexual content led them to rate casual sex less negatively than teens who did not view the programs (Bryant & Rockwell, 1994). In other studies, adolescents who view a lot of media are more likely to accept stereotypical sex roles (Walsh-Childers & Brown, 1993) and to believe that the unusual sexual behavior presented on talk shows is realistic (Greenberg & Smith, 2001; Strasburger & Furno-Lamude, 1997). One recent national survey actually found that 40% of teenagers said they have learned ideas about how to talk with their boyfriends or girlfriends about sex directly from media portrayals (Kaiser Family Foundation, 1998).

Given that the media are filled with sexual talk, behavior, and innuendoes and a lot of inaccurate information (Sutton et al., 2002), how do children and adolescents interpret such content? Does it have the same impact on a 7-year-old as on a 17-year-old? Clearly, the answer is no. The available research concludes the following:

- Young people bring their own unique knowledge and expectations to the viewing arena (Greenberg, Linsangan, & Soderman, 1993; Truglio, 1992).

- Although young children sometimes understand the jokes and innuendoes about sex (Kaiser Family Foundation/Children Now, 1996), there is usually an age-dependent ability to interpret sexual content (Silverman-Watkins & Sprafkin, 1983).

- Interest paid to and comprehension of sexual content is probably age dependent, although the lower age limits could be decreasing. One recent study of 8- to 13-year-olds found that most of them understood the sexual messages being portrayed and tuned in because they wanted to learn something about sex (Kunkel et al., 1996).

TABLE 5.8 Teenagers' Versus Adults' Perceptions of Sex on Television (in percentages)

Yes, TV gives a realistic picture about the following:	*Teenagers* (n = 1,000)	*Adults* (n = 1,253)
Sexually transmitted diseases	45	28
Pregnancy	41	24
Birth control	28	17
People making love	24	18

SOURCE: Adapted from Harris and Associates (1986).

- Sexual content is very appealing to teenagers (Hansen & Hansen, 1990; Sutton et al., 2001). Gender differences also seem to exist. Teen girls prefer more sexual content on television but often watch with their parents (Greenberg & Linsangan, 1993), whereas older adolescent boys choose more unsupervised hard-core sexual content in music lyrics and X-rated films (Buerkel-Rothfuss, Strouse, Pettey, & Shatzer, 1993; Greenberg & Linsangan, 1993). Girls who have not yet begun menstruating are much less interested in sexual content; conversely, girls who are more mature and more interested in sex seem to seek out sexual content in the media (Brown et al., 1993).

- Parents are very concerned about sexual content on television (Kaiser Family Foundation/Children Now, 1996).

- Many discussions about sex roles occur on television, with many focusing on the male sexual role and emphasizing a "recreational" orientation toward sex. In particular, the most frequently occurring messages depict sexual relations as a competition in which men comment on women's physical appearance and masculinity is equated with being sexual (Ward, 1995).

- Viewing soap operas, which are extremely appealing to many teens, may give viewers unrealistic and unhealthy notions about single motherhood (Larson, 1996). However, not all teenagers apparently interpret the same content in the same way (Greenberg, 1993). In a study of teenagers' reactions to Madonna's video "Papa Don't Preach," Brown and Schulze (1990) found that Black teens viewed the popular music video as a father-daughter story, rather than a story about teen pregnancy (see Table 5.8). Studying individual differences among children and teens who view the same media may represent the current "cutting edge" of media research.

Studies show that subtler aspects of human sexuality may also be affected (Donnerstein & Smith, 2001; Signorielli, 1993, 2001). For example, young children who watch 25 hours or more of TV demonstrated more stereotypical sex role attitudes than those who watched 10 hours or less per week (Freuh & McGhee, 1975). The frequent viewers thought that boys should play with guns and trucks and that girls should play with dolls. Numerous studies have shown that television cultivates such notions as "women are happiest at home raising children" and "men are born with more ambition than women," particularly among heavy viewers (Morgan, 1987). Even Saturday morning cartoons contribute to this traditional view of girls and women (Canonzoneri, 1984).

As the National Institute of Mental Health (NIMH) report concluded, the single most significant aspect of a child's learning about sex is the set of messages that relates to "normal" male and female characteristics and roles in life (E. Roberts, 1982). Although television has made some progress in this area—for instance, males outnumber females 2:1 currently instead of 3:1 in the 1970s (Gerbner, 1993)—even the independent women shown in current programming frequently depend on men for advice and directions, lose control more often than men, and become more emotionally involved. This has led one critic to charge that the traditional female roles are merely being "dished up in new guises" (Canonzoneri, 1984).

● WHY TEENAGERS MAY BE PARTICULARLY SUSCEPTIBLE TO SEXUAL CONTENT IN THE MEDIA

It is well known that teenagers sometimes resemble actors and actresses as they experiment with different facets of their newly forming identities and try on different social "masks." In particular, the idiosyncrasies of adolescent psychology seem to combine to conspire against successful use of contraception during early and middle adolescence (Strasburger & Brown, 1998). Teenagers often see themselves egocentrically as being actors in their own "personal fable" (Elkind, 1993) in which the normal rules (e.g., having unprotected sexual intercourse may lead to pregnancy) are suspended—exactly as on television. Even though 70% of teenagers, by age 16, have reached the final level of cognitive operational thinking described by Piaget (1972)—sequential logical thinking (formal operations)—they may still suffer from what Elkind (1984) calls "pseudostupidity": "The capacity to conceive many different alternatives is not immediately coupled with the ability to assign priorities and to decide which choice is more or less appropriate than others" (p. 384).

One major conclusion of the 1985 Guttmacher Report, which found that the United States has the highest rate of teenage pregnancy in 37 developed countries (despite the fact that American teenagers are no more sexually active than French or Canadian or Belgian teens), concerned the media (Jones et al., 1985). There are only two possible hypotheses to explain these data: Either American female teens are extremely fertile, or American teens do not use birth control as effectively as teens in other countries. In fact, these data confirm that American society limits access to birth control for teenagers in three vital ways—via their physicians (who are reluctant to prescribe it), their media (which are reluctant to mention it), and their school-based sex education programs (which are reluctant to talk about it) (Strasburger & Brown, 1998). Although rates of teen sex have decreased slightly in the 1990s (CDC, 2000c), the United States continues to have the highest teen pregnancy rate in the Western world (Cromer & McCarthy, 1999).

Given the content of current American television, one would expect that heavy viewers would believe that premarital sex, extramarital sex, rape, and prostitution are all more common than they really are (Greenberg, 1994; Strasburger & Furno-Lamude, 1997). Although teenagers are probably not as susceptible as young children to media violence, they may be more susceptible to sexual content. Indeed, they often believe that what they watch on television is real (Harris & Associates, 1986). This belief is actually highest among those who are heavier consumers of TV and among adolescent populations with the highest teenage pregnancy rates (see Table 5.8) (Harris & Associates, 1985). Regular exposure to sexy TV might alter teenagers' self-perceptions as well. They might be less satisfied with their own sex lives or have higher expectations of their prospective partners (Greenberg, 1994).

If, as Gerbner states, "daytime serials comprise the most prolific single source of medical advice in America" (Gerbner, Morgan, & Signorielli, 1982, p. 295), then teenagers, particularly females, are getting bad advice. One of the main messages from the soaps is that adults do not use contraception and, in fact, do not plan for sex at all. Being "swept away" is the natural way to have sex (Wattleton, 1987). Unfortunately, this message dovetails with adolescents' own ambivalence about sex and helps to explain why the leading reasons sexually active teens give for not using contraception are that sex "just happens" and there was "no time to prepare" (Harris & Associates, 1986).

Several studies support these manifestations of the "cultivation hypothesis." When college students were asked to identify models of responsible and irresponsible sexual behavior, they selected primarily media figures (Fabes & Strouse, 1984). And those who selected media figures as models of sexual responsibility had more permissive sexual attitudes and higher rates of sexual activity themselves (Fabes & Strouse, 1987). College students who were heavy viewers of soap operas estimated higher percentages of people in the real world who are divorced or have illegitimate children than did light viewers (Buerkel-Rothfuss & Mayes, 1981; Carveth & Alexander, 1985). In one study, pregnant teenagers were twice as likely to think that TV relationships are like real-life relationships than nonpregnant teenagers and that TV characters would not use contraception if involved in a sexual relationship (Corder-Bolz, 1981). And adolescents who identify closely with TV personalities and think that their TV role models are more proficient at sex than they are, or who think that TV sexual portrayals are accurate, report being less satisfied with their status as sexual virgins and with their own intercourse experiences (Baran, 1976a, 1976b; Courtright & Baran, 1980).

● MOVIES

As a medium, movies are probably less significant than television because they command much less time from the average teenager and are usually viewed with friends, thus allowing the process of socialization to temper whatever potential effects may exist. If teenagers see two movies per week at their local cinema, that still represents only 10% to 15% of the time they spend watching television in an average week. This does not imply that movies are not important, however (Steele, 2002). As many as 80% of all movies later shown on network or cable TV contain sexual content (Kunkel, Cope, Farinola, et al., 1999), and that content may be considerably more explicit in the initial theatrical release. There has also been a consistent trend toward more sexually suggestive and sexually graphic material being presented in movies (Greenberg et al., 1987; Kunkel, Cope, Farinola, et al., 1999; Nashawaty, 1999). The widespread prevalence of videocassette recorders—85% of American households have one (Nielsen Media Research, 2000)—also makes the local video shop an important consideration along with the local cinema.

In a survey of 15- to 16-year-olds in three Michigan cities, more than half had seen the majority of the most popular R-rated movies between 1982 and 1984, either in movie houses or on videocassette (Greenberg et al., 1986). Compared with prime-time television, these movies have a frequency of sexual acts or references that is seven times higher, with a much franker depiction than on television (Greenberg, Siemicki, et al., 1993). Moreover, for a society concerned with abstinence, it seems curious that there was an average of eight acts of sexual intercourse between unmarried partners per R-rated film analyzed, or nearly half of all the sexual activity depicted. The ratio of unmarried to married intercourse was 32:1 (Greenberg, Siemicki, et al., 1993). As Greenberg (1994) notes, "What television suggests, movies and videos do" (p. 180). Content analyses of the most popular movies of 1959, 1969, and 1979 demonstrate the trend toward increasing explicitness in depictions of sexual themes, but the themes themselves have remained stable: Sex is for the young and is an "action activity" rather than a means of expressing affection (Abramson & Mechanic, 1983). And, as on TV, intercourse and contraception are distant cousins, at best.

The years 1970 through 1989 represented the era of teenage "sexploitation" films. Hollywood pandered to the adolescent population, presumably because of demographic considerations: Teenagers constitute the largest moviegoing segment of the population. Such movies as *Porky's I, II,* and *III, The Last American Virgin, Going All the Way, The First Time, Endless Love, Risky Business, Bachelor Party,* and *Fast Times at Ridgemont High* have dealt with teenage sex. Although parents may complain about their teenagers' interest in such films, it is the adults making films in Hollywood (and the adult movie house operators allowing underage teenagers in to see R-rated films) who are ultimately responsible.

With the Baby Boom generation coming of age and producing children of their own, Hollywood seems to have returned to targeting the teen audience. In 1999, *American Pie* updated *Porky's* for the next generation. In it, four male high school seniors all make a pact to lose their virginity by prom night. Early in the movie, the main character, Jim (Jason Biggs) masturbates with an apple pie after his friends tell him that that's what intercourse feels like. The movie also features a scene of stripping and attempted intercourse, broadcast over the Internet (D'Angelo, 1999). Talk about contraception, or the risks of intercourse, is virtually nonexistent; yet the movie still struggled to get an R rating, rather than an NC-17, primarily because of the scene the movie derives its title from (Nashawaty, 1999). As one movie critic notes, the film is "pitched to the first generation of male and female adolescents who have been taught, from birth (mostly by MTV), to act as sex objects for each other" (Glieberman, 1999, p. 43). Other researchers feel that the distorted view of romance in contemporary movies popular with teens is at least as problematic as the overt sex (Pardun, 2001).

Nevertheless, since the 1980s, virtually every R-rated teen movie has contained at least one nude scene, and some, such as *Fast Times at Ridgemont High* and *Porky's,* contain up to 15 instances of sexual intercourse (Greenberg, Siemicki, et al., 1993). As one expert notes,

> The typical hour-long television program . . . will provide between two and three intimate sex acts, and most likely, there will be discussions/conversations about what someone is doing or has done, with the visual components quite rare. The typical 90-minute R-rated film, on the other hand, yields seven times that amount of sexual activity, with a large proportion made manifest through visual images. (Greenberg, Siemicki, et al., 1993, p. 56)

QUESTIONABLE LANGUAGE AND TASTE IN • MOVIES AND TELEVISION: A NEW TREND?

During the summers of 1998 and 1999, Hollywood seemed to be trying to stretch the boundaries of both the ratings and good taste. What is acceptable to the networks and the studios changes all the time, but during the past 5 years, the enter-

TABLE 5.9   A Chronology of Questionable Language on Prime-time TV

March 18, 1979	The PBS documentary *Scared Straight* brings prison language to prime-time.
February 26, 1984	Phoebe Cates's character on the miniseries *Lace* asks, "Which one of you bitches is my mother?"
January 22, 1990	Guns N' Roses let rip with four-letter words at the American Music Awards, including f—-.
September 10, 1990	The first appearance of the expression, "You suck!" on prime-time TV, in the CBS comedy *Uncle Buck*.
September 21, 1993	Andy Sipowicz yells, "You pissy little bitch!" in the series premiere of *NYPD Blue*. The same episode features the terms "d—-head" and "a—hole."
March 21, 1999	Whoopi Goldberg hosts the Academy Awards and uses the word "sh—" twice, as well as many double entendres.

SOURCE: Adapted from Rice (2000).

tainment industry has seemed less inclined to fear moral watchdogs in society (see Table 5.9). Films such as *There's Something About Mary; South Park: Bigger, Longer & Uncut; Austin Powers: The Spy Who Shagged Me; Me, Myself & Irene;* and *Freddy Got Fingered* have set new standards for what can be said, shown, or discussed on screen (see Exercises for a discussion of "taste"). For example, *Freddy Got Fingered* features scenes of the star masturbating a live horse and prancing around in the skin of a gutted deer and a costar being sprayed with elephant ejaculate (Robischon, 2001). Minute for minute, *South Park* may be the crudest movie ever distributed, with 399 words that Movie Index of Colorado Springs classified as "crude, obscene/profane or sexually suggestive" (Farhi, 1999). (Although *Pulp Fiction* contained 411 such words, it ran 154 minutes in length, compared with *South Park*'s 80 minutes.) Adult films such as Spike Lee's *Summer of Sam* and Stanley Kubrick's *Eyes Wide Shut* somehow avoided the "kiss-of-death" NC-17 rating and received R ratings instead. Even PG-13 films such as *Wild Wild West* contain conversations about penis size and breast texture and sights of Salma Hayek's bare buttocks (Hershenson, 1999).

One media critic feels that this has all contributed to a new "culture of disrespect" among children and adolescents, who are susceptible to the role-modeling influence of such programming (Walsh, 1994). Another prominent critic, commenting on the summer of 2000 that produced *Me, Myself & Irene* and *Road Trip,* commented, "The stinky-poo outrages of recent Hollywood fare have no higher agenda than coaxing rowdy laughter from randy teenagers. . . . Crass is mass market" (Ansen, 2000, p. 61). To date, no research examines the impact of "raunchy" content or language on children or adolescents.

PRINT MEDIA ●

Contemporary magazines reflect the same trend as seen in television and movies—a shift away from naive or innocent romantic love in the 1950s and 1960s (e.g., *Bachelor Father* and *My Little Margie* on TV, *Beach Blanket Bingo* and *Love Me Tender* in the movies) to increasingly clinical concerns about sexual functioning (Treise & Gotthoffer, 2002; Walsh-Childers, Gotthoffer, & Lepre, 2002). Content analyses demonstrate that by the 1970s, such mainstream magazines as *Ladies Home Journal, Good Housekeeping, McCalls,* and *Time* contained a threefold increase in the number of articles that discussed sexual functioning and a sixfold increase in sexual terms used (Bailey, 1969; Herold & Foster, 1975; Scott, 1986). Accompanying this change was a shift from discussion of sexual "morality" to concern about sexual "quality," a skepticism about virginity at marriage, and a liberalized view of extramarital sex (Silverman-Watkins, 1983).

In one of the handful of studies of print media that adolescents read, Klein et al. (1993) found that *Seventeen, Sports Illustrated, Teen, Time, Ebony, Young Miss, Jet, Newsweek,* and *Vogue* accounted for more than half of all reported reading (the survey was conducted before *Sassy* was introduced). Adolescents who read sports or music magazines were more likely to report engaging in risky behaviors. Many teenagers, especially girls, report that they rely on magazines as an important source of information about sex, birth control, and health-related issues (Kaiser Family Foundation, 1996; Treise & Gotthoffer, 2002; Wray & Steele, 2002).

Content analyses of *Seventeen* and *Sassy* have found that most of the stories in these two popular magazines contain very traditional socialization messages, including that girls depend on someone else to solve one's personal problems (Peirce, 1993), girls are obsessed with guys, girls are heterosexual, and girls are always appearance-conscious shoppers (Wray & Steele, 2002). *Sassy* initially featured content such as "Losing Your Virginity," "Getting Turned On," and "My Girlfriend Got Pregnant" (Brown & Steele, 1995). After an advertising boycott organized by the religious right, however, such content was withdrawn. In the mid-1990s, *YM* seems to have picked up where *Sassy* left off.

YM has undergone several name changes, from *Calling All Girls* to *Polly Pigtails* to *Young Miss* to its current moniker, which stands for "Young and Modern" and features such content as "Getting Intimate," a section sealed in a brown paper wrapper with information about sex (Carmody, 1994).

Kilbourne (1999) points out the trivialization of sex that occurs in women's magazines, both in their content and their advertising. For example, one print ad for jeans says, "You can learn more about anatomy after school" and shows a teenage guy groping a girl. According to Kilbourne, the print media give adolescent girls impossibly contradictory messages: be innocent, but be sexually experienced too. Teen magazines such as *Jane* are filled with articles such as "How Smart Girls Flirt," "Sex to Write Home About," "15 Ways Sex Makes You Prettier," and "Are You Good in Bed?" (Kilbourne, 1999).

In their defense, however, the print media are also far more likely to discuss contraception and advertise birth control products than broadcast media are (Walsh-Childers et al., 2002). A content analysis of teen magazines found that they devote an average of 2½ pages per issue to sexual issues (Walsh-Childers, 1997). Of sexual articles in teen magazines, nearly half (42%) concerned health issues (Walsh-Childers, 1997). However, much of the coverage is in the form of advice columns, and the overarching focus seems to be on decision making about when to lose one's virginity (Huston et al., 1998; Walsh-Childers, 1997).

● THE NATURE OF THE RESEARCH

Unlike the violence research, studies of the impact of sexy television and movies are, by necessity, considerably scarcer and more limited. Researchers cannot simply show a group of 13-year-olds several X-rated movies and then measure the attitudinal or behavioral changes that result. But a number of research modalities have yielded important data.

Content Analyses. These studies simply assay the amount of sexual material in current programming without addressing its effects. The first content analyses of sexual material on television were performed in the 1980s. Harris and Associates (1988) found that Americans in the late 1980s viewed more than 27 instances per hour of sexual behavior. Annually, that amounts to the networks transmitting 65,000 instances of sexual material per year during the afternoon and prime-time periods alone. From 1975 to 1988, the number of sexual behaviors on prime-time television doubled, the amount of suggestiveness increased more than fourfold, and sexual intercourse was portrayed for the first time (Harris & Associates, 1988).

Content analyses also found that rock music and music videos were becoming increasingly suggestive as well as graphic (Brown & Hendee, 1989; Prinsky & Rosenbaum, 1987; Sherman & Dominick, 1986). On Music Television (MTV), 75% of "concept" music videos (those that tell a story) involved sexual imagery, more than half involved violence, and 80% of the time the two were combined to depict violence against women (Sherman & Dominick, 1986).

In the 1990s, mainstream television programming became even more explicit in its depiction of sexual content (Huston et al., 1998). Yet the unhealthy trends established in the 1980s have also continued:

- More sex occurs between unmarried adults than married adults (Greenberg & Busselle, 1994; Kunkel et al., 1996; Lowry & Shidler, 1993; Sapolsky & Tabarlet, 1991).

- The risks of unprotected sex and teen sex (i.e., pregnancy and STDs) are rarely discussed (Kunkel et al., 1996; Lowry & Shidler, 1993).

- In the early 1990s, talking about sex was more common than sexual behavior, and intercourse was usually implied rather than shown (Kunkel et al., 1996). But that trend reversed later on (Cope-Farrar & Kunkel, 2002; Heintz-Knowles, 1996). Adding sexual talk and behavior together yields 8 to 10 incidents per hour of prime-time viewing (Kunkel et al., 1996; Lowry & Shidler, 1993).

- Sexual content increased from the late 1980s to 1991 to 15 instances per hour (Lowry & Shidler, 1993). A separate analysis found steady increases over a period of 20 years, from 1976 to 1996 (Kunkel et al., 1996). Two thirds of prime-time shows now contain some talk about sex or sexual behavior (Kunkel, Cope, Farinola, et al., 1999).

- During the so-called "Family Hour" (the first hour of prime-time TV), 75% of programs contained sexual content (Kunkel et al., 1996). Again, messages about the risk of pregnancy or AIDS, or the use of contraception, are rare.

Three content analyses have been done in the 1990s specifically examining shows most popular with children or adolescents. Greenberg et al. (1995) studied the sexual content of talk shows, which are popular with teens, and found that sexual activity, especially sexual infidelity, was one of the major issues discussed (see Table 5.10). Despite the sensitivity and the health-related nature of many of the sexual topics, experts were rarely heard on such shows (Greenberg & Smith, 2002). Ward (1995) analyzed the 12 most popular prime-time shows for children and teens and found frequent sexual references, a recreational philosophy toward sex, and an emphasis on the importance of physical attractiveness. Finally, Cope-Farrar and Kunkel (2002) performed the most comprehensive and recent analysis, examining the top 15 shows for teens ages 12 to 17 according to the Nielsen ratings (see Tables 5.1-5.3). More than 80% contained talk about sex or sexual behavior. Situation comedies featured 7 scenes per hour with sexual content, and shows with sexual material averaged 11 scenes per hour. Interestingly, for the first time in any content analysis, there was actually more sexual behavior depicted than talk about sex. Again, most sexual behavior (79%) occurred between unmarried characters, but only 6 portrayals of intercourse in just three program episodes were noted. Three fourths of all characters experienced no consequences associated with their sexual behavior. Only 14% of scenes with talking about sex and 3% of

TABLE 5.10 Major Issues on TV Talk Shows (N = 120 shows) (in percentages)

Issue	% of Shows
Parent-child relations	48
Dating	36
Marital relationship	35
Sexual activity	34
Abuse	23
Criminal acts	22
Sexual infidelity	18
Celebrities	10

SOURCE: Data from Greenberg et al. (1995).

scenes with sexual behavior involved discussion of sexual responsibility. The researchers concluded that it would be extraordinarily difficult for older children or adolescents to watch a show popular with their age group and not encounter numerous sexual messages, most of them unhealthy.

Soap Operas. Most researchers would agree that soap operas represent the most sensational, inaccurate, and popular view of adolescent and adult sexuality. Studies in the 1980s found that extramarital sex was portrayed 8 to 24 times more commonly than sex between spouses and that 94% of the sexual encounters depicted were between people not married to each other (Greenberg, Abelman, & Neuendorf, 1981; Lowry & Towles, 1989). Soap opera sex in the 1980s was impersonal, emotionless, and exploitative (Sprafkin & Silverman, 1982). Despite the fact that the mention or use of contraception was extremely rare, women seldom got pregnant, and no one ever got a sexually transmitted disease unless they were a prostitute or gay (Greenberg et al., 1980; Lowry & Towles, 1989). Homosexuals were rarely portrayed or were stereotyped as victims or as villains (Lowry, Love, & Kirby, 1987).

As with prime-time programming, soap operas have become even more sexually oriented and sexually explicit since the 1980s, but a small minority has chosen to portray sex more responsibly. Two recent content analyses provide greater understanding of trends in the 1990s (Greenberg & Busselle, 1994; Heintz-Knowles, 1996). Greenberg and Busselle (1994) analyzed 10 episodes of each of the five top-rated soaps (*General Hospital, All My Children, One Life to Live, Young and the Restless,* and *Days of Our Lives*) in 1994 and found an average of 6.6 sexual

TABLE 5.11 Sexual Content of Soap Operas (1996)

Behaviors	Frequency	Average per Hour
Passionate kissing	165	1.66
Verbal discussions about intercourse	66	0.68
Petting/caressing	30	0.31
Prostitution	27	0.28
Visual depictions of intercourse	17	0.19
Rape	13	0.14
Discussions of "safe sex," contraception, or AIDS	9	0.09

SOURCE: Adapted from Heintz-Knowles (1996).

incidents per hour, compared with 3.7 in a 1985 sample (Greenberg & Busselle, 1996). Sex was visually depicted twice as often as it was talked about. By now, nearly half the sexual incidents involved intercourse, usually between unmarried partners. Surprisingly, rape was the second most frequently depicted sexual activity, with a total of 71 incidents or 1.4 per hour. Contraception or "safe sex" was mentioned only 5 times out of 333 sexual incidents. The only mention of AIDS among the 50 episodes concerned the risk associated with intravenous drug use, not sex. And there was a single episode where a parent discussed sex with her teenage daughter.

A second content analysis in 1996 found that the amount of sexual content had stabilized at around six sexual incidents per hour but, again as with prime-time shows, there appeared to be a shift from talking about sex to showing more sexual behavior (see Table 5.11) (Heintz-Knowles, 1996). By 1996, sexual behavior was three times more likely to be depicted than merely talked about. Only 10% of sexual episodes involved the use of contraception or discussions about the risks of sexual activity. However, a few of the soaps were beginning to run major story lines with significant health-related content: *General Hospital* (ABC) was the first to feature a character with HIV, who at one point discusses with her partner the need to use condoms if they have intercourse. On *Young and the Restless* (CBS), a woman decides to get tested for HIV after learning about her husband's affairs. And on *All My Children* (ABC), a teenage couple becomes sexually active, and a wrapped condom is actually shown.

Unfortunately, teenage females are particularly avid viewers of afternoon soap operas; for years the sexiest soaps, *All My Children* and *General Hospital,* also commanded the largest teenage audience (Greenberg & Rampoldi, 1994; Lowry et al., 1987). The former contains 5.2 sex references per hour, the latter 3.1; most of the time these involve discussions of intercourse (Greenberg, 1994).

Higher rates of viewing soap operas by African American teens may expose them to greater amounts of sexual content (Greenberg, 1993). Soaps particularly popular with teenagers have increased their sexual content by 21% since 1982 and by 103% since 1980 (Greenberg, 1994). That trend may be coming to an end, however, with the appearance in 1999 of *Passions* (NBC), which has become the highest rated soap among teen viewers. Although criticized for having love-obsessed women with few goals in life beyond getting men, *Passions* contains nine teenage characters who have yet to have sex, smoke cigarettes, drink alcohol, or use bad language (Logan, 2000). In addition, nearly half of the show's characters are African American or Latino, at a time when Hollywood is being criticized severely for not providing more parts for minority actors (Shepard, 2000).

Advertisements. If advertisements had been counted in the longitudinal studies of sexual content on television, the results would have been significantly higher. From the time of the Noxema girl, who advised male viewers "to take it off, take it all off," to Brooke Shields's "nothing comes between me and my Calvins," to present-day ads for beer, wine coolers, and perfume, advertising has always used explicit visual imagery to try to make a sale (see Figure 5.8) (Kilbourne, 1993, 1999).

Teenage girls spend an estimated $5 billion a year on cosmetics alone (Graham & Hamdan, 1987). By 1977, one researcher found that nearly one third of all advertisements on prime-time TV "used as selling points the desirability of sex appeal, youth, or beauty, and/or those in which sex appeal (physical attractiveness) of commercial actors or actresses was a selling point" (Tan, 1979, p. 285). A similar study 8 years later of more than 4,000 network commercials found that 1 of every 3.8 ads relied on attractiveness-based imagery (Downs & Harrison, 1985). One byproduct of this kind of advertising is that women are subtly taught that their main goal in life is to attract men or serve as sexual prizes. If she is successful, can she possibly say no when he wants sex? And can he actually believe her (Brown & Steele, 1995)?

One by-product of the feminist movement of the 1970s has been that men are now being increasingly exploited for their sex appeal the way women once were (see Figure 5.12) (Svetkey, 1994). American media have become equal-opportunity exploiters.

In the 1990s, advertisers now seem to be wrestling with how to portray the images of both sexes. A recent series of advertisements show women with "attitude" (Leo, 1993). For example, an ad for Bodyslimmers shows a woman wearing a one-piece undergarment and reads, "While you don't necessarily dress for men, it doesn't hurt, on occasion, to see one drool like the pathetic dog that he is." A TV car ad has two women discussing whether men buy big cars because they are worried about the size of their penises: "He must be overcompensating for a . . . short-

Figure 5.12. Males in Sexy Ads

Instead of avoiding the exploitation of female sexuality in the media, advertisers in the 1990s and currently have chosen to exploit male sexuality as well.

coming?" says one. Then a handsome man drives up in a Hyundai Elantra, and her friend says, "I wonder what he's got under the hood" (Leo, 1993).

Modern advertising often features women's bodies that have been "dismembered"—just the legs or breasts appear (see Figure 5.13) (Kilbourne, 1999). Increasingly, little girls are sexualized (e.g., a shampoo ad reads, "You're a Halston woman from the very beginning" and shows a girl of about 5). A study of fashion and fitness advertisements in popular magazines found that females are more likely than males to be shown in submissive positions, sexually displayed, or be included in violent imagery (Rudman & Verdi, 1993). As Kilbourne (1999) notes,

> When sexual jokes are used to sell everything from rice to roach-killer, from cars to carpets, it's hard to remember that sex can unite two souls, can inspire awe. Individually, these ads are harmless enough, sometimes even funny, but the cumulative effect is to degrade and devalue sex. (p. 265)

What impact does this sexualization of American advertising have on adolescents? One can only speculate, but there are data that American adults seem to be

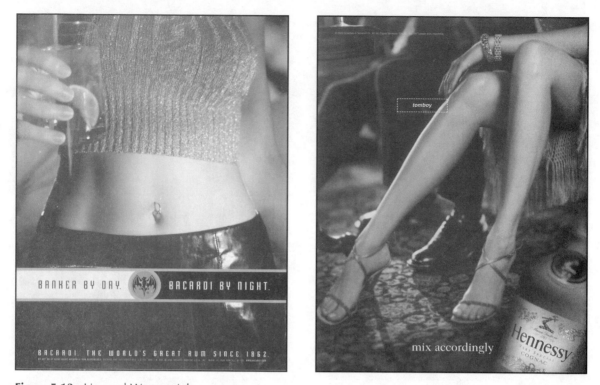

Figure 5.13. Unusual Women Ads

NOTE: According to Kilbourne (1999), women in advertising are often depersonalized and reduced to body parts. One very recent trend in advertising is the depiction of situations in which sexual orientation is uncertain.

having more sexual problems than ever before. In the most recent and comprehensive study since the Kinsey Report of the 1940s, 43% of women and 31% of men reported sexual dysfunction (defined as a lack of interest in or enjoyment of sex, performance anxiety, or inability to achieve orgasm) (Laumann, Paik, & Rosen, 1999). Could it be that media images are shaping people's reality of what their sex lives should be? If so, this would again represent the "cultivation effect" at work, which is known to be a strong factor in media influence (Gerbner, Gross, et al., 1994). Is it possible to measure up to the media's apparent sexual standard, where everyone is having great (harmless) sex all the time? Considerable qualitative research with adolescents will be needed before these questions can be answered authoritatively.

Correlational Studies. Clearly, according to content analyses, American television is both sexy and suggestive. Simple common sense would tell us that this is not healthy for children and younger adolescents. But some people want stronger evidence. Does all of this sexy content actually harm children, or is it merely fantasy and entertainment? Do teenagers who become sexually active at a younger age do

Figure 5.13. Continued

so because of exposure to sexy media, or do they simply prefer to watch such programming? Unfortunately, correlational studies are rare. In stark contrast to the
media violence literature, only six studies exist in which researchers have tried to
assess the relationship between early onset of sexual intercourse and amount of
sexual content viewed on television. Only one of these studies was longitudinal,
and four out of six are now more than a decade old. (A seventh recent but flawed
study found that African American female teens with greater exposure to rap music
videos or X-rated movies are more likely to have had multiple sexual partners and
test positive for an STD [Wingood & DiClemente, 1998; Wingood, DiClemente,
Harrington, et al., 2001].) However, all did demonstrate measurable effects:

- In a study of 75 adolescent girls, half pregnant and half nonpregnant, the
  pregnant girls watched more soap operas before becoming pregnant and
  were less likely to think that their favorite soap characters would use birth
  control (Corder-Bolz, 1981).

- A study of 391 junior high school students in North Carolina found that
  those who selectively viewed more sexy TV were more likely to have

begun having sexual intercourse in the preceding year (Brown & New-comer, 1991).

A study of 326 Cleveland teenagers showed that those with a preference for MTV had increased amounts of sexual experience in their mid-teen years (Peterson & Kahn, 1984).

- Data from the National Surveys of Children revealed that males who watch more TV had the highest prevalence of sexual intercourse and that teens who watched TV apart from their family had a rate of intercourse three to six times higher than those who viewed with their family (Peterson, Moore, & Furstenberg, 1991).

- A study of 214 teens ages 13 to 18 and their families found that there appeared to be no relationship between male virginity and exposure to R-rated or X-rated films, popular music, or music videos (Strouse, Buerkel-Rothfuss, & Long, 1995). However, for females there was a relationship between exposure to music videos and premarital sex. There was also an association between unsatisfactory home environments and premarital sex.

- A phone survey of 1,010 teens ages 14 to 19 in upstate New York found that listening to pop or hip-hop music or reading women's magazines was associated with having had sexual intercourse. It also found that adolescents spend nearly 8 hours each day with various types of media (Pazos et al., 2001).

To date, there has been no substantial longitudinal correlational study that links exposure to large amounts of sexy TV or movies with early onset of sexual intercourse. Such studies exist in other areas of media research (e.g., TV violence and aggressive behavior; amount of TV viewed and obesity). There is an urgent need for such a study (Huston et al., 1998; Strasburger & Donnerstein, 2000).

Experimental Studies. Severe constraints exist on studying any aspect of childhood or adolescent sexuality (Huston et al., 1998). For example, in 1991, U.S. Secretary of Health and Human Services Louis Sullivan canceled a planned 5-year, $18 million survey of 24,000 young people in Grades 7 through 11 because he was worried about the "inadvertent message this survey could send" (Marshall, 1991). The survey would have provided valuable information about teenagers' sexual habits and would have included several questions about their media habits as well. Fortunately, in 1994, the National Institutes of Health decided to fund the project, and it is currently being conducted and generating data (Resnick et al., 1997). However, in the entire survey, the only question about media use is how many hours students spend watching TV and videos, listening to radio, and so forth. This, despite the fact that nearly 100,000 teenagers and their families from around the country are being sampled, and unique data about media use and behavior could have been obtained. The Youth Risk Behavior Survey, sponsored by the CDC (2000c), studies more than 15,000 high school students nationwide, but again, no media questions are included, and nine states currently abstain from participating in this research.

Even in the new millennium, researchers are still fighting the old shibboleth that if you ask kids about sex, they will get ideas they would not otherwise have had (Strasburger, 1997c). Studies have examined the effectiveness of sex in advertising and programming: High schools girls shown 15 "beauty commercials" were more likely to believe that physical attractiveness was important for them than were girls shown neutral commercials (Tan, 1979). Male college students who viewed a single episode of *Charlie's Angels* were harsher in their evaluations of the beauty of potential dates than were males who had not seen the episode (Kenrick & Guttieres, 1980), and male college students shown centerfolds from *Playboy* and *Penthouse* were more likely to find their own girlfriends less sexually attractive (Weaver, Masland, & Zillmann, 1984).

Studies have also examined the impact of sexual content on attitude formation (Greenberg & Hofschire, 2000). For example, college students shown sexually explicit films reported a greater acceptance of sexual infidelity and promiscuity than controls did (Zillmann, 1994), and adolescents viewing only 10 music videos were more likely to agree with the notion that "premarital sex is acceptable" (Greeson & Williams, 1986). In two studies, college students' disapproval of rape was lessened by exposure to only 9 minutes of scenes taken from television programs and R-rated movies or viewing 5 hours of sexually explicit films over a 6-week period (Brown, Childers, & Waszak, 1990; Zillmann & Bryant, 1982). Finally, both male and female college students exposed to hour-long nonviolent X-rated videos over a period of 6 weeks reported less satisfaction with their intimate partners (Zillmann & Bryant, 1988). The researchers concluded, "Great sexual joy and ecstasy are accessible to parties who just met, who are in no way committed to one another, and who will part shortly, never to meet again" (Zillmann & Bryant, 1988, p. 450)—certainly an ominous finding for those interested in diminishing rates of adolescent sexual intercourse.

Obviously, studying college students is considerably easier than studying younger adolescents, particularly when sexual behavior is the variable being assessed. Although about half of high school seniors have engaged in sexual intercourse (CDC, 2000c) and adolescents are bombarded with sexual messages in the media, school administrators and parents are still reluctant to have their teenagers questioned about their sexual activities, even with the use of informed consent (Strasburger, 1997b).

Therefore, there is currently a return to small-scale laboratory and field studies, two of which have shown intriguing results. In the first, "massive exposure" to prime-time programming that deals with pre-, extra-, or nonmarital sex desensitized young viewers to such "improprieties." However, several factors militated against this: a clearly defined value system within the family, an ability to freely discuss important issues within the family, and active, critical viewing skills (Bryant & Rockwell, 1994). In the second, a small study of adolescents' interpretations of soap operas, Walsh-Childers found that teenagers' own sexual "schemas" influenced their perceptions of the characters' relationships (Walsh-Childers, 1991). Interestingly, mention of birth control did not have to be explicit to be effective. In fact, the use of the euphemism *protection* seemed to be preferable.

● PROSOCIAL SEXUAL CONTENT ON TELEVISION

One of the most appealing and practical approaches to address public health concerns about television has been dubbed "edutainment"—the practice of embedding socially responsible messages into mainstream programming (Brown et al., 2001). The Media Project represents a unique partnership between Advocates for Youth and the Henry J. Kaiser Family Foundation that works with the television industry in a collaborative fashion to increase the amount of accurate and prosocial sexual content on television. During the 1999 TV season, The Media Project worked with the producers of *Felicity* on a two-part episode about date rape. The Project encouraged the creation of a toll-free rape crisis hotline number to be displayed at the end of the episode, and the hotline received more than 1,000 calls directly after the show aired (Folb, 2000). In a small survey about a later episode that discussed birth control, more than one fourth of 12- to 21-year-olds surveyed felt they had learned something new about birth control and safe sex. The Project has also provided information for a *Jack & Jill* episode about an unwanted pregnancy, for a *For Your Love* episode about condom use, and for a *Get Real* episode about parent-child communication and teens becoming sexually active for the first time (Folb, 2000).

Collaborative efforts between the Kaiser Foundation and the producers of the hit show *ER* also resulted in successful story lines about the risks of human papilloma virus and the usefulness of emergency contraception (see Figure 5.14) (Brodie et al., 2001).

Such efforts demonstrate that the entertainment industry can occasionally be receptive to outside input and that healthier content can be introduced into mainstream television without government pressure or the threat of censorship.

● CONTRACEPTIVE ADVERTISING

One of the key findings of the 1985 Guttmacher Report was that America's high teenage pregnancy rate partially results from inadequate access to birth control

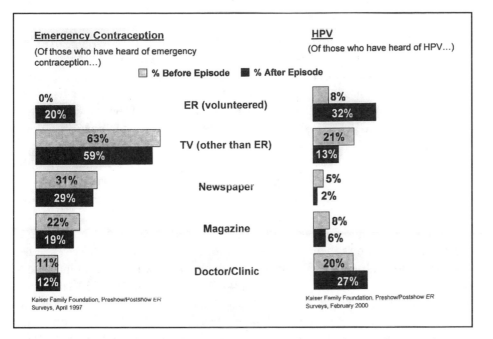

Figure 5.14. Viewers' Increased Knowledge after Storylines on the Hit Show *ER* about Emergency Contraception and about Human Papilloma Virus (HPV)

SOURCE: Brodie et al. (2001). Reprinted with permission from the Kaiser Family Foundation.

NOTE: A unique collaboration between the Kaiser Family Foundation and the producers of *ER* resulted in important health information about human papillomavirus (a sexually transmitted disease) and about emergency contraception being written into stories. This study illustrates the importance of mainstream media in disseminating information about sex and sexuality.

information and products (Jones, Forrest, Henshaw, Silverman, & Torres, 1988). Despite small decreases in rates of sexual activity and pregnancy among American teens in the late 1990s (CDC, 2000c), the United States still leads the Western world in teen pregnancy (Singh & Darroch, 2000). It seems odd, perhaps even hypocritical, that as the culture has become increasingly "sexualized" in the past 20 years, the one taboo remaining is the public mention of birth control. In 1985, the American College of Obstetrics and Gynecology (ACOG) made headlines when its public service announcement about teen pregnancy, entitled "I Intend," was banned from all three major networks. The one offensive line that had to be removed before the networks agreed to run the PSA said, "Unintended pregnancies have risks . . . greater risks than any of today's contraceptives" (Strasburger, 1989, p. 767). Network executives claim that such PSAs or advertisements for birth control products would offend many viewers.

The situation remains the same now in the new millennium as it did two decades ago. Yet there is no evidence to support this apparent prudishness. Birth control ads for nonprescription products air on many local TV stations around the United

States (e.g., KABC–Los Angeles) without complaints being registered. In addition, the 1987 Harris Report shows that a majority of the American public—including 62% of the Catholics surveyed—favor birth control advertising on television (see Table 5.6) (Harris & Associates, 1987). A 2001 study commissioned by the Kaiser Family Foundation found similar results (Mozes, 2001). On the other hand, the DeMoss Foundation spends more than $100 million a year on its anti-abortion "Life, What a Beautiful Choice" public service advertising campaign yet never mentions birth control (Murchek, 1994).

Would advertising of condoms and birth control pills have an impact on the rates of teen pregnancy or acquisition of HIV? The Guttmacher data (Jones et al., 1988) and other comparative data (Henshaw, 1998) seem to indicate that the answer is yes for teen pregnancy because European countries have far lower rates of teen pregnancy and far more widespread media discussion and advertising of birth control products. Furthermore, according to Population Services International, when Zaire began advertising condoms, there was a 20-fold increase in the number of condoms sold in just 3 years—from 900,000 in 1988 to 18 million in 1991 (Alter, 1994). In a relevant "natural experiment," Earvin "Magic" Johnson's announcement of his HIV infection was associated with a decline in "one-night stands" and sex with multiple partners in the subsequent 14 weeks in a Maryland study (CDC, 1993). It also resulted in increased awareness about AIDS (Kalichman & Hunter, 1992).

Would advertising birth control products make teenagers more sexually active than they already are? There is no evidence available indicating that allowing freer access to birth control encourages teenagers to become sexually active at a younger age (Reichelt, 1978; Strasburger & Brown, 1998). In fact, the data indicate the exact opposite: There are now five recent, peer-reviewed, controlled clinical trials showing that giving teens freer access to condoms does not increase their sexual activity or push virginal teenagers into having sex but does increase the use of condoms among those who are sexually active (Furstenberg, Geitz, Teitler, & Weiss, 1997; Guttmacher et al., 1997; Jemmott, Jemmott, & Fong, 1998; Kirby et al., 1999; Schuster, Bell, Berry, & Kanouse, 1998). Typically, teenage females engage in unprotected intercourse for 6 months to a year before seeking medical attention for birth control (Zabin, Kantner, & Zelnick, 1979). Organizations such as the AAP, the American College of Obstetricians & Gynecologists, and the Society for Adolescent Medicine have all called for contraceptive advertising on American television (AAP, 2001c; Society for Adolescent Medicine, 2000). Despite the hopes of many public health officials, the fear of AIDS may not be sufficient to increase teenagers' use of contraception. And in several longitudinal studies, the use of condoms has actually decreased among teenagers and young adults, despite widespread publicity (Kegeles, Adler, & Irwin, 1988; Ku, Sonenstein, & Pleck, 1993). In 2001, contraceptive advertising is rarely shown on national network programming (except for ads for Ortho-Tri-Cyclen, which mention only improvement in acne,

Figure 5.15
SOURCE: Copyright John Branch, *San Antonio Express-News*. Used with permission.

not pregnancy prevention) (see Figure 5.7) and very much subject to the discretion of local station managers. Thus, in our opinion, a major potential solution to a significant American health problem is being thwarted by a few very powerful but fearful people (see Figure 5.15).

PORNOGRAPHY ●

The relationship of pornography to behavior remains an important health issue as well as a controversial First Amendment issue (Donnerstein & Linz, 1994; Malamuth, 1993). Interestingly, print media are protected constitutionally by the First Amendment, whereas the broadcast media are subject to regulation under the 1934 Federal Communications Commission Charter. To date, cable television remains in a legal netherworld. For obvious reasons, there are no studies on the impact of pornography on children or adolescents.

Exposure

Teenagers have surprisingly ready access to a variety of R-rated and X-rated material. By age 15, 92% of males and 84% of females had seen or read *Playboy* or *Playgirl* in one study; by age 18, virtually all had (Brown & Bryant, 1989). Exposure to more hard-core magazines begins at an average age of 13.5 years, and 92% of 13-to-15 year-olds report having seen an X-rated film (Brown & Bryant, 1989). Of 16 popular R-rated films, Greenberg, Siemicki, et al. (1993) found that 53% to 77% of 9th and 10th graders had seen most of them. In a study of 522 African American 14- to 18-year-olds, researchers found that 30% had seen at least one X-rated movie within the past 3 months (Wingood, DiClemente, Harrington, et al., 2001).

Research

Current research involving adults seems to indicate that pornography itself is harmless unless violence is also involved (Strasburger & Donnerstein, 2000). In that situation, aggression might increase because there is a known relationship between portrayals of violence and subsequent aggressive behavior (Cline, 1994; Harris, 1994a, 1994b; Huston et al., 1992; Linz & Malamuth, 1993; Lyons, Anderson, & Larson, 1994; Malamuth, 1993; Weaver, 1994). The term *pornography* means different things to different people. The current state-of-the-art assessment subdivides the research according to content (Huston et al., 1992; Malamuth, 1993; Strasburger & Donnerstein, 2000).

Erotica. R- or X-rated material with implied or actual sexual contact but no violence or coercion. *Probably no antisocial effect* (Donnerstein, Linz, & Penrod, 1987). Wingood, DiClemente, Harrington, et al. (2001) did find an association between African American females having viewed X-rated movies and having more negative attitudes toward using condoms, having multiple sex partners, not using contraception, and having a positive test for chlamydia. This was a relatively small study that found an association, not a causal connection. It may represent a cultivation effect or its opposite: that teens who are more interested in sex tend to seek out more sexual media. Only a longitudinal correlational study will enable researchers to distinguish between the two.

X-Rated Material Degrading to Women. Nonviolent XXX-rated videos in which women are the eager recipients of any and all male sexual urges. *Highly controversial.* Most studies find no antisocial effect. But some researchers suggest that attitudes may be molded or changed by repeated exposure. In a study of college students, massive doses of pornographic films led to overestimates of uncommon sexual practices, decreased concern about the crime of rape, loss of sympathy for the women's liberation movement, and, among men, a more callous attitude toward sex (Zillmann & Bryant, 1982, 1988).

Violent Pornography. X-rated videos in which the woman victim is shown to be enjoying the assault or rape. *Known antisocial effects.* This is one of the most dangerous types of combinations—sex and violence—although it is probably the violent content that takes priority. Men exposed to such material show increased aggression against women in laboratory studies and increased callousness in their attitudes (Donnerstein, 1984; Linz & Malamuth, 1993). But men exposed to non-sexual violence can show the same effect as well (Huston et al., 1992).

Non-X-Rated Sexual Aggression Against Women. Broadcast or movie program-ming in which women are depicted as deriving pleasure from sexual abuse or assault. *Probable antisocial effects.* Such content may reinforce callous attitudes toward rape and rape victims.

Wilson, Linz, Donnerstein, and Stipp (1992) performed an interesting field experiment to investigate attitudes about rape. In 1990, NBC aired a made-for-TV movie titled *She Said No,* which concerned acquaintance rape. The researchers mea-sured audience responses to the movie to see whether it would decrease accep-tance of rape myths or date rape. Using a nationally representative sample, they randomly assigned 1,038 adult viewers to watch or not watch the movie over a special closed-circuit channel. When contacted the next day, the viewers answered questions about rape myths, which demonstrated that the movie had made an impact in altering perceptions of date rape. Considering these data, the reverse should be true as well. Another study correlated the viewing of wrestling on TV with date violence. Researchers studied 2,228 North Carolina high school students and found that watching was associated with having started a fight with a date and with other high-risk activities such as weapon carrying and drug use (DuRant, 2001).

One expert claims that much of sexy advertising is pornographic because it dehumanizes women, borrows the poses and postures of bondage and sadomas-ochism, and perpetuates rape myths (Kilbourne, 1999). Many ads seem to imply that women don't really mean "no" when they say it. In one ad, a woman is back-ing a woman against a wall. The ad says "NO" in big letters, and she is either laugh-ing or screaming. In small letters at the bottom is the word *sweat,* and the ad is for deodorant. Another ad, for a trendy bar in Georgetown, shows a close-up of a cocktail, with the headline, "If your date won't listen to reason, try a Velvet Ham-mer" (Kilbourne, 1993).

Sexualized Violence Against Women. R-rated videos that are less sexually explicit but far more violent than X-rated ones, often shown on cable TV or available in video stores. *Probable antisocial effects.* These do not involve rape but do contain scenes of women being tortured, murdered, or mutilated in a sexual context. This may be the single most important category for teenagers because it is more "main-stream" and represents an important genre of Hollywood "slice 'em and dice 'em" movies (e.g., *Halloween I-V, Nightmare on Elm Street I-V, Friday the 13th I-VIII, Texas Chainsaw Massacre I-II, Scream I-III,* etc.). Often, the title alone tells the tale: *Hide and Go Shriek, Kiss Daddy Goodbye, Return to Horror High, Slaughter High, The Dorm That Dripped Blood, Chopping Mall, Murderlust, Deadtime Stories,*

Splatter University, Lady Stay Dead, I Dismember Mama, Watch Me When I Kill, Lunch Meat.

Because sex is something that is not usually discussed or observed, except in the media, teenagers who are faithful viewers of such movies may be learning that acting aggressively toward women is expected and normal. Studies show that exposure to such material can result in densensitization to sexual violence, both for young men and women (Donnerstein et al., 1987; Mullin & Linz, 1995). However, such studies cannot always be replicated (Linz & Donnerstein, 1988; Weaver, 1994). As two prominent researchers note, "Our research suggests that you need not look any further than the family's own television set to find demeaning depictions of women available to far more viewers than pornographic material" (Linz & Donnerstein, 1988, p. 184).

● SOLUTIONS

Clearly, there is a strong case to be made for the impact of sexual content in a variety of media on young, impressionable preteens and teens (AAP, 2001c; Brown & Steele, 1995; Gruber & Grube, 2000). In a society that limits access to sexual information (e.g., sex education classes), teenagers will look to the media for answers to their questions. More important, the media will have a strong effect on teens without their even being aware of it, especially those whose parents do not inculcate in them a strong sense of "family values." Important questions get answered by the media: "When is it okay to have sex?" "How do I know if I am in love?" "Is sex fun?" "Is sex risky?" Unfortunately, as we have seen, the media answers to these questions are usually not the healthy or accurate answers.

What changes in media would give American youth a healthier view of sex and sexuality? A number of possibilities come to mind:

1. *Widespread advertising of birth control in mainstream media (e.g., TV, magazines, radio).* Advertising birth control represents one means of increasing teenagers' access to it. Such advertising needs to address the risks of pregnancy, not merely the cosmetic difference that birth control pills can make if a teenager has acne. Unless new products such as the morning-after pill are widely advertised, teenagers will not know about them or use them (see Figure 5.16). Comparative studies between the United States and Europe make it clear that countries that promote the use of birth control via advertising, sex education classes, and programming are rewarded with lower rates of teen pregnancy (Miller, 2000; Strasburger & Brown, 1998). Most national surveys have documented that adults favor birth control advertising (Harris & Associates, 1987), yet the media remain resistant. Given that five studies now prove that making birth control available to teenagers does

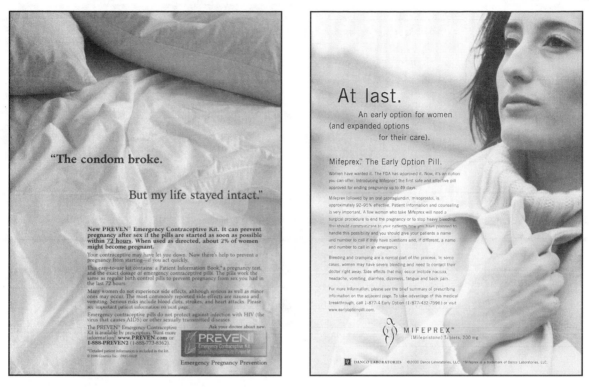

Figure 5.16. Print Ads for New Contraceptive Products
NOTE: Preven is an emergency contraceptive. Mifeprex is approved for first-trimester abortions.

not increase the risk of early sexual intercourse, there is no longer any excuse to withhold access to it (Furstenberg et al., 1997; Guttmacher et al., 1997; Jemmott et al., 1998; Kirby et al., 1999; Schuster et al., 1998).

2. *Greater responsibility and accountability of mainstream media for produc-ing healthy and accurate messages about sex and sexuality.* Entertainment indus-try executives need to realize that, like it or not, their product is educating American children and teenagers. Media have become one of the most important sources for sexual information for young people today. Yet what they view on television and in the movies is almost counterproductive to healthy adolescence: frequent premarital sex and sex between unmarried partners, talk about infidelity on talk shows, graphic jokes and innuendoes in the movies, rape myths, and sex-ual violence. Where is the depiction of sexual responsibility? Where is the talk about the need for birth control or the risk of STDs? Where are the depictions of condom use when they are most needed in modern society? Why aren't topics such as abortion, date rape, and rape myths portrayed and examined in greater detail? In the new millennium, the answer is that we cannot go back to the "golden age" of the 1950s, when sex was rarely discussed and Laura and Rob Petrie slept

TABLE 5.12 Guide to Responsible Sexual Content in Media

Recognize sex as a healthy and natural part of life.

Parent and child conversations about sex are important and healthy and should be encouraged.

Demonstrate that not only the young, unmarried, and beautiful have sexual relationships.

Not all affection and touching must culminate in sex.

Portray couples having sexual relationships with feelings of affection, love, and respect for one another.

Consequences of unprotected sex should be discussed or shown.

Miscarriage should not be used as a dramatic convenience for resolving an unwanted pregnancy.

Use of contraceptives should be indicated as a normal part of a sexual relationship.

Avoid associating violence with sex or love.

Rape should be depicted as a crime of violence, not of passion.

The ability to say "no" should be recognized and respected.

SOURCE: Strasburger (1995). Modified from Haffner (1987, pp. 9-11).

in separate beds on *The Dick Van Dyke Show,* despite being married. Nor should censorship be tolerated in a free society. Voluntary restraint and good judgment on the part of Hollywood and television writers, producers, and directors, however, would go far in improving the current dismal state of programming (see Table 5.12). A return to the "family hours" of protected programming between 7 p.m. and 9 p.m. would be one useful idea. Currently, *Boston Public,* which airs at 7 p.m., has featured such story lines as a high school girl trading oral sex for a boy's agreement to withdraw from a student council race, a girl tossing her breast pads away in the hallway, and another high school girl's sexual affair with one of the teachers. Unfortunately, as one TV critic notes, "Almost anything goes in primetime . . . TV says get used to it" (Salamon, 2000, p. 6WK).

3. *Better taste in advertising* (see Exercises for a discussion of "taste"). When sex is used to sell products, it is cheapened and devalued. Manufacturers who pay for advertising and companies that produce it need to recognize that they, too, have a public health responsibility to produce ads that are not gratuitously provocative, suggestive, or demeaning (see Figure 5.17). Kilbourne (1999) should be "must" reading for all account executives.

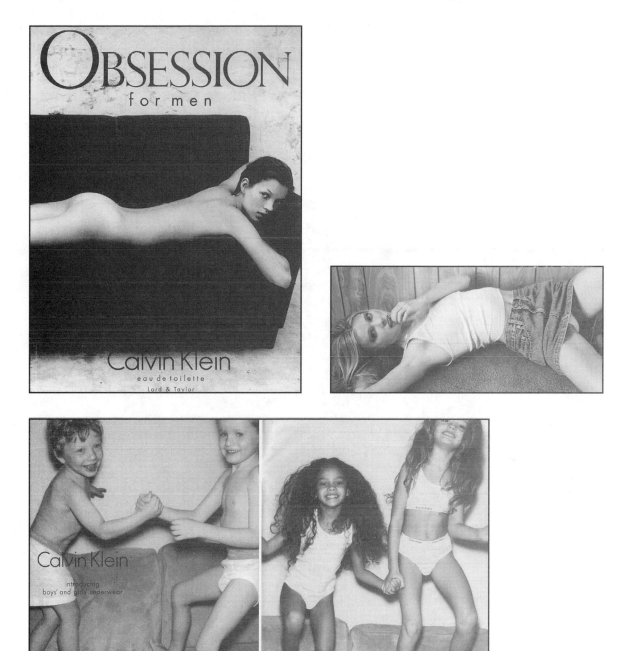

Figure 5.17. Three Different Calvin Klein Ads

Figure 5.18. Counteradvertising, Using Role Models
SOURCE: From the National Campaign to Prevent Teenage
Pregnancy, with permission.

4. *Incorporating the principles of media education into existing sex education programs.* Preliminary studies seem to indicate that a media education approach may be effective in decreasing children's aggressiveness (Huesmann et al., 1983) and teenagers' use of drugs (Austin & Johnson, 1997). There is no reason to think that helping children and teenagers decipher sexual content, the suggestiveness of advertising, and the conservatism of the broadcast industry regarding contraception would have anything but positive outcomes.

5. *More and better counteradvertising.* To date, only the National Campaign to Prevent Teenage Pregnancy has engaged in long-term efforts to counterprogram through the media (see Figure 5.18). Although no data exist about their success, the communications literature about drugs and media does contain several successful efforts involving counteradvertising against tobacco and illicit drugs with teens as the primary target audience (see Chapter 6 on drugs).

6. *More and better research.* Currently, although much is known about adolescent sexuality and the media, little is proven. There has yet to be a single longitudinal correlational study examining teens' exposure to media and changes (if any) in their sexual behavior. Fortunately, the National Institutes of Health has just recently funded four longitudinal studies of adolescents' sexual attitudes and behavior (National Institute on Child Health and Development [NICHD], 2000). The most ambitious will examine all media use, longitudinally over 5 years, among 5,000 teens ages 12 to 14 in North Carolina. They will be assessed both at home and in school. The other three studies will examine television only but will also be longitudinal in design and will try to establish if there is a causal relationship between television viewing and sexual behavior among teenagers (NICHD, 2000).

Four of the seven existing studies of media and sexual behavior are outdated, more than 10 years old, and have major defects (Huston et al., 1998; Strasburger & Donnerstein, 2000). New research should be interdisciplinary, using a variety of methods and a variety of populations, and should take into account developmental, gender, and ethnic differences (Huston, Wartella, & Donnerstein, 2000).

In 1998, the Kaiser Family Foundation sponsored an invitational conference concerning research needs in this area (Huston, Wartella, & Donnerstein, 1998). Many of the ideas could be expanded into other areas of concern, such as violence, drugs, and eating disorders. In addition to a large-scale longitudinal study of sexual behavior and media exposure, some of the other suggestions for future research included the following:

- How do different groups of children and teenagers view different sexual content? Do different groups use different types of media to find sexual content? Is that content interpreted differently? Are there developmental differences in how teens of different ages interpret sexual content? (A few preliminary studies of this kind have already been done [Greenberg, Linsangan, & Soderman, 1993; Kaiser Family Foundation/Children Now, 1996; Larson, 1996; Silverman-Watkins, 1983].)

- Do teens from different ethnic groups seek out programming unique to their own ethnic group?

- How do individuals negotiate sexual behavior in the media? What interpersonal contexts exist for sexual behavior? Do different media portray sexuality differently?

- Do media change teens' knowledge about sex and sexuality, their emotions concerning sex, or their attitudes? Regular adolescent viewers of soap operas could be recruited and be shown "future episodes" of their favorite program, which might be manipulated to show different messages, for example.

The barriers to doing this type of research are considerable (Huston et al., 1998; Strasburger, 1997b). School systems and parents need to grant access to researchers, and foundations need to fund such efforts. At present, only one foundation in the United States funds any research related to adolescent sexuality and the media—the Kaiser Family Foundation—but unfortunately, it does not fund the kind of basic "effects" research that still needs to be accomplished. The NICHD (2000) is currently funding four longitudinal studies of sexual behavior and attitudes. Other foundations need to recognize media research as a new and much-needed priority. In addition, society needs to accept the fact that teenagers should be able to give consent for such research on their own and that parents can be informed "passively" about ongoing studies (e.g., a letter explaining the research, along with the opportunity to withdraw the child if need be) rather than "actively" (e.g., having to send back signed permission forms) (Santelli, 1997; Strasburger, 1998b).

● CONCLUSION: UNANSWERED QUESTIONS

Despite this discussion, not all media are unhealthy or irresponsible for young people. Some shows have dealt responsibly with the issue of teenage sexual activity and teenage pregnancy: *Beverly Hills 90210, Dawson's Creek,* and *Felicity,* at times, and several others. Made-for-TV movies such as *Babies Having Babies* and *Daddy* have used extremely frank language to good, educational effect. The 1980s cop drama *Cagney and Lacey* contained one of the first instances of a TV mother talking to her son about responsibility and birth control. On *St. Elsewhere,* the only known mention of a diaphragm on prime-time TV was aired during the 1987-1988 season, although it required that the user be the chief of Obstetrics and Gynecology to accomplish it. But these are the exceptions rather than the rule on American television. And, unfortunately, it has not been the tragedy of teenage pregnancy or the high rates of early adolescent sexual activity that has blunted the red pencil of the network censors but rather the appearance of AIDS as a national health emergency. But here, too, there may be much educational programming made possible that will benefit teenagers. One example is the 1987-1988 episode of *L.A. Law* that discussed the risk of AIDS in heterosexual intercourse but also included good advice on birth control and choosing sexual partners (see Strasburger, 1989). How do adolescents process the sexual content that they view? Do different ethnic groups interpret the same content differently? Can teenagers learn abstinence or the need to use birth control from what they view in the media? Until the political and funding climate changes, and until adults understand that asking children and teenagers about sex will not provoke them into early sexual activity, we will simply have to speculate about many of these crucial issues.

As one author sadly notes,

I've often wondered what it would be like if we taught young people swimming the same way we teach sexuality. If we told them that swimming was an important adult activity, one they will all have to be skilled at when they grow up, but we never talked with them about it. We never showed them the pool. We just allowed them to stand outside closed doors and listen to all the splashing. Occasionally, they might catch a glimpse of partially-clothed people going in and out of the door to the pool and maybe they'd find a hidden book on the art of swimming, but when they asked a question about how swimming felt or what it was about, they would be greeted with blank or embarrassed looks. Suddenly, when they turn 18 we would fling open the doors to the swimming pool and they would jump in. Miraculously, some might learn to tread water, but many would drown. (Roberts, 1983, p. 10)

Exercises

1. *Taste.* A question about "taste": Whose "taste" do we mean? Ours? Yours? Hollywood's? This is a recurring problem in discussing the media and one we do not take lightly. In this volume, we have erred on the side of public health and psychology in discussing what is questionable "taste" and what represents "good" versus "bad" programming. Although we have tried to give examples, we have left the discussion purposefully vague because we acknowledge that taste can vary considerably. But when it comes to "bad" taste or "questionable" programming that is unhealthy, we would tend to agree with a paraphrase of Supreme Court Justice Potter Stewart's definition of pornography: "We know it when we see it."

   (a) Should the media be criticized on such grounds?

   (b) If so, whose "taste" should be used as the "gold standard"? Is an objective standard possible?

   (c) In making judgments about "taste," what sociocultural factors enter into the discussion?

2. *Prosocial Content.* How would you go about making a prosocial soap opera that would appeal to teenagers and young adults and contain sexually responsible language, discussions, and behavior but not lose the audience with a "goody-two-shoes" program?

3. *Sex Education.* The United States funds abstinence-only sex education ($50 million/year since 1996) as part of the Welfare Act of 1996. Should the government fund comprehensive sex education as well?

Figure 5.19

4. *Media Literacy.* Is there a media literacy approach to sex education that might work to decrease the impact of media on sexual attitudes and beliefs? What components would it have? How would sex education teachers be able to avoid "family values" types of issues if they discussed programming with sexual content?

5. *Doing Sexuality Research.* How could research be sensitively designed to assess what children learn from sexual content in the media?

6. *Contraceptive Ads.* Figure 5.19 shows two actual print ads for condoms. For what magazines would each be appropriate? Do the ads target different audiences? What other possibilities can you think of that might appeal specifically to all teenagers? To teenagers who are African American or Hispanic? To males? To females? Figure 5.16 shows actual print ads for emergency contraceptive pills and one for a product that produces an early medical abortion. How do these ads differ from other, "mainstream" ads? What is the target audience? Are these ads effective?

CHAPTER 6

DRUGS AND THE MEDIA

Joe Camel is little more than a child molester for the tobacco industry—seductive, predatory, lethal.

> —Editorial, *USA Today,* June 2, 1997

You don't see dead teenagers on the highway because of corn chips.

> —Jay Leno, when asked why he does commercials for Dorritos corn chips but refuses to do beer commercials. *TV Guide,* June 10, 1989

Whether we like it or not, alcohol advertising is the single greatest source of alcohol education for Americans.

> —Representative Joe Kennedy (D-MA),
> cosponsor of the Kennedy-Thurmond bill to require
> strict labeling of all advertisements for alcohol products.
> *American Medical News,* April 20, 1992

AUTHORS' NOTE: An earlier version of this chapter appeared in Singer & Singer, *Handbook of Children and Television*. Thousand Oaks, CA: Sage, 2001.

The so-called War on Drugs has been waged by the federal government for decades in a variety of locales except in the media (see Figures 6.1 and 6.2). In fact, at the same time that parents and school programs are trying to get children and teenagers to "Just Say No" to drugs, $10 billion worth of cigarette and alcohol advertising is very effectively working to get them to just say yes to smoking and drinking (Strasburger & Donnerstein, 1999). According to three recent content analyses, television programs, movies, and popular music and music videos all contain appreciable content depicting smoking, drinking, or illicit drug use (see Figure 6.3) (Christenson, Henriksen, & Roberts, 2000; Gerbner & Ozyegin, 1997; Roberts, Henriksen, & Christenson, 1999). Although there are few data showing that drug advertising or drug content has a direct, cause-and-effect impact on adolescents' drug use, numerous correlational studies speak to the impact of a variety of media on teenagers. Considering all of the studies done to date, there is sufficient evidence to warrant a total ban of cigarette advertising in all media, severe restrictions on alcohol advertising, and major changes in the way that cigarettes, alcohol, and illegal drugs are portrayed in movies.

● ADOLESCENT DRUG USE

Illegal drugs certainly take their toll on American society, but two legal drugs—tobacco and alcohol—pose a far greater danger to children and teenagers. Both represent significant "gateway" drugs and are among the earliest drugs used by children or teens. A child who smokes tobacco or drinks alcohol is 65 times more likely to use marijuana, for example, than a child who never smokes or drinks (National Institute on Drug Abuse [NIDA], 1995). And the effect is ongoing: A child who uses marijuana is 100 times more likely to use cocaine compared with abstaining peers (NIDA, 1995). The younger a child begins to use cigarettes, alcohol, or other drugs, the higher the risk of serious health problems and abuse carrying over into adulthood (Belcher & Shinitzky, 1998).

Every year, more than 400,000 Americans die from cigarette use—more than are killed by AIDS, alcohol, automobile accidents, murder, illegal drugs, suicide, and fires combined (Institute of Medicine, 1994)! An estimated 3,000 teenagers begin smoking each day, and about one third of them will eventually die from a tobacco-related illness (U.S. Department of Health and Human Services, 1994). New evidence concerning early smoking is alarming: Damage to lung cell DNA may occur, producing physiologic changes that may persist despite quitting smoking (Wiencke et al., 1999). Tobacco is the only legal product that, when used as directed, kills.

Increasingly, tobacco is being marketed overseas, particularly in Third World countries, with precipitous increases in smoking rates resulting (Mackay, 1999).

Figure 6.1. One Editorial Cartoonist's View of the "War on Drugs"
SOURCE: Reprinted with special permission of King Features Syndicate.

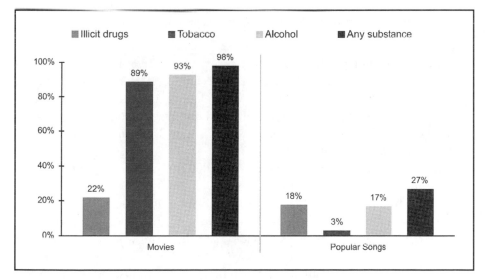

Figure 6.2. Substance Appearance in Popular Movies and Songs
SOURCE: Roberts, Henriksen, and Christenson (1999).

NOTE: The most recent and comprehensive content analysis of a variety of popular media found that tobacco, alcohol, and illicit drugs are very prevalent in movies that are popular with children and teens but considerably less prevalent in popular music. Percentages reflect the number of movies (200 total) and songs (1,000 total) in which substances appeared, whether or not they were used.

"All right, it's a deal. The four-letter words are in, the drug lyrics are out."

Figure 6.3
SOURCE: Copyright Sidney Harris. Used with permission.

America is the leading producer of cigarettes, exporting three times as many cigarettes as any other country (MacKenzie, Bartecchi, & Schrier, 1994). If current smoking rates continue, 7 million people in developing countries will die of smoking-related diseases annually. And one fifth of those living in industrialized countries will die of tobacco-related disorders (Peto, Lopez, Boreham, Thun, & Heath, 1992; "Tobacco's Toll," 1992).

Alcohol, too, is a killer, with more than 100,000 deaths annually in the United States attributed to excessive consumption (Doyle, 1996). It is the most commonly abused drug by children ages 12 to 17 years. Alcohol-related automobile accidents are the number one cause of death among teenagers, and alcohol consumption typically contributes to homicides, suicides, and drownings—three of the other leading causes of death (Comerci & Schwebel, 2000). Often, older children and preteenagers experiment with alcohol first, before other drugs. Drinking alcohol may contribute to premature sexual intercourse, lower grades, and experimentation with other drugs (Tapert, Aarons, Sedlar, & Brown, 2001). Youth who drink are nearly eight times more likely to use other illicit drugs than those who never drink (American Academy of Pediatrics [AAP], 1995a). And people who begin drinking as teenagers are two to three times more likely to be involved in an unin-

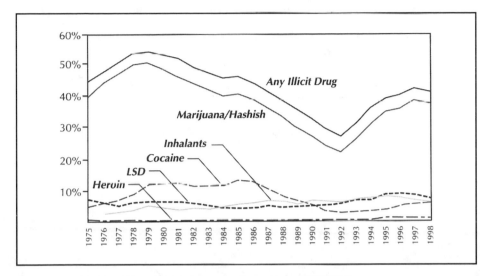

Figure 6.4. National Trends in Adolescent Drug Use, 1975-1998
SOURCE: Johnston, O'Malley, and Bachman (2001).

tentional injury while under the influence of alcohol (Hingson, Heeren, Jamanka, & Howland, 2000).

The best data regarding adolescent drug use come from the Monitoring the Future Study. The Youth Risk Behavior Survey (YRBS), sponsored every other year by the Centers for Disease Control and Prevention (CDC), also makes an excellent contribution to the field (CDC, 2000c). But the Monitoring the Future Study is unique: Nearly 45,000 students are surveyed annually, with equal numbers of males and females in the 8th, 10th, and 12th grades, at more than 430 public and private schools across the country. Funded by the NIDA, the study has been conducted annually since the mid-1970s by the Institute for Social Research at the University of Michigan (see Figure 6.4, Tables 6.1 and 6.2) (Johnston, O'Malley, & Bachman, 2001). No data are perfect, however. The Monitoring the Future study fails to capture high school dropouts, who may be using and abusing drugs at even higher rates than their school peers. It also depends on self-reports by teenagers. But no other collection of data is so extensive over as long a period of time.

Highlights include (Johnston et al., 2001) the following:

• High but slowly decreasing levels of smoking among teenagers. More than one third of American students smoke by the time they complete high school. Two thirds of teenagers have tried smoking, including nearly half of all 8th graders surveyed. Nearly 21% of 12th graders smoke daily. Overall, cigarette use increased by 50% among younger teens between 1991 and 1996, following a decade of relative stability. But in the past 4 years, it has been slowly declining. In addition, between 1995 and 2001, the percentage of students saying that there is "great risk" in smok-

TABLE 6.1 Adolescent Drug Use, 2001 (*n* = 13,300 12th graders) (in percentages)

Drug	Ever Used	Used During Past Year
Any illicit drug	53.9	44.4
Any illicit drug other than marijuana	28.5	19.8
Alcohol	79.7	73.3
Ever been drunk	63.9	53.2
Cigarettes	61.0	—
Marijuana	49.0	37.0
Smokeless tobacco	19.7	—
Amphetamines	16.2	10.9
Inhalants	13.0	4.5
Hallucinogens	12.8	8.4
Ecstasy	11.7	9.2
Other opiates	9.4	6.7
Tranquilizers	9.2	6.5
Cocaine	8.2	4.8
Steroids	3.7	2.4
Heroin	1.8	0.9

SOURCE: Adapted from Johnston, O'Malley, and Bachman (2001).

ing a pack a day of cigarettes rose from 66% to 73%. Other surveys have found that smoking among college students has risen in the 1990s (Wechsler, Rigotti, Gledhill-Hoyt, & Lee, 1998). The YRBS data indicate a significant increase in current smoking among U.S. high school students from 27.5% in 1991 to 34.8% in 1999 but some possible leveling off by the end of the decade (CDC, 2000b).

• High levels of alcohol use among teenagers. Although the percentage of "ever-users" decreased to 80% in 2000 from a high of 93% in 1980, 62% of high school seniors report having been drunk at least once, and 30% report having had five or more drinks in a row in the 2 weeks prior to being surveyed. These data are consistent between the Michigan study and the YRBS (CDC, 2000c). Interestingly, although athletes are ordinarily less likely to use illicit drugs other than anabolic steroids, male athletes are more likely to use alcohol (Aaron et al., 1995).

• A leveling off of illicit drug use among teenagers. Such use peaked at 66% in 1981 and declined to a low of 41% in 1992. Currently, more than half (54%) of 12th graders report having ever used an illicit drug. Nearly 30% have used an illicit drug other than marijuana.

TABLE 6.2 Trends in 12th Graders' Perception of Drugs as Harmful (in percentages)

How Much Do You Think People Risk Harming Themselves If They . . .	1980	1990	2001
Try marijuana once or twice	10.0	23.1	15.3
Smoke marijuana occasionally	14.7	36.9	23.5
Smoke marijuana regularly	50.4	77.8	57.4
Try LSD once or twice	43.9	44.7	33.2
Try cocaine once or twice	31.3	59.4	50.7
Try MDMA once or twice	—	—	45.7
Try one or two drinks of an alcoholic beverage	3.8	8.3	8.7
Have five or more drinks once or twice each weekend	35.9	47.1	43.6
Smoke one or more packs of cigarettes per day	63.7	68.2	73.3

SOURCE: Adapted from Johnston, O'Malley, and Bachman (2001).

- A leveling off in marijuana use among teenagers. Marijuana use peaked in 1979, when 60% of high school seniors reported ever having tried it. Now, about half of seniors have tried marijuana.

- Marijuana, cocaine, and heroin use bottomed out in the early 1990s but has risen among children and teenagers since then at all grade levels. This trend is now leveling off and may be in the process of reversing once again.

- A high rate of MDMA ("ecstasy") use; 11% of 12th graders report having used it.

- For all drugs, it is important to note that young adults and older adults have higher rates of smoking and alcohol use, and young adults have the highest rates of illicit drug use. But alcohol and tobacco are first used during adolescence in the majority of cases.

The United States is not alone in experiencing increasing rates of adolescent drug use. A recent survey of nearly 8,000 teens ages 15 and 16 throughout the United Kingdom found that nearly all had tried alcohol, half had engaged in binge drinking, 36% had smoked cigarettes within the previous 30 days, and 42% had ever tried an illicit drug, usually marijuana (Miller & Plant, 1996). In a survey of 10% of all 12- to 15-year-old schoolchildren in Dundee, Scotland, two thirds reported having consumed an alcoholic drink, and by age 14, more than half reported having been drunk (McKeganey, Forsyth, Barnard, & Hay, 1996).

● DETERMINANTS OF CHILD AND ADOLESCENT DRUG USE

A variety of factors have been implicated in the early use of drugs. Among adolescents, specific factors include poor self-image, low religiosity, poor school performance, alienation from parents, family dysfunction, physical abuse, and parental divorce (Belcher & Shinitzky, 1998; Schydlower & Rogers, 1993). The peer group has long been recognized as a unique risk factor in adolescence, and childhood temperament is gaining acceptance as another unique factor. A moody and negative child is more likely to be criticized by his or her parents, leading to a coercive model of parenting and a greater risk of early substance abuse. Interestingly, a recent comprehensive review of substance abuse in childhood and adolescence (Belcher & Shinitzky, 1998) failed to mention media influence as an etiologic force among young people initiating drug use (Strasburger, 1998a).

Peers. Peer pressure may play one of the most important roles in first drug use among young teens (Jessor & Jessor, 1977) but may also be involved in drug abstinence as well (Robin & Johnson, 1996). Teens who see their friends using drugs are more likely to partake themselves; teens who believe their friends are anti-drug are more likely to abstain. (Another, alternative, and as-yet untested hypothesis is that teens prone to drug use are more likely to search out like-minded peers.)

Regardless, the media may function as a kind of "super-peer," making drug use seem like normative behavior for teenagers (Strasburger, 1997c). Because teens are so invested in doing what is "normal" for their peer group, the media could represent one of the most powerful influences on them. Such a theory is a close first cousin to the cultivation theory proposed by Gerbner, Gross, et al. (1994). Media can represent a potent source of information for teens about a variety of health issues. For example, a study of 788 African American students in grades 5 through 12 found that television was the leading source of information about smoking (Kurtz, Kurtz, Johnson, & Cooper, 2001).

Peer pressure must also be placed in proper perspective:

Teens and preteens somehow get the idea that smoking makes one sexy, athletic, cool, or macho. The tobacco industry says these ideas come from their peers. No one asks where these peers—other kids—get these ideas. Yet about the only place in our society where these silly images occur is advertising. So-called peer pressure explains little. It is merely a clever term used to shift blame from the manufacturer and advertiser to the user. Like peer pressure, "parental example" does not just spontaneously occur. Parents of today started smoking as children, and no doubt had similar silly ideas about what smoking would do for their images. (DiFranza, Richards, Paulman, Fletcher, & Jaffe, 1992, p. 3282)

Family. Parents can be significant risk factors or protective factors, depending on the circumstances. Abused children have been found to be at increased risk for later substance abuse (Bennett & Kemper, 1994). Similarly, a "coercive" parenting style has been shown to lead to greater substance abuse and even delinquency in adolescence (McMahon, 1994). Genetically, alcoholic parents are two to nine times more likely to produce biological children who are alcoholic (Belcher & Shinitzky, 1998). The inherited risk probably also extends to other types of drug abuse as well (Comings, 1997). At the opposite end of the spectrum, growing up in a nurturing family with good communication with parents is a significant protective factor (Resnick et al., 1997).

Latchkey children are more likely to use alcohol, tobacco, and marijuana, perhaps because they are unsupervised or perhaps because they have unrestrained access to a variety of unhealthy media (Chilcoat & Anthony, 1996; Richardson et al., 1989). The media have sometimes been labeled "the electronic parents," and if parents fail to give their children appropriate messages about drugs, the media may fill the void with unhealthy information or cues.

Personality. One unusual study found that certain behavioral risk factors in 3- and 4-year-olds could predict adolescent drug use 10 or more years later (Block, Block, & Keyes, 1988). The researchers found that lack of self-control was apparent and predictive at an early age. Absence of resilience may also be important at a young age because resiliency (the ability to overcome adversity) is also protective (Resnick et al., 1997). Likewise, positive self-esteem and self-image, good self-control, assertiveness, social competence, and academic success are all positive resilience factors. The role of media in encouraging or diminishing resiliency is completely unknown. Different children may respond to the same depiction completely differently (Brown & Schulze, 1990). It is possible that children who are more "media resilient" are less likely to be affected by unhealthy portrayals in the media, but only one media education study has found this to be true so far (Austin & Johnson, 1997).

IMPACT OF ADVERTISING ON CHILDREN AND ADOLESCENTS ●

An interesting and unfortunate paradox exists in American media: Advertisements for birth control products, which could prevent untold numbers of teenage pregnancies and sexually transmitted diseases, are forbidden on two of the six major national networks. Yet all six networks frequently advertise products that cause disease and death in thousands of teenagers and adults annually—alcohol and cigarettes (see Figure 6.5) (Strasburger, 1997c).

Figure 6.5. Typical Cigarette and Alcohol Print Ads

NOTE: Smoking ads have used doctors and movie stars and currently tend to emphasize the independence of young women to smoke. Increasing attention is being paid to minority groups and the Third World. Alcohol ads typically target young males by using sex and rebellion.

Tobacco and alcohol represent two hugely profitable industries that require the constant recruitment of new users. With the death of 1,200 smokers a day and with thousands more trying to quit, the tobacco industry must recruit new smokers to remain profitable. Inevitably, these new smokers come from the ranks of children

Figure 6.5. Continued

and adolescents, especially given the demographics of smoking (50% of smokers begin by age 13, 90% by age 19) (U.S. Department of Health and Human Services, 1994). Big Tobacco has engaged in a systematic campaign to attract underage smokers for decades and then lied to Congress about it (Kessler, 2001). The alcohol industry has targeted minority groups and the young for years, particularly through promotion of sports and youth-oriented programming (Gerbner, 1990). Because 5% of drinkers consume 50% of all alcoholic beverages (Gerbner, 1990), new recruits are a must for the alcohol industry as well, preferably heavy drinkers.

Celebrity endorsers are commonly used, and older children and teenagers may be particularly vulnerable to such ads (Atkin, 1982; Atkin & Block, 1983; Zollo, 1995). Few commercials in the 1990s fail to employ some combination of rock music, young attractive models, humor, or adventure. "Beach babes," frogs, lizards, and dogs are all commonly seen in beer commercials. Production values are extraordinary: Costs for a single 30-second commercial may easily exceed those for an entire half-hour of regular programming, and 30 seconds' worth of advertising during the Super Bowl costs well over $2 million. Recently, a new form of alcoholic beverage has been dubbed "learner drinks for kids"—so-called "hard" lemonades, which contain about 5% alcohol. They, too, use fictitious cool guys such as "Doc" Otis and One-Eyed Jack and "make a mockery of the industry's claim that it doesn't market to kids," according to one expert (Cowley & Underwood, 2001).

A variety of studies have explored the impact of advertising on children and adolescents. Nearly all have shown advertising to be extremely effective in increasing youngsters' awareness of and emotional responses to products, their recognition of certain brands, their desire to own or use the products advertised, and their recognition of the advertisements themselves. In 1975, the National Science Foundation (1977) commissioned a report on the effects of advertising on children, which concluded,

> It is clear from the available evidence that television does influence children. Research has demonstrated that children attend to and learn from commercials, and that advertising is at least moderately successful in creating positive attitudes toward and the desire for products advertised. (p. 179)

Although the research is not yet considered to be scientifically "beyond a reasonable doubt," there is a preponderance of evidence that cigarette and alcohol advertising is a significant factor in adolescents' use of these two drugs (Altman, Levine, Coeytaux, Slade, & Jaffe, 1996; Center for Substance Abuse Prevention, 1997; Evans, Farkas, Gilpin, Berry, & Pierce, 1995; Grube, 1999; Grube & Wallack, 1994; Kessler, Wilkenfeld, & Thompson, 1997; Madden & Grube, 1994; Pierce, Choi, Gilpin, Farkas, & Berry, 1998; Pollay et al., 1996; Schooler, Feighery, & Flora, 1996; U.S. Department of Health and Human Services, 1994; Wyllie, Zhang, & Casswell, 1998). For alcohol, advertising may account for as much as 10% to 30% of adolescents' usage (Atkin, 1993b, 1995; Gerbner, 1990). Interestingly, a recent study of students' use of cigarette promotional items found that a similar figure applies to cigarettes as well: Approximately one third of adolescents' cigarette use could be predicted by their purchase or ownership of tobacco promotional gear (Pierce et al., 1998). Nevertheless, as one group of researchers notes,

> To reduce the argument regarding the demonstrable effects of massive advertising campaigns to the level of individual behavior is absurdly simplistic. . . . Rather, what we are dealing with is the nature of advertising itself. Pepsi Cola, for example, could not convincingly prove, through any sort of defensible scientific study, that particular children or adolescents who consume their products do so because of exposure to any or all of their ads. (Orlandi, Lieberman, & Schinke, 1989, p. 90)

Although there is some legitimate debate about how much of an impact such advertising has on young people and their decisions whether to use cigarettes or alcohol, advertising clearly works—or else companies would not spend millions of dollars a year on it. This leaves American society with a genuine moral, economic, and public health dilemma: Should advertising of unhealthy products be allowed, when society then has to pay for the disease, disability, and death that these products cause? Tobacco companies and beer manufacturers claim that they are simply influencing "brand choice," not increasing overall demand for their products (Orlandi et al., 1989). Moreover, they claim that because it is legal to sell their products, it should be legal to advertise them as well, and any ban represents an infringement on their First Amendment rights of commercial free speech (Gostin & Brandt, 1993; Ile & Knoll, 1990; Shiffrin, 1993).

Public health advocates counter that tobacco companies and beer manufacturers are engaging in unfair and deceptive practices by specifically targeting young people, using attractive role models and youth-oriented messages in their ads, and making smoking and drinking seem like normative behavior (Atkin, 1993a, 1993b; Kilbourne, 1993; Madden & Grube, 1994; Strasburger & Donnerstein, 1999; U.S. Department of Health & Human Services, 1994). For example, two recent studies of magazine advertising (which accounts for nearly half of all cigarette advertising expenditures) found that brands popular with teens were more likely than adult brands to be advertised in magazines with high teen readerships (King, Siegel, Celebucki, & Connolly, 1998). In fact, teen magazines have attracted an increasing number of cigarette ads since 1965 (Brown & Witherspoon, 1998). The fact that alcohol and tobacco manufacturers are trying to get adolescents to "just say yes" to cigarettes and beer at a time when society is trying to get them to "just say no" to drugs seems like a situation straight out of *Alice in Wonderland* (Kilbourne, 1993; Strasburger, 1997c). As we shall see, the available data strongly support the public health viewpoint.

CIGARETTES •

Impact of Cigarette Advertising

Cigarette advertising appears to increase teenagers' risk of smoking by glamorizing smoking and smokers (CDC, 1994c). Smokers are depicted as independent, healthy, youthful, and adventurous. By contrast, the adverse consequences of smoking are never shown. The weight of the evidence is such that in 1994, the U.S. Surgeon General concluded, "Cigarette advertising appears to affect young people's perceptions of the pervasiveness, image, and function of smoking. Since misperceptions in these areas constitute psychosocial risk factors for the initiation of smoking, *cigarette advertising appears to increase young people's risk of smoking*" (U.S. Department of Health & Human Services, 1994, p. 195, emphasis added).

In fact, some of the industry's advertising strategies are nearly Orwellian in their sophistication. In *The Weekly Reader,* a periodical sold in approximately 80% of all U.S. elementary schools and owned, at one time, by the same company that owned tobacco conglomerate RJR Nabisco, the following contradictory themes were seen in the early 1990s: Adults in positions of authority are trying to prevent teens from smoking (appealing to teens' sense of autonomy), laws are being enforced inconsistently, most teenagers smoke, smoking is highly pleasurable and relaxing, and teens intent on smoking will do so regardless of what adults try to do about it (DeJong, 1996). An expert in adolescent psychology could not have dreamed up a more effective "forbidden fruit" scheme to recruit new teen smokers. Recently, legislation originally brought by the U.S. Attorney General uncovered the fact that tobacco companies have specifically targeted teenage smokers as young as age 13 in an attempt to regain market share (Weinstein, 1998).

Perhaps, as a result, nearly half of eighth graders do not believe that smoking a pack of cigarettes a day represents a health risk (Johnston, Bachman, & O'Malley, 1994). Numerous studies show that children who pay closer attention to cigarette advertisements, who are able to recall such ads more readily, or who own promotional items are more likely to view smoking favorably and to become smokers themselves (Aitken & Eadie, 1990; Altman et al., 1996; Armstrong, de Klerk, Shean, Dunn, & Dolin, 1990; Biener & Siegel, 2000; CDC, 1992a, 1992b; Evans et al., 1995; Goldstein, Fischer, Richards, & Creten, 1987; Klitzner, Gruenewald, & Bamberger, 1991; Pierce et al., 1998; Sargent et al., 1997; Sargent, Dalton, & Beach, 2000; Schooler et al., 1996; Vaidya, Naik, & Vaidya, 1996; Vickers, 1992; While, Kelly, Huang, & Charlton, 1996). Teens who smoke are also more likely to believe messages in print ads for cigarettes (Hawkins & Hane, 2000). Among teenage girls, smoking rates increased dramatically around 1967, exactly the same time that women were being targeted by such new brands as Virginia Slims (Pierce, Lee, & Gilpin, 1994). Only a rare study can be found that concludes that tobacco advertising has no influence on children (Smith, 1989).

Beginning in the early 1990s, some important research has more clearly delineated the impact of cigarette advertising on young people. In 1991, two studies examined the impact of the Old Joe the Camel advertising campaign. In one, 6-year-olds were as likely to recognize Old Joe as the famous mouseketeer logo for the Disney Channel (see Figure 6.6) (Fischer, Schwart, Richards, Goldstein, & Rojas, 1991). Even at age 3, 30% of children could still make the association between the Old Joe Camel figure and a pack of cigarettes. In the second study, more than twice as many children as adults reported exposure to Old Joe. Not only were children able to recognize the association with Camel cigarettes, but they found the ads to be appealing as well (DiFranza et al., 1991). Not coincidentally, in the 3 years after the introduction of the Old Joe campaign, the preference for Camel cigarettes increased from 0.5% of adolescent smokers to 32%. During the same time period, the sale of Camels to minors increased from $6 million to $476 million, representing one quarter of all Camel sales and one third of all illegal cigarette sales to minors (DiFranza et al., 1991).

Other studies have provided important evidence as well. A California study documented that the most heavily advertised brands of cigarettes—Marlboro and Camel—are the most popular among teenage smokers (Pierce et al., 1991). A simi-

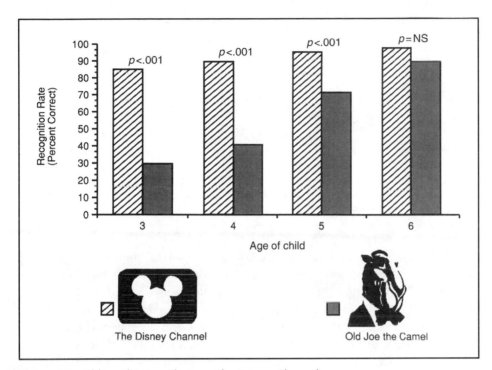

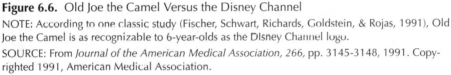

Figure 6.6. Old Joe the Camel Versus the Disney Channel

NOTE: According to one classic study (Fischer, Schwart, Richards, Goldstein, & Rojas, 1991), Old Joe the Camel is as recognizable to 6-year-olds as the Disney Channel logo.

SOURCE: From *Journal of the American Medical Association, 266,* pp. 3145-3148, 1991. Copyrighted 1991, American Medical Association.

lar national study by the CDC found that 84% of teenagers purchase either Marlboros, Camels, or Newports—the three most highly advertised brands in the United States in 1990 (see Table 6.3) (CDC, 1992a, 1992b). In England, the most popular brands of cigarettes (Benson & Hedges, Silk Cut, Embassy, and Marlboro) are likewise the mostly heavily advertised (Vickers, 1992).

Cross-sectional studies in the mid-1990s found that teenagers exposed to promotional items or advertising were far more likely to become smokers. A study of 571 seventh graders in San Jose, California, found that 88% of 13-year-olds reported exposure to cigarette marketing and that experimenting with smoking was 2.2 times greater among those who owned promotional items (Schooler et al., 1996). In a national sample of 1,047 adolescents ages 12 to 17 years, Altman et al. (1996) drew a similar conclusion. In rural New Hampshire, a survey of 1,265 6th through 12th graders found that students who owned promotional items were 4.1 times more likely to be smokers (Sargent et al., 1997). Evans et al. (1995) surveyed more than 3,500 California teens and found that receptivity to tobacco advertising exceeded exposure to family members and peers who smoke as a risk factor. In a unique longitudinal study of 529 Massachusetts teenagers, Biener and Siegel

TABLE 6.3   Is Cigarette Advertising Effective?

Advertising in $ Millions	Adolescent Brand Preference	Adult Brand Preference
1. Marlboro ($75)	1. Marlboro (60.0%)	1. Marlboro (23.5%)
2. Camel ($43)	2. Camel (13.3%)	2. Winston (6.7%)
3. Newport ($35)	3. Newport (12.7%)	3. Newport (4.8%)

SOURCE: Data from Centers for Disease Control and Prevention (1994) and Pollay et al. (1996). From Strasburger and Donnerstein (1999). Copyright American Academy of Pediatrics. Reprinted with permission.

(2000) found that those who owned a tobacco promotional item and could name a brand of cigarettes whose ad attracted their attention were nearly three times more likely to begin smoking in the next year than adolescents who did neither. Sargent et al. (2000) actually found a dose-response relationship between the number of cigarette promotional items owned by adolescents and their smoking behavior.

This is hardly an American phenomenon, however. In the United Kingdom, a survey of 1,450 students ages 11 and 12 years found that awareness of cigarette advertising correlated with smoking (While et al., 1996), as did a survey of nearly 2,000 students who were exposed to so-called passive cigarette advertising during an India–New Zealand cricket series televised in India (Vaidya et al., 1996). Unlike the United States, other countries have been more aggressive in banning cigarette advertising. In New Zealand, consumption fell after a complete ban on cigarette advertising (Vickers, 1992). In Norway, the prevalence of 13- to 15-year-old smokers decreased from 17% in 1975 to 10% in 1990 after an advertising ban was imposed (Vickers, 1992). In fact, an analysis of factors influencing tobacco consumption in 22 countries revealed that since 1973, advertising restrictions have resulted in lower rates of smoking (Laugesen & Meads, 1991).

Finally, a comprehensive 3-year longitudinal study of 1,752 California adolescents who never smoked found that one third of all smoking experimentation in California between 1993 and 1996 could be attributed to tobacco advertising and promotions (Pierce et al., 1998). This was the first study of its kind to use longitudinal correlational data that could yield cause-and-effect conclusions.

Several studies have documented that as the amount of cigarette advertising in a magazine increases, the amount of coverage of health risks associated with smoking decreases dramatically (Amos, Jacobson, & White, 1991; DeJong, 1996; Kessler, 1989; Warner, Goldenhar, & McLaughlin, 1992). Recently, researchers using a logistic regression analysis to examine 99 U.S. magazines published over a 25-year span (between 1959-1969 and 1973-1986) found that the probability of publishing an article on the risks of smoking decreased 38% for magazines that derived signifi-

TABLE 6.4   Does Cigarette Advertising Influence Editorial Content?

Magazine	Number of Magazine-Years	Probability of Coverage of Health Care Risks (%)
All magazines		
No cigarette ads	403	11.9
Any cigarette ads	900	8.3
Women's magazines		
No cigarette ads	104	11.7
Any cigarette ads	212	5.0

SOURCE: Adapted with permission from Warner, Goldenhar, and McLaughlin (1992). Copyright Massachusetts Medical Society. All rights reserved.

cant revenue from tobacco companies (see Table 6.4) (Warner et al., 1992). Women's magazines are particularly guilty. A study of *Cosmopolitan, Good Housekeeping, Mademoiselle, McCall's,* and *Women's Day* found that between 1983 and 1987, not one of them published a single column or feature on the dangers of smoking (Kessler, 1989). All but *Good Housekeeping* have accepted cigarette advertising. This occurred during the same 5-year period that lung cancer was surpassing breast cancer as the number one killer of women (Moog, 1991).

Why is tobacco advertising so effective? Aside from the sheer amount of money spent on it, creating a density of such advertising that is difficult to counteract, cigarette advertising may act as a "super-peer" in influencing teenagers that everyone smokes but them (smoking is normative behavior) and that they will instantly become more attractive to their peers if they do smoke (Strasburger, 1997c). Indeed, one group of researchers (Goldman & Glantz, 1998) has found that the only two strategies that are highly effective for preventing adolescents from smoking are showing the lengths to which the tobacco industry will go to recruit new smokers ("industry manipulation") and sensitizing teenagers to the risk of second-hand smoke. Both strategies involve "denormalizing" smoking (i.e., counteracting the myth that smoking is normative behavior for teens).

In 1998, the U.S. Attorney General negotiated what may be a remarkable settlement with the tobacco industry, calling for the payout of more than $206 billion to the states over the next 25 years, along with severe restrictions on marketing and advertising to children (see Table 6.8). Critics point to the fact that this figure represents a mere 8% of the $2.5 trillion that the federal government will lose over the same 25 years in health care costs related to smoking (Jackson, 1998). In addition, according to the Federal Trade Commission (FTC), the tobacco industry actually spent more money on advertising and promotions after the lawsuits were settled:

TABLE 6.5 Tobacco or Alcohol Content of G-Rated Children's Films

Film	Tobacco Use/ Exposure (seconds)		Alcohol Use/ Exposure (seconds)	
The Three Caballeros	Yes	548	Yes	8
101 Dalmations	Yes	299	Yes	51
Pinocchio	Yes	22	Yes	80
James & the Giant Peach	Yes	206	Yes	38
All Dogs Go to Heaven	Yes	205	Yes	73
Alice in Wonderland	Yes	158	No	—
Great Mouse Detective	Yes	165	Yes	414
The Aristocats	Yes	11	Yes	142
Beauty & the Beast	No	—	Yes	123

SOURCE: Adapted from Goldstein, Sobel, and Newman (1999).

$8.2 billion in 1999, a 22% increase from 1998 (Journal Wire Reports, 2001). Nevertheless, the now-substantial cigarette advertising research is hardly "moot" and may certainly have implications for alcohol advertising as well. For example, will there be future lawsuits against beer manufacturers by victims of drunk drivers or by the Attorney General to recover health care costs? In addition, the research may come back into play if the Attorney General settlement is overturned by a Congress that has traditionally been heavily influenced by tobacco money or by a federal court decision. What may replace the concerns about advertising and promotion is increasing alarm over the depictions of tobacco use in movies, music videos, and television programs—in a sense, the new "advertising" arena for tobacco companies.

Cigarettes in Television Programming, Music and Music Videos, and Movies

Smoking seems to be making a major comeback in the movies and, to a lesser extent, on television (see Figures 6.7 and 6.8).

Before the Surgeon General's landmark 1964 report on smoking, TV characters smoked nine times more frequently than in 1982 (Signorielli, 1990). By the early 1980s, only 2% of series stars smoked on TV (Breed & De Foe, 1983). However, this apparently healthy low percentage is deceptive: TV programs rarely showed characters refusing to smoke or expressing anti-smoking sentiments—probably so as not to offend the corporate advertisers whose parent companies also own tobacco

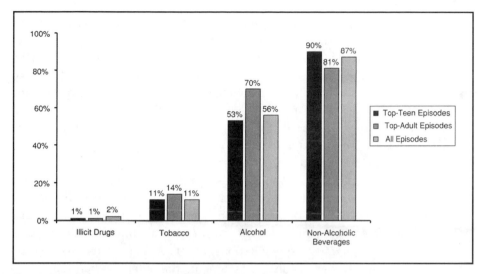

Figure 6.7. Substance Use on Television

SOURCE: Christenson, Henriksen, and Roberts (2000).

NOTE: Percentages based on 80 top-teen episodes, 80 top-adult episodes, or all 168 episodes.

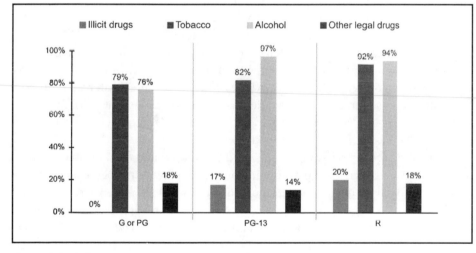

Figure 6.8. Substance Use in Movies, According to Ratings

SOURCE: Roberts, Henriksen, and Christenson (1999).

NOTE: Percentages based on 38 G- or PG-rated movies, 65 PG-13-rated movies, and 97 R-rated movies.

subsidiaries (Signorielli, 1990). By the 1990s, one of the latest content analyses shows that more young and middle-aged women are now depicted as smokers and that promotions for feature films constitute a new supply of smoking scenes (Gerbner & Ozyegin, 1997). In one analysis of the 1992 fall prime-time season, 24%

of programs contained smoking content, with only 8% of those scenes involving anti-smoking messages. Most of the smokers were high-status "good guys," rather than unsavory characters (Hazan & Glantz, 1995). The most recent content analysis of prime-time television found that 19% of programming portrayed tobacco use, with about one fourth of those depicting negative statements about smoking (Christenson et al., 2000). In music videos, one fourth of all Music Television (MTV) videos portrayed tobacco use, with the lead performer usually the one shown as smoking (DuRant et al., 1997).

Movies are providing tobacco companies with increasing opportunities for featuring smoking. Use of passive advertising—so-called "product placements"—has been extremely lucrative, although studio chiefs currently deny that this practice continues. The Philip Morris Company reportedly paid $350,000 to place Lark cigarettes in the James Bond movie *License to Kill* and another $42,500 to place Marlboros in *Superman II* (Consumer Reports, 1990). Direct payments for product placements of cigarettes ended in 1989 (Sargent et al., 2001), when the top 13 tobacco firms adopted the following guidelines to avoid federal regulation: "No payment, direct or indirect, shall be made for the placement of our cigarettes or cigarette advertisements in any film produced for viewing by the general public" (Shields, Carol, Balbach, & McGee, 1999).

Movies are also extremely popular with teenagers, who comprise 16% of the U.S. population but account for 26% of all movie admissions (Rauzi, 1998). Unique longitudinal research has shown that one of the most important factors in the onset of teen drug use is exposure to others who use substances (Kosterman, Hawkins, Guo, Catalano, & Abbott, 2000). Nowhere is that exposure greater than on contemporary movie screens. Two studies have linked adolescent smoking to the impact of actors and actresses who smoke on-screen (Distefan, Gilpin, Sargent, & Pierce, 1999; Tickle, Sargent, Dalton, Beach, & Heatherton, 2001).

Hollywood seems to use cigarette smoking as shorthand for a troubled or antiestablishment character, but the smoking or nonsmoking status of the actors themselves is also influential in whether their characters will smoke on screen (Shields et al., 1999). The list of prominent Hollywood actors and actresses puffing away on-screen is quite long: Julia Roberts in *My Best Friend's Wedding,* Al Pacino in *Any Given Sunday,* Michael Douglas in *Wonder Boys,* John Travolta in *Broken Arrow,* Brad Pitt in *Sleepers,* and Leonardo DiCaprio and Kate Winslet in *Titanic* (Roberts & Christenson, 2000). In the 1990s, there has been a new wave of content analyses performed, all of which have found that cigarette smoking in movies is a major occurrence and a continuing problem:

- Since 1960, the top-grossing films have shown movie stars lighting up at three times the rate of American adults (Hazan, Lipton, & Glantz, 1994).

- All 10 of the top-grossing films of 1996 contained tobacco use, and 17 of the 18 films in then-current distribution featured smoking (Thomas, 1996).

- In a study of the top 10 moneymaking films from 1985 to 1995, tobacco use was found in 98%. At least one lead character used tobacco in half of the films, and use was discouraged only one third of the time (Everett, Schnuth, & Tribble, 1998).

- In films between 1993 and 1997, male and female actors lit up about 40% of the time, which is 50% higher than in the general population. Leading women are as likely to smoke in movies aimed at teenage audiences (PG/PG-13) as in R-rated movies, whereas leading men smoke more often in R-rated movies. And young actresses are four times more likely to be featured smoking than older actresses (Escamilla, Cradock, & Kawachi, 2000).

- Even children's G-rated movies contain a surprising amount of smoking scenes. In fact, smoking has long been present in children's movies. Two reviews of 50 to 74 G-rated animated feature films released between 1937 and 1997 by five major production companies found that more than half portrayed one or more instances of tobacco use, including all seven films released in 1996 and 1997 (see Table 6.5) (Goldstein, Sobel, & Newman, 1999; Thompson & Yokota, 2001).

- In one of the two most recent studies of the 200 most popular movie rentals of 1996 and 1997, Roberts, Henriksen, and Christenson (1999) found that tobacco appeared in 89% of the movies, consistently across all genres (see Figure 6.2). Unlike real life, smoking rates in the movies have not changed between 1960 and 1990.

- In the other most recent study, researchers found that 85% of the 250 highest grossing movies released from 1988 to 1997 depicted characters using tobacco (Sargent et al., 2001). Although product placements are no longer paid for in Hollywood, the most highly advertised four brands of cigarettes in the United States accounted for 80% of the brand appearances in the films, which suggests an advertising motive still exists. This study represented the most comprehensive analysis of tobacco use in movies to date and found that more than half of the movies analyzed featured tobacco use by a major character. Of note for Hollywood producers and directors, tobacco use was not associated with box office success (Sargent et al., 2001).

Movie smokers tend to be White middle-class male characters, who are usually the heroes (Stockwell & Glantz, 1997). Smoking among males is associated with violent behavior and dangerous acts; among females, it is associated with sexual affairs, illegal activities, and reckless driving (Sargent et al., 2000). Movie depictions also tend to be very pro-smoking, with only 14% of screen time dealing with adverse health effects (Stockwell & Glantz, 1997). One study of the 100 most popular films spanning five decades found that smokers are depicted as more romantically and sexually active than nonsmokers and as marginally more intelligent (McIntosh, Bazzini, Smith, & Wayne, 1998).

● ALCOHOL

Research on Alcohol Advertising

Although the research on alcohol advertising is not quite as compelling as that on tobacco advertising, children and adolescents do seem to comprise a uniquely vulnerable audience. Like cigarette advertisements, beer commercials are virtually custom-made to appeal to children and adolescents: images of fun-loving, sexy, successful young people having the time of their lives. Who wouldn't want to indulge (see Table 6.6) (Kilbourne, 1993)? Using sexual imagery (Atkin, 1995; Kilbourne, Painton, & Ridley, 1985) or celebrity endorsers (Atkin, 1982; Atkin & Block, 1983; Friedman, Termini, & Washington, 1977) increases the impact of beer and wine ads on young people.

Content analyses show that beer ads seem to suggest that drinking is an absolutely harmless activity with no major health risks associated with it (Atkin, 1993a; Atkin, DeJong, & Wallack, 1992; Atkin, Hocking, & Block, 1984; Grube, 1993; Grube & Wallack, 1994; Madden & Grube, 1994; Postman, Nystrom, Strate, & Weingartner, 1988; Strasburger, 1993; Wallack, Cassady, & Grube, 1990). Yet more than one third of ads show people driving or engaging in water sports while supposedly drinking (Madden & Grube, 1994).

As with cigarette smoking, drinking alcohol is portrayed as normative behavior, with no adverse consequences. But unlike cigarette advertising, beer and wine ads are frequently featured on prime-time television: Children and teenagers view 1,000 to 2,000 of them annually (Strasburger, 1997c). Much of this advertising is concentrated in sports programming. In prime time, only 1 alcohol commercial appears every 4 hours; in sports programming, 2.4 ads appear per hour (Grube, 1995; Madden & Grube, 1994). In addition, alcohol advertisements are frequently embedded in sports programming, with banners and scoreboards featuring brand logos and brief interruptions of brand sponsorship (e.g., "This half-time report is brought to you by. . . ."), at a rate of about 3 per hour (Grube, 1995).

Such a density of advertising seems to have a considerable impact on young people. In one survey of fifth and sixth graders, nearly 60% of them could match the brand of beer being promoted with a still photograph from a commercial (Grube, 1995). Similarly, a sample of 9- to 10-year-olds could identify the Budweiser frogs nearly as frequently as Bugs Bunny (see Table 6.7) (Leiber, 1996). In one well-known survey of suburban Maryland children, 8- to 12-year-olds could list more brands of beer than names of American presidents (Center for Science in the Public Interest, 1988)! Rarely do young people see ads or public service announcements urging moderation (Madden & Grube, 1994). Perhaps as a result, nearly three fourths of American adults think that such advertising encourages teenagers to drink (Lipman, 1991).

TABLE 6.6   Seven Myths That Alcohol Advertisers Want Children and Adolescents to Believe

1. Everyone drinks alcohol.
2. Drinking has no risks.
3. Drinking helps to solve problems.
4. Alcohol is a magic potion that can transform you.
5. Sports and alcohol go together.
6. If alcohol were truly dangerous, we wouldn't be advertising it.
7. Alcoholic beverage companies promote drinking only in moderation.

SOURCE: Adapted from Kilbourne (1993).

TABLE 6.7   Are the Budweiser Frogs Effective Advertising? Commercial and Character Recall by Children 9 to 11 Years Old

Character	Slogan or Motto	% Recall (n = 221)
Bugs Bunny	"Eh, what's up Doc?"	80
Budweiser Frogs	"Bud-weis-er"	73
Tony the Tiger	"They're grrreat!"	57
Smokey Bear	"Only you can prevent forest fires."	43
Mighty Morphin' Power Rangers	"It's morphin' time!" or "Power up!"	39

SOURCE: Adapted from Leiber (1996). Copyright American Academy of Pediatrics. Reprinted with permission.

Considerable research exists that the media can make children more vulnerable to experimentation with alcohol (Grube, 1995; Grube & Wallack, 1994). This survey or cross-sectional research does not yield cause-and-effect conclusions, but a few examples of such research may demonstrate the extent of its findings:

- A series of survey studies by Atkin (Atkin & Block, 1983; Atkin, Neuendorf, & McDermott, 1983; Atkin et al., 1984) really began the investigations in this area. He found that adolescents heavily exposed to alcohol advertising are more likely to believe that drinkers possess the qualities being displayed in the advertising (e.g., being attractive or successful), have more positive beliefs about drinking, think that getting drunk is acceptable, and are more likely to drink, drink heavily, and drink and drive.

• Other studies have found that early adolescent drinkers are more likely to have been exposed to alcohol advertising, can identify more brands of beer, and view such ads more favorably than nondrinkers (Aitken, Eadie, Leathar, McNeill, & Scott, 1988; Wyllie et al., 1998).

• A 1990 study of 468 randomly selected fifth and sixth graders found that 88% of them could identify Spuds Mackenzie with Bud Light beer. Their ability to name brands of beer and match slogans with the brands was significantly related to their exposure and attention to beer ads. The greater the exposure and attention, the greater the likelihood that the children would think that drinking is associated with fun and good times, and not with health risks, and that the children expected to drink as adults. Their attitudes about drinking were especially conditioned by watching weekend sports programming on TV (Wallack, Cassady, & Grube, 1990).

Children begin making decisions about alcohol at an early age, probably during the elementary school years (Austin & Knaus, 1998; Wallack, Cassady, & Grube, 1990). Studies document that the media can make children more vulnerable to future experimentation with alcohol because children and adolescents do not develop adult-type comprehension skills to deal with media messages until about the eighth grade (Collins, 1983). Exposure to beer commercials correlates with brand recognition and positive attitudes toward drinking (Aitken et al., 1988; Austin & Nach-Ferguson, 1995; Wallack, Cassady, & Grube, 1990), and children who enjoy alcohol advertisements are more likely to drink earlier and to engage in binge drinking (Austin & Meili, 1994). Correlational studies indicate a small but positive (+0.15 to +0.20) relationship between ad exposure and consumption (Atkin, 1993a). In addition, advertising seems particularly related to initial drinking episodes, which, in turn, contribute to excessive drinking and abuse (Atkin, 1993a). As one expert concludes,

> The preponderance of the evidence indicates that alcohol advertising stimulates favorable predispositions, higher consumption, and greater problem drinking by young people.

Nevertheless, the evidence does not support the interpretation that advertising exerts a powerful, uniform, direct influence; it seems that advertising is a contributing factor that

> increases drinking and related problems to a modest degree rather than a major determinant. (Atkin, 1993a, p. 535)

But no media research is perfect. Researchers cannot willfully expose children or adolescents to a barrage of alcohol ads and watch who drinks or what brand of beer they choose in a laboratory setting any more than they can assess the effects of media violence by showing children violent movies and then giving them guns and knives to play with (Austin & Knaus, 1998). Most of the data are correlational (children who drink are more likely to have seen advertisements, for example, but heavy drinkers could conceivably choose to watch more ads).

Although there is always the possibility that adolescent drinkers search out or attend to alcohol advertising more than do their abstinent peers, this seems considerably less likely (Atkin, 1990; Grube, 1993). As one advertising executive notes,

> If greater advertising over time doesn't generate greater profits, there's something seriously wrong with the fellows who make up the budgets. (Samuelson, 1991, p. 40)

Furthermore, a few recent longitudinal studies do enable some important cause-and-effect inferences to be made. In an ongoing correlational study of fifth- and sixth-grade children, Grube and Wallack (1994) have found that those who are more aware of alcohol advertising have more positive beliefs about drinking and can recognize more brands and slogans. Their study is unique in that they discard a simple exposure model in favor of examining children's beliefs and behaviors only when they have processed and remembered alcohol advertisements. In their work, the finding of positive beliefs is crucial because that is what leads to an increased intention to drink, even when other important factors such as parental and peer attitudes and drinking behaviors are controlled (Grube, 1999).

In another recent study by Austin and Knaus (1998) of 273 third, sixth, and ninth graders in two Washington state communities, exposure to advertising and promotional merchandise at a young age was predictive of drinking behavior during adolescence. And an 18-month-long study of more than 1,500 ninth-grade students in San Jose, California, found that the onset of drinking alcohol correlated significantly with increased viewing of both television and music videos (Robinson, Chen, & Killen, 1998). This may point to the impact of both alcohol advertising (television) and role modeling (music videos).

There is also a small but demonstrable effect of exposure to advertisements on actual drinking behavior, among both teenagers (Atkin & Block, 1983; Atkin et al., 1984) and college students (Kohn & Smart, 1984, 1987). Other research is less powerful but also suggestive. For example,

- Since 1960 in the United States, a dramatic increase in advertising expenditures has been accompanied by a 50% per capita increase in alcohol consumption (Jacobson & Collins, 1985).

- In Sweden, a mid-1970s ban on all beer and wine advertising resulted in a 20% per capita drop in alcohol consumption (Romelsjo, 1987).

- In perhaps the best ecological study, Saffer (1997) studied the correlation between alcohol advertising on television, radio, and billboards in the 75 top media markets in the United States and the motor vehicle fatality rate. He found that greater density of alcohol advertising significantly increased the fatality rate, particularly for older drivers, and hypothesized that a total ban on such advertising might save 5,000 to 10,000 lives per year.

Alcohol in Television Programming, Music and Music Videos, and Movies

During the 1970s and early 1980s, alcohol was ubiquitous on American television. It was the most popular beverage consumed, and rarely were negative consequences of drinking shown or discussed (Breed & De Foe, 1981, 1984). Especially on soap operas, alcohol was depicted as being both an excellent social lubricant and an easy means of resolving serious personal crises (Lowery, 1980). Two initiatives tried to change this: new guidelines for the industry, written by the Hollywood Caucus of Producers, Writers, and Directors (Breed & De Foe, 1982; Caucus for Producers, Writers, and Directors, 1983), and the Harvard School of Public Health Alcohol Project in the late 1980s (Rothenberg, 1988). The caucus suggested that its members avoid (a) gratuitous use of alcohol in programming, (b) glamorizing drinking, (c) showing drinking as a macho activity, and (d) depicting drinking with no serious consequences. The Harvard Alcohol Project worked with major networks and studios to foster the notion of the "designated driver," and this device appeared in many story lines during the next few years.

Unfortunately, several content analyses demonstrate that alcohol is a problem that simply will not go away on prime-time television and in music videos. In fact, alcohol remains the most frequently portrayed food or drink on network television (Mathios, Avery, Bisogni, & Shanahan, 1998). In addition, a new study by the AAP suggests that the "designated driver" concept may be failing as well. A survey of 16- to 19-year-olds by the AAP found that 80% think that drinking is acceptable as long as there is a designated driver. Unfortunately, nearly half think that designated drivers can still drink (Tanner, 1998)! These data seem to confirm the Monitoring the Future findings that one fourth of all students surveyed had ridden in a car with a drinking driver in 1997 (O'Malley & Johnston, 1999).

A 1986 content analysis was the first to suggest that alcohol was still extremely common on TV and in the movies, despite the efforts of the Hollywood caucus: 100% of theatrical or made-for-TV movies and more than 75% of all dramatic series contained some mention of drinking (Wallack, Grube, Madden, & Breed, 1990). Of the 16 most popular R-rated movies in the mid-1980s seen frequently by teenagers, every film contained alcohol use, with an average of 16 episodes per film (Greenberg, Brown, & Buerkel-Rothfuss, 1993). Much of the alcohol use portrayed in both media was unnecessary to the plot, and drinking was still presented as being problem free. In addition, adolescent drinking is often treated in a humorous fashion, and teens frequently acknowledge a desire to drink as a symbol of adulthood (De Foe & Breed, 1988). Again, the impact of "normative drinking" must always be considered when adolescents are involved.

Several more content analyses have been done in the 1990s. Compared with earlier analyses, the first found that the frequency of drinking episodes has remained relatively stable: 6 per hour in 1991 versus 10 per hour in 1984 and 5 per hour in 1976 (Grube, 1993). Prime-time drinkers are usually familiar, high-status characters, and more than 80% of the prime-time programs examined contained references to alcohol (Grube, 1993).

In the second, Gerbner and Ozyegin (1997) found that alcohol remains the most commonly portrayed drug on American television, with one drinking scene occurring every 22 minutes, compared with one smoking scene every 57 minutes and illicit drug use every 112 minutes. On MTV, a viewer sees alcohol use every 14 minutes, compared with every 17 minutes in the movies and every 27 minutes on prime-time television. Popular movies are nearly equally rife with alcohol, with only 2 of the 40 highest grossing titles not containing alcohol depictions.

On prime-time television, 70% of program episodes depict alcohol use, according to the most recent content analysis (see Figure 6.7) (Christenson et al., 2000). More than one third of the drinking episodes are associated with humor, and negative consequences are shown in only 23%. A content analysis of music videos found that alcohol is portrayed in more than one fourth of videos on MTV and VH-1 (DuRant et al., 1997). In addition, alcohol is associated with increased levels of sex and sexuality—again, not a healthy association for teens pondering when and with whom to begin having sex.

The most recent study of movies examined 200 popular films from 1996 to 1997 and found that 93% of the movies contained alcohol depictions (see Figure 6.2). Even G- and PG-rated movies contained frequent references to tobacco and alcohol (see Figure 6.8) (Roberts, Henriksen, & Christenson, 1999; Yakota & Thompson, 2001). Although consequences of alcohol use were shown in 43% of the movies studied, only 14% depicted a refusal of an offer of alcohol and only 9% contained anti-use sentiments (see Figure 6.9) (Roberts, Henriksen, & Christenson, 1999). These findings were almost identical to another, separate content analysis of top-grossing American films from 1985 to 1995 (Everett et al., 1998).

Finally, one study cites certain media use as a possible cause of early alcohol use. Robinson et al.'s (1998) longitudinal study of 1,533 California ninth graders found that increased television and music video viewing are risk factors for the

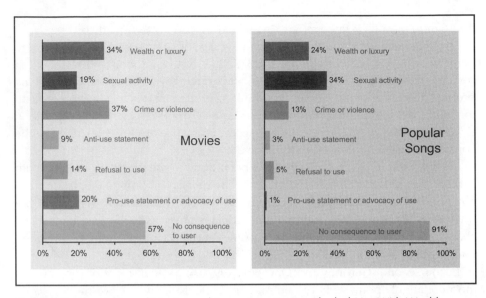

Figure 6.9. Percentage of Movies and Songs Associating Alcohol Use With Wealth, Luxury, or Sex

SOURCE: Roberts, Henriksen, and Christenson (1999).

NOTE: Based on the 183 movies and 149 songs that portrayed alcohol use. Alcohol use in movies and songs is usually associated with wealth, luxury, or sex and is rarely discouraged. In addition, the consequences of alcohol use are rarely depicted or sung about.

onset of alcohol use among adolescents. Odds ratios for television ranged from 1.01 to 1.18, and for music videos they ranged from 1.17 to 1.47, both statistically significant.

Further studies are needed. In particular, the continued presence or absence of product placements in movies and television programming needs to be determined, as does the behavioral impact of drug-oriented Internet advertising on children and teenagers.

● DRUGS

Illicit Drugs in Television Programming, Music and Music Videos, and Movies

Although illicit drugs are not advertised as tobacco and alcohol are, they still make a major appearance in programming seen by children and adolescents. Here, music videos and movies are the primary culprits, the ideal venues for adolescents to be influenced. On prime-time television, illicit drugs are rarely mentioned or shown, and illicit drug use is usually associated with negative consequences (Christenson et al., 2000; Roberts & Christenson, 2000). By contrast, the average MTV viewer sees illicit drugs once every 40 minutes, compared to once every 100 minutes in the movies and every 112 minutes on prime-time TV (Gerbner & Ozyegin, 1997). Addiction is rare, and addicts are portrayed as being evil rather than ill (Gerbner & Ozyegin, 1997). In their recent study of popular movies and songs from 1996 to 1997, Roberts, Henriksen, and Christenson (1999) found that illicit drugs appeared in 22% of movies and 18% of songs (see Figure 6.2). Rap songs were far more likely to contain references to illicit drugs than alternative rock or heavy metal. In movies depicting illicit drugs, marijuana appeared most frequently (51%), followed by cocaine (33%) and other drugs (12%). Currently, when the top movies portray drug use, no harmful consequences are shown 52% of the time (Christenson et al., 2000; Roberts & Christenson, 2000). On the positive side, 21% of movies include a character refusing to use drugs (Roberts & Christenson, 2000).

Marijuana does seem to be making a major comeback in Hollywood movies, thanks to movies such as *There's Something About Mary, Bulworth, Jackie Brown,* and *Summer of Sam* (Gordinier, 1998). Cocaine is featured in *The Last Days of Disco*, Woody Allen's *Deconstructing Harry,* and Spike Lee's *Summer of Sam*. And heroin use is depicted quite graphically in both *Trainspotting* and *Permanent Midnight* (Ivry, 1998).

What impact these depictions have on children or adolescents is conjectural at best. Such research is difficult to accomplish, but again, any media portrayals that seem to legitimize or normalize drug use are likely to have an impact, at least on susceptible teens. Clearly, far more research is needed in this crucial area.

A Word About Prescription and Nonprescription Drugs

During the past decade, there has been a virtual explosion of advertising for prescription drugs (see Figure 6.10). In 1993, prescription drug manufacturers spent $100 million on consumer-targeted advertising (Byrd-Bredbrenner & Grasso, 2000a); by 1999, they were spending nearly $2 billion (Woloshin, Schwartz, Tremmel, & Welch, 2001). Advertising of nonprescription drugs remains high, particularly for cold, flu, and headache remedies and heartburn medications (Byrd-Bredbrenner & Grasso, 2000a; Tsao, 1997).

Under new guidelines issued by the Food and Drug Administration (FDA) in 1997, prescription drug ads can now mention the specific drug being advertised (rather than having to say, "see your doctor") as long as the major health risks associated with the drug are mentioned and a toll-free phone number or Internet address is given (Byrd-Bredbrenner & Grasso, 2000a). As a result, ads for Meridia, Propecia, Viagra, and many other drugs are increasingly common, especially on prime-time television. Prescription drug ads can now be seen during 14% of all prime-time episodes (Christenson et al., 2000).

Figure 6.10

Ads for nonprescription drugs are even more common during prime-time TV: Fully half of all popular adult programs and 43% of all popular teen shows contain ads for over-the-counter medicines (Christenson et al., 2000). Most of these ads emphasize the quick, easy, no-risk approach to self-medication, what one researcher calls the "magic of medicine" perspective (Byrd-Bredbrenner & Grasso, 1999, 2000a). No wonder children in one older study reported that the first thing a person should do when he or she does not feel well is to "eat aspirin" and take medicine (Donohue, Meyer, & Henke, 1978). Half of the health or nutritional information in drug and food ads has been judged misleading or inaccurate (Byrd-Bredbrenner & Grasso, 1999, 2000a).

● **SOLUTIONS**

In a decade when "just say no" has become a watchword for many parents and school-based drug prevention programs, unprecedented amounts of money are being spent in an effort to induce children and teenagers to "just say yes" to smoking and drinking. Half of all the tobacco industry's profits come from sales of cigarettes to people who first became addicted to nicotine as children and adolescents (DiFranza & Tye, 1990). As one group of researchers suggests, the "discussion [should] be *elevated* from the scientific and legal arenas to the domain of ethics and social responsibility" (Orlandi et al., 1989, p. 92, emphasis added). Clearly, advertising and programming are creating a demand for cigarettes and alcohol among children and teenagers.

Discussed below are 11 ideas that, if implemented, could very well result in significant reductions in adolescent drug use without having a negative impact on any writer's or producer's First Amendment rights:

1. *More research.* Media research is difficult, sometimes tedious, and often expensive. However, considering how significant the impact of the media is on young people, more media research is desperately needed, including adequate funding for such efforts. Specifically, more longitudinal analyses of adolescents' drug use compared with their media use are needed, as well as studies of how teens process drug content in different media.

2. *Better dissemination of existing research.* A new Surgeon General's Report or National Institutes of Mental Health Report on Television by the year 2005 would be extremely useful to researchers, health professionals, parents, and policymakers and might provide the impetus for increased funding for media research.

3. *Development of media literacy programs.* Children and teenagers must learn how to decode the subtle and not-so-subtle messages contained in television programming, advertising, movies, and music videos (see Chapter 10). Parents need to begin this process when their children are young (ages 2-3 years), but school programs may be extremely useful as well. In particular, certain drug prevention programs have been extremely effective in reducing levels of adolescents' drug use (see Figure 6.11), but such programs must go far beyond the D.A.R.E. approach to include media literacy, peer resistance skills, and social skills building (NIDA, 1997; Schinke & Botvin, 1999). Although 80% of the nation's schools use the D.A.R.E. approach, currently there are no data that it actually works ("D.A.R.E. Redux," 2001). The United States is unique among Western nations in not requiring some form of media literacy for its students (AAP, 1999). Preliminary studies indicate that successful drug prevention may be possible through this unique route (Austin & Johnson, 1997). However, increased media literacy is not a substitute for needed changes in television and movie programming.

4. *A ban on cigarette advertising in all media and the restriction of alcohol advertising to "tombstone ads" in all media.* American society pays a high price for allowing tobacco and alcohol manufacturers' unlimited access to children and

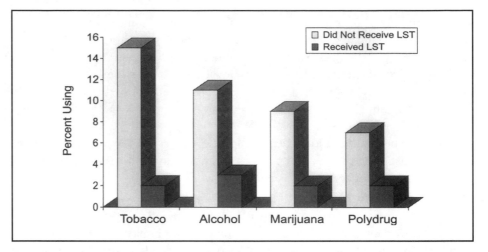

Figure 6.11. Follow-Up Results From Four Published Studies: 8th-Grade Drug Use and 12th-Grade Polydrug Use

SOURCE: Copyright Princeton Health Press. Reprinted by permission.

NOTE: An LST (life skills training) approach to drug prevention has shown dramatic decreases in adolescents' use of a variety of drugs, yet has not been implemented in many communities because D.A.R.E. (Drug Abuse Resistance Education) programs already exist. The LST approach is based on the work of Botvin (see Schinke & Botvin, 1999). By comparison, there is no evidence that the simplistic messages contained in the $226 million D.A.R.E. program have any impact, yet D.A.R.E. is used by 80% of school systems nationwide (Kalb, 2001).

adolescents, and the connection between advertising and consumption is significant. Any product as harmful as tobacco should have severe restrictions placed on it. Whether the recently negotiated tobacco settlement (see Table 6.8) will successfully accomplish this remains to be seen because the industry is actually spending more on advertising and promotion than ever before (Journal Wire Reports, 2001). Former FDA Commissioner David Kessler's solution is to reorganize the entire tobacco industry to remove the profit motive and to allow sales of cigarettes only in plain wrappers, without logos (Kessler, 2001). Several states have become emboldened by the tobacco settlement. In New York, Madison Square Garden removed a large Marlboro sign that was easily visible on television broadcasts. Other states are insisting that advertising be removed from sports arenas, and Minnesota's $6 billion settlement with the tobacco industry actually included a ban on product placements in movies (Brown & Witherspoon, 1998). But the United States as a whole remains far behind Canada, which recently legislated that more than 50% of each tobacco pack must feature a graphic representation of the hazards of smoking. The designs include photographs of cancerous lungs, damaged hearts, and stroke-clotted brains. Warning labels on American cigarette packs remain some of the weakest in the world (Newman, 2001). In alcohol advertising, tombstone ads involve showing the "purity" of the product only, not all of the qualities that the purchaser will magically gain by consuming it (see Figure 6.12). Such restrictions have already been endorsed by the FDA, the

TABLE 6.8   Some Features of the 1998 Tobacco Settlement

Payment of $206.4 billion from the tobacco industry to the states over the next 25 years, including $1.5 billion to fund research to reduce teen smoking

A ban on the use of cartoon characters in the advertising, promotion, or labeling of tobacco products

A prohibition on targeting youth in advertising, promotions, or marketing

A ban on all outdoor advertising, including billboards and signs in stadiums

A ban on the sale of merchandise with brand-name logos, such as T-shirts or backpacks

A ban on payments to producers of TV and movies for product placements

SOURCE: Adapted from *AAP News, 15*(1):4, January, 1999.

Figure 6.12. One Example of a "Tombstone" Ad for an Alcoholic Beverage
NOTE: Such advertising is limited to the inherent qualities of the product rather than the qualities the imbiber will "magically" acquire if he or she consumes the product.

Surgeon General, the AAP, and the American Medical Association and would address the deceptive and alluring quality of current advertisements (Strasburger, 1993). Legislation introduced by Senator Robert Byrd (D-WV) would also eliminate the tax deductability of money spent on alcohol advertising (Massing, 1998).

5. *Higher taxes on tobacco and alcohol products.* Taxes have a direct effect on consumption of products, particularly by teenagers (CDC, 1994c). Surprisingly, a recent study by the CDC suggests that the rate of gonorrhea, for example, could be decreased by nearly 10% simply by raising the beer tax by 20 cents per six-pack (CDC, 2000a). This is because of the well-known association between drinking alcohol and unsafe sexual practices, particularly among adolescents (MacKenzie, 1993; Tapert et al., 2001). Of course, when taxes are raised and consumption goes down, revenues accruing to state and federal governments decrease, people live longer, and the costs of Social Security payments go up. Although medical costs would decrease as well, this scenario represents a very complicated financial issue of whether society can "afford" less consumption of these unhealthy products.

6. *More aggressive counteradvertising.* Counteradvertising can be effective but only if it is intensive, well planned, and coordinated and uses a variety of media (see Figure 6.13) (Bauman, LaPrelle, Brown, Koch, & Padgett, 1991). To be truly effective, counteradvertising must approach both the occurrence rate and the attractiveness of regular advertising (Grube & Wallack, 1994). Some researchers speculate that the decrease in adolescent smoking in the mid-to-late 1970s may be attributable to a very aggressive, preban counteradvertising campaign in which one public service announcement (PSA) aired for every three to five cigarette ads (Atkin, 1993a, 1993b; Brown & Walsh-Childers, 1994; Madden & Grube, 1994; Wallack, Dorfman, Jernigan, & Themba, 1993). Unfortunately, part of the agreement that the tobacco companies made in accepting a ban on smoking ads was that anti-smoking ads would be eliminated as well (Gerbner, 1990). Currently, the density of public service announcements about alcohol has never remotely approached that of regular advertisements, nor are the production values comparable. Of the 685 total alcohol ads examined in one recent content analysis, only 3 contained messages about moderation and another 10 involved very brief public service announcements (e.g., "Know when to say when") (Madden & Grube, 1994). In another study of 1 week of television commercials from 1990, commercials promoting legal drugs and alcohol outnumbered network news stories and PSAs about illegal drugs by 45 to 1 (Fedler, Phillips, Raker, Schefsky, & Soluri, 1994). The best-known and most sophisticated example of aggressive counteradvertising is the campaign mounted by the Partnership for a Drug-Free America. Since 1987, $3 billion has been donated to create and air 600 anti-drug public service announcements (Partnership for a Drug-Free America, 2000). In a

Figure 6.13. Examples of Effective Counteradvertising

SOURCE: Used with special permission of the Partnership for a Drug-Free America.

NOTE: (a) The Partnership for a Drug Free America has created more than 600 anti-drug ads (although none have targeted alcohol or cigarettes). (b) Mothers Against Drunk Driving (MADD) billboard. The questions are the following: Does such advertising work (e.g., appeal to teenagers), and can it compete with the current density of mainstream advertising and drug content on TV and in movies?

study of nearly 1,000 public school students, ages 11 to 19, more than 80% recalled exposure to such ads, and half of the students who had tried drugs reported that the ads convinced them to decrease or stop using them (Reis, Duggan, Adger, & DeAngelis, 1992). Unfortunately, to date, not a single ad has aired dealing with either tobacco or alcohol. Some states have used part of the tobacco settlement money to fund large and aggressive counteradvertising campaigns, with good results. Florida, Massachusetts, and California have taken the lead in mounting aggressive campaigns (see Figure 6.14). In Florida, for example, a series of "Truth" ads that try to expose the tobacco industry as being manipulative and deceptive have resulted in decreased rates of smoking among teenagers (CDC, 1999; Sly, Hopkins, Trapido, & Ray, 2001). The ads are so hard-hitting that Philip Morris actually insisted that two be withdrawn. (As part of the industry's

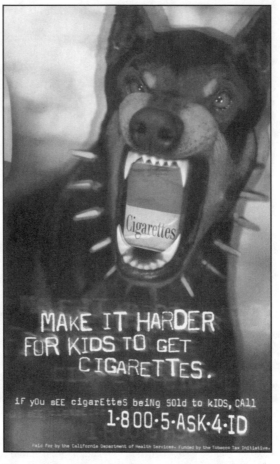

Figure 6.14. Example of a Counter-Ad From an Aggressive Anti-Smoking Campaign in California

$246 billion legal settlement, the nonprofit American Legacy Foundation was established, but it is not allowed to air ads that "vilify" tobacco companies.) In one ad, two teenagers carry a lie detector into Philip Morris's New York headquarters and announce that they want to deliver it to the marketing department. In the second ad, a group of teens in a large truck pull up in front of the headquarters and begin unloading body bags. One teen shouts through a megaphone, "Do you know how many people tobacco kills every day?" (Bryant, 2000). The two ads can still be viewed on the American Nonsmokers' Rights Foundation's Web site (www.no-smoke.org).

7. *Use of MTV and VH-1 as specific media outlets for targeting older children and adolescents with prosocial health messages about smoking, drinking, and drug use.* In the late 1990s, MTV began transforming itself from a music video

jukebox into what one critic calls "a programming service pandering to teens and their legions of base instincts" (Johnson, 2001). Programs such as *Jackass* and *Undressed* and nonstop spring break celebrations have replaced videos (Geier, 2001). Clearly, MTV is homing in on its youth market, but the producers need to accept "the fact that with the rewards of marketing to teens come special responsibilities" (Johnson, 2001). If society is serious about trying to minimize underage drinking and decrease teen smoking, then MTV and similar channels are one of the best places to start. Rather than rely on government-produced anti-drug advertising, MTV could develop its own unique brand of anti-alcohol and anti-smoking PSAs.

8. *Increased sensitivity on the part of the entertainment industry to the health-related issues of smoking, drinking, and other drug use in television programming, music videos, and movies.* A few programs popular with teens, including *Beverly Hills 90210* and after-school specials, have taken the lead in this area, but soap operas, MTV and VH-1, and movies need to follow their example. Cigarette smoking should not be used as a shortcut to dramatize the rebelliousness of a character, nor should alcohol be used to resolve crises. In addition, rock music lyrics should avoid glamorizing drinking or drug use (AAP, 1995a).

9. *Reassessment of the "designated driver" campaign.* Is it working, or do teenagers misunderstand it (Tanner, 1998)? Many public health experts question whether this campaign does not give everyone else accompanying the designated driver permission to drink excessively (Wallack, Cassady, & Grube, 1990).

10. *Revision of the ratings systems for both television and movies.* The current television ratings are not specific enough regarding content (Strasburger & Donnerstein, 1999) and lack any descriptors to denote drug use. Several studies show that parents would prefer a more specific, content-based system (Borgman, 1996; "The Ratings Wars," 1996). The movie ratings system, originally developed by Jack Valenti in the mid-1960s, has not been revised much since that time and tends to be overly skewed toward sexual content rather than violence or depictions of drug use.

11. *Campaign finance reform in Congress.* This recommendation may seem strange, contained within a chapter about the effects of media on young people, but three major industries arguably control much of what is media-related in Congress—the National Rifle Association (NRA), the beer and wine manufacturers, and the tobacco manufacturers—and none has the best interests of the nation's children at heart (see Figure 6.15). In 1996, for example, Seagrams was one of the top "soft money" donors to both the Democratic and Republican parties. Beer accounts for nearly 90% of all alcohol consumed in the United States. The largest brewer, Anheuser-Busch, is situated in the home congressional district of the

Figure 6.15

House minority leader and has contributed heavily to his campaigns. Anheuser-Busch also has lobbyists in every state capital as well. In 1996, the brewer contributed $400,000 to the Democratic Party. Not coincidentally, the Clinton administration failed to propose a single new tax or advertising restriction on beer or alcohol (Massing, 1998). Technically, Congress can control the media, but until Congress is liberated from its obligations to these special interest groups (Hitt, 1999), American media will remain unhealthy for young people.

Exercises

1. *Product Placements #1.* You are a movie director. The scene calls for a conversation between a police detective and one of his suspects in a murder investigation. They are sitting at a bar, drinking beer. How do you decide which beer they will drink? Are there any artistic elements involved in your decision (e.g., does one bottle of beer "look" better than another)? In all fairness, should you simply ask the actors which brand of beer they prefer? Should you ask your producer? How should everyday products be shown in the movies?

2. *Product Placements #2.* You are the new owner of a baseball team in Milwaukee. The makers of Old Milwaukee Beer come to you, asking if they can help build you a new scoreboard out in center field. You drink Old Milwaukee Beer yourself, and you were born and raised in Milwaukee. They offer to pay for the new scoreboard ($2 million), plus give you an annual fee of $750,000. Should you accept their offer? If, instead, you were a member of the Milwaukee City Council, should you allow this to happen? Would it be legal to ban such advertising from public ballparks? Would it be ethical if you were the director of sports broadcasting for a TV station to instruct the cameramen to avoid showing advertising logos whenever possible?

3. *Drugs and the Movies #1.* You are widely considered to be the heir-apparent to Scorsese and Tarantino. A recent graduate of the USC Film School and only 24 years old, you are now being offered a plum feature film directing assignment by a major studio, a big budget action-thriller with three major stars. But the film centers on an anti-hero. You, yourself, do not drink alcohol or smoke cigarettes, in part because your mother died from lung cancer and your father died from cirrhosis. How do you depict the anti-hero without showing him smoking or drinking and without consuming 10 extra pages of script? Will profanity alone accomplish your task?

4. *Drugs and the Movies #2.* You are a major Oscar-nominated film director in your 40s, but you have never made a film about the impact of drugs on society. You want this to be the overriding theme of your next film, which you will write, direct, and coproduce. You admired *Traffic* a great deal. You thought *Pulp Fiction* was overly violent but also made some interesting anti-drug points. On the other hand, you thought that *Blow* glamorized cocaine more than it cautioned against its use (or sale), although you would still very much like to work with Johnny Depp. Is it possible to make an "issue" film that shows a lot of drug use without glamorizing that use for certain audiences, such as teenagers?

5. *Drug Advertising #1.* Over-the-counter remedies are legal, often useful, and frequently used. How should they be advertised in a way that is both fair and accurate? Try designing some sample ads.

6. *Drug Advertising #2.* How could a researcher design a study to determine if the advertising of nonprescription and prescription drugs makes teenagers more likely to use cigarettes, alcohol, or illicit drugs?

7. *Adolescents and Alcohol.* According to national studies, more than 80% of teenagers have tried alcohol by the time they graduate from high school. If you are a filmmaker interested in doing a realistic film about contemporary adolescence, how do you deal with the issue of alcohol, remain socially responsible, attract an adolescent audience, and keep your artistic soul intact?

Figure 6.16

8. *Advertising Alcohol and Cigarettes.* (a) Try to create the most outrageous print ads you can think of for advertising alcohol and cigarettes. (b) Based on what you have learned in this chapter, analyze the two cigarette ads and two alcohol ads seen in Figures 6.16. (c) Figure 6.17 shows an actual ad for a new product entitled Bad Frog Beer. Does this ad target youth? If so, should restrictions be placed on where such ads can be displayed? (Note: This is based on an actual court case in New Jersey.)

Figure 6.17. Bad Frog Beer

NOTE: Until a court case was decided in 2000, Bad Frog Beer was marketed in New Jersey with a picture of a frog making an obscene gesture. The ad also states, "He just don't care" and "An amphibian with an attitude." This plays right into the hands of adolescents, who are attracted by advertising that makes drinking seem rebellious, cool, and anti-authoritarian.

9. *Counteradvertising.* Think of some creative counteradvertising ads dealing with cigarettes or alcohol that might be effective in preventing children from using these drugs. Design a study that would test their impact. How would such ads have to differ if the target audience was adolescents instead? How about Hispanic adolescents versus African American or White teens?

10. *Tobacco Policy.* If tobacco is a legal product, how can a ban on all tobacco advertising be justified?

11. *Drug Control Policy #1.* In January 2000, news reports revealed that the White House Office of National Drug Control Policy (ONDCP) had been reviewing scripts from the networks' most popular shows, including *ER, Chicago Hope,* and *Beverly Hills 90210.* Under an agreement involving a little-known $200 million government anti-drug ad campaign, networks that accepted government PSAs had to include matching messages in their programming (Lacey, 2000). Nearly $30 million in "credit" had been given to the networks by January 2000. The ONDCP did not ask for prior approval of scripts but did help writers and producers with information about drugs or anti-drug themes.

(a) Did this agreement violate the First Amendment?

(b) Should the government be involved in screening scripts for Hollywood?

(c) Isn't there a compelling public health interest in preventing drug use among citizens, especially children and teenagers? If so, what is wrong with the government aiding writers in creating anti-drug messages in mainstream programming?

(d) Does the entertainment industry have a responsibility to depict only wholesome "family values"?

12. *Drug Control Policy #2.* You are the newly appointed head of the Office of National Drug Control Policy (ONDCP) in the White House. Your mission is to cut the use of drugs in the United States by 20% within the next 4 years. Where do you start? With which drugs? Should you engage in discussions with the entertainment industry regarding their portrayals of alcohol and cigarettes? Should you engage in discussions with the tobacco and alcohol industries regarding their use of advertising? Does counteradvertising work? Should the government be in the business of counteradvertising? If so, which media would you target?

CHAPTER 7

EATING AND
EATING DISORDERS

Television presents viewers with two sets of conflicting messages. One suggests that we eat in ways almost guaranteed to make us fat; the other suggests that we strive to remain slim.

—L. Kaufman (1980, p. 45)

Research shows that virtually all women are ashamed of their bodies. It used to be adult women, teenage girls, who were ashamed, but now you see the shame down to very young girls—10, 11 years old. Society's standard of beauty is an image that is literally just short of starvation for most women.

—Author Mary Pipher,
People magazine, June 3, 1996

I never say a character is thin or fat because she will be cast as a thin person anyway. When you are dealing with the major actresses, all of them together might make up a size 14.

—Screenwriter Callie Khouri,
author of *Thelma and Louise, People* magazine, June 3, 1996

They want me to look like a girl, and I'm a woman. It's very hard nowadays. I think it's hideous. I don't read articles about men working out three hours a day and eating just vegetables.

—Actress Andie MacDowell,
Albuquerque Journal, October 27, 1998

TABLE 7.1   Some Facts About Figures

33-23-33 = average measurements of a model

36-18-33 = Barbie doll's measurements, if she were a full-sized human

5'4", 141 pounds = average American woman

5'9", 110 pounds = average model

33% = percentage of American women wearing size 16 or larger

$10 billion = revenues of the diet industry in 1970

$33 billion = revenues of the diet industry in 1996

SOURCE: Adapted from *People* magazine, June 3, 1996, p. 71.

Although sex, drugs, rock 'n' roll, and violence grab the headlines and represent major health concerns during childhood and adolescence, the media have an important impact on other areas of young people's health as well. Television can serve as an important source of information for young children and teens about foods and eating habits (Borzekowski, in press). Television nutrition—in particular, the impact of food advertising—and the image of women in programming and advertising are coming under increasing scrutiny as pediatricians and public health officials try to understand why more American children are becoming obese and why teenagers continue to suffer from a variety of eating disorders (see Table 7.1) (British Medical Association [BMA], 2000; Byrd-Bredbenner & Grasso, 1999, 2000c; Field, Camargo, Taylor, Berkey, & Colditz, 1999; Field, Cheung, et al., 1999; Horgen, Choate, & Brownell, 2001; Jeffery & French, 1998; Kilbourne, 1999; Kohl & Hobbs, 1998; Levine & Smolak, 1998; Ray & Klesges, 1993; Robinson, 1998).

National surveys have documented that the prevalence of obesity is increasing dramatically in the United States (Mokdad et al., 1999; Sokol, 2000). From 1991 to 1998 alone, the prevalence of obesity (defined as a body mass index > 30) has increased from 12% to 18% (Mokdad et al., 1999). (Body mass index, or BMI, is calculated by dividing weight in kilograms by the square of the height in meters. A BMI of less than 25 is desirable, and less than 18 indicates the possibility of an eating disorder.) More than 50% of American adults are now overweight (BMI > 25), and the number of overweight children has doubled in the past two decades (Yanovski & Yanovski, 1999).

The incidence of eating disorders among adolescents remains alarmingly high too. Anorexia nervosa occurs in as many as 1 in 100 to 150 middle-class females (Strasburger & Brown, 1998) and bulimia in as many as 5% of young women (BMA, 2000). Eating disorders may also include symptoms that fall short of full-blown disorders. For example, a recent study of nearly 2,500 middle school teens in North Carolina found that 10% of the girls and 4% of the boys reported vomiting or using laxatives to lose weight (Krowchuk, Kreiter, Woods, Sinal, & DuRant, 1998). Consequently, some researchers have looked accusingly at media portrayals of food to try to understand the frequency of these behaviors (Berel & Irving, 1998; Field, Camargo, et al., 1999; Field, Cheung, et al., 1999; Levine & Smolak, 2001; Shaw & Waller, 1995; Thompson & Smolak, 2001; Thompson, Heinberg, Altabe, & Tantleff-Dunn, 1999).

FOOD ADVERTISEMENTS ●

American children view an estimated 40,000 advertisements per year (see Table 7.2) (Kunkel & Gantz, 1992). More than half of such ads are for food (Brown & Walsh-Childers, 1994), especially sugared cereals and high-caloric snacks (Center for Science in the Public Interest, 1992; Hammond, Wyllie, & Casswell, 1999; Jeffrey, McLellarn, & Fox, 1983). On Saturday morning TV, 61% of commercials are for food, and more than 90% of those are for sugared cereals, candy bars, fast foods, chips, or other nutritionally unsound foods (see Table 7.3) (Center for Science in the Public Interest, 1992). Ads are cleverly constructed to get viewers to associate foods with happiness and fun, rather than taste or nutritional benefit (Scammon & Christopher, 1981).

Food advertising is big business. Americans spent $110 billion on fast food alone in the year 2000, more than on higher education, computers, or cars (Schlosser, 2001). During the 1998 fall season, the major networks averaged 8.5 to 10.3 minutes of advertising per hour (Horgen et al., 2001). Typically, advertisers spend more than $2.5 billion to promote restaurants and another $2 billion a year to promote food products on television (Horgen et al., 2001). Products such as Coke, Pepsi, potato chips, Doritos, Snickers, and Pop-tarts predominate, along with the fast-food chains. In one study of Australian 9- to 10-year-olds, more than half believed that Ronald McDonald knows what is best for children to eat (Food Commission, 1997).

Beginning in the 1960s, advertisers began to target children specifically with ads, reaping great financial rewards in return (Comstock, 1991b; Kunkel & Roberts, 1991). By 1998, the advertising industry was spending $2 billion on ads targeting children, a 20-fold increase from 1990 (Ethridge, 1999). After all, children and teens not only influence their parents' spending habits, but they also have their own money to spend. Teen Research Unlimited estimates that teenagers spend $140 billion a year (Span, 1999), and children under 12 spend another $25 billion (Ethridge, 1999) but may influence another $200 billion of spending per year (Horgen et al., 2001).

TABLE 7.2   Favorite Ads of Children and Teenagers
(*n* = 800 children ages 6-17)

1. Budweiser
2. Pepsi
3. Nissan
4. Nike
5. American Dairy Association
6. Coke
7. Barbie
8. Snickers
9. McDonald's
10. Hostess

SOURCE: Campbell, Mithun, and Esty, *National Study Reveals Kids' Favorite TV Ads* (press release), Minneapolis, MN, June 16, 1998.

TABLE 7.3   What Is Advertised on TV? (*n* = 17.5 hours; 108 ads)
(in percentages)

Food and restaurants	37
Low-nutrient beverages	16
Desserts and snack foods	15
Breads and cereals	11
Convenience entrees	6
Fruits and vegetables	4
Dairy products	2

SOURCE: Adapted from Byrd-Bredbenner and Grasso (2000b).

The problem is that children rarely see a food advertisement for broccoli (see Figure 7.1) (Goodman, 2000). Healthy foods are advertised less than 3% of the time (Kunkel & Gantz, 1991). A study of 52 hours of advertising during Saturday morning programming found that two thirds of the ads were for sugared cereals, sweets, or fats and oils, but none were for fruits or vegetables (Kotz & Story, 1994). A separate study found that 90% of ads on Saturday morning were for sugared cereal, candy bars, salty snack food, or fast food (Center for Media Education,

Figure 7.1

1998). A 1997 study of 900 commercials aired during 43 hours of children's programming (an extraordinary average of 21.1 ads/hour) found that about 45% of ads were for foods, with cereal, snack foods, and restaurants comprising the vast majority (Reece, Rifon, & Rodriguez, 1999). Taras and Gage's study (1995) also found nearly identical percentages. A 1998 sample of commercials broadcast during the top-ranked shows among 2- to 11-year-olds found that 40% of the food ads were for fast food and that public service announcements (PSAs) were virtually nonexistent (see Figure 7.2) (Byrd-Bredbenner & Grasso, 1999, 2000c).

As if this weren't bad enough, food ads often contain violence (62%), conflict (41%), and trickery (20%) (Rajecki et al., 1994). Cartoon characters abound and are incredibly effective. In Leiber's (1996) study of product recall among 221 children ages 9 to 11 years, cartoon characters were extremely efficient in getting children to recognize products (see Table 6.7). As an advertising icon, Ronald McDonald rates number two in the 20th century, second only to the Marlboro Man. Tony the Tiger and the Pillsbury Doughboy also made the top 10 list (Horgen et al., 2001). Worldwide, the McDonald's Corporation spends nearly $500 million a year on advertising, with approximately 40% of it targeting children (Horgen et al., 2001) (see Tables 7.4 and 7.5). Increasingly, McDonald's, Burger King, and others are engaging in toy tie-ins with major motion picture studios, trying to augment sales of fast food and attendance at children's movies (Sokol, 2000). In the only content analysis thus far to examine such advertising, Reece et al. (1999) found that nearly 20% of restaurant ads mentioned a toy premium in their commercials.

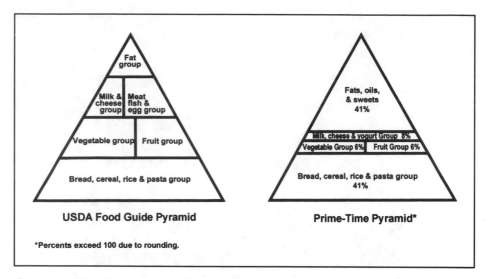

Figure 7.2. Two Conflicting Food Pyramids
SOURCE: From Byrd-Bredbenner and Grasso (1999). With permission from *International Electronic Journal of Health Education,* online at www.iejhe.org.

Only one study has examined food commercials aired during episodes of soap operas. Lank, Vickery, Cotugna, and Shade (1992) found that there were more ads for foods that were low in sugar or fat, but many of the foods advertised as being "low cholesterol" were, in fact, high in fat. Nearly half of the ads that promised good nutrition from their products were for flavored drinks with little nutrient value.

Not only are healthy foods rarely advertised on television, but PSAs are not used effectively to redress the nutritional misinformation being broadcast to children. One study of 20 hours of randomly selected programming over a 3-week period found no PSAs addressing nutrition (Wallack & Dorfman, 1992). Another study of 53 hours of Saturday morning cartoons found 10 nutrition-related PSAs competing with 564 advertisements for food (Kotz & Story, 1994). In Taras and Gage's (1995) content analysis of nearly 100 hours of children's programming, only 2.5 minutes were devoted to PSAs concerning nutrition-related topics. Of these, the messages were often as simplistic (and boring for children, compared with "real" ads) as "eat well," "don't ingest too much sugar," or "brush your teeth." In the most recent study, only 8 of the 900 ads aired during 43 hours of children's programming in 1997 were PSAs, less than 1% (Reece et al., 1999).

Although the industry cites the "when eaten as part of a nutritious breakfast" voice-over as fulfilling its obligations to consumers and their children, there is little evidence that such disclaimers actually fulfill their function (Liebert & Sprafkin, 1988; Muehling & Kolbe, 1999). Some children may understand the disclaimer

TABLE 7.4   Caloric and Fat Content of Selected Fast Food

Food	Calories	Fat (g)
McDonald's		
Big Mac	530	28
Quarter Pounder	430	21
Hamburger	270	9
Small French fries	210	10
Large French fries	450	22
Chicken McNuggets	430	26
Fajita chicken salad with lite vinaigrette dressing	250	10
Hard Rock Cafe		
Hamburger	660	36
Onion rings	890	65
Pizza Hut		
Cheese pizza, 2 slices	446	20
Pepperoni pizza, 2 slices	640	38
Arby's		
Roast beef sandwich	552	28
Jr. roast beef sandwich	233	11
Taco Bell		
Tacos (2)	360	22
Taco Bell salad w/o salsa	838	55
Kentucky Fried Chicken		
KFC Original Recipe, half breast	360	20
KFC Rotisserie Gold, 1/4	199	6

SOURCE: Adapted from *USA Today,* October 20, 1994, p. 7D and Hurley and Schmidt (1996). Reprinted from Strasburger and Brown (1998).

(Stutts & Hunnicutt, 1987), but by far the most important impact of the commercial is to intrigue the child with how "yummy" and "fun" the product is (Reece et al., 1999). Only 1% of children currently meet the U.S. Department of Agriculture's food intake guidelines set forth in the famous Food Guide Pyramid (see Figure 7.2) (Munoz, Krebs-Smith, Ballard-Barbash, & Cleveland, 1997).

TABLE 7.5   Fast Food and Kids

Kids ages 12-17:

spend $12.7 billion per year on fast food

eat 7% of all their meals at fast-food restaurants

visit fast-food restaurants an average of 2.13 times/week

46% say their favorite food ordered is a hamburger.

SOURCE: Adapted from Preboth and Wright (1999).

● THE IMPACT OF FOOD ADVERTISEMENTS ON BEHAVIOR

As discussed in Chapter 2, numerous studies have documented that young children under the age of 6 to 8 years are developmentally unable to understand the intent of advertisements and, in fact, frequently accept advertising claims as being largely true (American Academy of Pediatrics [AAP], 1995b; Atkin, 1982; Kunkel, 2001; Liebert & Sprafkin, 1988; Macklin & Carlson, 1999; Unnikrishnan & Bajpai, 1996; Young, 1990). Preteens, between ages 8 and 10 years, possess the cognitive ability to process advertisements but do not necessarily do so unless prompted (Brucks et al., 1988). Unfortunately, most research on young people's consumer behavior has been conducted by marketing researchers and remains unavailable to the academic community or to the public (Valkenburg, 2000).

What research is available clearly indicates that advertising is effective in getting younger children to request more junk food and to attempt to influence their parents' purchases (see Figure 7.3) (Galst & White, 1976; Goldberg et al., 1978; Liebert & Sprafkin, 1988; Ray & Klesges, 1993; Taras, Sallis, Patterson, Nader, & Nelson, 1989; Walsh, 1995). In fact, in the Taras et al. (1989) study, the amount of weekly television viewing of 3- to 8-year-olds actually correlated significantly both with children's requests for specific advertised foods and their caloric intake. Even brief exposures to TV food ads can influence children as young as preschool age in their food choices (Borzekowski & Robinson, 2001). Exposure to food ads also increases young children's snacking behavior (Bolton, 1983) and correlates with unhealthy notions about nutrition (Signorielli & Staples, 1997). One older study found that 70% of 6- to 8-year-olds thought that fast foods were actually more nutritious than foods cooked at home (Donohue, Meyer, & Henke, 1978). A much newer study of more than 21,000 children and adolescents nationwide has found that the prevalence of snacking has increased considerably during the past 20 years. By the mid-1990s, children were consuming 25% of their daily calories by snacking, compared with 18% in 1977, and teens consume 610 calories a day by snacking (Jahns, Siega-Riz, & Popkin, 2001). Even when important variables such

"...And upon being taken to a supermarket, you will remember and demand that brand. When I clap my hands you will awake..."

Figure 7.3

SOURCE: Jim Berry; reprinted by permission of Newspaper Enterprise Association, Inc.

as reading level, ethnicity, and parents' occupation and educational level are controlled for, fourth and fifth graders' television viewing correlates with poor eating habits (Signorielli & Lears, 1992).

Interestingly enough, the advertising industry's own "watchdog" group, the Children's Advertising Review Unit (CARU), was established in 1974 specifically to encourage the responsible advertising of children's products. CARU states that food ads should encourage good nutritional practices and show the product within the context of a balanced diet (Reece et al., 1999).

As might be expected, if advertising snack foods encourages snacking, advertising healthy foods can encourage more wholesome nutritional practices, even among children as young as 3 to 6 years of age. Several studies have shown that PSAs for fruits, vegetables, or products without added sugar increase the chances that children will make wiser nutritional choices (Galst, 1980; Goldberg et al., 1978; Gorn & Goldberg, 1982).

Cross-cultural studies show that similar problems vis-à-vis nutritional practices and advertising exist in Canada, Japan, Britain, New Zealand, and Australia (Goldberg, 1990; Ishigaki, 1991; Lewis & Hill, 1998; Public Health Association of Australia, 1999; Wilson, Quigley, & Mansoor, 1999).

By the late 1970s, this body of research was convincing enough to lead the Federal Trade Commission (FTC) to issue the following conclusion in 1981:

> The record . . . supports the following conclusions regarding child-oriented television advertising and young children six years and under: (1) they place indiscriminate trust in televised advertising messages; (2) they do not understand the persuasive bias in television advertising; and (3) the techniques, focus and themes used in child-oriented television advertising enhance the appeal of the advertising message and the advertised product. Consequently, *young children do not possess the cognitive ability to evaluate adequately child-oriented television advertising.* Despite the fact that these conclusions can be drawn from the evidence, *the record establishes that the only effective remedy would be a ban on all advertisements oriented towards young children, and such a ban, as a practical matter, cannot be implemented.* (FTC, 1981, pp. 2-4)

This was the closest that the American government has ever come to regulating advertising, specifically the advertising of sugared cereals to children. With the political landscape of the 1980s and the power of advertisers in America, however, the prospects for reform changed dramatically (Comstock, 1991b). Since the late 1970s, responsibility for the regulation of advertising has been moved from the FTC to the Federal Communications Commission (FCC). This has meant that advertising is now viewed more as a broadcasting issue than an issue of corporate responsibility. Questions about advertising are now about amount and placement of ads, rather than about the meaning, representation, and public health impact that they may have.

Given the current political and social climate in the new millennium, which seems to favor business over public health, the prospects for reform remain slim. Yet many researchers (Center for Media Education, 1998; Horgen et al., 2001; Strasburger, 2001b; Walsh, 1995), and public health groups such as the AAP (1995b) continue to believe that advertising directed toward children under 8 years of age is inherently deceptive and exploitative.

● FOOD IN TELEVISION PROGRAMMING AND MOVIES

Only a handful of content analyses have been conducted to study the portrayal of food in prime-time programming or in movies (Gerbner, Gross, Morgan, & Signorielli, 1980a; Jain & Tirodkar, 2001; Story & Faulkner, 1990; Sylvester, Williams, & Achterberg, 1993; Way, 1983). Perhaps this is because food advertising is such a powerful force on network and cable television and is therefore studied preferentially.

Food references occur nearly 10 times per hour on prime-time TV, and 60% are for low-nutrient snacks or beverages (Story & Faulkner, 1990). Snacking in television programming occurs as frequently as eating breakfast, lunch, and dinner combined (Gerbner et al., 1980a). The majority of food eaten by characters are sweets (Gerbner et al., 1980a; Story & Faulkner, 1990; Way, 1983). Borzekowski (in press) conducted the most recent study, a content analysis of the 30 highest rated programs, in 1997 among 2- to 5-year-olds, according to Nielsen data. Of the top 30, 47% were on network TV, 30% were on Nickelodeon, and 23% were on PBS. Each episode had at least one reference to food, and one third of the episodes contained 16 or more references. An average child would therefore see more than 500 food references per week during programming. Nearly one third of the references were to empty calorie foods high in fat, sugar, or salt. Another 25% of food references were to nutrient-rich foods that, however, were also high in fat, sugar, or salt.

Borzekowski (in press) was surprised to find that many popular children's programs contained a wide array of food choices (e.g., one episode of PBS's *Arthur* mentioned milk, cookies, apple juice, steak, corn on the cob, peanut brittle, raisins, soup, pears, watermelon, grapes, a banana, chocolate cake, pasta, lettuce, cereal, and orange juice). Of course, the amount of PBS programming "skewed" the sample somewhat, as did the choice of the youngest viewing population to study. Nevertheless, the authors of all of these content analyses concluded that the prime-time diet is inconsistent with healthy nutritional guidelines.

One unique study examined the four most popular sitcoms among Black audiences and among general audiences and found that the former contained 27% of actors who were overweight, compared with only 2% of the latter. This is significant given that a higher percentage of African Americans are overweight than members of the general population (Jain & Tirodkar, 2001). The study also found more food items displayed and a greater number of food commercials aired during the shows popular with African Americans—nearly 5 commercials per half hour, compared with 2.89 for the shows popular with general audiences (Jain & Tirodkar, 2001).

Only one content analysis has been conducted on the portrayal of food in films (Sylvester et al., 1993). An analysis of the 71 top-grossing films of 1991 revealed that more than two thirds of the films contained two or more major food scenes (see Table 7.6). Healthier, low-fat foods were most often depicted being used by more educated characters with higher socioeconomic status; overweight characters most often were seen consuming more high-fat foods.

FOOD ADVERTISED IN SCHOOLS ●

In the 1990s, advertisers have used any and all means possible to get messages in front of children and teens, including ads on schools buses, in gymnasiums, on

TABLE 7.6   What Do Movie Characters Eat? (frequency of occurrence)

	Food				Drinks	
Genre	Protein Foods	Bread/ Cereals	Fruits/ Vegetables	High-Fat Foods	Milk	Alcohol
Comedy (n = 29)	61	41	30	24	8	22
Drama (n = 23)	50	37	48	31	5	29
Action (n = 14)	6	4	3	1	1	2
Mystery	1	0	2	4	1	3

SOURCE: Adapted from Sylvester, Williams, and Achterberg (1993).

book covers, on athletic teams' warm-up suits, and even on cafeteria tray liners and in bathroom stalls (Brown & Witherspoon, 1998; Richards et al., 1998). This trend is not new, however. Trying to target schoolchildren dates back as far as the 1920s, when toothpaste samples were given away (Richards et al., 1998). What is new is that the age of children being targeted has decreased, reaching preschoolers by the 1980s (Richards et al., 1998).

According to a recent report from the U.S. General Accounting Office (GAO), 200 school districts have signed exclusive contracts with soft-drink companies to sell only those drinks in schools (see Figure 7.4) (Hays, 2000). Houston recently signed a contract with Coca-Cola worth more than $5 million over 5 years (Williams, 2001). Such agreements often specify the number and placement of soda vending machines, ironic given that schools risk losing federal subsidies for their free breakfast and lunch programs if they serve soda in their cafeterias (Williams, 2001). Textbook covers distributed by Philip Morris, Reebok, Ralph Lauren, and others now adorn students' textbooks.

Channel One was the first to invade the noncommercial sanctity of the schoolhouse, with 10-minute news programs interlaced with 2 minutes of commercials, in exchange for $30,000 worth of TV sets, VCRs, and satellite dishes (Bachen, 1998; Wartella & Jennings, 2001). By the end of their first year of operations, Channel One had agreements with 5,000 schools (Molnar, 1996). Currently, more than 8 million middle and high schools students watch Channel One in 12,000 schools, and advertisers pay $200,000 for ad time and the opportunity to target 40% of American teenagers for 30 seconds (Bachen, 1998; Johnston, 2001). According to the GAO report, Channel One now plays in 25% of the nation's middle and high schools (Hays, 2000). To date, it generates profits estimated at $100 million annually (Bachen, 1998). Channel One is also offering a $500 incentive payment to

Figure 7.4

teachers or administrators who can sign up a neighboring school or service (Golden, 2001).

Nearly 70% of the ads on Channel One are for food—mostly gum, soda, fast food, candy, and chips (Brand & Greenberg, 1994). Considering how controversial Channel One has been, it seems odd that more research has not been conducted on its impact (Bachen, 1998). Important research questions include the following (Bachen, 1998): (a) Do the students feel compelled to watch the ads? (b) Do they pay more attention to the ads on Channel One than they would to ordinary television ads? (c) Do the students feel that the products advertised are tacitly endorsed by the school? The most comprehensive study of Channel One (Johnston & Brzezinski, 1992) was funded by its owners at the time, Whittle Communications, which expressly forbid studying the impact of the advertising component.

A few studies have been conducted, however. In the first survey, students believed that the commercials told the truth about products (Bachen, 1998). Another survey found that about a third of students agreed that seeing the ads made them want to buy the products, and many did (Bachen, 1998). And Brand and Greenberg (1994) found that students who viewed Channel One rated products advertised higher than nonviewers did. They also found that the ads increased teenagers' intention to purchase the products advertised (although teens do not actually report purchasing them). Meanwhile, one study has found only a small benefit (3%) on a test of current events (Knupfer & Hayes, 1994).

Since the advent of Channel One, business concerns have not been content with only advertising in schools. Products have now become available in vending machines and in cafeterias throughout school systems, and many school districts now have contractual agreements with soft-drink manufacturers to stock only one brand (Molnar & Morales, 2000). One problem with this is that new research is beginning to question whether frequent consumption of soft drinks might lead to an increased risk of osteoporosis in teenage girls (Wyshak, 2000) and obesity in children and teens (Bellisle & Rolland-Cachera, 2001; Ludwig, Peterson, & Gortmaker, 2001). In addition, fast food is a known risk factor for obesity, and Taco Bell sells food in at least 3,000 school cafeterias, Subway in 650, and Pizza Hut in 4,500, among others (Oleck, 1994).

Is this merely free enterprise at work, or is it a violation of ethical principles to target schoolchildren where they are supposed to be learning basic subjects? Have the three "Rs" now become the four "Rs," with the fourth "R" being "retail" (Manning, 1999; Ward, 2000)? Critics have noted that there are five basic marketing practices that raise concerns (Richards et al., 1998; Wartella & Jennings, 2001):

1. Direct advertising in schools

2. Free or discounted products

3. Curriculum materials with corporate identification

4. Direct sales of products in schools

5. Fund-raising activities for schools

Consumers Union Education Services (1995) has published a report that is extremely critical of marketing in schools. The report urges parents and teachers to make schools "ad-free zones" and decries selling to a "captive" audience as a "perversion of education" (Consumers Union Education Services, 1995). Among its specific criticisms of school-based marketing are the following (Consumers Union Education Services, 1995):

1. It passes control of schools from teachers to corporations.

2. It promotes materialism among children and adolescents and means that young people have no safe haven from advertising.

3. Ads in schools carry an implied endorsement.

4. The purpose of education is not to get young people to feel good about products or corporations.

5. Promotional educational materials may have a biased viewpoint and may not be subjected to the same scrutiny as textbooks or other materials for classroom use.

6. Businesses should support schools without expecting any return on their money.

7. Young people are clearly influenced by in-school advertising, just as they (and adults) are influenced by other forms of advertising.

One of the leading critics of school-based advertising, Alex Molnar, heads the Center for the Analysis of Commercialism in Education at the University of Wisconsin at Milwaukee. He observes,

> There is a clear distinction between the purposes of marketing and education. Advertising makes no claim to telling the truth. Education attempts to tell the truth, and not because of a special interest but the interest of the entire community. The community and children don't come first in advertising. The sponsor does. (Krayeske, 1999)

DOES TELEVISION VIEWING ● INCREASE CHILDHOOD OBESITY?

Obesity is rapidly becoming a major concern among pediatricians and public health officials, not just in the United States but internationally as well. The World Health Organization (WHO, 1998) notes that this increase in obesity is worldwide. In the United Kingdom, one third of 15 year-olds are now overweight (BMI > 25), and 17% are obese (BMI > 30) (Reilly & Dorosty, 1999). These numbers have doubled among 6- to 17-year-olds during the past 20 years (Troiano & Flegal, 1998). Currently, one half of all adults in the United States are overweight or obese (Must et al., 1999). Obesity is thought to be responsible for 10% of health care expenditures in the United States (Koplan & Dietz, 1999), costing taxpayers an estimated $60 billion a year. Currently, 300,000 deaths annually can be attributed to obesity, putting it just behind smoking, with 434,000 deaths per year (Allison, Fontaine, Manson, Stevens, & VanItallie, 1999; Calle, Thun, Petrelli, Rodriguez, & Heath, 1999).

The serious health consequences of obesity have been known for decades, but newer ones have emerged as well (Dietz, 1998; Koplan & Dietz, 1999; Steinberger, Moran, Hong, Jacobs, & Sinaiko, 2001). Hypertension, lipid disorders and heart disease, and increased risk of diabetes are well-known medical morbidities of obesity in adulthood (Dietz, 1998; Strasburger & Brown, 1998), but recently the prevalence of Type II diabetes—previously thought to be almost exclusively an adult-onset disease—has risen dramatically among children and teenagers as well (Dietz, 2001; Pinhas-Hamiel & Zeitler, 2001). Obese children or teenagers are also at risk for a variety of orthopedic and respiratory problems (Strasburger & Brown, 1998). Nearly 60% of obese preteens have at least one risk factor (increased lipid levels, high blood pressure, or increased insulin levels), and one fourth have two or more (Freedman, Dietz, Srinivasan, & Berenson, 1999). Among obese adults, 80% have at least one of the following problems: diabetes, high cholesterol levels, high blood pressure, coronary artery disease, gallbladder disease, or osteoarthritis (Allison et al., 1999).

Unfortunately, obesity is associated with far more than medical problems, however. Studies also show that obese young women have lower incomes, are less likely to marry, and have completed less schooling (Gortmaker et al., 1993). By age 7, children have already learned norms of cultural attractiveness and are more likely to choose a playmate with a major physical handicap than one who is obese (Feldman, Feldman, & Goodman, 1988; Staffieri, 1967). A child or adolescent's self-concept is usually sufficiently tenuous that any physical characteristic that causes him or her to be different represents a potential threat to self-esteem (Davison & Birch, 2001; Dietz, 1998; Hill & Pallin, 1998; Strauss, 2000; Willis, McCoy, & Berman, 1990). By third grade, nearly one third of boys and girls have already tried to lose weight (Maloney, McGuire, Daniels, & Specker, 1989). A very recent study found an increase in depressive symptoms among nearly 1,000 third-grade girls with higher BMIs (Erickson, Robinson, Haydel, & Killen, 2000).

Along with aggression, obesity represents one of the two areas of television research where the medium's influence may rise to the level of cause and effect, rather than simply being contributory (AAP, 1995b), although this point remains hotly debated (Robinson, 1998). Five national studies, using cross-sectional data, have found a significant association between obesity and television viewing among children (see Figure 7.5). Of course, the causal arrow could run in either direction (Robinson, 1998). In other words, does television viewing cause obesity, or do obese children tend to be more sedentary and watch more television? But these five studies seem at least to provide "food for thought" on this issue:

1. Using National Health Survey data, Dietz and Gortmaker (1985) found that hours spent watching TV proved to be a strong predictor of obesity among both 6- to 11-year-olds and 12- to 17-year-olds. For each additional hour of average television viewing above the norm, the prevalence of obesity increased 2%. To exclude the possibility that children or teens watched more television because they were obese, the researchers chose children who were not obese at baseline but who became obese at follow-up (Dietz, 1993). A second, similar study conducted at the same time failed to duplicate these findings (Robinson et al., 1993) but involved a smaller sample and did not use national data (Dietz & Gortmaker, 1993).

Figure 7.5
SOURCE: Reprinted with special permission of Universal Press Syndicate.

2. In the National Children and Youth Fitness Survey, parents and teachers were asked to rate a child's activity level and television viewing time (Pate & Ross, 1987). Increased amounts of television viewing were directly and independently associated with the prevalence of obesity, and increased activity was inversely related (Dietz, 1993).

3. Gortmaker et al. (1996) observed a strong dose-response relationship between the prevalence of overweight and hours of television viewed in a national sample of 746 youngsters ages 10 to 15 years. The odds of being overweight were nearly five times greater for preteens and teens who viewed 5 hours of television per day compared with those viewing 0 to 2 hours per day.

4. Andersen, Crespo, Bartlett, Cheskin, and Pratt (1998) analyzed data from the Third National Health and Nutrition Examination Survey (NHANES III) on more than 4,000 children ages 8 to 16 and found that those who watched 4 or more hours of television per day had greater body fat and BMIs than those who watched less than 2 hours per day.

5. Crespo et al. (2001) also analyzed data from NHANES III and found that the prevalence of obesity was lowest among children watching less than 1 hour per day of television and was highest among those watching 4 hours or more a day.

Studies using smaller, regional samples have shown similar results as well (Armstrong et al., 1998; Locard et al., 1992; Obarzanek et al., 1994; Shannon, Peacock, & Brown, 1991). Taras et al. (1989) correlated television viewing with 3- to 8-year-olds' caloric intake but did not specifically study their weights. Two international studies are available as well: A cross-sectional study of more than 1,000 children ages 13 to 14 in Spain found that time spent watching television was significantly associated with BMI in girls and with body fat percentage in both sexes (Moreno, Fleta, & Mur, 1998). Among Mexican children and teens, the odds ratios for obesity were 12% higher for each hour of television viewing per day in a study of 712 adolescents ages 9 to 16 (Hernandez et al., 1999). In addition, at least two studies of adults have found that television viewing is positively associated with energy intake (Jeffery & French, 1998) and with BMI (Crawford, Jeffery, & French, 1999; Jeffery & French, 1998) among women (but not men).

Other studies have found that numbers of hours of TV watched is a strong predictor for high cholesterol levels in children (Wong et al., 1992) and that children who watch a lot of TV are more likely to have poor eating habits and unhealthy notions about food (Signorielli & Lears, 1992).

So the argument linking television viewing with obesity is persuasive but not conclusive. Television viewing probably contributes to overweight and obesity, but whether it is a major factor or a minor contributor remains unknown. Interestingly, the reverse can be shown to be true: If television viewing is reduced, a recent study documents that weight decreases among children (Robinson, 1999, 2000). Using a simple 18-lesson, 6-month classroom curriculum to reduce media use, Robinson (1999) demonstrated statistically significant decreases in third- and fourth-grade students' BMIs, skinfold thicknesses, waist circumferences, and waist-to-hip ratios (all important measures of adiposity). Among the students receiving the curriculum, there was less television viewing and fewer meals eaten in front of the television set than among the control students.

Why might the association between television viewing and obesity exist? Contrary to popular opinion, it only takes an excess intake of 50 Kcals a day to produce a weight gain of 5 pounds per year (Dietz, 1993). In other words, obesity is probably caused by small increments in daily caloric intake (or, conversely, small increases in sedentary activities), not massive binges of overeating. Therefore, even if television viewing exerts only a slight effect, it may be highly significant. Because obesity is caused by an imbalance of excess intake compared with energy expenditure (Yanovski & Yanovski, 1999), TV viewing may contribute in several ways:

1. *Displacement of more active pursuits.* As the leading leisure-time activity, television constitutes the principal source of inactivity for children and adolescents (Dietz, 1993). Children spend more time watching television than in any other activity except for sleeping (Roberts, Foehr, et al., 1999; Stanger, 1997). Williams's (1986) naturalistic study found that children participated less in sports activities once TV was introduced into their community. In the United States, data from the National Children and Youth Fitness Survey show that parents' and teachers' ratings of a child's activity level and time spent watching TV correlated directly with children's prevalence of obesity (Pate & Ross, 1987). Robinson's (1999) study showed convincingly that reducing the amount of television viewing leads to decreases in adiposity. Another recent study of obese 8- to 12-year-olds also found that reducing the amount of viewing and other sedentary behaviors resulted in decreased body fat and increased aerobic fitness (Epstein, Paluch, Gordy, & Dorn, 2000). One clever obesity researcher has developed a "TVcycle," a bicycle hooked up electrically to a television set so that the set would only work if the bicycle was being ridden. Six overweight 8- to 12-year-olds lost 2% of their total body fat in a preliminary study (Neergaard, 1999). Reducing total media time may be even more effective than increasing the amount of exercise in reducing weight (Epstein, Valoski, Vara, & Rodefer, 1995; Robinson, 2000). Clearly, if children and adolescents devoted just 1 hour a day to physical activities of the 3 hours they spend watching TV, their risk of obesity would diminish considerably.

2. *Increased energy intake.* Today's children and teens are more likely to eat in fast-food restaurants and consume more fried and high-fat foods than young people in the 1960s and 1970s (McGinnis, 1992). They also snack more frequently than ever before (Ritzer, 1993). Teenagers who watch more television tend to eat higher-fat diets (Robinson & Killen, 1995). A recent study of 91 parent-child pairs found that families who watch television during mealtimes tend to eat more pizzas, snack foods, and sodas and fewer fruits and vegetables (Coon, Goldberg, Rogers, & Tucker, 2001). In addition, older research indicates that ads for high-fat or high-calorie foods do influence children's eating habits (Gorn & Goldberg, 1982; Jeffrey et al., 1983). As we have discussed, television deluges young viewers with advertisements for food products and fast-food restaurants that provide marginal nutritional value at best. In addition, prime-time and Saturday morning programming models poor nutritional behavior for children. Time spent watching TV correlates with children's attempts to influence parents' food purchases, children's choice of snacks, the frequency of snacking while watching TV, and children's total caloric intake (Dietz, 1993; Taras et al., 1989). In a recent study of 209 fourth- and fifth-grade students, Signorielli and Lears (1992) found that heavy TV viewing was an extremely strong predictor of poor nutritional habits and that heavy viewers were far more likely to believe that food at a "fast-food" restaurant was as

nutritious as a meal prepared at home. Although no studies have specifically examined adolescents' television viewing and their food-buying habits, one study has found that both children and adolescents tend to consume higher-fat food products if they view a lot of television (Wong et al., 1992).

3. *Decreased energy expenditure.* Interestingly, a child's metabolic rate is actually lower while watching television than while resting quietly, according to one study (Klesges, Shelton, & Klesges, 1993), although these results have not yet been replicated (Dietz, 1993). But several studies do indicate that television viewing may adversely affect physical fitness (Dietz, 1993; Tucker, 1986; Robinson et al., 1993).

Recently, Horgen et al. (2001) have proposed a comprehensive theory to explain the pathway from food advertising to consumption and obesity (see Figure 7.6). Information is first "coded" and then later retrieved, in some ways similar to the effects of music videos on teenagers: First teens see the video, and then they hear the song associated with it and "flash back" to the video (Greenfield & Beagles-Roos, 1988). Children viewing advertisements associate certain likeable characters and memorable slogans—triggers—with certain products. Repetitive ads increase the association. Associations are then triggered when walking down a supermarket aisle or seeing a billboard. Any of these factors could lead to either a request to the parent to purchase the product or the child purchasing the product himself or herself. Once consumed, the product leads to increased calorie levels (because products advertised are usually unhealthy and high in fat or sugar). Assuming that exercise patterns remain stable, obesity results because of the imbalance between intake and expenditure.

It should be noted that four studies have found no statistically significant association between TV viewing and obesity (DuRant, Baranowski, Johnson, & Thompson, 1994; Robinson et al., 1993; Robinson & Killen, 1995; Tucker, 1986). Given that the correlations are consistently small, it is not surprising that some studies' data would not reach the level of statistical significance. The other problem is that it is difficult to get accurate self-reports of TV viewing or physical activity from children and adolescents (or their parents, for that matter). For these reasons, additional cross-sectional studies, or even longitudinal studies, may not be able to shed further light on this issue. What is now needed are experimental studies where the sole variable being manipulated is the amount of television viewed (Robinson, 1999). As one of the leading experts on television and obesity notes,

> The jury is still out on the question of whether television viewing is an *important* cause of overweight among children, although that should not stop parents and children from substituting less sedentary activities for sitting in front of the television, videocassette recorder, computer, and videogame. (Robinson, 1998, p. 960, emphasis added)

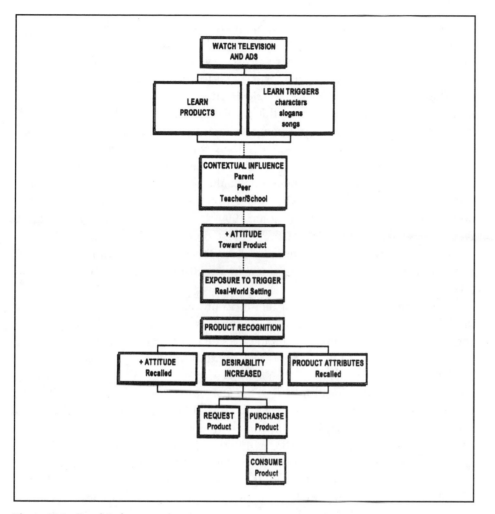

Figure 7.6. Food Pathway
SOURCE: Horgen, Choate, and Brownell (2001). Reprinted with permission.

EATING DISORDERS AND BODY IMAGE ●

One of the most exciting developments in communication research during the past decade has been researchers' increased interest in examining the role that the media play in women's health, specifically women's self-image and eating disorders. In 2000, the BMA (2000) issued a landmark report on the subject, and researchers such as Field, Kilbourne, Levine and Smolak, and many others have added considerably to our knowledge (Field, Camargo, et al., 1999; Field, Cheung, et al., 1999; Field et al., 2001; Levine, 2000; Levine & Smolak, 1996, 2001).

One of the first researchers to take an interest in this area was Kaufman (1980), who conducted a content analysis of eating behavior on television and observed that prime-time TV characters are usually happy in the presence of food. Yet food is rarely used to satisfy hunger. Rather, it serves to bribe others or to facilitate social introductions. As with other media, television seems to have an obsession with thinness: 88% of all characters are thin or average in body build, obesity is confined to middle or old age, and being overweight provides comic ammunition (Kaufman, 1980; Silverstein, Perdue, Peterson, & Kelly, 1986). On shows popular with teenagers, 94% of characters are below average in weight (Levine & Smolak, 1996). Some researchers have suggested that the presence of so many TV commercials for food, combined with other ads' emphasis on female beauty, fosters the development of eating disorders (Botta, 1999; Lavine, Sweeney, & Wagner, 1999; Ogletree, Williams, Raffeld, & Mason, 1990). Others have suggested that situation comedies could play a role because thin characters receive significantly more positive verbal comments from male characters than heavier female characters do (Fouts & Burggraf, 1999).

Interestingly, as the number of diet food product commercials has increased dramatically on network TV between 1973 and 1991, a parallel rise has occurred in eating disorders (Wiseman, Gunning, & Gray, 1993). Similar research by Silverstein and Perlick (1995) found that as thin models and actresses appeared more frequently in media from 1910 to 1930 and again from 1950 to 1980, eating disorders increased as well. In the 1990s, the diet industry tripled its revenues, from $10 billion a year to $36 billion (Kilbourne, 1999). Articles about dieting and exercise in women's magazines increased dramatically around the same time (Wiseman, Gray, Mosimann, & Ahrens, 1992) and now far outnumber similar articles in men's magazines (Nemeroff, Stein, Diehl, & Smilack, 1994). Studies have found that girls who read fashion magazines often compare themselves with the models in the ads and the articles, resulting in more negative feelings about their own appearance (Hofschire & Greenberg, 2001; Martin & Kennedy, 1994; Pinhas, Toner, Ali, Garfinkel, & Stuckless, 1999; Shaw, 1995).

Whether this is all cause and effect, effect and cause, or simply coincidental is arguable. As Kilbourne (1999) notes, there seems to be a very complicated connection between the diet industry and the real world. For example, a Weight Watchers ad shows a scrumptious piece of Boston cream pie, with the caption, "Feel free to act on impulse." Why would Weight Watchers want to tempt people to indulge in high-calorie desserts? Because it is actually in their best business interests for people to fatten up and then want to diet or to fail to lose weight, so that their revenues will continue to grow (Kilbourne, 1999).

Meanwhile, the exact specifications for thinness continue to diminish, almost yearly. A study of body measurements of Playboy centerfolds and Miss America contestants over a 10-year period found that body weight averaged 13% to 19% below that expected for age (Wiseman et al., 1992). Among Miss America winners

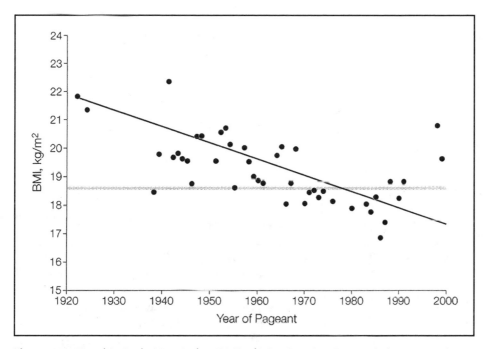

Figure 7.7. Trend in Body Mass Index (BMI) of Miss America Pageant Winners, 1922 to 1999

SOURCE: From the *Journal of the American Medical Association, 283,* p. 1569, 2000. Copyrighted 2000, American Medical Association.

NOTE: The gray horizontal line represents the World Health Organization's BMI cutoff point for undernutrition (18.5).

from 1922 to 1999, BMIs have declined significantly from 22 to less than 18, which signifies undernutrition (see Figure 7.7) (Rubinstein & Caballero, 2000). Two decades ago, the average American model weighed 8% less than the average American woman; today, she weighs 23% less (Kilbourne, 1999). In one study, adolescent girls described the "ideal girl" as being 5'7", 100 pounds, size 5, with long blonde hair and blue eyes (Nichter & Nichter, 1991)—clearly a body shape that is both rare and close to impossible to achieve.

Evidence is increasing that there are tremendous sociocultural pressures on today's girls and young women to try to attain body shapes that are unhealthy, unnatural, and dictated by media norms (BMA, 2000). Many researchers feel that this "internalization of the thin-ideal body image" has resulted in Western women's increasing dissatisfaction with their bodies and subsequent increase in eating disorders (see Table 7.7) (Field et al., 2001; Kilbourne, 1999; Levine, 2001; Stice, 1998; Thompson et al., 1999). But, as always, the research does not yield a simplistic "yes or no" answer. Probably the most conservative view is that there is now considerable evidence that the media influence body image and self-dissatisfaction among young girls and women. This may be, in fact, much more complicated than a sim-

TABLE 7.7 Influence of Women's Fashion Magazines on Girls
(n = 548 girls in 5th-12th grades)

Behavior	Infrequent Reader (%)	Frequent Reader (%)	p-Value
Dieting	34	45	.03
Dieting because of a magazine article	13	22	.02
Exercising to lose weight	48	64	.004
Exercising because of a magazine article	14	29	.001
Body image influenced by pictures	59	79	.001
Pictures make them want to lose weight	41	57	.004

SOURCE: Adapted from Field, Cheung, et al. (1999).

ple, linear relationship. Women unhappy with their body shapes might tend to read more fashion magazines, for example, which then reinforce their own low self-image. However, although the media may contribute to the development of eating disorders, there is not yet sufficient evidence to state conclusively that they are a major cause of them (Borzekowski, Robinson, & Killen, 2000; Levine, Piran, & Stoddard, 1999).

● DISORDERED BODY IMAGE

Body image has become an increasingly major concern of teenagers, especially females. Dissatisfaction seems to increase among young females and decrease among males during adolescence. As many as half of normal-weight teenage girls consider themselves overweight and have tried to lose weight (Krowchuk et al., 1998; Strauss, 1999). Television, movies, magazines, and music videos all display women with impossible bodies and put pressure on adolescent females to conform (see Table 7.8 and Figure 7.8) (American Association of University Women [AAUW], 1999; Field, Camargo, et al., 1999; Field, Cheung, et al., 1999; Field et al., 2001; Hofschire & Greenberg, 2002; Martin & Gentry, 1997; Signorielli, 1997; Tiggemann & Pickering, 1996; Wertheim, Paxton, Schutz, & Muir, 1997). Sitcoms such as *Friends* and *Ally McBeal,* soap operas, music videos, and films popular with teenagers may even expose young girls to potential role models who suffer from eating disorders themselves (Levine & Smolak, 1998). For example, one recent study of 837 ninth-grade girls found that the number of hours spent watching music videos was related to their assessment of the importance of appearance and their weight concerns (Borzekowski et al., 2000).

TABLE 7.8 **How Do Men and Women Perceive the Body Weight of Media Characters? (in percentages)**

Body Weight	TV Male	TV Female	Movies Male	Movies Female	Music Videos Male	Music Videos Female	Magazine Ad Models Male	Magazine Ad Models Female
Very thin	1	7	0	0	8	0	0	2
Thin	15	39	4	39	36	43	8	24
Average	65	41	76	58	44	36	58	39
Obese	6	1	4	0	0	0	0	0

SOURCE: Adapted from Signorielli (1997).

Figure 7.8. Thin models are the norm in most popular advertising. In some cases, such as the *Sports Illustrated* swimsuit issue, models are extremely thin yet large breasted, a combination that is extremely rare in real life.

TABLE 7.9   How Media Might Contribute to Eating Disorders

Emphasis on importance of appearance

Narrow definition of physical beauty

Creation of thinness as the "gold standard"

Linking thinness to success and beauty

Abhorrence of fat and fat women

Emphasis on dieting and fashion

Establishment of gender roles based on unrealistic expectations

---

SOURCE: Adapted from Levine and Smolak (1996).

There are four key components to the theory that sociocultural factors play an important role in body image and, perhaps, eating disorders as well (see Table 7.9) (Levine, Smolak, & Hayden, 1994):

1. Although the "ideal" woman has gotten increasingly thinner since the 1990s, the real woman has actually gotten heavier (Levine & Smolak, 1996; Rubinstein & Caballero, 2000).

2. Thinness has become associated with social, personal, and professional success (Guillen & Barr, 1994; Signorielli, 1997).

3. For teen girls especially, the "thin look" has become normative (BMA, 2000; Field, Cheung, et al., 1999; Moses, Banilivy, & Lifshitz, 1989; Signorielli, 1997).

4. Adolescent girls and grown women have been led to believe that thinness can actually be attained through dieting and exercising (BMA, 2000; Field, Cheung, et al., 1999; Guillen & Barr, 1994).

Advertisements on teen-oriented shows use beauty as a product appeal most of the time: 56% of the ads targeting females, compared with just 3% of the ads aimed at males (Signorielli, 1997). In movies, 58% of female characters have their looks commented on (Signorielli, 1997). Seventy percent of girls say that they want to look like a character on television (compared with 40% of boys), and half of those say that they did something to change their appearance as a result (Signorielli, 1997). Women are often caught up in the trap of living in a culture in which they are expected to be the objects of the male gaze but then having to compete with ultra-thin role models (Mulvey, 1975). In one interesting experiment, college women concerned about their body shape judged thin celebrities as thinner than they actually were, whereas women comfortable with their body shape judged them accurately (King, Touyz, & Charles, 2000). In another recent study, girls who wanted to look like media figures on television, in the movies, or in magazines were twice as likely to be very concerned with their weight, become constant dieters, and engage in purging behavior (Field, Camargo, et al., 1999; Field, Cheung, et al., 1999; Field et al., 2001). This was a large study, with a 1-year follow-up, of 6,770 girls ages 9 to 14 years in a national sample.

Magazines such as *Seventeen* enjoy readerships of upwards of 11 million girls and practically dictate that thin is in, fat is out, and you are no one unless you are impossibly thin with big breasts and small hips. Or, as one 15-year-old girl put it, "Everybody feels like they are not good enough, not pretty enough, not skinny enough. . . . Every time you open a magazine you always see beautiful people . . . you have to look good to be a good person" (Wertheim et al., 1997, p. 350). Several studies have found an association between reading popular teen or fashion magazines and the presence of weight concerns or symptoms of eating disorders in girls (Field, Cheung, et al., 1999; Hofschire & Greenberg, 2002; Stice & Shaw, 1994; Taylor et al., 1998). In a recent study of 548 girls in 5th to 12th grades, the majority were unhappy with their body weight and shape, and 69% reported that their ideal body was influenced by reading fashion magazines or other media (Field, Cheung, et al., 1999).

The most fascinating experiment examining teenagers and magazines was performed by Turner, Hamilton, Jacobs, Angood, and Dwyer (1997). Young college women were randomly assigned to a waiting room with two different sets of magazines before answering a survey about dieting and body image. They were exposed either to four fashion magazines or four newsmagazines. Those who chose a fashion magazine to read reported more dissatisfaction with their weight, more guilt associated with eating, and greater fear of getting fat. It is not surprising, then, that one ongoing meta-analysis of more than 20 experimental studies indicates that exposure to images of thin models causes an increase in a female's negative feelings about her body (Levine, 2001).

Many surveys have also found that adolescent females demonstrate exaggerated fears of obesity regardless of their actual body weight (Dietz, 1993; Moses et al., 1989; Story & Neumark-Sztainer, 1991). Girls become increasingly preoccupied with their weight during middle and late childhood and may even start dieting (Dietz, 1993). Nearly one third of third-grade girls have tried to lose weight; by sixth grade, this figure reaches 60% (Maloney et al., 1989). In a study of 326 adolescent females attending an upper-middle-class parochial high school, more than half of the underweight students described themselves as being extremely fearful of being obese, and more than a third were preoccupied with their body fat (Moses et al., 1989). A small study found that half of all sixth graders wanted to lose weight (Schur, Sanders, & Steiner, 2000) and that by age 8, many girls have already decided that weight control can improve their self-worth (Hill & Pallin, 1999).

People trust the media, especially television (Horgen et al., 2001), but the image that the media display of the "ideal" woman is increasingly distorted. Aside from the portrayal of "Roseanne" as being both overweight and hip and in control, both in her sitcom and her later talk show, there is a dearth of smart, successful, overweight female media role models. One attempt to buck this trend has been the British Broadcasting Corporation's 1985 ban on televising beauty pageants, labeling them "an anachronism in this day and age of equality and verging on the offensive" ("BBC Bans Beauty Contest," 1985).

Interestingly, the media themselves have taken up this concern as well, with a nearly overbearing obsession with the fluctuation in weights of Alicia Silverstone (*Clueless*), Calista Flockhart (*Ally McBeal*), the women in *Friends,* and female supermodels. Whether this degree of publicity about actresses' body weights is healthy or harmful remains to be tested.

● ANOREXIA NERVOSA AND BULIMIA

Several cross-sectional studies have found an apparent link between level of media exposure and likelihood of having an eating disorder or eating disorder symptomatology (Field, Camargo, et al., 1999; Levine, Smolak, & Hayden, 1994; Martin & Kennedy, 1994; Murray, Touyz, & Beumont, 1996; Stice, Schupak-Neuberg, Shaw, & Stein, 1994). Body-image disturbances seem to play an important role in patients with anorexia nervosa or bulimia, according to a recent meta-analysis of 66 studies (Cash & Deagle, 1997). How do such disturbances originate? Young women with eating disorders report that magazines and newspapers influence their eating habits and their concept of beauty, for example (Murray et al., 1996). They tend to overestimate body sizes in experimental situations (Hamilton & Waller, 1993; Verri, Verticale, Vallero, Bellone, & Nespoli, 1997; Waller, Hamilton, & Shaw, 1992; Waller, Shaw, Hamilton, & Baldwin, 1994). Field, Camargo, et al.'s study (1999) found a greater likelihood of purging behaviors among teens subscribing to a "media ideal" of beauty. Wanting to look like actresses or models on television, in movies, or in magazines doubled the risk of beginning to purge at least monthly. Elementary and middle school girls whose devotion to fashion magazines leads them to compare their bodies with fashion models report greater levels of dissatisfaction with their bodies and higher numbers of eating disorder symptoms (Levine, Smolak, & Hayden, 1994; Martin & Kennedy, 1994). Studies of college women find that those who most "internalize" the cultural bias toward thinness score higher on tests of body dissatisfaction and bulimia (Thompson et al., 1999).

Perhaps the most powerful link between media and eating disorders occurred in a naturalistic study (Becker, 1995, 1999). Three years after television was introduced into the Pacific isle of Fiji, 15% of teenage girls reported that they had vomited to control their weight. This contrasted with only 3% reporting this behavior prior to the introduction of TV. In addition, the proportion of teen girls scoring abnormally high on a test for disordered eating doubled. Three fourths of girls reported feeling "too big or fat" after the introduction of TV, and those who watched at least 3 nights per week were 50% more likely to feel that way and 30% more likely to diet.

Occasional studies do not find any correlation between eating disorders and exposure to fashion magazines (Cusumano & Thompson, 1997), television (Harrison & Cantor, 1997; Myers & Biocca, 1992), or other media (Barrett, 1997; Cash, Ancis, & Strachan, 1997; Champion & Furnham, 1999; Irving, 1990). Sometimes a study may find that one medium has no correlation with dysfunctional symptoms (e.g., television) but other media do (fashion magazines, music videos, soap operas, and movies) (Harrison & Cantor, 1997; Tiggemann & Pickering, 1996). These negative or variable findings may result from researchers' reliance on self-reports of media exposure or from the fact that teens are notoriously susceptible to the "third-person effect" (i.e., the belief that the media affect everyone but oneself) (Eveland et al., 1999). In addition, many "no effect" studies still report intriguing findings. Harrison and Cantor's (1997) study found that reading "fitness" magazines and having an interest in dieting accounted for a significant amount of the variance on their subjects' Eating Attitudes Test (EAT) scores, but watching popular shows on television did not. Yet Harrison's (2000) most recent study of 300 children ages 6 to 8 years at two Midwest schools did find a correlation between television viewing and symptoms of eating disorders.

So the media may play a role as a catalyst or intermediate influence, rather than as a direct and complete cause of eating problems, perhaps only in certain subgroups of young women (Harrison, 1998; Levine, Smolak, Moodey, Shuman, & Hessen, 1994). Or, it could be as simple as the media contributing to the formation of a woman's negative body image (BMA, 2000), which, if this occurs during early adolescence, makes a subsequent eating disorder more likely (Attie & Brooks-Gunn, 1989; Dietz, 1998). Unfortunately, little research has been done on male body images and eating disorders (Field et al., 2001; Levine, 2001). One study of boys' action figures between 1964 and 1998 found that although waist sizes have remained constant, chest and biceps measurements have ballooned (Pope, 1999). So boys and teenage males may suffer from sociocultural ideals that are completely opposite from those of girls and young women.

CONCLUSION   ●

Considerable data exist to justify the notion that the media make a significant impact on adolescents' eating habits, the occurrence of obesity during childhood and adolescence, and adolescents' and young women's self-images of their bodies and perhaps even contribute in some way to the development of eating disorders. Exactly what role the media play remains open to conjecture. Clearly there is some cultivation effect at work here (Gerbner, Gross, Morgan, & Signorielli, 1994): Girls and young women view beautiful, thin characters in the media and are led to believe that these impossible ideals are "normative" and they, themselves, are inadequate. But the research is certainly complex and incomplete at the present time, and considerably more work is needed (Levine et al., 1997).

● SOLUTIONS

Solving the twin problems of obesity and eating disorders in the United States is, of course, a mission impossible. Even ameliorating the apparent harm that some of the media do seems highly unlikely. But if media images of cigarette smoking, women in athletics, drunk driving, and violence against women can change dramatically over decades, why not the "impossibly thin" body image (Levine, 2001)? Why not the unhealthy food advertisements, particularly the ones targeting young children?

Congress has made one recent attempt to regulate advertising aimed at children, the Children's Television Act, passed in 1990. It limits advertising on children's programming to 10.5 minutes per hour on weekends and 12 minutes per hour on weekdays. But subsequently, more and more commercials are being compressed into that time period (Taras & Gage, 1995). By 1993, children were viewing 11% more commercials per hour than they had 6 years earlier, despite passage of the Children's Television Act (Taras & Gage, 1995). Although the quality of children's programming has probably improved (Jordan & Woodard, 1998; Taras & Gage, 1995), the extraordinary volume of advertising aimed at children and the deceptive nature of some of it have not.

Targeting children with unhealthy food advertisements may be just as unhealthy as inundating them with ads for alcohol or cigarettes (Williams, Achterberg, & Sylvester, 1993). It is possible to refrain from smoking or drinking alcohol but impossible not to eat (Horgen et al., 2001). Some public health groups such as the Center for Science in the Public Interest (CSPI) have been a thorn in the side of the food industry for many years and have successfully focused the public's attention on issues such as the fat content of movie popcorn and the poor nutritional choices available in fast-food restaurants (Horgen et al., 2001). Most recently, CSPI has suggested a tax on junk food (Jacobson, 2000). Michael Jacobson, the director of CSPI, notes that the food industry spends more than $33 billion a year to encourage people to buy their products, many of which are high in fat, sugar, or salt. McDonald's alone spends $1.1 billion a year. By contrast, the National Cancer Institute spends only $1 million a year in a futile attempt to urge Americans to eat more fruits and vegetables and thereby reduce their risk of cancer. A tax on junk foods could even the score considerably (Jacobson, 2000).

But the real power—to date, virtually unused—lies with the regulatory agencies of the federal government: the Federal Trade Commission, the Food and Drug Administration, and the U.S. Department of Agriculture. Recently, the Department of Agriculture sent a report to Congress stating that it should have the legal authority to set nutritional standards for all food and drink sold in schools (Brasher, 2001b). This would allow the Department of Agriculture to ban junk food in schools. However, it will take an act of Congress to give the department this discretionary power. According to Jacobson (1999), the food industry may be even more difficult to deal with than the tobacco industry. It contains at least 78 different lobbying groups, ready to protect the industry's interests. In a sense, this issue represents a classic public health struggle in the United States: the "rights" of free business versus the public health of certain populations in society. In the past, when children are involved, their interests take precedence, and government policy is modified accordingly (Kunkel & Roberts, 1991). But those days may have ended (Kunkel, 1998).

Where does one draw the line between the free marketplace and the public health of children and adolescents? Probably, it should be drawn at the schoolhouse door. Apologists for Channel One say that schools gain valuable technological equipment they can ill afford without sacrificing anything. After all, children and teenagers are already exposed to an environment that is saturated with advertising, and many of them do not even pay attention to the 2 minutes a day of advertising broadcast on Channel One (Bachen, 1998). But the line needs to be drawn somewhere, or else we will soon be selling space on our children's diapers to commercial advertisers. The Consumers Union Education Services (1995) is probably correct in their opposition to Channel One and similar ventures (Johnston, 2001). The "three Rs" should not include "retail." In Maryland, lawmakers have debated a proposal to prohibit advertising in public schools and to prevent schools from entering into exclusive agreements with soft-drink companies such as Charles County's recent 10-year, $6 million contract with Coca-Cola (LeDuc, 2001). Theoretically, issues such as these that involve common sense should not have to be legislated, but obviously, in modern America, that is no longer true.

Again, as with other issues such as media violence, alcohol and tobacco advertising, and inappropriate sexual content, it is extraordinarily difficult to change the producers of such media. It would be easier to change the consumers: children and teenagers. For example, children as young as 6 to 9 years can be taught to discriminate between information and selling techniques presented in commercials (Pearson & Lewis, 1988). Although prevention programs targeting diet and activity have been relatively unsuccessful at reducing obesity (Resnicow & Robinson, 1997; Robinson, 1998), a simple program to reduce the total amount of television viewed by children has resulted in decreased measures of adiposity (Robinson,

1999, 2000). Similarly, a 12-week program that made TV viewing contingent on pedaling a stationary bicycle resulted in both less time spent viewing TV and reductions in total body fat (Faith et al., 2001). Media education programs could also target eating disorders as an important issue, and a few already have (Levine et al., 1999).

Media education classes can encourage young people to analyze critically and decode the images they view (see Chapter 10). Sociocultural factors may be modifiable if they are recognized and discussed, particularly with the peer group present (Levine, 2001; Levine & Smolak, 2001; Shaw & Waller, 1995; Story & Neumark-Sztainer, 1991). At Stanford University, a college course titled "Body Traps: Perspectives on Body Image" resulted in students significantly decreasing their body dissatisfaction and their symptoms of disordered eating (Springer, Winzelberg, Perkins, & Taylor, 1999). Other experimental work with college students has also been successful in changing notions of body image (Levine et al., 1999; Posavac, 1998; Rabak-Wagener, Eickhoff-Shemek, & Kelly-Vance, 1998). Even at the high school level, media education courses can successfully alter high school students' perceptions of media images and their internalized standards of thin beauty (Irving, DuPen, & Berel, 1998; O'Dea & Abraham, 2000). To date, there are 42 different published and unpublished reports of prevention programs in elementary, middle, and high schools. Of these, two thirds showed positive changes in at least one measure of attitude or behavioral change (Levine & Smolak, 2001).

Rather than being part of the problem, the media could become part of the solution. Media are, after all, crucial sources of important information, some of it health related (BMA, 2000; Harris, 1994a). Media could be instrumental in raising awareness about eating disorders and providing information about where and when to seek help (BMA, 2000). Some American companies such as Lands End intentionally use models who are more "plus sized," and there are experimental data that teenagers' self-images can improve with more realistic advertising (see Figure 7.9) (Crouch & Degelman, 1998). Music videos can also buck the trend of showing beautiful women wholly subservient to men. One prime example of this is a recent video by TLC, "Unpretty." A young woman is shown going to a cosmetic surgery clinic at the urging of her boyfriend for a breast enlargement procedure, but at the last minute, she tears off the hospital gown, runs out, and dumps him. In a secondary story line, a plump adolescent girl is shown gazing longingly at pictures of ultra-thin magazine models that she has pasted on her walls. She even cuts out a picture of her own face and tapes it over a model's face. But at the end of the video, she tears the pictures off the wall and decides to accept herself as she is (Arnett, 2001). This is powerful counterprogramming, indeed!

After the BMA report was issued, the British government held a Body Image Seminar, a summit meeting attended by heads of the fashion industry and media. Editors of the leading women's and teen magazines in Britain announced that they would adopt a new voluntary code that will prohibit pictures of ultra-thin models

Figure 7.9. Only occasionally are women's fashion businesses brave enough to advertise large-sized products or to use fuller-sized models in their ads.

and celebrities in their publications (Frean, 2000). Changing the way that various media portray beauty and thinness will take a true cultural shift and will not be easy to accomplish. But the rewards of healthier young women, with healthier self-images, throughout the Western world would be astounding (BMA, 2000).

Exercises

1. For 1 week, watch your normal television programs but keep a log of the commercials shown during the breaks. Try to show a link between the type of show and the type of advertising. What types of foods are being advertised? What types of body types are displayed in the advertising?

2. Given the current epidemic of obesity in the United States, should governmental limits be placed on fast-food advertising? Should warning labels be placed on sugar-sweetened cereals and drinks or on high-fat foods?

3. If the U.S. government were to convene a Body Image Seminar as the British government did, what would the result be?

4. Name your favorite five television actors and actresses. Would you still like/ watch them if they weighed 30 pounds more than they currently weigh? Does being overweight or obese ever "help" an actor or actress (hint: Renée Zellweger/Bridget Jones, Robert DeNiro/Jake LaMotta)? Fat people are often depicted in comical ways on television and in movies. Are there ever any good traits attached to being fat?

5. You are the new female editor-in-chief of *Sports Illustrated* magazine. The previous editor-in-chief (a male) was recently fired because revenues have been sagging during the past year. You know that the swimsuit issue is, by far, the leading revenue-producer for your magazine, but you have two preteen daughters at home and are very familiar with the recent literature on body image and eating disorders. In fact, you had some bulimic symptoms in college for a year or two before getting counseling. How do you handle the swimsuit issue?

6. You are the president and CEO of the leading public health nonprofit association in the country. Your goal for this year is to devise a campaign that will inform parents and children about healthy nutritional practices and educate them about how unhealthy it is to eat at fast-food restaurants frequently. What sort of public campaign do you envision?

7. McDonald's is the leading producer of fast food in the world. It could be argued that McDonald's is also one of the leading causes of the new epidemic of obesity in the United States. At the same time, the Ronald McDonald Children's Charities contribute millions of dollars a year to children's hospitals around the country and provide funds for the housing of children and teens undergoing treatment for childhood cancers. Does McDonald's do more good than harm for American society? Could McDonald's do a better job of informing the public about healthier food choices it serves? Can a business that produces a product that is unhealthy compensate for it through its good deeds? What about other businesses, such as the alcohol industry? The tobacco industry? The makers of *Pokémon*?

8. If product placements are now viewed as being unethical in the movie industry, should toy placements in fast-food restaurants be allowed? What about movie advertisements on soft-drink cups in fast-food restaurants?

9. If a tattoo parlor devised an agreement with a major corporation to tattoo advertisements on human bodies, with payments for the individuals being tattooed (size of payment dependent on how visible the tattoos are), what should be society's stance in allowing or forbidding such tattoos?

10. If the tobacco industry can be held liable for billions of dollars worth of damages for the health-related illnesses that tobacco causes, should the fast-food industry be held accountable as well?

CHAPTER 8

ROCK MUSIC AND MUSIC VIDEOS

Sex sells in America, and as the advertising world has grown ever more risqué in pushing cars, cosmetics, jeans, and liquor to adults, pop music has been forced further past the fringes of respectability for its rebellious thrills. When Mom and Dad watch a Brut commercial in which a nude woman puts on her husband's shirt and sensuously rubs his after-shave all over herself, well, what can a young boy do? Play in a rock 'n' roll band and be a bit more outrageous than his parents want him to be. Kids' natural anti-authoritarianism is going to drive them to the frontiers of sexual fantasy in a society where most aspects of the dirty deed have been appropriated by racy advertising and titillating TV cheesecakery.

—Terence Moran,
The New Republic (1985, p. 15)

What else can you rap about but money, sex, murder or pimping? There isn't a whole lot else going on in our world.

—Rapper Ja Rule,
Newsweek, October 9, 2000, quoted in
Samuels, Croal, and Gates (2000, p. 61)

When Little Richard sang, "Good golly, Miss Molly/Sure likes to bawl/When you're rockin' and rollin'/You can't hear your mama call!" in 1959, he was not singing about a young woman with hay fever and middle ear problems. Nor was the Rolling Stones's 1960s hit "Let's Spend the Night Together" about a vacationing family planning to stay at a Motel 6. In fact, the producers of *The Ed Sullivan Show* insisted that the Rolling Stones change the lyrics to "Let's spend some time together" before they could even appear on the show. And, perhaps the most famous ambiguous rock song ever recorded—"Louie, Louie" by the Kingsmen—was played speeded up, slowed down, and backwards before the Federal Communications Commission decided in 1962 that it was "unintelligible at any speed" (Marsh, 1993; Moran, 1985). Rock lyrics and rock music have always been controversial and problematic to adult society (see Figure 8.1) (Arnett, 2001; Christenson & Roberts, 1998; Strasburger & Hendren, 1995).

Of course, suggestive song lyrics did not originate with 1950s rock 'n' roll. From Cole Porter ("The Lady Is a Tramp," "Let's Do It") to 1930s country music singer Jimmy Rodgers ("If you don't wanna smell my smoke/Don't monkey with my gun") to classic blues songs such as "Hootchie Cootchie Man" and lyrics such as Mamie Smith's "You can't keep a good man down," American songwriters and singers in the 20th century have seemed obsessed with seeing how much they can get away with (Arnett, 2001). Yet, there is no question that lyrics have gotten more provocative and explicit in the past five decades (see Figure 8.2) (Fedler, Hall, & Tanzi, 1982; Strasburger & Hendren, 1995; Robischon, Snierson, & Svetkey, 1999; Schwarzbaum, 2000). Between 1980 and 1990 alone, implicit sexual references decreased 20%, whereas explicit language increased 15% (Christenson & Roberts, 1998). In other words, rock music is becoming much more graphic and much less subtle. On the other hand, to a certain extent, rock 'n' roll must be provocative, anti-establishment, and disliked by adults. Rock music is an important badge of identity for adolescents and an important activity for them (Hansen & Hansen, 2000).

Perhaps even more, rock 'n' roll music, music videos, and the entire MTV culture represent the latest of what could be considered an ever-growing line of "media panics"—adults and society in general tend to fear each new medium as it becomes developed (Starker, 1989). Some date this tendency as far back as the banishing of storytellers from Plato's Republic. Others point to more recent historical concerns, ranging from the impact of nickelodeons, romance novels, and comic books earlier in the 1900s to the Internet and rap music later in the century (Starker, 1989). With each new medium, similar concerns emerge: loss of control, increased sexual activity, inattention, increased aggression. Baby Boom parents can remember their parents asking, "What is rock 'n' roll doing to our children?" in much the same way that parents today question what Eminem is doing to theirs (and why should he be allowed to do so?).

Figure 8.1

Figure 8.2
SOURCE: Reprinted with special permission of King Features Syndicate.

What is also unique in considering the effects of rock music on adolescents is that it is an aural medium and one in which exposure does not typically begin until late childhood or early adolescence. Presumably, teenagers will have developed greater critical faculties and be less susceptible to media influences at age 14 than at age 4. That is not necessarily the case with music videos, which are visual (and therefore as potent as television) and are popular with preteenagers as well. Some critics feel that during adolescence, music becomes the preeminent medium when discussing the media's impact on young people (Christenson & Roberts, 1998; Larson, Kubey, & Colletti, 1989). We feel that there is ample evidence that television remains important, with the addition of the powerful new element of music videos (Roberts, Foehr, et al., 1999).

● ROCK 'N' ROLL MUSIC

The terms *rock music* and *popular music* will be used interchangeably to indicate music currently listened to by teenagers. Such music includes *hard rock, soft rock, punk rock, heavy metal, rap, grunge, salsa,* and *soul music.* Different genres of music are popular with different racial and ethnic groups, although there is considerable crossover (see Table 8.1). Teenagers' choice in music helps them to define important social and subcultural boundaries (Christenson & Roberts, 1998). Although there is more crossover between music types than ever before, in the interests of simplicity we will maintain these "older" genres rather than trying either to coin new terms or to use terms that will not last.

Heavy Metal Music. Of all the types of music that teenagers listen to, heavy metal and rap music have elicited the greatest concern. Once considered as only a fringe category of rock music, heavy metal is characterized by the loud, pulsating rhythm of electric bass guitar and drums and the seeming obsession with themes of violence, dominance and abuse of women, hate, the occult, Satanism, and death (see Table 8.2) (Arnett, 1991). In some ways, *heavy metal* is an outdated term, but it is one that remains familiar to many (see Figure 8.3). Concerns escalated in the 1980s when themes of violence and the occult began to appear more frequently in lyrics (Gore, 1987; Hansen & Hansen, 2000). Groups such as Metallica, Black Sabbath, Megadeath, Slayer, and AC/DC gained increasing notoriety. In 1989, the group Guns-N-Roses reported a 2-year income of more than $20 million ("Entertainers Have the Last Laugh," 1990). The 1980s form of heavy metal (Motley Crüe, Poison) evolved into a more stylized early '90s form (Metallica, Tool) and finally added more rhythm from rap music (Limp Bizkit, Korn, the Deftones) to achieve mainstream status once again. Now, it could just as easily be termed *rap/metal* or *heavy rap.*

In one study, heavy metal fans were found to be higher in machismo and were more likely to overestimate the frequency of people with antisocial attitudes and behaviors and people involved in sex, drugs, and the occult in the general population. Likewise, punk rock fans were found to be less accepting of authority (Hansen & Hansen, 1991a, 2000).

TABLE 8.1 Teenagers' Tastes in Modern Music (*N* = 2,760 teens 14-16 years of age; 68% White, 32% Black) (in percentages)

Favorite Music Type		Groups Most Often Named	
Rock	31	Bon Jovi	10
		U2	2
Rap	18	Run DMC	6
		LL Cool J	4
		Beastie Boys	4
Soul	18	New Edition	3
Heavy metal	13	Motley Crüe	2

SOURCE: Adapted from Klein et al. (1993).

TABLE 8.2 Sample Death Metal Song Titles

"Staring Through the Eyes of the Dead"

"F——- With a Knife"

"Stripped, Raped and Strangled"

"She Was Asking for It"

"Force Fed Broken Glass"

SOURCE: All from Cannibal Corpse CD, *The Bleeding,* copyright 1994, Maggot Music.

Figure 8.3
SOURCE: Tribune Media Services, Inc. All rights reserved. Reprinted with permission.

One reason for the apparent upswing in popularity of heavy metal music may be that mainstream rock 'n' roll music has now been almost completely co-opted by ordinary adult society. Hardly a commercial goes by on network television that is not set to mainstream rock music. In the late 1990s, even the Beatles sold out to Madison Avenue.

The relationship between heavy metal music and violence committed by its fans has always been problematic (Cole, 2000). Consider, for example, these lyrics from "F——— With a Knife" by Cannibal Corpse:

> She liked the way it felt inside her
> F—— her, harder, harder
> Stick it in
> Rip the skin
> Carve and twist
> Torn flesh
> I cut her crotch
> in her ass
> I stick my c——
> Killing as I cum
> (Lyrics by Chris Barnes, ©1994 Maggot Music)

As heavy metal shades into rap, songs include provocative titles such as "S&M" by 2 Live Crew, "Stripped, Raped and Strangled" by Cannibal Corpse, and "Smack My Bitch Up" by Prodigy (Mediascope, 2000a, 2000b). Both heavy metal and rap seem to pride themselves in explicit and sexually violent themes (see Figure 8.4) (Mediascope, 2000a, 2000b). Given the enormity of the problem of domestic violence, even a slight causal connection with heavy metal or rap music would be highly significant. In the United States, domestic violence is the number one cause of injury to women (Commonwealth Fund, 1993). One woman is raped every 2 minutes in the United States, one in seven has been raped in her lifetime, and 30% of women murdered in the United States are killed by their husbands, ex-husbands, or boyfriends (U.S. Department of Justice, 1996). Because more than 40 years of research attest to the learning of aggressive attitudes and behaviors through the media (Donnerstein, Slaby, & Eron, 1994), these concerns seem warranted, although the available research may not yield many conclusions about music per se.

Yet a few studies are illuminating. One study of 121 high school students found that heavy metal fans had more thoughts of suicide than did nonlisteners but that the music had a positive effect on mood (Scheel & Westefeld, 1999). Another study compared data on heavy metal magazine subscriptions and suicide rates in all 50 states. The higher the subscription rate, the higher the suicide rate, and this single factor accounted for 51% of the variance in youth suicide (Stack, Gundlach, & Reeves, 1994). Other studies have found that exposure to heavy metal lyrics

Figure 8.4. Cover Art for Marilyn Manson's 1998 CD titled *Mechanical Animals*

The image is of "Manson as an anorexic, silver-skinned alien, with breasts and airbrushed genitals" (Browne, 1998, p. 84).

increases males' sex-role stereotyping and negative attitudes toward women (although classical music is more sexually arousing!) (St. Lawrence & Joyner, 1991).

All in all, the research seems divided on this issue. Heavy metal may be a "red flag," but adolescent suicide seems to be more closely related to personal and family circumstances (Scheel & Westefeld, 1999). However, the music could nurture suicidal tendencies already present in the subculture of heavy metal (Stack et al., 1994). Roe's (1995) theory of "media delinquency" is that teens gravitate toward objectionable lyrics and other media content simply because they are alienated, rather than the lyrics actually causing the alienation.

Some parents and parent groups have advocated censorship, but clearly that is not an acceptable or legal solution (American Academy of Pediatrics, 1996; Strasburger & Hendren, 1995). In October 1992, the U.S. Supreme Court let stand lower court rulings that declared that heavy metal rock star Ozzy Osbourne's free speech rights protected him against lawsuits brought by the parents of two teenagers in Georgia and South Carolina who had committed suicide after listening to his song, "Suicide Solution" (*Albuquerque Journal,* October 14, 1992). Two other suicides have been attributed to alleged subliminal messages of "do it" in Judas Priest's song, "Beyond the Realms of Death" ("Families Sue Band," 1990). In all such cases, lawsuits against the recording artists have failed.

Heavy metal fans and sympathetic critics argue that the lyrics are provocative but also symbolic and ironic (Brunner et al., 1999). Admittedly, it is sometimes difficult to understand how such lyrics as Rammstein's "Red welts on the white skin/I'm hurting you/And you are loudly whimpering/Now you are scared" should qualify for lofty literary status. Or from Insane Clown Posse: "I looked into her eyes/And she was scared as hell/I knew she was a snitch/So I cut off her tongue." *Hate rock* may be a more apt term for such music, rather than heavy metal (Brunner et al., 1999). At the same time, listeners actually misinterpret songs such as "Suicide Solution," according to one study. The song concerns the evils of alcohol, equating drinking with committing suicide, but does not advocate suicide (Hansen & Hansen, 1991b). In addition, the argument is certainly true that most Nine Inch Nails fans do not typically commit murder and mayhem. As one researcher notes,

> Not every kid that listens to a suicide song is going to commit suicide. Not every kid that listens to a song that talks about killing a policeman is going to go shoot at a policeman. On the other hand, there are kids who have done that who were inspired by a particular song. They tell me they're inspired. That the music speaks to them, to their anger and resentment, to the hate. (Cole, 2000, p. A5)

Rap Music. Rap music has its roots in Black culture and is characterized by talking to a musical beat. At times, it is angry and violent (e.g., gangsta rap). Many rappers, including Snoop Doggy Dogg, Tupac Shakur, and Dr. Dre have had well-publicized encounters with the law (Hirschberg, 1996; Leland, 1993), and both Shakur and Biggie Smalls were eventually gunned down in 1996 in well-publicized murders. Critics note that "hard-core rap music is now driven almost exclusively by sex, violence, and materialism" (Samuels et al., 2000, p. 62). Lyrics can be extremely sexy or just plain misogynistic and sexually violent. Rap star Juvenile has a song titled "Back That Azz Up." In Eminem's "Kim," the protagonist cuts his wife's throat and locks her in the trunk of his car. Mystikal raps, "Came here with my d—k in my hand/Don't make me leave here with my foot in yo' a—" (Samuels et al., 2000).

As with heavy metal, rap lyrics have invited considerable controversy. Rap has drawn criticism for years. In 1988, N.W.A. issued a song titled "F—K Tha Police." Not to be outdone, in 1992, Ice-T's song "Cop Killer" contained the lyrics, "I'm 'bout to bust some shots off/I'm 'bout to dust some cops off" and a chant of "Die, Die, Die, Pig, Die!" Ice-T's song was actually a rap/rock amalgam, with a rap performer fronting a speed metal band called Body Count. Police organizations from around the country demanded the recall of the recording (Leland, 1992). According to one version of the events, Warner Brothers Records refused to issue a recall, but Ice-T asked that the track be removed from all future productions of the album. A second version of the story is that Warner Brothers made it clear that Ice-T needed to "voluntarily" remove the song from the album. Given that Ice-T eventually left the label, the latter version is probably more accurate (Christenson & Roberts, 1998).

What separates rap from heavy metal is its newfound and widespread appeal. One study found that only 26% of rap fans were Black (Bryson, 1996). In 2000, 6 of the top 20 albums were rap records. All had parental advisory warnings (Samuels et al., 2000). The latest rap phenomenon is also the most controversial: Eminem. His album *The Marshall Mathers LP* sold 7.92 million copies in 2000 and was the number two album in America, after 'N Sync's *No Strings Attached* (Willman, 2001). The album features such lyrics as "New Kids on the Block sucked a lot of d—/Boy-girl groups make me sick/And I can't wait 'til I catch all you faggots in public/I'ma love it" (Schwarzbaum, 2000). His newfound prominence, despite some of the most racist, sexist, and homophobic lyrics ever to grace popular music, led the editors of *Entertainment Weekly* to run a cover story titled "Lewd Awakening" (Schwarzbaum, 2000). One of their lead critics notes,

> The fence that separates the decent from the indecent has so many holes in it (what is Granny Klump doing to Buddy Love in that Jacuzzi during prime time?) that homophobes, racists, misogynists, and common potty mouths step right through, unchallenged. Smirking all the way to the bank, they're indistinguishable from arts and innovators of real, if disturbing, substance. (Schwarzbaum, 2000, p. 22)

Rap music is not unidimensional, however. At times, it can also be prosocial, embracing such traditional social values as nurturing, education, and self-sufficiency (Leland, 1992). One observer compares the "sexual speak" of Black women rappers to the "blues" tradition of struggling for empowerment (Perry, 1995) (although explaining what tradition violent male rappers represent may be a bit more difficult). Furthermore, no other music style has so many anti-drug songs (Pareles, 1990). And rap music has contained several responsible songs about sex (e.g., "Safe Sex" by Erick Sermon, Salt 'n Pepa's "Let's Talk About Sex," and Weatoc's "I've Got AIDS") (Perry, 1995).

HOW TEENAGERS USE MUSIC ●

Consumption. As television viewing begins to wane during mid-to-late adolescence, listening to rock music increases, although television remains the predominant medium throughout childhood and adolescence. In one survey of 2,760 teens ages 14 to 16 in 10 different urban Southeast centers, listening to music averaged 40 hours per week (Klein et al., 1993). In a survey of California teens, consumption was lower—2½ to 3 hours per day—although the total average daily time spent

TABLE 8.3   Adolescents' Daily Media Use

	7th Grade (Hours/Minutes)	11th Grade (Hours/Minutes)
Watching television	1:40	2:00
Watching TV news	27	30
Watching music videos	41	23
Total TV time	2:56	2:53
Reading for school	57	1:09
Reading for pleasure	47	29
Total reading time	1:44	1:38
Listening to radio	1:25	1:43
Listening to music	1:04	1:29
Total music time	2:29	3:12
Total broadcast media time	7:09	7:43

SOURCE: Adapted from Christenson and Roberts (1990).

with broadcast media was 7 hours (see Table 8.3) (Christenson & Roberts, 1990). In the most recent survey, a national sample of 3,155 children ages 2 to 18, older children and teens spent 6 hours and 43 minutes a day with media—56% of the total time with TV, 22% with music (Roberts, Foehr, et al., 1999). Often, music is used as a background accompaniment to doing homework, driving, or talking with friends. There is no evidence that music media exert a displacement effect on other activities such as schoolwork (Christenson & Roberts, 1998), although there are several suggestive studies that teens who spend more time listening to music tend to do less well academically (Burke & Grinder, 1966; Larson & Kubey, 1983) and that students who study while listening to rock music exhibit lower comprehension of the material than students studying in silence or listening to classical music (LaVoie & Collins, 1975). However, with the exception of the comprehension study, these studies do not establish cause and effect, only associations. Given the importance of popular music in adolescents' lives, the lack of research into its effects on academic performance seems rather surprising.

Why Adolescents Like Rock Music. The uses (and abuses) of popular music are myriad. Main categories include the following:

- Relaxation and mood regulation

- Social (partying, talking with friends, playing)

- Silence filling (background noise; relief from boredom)

- Expressive (identification with a particular sound, lyrics, or musical group)

When teenagers are asked about the appeal of rock music, they respond that they are most interested in "the beat," not the lyrics. Yet even if lyric content remains unimportant to them on a conscious level, that does not exonerate provocative lyrics or dismiss the possibility that teens can learn from them. As two experts note, "We don't drive down the freeway in order to see billboards, but we see them and we acquire information from them" anyway (Christenson & Roberts, 1990, p. 28).

Music does play an important role in the socialization of adolescents. It can help them identify with a peer group (Roe, 1990) or serve as an important symbol of anti-establishment rebellion (Strasburger, 1997a, 1997c). The performers of popular music also have a significant role in adolescent development as potential role models. And with adolescent consumers estimated to have $140 billion worth of purchasing power (Span, 1999) mainstream advertising is now saturated with rock 'n' roll music. In fact, as one critic asserts, rock 'n' roll has actually become the voice of corporate America (Frith, 1992). But questions regarding the influence of popular music on adolescents need to be qualified by such information as the following: "Which music?" "Which adolescents?" "At what stage of development?" "With what coping abilities and environmental stresses?"

The anti-establishment nature of rock music and its importance in adolescent identity formation are complex issues (Arnett, 2002). One view is that "young people use music to resist authority at all levels, assert their personalities, develop peer relationships and romantic entanglements, and learn about things that their parents and the schools aren't telling them" (Lull, 1987, p. 152). Another critic maintains that the critical job of music is to divide the cultural world into us versus them (Grossberg, 1992). This is similar to the "media delinquency" theory of music (Roe, 1995). Only one experimental study addresses this issue directly: a longitudinal study of Swedish youth and rock music (Roe, 1984). Early converts to rock music (age 11) were more likely to be influenced by their peers and less influenced by their parents than were older adolescents. Because this was a longitudinal study, the investigator could use statistical analyses to demonstrate that it was the early age of music involvement that predicted the increased influence of the peer group over parents.

On the other hand, most rock 'n' roll—aside from heavy metal and gangsta rap—is surprisingly mainstream in its value orientation (Christenson & Roberts,

1998). Romantic love is still the most prevalent theme, despite the fact that the lyrics have become more explicit and the treatment of love is less romantic and more physical (Fedler et al., 1982). In addition, a more modern or revisionist view of normal adolescent psychology would say that the Sturm und Drang ("storm and stress") of adolescence is inaccurate and that most teenagers never consciously identify rock music as a way of driving a rift between themselves and their parents (Christenson & Roberts, 1998).

One content issue currently being closely examined is the frequency with which drugs are mentioned in contemporary rock music. Again, the music industry's fascination with smoking, drinking, and illicit drugs is hardly new. Roger Miller sang "Chug-a-lug" back in 1964, and Jimmy Buffet made "Margaritaville" extremely popular in 1977 (Cooper, 1991). Lyrics about smoking are a bit rarer but date back at least as far as Tex Williams's 1947 song, "Smoke! Smoke! Smoke! (That Cigarette)" (Roberts & Christenson, 2000). And, of course, the 1960s and 1970s were the heyday for illicit drugs, with references sprinkled throughout popular songs by groups such as the Beatles, the Rolling Stones, and Jefferson Airplane (Ward, Stokes, & Tucker, 1986).

But drug-oriented lyrics seem to be making a comeback in the 1990s. In addition, highly publicized drug use by musicians has been a continuing issue since the 1960s because of the potential role-modeling effect (Christenson & Roberts, 1998). Until recently, the only analysis of music lyrics was done in 1977, of top-rated country-and-western songs and alcohol use (cited in Roberts & Christenson, 2000). It found considerable ambivalence about drinking in country songs. Alcohol use always causes problems but also represents an important way to escape problems ("I went to hell when you left me, but heaven's just a drink away"). In 1999, Roberts, Henriksen, and Christenson (1999) examined the 1,000 most popular songs from 1996 to 1997 and found that 17% had references to alcohol (75% of all hip-hop songs) and that there was rarely a mention of the negative consequences of drinking (9%) (see Figures 8.5-8.7). Tobacco or smoking in song lyrics was even rarer: only 3% of the 1,000 songs, although rap and hip-hop songs frequently mentioned it (64%). A larger percentage of songs mentioned illicit drugs (18%). Again, there was a major difference across genres, with 63% of rap songs mentioning drugs, compared with only 1% of country songs. Marijuana was the most common illicit drug, accounting for two thirds of all the references. Unfortunately, both alcohol and illicit drug use were frequently mentioned in positive contexts, associated with sex, romance, wealth, or luxury (Figure 8.7 and Table 8.4) (Roberts, Henriksen, & Christenson, 1999).

The following case vignettes illustrate the important role rock music can play in the life of an adolescent and how one cannot talk about the effect of such music without talking about particular individuals (Strasburger & Hendren, 1995).

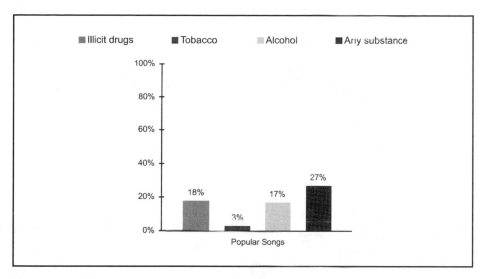

Figure 8.5. Substance Appearance in Popular Songs

SOURCE: Roberts, Henriksen, and Christenson (1999).

NOTE: Percentages reflect the number of songs (1,000 total) from 1996 to 1997 in which substances appeared, whether or not they were used.

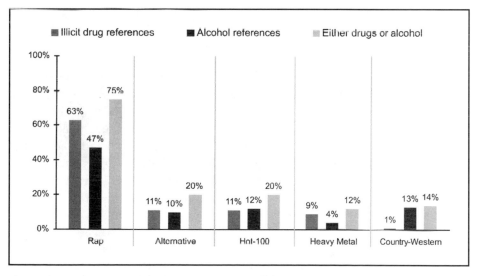

Figure 8.6. Percentage of Songs With Substance References by Genre

SOURCE: Roberts, Henriksen, and Christenson (1999).

NOTE: Based on 212 rap songs, 211 alternative rock songs, 212 hot-100 songs, 211 heavy metal songs, and 212 country-western songs popular in 1996-1997.

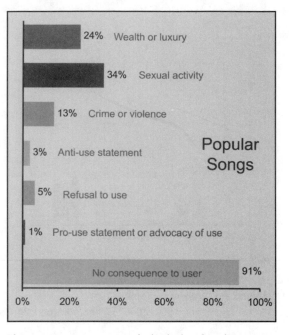

Figure 8.7. Percentage of Alcohol-Related Songs Associated With Certain Themes

SOURCE: Roberts, Henriksen, and Christenson (1999).

NOTE: Based on 149 popular songs in 1996-1997 that portrayed alcohol use.

Case 1

Sean was a 16-year-old emotionally reserved boy whose parents ended their marriage in an acrimonious divorce 3 years earlier. Because of parental fighting, Sean saw little of his father, and when he did, they usually had a fight about the father's young girlfriend. Sean was extremely interested in the martial arts and heavy metal music. After school, he often went into his room and read martial arts books while listening to groups such as Metallica and Slayer. He reported feeling less alone and angry after this, although it upset his conservative mother. Sean has never been violent although he continues to be emotionally reserved and socially withdrawn. Currently, he is attending law school.

Case 2

Owen was a 15-year-old boy whose parents are bright university professors, who were adolescents during the 1960s. They became concerned that Owen might be involved with drugs because he was very interested in acid rock and the music associated with the drug culture in the 1960s. Owen was bright but not doing well in school. He said he found it difficult to do as well as his successful parents. He tried recreational drugs but stopped drug use around age 17.

TABLE 8.4 The Context of Substance Use in Song Lyrics (in percentages)

Context	Alcohol	Illicit Drugs
Negative effects on the community	1	8
Desire or attempt to quit	3	5
Addiction	2	7
Seeking treatment or help	1	2
Sobriety or being straight	3	3
Intoxication or being high	24	44

SOURCE: Roberts, Henriksen, and Christenson (1999, p. 40).

Currently, he is attending a liberal arts university and identifies with the "artsie liberal types" there.

Case 3

Kurt was a 17-year-old boy whose parents divorced when he was young. He had limited contact with his alcoholic father. Kurt always had trouble in school and also had some minor trouble with the law. He became involved in a satanic cult where he and others frequently listened to heavy metal rock. He was hospitalized in an adolescent psychiatric hospital after a suicide attempt. While there, he admitted to being involved in several human sacrifices as part of the satanic cult.

Adolescents' Comprehension of Song Lyrics. If there is "good" news about the increasingly explicit lyrics of popular music, it is that many teenagers do not know the lyrics or comprehend their intended meaning. For example, in one study, only 30% of teenagers knew the lyrics to their favorite songs (Desmond, 1987; Greenfield et al., 1987). Even if the students knew the lyrics, their comprehension varied greatly. For example, only 10% of fourth graders could correctly interpret a Madonna song, none could correctly interpret a Springsteen song, and nearly 50% of college students thought that "Born in the U.S.A." was a song of patriotism, not alienation (Greenfield et al., 1987). Other studies have found similarly low rates of lyric knowledge or comprehension (Denisoff & Levine, 1971; Leming, 1987; Prinsky & Rosenbaum, 1987).

Heavy metal music devotees seem to be the exception. In Greenfield et al.'s study (1987), 40% knew the lyrics to their favorite songs. Other studies have found that such teenagers are more likely to listen closely to the lyrics, to feel that the music represents a very important part of their life, and to identify with the performers (Arnett, 1991; Wass et al., 1988).

Comprehension of lyrics increases with age (Strasburger & Hendren, 1995). Even so, whereas adults frequently identify such themes as sex, drugs, violence, and satanism in current rock music, teenagers tend to interpret their favorite songs as being about "love, friendship, growing up, life's struggles, having fun, cars, religion, and other topics that relate to teenage life" (Prinsky & Rosenbaum, 1987, p. 393).

Of course, these studies assess comprehension using an adult norm (Christenson & Roberts, 1998). Theoretically, the adult interpretation could be incorrect, or the incorrect interpretation could still be having significant behavioral impact. In addition, the small percentages of teens who actually do know the lyrics or comprehend their meaning might be precisely those who are at highest risk. Alternatively, those who comprehend the lyrics might then be able to reject the implied values. For example, half of a small sample of academically gifted 11- to 15-year-olds said that music had influenced how they thought about "an important topic," but 70% rejected lyrics that seemed to condone casual sex (Leming, 1987). These are teenagers who might be relatively more "media resistant." A teenager's current level of development and current level of stress could lead him or her to be more susceptible to particular lyrics—for example, a teenager contemplating her first sexual intercourse might be more interested in sexy lyrics; a depressed teen might seek out songs of alienation (Christenson & Roberts, 1998).

Behavioral Impact of Lyrics. To date, there are no studies that document a cause-and-effect relationship between sexy or violent lyrics and adverse behavioral effects. However, half of mothers with children in public schools believe that violence in rap music contributes significantly to school violence (Kandakai, Price, Telljohann, & Wilson, 1999). And the well-known fascination of Columbine killers Eric Harris and Dylan Kliebold with Marilyn Manson and other rock antiheroes makes the public worry about the safety of music as a form of entertainment for their children (Strasburger & Grossman, 2001).

In addition to the two behavioral studies already discussed, there are, however, other studies that indicate that a preference for heavy metal music may be a significant marker for alienation, substance abuse, psychiatric disorders, or risk-taking behaviors during adolescence (King, 1988; Klein et al., 1993; Scheel & Westefeld, 1999; Stack et al., 1994; Tanner, 1981; Weidinger & Demi, 1991). Some of their findings are as follows:

• Young adolescents who felt alienated from school life were more likely to prefer heavy metal music in one early study (Tanner, 1981).

• Among teenagers in a hospital psychiatric unit, 59% of those admitted for chemical dependency rated heavy metal as their musical preference. Many of

Figure 8.8. Voluntary Label Affixed to Record Albums by Record Manufacturers

them were also involved in violence, stealing, and sexual activity. A second group of patients with psychiatric disturbances but less substance abuse rated heavy metal as their first choice 39% of the time. By contrast, only 17% of patients with primarily a psychiatric disorder rated heavy metal as their top choice, and they were less likely to be involved in conduct-disordered behavior (King, 1988). A survey of 60 teens admitted with dysfunctional psychosocial behaviors to a different psychiatric unit found similar results (Weidinger & Demi, 1991).

- A survey of more than 2,700 teens ages 14 to 16 found that White male adolescents who reported engaging in five or more risk-taking behaviors (e.g., smoking cigarettes, drinking alcohol, cheating in school, having sex, cutting school, stealing money, smoking marijuana) were most likely to name a heavy metal group as their favorite (Klein et al., 1993). The relative risk for engaging in five or more risky behaviors was 2.1 for girls and 1.6 for boys, respectively. Discussing music preferences with teenagers—indeed, discussing preferences for a variety of different media—could serve a useful screening tool for primary care physicians and mental health professionals (Brown & Hendee, 1989). It could also help them understand both the cultural milieu their patients live in and their patients' own unique psychology.

Of course, until a longitudinal correlational study is performed, it is equally possible that alienation leads to a preference for heavy metal music rather than the reverse. Roe's (1984) study comes the closest to answering this argument. His study found that alienation from the mainstream culture precedes rather than follows a taste for music such as heavy metal. This seems to reinforce the notion of heavy metal music as a "marker" but not a "cause" of antisocial adolescent behavior (Roberts & Christenson, 2001).

Effects of Parental Advisory Labels. Since 1985, recording companies have been voluntarily adding parental advisory labels to record albums, tapes, or CDs that they judge to be violent, sexually explicit, or potentially offensive (see Figure 8.8). Record companies are given the alternative of printing such lyrics on album jackets as consumer information for parents (Parents Music Resource Center, 1985). There has been a great deal of controversy about whether the labeling would result in the recordings becoming more or less appealing to adolescents.

As mentioned previously, several studies have found that most students cannot accurately describe the themes of their favorite songs and are usually unaware of the content or meanings of the lyrics. This raises the concern that labeling the album will call attention to the very themes that parent groups object to. Teenagers might then respond in one of two different ways: avoiding the albums (the "tainted fruit" theory) or finding them more appealing (the "forbidden fruit" theory) (Christenson, 1992a). In addition, printed lyrics on the jacket cover might make previously indecipherable lyrics easily accessible. (Imagine, for example, if the Kingsmen had published the lyrics of "Louie, Louise" on their album cover.) Only one experimental study has dealt with the issue of labeling. In it, young adolescents were asked to evaluate the same music, labeled and unlabeled (Christenson, 1992a). The adolescents liked the labeled music less well, but the impact was limited. The adolescents reacted primarily to the music per se, rather than the lyrics.

Regardless of the research, the music industry does not seem interested in complying with any restrictions on its products, including parental advisory labels. The Federal Trade Commission report of 2001 found that all five major recording companies placed advertising for explicit music on television programs and magazines with substantial under-17 audiences. In addition, ads for such music usually did not show the parental advisory label, or it was too small to be read (Federal Trade Commission, 2001).

Conclusion. Overall, the research is incomplete on rock music and music lyrics, but if any conclusion can be drawn, it is that although rock music has become increasingly more graphic in content—particularly rap and heavy metal—different teenagers respond to lyrics differently, depending on their own unique psychological, social, and developmental makeup. Very rarely, certain types of music could act as a catalyst for violence in someone who is already psychologically disposed toward it. But at the same time, there are clearly few reasons to forgive some of the increasingly misogynistic and violent lyrics in some music genres.

● MUSIC VIDEOS AND MUSIC TELEVISION (MTV)

Things seen are mightier than things heard.—Alfred Lord Tennyson (cited in Roberts & Christenson, 2001)

As a visual medium, music videos are compelling. Not only do they possess the impact of ordinary television, but they could be even more powerful. Although music lyrics may be ambiguous or difficult even to hear or understand, there is no

Figure 8.9
SOURCE: Reprinted with special permission of King Features Syndicate.

mistaking a scene of graphic violence or a couple cavorting in bed together (see Figure 8.9) (Mediascope, 2000a, 2000b).

Music videos represent a unique form of broadcast media—impressionistic, nonlinear, and one that is immensely popular with teenagers and preteenagers (Christenson & Roberts, 1998). Again as with music lyrics, although few cause-and-effect studies exist, music videos seem capable of influencing teenagers' ideas about adult behavior and, potentially, even modifying their own behavior. Although adolescents seem to appreciate primarily the music, the addition of sexual images seems to increase their excitement (Zillmann & Mundorf, 1987). Sexual content, in particular, seems to appeal to young people (Hansen & Hansen, 1990, 2000).

In addition, MTV and music videos have defined an entire generation, the MTV generation: what's "hot," what's "cool," what's "in," and what's "out" are played out every day and night on the TV screen. Adolescent girls may use music lyrics and videos to come to grips with their own sexual identities (Brown & Steele, 1995). Many critics are concerned that the power of the music and lyrics becomes magnified when visual images are added to them, increasing the risk of deleterious effects on young people (Strasburger & Hendren, 1995). Such concern seems justified, given that numerous studies have documented television's potential harmful effects in the areas of violence, smoking and drinking behavior, and risky sexual activity (Strasburger, 1993, 1997a, 1997c; Strasburger & Donnerstein, 2000).

In the 1980s and early to mid-1990s, Music Television (MTV) comprised performance videos, concept videos, and advertising. In a performance video, a musical performer or group sings the song in concert or in a studio. Roughly half of all music videos are performance videos. A concept video consists of a story that goes along with the song, which may or may not add a plot to the lyrics.

Although performance videos can occasionally be outlandish (e.g., David Lee Roth's attire or his masturbating onstage with a huge inflatable phallus in the video "Yankee Rose"), there is no evidence that such videos have demonstrable behavioral impact (American Academy of Pediatrics, 1996). Such depictions are roughly the equivalent of Elvis Presley gyrating his hips in the 1950s. Rather, it is the concept videos that have attracted much of the criticism for promoting violence, sexual promiscuity, and sexism. Concept videos are strongly male oriented, and women are frequently worshipped as upper-class sex objects (e.g., Billy Joel's "Uptown Girl" or The Thunderbirds's "Wrap It Up"). Rock stars also serve as potential role models for impressionable children and young adolescents. When Madonna sings, "Papa don't preach/I'm in trouble deep/Papa don't preach/I've been losing sleep/But I made up my mind/I'm keeping my baby" while dancing around looking like a thin Marilyn Monroe, it becomes that much more difficult to convince a pregnant 14-year-old that having a baby would be a severe hardship. One national columnist called it "a commercial for teenage pregnancy" (Goodman, 1986). George Michael's "I Want Your Sex" combines striking sexual imagery with explicit lyrics ("Sex is natural/Sex is good/Not everybody does it/But everybody should"). It also includes the disclaimer, "This song is not about casual sex. . . . Explore Monogamy." Of course, if the equivalent ploy were tried with cigarette labeling, the disclaimer might read, "Caution: Cigarettes may be hazardous to your health, but only if you smoke them."

Common themes in concept videos include, in order of occurrence, the following: visual abstraction (use of special effects to produce odd, unusual, or unexpected representations of reality), sex, dance, and violence or crime (Baxter, De Riemer, Landini, Leslie, & Singletary, 1985). Music videos have also been shown to contain nihilistic images in 44% of the concept videos studied (Davis, 1985). This includes themes of destruction, death, ridicule of social institutions, and aggression against authority. As such, they seem to play on the presumably rebellious nature of the adolescent audience.

Advertising on MTV parallels prime-time advertising in that sex is used to sell every sort of product (Strasburger, 1997a, 1997c). Although birth control ads are occasionally aired on MTV (and the network was one of the first in this regard), such ads are not nearly as widespread as they should be, considering the target audience and the need. Meanwhile, alcohol advertising is particularly prevalent. Given the amount of alcohol and tobacco use in mainstream videos (DuRant, Rome, et al., 1997), some critics might say that the videos themselves have become advertisements. Speech patterns, fashion trends, and even certain behaviors have become "advertised" via music videos. Consumerism reigns supreme. Although occasional public service announcements (PSAs) are aired, discussing drugs or AIDS or the need to vote, they are heavily outnumbered by beer commercials and ads that exploit female sexuality.

More recently, MTV has "transformed itself from a kind of video jukebox into a programming service pandering to teens," according to one critic (Johnson, 2001). Music videos are aired in the early morning and again on the hit afternoon show, *Total Request Live.* But much of MTV's airtime is now taken up with programming such as *Jackass,* a stunt show; *Undressed,* a very sexually explicit soap opera aired late at night; and the annual spring break marathon. Other music-oriented channels, such as VH-1 and Black Entertainment Network (BET), have taken up the video slack. Still, MTV remains the prototype of a medium designed almost exclusively to attract teenage viewers.

Consumption. Music video has become a pervasive and influential form of consumer culture and has altered the television viewing, music listening, and record-buying habits of the young people who constitute its audience (Burnett, 1990). With 76% of American households receiving cable TV (Nielsen, 2000), most teenagers have access to MTV and may spend as many as 2 hours a day watching it (Sun & Lull, 1986), although most studies report closer to 30 to 60 minutes per day (Christenson & Roberts, 1998; Mediascope, 2000a, 2000b). According to a recent study, music videos are watched more by girls than boys, more by Black teens than by Hispanic or White teens, and more by lower-income teens than by others (Roberts, Henriksen, & Christenson, 1999).

MTV grows by more than 5 million households a year; by the early 1990s, it was available in 55 million homes (Christenson & Roberts, 1998; Polskin, 1991). It is also available in 40 countries overseas, reaching more than 194 million households (Polskin, 1991). As a commercial medium, its profits are projected to be more than $100 million. The effects of MTV's advertising content are considerable and have been examined in detail elsewhere (see Strasburger, 1993).

Content. From the advent of MTV, content analyses have shown that music videos are rife with sex, drugs, and violence. Surprisingly, they are relatively tame when it comes to profanity (see Tables 8.5 and 8.6) (Center for Media and Public Affairs, 1999), with perhaps the exception of recent rappers such as Eminem.

In the mid-1980s, the first content analyses showed that the characters portrayed in concept music videos were primarily White and male (Sherman & Dominick, 1986). Episodes of violence occurred in 57% of concept videos, with White males most likely to be the aggressors. Wrestling, punching, and grabbing were the most common forms of aggression, and the outcome of the aggression was rarely shown. Sexual intimacy appeared in more than three quarters of the music videos studied and was more implied than overt. Half of all women were

TABLE 8.5   Scenes With Profanity in Various Media

Medium	Hardcore Profanity	Mild Profanity	Coarse Expressions
Broadcast TV	3	1,032	429
Basic cable TV	0	268	42
Premium cable TV	175	161	46
Movies	788	910	235
Music videos	0	136	24

SOURCE: Center for Media and Public Affairs (1999).

NOTE: Sample included 284 broadcast shows during 1998-1999 season, 50 of the highest rated made-for-TV movies, 188 music videos on MTV, and the 50 top-grossing films for 1998.

TABLE 8.6   Dirty Dozen Music Videos

Title	Artist	Number of Scenes With Profanity
"What's So Different"	Ginuwine	7
"Wrong Way"	Sublime	3
"No Scrubs"	TLC	3
"Here We Come"	Timbaland	3
"Flagpole Sitta"	Harvey Danger	3
"Changes"	2Pac	2
"Ghetto Superstar"	Pras	2
"Gimme Some More"	Busta Rhymes	2
"Slippin'"	DMX	2
"How Do I Deal"	Jennifer Love Hewitt	2
"My Name Is"	Eminem	2
"Under the Bridge"	Red Hot Chili Peppers	2

SOURCE: Adapted from Center for Media and Public Affairs (1999).

dressed provocatively and were often presented as upper-class sex objects. Furthermore, most of the violent videos also contained sexual imagery, usually involving violence against women.

Another 1980s content analysis found that nearly 60% of concept videos contained sexual themes, and more than half contained violence (Baxter et al., 1985).

TABLE 8.7   Content of Music Video Genres (*N* = 203 videos) (in percentages)

Category	Rap	Hip-Hop	Rock	R&B	Country
Profanity	73	17	2	0	0
Guntalk	59	8	6	2	5
Alcohol	42	17	8	15	24
Violence	36	0	22	6	19
Female "sexdance"	25	58	8	31	8
Heavy cleavage	15	25	6	17	30
Simulated intercourse	9	42	2	13	3
Fondling	7	42	14	22	8

SOURCE: Data from Jones (1997).

In one analysis of sexism in rock videos, more than half portrayed women in a condescending manner (Vincent, Davis, & Bronszkowski, 1987).

Women have never fared very well on MTV, and that continues into the 1990s and the present. A content analysis of 100 videos on MTV found that women are often portrayed as "bimbos" (Gow, 1993). Men are portrayed nearly twice as often as women, but women are engaged in more sexual and subservient behavior (Sommers-Flanagan, Sommers-Flanagan, & Davis, 1993). One critic feels that MTV creates a "dreamworld" in which all women are nymphomaniacs, waiting to be ravaged (Jhally, 1995). Music videos separate women into body parts (Jhally, 1995), just as mainstream advertising often does (Kilbourne, 1999). Consequently, the viewer sees erotic images, but not a whole person: sex without the humanity. According to one expert, "If there is such a thing as a typical music video it features one or more men performing while beautiful, scantily clad young women dance and writhe lasciviously" (Arnett, 2001, p. 256). Commercials shown on MTV tend to mimic the programming as well, so that female characters are seen less frequently than males but then are displayed as sex objects wearing skimpy clothing (Signorielli, McLeod, & Healy, 1994).

During the past decade, rap and hip-hop music videos have moved to the forefront of parents' concerns (Kandakai et al., 1999). Such videos contain more violence, guns, sex, alcohol, cigarettes, and profanity than any other form of music videos (e.g., rock, country, etc.) (see Table 8.7) (DuRant, Rich, et al., 1997; DuRant, Rome, et al., 1997; Jones, 1997). Of all the music video channels, BET is highest in depicting videos with sexual imagery and sex-role stereotypes, probably because it shows rap and hip-hop videos (DuRant, Rich, et al., 1997; DuRant, Rome, et al., 1997; Hansen & Hansen, 2000; Tapper, Thorson, & Black, 1994). When violence is depicted, it is usually the attractive lead singer/role model who is involved (Rich, Woods, Goodman, Emans, & DuRant, 1998). In one analysis of rap music videos, there was frequent talk about guns (59%), drug use (49%), profanity (73%), grabbing (69%), alcohol use (42%), and explicit violence (36%) (Jones, 1997). In another analysis of all forms of music videos, across several different TV channels, rap videos were by far the most violent (DuRant, Rich, et al., 1997). Even women were shown engaging in violence (41%) or carrying weapons (34%), and Black males were overrepresented in their levels of violence and weapon carrying. Interestingly, videos that had high levels of eroticism did not contain violence (the "Make Love, Not War" effect commented on by one observer) (Strasburger, 1997a). Overall, nearly one fourth of all videos across all genres contained overt violence, and a similar number depicted weapon carrying (DuRant, Rich, et al., 1997).

What about drugs? An analysis of 518 music videos on four different channels found that MTV displayed more tobacco use (25% of all videos), with rap videos leading the way (30%) (DuRant, Rome, et al., 1997). All four channels—MTV, VH1, Country Music Television (CMT), and BET—showed videos that depicted alcohol usage between 18% and 25% of the time. Typically, the lead performer is the one shown smoking or drinking, and much of the alcohol use is combined with sexual elements. As a result, the authors conclude, even a casual observer may be exposed to substantial amounts of glamorized drug use (DuRant, Rome, et al., 1997).

Comprehension. Music videos are more than just television plus music. They are self-reinforcing: If viewers hear a song after having seen the video version, they immediately "flash back" to the visual imagery in the video (Greenfield & Beagles-Roos, 1988). Obviously, the impact music videos have is dependent on how the viewer interprets them. New evidence suggests that teenagers are a diverse group whose perceptions cannot always be predicted. For example, adolescent viewers of a Madonna video, "Papa Don't Preach," differed in how they interpreted the story elements based on their sex and race (see Table 8.8) (Brown & Schulze, 1990). Black viewers were almost twice as likely to say the video was a story of a father-daughter relationship, whereas White viewers were much more likely to say it was about teenage pregnancy. A similar study of Billy Ocean's video, "Get Outta My Dreams, Get Into My Car," found that children tended to be very concrete in interpreting the video (Christenson, 1992b). Some even said the video was about a man and his car, whereas slightly-older 12-year-olds saw the video in more abstract terms, focusing on the relationship between the man and the woman. These studies suggest that both cognitive development and social background play a role in how teenagers and preteens process music videos.

Watching music videos—particularly MTV—may differ from watching "regular television" or listening to the radio for the average adolescent. Music videos and MTV represent an entertaining diversion, rather than a means of mood control or a

TABLE 8.8   Do Teenagers View Madonna Music Videos Differently?
Reactions to "Papa Don't Preach," by Race and Sex (in percentages)

Primary Theme	Black Males (n = 28)	Black Females (n = 40)	White Males (n = 54)	White Females (n = 64)
Teen pregnancy	21	40	56	63
Boy-girl relationship	21	5	15	5
Father-daughter relationship	43	50	22	25
Independent girl making a decision	14	5	7	8
Part of theme deals with pregnancy	43	73	85	97

SOURCE: Adapted from Brown and Schulze (1990).

social lubricant (Christenson & Roberts, 1998). If teenagers admit to learning anything from the medium, it is what's "hot," music- or fashion-wise, rather than learning social values. This is classic "social desirability bias" and "third-person effect" (i.e., the media influence everyone else but me) (Eveland et al., 1999). It is also typical of normal adolescent psychology at work: After all, admitting that the media influence your values or ideas would mean that you are not invulnerable after all. So MTV provides pictures of attractive people and, in many ways, functions as a style show. Yet 10- to 12-year-olds recognize that some of the sexual imagery and objectionable language may not be appropriate for them (Christenson & Roberts, 1998), so some value-laden material must be getting through as well.

Behavioral Effects.   As with television in general, the amount of direct imitation of music videos or MTV is rare, but when it occurs, it makes national headlines. Such was the case when MTV's infamous show *Beavis and Butthead* allegedly inspired a 5-year-old Moraine, Ohio, boy to set fire to his family's mobile home, killing his 2-year-old sister ("Mom Says MTV's 'Beavis,'" 1993). The incident followed earlier reports that three girls in western Ohio had also started a fire while imitating a scene from the show (Hajari, 1993). Although *Beavis and Butthead* is a cartoon, not a music video, it was prominently featured on MTV, and much of the show involved the two main characters commenting on music videos. In response, MTV promised to delete "all references to fire" from future episodes and moved *Beavis and Butthead* to a late evening time slot (Hajari, 1993).

More recently, Jason Lind, a 13-year-old Connecticut boy, was hospitalized for 5 weeks with second- and third-degree burns after imitating an MTV personality who set himself on fire during a stunt show titled *Jackass* ("Jackass Imitation

Stunt," 2001). In the show, the host wore a fire-resistant suit and lay across a barbe-cue grill while the cast shot lighter fluid onto the flames. The teenager reenacted the stunt with friends in one of their backyards. Although MTV apologized to the family, it accepted no responsibility or blame for the incident. A second such inci-dent occurred in Florida with a 12-year-old boy getting severely burned (Geier, 2001).

As one observer sums it up,

> More than a week has passed since MTV's one-time-only broadcast of Madonna's new video "What It Feels Like for a Girl," but as of press time no one has stolen two cars, collided with multiple vehicles, run down street-hockey players, held up an ATM patron, torched a gas station, pointed metallic squirt guns at cops, and crashed head-on into a pole. Yet. (Geier, 2001, p. 10)

Despite the rarity of direct imitation, there is now significant evidence that even brief exposure to music videos can "prime" viewers' schemata and influence their social judgments (Hansen & Hansen, 2000). Outcomes depend on content. For example, exposing college students to videos with antisocial themes produces a greater tolerance of antisocial behavior. Showing them videos with sex-role ste-reotyping produces greater acceptance of such attitudes and behavior (Hansen & Hansen, 2000).

Hansen and Hansen (2000) use the following example to illustrate the impact of music videos: Imagine that Johnny, a teenager, watches a lot of MTV and BET because he enjoys rap music. Because rap videos tend to portray women as sex objects, Johnny's social schemata for women will be "primed" frequently. He enjoys the videos, so his sex object schema for women will be positively rein-forced as well. Yet if you were to ask Johnny if he thought music has influenced his attitudes or behavior, he would say no and would be giving an honest—although inaccurate—answer. In this way, music and music videos, in particular, work to prime individuals who are totally unaware of what is occurring.

Several experimental and field studies have been conducted. Music video exposure is correlated with an increase in risky behaviors among teens (Klein et al., 1993; Roberts, Dimsdale, East, & Friedman, 1998), although only one study has documented a cause-and-effect relationship (Robinson et al., 1998).

The largest body of research concerns violence in music videos and its possible impact on a young audience:

- Desensitization appears to occur on both a short- and long-term basis after viewing music videos (Rehman & Reilly, 1985).

- Even brief exposure to music videos with antisocial content can lead to greater acceptance of antisocial behavior (Hansen & Hansen, 1990).

- In a recent study, 46 inner-city Black males, ages 11 to 16 years, from Wilmington were divided into three groups: The first group was exposed to a half-hour of rap videos, complete with shootings and assaults; the second viewed non-violent rap videos; and the third saw no videos. The teens were then given two different scenarios: one to test for their propensity for violence, the other to determine their attitude about academics. Those who had viewed the violent videos were significantly more likely to condone violence in the theoretical scenario, and both groups of teens who viewed the rap videos were less likely to approve of high academic aspirations (Johnson, Jackson, & Gatto, 1995).

- Several studies have documented changes in music video viewers' attitudes toward women (Johnson, Adams, Ashburn, & Reed, 1995; Peterson & Pfost, 1989; Reid & Finchilescu, 1995). A study of 144 college males found that viewing videos containing violence and eroticism resulted in less aggressive attitudes toward women than viewing videos that were violent but without eroticism (Peterson & Pfost, 1989). An alarming 40% indicated some interest in committing rape if they could be assured of not being caught and punished. A similar study found that misogynous videos facilitated sexually aggressive attitudes among college males (Barongan & Hall, 1995). Effects are not limited to males, however. In a study of African American teen females, viewing rap videos led to increased acceptance of teen dating violence (Johnson, Jackson, & Gatto, 1995). Rap videos may also foster unfavorable attitudes toward Black women among Whites, especially if the videos are sexually suggestive (Gan, Zillmann, & Mitrook, 1997; Su-Lin, Zillmann, & Mitrook, 1997).

- Eliminating access to MTV in a locked treatment facility decreased significantly the number of violent acts among the adolescent and young adult inmates (Waite, Hillbrand, & Foster, 1992).

Unfortunately, fewer researchers have examined the issue of sex and sexuality in music videos. Two experiments have found that R-rated sexual images increase viewers' approval of music videos, whereas the combination of sex and violence decreases their approval (Hansen & Hansen, 2000; Zillmann & Mundorf, 1987). Cross-sectional studies of teen females seem to indicate that exposure correlates with unhealthy body image, greater sexual permissiveness, and attitudes more accepting of sexual harassment (Borzekowski et al., 2000; Brown & Newcomer, 1991; Strouse & Buerkel-Rothfuss, 1987; Strouse et al., 1995; Tiggemann & Pickering, 1996). For example:

- A study of nearly 1,000 ninth-grade girls in California found that hours spent watching videos was significantly related to the girls' perceived importance of their appearance and their weight concerns (Borzekowski et al., 2000).

- In another study of 214 teenagers, ages 13 to 18 years, which surveyed the teens and their families about media use, male virginity was unrelated to viewing R- or X-rated movies, music choices, or music video exposure. However, there was a strong relationship between music video exposure and premarital permissiveness for females, which was even stronger if their home environment was unhappy (Strouse et al., 1995).

- In a different study, 7th and 10th graders who were exposed to only 1 hour of selected music videos were more likely to approve of premarital sex than were adolescents in a control group (Greeson & Williams, 1986). In addition, the 10th graders exposed to the videos showed less disapproval of violence.

- Only two longitudinal studies exist. A report of 522 African American females and their exposure to music videos found an association between heavy viewing of rap videos (up to 20 hours per week or more) and increased likelihood to test positive for a sexually transmitted disease, to report not using condoms, to have multiple sexual partners, and to have engaged in other high-risk activities (Wingood et al., 2001).

- A different longitudinal study (yielding potentially cause-and-effect data) of adolescent media use and its impact on alcohol found that music videos held the strongest correlation for beginning to drink alcohol for teens (Robinson et al., 1998). Among more than 1,500 ninth graders, the odds ratio for early alcohol use among heavy music video viewers was 1.31. In fact, music videos exceeded network television as an influence on early adolescent drinking.

Obviously, this is not a comprehensive body of research. Far more research is needed. But these studies have added to the vast body of research done on media violence in revealing important effects, even with limited amounts of exposure.

● CONCLUSION

Despite the fact that rock 'n' roll is practically middle-aged, and MTV just turned 20 in 2001, research on popular music and music videos is in its infancy. There has been surprisingly little research about either, despite massive public concern about violent or sexually suggestive lyrics and videos. In addition, little attention has been paid to how these immensely popular media might be harnessed to provide prosocial or health-related messages. Of course, the question would still remain, Whose prosocial or health-related messages should be dramatized? To date, no cause-and-effect studies exist to link either music or videos with violent or sexually promiscuous behavior, and only one links viewing music videos with an increased risk of early alcohol use during adolescence. Clearly, for a small minority of teenagers, certain music may serve as a behavioral marker for psychological distress. The most important questions to ask before drawing any conclusions about the effects of rock music or music videos on teenagers are, "Which music?" and "Which adolescents?"

Exercises

1. Go around the room and ask everyone to sing (or say) the lyrics to their favorite song. Do the results concur with the research (only 30% of you should be successful)? Discuss Bruce Springsteen's "Born in the USA." What is it about? How much of the lyrics can you remember? Then read the study by Greenfield et al. (1987).

2. Why should some children and adolescents be more susceptible to the influence of rock music lyrics or music videos than others? What factors might determine vulnerability?

3. Consider the lyrics of Eminem (or the much older lyrics of 2 Live Crew). Is there a line that has been crossed in popular music? Are there some lyrics that should—for reasons of public safety, for example—never be tolerated? Racist lyrics? Anti-Semitic lyrics? Can objectionable lyrics be made less objectionable by the artist saying that he or she is merely trying to be "ironic"?

4. You are the newest executive producer at MTV, having just been hired away from a very successful gig at *Rolling Stone* magazine. You want to "make your mark" with new, insightful, controversial, and preferably very highly rated programming on the station. You are asked to devise a new half-hour show that will air during prime time. What ideas do you have? Does it make any difference that you are 23 years old and still have a 15-year-old sister back home who adores you and watches 3 hours of MTV a day?

5. Design an anti-drug PSA specifically for an MTV audience. Design a public health campaign specifically for an MTV audience.

6. You are a producer for the Big Label record company. You discover a raw new talent in Anthony, New Mexico, who has a song about killing cats because they are evil and spread disease. (You may laugh, but this is an issue that is considerably more complicated than it appears on the surface. You see, your singer lives in southeast New Mexico, where cats sometimes spread the plague. So he has something of a point, although the number of cases is limited to a handful per year, and they are easily treatable if diagnosed in time. On the other hand, hantavirus, which is spread by deer mice that could be hunted and killed off by

cats, is endemic in northwest New Mexico and is much more common and far more likely to be fatal. However, your singer doesn't appreciate cats' ability to limit the rodent population.) At any rate, the song has a good beat, so you don't worry too much about the lyrics. It hits the Billboard Top 100 in early October and by the end of October, the Humane Society of America reports that thousands of cats have been killed or tortured. The Ancient Egyptian Anti-Defamation League complains that cats should be considered sacred, not evil. Both sue you, the singer, and your company. What is your defense?

7. You are a Baby Boom parent, a child of the 1960s. You were tear-gassed in college while marching against the war in Vietnam. You may or may not have experimented in college with illegal drugs, depending on who is doing the asking. You are now married (for the second time) and have a 13-year-old son who thinks that Eminem is "cool" and who wants to buy his latest CD. Do you let him? What do you tell him?

CHAPTER 9

THE INTERNET

Edward Donnerstein

The introduction of computer technology into children's lives parallels the introduction of previous waves of new media technology throughout the past century, and many lessons can be learned from the history of media research about the effects of computers on children.

—E. Wartella and N. Jennings (2000, p. 31)

One never knows whether one is interacting with a "real self" or with someone's alternative identity. . . . the distinction between fantasy and reality is truly blurred.

—K. Subrahmanyam, R. Kraut, P. Greenfield, and E. Gross (2000, p. 138)

It is estimated that the online pornography industry will reach $366 million by 2001.

—M. Griffiths (2000)

Figure 9.1

Throughout this book, we have discussed the impact that various media have on children's and adolescents' behavior, values, and beliefs. We have seen the enormous ability of the media to transcend the influence of parents and peers in providing information (sometimes correct, but often not) about the world in which we live. The interesting thing about the research and findings we have discussed is that in many ways, it has dealt with fairly traditional media forms such as television, film, radio, music, and print. But the media have changed. Newer technologies—in particular, the Internet and interactive video games—have created a new dimension for researchers to consider when they examine the effects of both problematic content (violence and sex) and educational content. Just like the potential effects of video games discussed in Chapter 4, the Internet is highly interactive, suggesting that the effects could be stronger than those for television or other traditional media (Paik, 2001). There are some researchers (Tarpley, 2001) who see the Internet as the most interactive of our current media (see Figure 9.1).

Unlike traditional media such as TV, radio, and recorded music, the Internet gives children and adolescents access to just about any form of content they can find. For the first time, youth will be able (with some work) to have the ability to view almost any form of sexual behavior, violent content, or advertisement. Unlike years past, this can be done in the privacy of a child's bedroom with little knowledge of their parents. A Time/CNN ("Children and the Internet," 1999) survey of teenagers reveals some interesting findings on the use of and concerns about the Internet among this age group:

- 82% use the Internet
- 75% believe that the Internet was very or/somewhat responsible for the school shooting in Colorado
- 44% have seen X-rated content
- 62% say parents know little or nothing about the Web sites they visit

When children and adolescents were asked to indicate what are the most influential sources of information for them in making decisions, the media in all their components exceeded parents and schools. Most interesting for our current discussion is that the Internet was considered more important than fathers (Kaiser Family Foundation, 1999a). As we have seen throughout this book, the media play a powerful role in the socialization of children and adolescents. There is every reason to expect that newer technologies such as the Internet and interactive games (see Chapter 4) will be a significant "player" in their developmental progress.

For decades, parents and others have been consistently concerned about the potentially "harmful" influences of exposure to sexual and violent media content. The major difference today compared to those concerns in the past is a technology about which children and adolescents are often more sophisticated and knowledgeable than their parents are. Too often we hear of computer-phobic adults who possess little knowledge of this expanding technology. Such resistance to the technology, combined with a limited knowledge base, will make solutions to potential problems (such as easy access to sexual images) even more difficult. Furthermore, when policy and advocacy groups attempt to inform parents of the Internet, it does little good to tell them to contact "www.hereforhelp.com" when they are often ignorant about these terms and World Wide Web usages.

Before discussing this "new" addition to our media world, it is important to point out a few differences in our knowledge base with regard to the Internet and more traditional media. First, the research on effects, both positive and negative, is limited. Not only is the technology new, but so is our research base. Second, content analysis is not only limited but, one may argue, also extremely difficult to conduct due to the problems of determining a proper sample. Finally, the solutions to deal with harmful effects are further complicated by the global nature of this medium. In many ways, this is both a new medium and a new research focus. We can expect in the next edition of this book a wealth of information on the positive and negative impact of exposure to the Internet on children and adolescents. In the interim, we will look at what we currently know and speculate from past knowledge and theory about what may be the outcomes.

● THE INTERNET: WHAT IS IT?

Very often we refer to the Internet more generally as the Net. This expanding technology is simply a vast group of computer networks linked around the world. It has a number of various components that are familiar (at least in terminology) to most of us, and these components have the ability to deliver an enormous array of information. These include the following:

1. E-mail for electronic communication. Many would agree that this is certainly one of the most popular forms of communication in today's society. Even this simple and everyday form of technology has changed in recent years, with the ability to send voice, video, and other forms of attachments around the world in an almost instantaneous manner.

2. Bulletin board systems for posting of information on almost any topic one could imagine.

3. Chat groups that can be used for real-time conversations. For many adolescents, it is the global equivalent of a "free" conference call. However, unlike the traditional conference call, you can choose your topic, person, and time in any manner you desire.

4. The World Wide Web, which combines visuals/sound/text together in a manner that allows linkages across many sites that are related to a particular topic. These topics obviously can be those related to sex, violence, drugs, or any other content for which we may have concerns.

The introduction of the World Wide Web (WWW) to the Internet increased its popularity and use. Most Web browsers (e.g., Internet Explorer, Netscape) now do more then just surf the Web. Today, these powerful integrated programs deal with e-mail, video streaming, newsgroups, and more.

Many people can now conduct many of their daily activities on the Web. Our banking, airline reservations, weather and news reports, sports scores with live transmissions, and almost anything we can think of can be found, accessed, interacted with, and saved within the World Wide Web.

The popularity and sophistication of the Internet are due to the increase in powerful search engines. A search engine, such as Excite, Lycos, Alta Vista, and Google, is a server that searches other servers in a systematic manner and indexes

Figure 9.2. Listing of Disney World Hotels Using the Search Engine Google

its findings in a database. There is basically nothing on the Web that cannot be found by one of these engines. Interested in going to Disney World? Need a hotel? Just go to a search engine such as Google and type in the words "Disney World Hotels" and, as shown in Figure 9.2, you will have in less than a second 142,000 Web sites you can access with more information than you could ever imagine. Take a virtual tour of your selection, book the room, and print out a map with explicit directions on how to get to your hotel from the airport. Of course, you also can book your travel (airline, car rental) with the same ease and speed.

It is important to note that the Web and other Internet components are extremely informative and useful. This is one technology that we want our children to have access to and be knowledgeable about. It is exceedingly educational and almost indispensable in today's society. Like any new technological advance, it will have some downsides, but these negatives should in no way be considered a barrier to continued advancement and teaching of children and adults about its vast usefulness and value. We strongly emphasize that in all respects, the Internet is a very powerful information and instruction technology that we must continue to develop. We want the reader to continue to keep this in mind because many of the things we will discuss in this chapter deal with a small part of the Net that we might consider potentially "harmful" to children. Though a small fraction of the materials available, such content must be discussed because, unlike with other technologies, it is much easier to search and find than in the past.

● IS THE NET BEING USED?

Much of our discussion on the Internet would be meaningless if its use by children and adolescents was nonexistent. This is not the case, however. In a report on media use in the home, a Kaiser Family Foundation (1999a) study found that 69% of children live in homes with computers, and 45% of these homes have some form of Internet access. Overall use of the Internet has increased 50% a year since 1990. Between 1999 and 2002, there was an expectation of a 155% increase in use among 5- to 12-year-olds and 100% among teens (Paik, 2001). There is every indication that 50% of children, even as young as age 5, will be "online" within the next few years.

The Internet is a technology that seems to differentiate, at least for now, the young from the old. In its most recent survey of online use, the Pew Foundation (2001) found that only 15% of people 65 and older are online, compared with 75% of those in the 18 to 29 age bracket. Children and adolescents in the 9- to 17-year-old range are also regular users according to surveys (Kaiser Family Foundation, 1999a), and youth actually prefer their computers to more traditional media such as television or phones. Of course, this should not come as a surprise to many of us because the computer is now both a television and a phone.

More recent analyses are beginning to indicate that children and adolescents are spending more of their time with computers and less time with television (Subrahmanyam, Kraut, Greenfield, & Gross, 2001). In addition, more computer time is spent in activities such as games, chat rooms, e-mail, and Web surfing than in school-related activities (Kaiser Family Foundation, 1999a). Communication with others (e-mail) is perhaps the major reason for Internet use (Subrahmanyam Kraut, et al., 2001). There is also the possibility of communication with strangers through use of Usenet newsgroups, listservs, and chat groups.

Will the Internet, with all its varying components, replace television as the media of choice? A recent study by the National Association of Broadcasters (NAB, 2000) indicates that a faster Internet connection will draw people more deeply into the Web—and away from their TV and radio. In the average American home (without a broadband Internet connection), individuals spend about a third of their "media time" with television, followed by radio at 28%. The Internet is only at 11%. But in homes with broadband access, such as a cable modem or DSL, people typically spend 21% of their media use online, close to the 24% of the time spent watching television and 21% listening to radio.

Is the television dead? No, not really. But as technology changes and high-speed connections become more popular (and less expensive), the computer and the Internet may replace other media as the main source of entertainment and information. Live video transmissions are now routine, and our ability to access full-length violent movies, video games, and anything else we desire in entertainment "on demand" is right around the corner.

CONCERNS ABOUT THE NET ●

We can certainly see that the Internet is increasing in popularity. One of the issues of concern, however, is that this is a medium in which youth are currently not only heavier users than their parents are but also are more sophisticated in its applications. It is also a medium over which parents often have little control, few rules for use, and minimal supervision. Nevertheless, about half of parents believe that being online is more positive then watching TV (Tarpley, 2001) (see Figure 9.3). Perhaps they are unaware (see Tarpley, 2001) of the following:

- Of the 1,000 most-visited sites, 10% are adult sex oriented.

- Forty-four percent of teens have seen an adult site.

- Twenty-five percent of teens have visited a site promoting hate groups.

- Twelve percent have found a site where they receive information on how to buy a gun.

- Many child-oriented sites have advertisements. The Federal Communications Commission (FCC) does not regulate the Net, and as we know from previous chapters, children are more susceptible to ads then adults are.

- Violent pornography has increased over the years in both newsgroups and Web sites, and access to violent pornography has become easier (Bjornebekk & Evjen, 2000).

Even if parents were aware of these data, so much of online activities of children and adolescents are done alone, in an anonymous context, and without (as we have already noted) parental supervision. The messages of concern on the Internet do not differ from those of traditional media: those involving sex, violence, sexual violence, and tobacco and alcohol advertisements. The effects from exposure we would expect to be at least the same, if not enhanced. The interactive nature of the Internet, which can lead to more arousal and more cognitive activity, would suggest that influences such as those found from media violence would be facilitated (see Huesman, 1998, and Chapter 3, this volume). More important, the easy access to materials, which should be extremely limited for children and adolescents, is now readily obtainable with the power of search engines and the

Figure 9.3
SOURCE: Reprinted with special permission of King Features Syndicate.

Internet. Perhaps our discussion of sex on the Internet will make this more apparent.

● SEX ON THE NET: A PRIMARY CONCERN

One of the most controversial Internet content categories is sexual material, which has raised concerns about child exploitation (see Figure 9.4). Such material ranges from photographs to the Net equivalent of "phone sex," sometimes with a live video connection. Sending of sexual information over e-mail or posting on bulletin boards by those targeting children has been a critical issue. Adult Web sites that feature "hard-core" sexual depictions are of equal concern. One estimate is that such sites are a half billion-dollar industry and that half of the spending on the Internet is in this area. Some suggest that it is the "king" of advertising and that it is one of the most frequent type of sites searched for by users (Griffiths, 2000). In their discussion of the potentially harmful effects of children's exposure to sexual media, Malamuth and Impett (2001) make note of the easy access via the Internet to sexually explicit materials by users ages 9 to 15. This is not to imply that children did not seek out and find sexual content before the Internet. Today, the process is

Figure 9.4
SOURCE: Copyright Steve Breen and Copley News Service. Used with permission.

easier, faster, more anonymous, and likely to bring to the computer screen anything a child wants.

Search engines, such as Google, allow the user to type in words and word combinations that ask the computer to search for almost any sexual content. If we take for a moment the curiosity of a 12-year-old and let his or her fingers (and mouse) do the walking, one can see how easy the process works. For example, if we use our search engine to type in the words "Sex Pictures," we see in Figure 9.5 that in less than 1 second, we are given a list of almost 2 million sites that contain these words and most likely the pictures that our 12-year-old is seeking. If the child then accesses one of these sites, as shown in Figure 9.6, it is not "officially blocked" to minors unless certain blocking software is implemented (though often not entirely effective). Most sexually explicit adult sites merely indicate that the site (a) contains sexually explicit pictures, (b) may be offensive to users, and (c) the user must be at least 18 years of age; if not, the user is supposed to exit the site immediately. Needless to say, a high percentage of sexually curious adolescents, and even children, will simply click their mouse and indicate they are of age and enter the adult site. Once within one of these sites, the user can link into other similar sites offering samples of pictures, text, and video of a "hard-core" sexual nature, as shown in Figures 9.7 and 9.8. The great sophistication of search engines also allows for the searching of web sites on (a) bestiality, (b) child pornography, (c) rape and bondage, and (d) teen sex.

Figure 9.5. Listing of Sex Picture Sites From Google

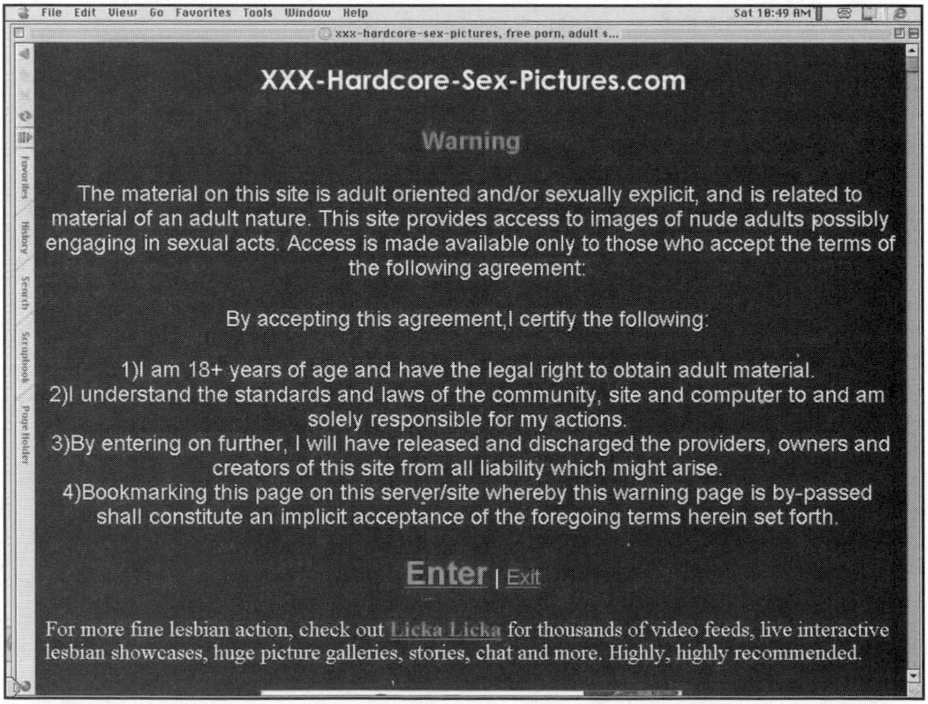

Figure 9.6. Warning Information Provided on a Typical Adult Internet Sex Site

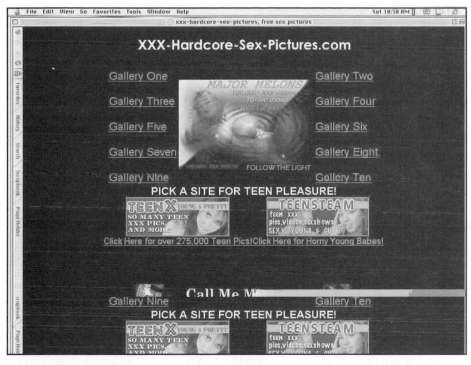

Figure 9.7. Entrance to an Adult Internet Sex Site

Figure 9.8. Pictures From the Adult Sex Site

Figure 9.9. The Site You Will Find When Requesting Whitehouse.com Rather Than Whitehouse.gov

Search engines exist to help, but the typical Internet user is not going to come in contact with inappropriate content without making a conscious decision to find these sites. However, in recent years, it has become known that certain adult sites have used address codes that are quite similar to popular Internet Web sites, often-times leading the user unknowingly into an area he or she did not wish to visit. For example, if children are looking for information about the White House and then type www.whitehouse.com instead of www.whitehouse.gov (not an unlikely mistake in our dot com world), they will find themselves linked to an adult site, as shown in Figure 9.9.

The speed and anonymity of Internet technology have led users to a variety of ways in which traditional sexual activities can now be supplemented by the Internet. Griffiths (2000) describes five major types of sex-related use of the Internet:

1. *The search for sexual educational materials.* Sites related to sex education and healthy sexual interactions are readily available.

2. *The buying or selling of sex-related goods.* This can be done in online sex shops in an atmosphere of almost total anonymity. As we noted earlier, the sex industry is one of the most popular types of sites visited by adults and frequented by adolescents. Even the buying of Viagra can be done online.

3. *Seeking out materials for entertainment or masturbatory purposes*. The individual can also digitally manipulate images in sophisticated programs. Virtual partners, including children, are now part of the interactive environment. Within a legal context, virtual child pornography will be difficult to manage given the fact that no "real" under-age child actually exists.

4. *Seeking out sexual partners for long-term or short-term relationships and encounters*. Everything from dating or matchmaking services to advertised prostitution are now available with the typing of a few words and the click of a mouse.

5. *Illegal seeking out of individuals for sexually related Internet crimes* (sexual harassment, cyberstalking, children).

There have been discussions recently (see Griffiths, 2000) of the possibility of some form of sexual addiction occurring with the proliferation and use of sexually related Internet sites. One argument is that the anonymity of the Internet could foster such addiction. However, the research does not demonstrate that such addiction occurs, and if it does it is a relatively small minority of users who are affected. There is no question, however, that this is one area that needs further study (Griffiths, 2000).

Unlike our knowledge of other media systems such as TV, we are only beginning to explore the usage, content, and effects of Internet access among children. A recent Kaiser Family Foundation report on sexual media content (Huston et al., 1998) called for the start of systematic research into these areas. We believe that this is essential given preliminary surveys on the use of and access to the Internet among children and adolescents and the availability of sexual content of such a diverse nature.

OTHER AREAS OF CONCERN ●

Concerns about children's and adolescents' use of the Internet is not limited to sexual content (see Donnerstein, 1998). Another perceived danger comes from information on satanism and religious proselytizing, as well as drugs and gambling. Religious cults, which only a few years ago would have had a limited audience, can now reach out to a worldwide following. Offshore gambling is now a major e-commerce business. We no longer need to go to Las Vegas to place a bet; offshore casinos do the same thing, as well as presenting online slots, craps, and poker. A credit card or a money order (something teenagers can purchase) allows access to any one of hundreds of offshore casinos.

Figure 9.10
SOURCE: Copyright Mike Luckovich and Creators Syndicate. Reprinted with permission.

Terrorism is another issue of concern. Some online archives provide instructions for making bombs or other weapons. The teenage school killer in Oregon, John Kinkel, described himself in his e-mail profile as someone who liked "watching violent cartoons on TV, sugared cereal, throwing rocks at cars," and his favorite occupation was "surfing the Web for information on how to build bombs."

The proliferation of hate speech and hate groups has also become easily accessible on the Web. Not only is the reach of White supremacist groups changing, but so are their targets. According to a report from the Southern Poverty Law Center (1999), Internet hate groups have risen more than 60% in recent years. Mark Potok of the center notes,

> The movement is interested not so much in developing street thugs who beat up people in bars, but college-bound teens who live in middle-class and upper-class homes. It has become the propaganda venue of choice. It allows Klansmen who a few years ago could reach only 100 people with a poorly produced pamphlet to reach an audience in the millions. (Southern Poverty Law Center, 1999)

Alcohol and tobacco advertisements and Web sites dedicated to smoking and drinking are another problem. Many of these sites use promotional techniques that are considered quite appealing to adolescents. In a recent report in this area, the Center for Media Education (1999) identified numerous sites dedicated to smoking and alcohol use that would be influential to teens, and found that these sites were not readily shielded by blocking software (a concern we will address in a later section). We have seen in previous chapters the strong influence of advertising on both children and adolescents. The enforcement of government regulations with respect to tobacco and alcohol has been of significant help with respect to more traditional media such as television. This has not been the case with respect to the Internet and, as we discuss later, is not likely be an effective tool to combat advertising that exists within a global context.

Children's privacy is another major issue. In a series of reports from the Center for Media Education (2001), there is growing concern that many Web sites, even those aimed directly at children (under age 13), are requesting personal information without asking for parental permission. In fact, less than 25% asked children for their parents' permission to disclose information such as e-mail addresses, phone numbers, home addresses, and information about their parents. According to the Annenberg Public Policy Center (2000), more than 50% of children are willing to give out information about their parents in exchange for a free gift offered on a Web site. The standard advertising techniques discussed in Chapter 2 seem to be just as appealing when children surf the Web. Recent governmental regulations have slowed this steady tide of invading children's privacy, but concerns still exist.

We should emphasize the Internet also has the ability to promote prosocial effects. According to Mares and Woodard (2001), it is a promising medium for three major reasons. First, it is not that expensive for a small nonprofit or educational group to reach a large and even global audience. No other medium has this ability at the relative cost of the Internet. Second, it can target a specific narrow audience. The ability of the Web to be selective and to gather information from users allows for the tailoring of specific Web pages to a target audience. Finally, it is interactive, allowing for changes to be made in the site. The major problem is that few children are using these prosocial sites, and they are still relatively uncommon on the Web.

SOLUTIONS TO INTERNET CONCERNS ●

In thinking about solutions to children's and adolescents' access to inappropriate Net content, there are three major approaches. The first is government regulation restricting the content. The second is technology, including blocking software and some form of rating system. Third, and we believe the most important, is media

literacy for both parents and their children as to the benefits and sometimes problems of the Internet. The issue of media literacy is discussed in more depth in the
next chapter.

Government Regulation

Within the United States, the First Amendment protects offensive speech from
censorship, including sexually explicit materials. In general, the U.S. courts have
struck down most content restrictions on books, magazines, and films. There are,
of course, exceptions such as "obscenity," child pornography, and certain types of
indecent material depending on the time, place, and manner of the presentation.
In 1996, Congress passed the Communcations Decency Act, a bill to deal specifically with Internet content regulation primarily in the area of pornography.

The bill took as its premise a number of questions that are to be considered with
regard to the issue of the protection of children. First, is access to Internet pornography easy for children? The answer is probably yes, if the individual has some
computer savvy. As we discussed earlier, sophisticated search engines make the
search rapid and extensive. Second, is access to pornography accidental? Except
for the typing errors, the answer is probably no. Finally, is access to this type of
material harmful? This is difficult to assess and depends on many factors, as discussed in previous chapters. Nevertheless, most of us would agree that we should
certainly monitor and protect children from these unwanted sites.

The Supreme Court of the United States ruled on the Communications Decency
Act in 1998 and, as expected, held it to be unconstitutional and an infringement on
freedom of speech. Likewise, other courts have noted that service providers, such
as America Online, could not be held liable for the sending of pornographic materials over the Internet. It is obvious that the courts are well aware that government
regulation in this area would be difficult or near impossible given not only the vast-
ness of materials available but also the global scope of the Internet.

Blocking Technology

Another solution has been the development of software that is designed to
block unwanted sites. This blocking software can block known adult sites, for
instance, or any site containing predetermined words such as *sex, gambling,* and
other unwanted content. A number of these types of software are available that
perform these and other functions.

But none of these blocking systems are completely effective. The Web changes
quite rapidly, and software designed for today may not be entirely appropriate
tomorrow. In one test of the effectiveness of blocking adult sites (Consumer Reports, 1999), it was found that one program was able to block out 18 of 22 selected
sites. Other programs were able to block about half the adult sites, and one of the

tested programs did not block any of the sites. Furthermore, those blocking e-mail or chat group communications were often defeated by either transposing letters or renaming the Web browser on the hard disk.

In a more recent test of these products by Consumer Reports (2001), there was some improvement in the ability of this type of software to block objectionable materials that contain sexually explicit content or violently graphic images or that promote drugs, tobacco, crime, or bigotry. Far more troubling, however, was the finding that a filter appeared to block legitimate sites based on moral or political value judgments. Given the filtering of certain word strings or known sites, extremely educational Web pages are also blocked. As the report rightfully concludes, filtering software is no substitute for parental supervision.

Media Literacy

The role of parents in working with their children and becoming familiar with this technology is critical. Children can be taught "critical viewing skills" in their schools so that they learn to better interpret what they encounter on the Web. The same techniques used to mitigate media violence or the appeals of advertisements can also be effective in this area. In addition, a large number of professional organizations concerned with the well-being of children and families have begun to take a more active role in reducing the impact of harmful Internet content (e.g., American Academy of Pediatrics, American Medical Association Alliances). Within this new arena of technology, we should take a lesson from our findings on media violence interventions. Research on intervention programs has indicated that we can reduce some of the impact of media violence by "empowering" parents in their roles as monitors of children's television viewing. These studies indicate that parents who view programs with their children and discuss the realities of violence, as well as alternatives to aggressive behaviors in conflict situations, can actually reduce the negative impact (increased aggressiveness) of media violence (i.e., Donnerstein, Slaby, & Eron, 1994). The same types of positive results could be obtained when parents begin to monitor, supervise, and participate in their children's Internet activities. Chapter 10 examines the possibilities of media literacy in more detail.

ON THE POSITIVE SIDE ●

As we noted at the start of this chapter, the Internet can be extremely beneficial as both an educational teacher and tool for positive development. Although we have alluded to the small fraction of Web sites that can create problems for children and adolescents, we cannot overlook the immense benefit of this technology. We do

Figure 9.11. MaMaMedia Site

not want to leave the reader with any hesitation about the positive aspects of this technology. The Internet is perhaps the greatest teaching tool we have ever encountered, and its impact on children and adolescents undoubtedly will be to enrich their lives in immeasurable ways. Therefore, it seems appropriate to end this chapter on a more positive note.

In a recent report on children and computer technology, the Packard Foundation (2000) notes the wide variety of positive effects that the Internet and computers can have on children. There are numerous Web sites that allow children and teens to explore the world and create art and literature. Many of these nonprofit sites are among the most popular sites accessed by this age group. Montgomery (2000) has examined a number of these sites and their potential for children's education.

There are Web sites that foster creativity. For instance, MaMaMedia (see Figure 9.11) allows children to create their own digital stories, make digital drawings that include music and animation, and learn word meanings. There are Web sites that focus on social issues. Yo! Youth Outlook (see Figure 9.12) has created a site that discusses current social issues that teens can relate to in their own lives. Sesame Workshop offers children an array of educational opportunities, including games and stories. Among the most popular sites for children are PBS Online, Discovery Online, Nickelodeon, and the child version of Yahoo, Yahooligans (see Figure 9.13).

Figure 9.12. Yo!Youth Outlook Site

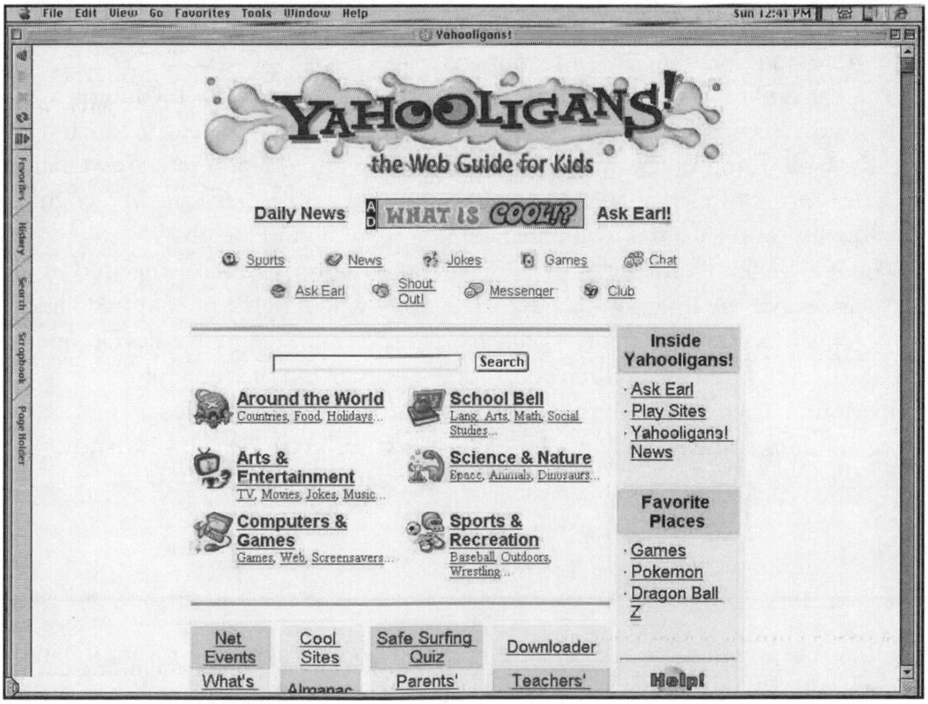

Figure 9.13. Yahooligans Site

The Internet can also be an effective learning tool that can facilitate academic achievement. Roschelle, Pea, Hoaddley, Gordin, and Means (2000) have noted that learning is most effective when four fundamental characteristics are present. The first is active engagement. There is no question that computer-mediated teaching is highly effective in this area, and the Internet allows students to be anything but passive. The constant interactive nature of the Internet is a highly efficient tool for positively engaging students in the learning process.

A second characteristic is that of learning through group participation. Although on one level, we may think of "surfing the Net" as an individual type of activity, many group-oriented activities are not only possible but highly engaging on the Internet. Many types of learning networks already developed have been shown to be effective teaching models in the classroom.

A third major characteristic is learning through frequent interaction and feedback. There should be no disagreement that computer-mediated learning is ideal for this form of instruction. The research in this area supports the position that children's and adolescents' use of Internet-based activities can increase motivation, a deeper understanding of concepts, and a stronger motivation to engage in difficult assignments.

Finally, the Internet provides an ability to learn through connections to real-world contexts. The vast array of Internet Web sites allows students the ability to explore almost any concept in interactive multimedia context. Equally important, as Roschelle et al. (2000) note, the Internet allows students the ability to have exposure to ideas and experiences that would have normally been inaccessible with more traditional modes of learning.

The Packard report (Packard Foundation, 2000) also finds that the Internet can be a positive component in children's lives by enabling them to keep in touch with friends, family, and others to form communities with common interests. Finally, with the advent of media literacy, children should be able to learn and recognize high-quality Web sites that will enhance their leaning and creativity.

There is general agreement that considerably more research is needed in all these areas, but the Internet is a new technology with a rich array of possibilities. Its potential for positive impacts on learning, social and cognitive development, and the overall future of children's and adolescents' lives is just emerging. We need to explore and continue our examination of all these possibilities as more and more children come online and the technology itself changes and expands.

● CONCLUSION

The Internet is without question an innovative and exciting tool for information and education. It is a technology that will become more accessible worldwide over the years and will only improve in its capacity to stimulate and enrich our lives. We need to understand its potential for increasing our children's educational opportunities while recognizing its limitations and dangers. These dangers, however, are not going to be easily remedied through traditional solutions such as governmental regulation. The Internet is a technology that necessitates parental involvement and leadership. With such involvement, it is very likely that both children and parents will experience the Internet as a new and enriching environment in which to interact.

Exercises

1. The Internet can be used for an array of activities from instructional to entertaining. Consider an activity you normally do in which you have not yet used the Internet, such as taking a trip or buying tickets to a concert. Try doing the same activity with the help of the Internet. Was the process faster? Did you obtain more useful information? Was the Internet a better source for this activity than your normal procedure?

2. If you have blocking software or a service provider (AOL) that allows you to restrict particular content, try the following: Select a topic that might be controversial such as drugs or gambling. Perform a search on this topic with and without the blocking activated. Is there a significant difference in the quantity and quality of the information you find?

3. One suggestion for restricting children's access to inappropriate material on the Internet is a rating system similar to that applied to TV content. Could a system of this type be effective with the Internet? Given the global nature of the Internet, would it be possible to define a universal rating system for violence or sex? What might be an appropriate rating system?

4. We indicated in this chapter that the Internet should be used to facilitate learning in the classroom. Design a curriculum for high school students that relies entirely on the Internet. How would it differ from traditional modes of instruction? How might you evaluate its effectiveness?

5. Figures 9.11 through 9.13 illustrate examples of Web sites that are of educational value for children. What other sites can you find? Why would you consider the sites you find to be particularly beneficial for children?

CHAPTER **10**

MEDIA LITERACY
What? Why? How?

Bob McCannon

The most fascinating thing about dusk is the lack of demarcation. It is one long smooth transition. By contrast, life, especially TV life, seems constantly to insist on more lines, more borders, TV expects you to shift entirely each half hour . . . demanding laughter, fear or sadness . . . . We complain incessantly about the "fast pace of modern life," and say that we have "no time." But we have lots of time, or every study wouldn't show that we watch three or four or five hours of television a day. It's that time the way it really works has come to bore us. Or at least make us nervous, the way that silence does, and so we need to shut it out. We fill time, instead of letting it fill us.

—Bill McKibben (1992, p. 72)

If information is the coin of the realm, only the media literate will share in the riches.

—Dierdre Downs (1994)

Generally defined as the ability to analyze, access, and produce media, media literacy education holds great promise for individuals to lead more examined and rewarding lives. (Many other definitions of media literacy exist. One of the most complete and interesting comes from Art Silverblatt; it is included in Appendix C at the end of this book.) Although a relatively new and sprawling field, noteworthy media education exists in about a dozen countries. Australia and England have highly developed and complex standards and programs, and Ontario, Canada, made media literacy mandatory in 1987. Although, in one form or another, media education is a desired standard in most states of the United States (Silverblatt, 2001), it is taught in varying intensities, with limited efforts and, in general, minimal success. Even where it is a strongly mandated educational standard, in Australia, England, Ontario, and states such as New Mexico, the decentralized nature of school systems and reform movements creates uneven emphases. Thus, media literacy is young, research is incomplete, and agreement is sporadic. Nonetheless, the movement is flourishing.

Proponents believe that although people enjoy media and interact with media in complex ways and, sometimes, discuss media, most of them could benefit greatly from a formal study. And even though media education has always been important, the modern communications revolution and the consolidation of global media monopolies make media literacy an essential skill for families and citizens.

Media literacy holds out a promise for understanding, empowerment, health, and success for children, adults, and communities. It also creates the possibility that more citizens could play active roles in civic affairs, enhancing democracy. Like anything else, media literacy can be done poorly and achieve negligible or negative results, but when taught effectively, it can move people from cynicism to skepticism and from passivity to power.

There is a spectrum of media literacy "experts" and a much wider and more diverse spectrum of media experts. One finds the latter in media education, communications, film study, medicine, psychology, and many other disciplines, even "media ecology" (Neil Postman's graduate department at New York University). Some of these experts believe their methods and their opinions are the only paths to success, branding others with labels such as "protectionists," "apologists," or even, Luddites. Some emphasize media production and media appreciation. Others emphasize media criticism. Some emphasize media production. A few media literacy experts earn money working for media corporations, writing sponsored curricula and holding media-sponsored events. At the other end of the financial spectrum, some make it a point to take no money from "Big Media." Others take media money but disclose these earnings. Credibility has become a media literacy "expert" issue.

Some media educators believe that media literacy should be value neutral. Others emphasize it as a focus for media advocacy and social justice, and/or a stimulant for cultural change. Debates rage within the field, and, not surprisingly, most of the participants use hyperbole, ad hominem, and other techniques of persuasion as only students of such can, making for an interesting field of study.

Most practitioners of media education emphasize a number of similar goals. Media education should enrich lives, leading students to a more complex understanding of media compositions, effects, forms, and aesthetics. Students learn how to evaluate, influence, and produce their media culture. It is hoped that this process leads to deeper appreciation of some media and a devaluation of others. It is equally hoped that it leads students to become better parents and more effective citizens.

Much criticism, research, and curriculum development precede this book, and this chapter cannot mention all the important media education pioneers, but initiates could do worse than to visit the works of the following group, which represents a full spectrum of media criticism and pedagogy: Neil Postman, Len Masterman, Robert McChesney, Elizabeth Thoman, Mark Crispin Miller, Art Silverblatt, Barry Duncan, Roderick Hart, John Pungente, Naomi Klein, Kathleen Tyner, Gerry Mander, David Considine, Bill McKibben, Jerome and Dorothy Singer, Peter DeBenedittis, Sut Jhally, David Buckingham, George Gerbner, Rénee Hobbs, Noam Chomsky, and Robyn Quin.

This chapter hopes to give the reader a taste of the general rationales, skills, and strategies used in media literacy as experienced and practiced by the New Mexico Media Literacy Project (NMMLP), a leader in the United States. The NMMLP model is highly inclusive and mildly protectionist. It emphasizes a technological process within an active, dialogue-based classroom that stimulates critical thinking, personal examination and growth, media production, personal activism, and social advocacy. In a phrase, students gain freedom as they grow in their ability to analyze, access, and produce media.

● McLUHAN'S GLOBAL VILLAGE: WHAT HAPPENED?

When congressional leaders passed the Communications Act of 1934, they expected television to become the university of the airwaves, ushering in a period of universal education and art, imbuing democracy with pride and participation. Marshall McLuhan suggested that the coming electronic media revolution would provide children and parents with a global village of increasingly rich media choices, an era that would amplify dignity, heighten freedom, and supplement education.

Decades later, the jury is still out, but a short-term evaluation would hazard a contrary evaluation. Congress mistakenly assumed that television would be noncommercial, and McLuhan did not take into account that globalization would place an ever larger premium on sex and violence or what the industry calls "romance" and "action." Hardly anyone foresaw that today's global utopia would involve massive corporate targeting of children.

Although many children profit from the small amount of excellent media fare that is available, it is safe to say that too few kids are living in McLuhan's utopia. Bill McKibben (1992), in his seminal *The Age of Missing Information,* suggests that the global village "is, at most, a global convenience store" (p. 54). Most of today's children choose from a media menu of adult movies in which characters increasingly smoke and drink, dark cartoons, "extreme" sports, endless sitcoms, bizarre "reality" programming, and the increasing violence, coarseness, and sexual distortions of Jerry Springer, the World Wide Wrestling Federation, MTV, the video game industry, Hollywood, and, of course, the Internet. This menu is long on chauvinism, impulsiveness, and the sale of addictions but short on education.

McKibben (1992) notes that instead of a village of enriching media choices, today's youth grow up in a very simple world,

> all of which can be understood by nineteen-year-olds and ninety-year-olds; all of which can be understood in a matter of seconds by someone who switched them on halfway through . . . . And the problem is not that it exists—the problem is that it supplants. Its simplicity makes complexity hard to fathom. (p. 52)

Many children live in a culture where complexity has been reduced to a sports metaphor, a world of winners and losers, black and white, where decisions are made with little thought for nuance, complexity, or reflection. This simplistic fantasy evinces a materialism that is presented as the answer to every human complexity. That the commercially driven culture bombards young children with increasingly powerful simplicity is beyond question. That many parents worry about their children's media "diet" is also evident. That too few take decisive action to prepare their young for a mediacentric world seems understandable, yet consequential (see Figure 10.1).

Such inattention to hypercommercialism is clearly shown by the way U.S. citizens handle their debts. The average child sees thousands of advertisements for credit cards, many of which feature parents using credit cards to buy things for their young. Irrespective of credit card company claims that their ads target adults, and keeping in mind that television advertising is probably the most powerful communication that modern technology can create, consider what might be the effect of the following ad.

A long-running (hence successful) Visa ad begins with an attractive little girl, about 8 years old, walking with an elephant that is on a leash. High production values characterize scenes showing delightful close-ups of the girl as she plays with the elephant. It sprays water on her with its trunk and, at her command, stands up on its hind legs. It pours her a cup of tea with its trunk. She climbs on it, plays in the park with it, and together they watch other elephants on TV (see Figure 10.2).

Figure 10.1
SOURCE: Copyright Steve Breen and Copley News Service. Used with permission.

Figure 10.2

They stand on their heads together, communicate with each other, and obviously love one another. When the little girl goes to school, the elephant is sad and follows the school bus, pulling the fence to which it was tied. To an intimate piano score that slowly builds to a climax, the voiceover says the following:

Young girl's voice: I wish I had an elephant, who would always play with me . . . would always be my friend . . . who'd sit and share some tea with me. "How are you today, Mrs. Mulloy?" An elephant, an elephant . . . an elephant and me. "Bye, bye." But wishes are like elephants, they're bigger than can be (here the elephant dissolves, disappearing; the little girl is sad.)

Visa announcer (powerful, rich, all-knowing, echo-laden, male voice): OK, maybe you can't give her everything her heart desires (father looks at her worriedly), but with the humongous purchase power of the new Visa Platinum card (girl and dad at counter with card, purchasing), maybe you can (the girl has the elephant back). . . . And besides, you'll never know what she will want next. (Little girl is appears, walking a zebra—a close-up of her face follows with her giving a cute shrug.) Visa Platinum, it's everywhere you want to be (the ad can be viewed at www.nmmlp.org).

The *manifest text* of the ad (the superficial intended message) targets the fathers of the world, many of whom are single and/or feeling varying degrees of guilt about how little time they spend with their daughters. The main objective of the ad, however, probably is its *latent subtext* (the less obvious message). It targets little girls. Of course, the brilliance and uniqueness of this ad lie in its success in targeting both groups while the former seldom consider that it targets the latter. That keeps adults unaware of the true target, but if the ad's main target was fathers, the dad would have played a larger role, and, perhaps, his voice would have been included.

Visa, like the rest of Madison Avenue, knows that to create brand loyalty, they must "make friends" with consumers when they are young. R. J. Reynolds demonstrated this with Joe Camel, which became as well known to 6-year-olds as Mickey Mouse, boosting teen use of their cigarettes to record highs. How common is such targeting?

Consider conservative columnist George Will (2001). Will speaks out against cradle-to-grave advertising and commercialism in schools, rightly noting the amoral zeal of corporations that target ever younger children:

Children, according to one ebullient marketer, are "born to be consumers," they are "consumer cadets" in whom "the consumer embryo begins to develop in the first year of existence." Excited by evidence that children as young as 12 months are capable of "brand associations," and guided by the principle of KGOY (kids getting older younger), marketers study "marketing practices that drive loyalty in the preschool market" and "the desires of toddler-age consumers." (p. A-18)

Thousands of Visa, Mastercard, and American Express ads condition people from the earliest age to a fantasy-based reality. The average family now owes $7,000 on a total of 10 credit cards, at an average interest rate of 18.9% (Association of Independent Consumer Credit Counseling Agencies [www.aicca.org]), which is up from 18% just 4 years ago. Many of these families could get lower interest rates by simply walking to their local bank. Even more ominous is the increase in advertising for "payday" loans and automobile "title" loans, which charge anywhere from 200% to 500% for their loans! Debt is a major factor in creating the advertising fantasy culture.

More important, the Visa example shows the interaction of media messages within the culture through the conditioning of children and teens in a way that influences them toward impulse buying and compulsive consumption. Compulsive behavior is related to habituation. Habituation is related to addictive behavior, and addiction seems to be related to brand loyalty.

Children increasingly rely on heavily advertised addictive substances. Indeed, media emphasizing impulsiveness, compulsivity, and habituation dominate youth culture. Gambling and debt plague young adults. Youth depression, obesity, poor nutrition, and eating disorders seem directly related to the media culture (Kubey & Csikszentmihalyi, 1990). "Apprehension and cynicism can replace healthier habits of mind such as curiosity and skepticism" (Hart, 1994, p. 21). Anxiety seems to derive from the intensification of violence in youth culture. There is a strong "causal inference" that media are in some part causing aggression (Centerwall, 1992; Comstock, 1991a; University, 1996). As we have seen in other chapters, media can encourage exploitation of the young and, of course, the elderly, women, and minorities as well (Huston et al., 1992).

Many important factors cause violence and youth problems, and the degree to which media are a cause is controversial. However, one thing is certain. The percentage of children who are defined as being "at risk" continues to grow and now includes nearly half of our young people (Carnegie Council on Adolescent Development, 1995), and media are a preventable cause.

At this point, some readers might be tempted to ask, "Isn't this mere media bashing? Isn't it anti-capitalist? Isn't it protectionist?" The answers to those questions define NMMLP's approach to media literacy. Some media need to be criticized. If that is bashing, so be it. The term *bashing* is often used but seldom defined. If not defined, the term is meaningless.

Capitalism supposedly depends on free enterprise, which involves competition and free choice. If Visa can condition people through its monopoly of the culture's media, such information needs to be brought to the culture (i.e., students and consumers). To do so is an attempt to protect, just like all education. The objectives of most media literacy programs are, in one form or another, somewhat protectionist. Used in this manner, the term *protectionist* does *not* mean didactic, teacher centered, or tyrannical. NMMLP believes in listening to students and honoring their opinions as an essential part of the media literacy process.

Let us consider another media example. Two boys drive a truck to the Philip Morris factory. They are looking for the Marlboro Man. The guard tells them that he died. They are disappointed and ask, "Is his horse still alive?" The guard says, "No." They inquire about directions to his grave and the location of his equipment, all to no avail. The guard makes them drive on, and as they drive off, one is heard saying to the other, "We came all the way to Marlboro country and there is no Marlboro Man." The other responds with, "Yeah, I wonder what killed him."

This advertisement is entertaining, wonderful, and unique. It stands in stark contrast to the tobacco companies' media monopoly. It uses the advertising industry's own weapons to present another point of view that some would say is the truth. It has humor, technology, and rebellion. If there were enough such ads, they would represent competition for Big Tobacco's advertising billions, but, of course, there are very few. In the television credit card market, there is no opposing view. Such corporate monopolies are common on television—for example, soft drinks, fast food, sugar, gambling, and violence.

Compounding the situation is democracy's decreasing functionality (Hart, 1994). In a healthy republic, useful information motivates active citizens and, parenthetically, their representatives. The political process in the United States is increasingly typified by a news media in which "mainstream journalism has fallen into the habit of portraying public life as a race to the bottom—in which one group of conniving, insincere politicians ceaselessly tries to outmaneuver another" (Fallows, 1996, p. 7). One only needs to look at voter participation statistics to see the result of media's effect on the polity. Ever more sensational news and negative campaign ads reinforce cynicism, and young adults drop out of the process.

Media literacy strives to emphasize active, mediacentric strategies for dealing with a media culture that seems to be growing more inimical to kids and democracy. When students learn about the effect and nature of political ads, they take an interest in their school and community issues. When they make their own media campaigns, their optimism can be reborn.

Media literacy can reveal advertising's fantasy world to students and adults as nothing else can. In New Mexico, hundreds of thousands of students are deconstructing the addictive media world of debt, sugar, drugs, gambling, and wasteful materialism. They seek to understand the narrow world of mainstream corporate media. They are becoming less likely to spend their adult lives in service to Visa, the casinos, Coke, McDonald's, and Budweiser.

Then, these students tell their own stories. And, ironically, these children, when they become parents, are more likely to talk, read, and play with their children.

● STEP ONE: BECOME INFORMED

Learning about problems does not contribute to cynicism. It engenders skepticism. Cynicism immobilizes; skepticism activates. Cynicism promotes escape; skepticism promotes purposeful activity. Skepticism is a tool that conquers propaganda and spin. Cynicism is defeatist. Skepticism is liberating. As one student put it, "*Teen* magazine wants us to feel like we suck, so they can sell us more clothes, diets, hair products and cosmetics" (McCannon, 1996).

Students, parents, and policymakers need to learn the results of media effects research. Information is power; it motivates students, parents, educators, and the health community to promote wiser media usage. It is an integral part of media literacy.

The Carnegie Council of Adolescent Development's (1995) study, *Great Transitions: Preparing Adolescents for a New Century,* 9 years in the making and one of the most thorough studies of America's youth, concludes that media's "effects have been established during decades of research" (Carnegie, 1995, p. 54). This is crucial knowledge because today's media environment is heavily censored.

Censorship here refers to the manner in which our media are produced, the recent revolution that now finds a handful of corporations controlling most entertainment and news. The mainstream electronic news media seldom report complex stories (which they interpret as boring). They tend to report sensational stories that produce good ratings. And they seldom report information that is critical of themselves in any persuasive or systematic fashion. O. J. Simpson, Lady Diana, and Elián Gonzalez get the press, but most parents are unconvinced that there is a substantial body of research showing that television's "passive consumption leads to attention deficits, nonreflective thinking, irrational decision making, and confusion between external reality and packaged representations" (Carnegie Council on Adolescent Development, 1995, p. 116).

Parents need to know that fantasy (media) violence contributes to reality violence (Singer, Zuckerman, & Singer, 1980). More ominous are the studies that have shown that children who frequently view violent media are desensitized to the effects of violence and the suffering of victims while these children develop a "mean world syndrome in which they feel people cannot be trusted, and the world is inordinately scary" (Torney-Purta, 1990, p. 457). Unfortunately, few parents hear about such research. George Gerbner spent 27 years as dean of the Annenberg School of Communication researching these theories, yet he is rarely seen on mainstream television.

Research documenting the desensitization of children surprises most parents. Why? Because Dan Rather and Peter Jennings find it inconvenient to repeat such findings. How many parents know there are approximately hundreds of scholarly studies connecting watching violence to aggressive behavior. About 20 studies dispute that correlation, most of which were paid for by the television industry. What else should parents know? Film critic and media analyst Michael Medved has coined the phrase "a generation of despair" referring to the cynicism of today's youth. He documents the number of depressing movie themes and the lack of movie heroes in *Hollywood vs. America: Popular Culture and the War on Traditional Values* (Medved, 1992). Other negative outcomes of adolescent media consumption include obesity, malnutrition, obsession with thinness, inability to bond with peers, and lowered academic achievement (Carnegie Council on Adolescent Development, 1995, p. 116).

This is important information, but in an era when global entertainment conglomerates own and censor the news, you will seldom find this information presented on their networks. Murders, hurricanes, and celebrities are reported in intimate detail, but one has to look hard for media effects research. This is a wonderful opportunity for media literacy advocates and activists. They are in high demand to talk to students, run in-services, and facilitate workshops. More and more conferences are looking for keynotes that say what is seldom heard in the mainstream news. It is a fresh, new perspective that resonates with audiences. Students are anxious to help solve society's problems; they sense that they are not being told the whole story. It is liberating for them to learn the methods and issues of media literacy.

STEP TWO: A MEDIA LITERATE ADVOCATE ●

A *media literate advocate* is someone who has learned the skills of media literacy, a person who negotiates meaning with media perceptively, actively, and systematically (see Appendix A at the end of this book for a partial list of skills). A *media literate advocate* accepts learning the issues of media literacy as a lifelong task, intimately connected to the cultural, historical, political, and social contexts of her or his time. Dozens of issues are media related, including addictions and health, racism, sexism, violence, democracy, more enjoyable and valuable media, media monopolies, body image, self-esteem, corporate power, employment, prices, wages, quality of life, stereotyping, education, neighborhood projects, and much more. *Media literate advocates* choose an activist role, advocating for change in the social, political, artistic, or philosophical realm of their choice. Such advocates accept the assumption that media education and media advocacy should be a major component of life, education, child rearing, personal satisfaction, financial independence, and sustainable communities. *Media literate advocates* study and teach media literacy but also are part of the solution to media-accentuated problems.

Information age citizens need media literacy skills and content to understand the methods, variety, and size of the Big Media system that is competing for our attention, controlling our democracy, and shaping our cultural perceptions of reality. In just the past 15 years, the corporate world has learned the invaluable importance of large public relations (PR) campaigns. (Public relations firms' size, influence, and activities have undergone massive increases in just the past 15 years. This is problematic, because public relations are by definition designed to influence society by working in the background, unnoticed, stealthily. More people now work in PR than in advertising [Stauber & Rampton, 1995].) Corporations are spending billions of dollars on PR to control the content of the news and information environment (Stauber & Rampton, 1995). During that same 15 years global media have been consolidated; just a few organizations control most of our information. This power allows them to shape lifestyles, brands, and politics. Such power, exceeding by a factor of 10 that of global media just a decade ago, is one of the paramount crises of our time, and it creates a central contradiction for society—"the contradiction between a highly concentrated, advertising saturated, corporate media system and the communication requirements of a democratic society" (McChesney, 1999, p. ix). For students and citizens to understand the extent and power of such influence is not easy when immersed in an advertising culture, especially when schools increasingly adopt corporate curricula that present students with the greatness of their brands.

Should one trust an environmental curriculum from Shell Oil? It recommends the widespread use of internal combustion engines. Exxon's school curriculum praises itself for cleaning up the Alaskan oil spill but avoids discussion of the spill itself. A *Consumer Reports* study found that 80% of sponsored educational materials (SEMs) are based on incomplete information or are biased toward the corporation. Wal-Mart, Nike, and many other corporations make curricular materials. None mention sweatshops or abuse of child labor. Students express surprise at the details of child labor abuses from both the 19th century and today because this information is not readily available in their culture. Seldom have they considered the possibility that Chinese girls work in terrible conditions for 90 hours per week at 30 cents an hour with no overtime pay.

Philip Morris sponsors 4-H clubs and, amazingly enough, prevention curricula. The word is out in corporate boardrooms. PR can furnish control, and part of that strategy is to target younger citizens. The schools' captive audiences are needed to create politically complacent and economically brand-loyal consumers.

Media literacy turns the monopolistic power of media on its head. For example, most people have seen the Philip Morris feel-good "people" advertising campaign.

Philip Morris employees seem to be everywhere (even Kosovo), saving poor African American boys, pregnant girls, flood victims, battered women and children, and so on. However, the power of Philip Morris's campaign can be transformed in a moment when one analyzes these ads, particularly with a deconstruction of a Virginia Slims ad showing an African American woman saying, "Never let the goody-two-shoes get you down, find your voice, smoke Virginia Slims" (nmmlp.org). Philip Morris's Marlboro man looks powerful on his horse, until the words, "Bob, I have emphysema" appear across them. Thus, the very extent of the media monopolies' power can work for media literacy.

Media literate advocates are most concerned for our young, those least able to fend for themselves in a "hypermediated" culture—one that is distinguished by the intensity of exposure to the newer mass media. Some authors believe that the United States is the only *hypermedia* culture. Media education, therefore, should begin at home. It is the responsibility of health professionals and parents to understand the nature and power of media and, also, its ability to change culture. Carnegie suggests that the world of the young

> cannot be understood without considering the profound influence of the mass media, especially television, but also movies and popular music . . . shaping young people's attitudes and values about acceptable behavior, their perceptions of what kind of society they live in, their place in society, and their expectations of the future. (Carnegie Council on Adolescent Development, 1995, p. 115)

Thus, understanding the *pace* of change is a key to this effort. Only in the past decade has the public relations industry come of age, affecting the quality of children's culture, agriculture, the environment, and our political systems. Ten years ago, soft money contributions to political parties were negligible. In the presidential election of 2000, corporations gave almost a billion dollars in soft money to U.S. political parties; most was spent on television advertising. *This singular fact affects all aspects of our media system and, ultimately, all parents, citizens, and young people.*

Today, students of all backgrounds are fascinated by the media issues of censorship and media monopoly.

MEDIA LITERACY: UNDERSTANDING THE ●
TRADE-OFFS, THE OPPORTUNITY COSTS

Media literate advocates support the idea that all media, especially television, movies, video games, and the Internet, have important *strengths and weaknesses.* Families need to understand these trade-offs. Trade-offs can be as simple as a Dr.

Pepper commercial that has a humorous, entertaining, and humane story of sportsmanship embedded in its addictive and malnutritive message. If children are to have a healthy media "diet," families should discuss such trade-offs on a regular basis. As media choices multiply, and electronic mass media increasingly blur the differences between education and entertainment, families must regulate the media diet of young children. In this manner, media literacy becomes a form of family activism that teaches children the difference between human and inhuman, between reality and fantasy.

As Carl Sagan (1995) noted shortly before his death, modern technology is leading our citizens to accept the paranormal as the normal. The Carnegie Council on Adolescent Development (1995) notes that a combination of influences is

> merging signals from telephone, television, high-capacity storage media . . . and multimedia computers into a single medium capable of receiving enormous amounts of information. *As the potential—both positive and negative—unfolds,* one thing is clear: cyberspace has the potential to transform education, health care, and many of the vital aspects of life, including the experience of growing up. (p. 115, emphasis added)

Big Media (the handful of huge transnational media conglomerates that in the past decade have come to monopolize media) are increasingly able to either expand or limit the horizons of children and adults.

Everyone needs to consider the benefits and drawbacks to the new media system. Media literacy can encourage such a discussion. Why does Disney buy ABC? Does it produce better movies or merely more powerful marketing of mediocre movies? Does Viacom's ownership of CBS, VH1, and MTV mean more or less variety for young music fans? When a single company can own thousands of newspapers and radio stations, hundreds of TV stations, dozens of networks, magazines and book publishers, plus movie studios, cable systems, and satellites, does it add up to more freedom of choice or less? More political power or less? A better life, job, or environment? More rights or less? Are these merged, huge corporations really capitalism? Do they merge to promote risk taking and free enterprise, or are they monopolies, working in concert with their big corporate advertisers for dictatorial control of world markets and culture and politics?

Thus, children need media literacy's skills, content, and goals to better understand the trade-offs involved in consuming any medium. Learning trade-offs and guiding a child's media education are formidable tasks, tasks that require some commitment. After all, there is so much to learn, and television and video games are such convenient and entertaining baby-sitters. Parents and health professionals need to walk the walk, not only because they are role models but also because changing the media habits of an entire culture is worthwhile precisely *because* of the enormity of the problem.

AN OPPORTUNITY FOR ACTIVISTS ●

Solutions to global media monopoly are becoming more accessible. Creation of media, a crucial part of media literacy, is increasingly feasible as powerful desktop technologies come of age. They offer media literacy professionals an avenue for the creation of "alternative" media, media that are not controlled by the global juggernauts. Media that stimulate the creativity of youth can now be created, inspiring children, exposing more rewarding lifestyles, and modeling positive cultural expectations.

Alternatives to mainstream media are increasingly having a beneficial effect on our culture. They are a major reason for the current interest in media literacy. Indeed, they are a reason for the existence of the book you are holding. Media educators should teach the value of NPR, *Frontline, The National Review, The Nation, The Washington Times, Mother Jones,* Tom Paine.com, PR Watch.org, Adbusters.org, Adcritic.com, and the growing plethora of alternatives.

In this struggle, we can learn from our neighbors; many nations are far ahead of the United States in media education. Other countries are trying to create more rational media cultures. "Most other developed nations use television more prudently than the United States, particularly with regard to the welfare of their children" (Huston et al., 1992, p. 5). Australia, parts of England, Germany, Brazil, New Zealand, and Canada have been teaching media literacy for several decades. They have discovered the value of identifying examples of media use and exploring the contexts, commerce, and meanings of media. They study media issues with children and provide positive uses of media technology for students to tell their stories. In the United States, many worthwhile examples are emerging.

In the "worst" parts of Chicago, inner-city youth, calling themselves *Video Machete,* document the extent of police brutality, capturing incidents and interviewing survivors and relatives. At-risk youth in Santa Fe's Academy of Communication Arts and Technology create full-fledged PR campaigns to pass legislation, document environmental threats, and obtain furniture for orphanages. Taos students put media awareness messages into plays that they perform for students in juvenile detention centers. High school students across the country create complete educational curriculum packages and publicity campaigns with an anti-smoking theme for their elementary clusters.

FAMILY MEDIA LITERACY: A MEDIA DIET—SOME GUIDELINES ●

The home must be the heart of media-literate advocacy. Consuming media is like consuming food, both good and bad. Nothing is simple; few foods are completely

Figure 10.3
SOURCE: Copyright John Trever, *Albuquerque Journal*. Reprinted with permission.

good or bad. Likewise, consuming any piece of media is usually good *and* bad. Nonetheless, as we have seen, media, as consumed by most children today, are having significant deleterious effects, and parents are far more aware of their children's nutritional needs than their media requirements. Few parents let children create their own candy or alcohol diets, but many parents exert little control over their children's media consumption. The following are guidelines that can protect children but, more important, teach valuable skills, as well as add to the bonds between parents and children. These guidelines should be passed on to young parents and teachers. Presentations or handouts at the PTA, on parents' night, in church, or at teacher-parent meetings are valuable and appreciated by most parents.

Parents should play and read with children as much as possible. Children's brains and attitudes develop best in active engagement, so involve them in activities that require decision making and creativity. Although some studies indicate that watching screens is not necessarily a simple cognitive task, watching some types of content can habituate the child and can produce shorter attention spans. Encourage many kinds of activity, including reading, a valuable form of cognition that lengthens attention spans.

One of the young brain's *best developmental activities is talking* with caring adults, so maximize story creating, storytelling, questioning, and explaining within the family. Develop games such as "if," "make believe," or "guessing." Create regular activities such as describing daily activities during conversations at mealtime. Mealtimes and other times during the day should be regular and expected *TV-free zones* that the whole family agrees on.

Next, *limit consumption of screens,* such as TV, movies, and video games, especially those that are violent, hyperstimulating, stereotypical, or mindlessly repetitive. These limit the potential of children and influence them toward at-risk behaviors. Avoid first-shooter video games that some think condition aggressive impulses and many think are desensitizing. Several studies have shown that limiting TV correlates with decreased aggressiveness and increased physical fitness. Minimize video games. Remember, just because a child can do the same task faster in a video game does not mean the child has gained any new skill, and it may mean the child has simply become more habituated to the game (and the violence).

Allow no television until the child is age 2. The American Academy of Pediatrics, after a great deal of study, recommended this policy in 1999. First, the tendency to use TV to pacify the child is strong. Second, consider brain development and relationships. Much nurturing and bonding should go on during this part of a child's life. Even more ominous, some research indicates that "watchers" develop less mass in critical parts of the brain than "doers" (DeGaetano & Bander, 1996). Think about the difference in brain stimulation between a child who goes swimming or a child who watches another child go swimming on TV. It is highly beneficial to encourage active play for young children (Healy, 1991).

After age 2, do not *proscribe* media but rather *provide a lifestyle* that engages children in a variety of beneficial activities. Merely banning screens can create the forbidden fruit syndrome. Literally hundreds of family activities are healthier than having everyone in their own room watching their own TV screen. Activity lists are available from many publishers, TV Free America, and nmmlp.org.

Plan carefully, and discuss media choices with your children. Point out that media are carefully created products with good and bad consequences. Help children to understand that all media sell things. Such an investigation creates valuable skills that can be applied to most of life's decisions. There are many beneficial children's stories in all media. Some organizations, such as the Coalition for Quality Children's Television, have qualified people to "rate" children's books, movies, videos, games, and Web sites. It is ironic that in the United States, we let the movie industry "rate" movies and the TV industry rate TV programs. It is not this way in some other countries.

Analyze all communication. Applying skills or "tools" of analysis stimulates abstract critical thinking and higher-level cognition. There are systems of analytic tools. One is called the "language" of persuasion, which is used in many states (see Appendix B). Several of these tools are given below as examples. They are skills that can be applied to all communication, everything from advertising to asking Mom for the car keys to negotiating with a boss for a raise. They are fun, and children develop valuable habits of mind.

Censor unsatisfactory media and provide appropriate media. This is an essential process by which children learn a functional and stable value system. Select media content that is appropriate for your child. This can be difficult because much electronic media operate in the brain's visual "reaction" center. Reaction is quicker and requires less effort than "thinking." Many electronic media tend to exploit and reinforce knee-jerk reactive cognition. It is important to teach children that higher-level cognition (i.e., thinking) is harder, takes longer, and happens in a different part of the brain than reaction. Many experts believe that these "metacognitive" (thinking about thinking) abilities are important characteristics of successful people. Parents can plan an enjoyable and rewarding family media environment that stimulates higher-level cognition. Remember, it is not necessarily easy to create an effective abstract thinker. That is why there are so few of them, but, eventually, your young adult will thank you for your persistence.

Emphasize neocortical development. Parents can choose to develop the language centers of the child's neocortex (the newest part of the brain), the part that controls abstract thinking and language skills, by emphasizing critical consumption. Talking and playing with young children is one of the best ways to stimulate abstraction. Screens, on the other hand, are strangers that are powerful and passive teachers. Always consider, "What and how are the screens teaching?" As parents model such behaviors, children learn habits of mind. Many advertising people confirm the ability of media to sell. Programs, movies, and video games are always selling attitudes, modes of thinking, and behaviors. Try to avoid letting the stranger have uncriticized, unauthorized, or monopolistic access to children.

Try to watch as a family and discuss the shows you have selected, both as you watch them and after you watch them. Do not let young children have televisions or computers attached to the Internet in their own rooms.

Build your child's value system. Don't follow Nike's advice and "Just do it"; rather, "think about it." Noted psychiatrist and researcher Brandon Centerwall says, "A child *must* develop a functional value system or that child *will be* pathological as an adult" (McCannon & Hizel, 1995, p. 12). According to Centerwall (cited in McCannon, 1998), the mental health profession is in agreement that a functional value system *must have* a source of values that has the following characteristics:

(a) *Consistency:* The value system can be liberal or conservative, but the values promoted cannot be constantly changing. It cannot be permissible to hit Alex on Monday but not on Tuesday.

(b) *Security:* The source of values must be able to protect the child, or the child will not value the system.

(c) *Enforcement:* The source of values must be able to enforce the value system, or the child will not respect the value system.

(d) *Responsive:* The source of values must be loving and frequently available for the child—in joy, sickness, celebration, discipline, learning–providing many repetitions. The total amount of time spent reinforcing values with the child is important.

Television, video games, and movies, as generally composed, exhibit a huge range of value systems and thus are not consistent. (Some argue that television *is* consistent in the way it treats violence, sex, minorities, and more, but this author accepts Centerwall's point that media present kids with a bewildering array of value systems.) They cannot protect children or enforce values, and they care for little except profit (McCannon, 1996). They do not, therefore, provide healthy mental development. One hopes that such media are not the regular source of a child's values. Families are, therefore, in competition with the entertainment industry for the mental health of their children.

Whenever possible, families should *prerecord television.* This allows two important things to happen:

1. The program can be *stopped* for discussion. This is important for young children (ages 3-7) because small children have great difficulty distinguishing fantasy from reality. Adults help interpret the world, providing knowledge and security. (Centerwall, cited in McCannon, 1998). When interpreting or discussing, it is also a time for everyone to practice "tools" of analysis (below). For example, when watching a Disney movie, and a character kills another character, one could stop and ask questions such as, "What was the problem? How else could they have solved their problem? Who will be sorry? Who will want revenge? Who will pay for the funeral? Is this hyperbole? How is it a simple solution?"

2. Fast-forward through the commercials. Commercials are the most powerful media messages. They are front-end loaded with emotional material to "grab" your attention. Paying attention to ads also typically means "stopping thinking." Experts estimate that children normally see 400,000 to 700,000 commercials by age 18. That is many repetitions of "stop thinking" (McCannon & Hizel, 1995). The mythical "average" American watches television for about 8 to 12 continuous years (depending on whose statistics are used). Using 10 for a median estimate, the average person watches television for the staggering equivalent of 30 years of 8-hour work days or more than 60% of a person's leisure time (Kubey & Csikszentmihalyi, 1990). That is a great deal of advertisements.

Mel Levine, an attention deficit disorder expert and renowned pediatric developmentalist, suggests, "Ads are powerful conditioning to stop thinking; the ad barrage is an important factor in the increasing distractibility of our students" (cited in

McCannon & Hizel, 1995, p. 13). Thus, it would seem that fast-forwarding through the commercials and, instead, discussing the subject of the video is an important way to *build* a child's ability to concentrate.

Allow children many opportunities for *nondirected play*. Develop imagination and self-reliance. Build a regular time into the day for children to entertain themselves. Can you make a house out of sticks in the backyard?

Investigate caregivers and schools. Avoid baby-sitters, daycare centers, and teachers (if possible) that use television to keep kids quiet. The tendency to use TV as a baby-sitter is powerful not only in caregiving centers but also in schools. As frequently used (with small screens and little discussion), educational television is often a scholastic oxymoron, but it keeps the students quiet. (This should warn us about the power of the medium to condition normally active kids to watching.) Talk with the child about her or his day, and do not hesitate to question a school's use of television.

This brings up an important school/media issue. About 40% of U.S. schools have institutionalized a form of television called Channel One. Channel One gives TV monitors and wiring to schools in return for exposing the kids to a 12-minute "news" program that contains 2 minutes of commercials. The news is more like *Entertainment Tonight* than the *Jim Lehrer News Hour,* and many of the news stories look like ads. Some researchers have found that only 20% of Channel One's airtime is devoted to news, with the rest going to sports, ads, new TV programs, celebrities, and movies. But that is the good news.

The bad news: Kids are forced to watch ads for sugar, fat, caffeine, violent movies, and other things of which many parents would disapprove, except the parents usually have no knowledge of Channel One's content. Most important, few parents are aware that 12 minutes per day add up to about 1 week of schooling. Because wealthier schools tend to be among the 60% of schools that turn down Channel One, it is mostly poor students who lose 7 weeks of schooling in a Channel One district. When one figures the total costs that go into building schools, paying staff, and providing transportation, equipment, insurance, retirement, and so on, the 7 weeks devoted to Channel One's questionable news and commercials cost many times the value of its small TV monitors and wiring. Some parents have started movements to remove Channel One and/or keep it out of their schools.

Another guideline for family and health professionals is to *increase constantly their level of media knowledge*. The culture surrounding children used to be created when kids interacted with people. Now youth culture is created by huge multinational corporations that are motivated almost entirely by profit. Their PR departments work overtime to mislead children and parents about the effects of their media on children. Fortunately, there are many wonderful publications, bibliographies and newsletters (NMMLP publishes resources, and its Web site [nmmlp.org] links to others), magazines, videos, medical groups, and Web sites devoted to media education, getting out the untold story. The resource guide at the end of this chapter should enable one to get started. For example, suppose you came across the following ad from *TV Guide*, one of the largest subscription magazines in the world, and it was part of a huge, multimedia advertising campaign from ABC television. The campaign featured many television ads as well as radio and print ads. Teach your children (and students) to talk back to ads such as these, discussing what stories are not being told and what techniques of persuasion are being used. Some organizations such as *Consumer Reports* have contests for children on how to talk back to ads (see nmmlp.org).

The following ad was all text, a full page with black text on an orange background, with an ABC logo at the bottom. The exact title and text follow with possible discussion questions and comments (talking back to the ad) added in italics. The comments attempt to mimic the style of the ad.

TV IS GOOD.

Who is paying for the ad? ABC. Why? Is ABC's viewership down? (It was.) For whom is TV "good?" ABC's leaders? What is the salary of the CEO of ABC (Disney) or Peter Jennings? Ted Koppel?

For years the pundits, moralists and self-righteous, self-appointed preservers of our culture have told us that television is bad.

This is name-calling or ad hominem attack: Critics of TV also include the vast majority of parents, teachers, the health community, and researchers. What is it about this research that makes "Big Media" people crazy? They do not like to hear about the media effects research!

This part of the ad "stacks the deck": Few critics condemn all of TV; most recognize that TV can be wonderful and educational. This technique is also called "straw man," where you claim your opposition says something but you hyperbolize it, so that you can more effectively attack it.

It is also simplifying a complex problem to the level of idiocy in the hopes of persuading some simple people directly and getting the somewhat brighter people to laugh at the supposed "irony." This kind of simple irony is most often used these days by those trying to sell people products like Sprite or Seven-Up or Millers beer by getting people to laugh at stupidity, or themselves, or themselves being stupid, flattering them that they are in the "in-crowd" that gets the joke—which is a laughable notion, logically, but not emotionally. Thus, it is a "plain-folks" appeal. The only bad thing about plain-folks appeals is that they suggest that to be plain or average or, in the case of this ad, to be stupid is a worthwhile goal.

They've stood high on their soapbox and looked condescendingly on our innocuous pleasure. They've sought to wean us from our harm-

less habit by derisively referring to television as the Boob Tube or the Idiot Box.

Innocuous? Harmless? Parents spend 60% of their leisure time watching screens. Most of them could have gone to night school and become a lawyer, accountant, or teacher 10 times over with just half of that time.

It is good, though, to see that the industry recognizes that it is a HABIT, because habits are right next to addictions, and because about half of parents spend less than 38 minutes a week talking to their children while spending more than a thousand minutes watching TV, it is good to see official recognition from the TV industry that television is possibly addictive.

It would also be nice to see the TV industry recognize that parents are spending too little time doing things with their kids, like playing with them and reading with them.

Well, television is not the evil destroyer of all that is right in this world. In fact, and we say this with all the disdain we can muster for the elitists who purport otherwise–TV is good.

This technique is many things but, most of all, repetition: It is one of the most unfortunate characteristics of bad television, horrible movies, and worse advertising. It simply means that the person who wrote this copy was not creative enough to think of any other reasons, possibly because the argument is so "ironic" or, perhaps, moronic? It is also why we see so many car chases and so many people jumping through windows.

It also reminds us of a necessary ingredient of all propaganda, the truth. If there were no truth in propaganda, we would not value it. Thus, there is truth here. There is much good about television.

This is also a wonderful psychological ploy. We all feel guilty about the amount of time we spend with TV. This statement uses our guilt to build a defensive reaction . . . for the benefit of ABC.

TV binds us together. It makes us laugh. Makes us cry. Why, in the span of ten years, TV brought us the downfall of an American president, one giant step for mankind and the introduction of Farrah Fawcett as one of "Charlie's Angels."

Television has brought us much that we love and value, but television also does NOT tell us much, especially where its interests are concerned. For example, the Telecommunications Act of 1996, according to Bob Dole, gave $75 billion to the TV industry that should have been given to the taxpayers.

During the 9 months that that bill was before Congress, only one story appeared on the evening news, and it was NOT on ABC.

That $75 billion would have provided health care for all Americans (who do not have it) for 2 years. Why didn't ABC tell us? Maybe because they were the beneficiaries of this giveaway, this giant hunk of corporate welfare to the networks?

But, not to worry, ABC will give us invaluable info about the remake of Charlie's Angels dozens of times when it comes out and, if we are lucky, they'll eventually play it for us, with only two zillion commercial interruptions.

Can any other medium match TV for its immediacy, its impact, its capacity to entertain?

No, no other medium can, and when TV does something great, it enriches us all. It is just too bad that it happens so seldom.

Who among us hasn't spent an entire weekend on the couch, bathed in the cool glow of a Sony Trinitron, only to return to work recuperated and completely refreshed?

This is called the Big Lie technique. It flies in the face of most of our experience. Who can compare a weekend where one has repainted the house, taken the family camping, done the research paper, gone jogging, or, even, had friends over? Who would compare these truly valuable experiences with a weekend of being a couch potato? But, then again, maybe we're missing the point. Perhaps this is really sophisticated satire.

And who would dispute that the greatest advancement in aviation over the last 10 years was the decision to air sitcoms during the in-flight service?

Help! Who hired this person to write this copy? Sitcoms on airplanes?? Good heavens, next this ad will be talking about remote controls.

Why, then, should we cower behind our remote controls? Let us rejoice in our fully adjustable, leather-upholstered recliners. Let us celebrate our cerebral-free non-activity.

Celebrate cerebral-free activity? Why not celebrate something truly great, like that which distinguishes us from the animals, you know, like . . . cerebral activity! Like humanitarian activity . . . charities . . . saving the environment . . .

Let us climb the highest figurative mountaintop and proclaim, with all the vigor and shrillness that made Roseanne a household name, that TV is good. ABC.

> *Now there is a winning metaphor for excellence, Roseanne. She was a model of intelligence, subtlety, self-discipline, and wit (never a sight gag or pratfall). We might ask ourselves, what does this kind of humor say about ABC's opinion of the intelligence of the average reader of TV Guide?*

It is hoped that one can see from this light-hearted deconstruction (media analysis) that talking back to ads can be valuable and fun. It helps to reveal the stories that the ad is omitting but also those that it does not want told. Engage children and students in discussions of consumerism, compulsion, habituation, addictive lifestyles, stereotyping, simple solutions, and other values promoted by many media storytellers.

If you run into teen rebellion, don't browbeat the teen. Recognize that teens have a right to their opinions, and enjoy the discussion opportunities that such deconstructions present. Know that you are planting seeds that will grow in the future.

Give the young a sense of pride in having skills of analysis, access, and production. If possible, suggest to them that being different is all right. After all, the average newspaper is written at a sixth-grade reading level. Inspire students to want to be above this "average." Parents who have followed the above procedures report that their children are more popular because they are interesting and creative, and they do better in school. Do not buy into the myths promoted by the media industry, PR people, and their media literacy retainers:

Myth number one: Children are handicapped if they grow up having watched less television than their peers have. On the contrary, children who grow up in a good family life with the advantages of bonding and an active entertainment culture can have greater skills, creativity, discipline, manners, success, and satisfaction.

Myth number two: Watching television is just as good as reading. Believe it or not, a number of "media literacy" people (most of whom are supported by the television industry) say this. Be confident that reading happens in a different part of the brain than watching, involves greater recall, creates more and deeper comprehension, and generates longer attention spans than most screen watching.

Finally, talk, play, and read with children. Interact with them in constructive and meaningful ways. Research suggests that there is a big difference between watching screens for 1 hour per day or less and 3 hours per day or more. That difference could translate into more confidence, better grades, better jobs, more successful lifestyles, healthier relationships, more stable families, and less jail time.

MEDIA LITERACY FOR SCHOOL AND FAMILY ●

As noted, many school media literacy programs and groups have blossomed during the past several decades. Australia, Canada, and parts of the United Kingdom, Germany, and Latin America have media literacy as parts of their school curricula. In the United States, the movement is more recent. Most of these programs emphasize higher-level cognitive skills, media issues, and media production. This chapter will emphasize the programs in New Mexico, one of the first U.S. states to adopt a mandatory media literacy requirement, as a model; many other models exist, and links to many of them can be found at www.nmmlp.org.

The media literacy part of that overused school administrator phrase, developing "critical thinking," lies in applying abstract concepts to concrete examples from one's immediate experience. Critical thinking about media functions in a similar and positive manner.

1. It develops *skills* that are abstract concepts or "tools" that can be applied to media analysis, access, and production (D. G. Singer & J. L. Singer, 1994, 1998). Students learn the questions to ask, research answers, and, if necessary, hypothesize possible answers. They discover meanings and learn to think for themselves. They also can gain positive affective results from a media literacy regimen in how they view and use television (Singer et al., 1980).

2. It discusses *media issues* that are cultural subthemes affected by media, giving students valuable windows into the censored world of mainstream media, allowing for personal growth and critical cultural autonomy (Kilbourne, 1999; McChesney, 1994).

3. It posits *strategies of activism* that become increasingly essential in a culture that seems to be becoming less active (Healy, 1991; McKibben, 1992; Schechter, 1997).

These areas are explored in media literacy trainings and materials. As examples, three of the most important media literacy *skills* (Aufderheide, 1992) or "tools of analysis" are explored in depth below. Each is accompanied by an example.

These tools can aid an investigation of any media-related issue. Several important media issues will be used as examples: (a) passivity, cynicism, and apathy that surround government, civic issues, and volunteerism in America; (b) the construction of advertising; and (c) the tendency of advertising to promote habituating or addictive lifestyles.

● TOOLS OF MEDIA ANALYSIS

Tool 1: Media Create Culture

Every time one experiences a medium, one would be well served to ask, "What kind of culture does this create?" and "What stories does this media example leave untold?" Technology ubiquitously immerses us in powerful media of communication, and society consumes these media out of habit and choice. In the same way that a fish probably ignores water, people tend to ignore the changing cultural power of media (Jhally, cited in Boihem & Emmanoullides, 1996). As George Gerbner (1995) notes,

> A child today is born into a home in which television is on an average of more than seven hours a day. For the first time in human history, most of the stories about people, life and values are told not by parents, schools, churches, or others in the community who have something to tell, but by a group of distant conglomerates who have something to sell. (p. 115)

Ralph Nader (2000) takes this one step farther:

> Our children are now exposed to the most intense marketing onslaught in history. From the age of 9 months to 19 years, precise corporate selling is beamed directly to children separating them from their parents, an unheard of practice formerly, and teaching them how to nag their beleaguered parents . . . . They teach them how to crave junk food, thrill to violent and pornographic programming, and interact with the virtual reality mayhem. The marketeers are keenly aware of the stages of child psychologies, age by age, and know how to turn many into Pavlovian specimens powered by spasmodically shortened attention spans as they become ever more remote from their own family. (p. 3)

Unfortunately, as Nader (2000) goes on to say, "This commercial traffic makes children even more vulnerable to the streets" (p. 4).

Understanding how the new media conglomerates manipulate children, communities, and democracy gives us *the opportunity to take back our culture,* leading the next generation to become even more media literate, reflective, aware, and determined citizens (Fallows, 1996).

The first step in taking back culture is to understand how the culture is changing vis-à-vis journalism and democracy. Most citizens are aware that political campaigns and news coverage have changed. Some are uncomfortable with the periodic avalanches of negative and deceptive television campaign ads.

People, however, seldom consider the political power television gives to media managers and their sponsors, corporations. Consider what would happen if

United Airlines ran ads about corrupt and shoddy Delta Airline mechanics. Think what would happen if Delta retaliated with ads implying that United pilots drank heavily, showing pictures of airliners crashing in great fireballs! Would anyone fly on these airlines? Probably not, and today few people vote, probably out of TV-induced cynicism (Hart, 1994).

Consider another example. It is indisputable that for the past 20 years, the political power of monopolistic corporations has been on the rise. Many Americans read in their history books about John D. Rockefeller's Standard Oil and other trusts abusing competitors, buying political power, and, finally, causing some progress—anti-trust legislation—which eventually broke up Rockefeller's empire, restoring competition and a semblance of fairness to the oil industry. Currently, however, much of Standard Oil has been put back together; we have high energy prices and reports of marketplace gouging. Evidence seems to exist that natural gas and electric companies are overcharging; oil company profits are at an all-time high; and yet, most of our news coverage centers on the OPEC cartel and supposed shortages of supply. During the presidential debates of 2000, this subject hardly came up. Energy independence and, particularly, alternative ways to create energy, such as solar and wind power, were not discussed at all. Such subjects are rarely seen in the mainstream news.

Such "censorship" in the media creates an opportunity for media-literate advocates. As the oil, gas, mining, and nuclear industries are increasingly able to create the cultural context in which we discuss the energy "crisis," stories such as the recent one on *USA Today*'s front page (Bowles, 2000) give media literacy teachers and their students a powerful opportunity to investigate news "censorship."

Headlined "Fuel Crisis: Energy Crunch the Worst in 25 Years," the story mentions all of the following as solutions to the "crisis": oil drilling in Alaska, releasing oil from U.S. reserves, more offshore oil drilling, weather-stripping windows, turning down thermostats, more wood stoves, and using more home generators (an interesting notion for fuel savings).

Applying their first skill, students ask what stories were not told. They discover that there was no mention of some viable ways to aid the situation, such as imposing the same fuel economy standards on light trucks and SUVs that are now in place on cars. It did not mention wind, solar, cogeneration of energy, hybrid cars, and other sources of power that are feasible with today's technology. The students soon became intrigued by why such news anomalies exist and began to research news programs, politics, and the energy crisis, planning to make their own media messages about energy solutions. This is the power of media literacy, empowering students in the real world—their culture.

In another area, some Americans realize just how little "news" there is in the news, but too few take action. Others fit into the pattern observed by several scholars whereby people watch more, know less, but *feel* like they know more (Hart, 1994; Schechter, 1997). Many others refuse to watch the news, and why should they? "Journalists present public life as a depressing spectacle" (Fallows, 1996, p. 8). Neil Postman (1985) speculates that "embedded in the surrealistic frame of a television news show is a theory of anticommunication . . . that abandons logic, reason, sequence and rules of contradiction" (p. 105). Robert MacNeil (1983) of the *MacNeil-Lehrer News Hour* speculates that TV news has to

> keep everything brief, not to strain the attention of anyone, but instead to provide constant stimulation through variety, novelty, action and movement . . . pay attention to no concept for more than a few seconds . . . complexity is to be avoided . . . nuances are dispensable . . . visual stimulation is a substitute for thought, and verbal precision is an anachronism. (p. 2)

A media-literate public would beware of such signs of simplicity and emotionalism. Students should be taught that the "license they [journalists] have to criticize and defame comes with an implied responsibility to serve the public . . . to make journalism more useful [and] public life stronger" (Fallows, 1996, p. 270). If taught in school, coupled with investigation of media, this would be empowering information, real news, even. Citizens might demand that they hear about the obligations of journalists more often in the mainstream press. Such stories could lead to demands for better news, perhaps even electoral reform.

Citizens might even form organizations; they could help their local educators understand the extent of the tabloidization of the news, and they could in turn teach students the skills, wisdom, and discernment to combat cynicism and, perhaps, even reaffirm Jefferson's "miracle" of democracy.

By investigating the local news, students can learn that the local TV news is a cash cow that often treats advertisers with kid gloves. They learn that the news without fail will tell when a man robs a bank but seldom tells when banks rob the people.

Most citizens know that Bonnie and Clyde robbed banks, but few know that the savings and loan scandal of the 1980s cost the taxpayers of America more than $600 billion. Not many know how it happened or why. Almost none think of this as a massive corporate welfare bailout, and the vast mass of Americans are not aware of what else that $600 billion could have bought.

With media literacy, children learn about stereotyping, bias, and simple solutions. They discover the difference between entertainment and news (and cohost chitchat). They evaluate the importance of murders, disasters, and car accidents (always covered) and good things going on in neighborhoods (almost never covered). Most important, they discover that they can make their own news. Many students in New Mexico, tired of seeing stories about drugs and guns in their schools, make "real" stories about successful students, interesting programs, and great teachers; they learn that they can tell their stories, valuable stories that are seldom covered in the media, and, frequently, their stories appear on the local news!

Media-literate advocates can teach about how news is censored by large corporations that have an interest in telling citizens what the corporations want them to know. Kids learn about video news releases (VNRs), made by corporations and masquerading for as much as 25% of news. Media literacy students study Robert McChesney (1997), who teaches how our news is mostly based on violent events, celebrities, and "fluff" rather than "long term social issues that are critical for society" (p. 16). They learn that people are conditioned to fluff because fluff sells products.

> Indeed, in what stands as perhaps the most damning statement one could make about the news media, some studies have suggested that the more a person consumes commercial news, the less capable that person is of understanding politics or public affairs. (McChesney, 1997, p. 17)

Armed with such knowledge, skills, and active strategies, students, parents, teachers, and health professionals in conjunction with media literacy professionals can use technology to recommit our culture to democracy as a positive and vital activity in which citizens should take part to maintain their own freedom (Fallows, 1996). Thus, studying the media literacy of journalism could change the news and revitalize our democratic institutions.

We live in a democracy, the rarest of all forms of government. Quality knowledge is an essential ingredient of freedom. If the rise of media globalism signifies a new censorship, a censorship supporting a political arrangement whereby "people have the right to vote, but political and economic power is resolutely maintained in the hands of the wealthy few" (McChesney, 1999, p. 79), it is up to media-literate advocates to help preserve our most fragile of governmental systems. We can rekindle students' interest in public affairs, and we must. As former Federal Communications Commission Chairman Newton Minow (1995) said, "Our children are the public interest; living and breathing, flesh and blood" (p. 175).

Tool 2: Media Use Identifiable Techniques That Can Be Deconstructed

Media are constructed very carefully and yet disguise this fact, multiplying their powerful and predominantly unacknowledged effects. The most powerful media are advertisements. Television ads cost about a million dollars, which is more expensive than most movies (few movies cost $2 million per minute). National ads are tested in focus groups with sophisticated techniques.

This writer is lucky enough to travel the country and show ads to people of all ages. When he shows the Coke polar bear to adults and teenagers, they enjoy it, but when he shows it to elementary students, they usually become uncontrollable for a minute or two. The excitement level is so high that they just have to talk to one another, presenting an interesting discussion opportunity for the author and the students. Together they figure out why the ad is so enjoyable. That is the media literacy "hook." The students learn about the type of animation, the imagery, the myths and assumptions about polar bears and Coke, the cost, the fact that the ad has no words, the cultural context that Coke seeks and enjoys, and the unconscious emotional transfer from the bear to the Coke logo. The untold story also comes out–the health, drug, and nutrition story that Coke does not want to tell as well as the inexpensive raw materials that create a Coke, despite the expensive price of Coke. Gradually, the students understand why *Advertising Age* gave the polar bear ad the year's best ad award of 1994.

Ad agencies routinely spend dozens or even hundreds of millions of dollars to buy time and places for ads. The end product of this expensive process is quite simply the most powerful communication that humans can create. It is so powerful that kids are drinking Coke instead of milk, helping to cause what the Centers for Disease Control and Prevention (CDC) call an epidemic of diabetes, rickets, and osteoporosis among youth. Coke's cultural influence is so powerful—its censorship so complete—that the average person never considers the diuretic and calcium-leaching properties of this addictive drug-laden beverage. Media literacy's "magic" is that it can cause students to enjoy learning this kind of unhealthful information.

Interestingly enough, powerful media depend on an unlikely dichotomy. "Like most other propaganda, advertising must pervade the atmosphere; for it wants, paradoxically, to startle its beholders without really being noticed by them" (Miller, 1988, p. 11). In surveys, most Americans will say that advertising is powerful but that it affects them very little. In other words, "It affects others."

Analyzing or "deconstructing" the cultural narrative created by media is the key to breaking through such conditioning. Deconstruction fascinates those of us who are immersed in a hypermediated culture, and it is a subtle way to focus attention on the power of media without causing defensiveness. One of the easiest ways to analyze media is to deconstruct an advertisement. "Studies estimate that, counting all the logos, labels and announcements, some 1,600 ads flicker across an individual's consciousness daily" (Savan, 1994, p. 1).

This is a natural human condition because the average person, on reaching his or her 18th birthday, will have seen at least 350,000 television ads–each one telling a story, each a little narrative, usually with a happy ending. Aided by the fact that the cost of each ad is tax deductible (corporate welfare notwithstanding) such cultural omnipresence builds a universal fascination. A growing number of television programs feast on this magnetism: the best ads of 2001, Europe's best ads, the hottest ads from Tuesday, and so on. Thus, media literacy has a powerful and natural vehicle for the inculcation of skills.

A formula for the quick deconstruction of an ad (and most media) asks for technical, economic, cultural, ethical, social, and health evaluations by the student, all of which involve critical thinking.

A Quick Deconstruction

- Who paid for the media? Why?
- Who is being targeted? Age? Ethnicity? Wealth? Profession? Interests?
- What text, images, or sounds lead you to this conclusion?
- What is the text (literal meaning) of the message?
- What is the subtext (unstated or underlying message)?
- What kind of lifestyle is presented? Is it glamorized? How?
- What values are expressed?
- What tools or techniques of persuasion are used?
- Is there a historical, cultural, literary, or other context used by the example?
- In what ways is this a healthy and/or unhealthy media message?
- What related stories are not told by this media example?

As an example, the above quick deconstruction formula is used below with the following magazine ad:

Figure 10.4

An alcohol company paid for the ad. Why? It sells an expensive product that no one "needs"; hence, it must advertise a great deal. The picture would indicate that the targets are young males; it is hard to tell, but probably Caucasian. The textual message devalues relationships with women and suggests substituting whiskey for girlfriends. It suggests a cultural, media, and historical context for male drinking (most action movies) and the ad's targets are part of that cultural subgroup that participates heavily in drinking as a macho bonding ritual, possibly college men (a big market).

The subtextual message is probably aimed at middle and high school boys. It says that girls are a pain; they cannot be relied on, but Jim Beam will always be your "real friend." Alcohol companies have the same problem that cigarette companies have. They must make their customers brand loyal by ages 10 to 16 because kids decide whether to drink or not by then, so the psychological ploy that girls don't measure up works well with kids of middle school age. Those boys are having difficulty with the female sex in general and dating in particular.

Repetition! Glamorization of the "party" lifestyle is a value that must be repeated endlessly by alcohol companies because the related untold stories reveal major disadvantages of the drug. Alcohol is not needed. About two thirds of the population drink little or not at all. Nondrinkers are just as happy as the drinkers are, and they think big drinkers are uncool, wasteful, and unattractive. Drinkers are poorer because booze is expensive. After the initial drug high wears off, many people feel worse because alcohol is a depressant. Other disadvantages include, but are not limited to, the following: headaches and worse, sexual mistakes, car accidents, rapes, crimes, and child abuse.

The average person sees 100,000 alcohol ads (in all media) by the time he or she is age 18. That is definitely a hypermediated commercial culture, the power of which can be seen by asking, "Will the average child have heard 'I love you' a hundred thousand times before he or she is 18?"

Jim Beam's other techniques include a variety of male symbols, card stacking, and straw men. The use of a black-and-white photo indicates casual fun and, perhaps, helps to spread the ethnicity a bit. The glass is above the camera and foreshortened to add power to the drink. The dark colors add freshness and reality to the bottle, which has phallic power and incredible lighting. The former suggests in powerful terms that alcohol provides status, success, friendship, and dependability; the latter suggests that such benefits derive from a loving, nurturing, and mystically powerful source.

Last, the white print at the bottom of the page, which is so small only good eyes can read it on the original, says, "Real friends drink together responsibly." This is a technique called the Big Lie. One could find several reasons for that copy, but it is fun to ask kids to define responsible drinking and, then, carefully introduce the idea that 7% of the population are alcoholics and then ask carefully (some parents are alcoholics) if alcoholics drink responsibly. When kids find out that approximately 50% of the booze is consumed by that 7%, many conclude that Jim Beam makes half its money from irresponsible drinking. The students frequently ask, "Is Jim Beam really serious about responsible drinking?"

This is not a healthy message. For those who value loving relationships and friendships based on respect, the ad is an unfortunate addition to youth culture. Binge drinking among high school and college students, particularly among women, is increasing rapidly.

One can see from this example that analysis of media messages depends on recognizing their constructed nature. Television ads provide an excellent source of material for deconstruction precisely because they are short, yet they are constructed carefully, scene by scene. Each scene is discussed by highly paid professionals for months. One cannot possibly spend as much time and effort in *deconstruction* as the ad agency, client, focus group testing firm, and production company spent in *construction*. Remember that television ads are made more carefully than movies. The following is a possible scenario for the construction of a national television ad.

1. The rough outline is brainstormed by agency and/or client "creative" people.

2. Scenes are discussed with advertising agency account managers and experts; improvements are suggested.

3. Improved scenes, rough drawings, and a script are discussed with the client.

4. Computer storyboards of the scenes are generated and discussed.

5. The new scenes are shown to the client with more discussion.

6. Improved storyboards of scenes are created with actor descriptions and finalized script. It is gone over with the production company and the casting crew.

7. Actors are hired, based on the descriptions; backgrounds made; locations selected; costume, lighting, sound, animation, and technical experts hired.

8. The scenes are rehearsed.

9. All scenes are shot numerous times on *film* with full crews, lights, camera, and action.

10. Scenes are mixed into a rough-cut mix in an editing studio.

11. The scenes are reviewed; impact is assessed by the production company and the ad agency. A second rough cut is prepared.

12. The scenes are discussed with the client. A third mix is prepared.

13. The scenes are shown to focus groups and discussed; changes may be made.

14. The scenes are test marketed; changes may be made.

15. The scenes in finished ad form begin running. The client monitors sales. The length of an ad's run is assessed in terms of sales and brand affection, which determines how long the ad runs.

16. For special uses, such as Channel One, a new mix may be created (McCannon & Hizel, 1995, p. 7).

Note that the scenes have been discussed by highly paid and trained people at least 10 times. *Nothing is accidental.* This information surprises many students and adults.

Other questions for students to answer include the following: How long is the ad? How many scenes are there? What is the purpose of each scene? Why are they in a particular order? Why are some so short and others longer? Most ads have a "key" scene, the longest and most important for establishing the client's message. What is the target market of the ad? In what ways unique to video does this ad sell the product to the target?

It is also valuable for students to produce media; production of media can provide valuable insights. Production can be video, but it also can be posters, cereal boxes, newsletters, magazines, radio, or other media. An especially valuable production exercise is the production of *anti-ads* or counter-ads. These can be public service announcements, spoof ads, or ad satires.

Creating counter-ads allows students to talk back to deceptive or harmful media messages and to experience some control over these powerful cultural icons. Counter-ads can also be very effective educational devices (Atkin, 1993a; Grube & Wallach, 1994). Counter-ad tobacco campaigns have reduced teen smoking in several states (CDC, 1999; Siegel & Biener, 2000; Wallack et al., 1993). Anti-ads can be parodies of advertisements. They deliver more truthful or constructive messages yet use the same persuasion techniques as the real ads. By creating counter-ads, students can apply media literacy skills to communicate positive messages in a fun and engaging exercise.

Creating Counter-Ads

The simplest way to create a counter-ad is to alter a real ad (magazine or newspaper ads work best) by changing the text or adding graphic elements; young students can just write or draw over the original ad or paste new materials onto it. An example: Change "Come to Marlboro Country" to "Come to Marlboro's Graveyard" and add a few tombstones to the landscape. A counter-ad can also be created by drawing a new image, copying the design and layout of a real ad. Collage techniques work well, too. For radio or TV counter-ads, students can write scripts and read them to the class, or take it a step further and record or videotape their counter-ads. Here are some battle-tested tips for making effective counter-ads:

- *Analyze.* Look at several real ads and try to figure out why they are effective. The best counter-ads use the same techniques to deliver a different message.

- *Power.* Your message has to break through the clutter of all the real ads that people see or hear. Think about what makes an ad memorable to you. What techniques does it use to grab your attention? Use them.

- *Persuade.* Use the same persuasion techniques found in real ads—such as humor, repetition, or flattery—to deliver your alternative message.

- *Pictures.* Visual images are incredibly powerful. People often forget what they read or hear but remember what they see. The best counter-ads, like the best ads, tell their stories through pictures.

- *Rebellion.* Advertising targeted at young people often appeals to a sense of youthful rebellion. Effective counter-ads expose misleading and manipulative advertising methods and turn teens' rebellious spirit toward the corporate sponsors who use these methods.

- *"KISS"–Keep It Short and Simple.* Use only one idea for your main message. Focus everything on getting this message across.

- *Plan.* Try to think of everything—words, images, design—before you begin production. Make sketches and rough drafts before you start crafting the final product.

- *Practice.* If you are going to perform a radio or TV script (and especially if you are making an audio recording or video), your cast and crew will need to rehearse. Then, rehearse it again.

- *Teamwork.* Working in a team can lighten your workload and spark creativity. Brainstorm ideas as a group. Make sure all members share responsibility for the work.

- *Revise.* When you think you are finished, show your counter-ad to uninvolved people for feedback. Do they understand it? Do they think it is funny? Use their responses to revise your work for maximum impact.

- *Distribute.* Your ideas were meant to be seen! Make copies of your counter-ads and post them around your school. Get them published in your school newspaper. Show your videotape to other kids and adults. Your counter-ad can stimulate needed discussion and debate around media and health issues.

- *Have fun!* Making a counter-ad is an enjoyable way to learn about media and health, to be creative, and to express your views. Enjoy it!

In more sophisticated analyses, one should consider the cultural context and *feelings* that each scene creates. Television needs to make people feel emotions. Both Leslie Savan and Mark Crispin Miller present brilliant media critiques, and they detail specific tools for deconstructing advertising's subtle emotional pitches. Miller (1988) suggests that television uses "preemptive irony" to induce you to "prove your superiority to TV's cheap and dirty messages, not by criticizing or refusing them, but by feeding on them, taking in their oblique assurances that you're too smart to swallow any of it" (p. 15). In such a way, one might explain the cross-generational success of *Comedy Central,* Dave Letterman, Dana Carvey, pro-wrestling, and Beavis and Butthead.

One of Savan's (1994) cardinal rules for deconstructing ads is *"follow the flattery"* (p. 10). Flattery can be defined as "telling or implying that your target is that which makes them feel good, often what they want to be" (McCannon & Williams, 1997, p. 10), and surely, an attractive, sophisticated, charming, and intelligent reader such as yourself will perceptively understand how often this technique is used.

Adding to flattery's impact is the unnoticed nature of modern advertising. "People don't attend to advertising; it is more of a subconscious or subliminal effect," said Fred Baker (cited in Miller, 1988, p. 17). He should know; he is senior vice-president of McCann-Erickson, one of the largest advertising agencies. Several other renegade advertising executives have written valuable books about the subject. One suggests that "conscious awareness appears [to be just] a minute fragment of what is available in the memory" (Key, 1989, p. 37).

Electronic ads depend on the fact that consumers have little time to analyze them before the next ad appears. One must consider the speed and power of quickly changing scenes and visual images. They overwhelm the neocortex or "thinking" part of the brain. Gerry Mander (1978), another former advertising executive and a radical in the media movement, discusses advertising and the permanency of television images in the human mind. Take one of his tests; think about landing on the moon. What image comes to mind? Did you have any choice about "seeing" Neil Armstrong?

Media literacy can consider these and many more factors, looking at electronic media scene by scene. Students learn that when television runs at 30 pictures per second, the cognitive part of our brain cannot keep up; thus, we see motion. As they reflect on one quick scene, another is washing its message out of short-term memory. People are left with advertising's goal–unnoticed stimuli; the viewer becomes the product, "slowly recreated in the ad's image" (Savan, 1994, p. 7). Advertising imprints us, the product, with the embedded notion that satisfaction comes from things that can be bought and sold (Leiss, Kline, & Jhally, 1990). The failure of the conscious mind to reflect on fast-paced televised information says a great deal about the character of image-based media versus text-based media for conveying detail, complexity, and useful synthesized knowledge. This is a valuable discussion for students. Have them bring in and discuss their examples of "best" media.

Students can also deconstruct the difference between watching and doing. Recent research on the brain's formation also sheds light on the difference between "watching" and "doing" (i.e., *active and passive processing*). Jane Healy's (1991) valuable synthesis of neurophysiology and education, *Endangered Minds*, spotlights 30 years of work by Dr. Marion Diamond and other neurophysiologists who believe that young brains grow in response to active participation in learning. They further believe that watchers wind up with less mass–neurons, dendrites, and support cells–in the parts of their brains that manage higher-level cognition. "We know that environments shape brains; all sorts of experiments have shown that it happens [creating] profound differences, depending upon what is being taken in through the senses" (Healy, 1991, p. 51). Adults who worry about the chilling possibility that using screens as a baby-sitter could negatively affect their children should, perhaps, take a conservative approach until more definitive research is done.

Tool 3: All Media Contain Ideological and Value Messages

Value messages can be intended or unintended. *Manifest text* messages are those messages that the producer wants the viewer to consider. *Latent subtexts* are messages that the creator would prefer the viewer to absorb unconsciously. Messages can be positive or negative, healthy or unhealthy, and, as we have seen, messages usually target specific groups, a target market.

The back cover ad (see Figure 10.5) appeared in *Sports Illustrated for Kids*, a magazine that targets elementary school boys.

The written text is illustrated with graphic text, 10 cartoon pictures and characters that convey the message for those boys who cannot or will not read it. The written text of the ad follows.

> So there I was going to a cool party at my new school . . . and I didn't know anybody. [picture of fearful boy who is shaking] I mean I was SHAKING IN MY SHOES! [the shoes have a cute face that says, "This guy's nervous"]

Figure 10.5

I felt like I was from another planet. Then, the cap'n of confidence shows up with my ALL-TIME FAVORITE CEREAL!

Thanks to that delicious crunchberries BLAST and the help of CAP'N CRUNCH, I was ready to PARTY.

AND I DID. [largest font size on page]

Made a ton of friends and we DANCED OUR BRAINS OUT!

You and the CAP'N MAKE IT HAPPEN! CRUNCH [happy boy says, "YUM!"] (*Sports Illustrated for Kids,* 1996)

Some think this to be a benign message from Cap'n Crunch–just harmless fun. Others suggest the ad uses the rebellion of an unhealthy lifestyle and drug-based priorities to excite elementary school boys with the "cool" party lifestyle. A deconstruction might go something like this: "Cure your insecurity by ingesting a nonnutritional sugary substance that gives you a blast! Party! Dance your brains out! You need a substance to make friends! You and the substance make it happen!" Make what happen? In a country in which "obesity has increased fifty-five percent among children, and high school girls get half the exercise that they did a decade ago, the propensity for malnutrition is epidemic and the consequences for health care are enormous" (CDC, 1995, p. B1).

Is the "party" lifestyle a value to reinforce with young children when smoking, binge drinking, and drug use among teens are at dangerous levels? Media literacy helps parents and children understand the hedonistic values contained in such ads that use rebellion and pseudo-sophistication to sell a product that is merely sugar masquerading as food.

All ads and most media can be interpreted in this manner. Many positive and negative value messages, appearing as texts and subtexts, are seldom analyzed. With practice, students become better at quickly recognizing the values of gender, ethnic, lifestyle, and age stereotyping. They can differentiate gratuitously violent and sexual messages from similar messages that advance a valuable concept (*Lethal Weapon* vs. *Hamlet*). Students can discuss the promotion of confident incompetence, the denigration of the natural world, the emphasis on rebellion for the sake of rebellion, and the subtle and not-so-subtle marketing of addictions.

A particularly egregious value system involves the generally unrecognized discrimination against women primarily practiced by alcohol companies, particularly Budweiser. Consider a few recent examples from Budweiser ads: A woman is in the way of your pool shot. Ask her to move? Why bother, when you can knock her out of your way with your pool cue?

It is a cold winter night, the man is out of money, but he needs his Bud Light. What to do? It's obvious: make a trade–his girlfriend's winter coat for the beer, leaving her shivering while he makes fun of her.

Two adolescent-looking actors sneak into a figure painting class. When the model takes off her clothes, they pull out beer and binoculars, the better to leer at her. It's a party, until a spoilsport teacher–female, of course, because in Bud's young adolescent world, most women are a drag, mean, or dumb–tells them to "get out." A middle school fantasy, you say? Of course.

In another, a male expresses eternal love for his girlfriend, saying that he will die for her, yet when she asks for one of his beers, he refuses. In Bud ads, men regularly hide from wives to drink; they lie to beautiful wives who want them to come home. They "accidentally" spray beer into beautiful women's faces, yet don't try to move the bottle away, and they send them careening down a hillside, rolling over and over while trapped in a Porta Potty.

Thus, we have a bizarre reversal of an older beer marketing strategy. Beer ads used to say that beer would get the girl. Now, beer companies frequently tell young men that women are not necessary because they are not worth the trouble. Like the Jim Beam ad, why bother with a relationship? It's too much trouble. Just drink! Many male students have deconstructed these ads (which they had seen countless times before) and found it to be surprising and valuable to figure out various interpretations of the ads' meanings.

● HOW EFFECTIVE IS MEDIA EDUCATION?

The anecdotal information surrounding media education is persuasive. Popularity of media literacy and demand for media literacy presentations and workshops are rising dramatically. Publishing and marketing houses such as the Center for Media Literacy, which was founded by media literacy pioneer Liz Thoman, and the Media Education Foundation, run by Sut Jhally, are prospering.

Interestingly, one finds the ironic and disturbing phenomenon whereby *most major media curricula are currently being produced by large global media corporations* such as Primemedia and AOL-Time-Warner-Turner. Although there is much to value in these curricula, one has to ask if this is the fox guarding the hen house. One must question the motives of these global media monopolies, motives beyond their PR gains. What will be the effect of Big Media pouring money into a few relatively sympathetic media literacy groups and organizations? Big Media's interest in media literacy, like nothing else, reveals both the importance of media education and the high level of student, administrative, and citizen satisfaction with media literacy.

A small but growing body of research indicates the importance of school-based media literacy. Studies suggest that such education can, in fact, produce less vulnerable children and adolescents (Dorr, Graves, & Phelps, 1980; Huston et al., 1992; Singer et al., 1980). Studies of media literacy programs that attempt to educate children about advertising, for example, have been shown to be effective in increasing their critical viewing skills and abilities to critically perceive advertising (Feshbach, Feshbach, & Cohen, 1982; Roberts et al., 1980).

Erika Austin found that "a media literacy training program for children as young as third grade can reduce expectancies and a propensity toward unhealthy behavior, in this case underage alcohol use, by affecting children's decision-making processes" (Austin & Johnson, 1997, pp. 35-36). Others have found a "protective" effect of media education (Huston et al., 1992). Several programs have been implemented with successful results (Dorr et al., 1980; Huesmann et al., 1983; Singer et al., 1980; D. G. Singer & J. L. Singer, 1994). Robinson (1999; Robinson, Saphir, Kraemer, Varady, & Haydel, 2001; Robinson, Wilde, Narracruz, Haydel, & Varady, 2000) found that relatively simple media literacy programs had positive results with young children. As some of these studies indicate, "protectionist" programs offer significant opportunities for media literacy research, and, after all, aren't most citizens and parents ultimately interested in protecting children?

In New Mexico, the New Mexico Tobacco Use Prevention and Control Program (TUPAC) began in 1997. In 4 years, the program visited approximately 90 schools, reaching approximately 20,000 middle school students. A 90-minute multimedia presentation evolved. It explains the techniques and tactics used by advertising to create impulsive and compulsive consumption: credit cards, apparel, cosmetics, diet, body image, alcohol, and tobacco.

Students are presented with two different worlds: fantasy and reality. The presentation tries to convey that advertising tells only one of many possible stories, and that it can be deceptive, self-serving, and a bad economic deal for consumers. The students are moved to anger at the profits and lies of these corporations. The path of teen rebellion becomes a tobacco-free lifestyle. The presentation uses Madison Avenue's own selling techniques: humor, sound, graphics, rebellion, hyperbole, and selected prevention facts.

Posttests given to about 700 students at 14 schools 1 week after the presentations revealed that 73% of nonsmokers were less likely to smoke as a result of seeing the presentation; 64% of smokers had considered quitting, and 54% of smokers had actually tried to quit. Equally significant, 53% of students said they were angry at tobacco companies for using misleading advertisements, and 97% of students felt tobacco companies did not care about their welfare.

In 1998, the presentation was expanded to a 3-day curriculum, and a pilot study with third and fourth graders determined that media literacy could be effective for treating and preventing addictive and compulsive behavior. During the 1999-2000 school year, four New Mexico prevention studies indicated that media literacy prevention programs were educational, enjoyable, and effective.

A Safe and Drug Free Schools and Communities program implemented *Media 2000* at six New Mexico schools (including two at-risk schools). The program included curriculum materials with the CD-ROM, *Media Literacy: Reversing Addiction in Our Compulsive Culture,* and grade-specific lesson plans. The lesson plans addressed issues of alcohol, tobacco and other drug use, violence, nutrition, relationships, and body image. In addition, faculty in-services and presentations to parents raised community awareness. Statistical analysis of surveys showed that media literacy prevention presentations caused students to question the reality of what they saw in the media, especially in alcohol and tobacco advertising, and students were less likely to identify favorably with the people they saw on TV. In other words, the fantasy world of advertising became less desirable.

A 1999-2000 study with four Santa Fe middle schools introduced media literacy skills in relation to the portrayal of alcohol. After all-school assemblies, students volunteered to join after-school "Ad-Buster" clubs and produced counter-ads designed to counter peer pressure to drink alcohol. A total of 185 student-produced counter-ads went head-to-head with Budweiser and the other beer companies on the cable channels that kids watch. The counter-ads aired on MTV, TNT, USA, Nickelodeon, and the Discovery Channel. Students showed a significant change in their attitudes and were less likely to identify with the images and portrayals seen in alcohol advertising.

In 1999, a State Incentive Grant developed a substance abuse prevention program, Strategies for Success, within the contexts of media literacy and language arts education. A total of 1,360 students at six different middle schools in New Mexico in Albuquerque, Rio Rancho, and Portales took part.

The goals of the Strategies for Success program were the following:

- Identify different types of media

- Learn and apply transferable media literacy skills

- Analyze media using specific media literacy skills

- Counteract negative advertising

- Produce spoof ads and commercials

- Evaluate media by presenting skits/plays to parents and school

- Resist negative messages and imagery

- Recognize and understand different types of advertising and images

- Question the different contexts of ads and images (cultural, social, or political)

- Devalue advertising messages that promote addictive and risky lifestyles

- Distinguish between impulsive, compulsive, and addictive ads and behaviors

- Enjoy learning important information in a very active and challenging manner

Media literacy trainings, in-services, and parents' night presentations and activities were designed to involve the whole community. The curriculum complemented the Language Arts Standards and Benchmarks of the New Mexico State Department of Education. The schools received a copy of *Media Literacy: Reversing Addiction in Our Compulsive Culture* CD-ROM; a copy of the *Understanding Media* CD-ROM; and the video, *Just Do Media Literacy*. In addition, each school received multidisciplinary lessons, and each student received a copy of the activist guide *Standing Strong, Fighting Back*. The 6-day curriculum unit and three booster sessions were incorporated into sixth-grade language arts classes. The lessons had three skills objectives–language arts, media literacy, and prevention.

After the units and booster sessions were administered, comprehensive pretest/posttest analyses showed a marked *decrease* in favorable attitudes toward alcohol lifestyles, alcohol and tobacco companies, and tobacco use. Posttests of the comparison schools showed an *increase* in these attitudes, possibly reflecting the success of alcohol advertising. It would seem that media literacy helps to protect children from the alcohol company's barrage of goofy guys and cartoons that glorify drinking as the path to success.

All of the participating schools stated that students, teachers, and parents were happy with the units. Though not required, the schools are repeating the lessons in succeeding years. Interestingly enough, some schools' language arts teachers were initially cool to the idea of adding something else to their busy schedule. After the program, the same schools actually did extra media literacy activities. Because of the success of these programs, NMMLP has just released a CD-ROM-based K-12 health curriculum, and is about to release (2001) a 4-year project, a K-12, multidisciplinary, thematic, critical thinking curriculum.

In summary, it could be that media literacy might be an effective school-based, protective strategy, but more research is needed (see Chapter 11, this volume).

CONCLUSION: DOING MEDIA EDUCATION ●

Media literacy can be effective in the community as well as in schools. Because global media corporations have replaced many extended families and neighborhood groups, we need to revitalize our communities. Media literacy can produce a revolution. Media awareness can be the spark that explodes parental interest in children. Media literacy works best from the grassroots. Although schools are important, schools alone will not create a cultural revolution. New Mexico's program has been a "bottom-up" revolution. Media literacy activists are targeting the medical community, parents groups, the media community, businesspeople, foundations, chambers of commerce, politicians, film festivals, advertising executives, neighborhood associations, daycares, and other professional groups. Media literacy can build wide coalitions.

Making media literacy work is hard but rewarding work. Several factors can help lead to success, but perhaps the most valuable and necessary one is to create and deliver entertaining, educational, and inspirational presentations. The measure of a presentation or workshop's effectiveness should be "repeat business." In other words, is the presenter invited back to present again? Good presenters take the audience's perceptions into account and avoid getting carried away with missionary zeal, just like good teaching is student based with constant dialogue, with the teacher listening to the students' opinions, recognizing that everyone negotiates different meaning from media. Thus, although knowledge of media issues and skills is important, delivering the "most intellectual" presentation is less important than interacting with and inspiring one's students.

Another key point is to *use media* when talking about media. This axiom is not chiseled in stone; some people, like Neil Postman, can captivate audiences with the eloquence of the spoken or written word. Most of us, however, would do well

Figure 10.6

to take concrete examples to augment our workshops. A computerized hyper-media database allows presenters great flexibility. CD-ROM technology, combined with a computer and projector, puts hundreds of media examples and interpretations "just a mouse click away." It is ideal technology for leading Socratic seminars or giving multimedia presentations. CD-ROMs (see Figure 10.6) contain hundreds of examples and hundreds of pages of text.

When teaching media literacy (or anything, for that matter), one should recognize that mass electronic media can condition people to respect simplicity and emotional responses. The teacher or community activist has, therefore, an opportunity to emphasize complexity and metacognition but, at the same time, use media to provide emotional peaks and valleys, especially the humor that most people have come to expect, respect, and demand from their media.

Publicity is important for the community activist. Publicize upcoming events. When possible, use personal means, such as phone calls. A call to an important doctor, businessperson, reporter, legislator, educator, or other influential person can turn a small workshop or presentation into a large success. Remember that no group is too small or unimportant. Small groups offer the opportunity to have a conversation instead of a presentation, an opportunity for the presenter to listen, which is what good media literacy involves. Try never to be discouraged. A first presentation in an area might have a small attendance, but a good workshop will bring more opportunities with larger audiences.

Publicize Success. The following quotation from a media-literate student appeared on the front page of the *Los Angeles Times* in a story about a media literacy organization: "I still watch television, but I'm more careful. I watch it less and, when I do, I pay more attention. I've learned that everything you see has been planned for weeks, even years. And most of the time they are trying to sell you something" (Puig, 1995, p. A1). This publicity bonanza resulted from a simple press release.

Network. Whether working with a school or the community, make connections between people and organizations. Set up meetings; use the Internet; build coalitions. One can take the media literacy revolution to the streets; the task is formidable, but so was the struggle against Big Tobacco. That war is continuing, but significant gains have been made by dedicated, networked activists. In the coming decades, as the power of media corporations continues to increase, people will have to decide whether to be free, aware of their consumption of media, and knowledgeable of media's effects or, on the other hand, be Aldous Huxley's highly conditioned inhabitants of *Brave New World,* people "who do not have to be coerced, because they love their servitude" (Huxley, 1932, p. xv).

Thus, in the words of George Gerbner (1998), "Don't agonize . . . *Organize!*" Knowledge and activism are the keys, and, fortunately, the task is important, educational, entertaining, and satisfying.

Exercises

1. Read an article or view a video clip. Establish a "spectrum" of possible opinions about the example by writing down a spectrum of people who would have different reactions to that article. (Remember, people negotiate their own meanings from media, and all honest reactions should be honored). Example: Bill Clinton, Jerry Falwell, Tipper Gore, George W. Bush, Eminem, and Bart Simpson. When you have your list, assign a name to different students and have them write a paragraph deconstructing a piece of media *from that person's point of view.* Use "A Quick Deconstruction" (mentioned earlier in this chapter) for your guide. This is a valuable exercise that circumvents the reluctance of kids to express different points of view due to peer pressure. Amazing things happen when a lover of Comedy Central has to deconstruct *South Park* from the point of view of Tipper Gore or Neil Postman.

2. Take a news article or story. Analyze 10 key words for bias. Then, change the words. See how that can change the story. Make a list of the related ideas that

the story did not mention. Discuss why that might be the case. Write a script for another news story covering omitted issues that you think are important.

3. Establish a definition of news (information useful to citizens in our democracy). View a national network television news program. List the stories. How long was each? How much news fits the definition? How did each story make you feel? How many of the stories cause one to feel anxious? How many were "mayhem" (murders, disasters, typhoons, floods, tornadoes, repeat stories about older mayhem stories, etc.)? How useful are these stories to the average person? How many of the other stories are? What vital information do the stories leave out? Which were the most "enjoyable?" Were the most enjoyable ones valuable for citizens in a democracy? Were any of the stories truly educational? How much of the half hour is advertising? What were the advertisements? Note: Neil Postman's theory is that bad news makes people anxious, and anxious people buy more pain relievers, insurance, and the other stuff advertised on the news. Make lists of the nation's and world's most pressing problems. What did the program leave out? Were any addressed in meaningful detail? What led the news? Was it the most important issue? If not, why was it first?

4. View a local news program. Many of the questions above also apply. How much of the half hour is local news? How much was repeated national news? How much was advertising? How much was sports? How much was weather? Is all of the weather useful? Did the hosts spend some time in "chitchat?" How much? Were there any "fluff" stories (cute and emotional but useless–kitten rescued from tree)? Did any stories seem to benefit a corporation (as much as 25% of news stories are VNRs-video news releases from corporations)? Make a list of the most important issues in your community for you, your school, or your neighbors. Were any of them addressed? Again, make your own news program. Visit a local television station. Take a tour. Or have a representative come to your class. Ask the news manager questions about their program. Compare the local television news program to a newspaper for content, detail, variety, depth, and usefulness. Think about the process of reading a newspaper versus watching TV news. In which process do you think the individual consumer has more freedom? Learns more? Has more interest? Why? Is it the same for everyone? Which medium is better for voters? Democracy? Seek out some alternative sources of media and apply the same questions, making comparisons between the mainstream and independent media sources.

5. Bill McKibben (1992) insightfully and humorously observes the current explosion of information that has transformed our cultural landscape. He also concludes that, despite our having access to more information than any other culture in history, "we also live in a moment of deep ignorance, when vital knowledge that humans have always possessed about who we are and where we live seems beyond our reach" (p. 9). McKibben refers to this condition as an

Unenlightenment, an age of missing information. One can test this theory in many ways, but here are a few. Watch a nature program with time lapse photography of plants exploding before your very eyes or view an SUV commercial that takes place in a natural setting. What meaning is sent about the natural world in these media mesages? As the SUV chews its way across fields, climbs mountains, and blasts through forests, what is said about ecology, the delicate balances that maintain life? What message is sent about how to enjoy nature? Or the kind of stimulation that brings pleasure? Or conservation of resources? Or whether there are any limits to man's enjoyment of nature? Next, grow a plant from a seed. Keep a detailed log. What does growing a plant teach about limits? What happens if the plant does not get enough water or light or nutrients? Or too much? Which teaches the truer lesson about limits, the fantasy world of advertising or the natural world of growing the plant?

CHAPTER **11**

TEN ARGUMENTS IN FAVOR OF SOLUTIONS

This instrument can teach, it can illuminate; yes, and it can even inspire. But it can do so only to the extent that humans are determined to use it to those ends. Otherwise it is merely wires and lights in a box.

—Edward R. Murrow (1958, p. 12)

Values are not, and will not be, inculcated by the family, the church, or other social institutions in either the present or the future. They are, and will be, inculcated by the visual and electronic media.

—Lester Thurow (1996, p. 277)

TABLE 11.1 How Much Do Children and Teens Know About Current Events?

Percentage of 10- to 17-year-olds who knew or could name . . .	
One of the women justices on the Supreme Court	6
The Speaker of the U.S. House of Representatives	23
The Vice President of the United States	58
versus	
Who Dennis Rodman is	75
The family characters on The Simpsons	95

SOURCE: Adapted from Stanger (1998).

A vast literature now exists that attests to the power of the media in influencing children's and adolescents' beliefs and, potentially, their behavior as well. Television can be a powerful teacher. The only question is, what is it teaching? (See Table 11.1.) As one eminent group of researchers notes,

> The question of "which comes first" is misleading and irrelevant. People are born into a symbolic environment with television as its mainstream. Children begin viewing several years before they begin reading, and well before they can even talk. Television viewing both shapes and is a stable part of lifestyles and outlooks. It links the individual to a larger if synthetic world, a world of television's own making. (Gerbner, Gross, et al., 1994, pp. 23-24)

Unfortunately, American media currently contribute more to adverse health outcomes than to positive or prosocial ones, but it does not have to remain this way. Listed below are 10 potential solutions that would either significantly improve the media or would help immunize children and teenagers against their harmful effects.

1. IMPROVING PROGRAMMING QUALITY ●

Although the United States was the first nation in the world to have television, it is unique in lacking any clear public policy regarding it (Kunkel & Wilcox, 2001; Paik, 2001; Palmer, 1988). American television was established and regulated according to the Communications Act, passed by Congress in 1934. The preamble to that act states that the public owns the airwaves, which are leased back to the networks to produce programming *in the public's best interests.*

Many critics of American television now feel that the programming produced is almost extraneous to the real purpose of television, to deliver the audience that advertisers want (Flint & Snierson, 1999). As a result, the major networks have abandoned their mass audience and chosen to concentrate on White, urban teens and young adults—so-called "upscale audiences" with real purchasing power. For example, the WB's *Felicity* has ratings similar to the network's two highest rated African American series, yet the former commanded $80,000 per 30-second commercial spot versus less than $40,000 for a spot during the African American series (Flint & Snierson, 1999). Clearly, business decisions rule the networks, not a desire to create programming that will enrich viewers' lives. Writers, directors, and producers who howl about the encroachment on their First Amendment rights whenever public health activists or senators criticize TV remain curiously quiet about the impact that Madison Avenue has had on their writing.

Although the Hollywood and New York creative communities see little problem with the quality of their product, the research literature and most parents would disagree. American media are the most graphically violent and sexually suggestive in the world. At present, the networks and studios have virtually no incentive to create more educational and healthier programming, other than vague threats from Congress and the risk of noncompliance with the Children's Television Act of 1990. That legislation requires local television stations to air "educational and informational" programming for children and to keep records of this content. (The terms *educational* and *informational* were left vague, perhaps intentionally so. Who is to judge what is "educational"? Viewers? Congress? The FCC? A panel of educators?) Nevertheless, that did not stop TV stations from asserting that they knew what *educational* meant (see Figure 11.1). In 1993, several stations submitted the following description of the cartoon *Yogi Bear* to support that it was "specifically designed" to serve children's educational needs:

> Yogi Bear: Despite the fact that the program is entertaining, it nevertheless does teach certain moral and ethical values such as not to do stupid things or you will have trouble; don't take what doesn't belong to you or be prepared to face the music. (Kunkel, 1998, p. 45)

Interestingly, the entertainment industry seems to have an intrinsic grasp of this issue. Hollywood is quick to point out its exemplary works, such as *Schindler's List, Boyz N the Hood,* or the old *Cosby Show,* as being pro-humanitarian, anti-violence, and demonstrating positive values. According to the creative community, such works ennoble our society. But if that is the case (as we believe it is), surely other programming can have significant negative effects (see Figure 11.2). The media street is not one-way.

Figure 11.1
SOURCE: Copyright Gary Markstein and Copley News Service. Used with permission.

Figure 11.2
SOURCE: Mike Smith; reprinted by permission of United Feature Syndicate, Inc.

One frequently heard complaint from people in the entertainment industry is that they are simply "giving people what they want," and sex and violence "sell." For many years, local newscasters have reportedly used the rule of thumb "if it bleeds, it leads." Yet, there is significant evidence to the contrary that the industry chooses to ignore. Gerbner, Morgan, and Signorielli (1994) compared Nielsen ratings of two samples containing more than 100 programs each: one sample with only violent programs, the other with only nonviolent programs. The nonviolent programs had a higher overall rating and market share. Similarly, a movie industry study found that PG-rated movies were three times more likely to gross $100 million than R-rated films were (Giles & Fleming, 1993). Similarly, another study that examined the success or failure of 2,000 films between 1988 and 1997 found that G-rated films were eight times more profitable than were R-rated films, yet 55% of all films produced were R rated, compared with only 3% G ratings. In a recent study, researchers adjusted the violent content in several films and found that cutting out the violence increased the films' enjoyability for college women but did not affect men's enjoyment of them (Berry et al., 1999). Finally, public opinion polls document that the entertainment industry is simply wrong in their assumptions about what people want. More than 80% of the American public feel that the amount of violence in movies is a serious problem, for example, and 75% of parents say that they have either turned off a television program or left a movie theater because of the violence being shown (Mediascope, 2000a).

Nevertheless, the creative community needs positive as well as negative incentives. One such positive incentive was the gift of $70 billion worth of publicly owned airwaves to broadcasting companies free of charge. In 1999, Congress gave away additional airspace so that television stations could go digital. According to a former president of NBC News, Lawrence Grossman, this represented "one of the biggest financial coups of the century" (Grossman, 1999, p. 53).

Despite this apparent windfall, children's programming needs specific funding. Increased funding for children's TV could come from either a national tax on television sets annually (Britain funds the BBC with a $75/set tax/year) or a 10% windfall profits tax on children's toy manufacturers and food producers who use advertising to help sell their products to children. Sales of Mighty Morphin Power Rangers paraphernalia in the mid-1990s reached $1 billion in 1995, for example (Meyer & Tsiantar, 1994). After expenses for personnel, production, and marketing, perhaps the profits were $350 million. A 10% windfall tax would have generated $35 million for a children's television trust fund.

Other countries have given far higher priority to daily educational programming for children and adolescents—most notably, Great Britain and Japan. They have accomplished this by adequately funding their public television stations (Palmer, 1988). By contrast, in the United States, there is not a single hour of daily educational programming for children on any of the six major commercial networks (the last such show was *Captain Kangaroo*). The Corporation for Public

---

TABLE 11.2 Joint Network Standards on TV Violence

Endorses voluntary limits on

Gratuitous or excessive violence

Glamorous depictions of violence

Scenes showing excessive gore, pain, or physical suffering

Scenes showing uses of force that are "on the whole" inappropriate for a home-viewing medium

Replicable, unique, or "ingenious" depictions of inflicting pain or injury

Portrayals of dangerous behavior or weapons that invite imitation by children

In children's programs: realistic portrayals of violence that are unduly frightening

Gratuitous depiction of animal abuse

Encourages

Portrayal of the consequences of violence

Scheduling all programs with regard for the likely composition of the intended audience

Urges caution

In stories and scenes showing children as victims

In themes, plots, or scenes that mix sex and violence (e.g., rape)

SOURCE: News release, Senator Simon's office, Washington, DC, December 1992.

Broadcasting, which controls PBS, is woefully underfunded and, of course, has to program for adults as well as children. Yet, more often than not, public broadcasting is fighting Congress to keep its budget from being cut rather than being expanded.

Some observers have suggested that children and adolescents deserve their own separate, commercial-free, educational channel—a Children's Television Network (Strasburger, 1988). Currently, 76% of households in the United States have cable TV (Nielsen Media Research, 2000). In fact, one fourth of children have a cable hookup in their own bedrooms (Roberts, Foehr, et al., 1999). If current predictions are correct (Waters & Beachy, 1993), 500 channels will be carried into most households within the next decade using fiber-optic phone lines. If so, at least 10 to 20 such channels could be reserved for commercial-free, age-specific, educational programming for children and adolescents.

Broadcasters have a variety of ways that they could improve the current state of American programming. First, they could adhere to their own, voluntary guidelines regarding portrayals of violence (see Table 11.2). Second, they could adopt analogous, voluntary guidelines regarding portrayals of sex and sexuality (see Table 11.3) and cigarettes, alcohol, and other drugs. Movie, video game, and music

TABLE 11.3 Guide to Responsible Sexual Content in Media

Recognize sex as a healthy and natural part of life.

Parent and child conversations about sex are important and healthy and should be encouraged.

Demonstrate that not only the young, unmarried, and beautiful have sexual relationships.

Not all affection and touching must culminate in sex.

Portray couples having sexual relationships with feelings of affection, love, and respect for one another.

Consequences of unprotected sex should be discussed or shown.

Miscarriage should not be used as a dramatic convenience for resolving an unwanted pregnancy.

Use of contraceptives should be indicated as a normal part of a sexual relationship.

Avoid associating violence with sex or love.

Rape should be depicted as a crime of violence, not of passion.

The ability to say "no" should be recognized and respected.

SOURCE: Strasburger (1995). Modified from Haffner and Kelly (1987).

producers could consider such guidelines as well. When 85% or more of contemporary movies contain tobacco use (Escamilla et al., 2000; Everett et al., 1998; Sargent et al., 2001), there is considerable room for improvement. All too often, movie characters are shown smoking either because the actors themselves are smokers or because the writers want to demonstrate a character quirk (Shields et al., 1999). Smoking needs to be "de-normalized" (Males, 1999). Third, producers and advertisers need to adopt a more responsible attitude toward the depiction of extremely thin women as role models in programming, music videos, and advertising (Kilbourne, 1999). A wider variety of more realistic body shapes needs to be displayed (British Medical Association, 2000). Fourth, the industry could do a far better job of depicting racial and ethnic diversity in its programming. Although Bill Cosby made huge gains for Blacks and Black-themed shows in the 1980s, by the 1999 season, the prime-time scene was remarkably "White" (Bogle, 2001). Only 10% of characters on entertainment programs were African American, a decrease from 18% during the 1993-1994 season. Hispanic characters accounted for less than 4% of all roles, yet Hispanic Americans make up more than 11% of the U.S. population (Farhi, 1999; Flint & Snierson, 1999). Finally, station managers could try to exceed the basic requirements of the Children's Television Act by broadcasting even more educational programming for children, something that few broadcasters have chosen to do (Kunkel, 1998).

Beginning in the fall of 1997, the Federal Communication Commission's (FCC's) new rules went into effect, which declared that television stations must do the following (Hill-Scott, 2001):

- Serve the educational and information (E/I) needs of children under age 16

- Air a minimum of 3 hours per week of educational or informational programming between the hours of 7 a.m. and 10 p.m.

- List the E/I symbol in program guides

- Provide a written statement about educational and informational objectives, to be filed quarterly with the FCC (Form 398)

However, compliance with these rules is almost completely voluntary because not a single TV station has ever lost its license by failing to do so. Furthermore, broadcasters can air less than 3 hours per week of E/I programming if they can demonstrate that they are serving the child audience in other ways (Jordan, 2001). How have broadcasters reacted to these new rules? In 1998, an analysis of the programming on the six national networks found that 36% of the programs offered as E/I had minimal educational content (Jordan, 1998). A year later, that figure had dropped to 17% (Woodard, 1999). Currently, the figure is back up to 23% (Jordan, 2000). But there are other concerns as well:

- E/I programs are the most likely to be preempted: 46% of the time in the Philadelphia market, for example (Hill-Scott, 2001).

- Local stations tend to keep to the minimum level of 3 hours per week (Jordan, 2000).

- The "E/I" symbol is not widely used or recognized, and parents are not even aware of its meaning or significance (Schmitt, 2000).

- Only 7% of the E/I programs are for preschoolers, who probably need this content the most. Programs are aimed more at elementary school children (57%) and teens (36%) (Jordan, 2000). Could this possibly have something to do with associated advertising revenues?

- Although 77% of the programs studied met the E/I guidelines, only 20% were deemed "highly educational" (Jordan, 2000).

Some critics feel that the "conventional wisdom" in Hollywood is wrong and that it prevents writers and producers from making better television programming for children and teens. For example, Jordan and Woodard (1998) point out four myths that are widely held within the industry:

1. Children outgrow educational programming by the time they are 6.

2. The only way to provide educational programming for older children is to focus on social concerns and avoid academic content.

3. Educational programming is more expensive to create than entertainment programming.

4. It is preferable to target an audience of boys than an audience of girls or a mixed audience.

Others feel that the Children's Television Act has been effective in creating better programming alternatives for children, if only to alert station managers that they can no longer ignore the interests of their youngest viewers (Hill-Scott, 2001). Yet some estimates put the amount of child-oriented television programming on all network and cable channels at 1,000 hours per week (Jackson, 1999). Why be satisfied with only 3 hours of educational programming per week per channel? Other countries do far more (Strasburger & Donnerstein, 1999, 2000). Given that television stations were originally licensed by the FCC to produce programming in the public's "best interests," mandating an hour a day for children does not seem excessive or harsh (Strasburger & Donnerstein, 1999, 2000).

● 2. IMPROVING ADVERTISING

Advertising exists to sell products. Without public pressure and federal regulations, businesses would arguably do whatever it takes to sell their products and satisfy their stockholders. During the past two decades, the total number of commercials per hour has skyrocketed from 11 to 40 per hour (Byrd-Bredbrenner & Grasso, 2000b). There are two primary reasons for this increase: the elimination of the voluntary Code of the National Association of Broadcasters (NAB), which permitted only 9½ minutes of advertising per hour of prime-time television, and the decrease in average commercial length, from 30 seconds in the mid-1970s to 22 seconds currently. At present, nearly 15 minutes per hour of prime-time TV is devoted to commercials (Byrd-Bredbrenner & Grasso, 2000b).

The recent explosion of commercialism within school systems is a by-product of the corporate drive to reach consumers as young as possible. In this case, many school administrators and teachers are aiding and abetting big business. But what happens when the products are potentially harmful, or the audience is unable to decipher properly the advertisements being broadcast? Currently, the food and alcohol industries account for nearly 16% of the $73 billion mass media advertising market, second only to the automobile industry (Byrd-Bredbenner & Grasso, 2000b). Does society have a duty to children and teenagers to protect them against unfair exposure to advertising or exposure to legitimate advertising for unhealthy products (Strasburger, 2001b)?

Alcohol and Cigarettes. As U.S. Supreme Court Justice Tom Clark once said, there is no war between the Constitution and common sense (Shiffrin, 1991). Compelling public health interests exist in protecting at least children and adolescents against the advertising of cigarettes and alcoholic beverages, for example. Because advertising of these products represents "commercial speech," it is not automatically protected under the First Amendment (Ile & Knoll, 1990; Shiffrin, 1991). In fact, commercial speech received no protection under the First Amendment until a court decision in 1976. Few industry spokespersons would challenge the constitutionality of the Public Health Act of 1969 that banned televised commercials for cigarettes. Furthermore, tobacco and alcohol advertising could be banned as being "unfair and deceptive," given its appeal to underage drinkers and smokers. The Federal Trade Commission (FTC) is already empowered by Congress to restrict such advertising.

The one significant drawback to a broadcast ban on alcohol advertising is that from a public health viewpoint, it would be unwise if the ban also eliminated effective counteradvertising. Many public health advocates feel that the Public Health Act of 1969 actually did more harm than good by eliminating minute-for-minute, aggressive counteradvertisements that were just beginning to be effective in diminishing the public's consumption of cigarettes (Atkin, 1993a; Grube & Wallack, 1994). A reasonable alternative would be to insist on tombstone advertising (i.e., ads that show the product only but do not depict the qualities that the drinker might acquire). This would avoid the party dogs, the Swedish bikini team, and the entire humorous mythology that is allowed to surround drinking and getting drunk. Preteens and teens are unusually sensitive to these images and the fact that alcohol ads "normalize" drinking. Similarly, legislation to eliminate the tax deductability of alcohol advertising might be successful in decreasing consumption (Massing, 1998).

On the other hand, cigarette advertising has become so deceptive and harmful that it justifies a ban in all media, including promotional activities aimed at adolescents (American Academy of Pediatrics [AAP], 1995b, 2001b; Gostin & Brandt, 1993; Kessler, 2001). Researchers are closing in on establishing a causal connection between tobacco advertising and marketing and onset of adolescent smoking. In the latest study, adolescents who owned a tobacco promotional item and could name a brand of cigarettes whose advertisements attracted their attention were more than twice as likely to have begun smoking a year later (Biener & Siegel, 2000). The tobacco settlement of 1998 may help considerably in these regards. Cigarette manufacturers agreed to discontinue billboard advertising and sponsorship of sports teams or any events where children may be attending. In Minnesota, the $6 billion settlement with the tobacco industry actually included a ban on cigarette product placements in movies (Brown & Witherspoon, 1998). Tobacco companies must also contribute to educational campaigns to prevent teens from smoking and research to help smokers quit. Finally, Joe Camel was retired, as was wearing apparel with tobacco logos (Horgen et al., 2001). However, to date the tobacco settlement has had little demonstrable impact on either the amount of cigarette advertising in magazines or on the exposure of young people to such advertising (King & Siegel, 2001). All of this may sound like society is headed in a healthier direction, except for one very interesting fact: According to the FTC, the tobacco industry has actually spent more on advertising and promotion postsettlement—a record $8.2 billion in 1999, which was a 22% increase from 1998 (Journal Wire Reports, 2001). So, this story is far from over.

Recently, the National Institute on Drug Abuse (NIDA) embarked on a $178 million media campaign, which may grow into a $1 billion 5-year effort (Brown & Witherspoon, 1998). Unfortunately, this amount of money pales in comparison with the $8 billion spent annually on tobacco advertising and the $2 billion spent annually on alcohol advertising (Strasburger, 2001a). In addition, the National Youth Anti-Drug Media Campaign will target illicit drugs only, not mainstream drugs such as tobacco and alcohol. The grand total is $178 million a year to combat illegal drugs versus $10 billion a year to entice children, teens, and adults to use legal drugs. This illustrates a key point in this discussion: When public health comes into conflict with economic health, the latter usually wins, especially when the federal government is involved.

Toys. Although the Children's Television Act of 1990 limited the amount of commercial time on children's television to no more than 10.5 minutes per hour on weekends and 12 minutes per hour on weekdays, it did not specifically ban socalled program-length commercials (programs like ABC's 1969 cartoon *Hot Wheels,* a cartoon based on toy cars) (Allen, 2001). Such commercials still exist, the most notorious of them being *Pokémon,* which is built around a product (Pokémon cards) and actually encourages viewers to collect all the cards.

The major advertisers on children's television—Hasbro, Mattel, Kraft, General Foods, and Kellogg—spend about $1 billion a year (Alexander, 2001). All European countries place far more severe restrictions on advertising to children than the United States does (Valkenburg, 2000). As the HBO/Consumer Reports series *Buy Me That* so eloquently illustrates, advertising for toys must show them realistically and fairly. The industry's watchdog organization, CARU (Children's Advertising Review Unit), needs more teeth in its ability to reign in its voluntary members. Likewise, the FTC needs greater political support, especially from Congress, to act against unfair or deceptive advertising aimed at children.

Food Commercials. Advertising of food products that are nutritionally unsound must also be severely curtailed if American parents are truly motivated to improve their children's health (Strasburger, 2001b). The most appropriate place to do this would be on Saturday morning TV, which currently is filled with ads for heavily sugared cereals and calorically dense snack foods (Borzekowski, 2001). Research shows that even brief exposures to televised food commercials can influence children as young as preschoolers in their food choices (Borzekowski & Robinson, 2001). If the tobacco settlement included doing away with Joe Camel and other cartoon characters, should not cultural icons such as Ronald McDonald and Tony the Tiger be forced to retire as well (Horgen et al., 2001)? Some critics have even suggested a tax on junk food, which might even up the remarkable disparity between what the National Cancer Institute spends to influence people to eat sensibly ($1 million a year) and what the food industry spends to encourage people to eat food that is high in fat, sugar, or salt ($33 billion a year) (Jacobson, 2000).

Just as with the debate about alcohol and cigarette advertising, the alternative to banning or restricting junk food advertising is to promote aggressive counter-advertising. Such ads are effective, and the government could require food companies to provide money for equal airtime for messages about what constitutes healthy nutrition (Horgen et al., 2001). However, with more than 78 lobbying groups and trade associations to protect its interests, the food industry is not likely to acquiesce to such a requirement without a major fight. But "quieter" avenues for change exist: Tax deductions for advertising expenses of unhealthy foods could be eliminated, or conversely, increased tax deductions could be given for advertising expenses of healthy foods (Horgen et al., 2001).

Schools. Advertising in schools is one of the most current and controversial issues in media studies (Strasburger, 2001b). Channel One's efforts have been nearly dwarfed by stories such as Dr. Pepper paying $3.45 million over 10 years to a Texas school district for advertising space in gyms, stadiums, and even on school rooftops, or a $200,000 high-tech scoreboard at Sycamore High School in Cincinnati, which has space for 17 advertisements on rotating panels (Wartella & Jennings, 2001). One school district in Colorado Springs signed a 10-year, $8 million deal with Coca-Cola, complete with a consumption clause. When the students were not drinking up to standards, a district administrator wrote a memo to area principals asking them to allow Coke in the classrooms (Manning, 1999). By 2001, 200 of the nation's 12,000 school districts had exclusive contracts with soft-drink companies (Brasher, 2001a). A new proposal by the U.S. Department of Agriculture would require that all food sold in schools meet nutritional standards and thus would put an end to such contracts and to vending machines filled with junk food (Brasher, 2001a). In Maryland, lawmakers have proposed prohibiting all advertising in public schools, including exclusive contracts with soft-drink companies after Charles County signed a 10-year, $6 million deal with Coca-Cola (LeDuc, 2001).

This issue seems to polarize people into two large groups. On one side are those who believe that advertising is everywhere, public schools are chronically underfunded, and therefore "no harm, no foul." Even teachers can subscribe to this philosophy: "You just don't turn down a deal that will bring $20,000 a year to your school," according to one (quoted in Manning, 1999, p. 12). In vocal opposition are those who believe that schools should be "commercial-free zones" whose primary and sole purpose should be to educate children, not to sell them out to the highest bidder (Richards et al., 1998). Occasionally, school systems turn down lucrative deals. At Berkeley High School, Pepsi offered the school $90,000 and a fancy scoreboard in exchange for a vending machine deal. The school said no. Nearby, San Francisco approved the first Commercial Free Schools Act in the country (Manning, 1999). However, good national data about how American parents and other adults feel about this issue do not currently exist. Many parents are simply unaware of how much advertising already exists within their own school systems.

Probably the most insidious example of commercialism within schools is sponsored educational material (SEM), which can come in the form of posters, videos, magazines, or computer software. Nearly 80% contain biased or incomplete information that favors the company (Manning, 1999). For example, an environmental curriculum video by Shell Oil touts the virtues of the internal combustion engine and opines, "You can't get to nature without gasoline or cars" (Manning, 1999, p. 17). Clearly, given the educational mission of schools and teachers, SEMs have no place in classrooms, no matter how poorly funded the school district is. As for the other in-school practices, unless one philosophy wins out over the other, more research will be needed to determine the exact impact of Channel One and other advertising on the students.

● 3. PERCEIVING MEDIA VIOLENCE AS A PUBLIC HEALTH THREAT

Media violence is not the leading cause of violence in society, but it is the most easily remediable cause. Estimates place the contribution of media violence to real-life violence at between 10% and 30% (Comstock & Strasburger, 1993). Other factors are certainly significant: poverty, racism, unique personality factors, and so on. Nearly all children have witnessed real-life violence during their childhood. In one study of 175 children ages 9 to 12 who attended an urban pediatric clinic, 97% of children had seen violence, including 31% witnessing someone being shot, stabbed, or killed (Purugganan, Stein, Silver, & Benenson, 2000). But the media present numerous, compelling examples of violence vicariously, and these too have an impact. In one recent study, demographic variables, parental monitoring, television-viewing habits, and exposure to real-life violence explained nearly half of 2,245 children's self-reported violent behaviors (Singer et al., 1999). In another,

Figure 11.3
SOURCE: Copyright Mike Thompson and Copley News Service. Used with permission.

the only significant predictor of attitudes toward media violence was the amount of television viewed (Hough & Erwin, 1997).

The battle over media violence and its impact on society has been raging for half a century (see Figure 11.3). In 1954, Senator Estes Kefauver, chairman of the Senate Subcommittee on Juvenile Delinquency, was the first public official openly to question the need for violence in television entertainment. The television industry replied that perhaps some risk existed but that more research was needed (Liebert & Sprafkin, 1988). Now, hundreds of research studies later, the entertainment industry continues to deny that television programs, movies, or video games have any impact on children or adolescents (Wartella, Olivarez, & Jennings, 1998). Yet of those many studies, only a handful have shown no effect. No other area of media has been so thoroughly researched, with such convincing results (AAP, 2001b; Bushman & Anderson, 2001; Eron, 1995; Strasburger & Donnerstein, 2000; Villani, 2001). And this is all the more remarkable given that social science research is notoriously difficult to conduct and that positive findings are often hidden among the clutter of many other variables (Comstock & Strasburger, 1993). In fact, one of the most expert researchers in the field is convinced that the evidence link-

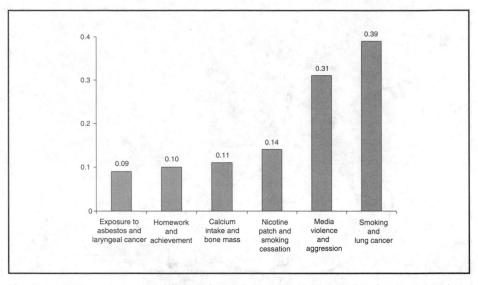

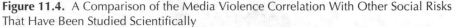

Figure 11.4. A Comparison of the Media Violence Correlation With Other Social Risks That Have Been Studied Scientifically

SOURCE: From Bushman and Huesmann (2001, p. 235). Reprinted with permission from Sage.

How strong is the association between media violence and real-life violence? Some researchers feel that the relationship rivals the association between smoking and lung cancer.

ing media violence to aggressive behavior is nearly as strong as the evidence linking smoking to lung cancer (see Figure 11.4) (Bushman & Huesmann, 2001).

In the 1990s, America experienced an outbreak of schoolyard shootings, which sometimes seemed nearly epidemic in proportions. From Jonesboro, Arkansas to Springfield, Oregon to Littleton, Colorado, teenagers were running for their lives almost monthly on the national news. Although it brought the issue of media violence to the forefront once again, the school shootings continue to be minimized by the government and misunderstood by parents and educators (see Figure 11.5). In fact, although there is a one in two million chance of being killed in school, 71% of Americans feel that a shooting is likely in their school (Brooks, Schiraldi, & Ziedenberg, 2000). At the same time, Baby Boom parents cannot ever remember feeling threatened when they attended school, and even one school shooting death in any given year seems too high (Strasburger, 1999). There are several important points to consider (Strasburger & Grossman, 2001):

1. Nearly all of the many shooters were exposed to and enamored of various forms of media violence. Although a *New York Times* study of the 102 teen and adult rampage killers from 1949 to 2000 found that only 13% had an interest in violent media (Fessenden, 2000), this statistic may be misleading. The findings were based on self-reports of media use. Because of the "third-person effect," many

Figure 11.5
SOURCE: Copyright John Trever, *Albuquerque Journal*. Reprinted with permission.

people, especially teenagers, deny that they themselves are ever influenced by the media (Eveland et al., 1999).

2. "Justifiable" violence is the most commonly portrayed type of violence on television and in movies, and it is also the most powerfully reinforcing (Bushman & Huesmann, 2001; Willis & Strasburger, 1998). After his arrest, 16-year-old Luke Woodham of Pearl, Mississippi, was quoted as saying, "I am not insane. I am angry. I killed because people like me are mistreated every day. I did this to show society push us and we will push back. Murder is not weak and slow-witted; murder is gutsy and daring" (Nationline, 1997, p. 3A). Where else but in the media would he have learned such distorted notions?

3. American media are unique in portraying "funny violence." One of the Littleton killers supposedly laughed at a student hiding under a cafeteria table and yelled "Peek-a-boo" before shooting her in the face.

4. Guns and weaponry are glorified on television, in movies, and particularly in violent video games such as *Doom* and *Quake*. On any given day, one out of every four boys will be playing a video game such as *Doom* or *Duke Nukem* (Roberts, Foehr, et al., 1999).

Are we teaching children how to kill? That is the provocative question asked by Lt. Col. (ret.) David Grossman, a former West Point Psychology Professor and Army ranger and consultant to law enforcement agencies around the world (Grossman, 1995; Grossman & DeGaetano, 1999). In the Paducah, Kentucky, shooting, 14-year-old Michael Carneal walked into his school, opened fire on a prayer group, but never moved his feet, never fired very far to the left, right, or up or down. He simply fired once at everything that popped up on his "video screen." In law enforcement or the military, the normal response is to fire at one target until it drops, then move on. But in video games, you fire at each target only once, which is what Carneal did. In addition, although he had never fired an actual gun in his life, Carneal's eight shots had eight hits, all head and upper torso, with the result that three teens were killed and one paralyzed (Grossman & DeGaetano, 1999).

Similarly, in Jonesboro, Arkansas, only one of the two boys had any experience with real guns, but both were avid video game players. With a combined total of 27 shots from more than 100 yards, they hit 15 people. Dylan Klebold and Eric Harris, the Columbine killers, were likewise obsessed with video games. In fact, Eric Harris had reprogrammed his edition of *Doom* so that it looked like his neighborhood, complete with the houses of people he hated (Grossman & DeGaetano, 1999).

In the United States, video game revenues now exceed $10 billion, and children who have home systems average about 90 minutes per day (Federman, Carbone, Chen, & Munn, 1996). Many experts feel that the mechanical, interactive quality of "first-person shooter" games such as *Doom* or *007 Golden Eye* make them potentially more dangerous than movie or television violence. The most violent of these games use operant conditioning to teach young people to kill. The military uses adaptations of similar games to teach new recruits to kill (Grossman, 1995; Grossman & DeGaetano, 1999). After all, killing is not a natural human endeavor. In World War II, soldiers only fired at their targets 15% of the time. By the Vietnam War, that rate was up to 95% because the military had learned that it could condition recruits to fire at human targets using MACS (Multipurpose Arcade Combat Simulators), essentially supercharged Nintendo games (Grossman, 1995).

Are the schoolyard shootings the direct result of violent media? No. The causes are almost certainly multifactorial: Disturbed adolescents who are influenced by violent media and who go unnoticed by overburdened schools, teachers, and parents get access to guns and start firing at their teachers and classmates (Strasburger & Grossman, 2001). At present, perhaps the most accurate observation would be that violent media may serve as a catalyst for a few selected individuals who are already predisposed toward violence and have both the motive and the opportunity to do harm (see Figure 11.6). But teenagers do not necessarily need guns to kill. In January 2001, a 13-year-old boy was found guilty of murdering a 6-year-old girl. He said he was imitating wrestling moves he had seen on *WWF Smackdown* by Dwayne "The Rock" Johnson. The boy weighed 180 pounds, the girl 48 pounds; he pummeled her to death ("Conviction Urged," 2000). Young boys are

Figure 11.6
SOURCE: Copyright John Branch, *San Antonio Express-News*. Used with permission.

not inherently violent (Pollack, 1999). But certainly violent media have to represent one of the more easily remediable influences on violent or aggressive behavior in society. In addition, the media need to recognize the risk of imitative violence after reporting on such violent incidents (Kostinsky, Bixler, & Kettl, 2001).

Where should society start in addressing such a difficult and far-reaching issue? First and foremost, media violence should not be marketed to children. Yet a September 2000 report issued by the FTC found that the entertainment industry is guilty of doing exactly that (FTC, 2000). For example, of 44 movies rated R for violence, 35 (80%) were targeted to children under 17, according to the studios' own marketing plans. The plan for one violent R-rated film stated, "Our goal was to find the elusive teen target audience and make sure everyone between the ages of 12-18 was exposed to the film" (FTC, 2000, p. iii). Half of movie theaters surveyed admitted teens ages 13 to 16 to R-rated films without an accompanying adult. But no medium was entirely blameless. Of 55 music recordings with the "parental advisory" label, 15 (27%) specifically targeted teenagers. Of the 118 video games with an M (Mature) rating for violence, 83 (70%) targeted children under 17 (FTC, 2000). Although a follow-up report 6 months later found some improvement within the movie and video game industries, the music industry had made no changes. All five major recording companies continue "routinely" to advertise music with explicit content in magazines with significant teen readerships and on after-school TV shows popular with teens (FTC, 2001).

Second, children and teens should not have access to violent media, especially violent video games. In 2000, Montgomery Ward and Sears announced that games with an "M" rating such as *Mortal Kombat* and *Resident Evil* would not be sold at their stores (Keith, 2000). This was a completely voluntary decision that did not require local, state, or federal legislation.

Third, the National Television Violence Study (NTVS) provides an excellent roadmap for dealing with media violence on the big and little screens (Federman, 1998; Wilson, Kunkel, et al., 1999):

For the television and movie industry:

1. Accept some responsibility for the programming produced (see Figure 11.7). Accept responsibility for and discontinue the deceptive marketing practices documented in the FTC report of September 2000.

2. Produce more programs with less violence.

3. Show violent acts being punished.

4. Show the consequences of violence.

5. Show less justification for violent actions.

6. Place greater emphasis on anti-violence themes when violence is depicted.

7. Develop more prosocial cartoons and other programming for preschool children.

For policymakers:

1. Recognize the importance of context in assessing media violence (see Figure 11.8).

2. Accept that there is a cohesive body of research that documents certain risks associated with beaming media violence at young people. The U.S. Surgeon General's Scientific Advisory Commission (1972), the National Institute of Mental Health (Pearl et al., 1982), the American Academy of Pediatrics (1995b, 2001b), the American Medical Association (1996), the American Psychological Association (1993), the Centers for Disease Control and Prevention (CDC, 1991), and the National Academy of Sciences (Reiss & Roth, 1993) have all issued reports calling the nation's attention to the dangers of media violence. These are all groups with public health at the center of their mission. Yet many in the entertainment industry continue to deny that there is any cause for concern (Kunkel & Wilcox, 2001).

3. Continue close scrutiny of the amount of violence on TV and in movies. The NTVS should probably become an annual content analysis, expanded to include movies, video games, and music videos and funded by Congress or by the industries themselves.

TABLE 11.4 Gun Deaths: United States Versus Other Countries

United States	36,000	(1995)
Canada	1,189	(1994)
United Kingdom	277	(1994)
Japan	93	(1995)

SOURCE: Data from *AAP News, 15*(6), 6, 1999.

TABLE 11.5 Handguns and American Youth

The United States leads all industrialized nations in homicides, with four times the next highest rate (9.8 per 100,000). Firearms are involved in 68% to 75% of all homicides, mostly handguns.

Although Americans say that they are purchasing handguns for protection, guns in the home are 43 times more likely to kill a family member than an intruder.

Half of adolescent males and nearly one fourth of adolescent females report that they could easily obtain a handgun if they so desired. Nearly 6% of students carried a gun to school during the 30 days prior to the 1997 Youth Risk Behavior Survey.

One fourth of the violent incidents on television involve use of a handgun.

SOURCE: Data from Hennes (1998), Cohall and Cohall (1995), Kellerman and Reay (1986), Callahan and Rivara (1992), Centers for Disease Control and Prevention (1997), and Wilson et al. (1998).

For parents:

1. Be aware of the risks involved in viewing media violence.

2. Be aware of a child's developmental maturity in considering or allowing him or her to view media violence.

3. Recognize that certain violent cartoons (despite their benign appearance) are not healthy for young children to view.

Finally, the issue of guns is separate but very much related. America has always had a love affair with guns. But it pays a very high price, indeed (see Tables 11.4 and 11.5). A child growing up in the United States is 12 times more likely to die from gun violence than a child in any of 25 other industrialized nations is, and three fourths of all murders of young people under the age of 14 years around the world occur in the United States (see Figure 11.9) (CDC, 1997). Every 2 years, guns kill more people in the United States than were killed in the Vietnam War. In fact, there are more guns in the United States (220 million) than there are households

© 1999 BORGMAN—CINCINNATI ENQUIRER

Figure 11.7
SOURCE: Reprinted with special permission of King Features Syndicate.

PREDICTED EFFECTS OF HOW CONTEXTUAL FEATURES CAN AFFECT THE RISKS ASSOCIATED WITH EXPOSURE TO TV VIOLENCE			
	HARMFUL EFFECTS OF TV VIOLENCE		
	LEARNING AGGRESSION	FEAR	DESENSITIZATION
CONTEXTUAL FEATURES			
Attractive Perpetrator	▲		
Attractive Victim		▲	
Justified Violence	▲		
Unjustified Violence	▼	▲	
Conventional Weapons	▲		
Extensive/Graphic Violence	▲	▲	▲
Realistic Violence	▲	▲	
Rewards	▲	▲	
Punishments	▼	▼	
Pain/Harm Cues	▼		
Humor	▲		▲

Note: Predicted effects are based on review of social science research by NTVS staff on the different contextual features of violence. Blank spaces indicate NTVS staff's view that there is no relationship or inadequate research to make a prediction.

▲ = likely to increase the outcome
▼ = likely to decrease the outcome

Figure 11.8. Predicted Effects of How Contextual Features Can Affect the Risks Associated With Exposure to TV Violence
SOURCE: National Television Violence Study (Wilson et al., 1998). Reprinted from the Federal Trade Commission (2000).

Figure 11.9
SOURCE: Copyright Mike Keefe, *Denver Post*. Used with permission.

(200 million) (Diaz, 1999). According to federal data, nearly 10% of high school males carried a gun to school within 30 days of being surveyed (CDC, 2000c). Two thirds of the guns used in school shootings since 1974 came from the shooters' own homes or the home of a relative (Jackson, 2001). Given all these statistics, it is entirely possible that the Supreme Court will one day have to weigh in with its interpretation of the Second Amendment's "right to bear arms" (see Figure 11.10) (Thomas, 2001). Yet keeping guns out of criminals' hands will not solve the problem of school shootings or juvenile homicide or suicide. Because part of the decision to carry a gun depends on how safe a teenager feels (Ash & Kellerman, 2001), the media may indeed play an important role. Gerbner has shown that heavier viewers of television tend to believe in a "mean and scary world" (Gerbner, Gross, et al., 1994) and might therefore be more likely to carry a gun.

What also links adolescent homicides to American media is the glamorization of guns, which appear in one fourth of all violent interactions on television (Wilson et al., 1998). Although there are no specific data linking viewing gunplay in the media with actual gun-related offenses in real life, the connection seems logical, at least to one TV critic:

> On average, a violent crime is committed [in the United States] every seventeen seconds. The entertainment industry alone cannot be blamed for this, any more than guns alone, and not the people who pull their triggers, can be blamed for gun-related deaths. But the connections are inescapable. If there were fewer guns, fewer people

Figure 11.10
SOURCE: Copyright Jimmy Margulies, *Hackensack Record*. Used with permission.

would be shot to death; if there were fewer violent images, fewer people might be moved to seek violent solutions. (Auletta, 1993, p. 46)

● 4. CREATING A UNIFORM RATING SYSTEM FOR ALL MEDIA

The first ratings system, of movies, was created in 1968 as a joint venture between the Motion Picture Association of America (MPAA) and the National Association of Theatre Owners (see Figure 11.11). Interestingly, it quickly followed two Supreme Court decisions that upheld the power of states to regulate children's access to media otherwise protected by the First Amendment (*Ginsberg v. New York,* 1968; *Interstate Circuit v. Dallas,* 1968). Although the system is voluntary, most films are rated. Ninety percent of parents are aware of the ratings system, and more than half approve of it (Federman, 1996). However, a significant percentage of parents disagree with the ratings for particular movies (Walsh & Gentile, 2001). In addition, parents and public health organizations are overwhelmingly in favor of a content-based ratings system for all media (Cantor, 1998c; Greenberg & Rampoldi-Hnilo,

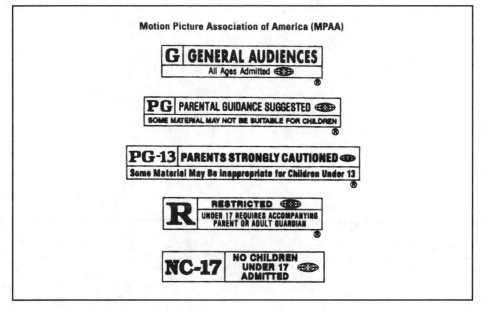

Figure 11.11. MPAA Movie Ratings

2001; Hogan, 2001). The current movie ratings are as follows (see Figure 11.12) (Federman, 1996; FTC, 2000):

G: General audiences—all ages admitted.

- Signifies that the film contains nothing that most parents will consider offensive, even for their youngest children. No nudity, sex scenes, or scenes depicting drug use.

- Recent examples: *Chicken Run, Fantasia 2000.*

PG: Parental guidance suggested—some material may not be suitable for children.

- May contain some material that parents might not like their young children exposed to, but explicit sex scenes or scenes of drug use are absent. However, nudity may be briefly seen, and horror and violence may be present at "moderate levels."

- Recent examples: *The Adventures of Rocky and Bullwinkle, Disney's The Kid.*

PG-13: Parents strongly cautioned—some material may be inappropriate for children under 13.

- "Rough or persistent violence" is absent, as is sexually oriented nudity. There may be some scenes of drug use but one use (only) of a common sexually derived expletive.

- Recent examples: *Mission Impossible 2, The Perfect Storm, Castaway.*

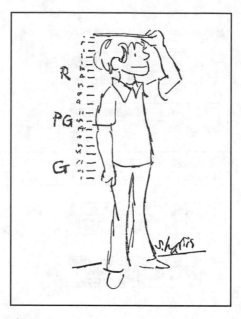

Figure 11.12
SOURCE: Copyright Sidney Harris. Reprinted with permission.

R: Restricted, under 17 requires accompanying parent or adult guardian.

- May contain some adult material. May contain "hard" language, "tough violence," sex or nudity, or drug use. Consequently, parents are urged to learn more about the film before taking their children to see it.

- Recent examples: *Traffic, Gladiator, The Patriot, Me, Myself & Irene, Billy Elliot.*

NC-17: No one under 17 admitted.

- May contain material that the ratings board feels is "patently adult," and therefore children 17 and under should not be viewing it. May contain explicit sex scenes, considerable sexually oriented language, and/or scenes of excessive violence.

- Recent example: *Requiem for a Dream* (older examples: *Showgirls, Kids*).

There are several problems with the MPAA system. Initially, the ratings were evaluative only, not descriptive (see Table 11.6). Parents would be given only the "PG" or "PG-13" symbol without being told exactly what content was problematic. For certain parents, offensive language could be more of an issue than scenes with brief nudity, for example. Recently, however, and with very little public fanfare, the MPAA added descriptive information below the symbols (e.g., *Hannibal* is

TABLE 11.6 Examples of Descriptive and Evaluative Ratings

Descriptive	Evaluative
Contains some violence	Parental discretion advised
Nudity/sex level 3	Teen: ages 13+
Violence: blood and gore	R: restricted
Language: mild expletives	Adults only
Contains extreme violence	Mature: ages 17+
BN: brief nudity	PG: parental guidance

SOURCE: Federman (1996). Reprinted with permission.

rated R for "strong gruesome violence, some nudity, and language"). But the descriptions do not always accompany the rating, nor is the print always large enough to be deciphered by the average parent with average eyesight.

Sometimes, decisions by the ratings board defy explanation. The movie *Billy Elliot* was a fine film for children and teenagers, except for repeated use of the "f" word. Despite the fact that the word was spoken in a northern English accent so thick that it was barely decipherable, the film received an R rating, putting it out of reach of many teens who would have enjoyed seeing it. *Hannibal,* a gory sequel to *Silence of the Lambs,* was rated R, not NC-17. As critic Roger Ebert noted in his review, "If it proves nothing else, it proves that if a man cutting off his face and feeding it to the dogs doesn't get the NC-17 rating for violence, nothing ever will" (Ebert, 2001, p. 4). The board is also notoriously susceptible to negotiation with the industry. Thus, the movie *South Park: Bigger, Longer & Uncut* received an R rating only after it was rated five times as NC-17. "God's the biggest bitch of them all" qualified the film for an R rating, whereas "God f—ing me up the a—" would have merited an NC-17 (Hochman, 1999). Even the makers of the film were surprised that their film escaped with just an R rating (Hochman, 1999).

Many observers have felt that the MPAA rates more harshly on sex than on violence, which is the exact reverse of what European countries do (Federman, 1996). Any depiction of sexual activity is likely to earn a picture an R rating, whereas a PG-13 movie can contain an appreciable amount of violence. Films that were extremely violent, such as *Natural Born Killers* and *Pulp Fiction,* received R ratings, whereas *Showgirls,* which had graphic sexuality and some nudity but only brief violence, received an NC-17 rating (Federman, 1996). Even former members of the MPAA ratings board have serious problems with how this is decided (Waxman, 2001a).

Other problems with the MPAA system are that through the years, the industry has tolerated significant drug and violent content in G- and PG-rated movies,

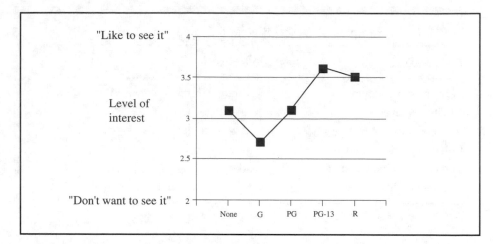

Figure 11.13. Effect of MPAA Ratings on Older Children's Interest in a Movie
SOURCE: Cantor (1998c, p. 64). Used with permission.

despite its own guidelines. Of all the animated feature films produced in the United States between 1937 and 1999, 100% contained violence, and the portrayal of intentional violence increased during this 60-year period (Yokota & Thompson, 2000). Two studies of G-rated children's films released between 1937 and 1997 have found that nearly half displayed at least one scene of tobacco or alcohol use (Goldstein et al., 1999; Thompson & Yokota, 2001).

Several studies have noticed that the age-based ratings simply encourage children, especially boys, to seek "older" fare (see Figure 11.13) (Cantor, 1998c). When ratings are based on age rather than content, the "forbidden fruit theory" seems to become operational (Bushman & Stack, 1996).

There is also the problem of "enforcing" the ratings system. As was discussed above, half of movie theater operators surveyed confessed that they admit teens under 17 to R-rated movies without an accompanying parent or guardian (FTC, 2000). Even if theater owners were more conscientious, today's multiplex theaters allow children and teens to pay for a PG movie and switch to an R movie with minimal chances of being caught. There is some evidence that this trend may be changing, however. A 2001 study by an industry research firm found that films may lose as much as 40% of their potential opening-weekend earnings if they are rated R (Waxman, 2001b). Films that might appeal to teens, such as *The Mexican, Tomcats,* and *Freddy Got Fingered,* were particularly at risk. Researchers who polled 1,500 people per week found that increasingly teens were being turned away at such R-rated movies (Waxman, 2001b).

The television industry has lagged far behind the motion picture industry in developing a ratings system. Nearly 30 years after the MPAA system was introduced, the networks began rating their shows but only after considerable pressure from parents, advocacy groups, and the federal government (Broder, 1997; Hogan,

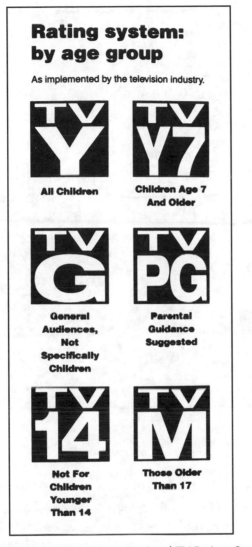

Figure 11.14. Current National TV Ratings System
NOTE: These ratings are voluntary and self-administered.

2001). In fact, it took congressional legislation to accomplish it. In 1996, the Tele-communications Act mandated that new television sets be manufactured with a V-chip and that television programs be rated so that the chip could be programmed accordingly (see Figure 11.14). Like the MPAA ratings, the TV ratings system also has many flaws (see Figure 11.15). News and sports programs are not rated. Initial age-based ratings had to be supplemented with content descriptors (see Table 11.7). Many public health groups suggested that the system should have been modeled after the premium cable channels' practice of indicating the level of sex,

Figure 11.15
SOURCE: Reprinted with special permission of Universal Press Syndicate.

violence, and coarse language in each program (Cantor, 1998c; Mediascope, 2000b).

However, even after descriptors were added, studies show that the system is still not working properly. NBC refuses to use the content descriptors in its ratings. The current categories are not specific enough regarding content, and the contextual impact of violent or sexual references is completely ignored. For example, certain content becomes lost to the highest rating: A TV-M program with an "S" for sexual content may contain violence at a TV-14 level but is not given a "V" for violent content. In addition, parents may be tempted to place inappropriate faith in the rating "FV" for fantasy violence, even though research shows that this represents some of the most potentially detrimental programming for young children (Cantor, 1996; Federman, 1998). Finally, the ratings are completely voluntary, and two recent studies reveal that producers are not always conscientious about rating their own programs (Greenberg, Rampoldi-Hnilo, & Mastro, 2000; Kunkel et al., 1998). Nearly 80% of shows with violence and more than 90% of shows with sex do not receive the V or S content descriptors (Kunkel et al., 1998) (see Figure

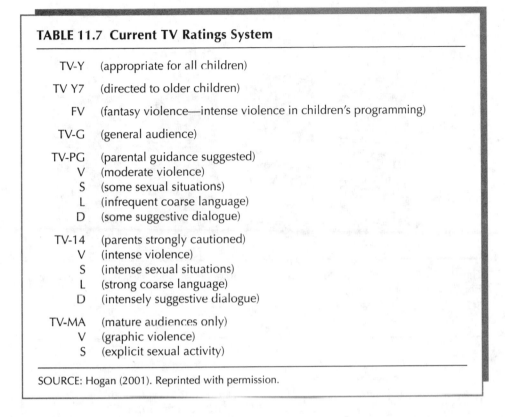

TABLE 11.7 Current TV Ratings System

TV-Y	(appropriate for all children)
TV Y7	(directed to older children)
FV	(fantasy violence—intense violence in children's programming)
TV-G	(general audience)
TV-PG	(parental guidance suggested)
V	(moderate violence)
S	(some sexual situations)
L	(infrequent coarse language)
D	(some suggestive dialogue)
TV-14	(parents strongly cautioned)
V	(intense violence)
S	(intense sexual situations)
L	(strong coarse language)
D	(intensely suggestive dialogue)
TV-MA	(mature audiences only)
V	(graphic violence)
S	(explicit sexual activity)

SOURCE: Hogan (2001). Reprinted with permission.

11.16). For example, an episode of *Walker, Texas Ranger* featured the stabbing of two guards on a bus, an assault on a church by escaped convicts threatening to rape a nun, and a fight scene in which one escapee is shot and another is beaten unconscious. It did not receive a V descriptor. In addition, 80% of children's programs with violence do not receive the FV descriptor (see Figure 11.17) (Kunkel et al., 1998).

To add to all of this confusion for parents, the gaming industry began by using two different systems, one for video games and the other for computer games. The former won out, but it bears little resemblance to the movie and TV ratings systems (Walsh & Gentile, 2001): E (everyone), T (teen), M (mature), and AO (adults only) (see Figure 11.18). Finally, the music industry uses a single rating system, "Parental Advisory: Explicit Lyrics." It, too, is voluntary and does not distinguish among lyrics that are explicitly violent, sexual, or profane (Federman, 1996).

All of these disparate systems rely on the integrity, honesty, and judgment of the producers of the program, except for the MPAA system, which has an independent board, comprised of parents, that confers the rating. However, even then, the independence of the board is sometimes questionable, and the lack of expert membership is often apparent (Federman, 1996; Waxman, 2001a, 2001b). These separate and noncompatible systems have been developed with very little input from the

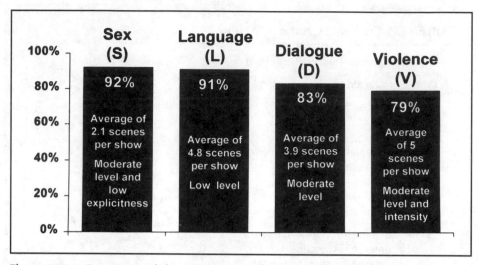

Figure 11.16. Percentage of Shows With Sex, Violence, or Adult Language That Did Not Receive a Content Descriptor
SOURCE: Kunkel et al. (1998). Reprinted with permission.

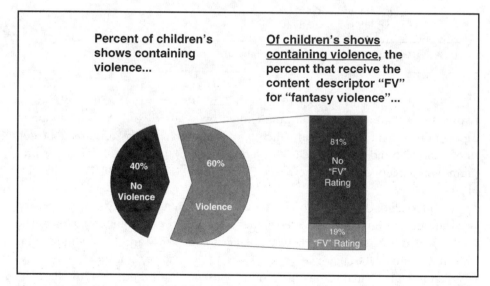

Figure 11.17. Percentage of Children's Shows Containing Violence
SOURCE: From Kunkel et al. (1998). Reprinted with permission.

public, the medical community, or the academic community (Walsh & Gentile, 2001). One recent "test" of the ratings systems found that parents frequently disagree with the industry in the ratings applied to different media, particularly when violent content is involved. Only half of parents surveyed agreed with the G rating

Figure 11.18. Original Video Game Ratings

NOTE: Now an "E" category has been added for "Everyone." The "AO" rating is almost never used.

TABLE 11.8 Should This Movie Have Been Rated PG?
          (no, according to many parents)

Austin Powers: The Spy Who Shagged Me

Charlie's Angels

Little Nicky

Nutty Professor II: The Klumps

She's All That

The Wedding Singer

SOURCE: Walsh and Gentile (2001).

---

given to popular movies, and more than a third disagreed with PG ratings (see Table 11.8) (Walsh & Gentile, 2001).

The solution here should be readily apparent: a single, uniform, content-based ratings system that could be applied to all media that children and teenagers use (Greenberg & Rampoldi-Hnilo, 2001; Hogan, 2001; Walsh & Gentile, 2001). The current "alphabet soup" of ratings systems is too confusing for parents to learn and apply and is even difficult for researchers to study (Greenberg et al., 2000). In addition, the voluntary nature of the current ratings systems is too easy for producers to exploit. The temptations are ever present to downcode a product to capture a larger audience (or, ironically, upcode it) or to depict increasingly edgy sexual, violent, or drug-taking behavior (Walsh & Gentile, 2001). An external ratings board, with representation from the various industries, along with parents, health professionals, and academics, would put the United States on par with many other Western countries (Federman, 1996). In addition, such a move would inevitably lead to a societal discussion of cultural values—What should we rate most heavily against? How do we define *quality* and *educational*?—that, in itself, would be therapeutic.

5. IMPROVING THE PORTRAYAL OF SEX AND SEXUALITY IN THE MEDIA

In the United States today, there is no more powerful sex educator than television (Strasburger, 1995). Nor is television a particularly responsible one at that. On prime-time TV and afternoon soap operas, sex is frequently casual, unplanned, a giggle, an arched eyebrow, a joke, or a gesture. It is a subject for titillation rather than a serious matter (*Temptation Island* being the most recent example) (Roush, 2001). There is little or no mention of abstinence, responsibility, the risk of sexually transmitted diseases (STDs), or the risk of pregnancy. When sex is used to sell everything from beer to perfume to hotel rooms, teenagers begin to think that having sex, even at a young age, is normative behavior. Yet not every teenager is obsessed with sex, nor are most teenagers "hormones with legs" (Leo, 1998).

America does not have the most sexually explicit media, but it does have the most sexually suggestive media, and children and teenagers clearly learn about sex and sexuality from what they view. Many critics feel that American adults remain "hung up" about sex. It attracts them in the media, and they will gladly watch sexual content; but children and teenagers must remain sheltered. American culture has never felt comfortable with sex or sexuality, from the days of the Pilgrims to modern times (Brown et al., 2002). Certainly, the United States is the only Western nation that rates more heavily against sex than violence in mainstream media (Greenberg & Rampoldi-Hnilo, 2001). Our European counterparts tend to have a healthier outlook on sex and teenagers. One recent study of teenagers in the Netherlands, France, and Germany concluded,

> In the countries studied, adolescents are valued, respected, and expected to act responsibly. Equally important, most adults trust adolescents to make responsible choices because they see young people as assets, rather than problems. That message is conveyed in the media, in school texts, and in health care settings. (Kelly & McGee, 1999, p. 11)

Unfortunately, at a time when sex education programs are scaling back their range of topics to "abstinence only," sexually suggestive content on prime-time television is increasing (Kunkel, Cope-Farrar, Biely, Farinda, & Donnerstein, 2001). The result is that children and teenagers are being trapped in a conspiracy of silence about birth control and misinformation about human sexuality. Admittedly, these are all strong statements and certainly arguable, but there are several recent studies to support them:

1. Although some parents claim that sex education belongs exclusively at home, one third of 15-year-old girls say that neither parent has ever talked to them

about pregnancy, and half report that neither parent has ever discussed STDs or contraception (Alan Guttmacher Institute, 1994). In fact, more than half of teens in one survey felt that their parents had failed miserably in providing sex education at home (Kaiser Family Foundation, 1996).

2. Television and other media may function as a "super-peer" in pressuring young teens into having sexual relationships. In one poll, four times as many teens said that they felt pressure from the media to begin having sex than pressure from friends (Roper Starch Worldwide, 1994). In the Kaiser study, one third of teens felt that the media encourage teens to begin having sex (Kaiser Family Foundation, 1996).

3. Children and teens view nearly 14,000 sexual references and innuendoes on TV, but less than 175 refer to responsible sexuality (Harris & Associates, 1988). The amount of sexual content has increased significantly on prime-time television, from 66% of shows having at least one reference to sex in 1998 to 75% of shows in 1999-2000 (Kunkel et al., 2001). Sex is mentioned in four out of five sitcom episodes. Yet only 10% of programs refer to the risks or responsibilities involved in a sexual relationship (Kunkel et al., 2001).

4. The nature and content of sex education programs in schools are changing dramatically, focusing more on abstinence and less on comprehensive sex education (Darroch, Landry, & Singh, 2000). In one survey of public school superintendents in 1999, only 14% reported having a comprehensive sex education program, whereas 51% had an "abstinence-plus" policy and 35% had an abstinence-only policy (Landry et al., 1999). The federal government now funds abstinence-only programs to the tune of $50 million per year, but discussion of contraception or safe sex is forbidden (Schemo, 2000; Wilson, 2000). In fact, one study of health education instructors who teach specifically about HIV and AIDS discovered that only one third feel that they can discuss how to use condoms correctly (CDC, 1996). Yet an overwhelming majority of American adults favor the teaching of contraception information as well as abstinence in school programs: 93% in a 1999 nationwide survey of 1,050 adults (Sexuality Information and Education Council of the U.S. [SIECUS], 1999).

TV and movie producers and writers need to accept greater responsibility for the sexual dialogue and behavior they depict and understand that they have become, in fact, sex educators for young people in America (J. D. Brown, 2000a, 2000b; Brown, 2001; Brown et al., 2002). Some have. In the latest Kaiser report, 30% of teen shows included references to sexual risks and responsibilities, compared with only 10% of other programs (Kunkel et al., 2001). *Felicity* aired an episode in which the lead character went to the college health service and received a very explicit discussion about condoms, including a demonstration of how to put one on. *Dawson's Creek* aired an extremely sensitive story line about a teenage male trying to come to grips with his homosexuality. Hollywood writers and producers are fully capable of responding to the public's needs in a very creative fashion, if the New York network executives will allow them to. Unfortunately, the networks choose not to when the issue is birth control advertising. Of the six major networks, only three currently permit advertising for condoms, and then only if the ad is confined to emphasizing protection against HIV, not pregnancy prevention. ABS has aired ads for the birth control pill Tri-Cyclen, but only their effect on acne is ever mentioned, not their use as a contraceptive.

Birth control needs to be featured prominently in programming, and advertising for birth control products must be accepted, especially in programming popular with teenagers (e.g., MTV) (Society for Adolescent Medicine, 2000). Media represent one important access point for teenagers to get information about birth control. Yet the networks seem to subscribe to the old-fashioned myth that if you give teens information about or access to contraceptives, that will somehow lead them into becoming sexually active earlier (Strasburger & Brown, 1998). In fact, according to the most recent survey of 1,050 adults nationwide, more than 80% support giving teenagers information about birth control (SIECUS, 1999). In addition, there are now five peer-reviewed studies on the effects of programs that allow greater access to birth control for teenagers. All five show no increase in rates of sexual activity or earlier onset of intercourse (Furstenberg et al., 1997; Guttmacher et al., 1997; Jemmott et al., 1998; Kirby et al., 1999; Schuster et al., 1998).

On the other hand, school officials and educators need to recognize the impact of the media on students, incorporate media discussions into sex education programs, and widen the scope of sex education programs beyond abstinence. Otherwise, the media will continue to perform the job that schools should be doing, albeit in a much more haphazard and irresponsible way.

● 6. CONDUCTING MORE RESEARCH

Although the violence research is extensive and conclusive, other research is incomplete or insufficient. In addition, much more information is needed about how to mediate harmful effects of the media and how different children and teenagers may process the same content differently. Finally, a surprising amount of ecological research about teenagers continues to ignore the impact of the media on them. In one of the most remarkable studies to date, the National Longitudinal Study of Adolescent Health (ADD Health) has surveyed nearly 100,000 students in schools across the country in Grades 7 through 12, with about a third of the students participating in at-home interviews as well (Loewenson & Blum, 2001). Yet there is only one media question on the in-school questionnaire (how much time is spent watching television or videos on an average school day) and only five questions on the in-home survey (separate questions on hours spent watching television, watching videos, playing video or computer games, and listening to the radio). Similarly, a recent review of gun-carrying among teenagers fails to mention even the potential influence of television, movies, or video games (Ash & Kellerman, 2001). Likewise, a supposedly comprehensive review of why teens use drugs completely neglects to cite the influence of advertising and of movies and television (Belcher & Shinitzky, 1998). It would seem difficult to understand adolescent culture and high-risk behaviors without an in-depth assessment of their media consumption and their attitudes that could be derived from media (cultivation effect). Specific new studies that could be conducted include the following:

- A violence prevention project with a prominent media component. Many violence prevention projects are now being funded, but few employ media education as a vital component. Activities might include visiting a TV or movie set, having a stunt man explain how fights are choreographed, watching and discussing a variety of violent media (TV, movies, videos, video games, etc.), trying to design an anti-violence PSA, having students do their own content analyses of various media, and so on.

- Ongoing content analyses of violence and sex in television programming, movies, and rock music lyrics. Kunkel et al.'s analyses (Kunkel, Cope, Farinola, et al., 1999; Kunkel et al., 2001) are now planned for every 2 years, funded by the Kaiser Family Foundation. However, the National Television Violence Study (NTVS)—the most exhaustive content analysis of American television ever conducted—has been disbanded because of lack of funding. It, or a similar effort, needs to be re-funded.

- A longitudinal study of consumption of sexy media and subsequent sexual behavior. Four of these are now ongoing (NICHD, 2000). The most ambitious will examine all media use, longitudinally over 5 years, among 5,000 teens ages 12 to 14 in North Carolina. The teens' media habits will be assessed both at home and in school. The other three studies will examine television only but will also be longitudinal in design and will try to establish if there is a causal relationship between television viewing and sexual behavior among teenagers (NICHD, 2000).

- Continued studies on the possible relationship between media exposure and eating disorders. Similarly, more information is needed about the impact of media on obesity. Does the relationship between TV viewing and obesity exist, for example, because children are not participating in more active pursuits, because they are learning unhealthy nutritional practices, or because they are snacking while they are watching TV?

- A longitudinal study of the impact of rock music on adolescent behavior and attitudes, particularly depression and suicide, antisocial behavior, smoking and drinking, and sexual behavior.

- A content analysis of health-related behaviors in music videos.

- An updated content analysis of violence and sex in music videos.

- New and updated studies of how children and adolescents react to and process different forms of advertising. Virtually all of the basic research in this area was conducted more than 20 years ago.

- An assessment of in-school advertising and commercialism and their effects on school policies and on students. Are children and teens influenced by in-school advertising? How do they process it? How are decisions made by key school personnel to allow in-school advertising and marketing to take place?

- Further research on the importance of individual responses to different media, why such variations occur, and what can modify an individual's response to media content. For example, Brown and Schulze (1990) found that teens interpreted Madonna's video, "Papa Don't Preach," completely differently, depending on their sex and race. Bryant and Rockwell (1993) found that massive exposure to prime-time programming with sexual content may desensitize young viewers to premarital sex but that several factors can mitigate against this: a clearly defined value system and an ability to discuss freely important issues within the family, as well as active, critical viewing skills.

- More research that would help to establish the effectiveness of media education programs. What components are essential? What is the minimum "dose" needed? Are all areas of health-related behavior equally susceptible to this kind of approach?

Of course, such research would require far more generous funding from government agencies and private foundations than is now available. Currently, the Kaiser Family Foundation and the William T. Grant Foundation have assumed the leadership in funding research efforts in media, particularly questions about sexual behavior and attitudes. Other national foundations will need to pick up their fair share.

In addition, sufficient new data exist since the 1982 National Institute of Mental Health (NIMH) report was issued to warrant a 2005 NIMH report on media and its impact on children and adolescents (AAP, 2001a). The Surgeon General's Report in 1972 was extremely influential, as was the NIMH report a decade later. But nothing has been generated since then that serves as a synthesis of the research.

7. INCREASING MEDIA EDUCATION FOR CHILDREN ●

In 1900, to be literate meant that a person could read and write. In the new millennium, to be literate means that a person can read, write, and interpret a wide variety of media, including television, movies, videos, video games, and the Internet (Rich, 2001). Literacy has been redefined in the past 100 years, and children now need to learn more than simply the three "Rs." A media-literate person realizes that all media messages shape our understanding of the world, that such messages are carefully constructed, that individuals interpret media differently, and that the mass media represent a very powerful economic and social force in contemporary society (AAP, 1999).

Media education involves "de-mystifying" the media for young children (Brown, 2001; Potter, 2001; D. G. Singer & J. L. Singer, 1998; J. L. Singer & D. G. Singer, 1998). For example, children can observe how a "fight" is choreographed and see how the actors are not really hurt. They can learn about who controls certain media and why certain messages are presented (or are not presented). They can deconstruct alcohol and tobacco advertising and see how some of the messages presented are deceptive or manipulative. Anyone who has ever participated in such an exercise comes away with a renewed sense of self-empowerment. In Albuquerque, the nationally recognized New Mexico Media Literacy Project (www.nmmlp.org) trains educators for free to conduct such exercises with their students (see Chapter 10).

The United States lags far behind other Western nations in its lack of school-based media education programs for children and adolescents (Potter, 2001). Ontario, Canada, and most of Australia mandate media education for all school-children. Many other countries incorporate it into various parts of the school curriculum, including Great Britain and some Latin American countries (Brown, 2001). A few states in the United States have shown some interest in early elementary school programs (Kubey & Baker, 1999).

Media education is exciting for two completely different reasons: (a) it holds the promise that children and teens can be successfully "immunized" against unhealthy media effects, and (b) it is relatively uncontroversial, supported by both the entertainment industry and public health advocates.

Many studies suggest that media literacy can exert a protective effect against unhealthy attitudes learned from the media (Huston et al., 1992). For school-based programs, several different types of curricula have been developed: At Yale, the Singers developed an eight-lesson critical viewing curriculum for third through fifth graders, designed to teach them how television programs are produced, how special effects are accomplished, how television reality differs from real life, how stereotypes are portrayed on TV, and how TV violence is unreal (Singer et al., 1980). Dorr at UCLA developed a similar curriculum (Dorr et al., 1980). Both have been extensively and successfully field-tested. In Los Angeles, the Center for Media Literacy has developed a four-session curriculum for parents, titled "Parenting in a TV Age," and an eight-lesson program for children, "TV Alert: A Wakeup Guide to Television Literacy" (Center for Media Values, 1992). Also, Home Box Office and Consumer Reports have pioneered a series of shows including *Buy Me That!* and *Buy Me That Too,* which teach children about television commercials and consumerism. At Yale, the Singers have also developed an effective adolescent health education mini-curriculum using five episodes of *Degrassi Junior High* with teens and preteens in Grades 5 to 8 (Singer & Singer, 1994). Finally, the New Mexico Media Literacy Project has recently developed several CD-ROMs, including a K-12 curriculum for teachers contained on a single CD-ROM (see Chapter 10, this volume, by McCannon). Are such curricula effective? Obviously, much depends on how *effectiveness* is defined. All of the curricula mentioned above have been extensively tested, and increased levels of knowledge among students can be demonstrated.

Certain media education programs have gone even further and have successfully targeted specific areas of concern. In 1983, Huesmann and Eron developed a curriculum to counter some of the adverse effects of televised violence and successfully pilot-tested it. First and third graders who completed the program experienced changes in their attitudes about TV violence and in their own level of aggressive behavior as rated by their peers (Huesmann et al., 1983). Two recent studies have found a change in children's attitudes regarding intention to drink alcohol after a media education program (Austin, Pinkleton, & Fujioka, 2000; Austin & Johnson, 1997).

Most recently, Robinson (1999; Robinson, Saphir, et al., 2001; Robinson, Wilde, et al., 2000) has used a very simplified media intervention program to show demonstrable decreases in (a) obesity, (b) children's requests for toys, and (c) aggressive behavior. In his program, third- and fourth-grade students received an 18-lesson, 6-month classroom curriculum simply designed to reduce television, videotape, and video game use. Although not a full-blown media education program per se, the curriculum did include lesson plans to teach children to become more "intelligent viewers" and strategies for parents as well. Compared with controls, children receiving the intervention demonstrated significantly less aggressive behavior and verbal aggression (Robinson, Wilde, et al., 2001); decreases in body mass indices (BMIs), skinfold thicknesses, waist circumferences, and waist-to-hip ratios (all important measures of adiposity) (Robinson, 1999); and less requests made to their parents for toys (Robinson, Saphir, et al., 2001).

But good media education programs do not necessarily have to be school based. Parents can play an important role in creating media-literate children but only if they watch TV and movies with their children and discuss, explicitly, what is being viewed. Organizations such as the National Institute on Media and the Family, based in Minneapolis, have successfully demonstrated that parent education programs can teach parents to monitor their children's media use and provide them with alternatives to watching TV (Walsh, 2000). A number of popular books are also available to help teach parents such skills (Chen, 1994; DeGaetano & Bander, 1996; Grossman & DeGaetano, 1999; Murphy & Tucker, 1996). The American Academy of Pediatrics has recently developed the Media Matters campaign, which teaches pediatricians about media effects and gives them the training to teach other health professionals and parents (Hogan, 2000).

Currently, media literacy is an area of intensive research among communication specialists and may yield exciting new approaches in the next decade for mitigating the harmful effects of the media on youth. It also makes perfect sense in a society that prides itself on personal freedom, is unenthusiastic about censorship, but tends to be rather apathetic about public health issues if business concerns are involved. Research funding is a problem, however. Wholehearted commitments will be needed from the federal government, private foundations, schools, and parents if further research is going to be accomplished.

8. INCREASING MEDIA EDUCATION FOR ● PARENTS AND HEALTH PROFESSIONALS

According to the media industry, if there are any untoward effects from TV, movies, and rock 'n' roll, it is only because children and adolescents are not being properly supervised and monitored. TV sets have on/off switches, movies and CDs have ratings, and the Internet has NetNanny. Of course, given the penetration of media in American society, this argument may strike some as ridiculous. And certainly it would be far easier for parents to supervise their children if there were healthier programs from which to choose.

Nevertheless, parents are guilty of using the TV as an electronic baby-sitter and of underestimating the influence that the media may be having on their children (see Figures 11.19a-11.19b) (Strasburger, 1995). Two national studies have found that a surprisingly large number of children and teenagers have television sets in their own bedrooms (see Figure 11.20): approximately 25% of young children, 50% of older children, and nearly two thirds of teenagers (Roberts, Foehr, et al., 1999; Woodard & Gridina, 2000). In a regional study of 1,200 Boston-area sixth and seventh graders, 54% of them reported that they had TV sets in their bedrooms (Wiecha, Sobol, Peterson, & Gortmaker, 2001). Although parents express a great deal of concern about media influence, especially television, they still allow their children to spend nearly 6½ hours a day using media (see Figures 11.21 and 11.22)

Figure 11.19
SOURCE: Reprinted with special permission of King Features Syndicate.

(Woodard & Gridina, 2000). The amount of coviewing that parents do is debatable. In surveys, parents know that they are "supposed" to coview, but there are no reports corroborated by either children or technology. In one recent study, 87% of the 1,235 parents surveyed reported coviewing at least "sometimes," which seems an inflated figure (Woodard & Gridina, 2000). In other surveys, when parents are asked if they coview consistently, less than half say yes (Stanger, 1998; Valerio, Amodio, Dal Zio, Vianello, & Zacchello, 1997). In the recent Boston study, 42% of the students reported that their parents set no limits on their television viewing (Wiecha et al., 2001). All of this adds up to more television viewing. In the Boston study, for example, students with TV sets in their bedrooms, or whose parents set no limits on viewing, reportedly viewed an average of an hour a day more than their peers did (Wiecha et al., 2001).

Parents also need to appreciate that they may role-model television-watching behavior for their children. If parents commonly eat meals in front of the TV set, their children will too. In a recent survey of 287 schoolchildren in Houston, 42% of dinners eaten at home involved TV viewing. Overweight children were more likely to be eating dinner in front of the TV than normal-weight children were (Belchak, 2000).

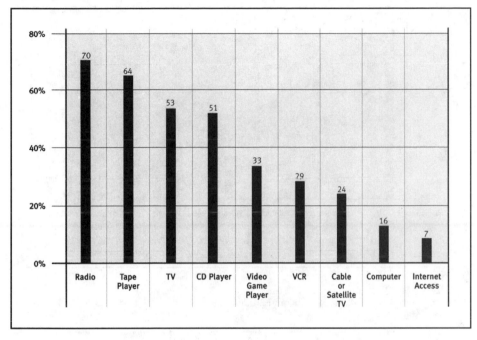

Figure 11.20. Media in the Bedroom

SOURCE: From Roberts, Foehr, Rideout, and Brodie (1999). Reprinted with permission of the Kaiser Family Foundation.

NOTE: A national survey of 3,155 children, ages 2 to 18. Among children 8 and older, 65% have a TV set in their bedroom.

Health professionals could also benefit from appreciating the negative and positive influences that the media may be having on their patients (Hogan, 2000, 2001). A recent study of the 209 accredited pediatric residency programs in the United States found that only 28% offered formal training to residents and medical students about media (Rich & Bar-on, 2001). Although this figure has increased from 14% in the mid-1980s (Smith, Fosarelli, Palumbo, Loening, & Melmed, 1986), it still seems very low, given the AAP's 20-year interest in this issue (11 policy statements issued since 1984). About half of residents were encouraged to discuss media use with parents (Rich & Bar-on, 2001).

Pediatricians and family practitioners, in particular, should take a careful television history when they see patients with any of the following problems (Strasburger, 1997c):

- aggressive behavior in school
- learning difficulties
- obesity

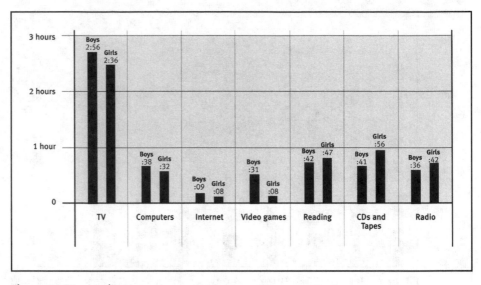

Figure 11.21. Media Use

SOURCE: From Roberts, Foehr, Rideout, and Brodie (1999). Reprinted with permission of the Kaiser Family Foundation.

NOTE: In the same national survey, television remains the preeminent medium. However, among 8- to 18-year-olds, 55% of boys and 23% of girls play video games daily, and 17% of boys spend more than an hour.

- depression
- suicidal ideation
- eating disorders

Specific counseling recommendations for families with children and teenagers include the following (AAP, 2001a):

1. Parents should be advised to limit their children's total media time to no more than 1 to 2 hours per day. Obviously, alternative activities must be provided and should be strongly encouraged.

2. Parents need to monitor what shows their children and teens are watching. Shows should be prosocial, and not violent, sexually suggestive, or beyond their children's developmental levels. Parents who continue to use the TV set as an electronic baby-sitter should at least carefully select prerecorded or rented tapes to be shown on the videocassette recorder rather than letting their children play "channel roulette." But depriving children of a parent to coview with makes it far less likely that children will distill prosocial messages contained in programming they are viewing (Friedrich & Stein, 1975; D. G. Singer & J. L. Singer, 1998; J. L.

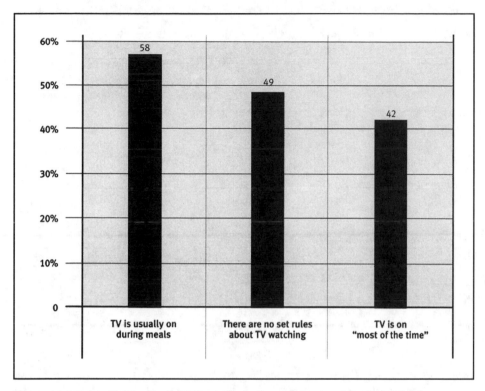

Figure 11.22. Media Use in the Home, According to a National Study of Children Ages 2-18

SOURCE: From Roberts, Foehr, Rideout, and Brodie (1999). Reprinted with permission of the Kaiser Family Foundation.

NOTE: In the Kaiser survey, 95% of children older than 7 and teens report that they almost never watch TV with their parents. Even parents of 2- to 7-year-olds report that 81% of the time, their children are watching TV without them.

Singer & D. G. Singer, 1998). How important are parents in determining the impact of media? A recent study of 2,245 third through eighth graders in Cleveland found that the combination of demographic variables, parental monitoring, TV-viewing habits, and exposure to real-life violence accounted for 45% of children's self-reported aggressive behaviors (Singer et al., 1999).

3. Parents of teenagers need to realize that they can counteract the overly sexual or violent nature of much television programming, including music videos, but only if they watch such content with teens and explain their own views. Clear explanations of parents' values and expectations—even if they are conservative ones—are useful and protective for teenagers. Increasingly, it seems, parents are unaware of their teenagers' risky behaviors (see Table 11.9) (Young & Zimmerman, 1998).

TABLE 11.9 Are Parents "Clueless" About Their Teens' Risky Behavior? (in percentages)

Behavior	Student Admits to Being Involved (n = 89)	Parents Think Their Teen Is Not Involved (n = 96)
Carrying a weapon to school	25	98
Suicide attempt	22	98
Sexual intercourse	58	98
Alcohol use	55	95
Marijuana use	38	97

SOURCE: Adapted from Young and Zimmerman (1998).

9. USING MEDIA TO CAMPAIGN FOR HEALTH AND PROSOCIAL PURPOSES

Health Campaigns. Clearly, if the media can teach children that violence is justifiable or that drinking alcohol is normative behavior for teenagers, then the media can also teach young people to respect their parents, understand people of different racial or ethnic backgrounds, avoid violence at all costs, and avoid harming nature. Special interest groups are certainly not shy about exploiting the media for their own purposes (see Figure 11.23a). Although using the media for prosocial purposes has some unpleasant Orwellian possibilities, so little has been done in this regard that there seems little danger of abuse in the near future (see Figure 11.23b). Radio, in particular, seems nearly totally unexplored as a way of positively influencing teenagers, even though teenagers spend an average of an hour a day listening to it (Roberts, Foehr, et al., 1999).

To date, however, the success of public health media campaigns has been mixed. A $32 million AIDS campaign in Great Britain accomplished little more than raising general anxiety about AIDS, for example. Similarly, the CDC spent millions of dollars mailing an "Understanding AIDS" brochure to every household in the United States, but the brochure probably failed to reach those at highest risk of contracting HIV infection (Brown & Walsh-Childers, 1994). Clearly, health campaigns are not without controversy. Many people feel that they result in a tremendous waste of money; that advertising messages will never deter teens from using drugs or having sex; that prosocial messages belong in programming, not on billboards; and that the ads themselves may send mixed messages by combining scare tactics with sexy models (Brown & Witherspoon, 1998).

Figure 11.23. Examples of Two Opposing Public Health-Related Media Campaigns

However, there are some success stories. A $2 million television and radio campaign in Vermont in the early 1990s cut rates of teen smoking by 35% (Flynn et al., 1994). A 4-year, $50 million anti-smoking campaign in nearby Massachusetts resulted in a 50% reduction in the onset of smoking among young adolescents (Siegel & Biener, 2000). A 1988 media campaign in Maryland contributed to reducing teen pregnancies by 10% in Baltimore, where rates had been among the highest in the nation (Brown & Steele, 1995). The $7 million a year Baltimore campaign used TV ads, billboards, and ads on the sides of buses to target 9- to 14-year-olds with messages such as "VIRGIN: Teach your kids it's not a dirty word." In California, the state government spent $14.5 million annually to go toe-to-toe with the cigarette industry on billboards, and sales have declined three times faster than elsewhere in the country (Adelson, 1994).

Most campaigns subscribe to the "health belief model"—that is, if the individual knows the facts, he or she will choose a healthier alternative. Such a strategy is relatively easy for advertisers to exploit: The model is based on the assumption that the victim is to blame. It clears advertisers' consciences and allows them to continue to spend billions of dollars to encourage unhealthy consumption. To break this cycle, fundamental public policy changes are needed that will make it easier for people to adopt healthier behaviors (Brown & Walsh-Childers, 1994; Wallack et al., 1993).

Successful media campaigns share several features: (a) messages target specific groups, (b) multiple media are used, (c) campaigns are long enough to saturate the community, and (d) the campaigns are complemented by other programs in schools and communities and the messages are reinforced by parents and friends (Brown & Steele, 1995). Teenagers advise public health advocates not to preach and to use examples of real people. For example, an anti–drunk driving campaign in North Carolina that used teen focus groups came up with a poster that used a photograph of a cemetery funeral scene, with the following caption: "I bought the beer. But my best friend paid for it" (Brown & Witherspoon, 1998).

The Partnership for a Drug Free America (PDFA) was the first to initiate a large-scale anti-drug advertising campaign, with its famous "this is your brain/this is your brain on drugs" frying egg ad. Only one study has tested the effects of this campaign, but it did find that 75% of nearly 1,000 middle and high school students reported that they had decreased, stopped, or been convinced never to begin drug use (Reis et al., 1994).

The most current public health campaign is the National Institute of Drug Abuse's (NIDA) anti-drug initiative. NIDA has allocated nearly $200 million for the first year of an intended 5-year public media campaign against drug use. The campaign will be designed by Porter Novelli, a mainstream advertising firm, and will use a variety of media to target youth with anti-drug messages (Kelder, Maibach, Worden, Biglan, & Levitt, 2000). As mentioned previously, however, the target of this campaign will be illicit drugs, not tobacco and alcohol (see Figure 11.24). Public health advocates are quick to point out that commercials promoting drugs and alcohol outnumber PSAs by 45:1 (Fedler et al., 1994).

There are some interesting "renegade" campaigns, however, that are willing to battle corporate America. One of these is the "Truth" anti-tobacco campaign, a 5-year, $150 million per year project funded by the American Legacy Foundation in Washington, D.C. One ad, which aired during the 2000 Summer Olympics, showed teenagers at clubs and beaches, surrounded by body bags instead of friends. The ads target teens with messages that their age group is being manipulated into buying cigarettes by Big Tobacco (Livni, 2000).

Health Campaigns Incorporated Into Programming. Many health advocates feel that campaigns are not as effective as convincing Hollywood writers and producers to incorporate health messages into existing programming, sometimes referred to as "edutainment." However, some of the topic areas could conceivably alienate potential advertisers, such as "safe sex" (Brown & Witherspoon, 1998). Perhaps the first and most successful example of this was the Harvard Alcohol Project, which convinced the TV industry to use the new concept of a "designated driver" in more than 80 different program episodes (Rothenberg, 1988).

For the past 5 years, FOX-TV has organized the Soap Summit in Hollywood, a meeting of writers, producers, and network executives at which the CDC and

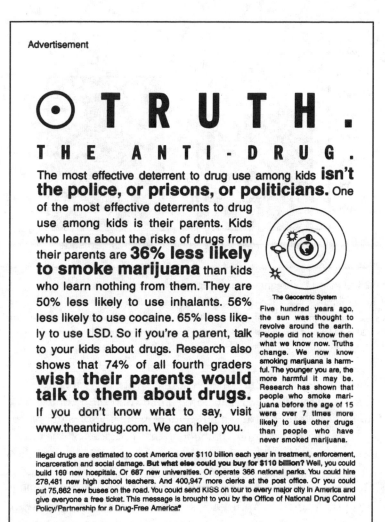

Figure 11.24

SOURCE: Reprinted by special permission of the Partnership for a Drug Free America.

other experts present information about current health issues in hopes of inspiring new plot lines. In October 2000, ABC's *One Life to Live* aired an episode "Viki's Breast Cancer," which stressed the importance of early detection and mammograms (Belchak, 2001).

One experimental study and two studies of prime-time shows have actually tested whether embedding health messages in mainstream programming works. In the experiment, Walsh-Childers (1991) used three different versions of a soap opera: In one, a couple did not discuss using contraceptives; in another, they discussed using "protection"; and in a third, the female explicitly asked, "Did you

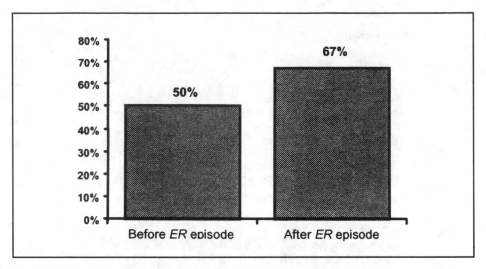

Figure 11.25. *ER* and Emergency Contraception

SOURCE: Kaiser Family Foundation (2000a, 2000b). Used with permission.

NOTE: A successful example of "edutainment." The Kaiser Family Foundation and the writers and producers of the hit show *ER* collaborated on a story element that included a discussion of emergency contraception.

bring a condom?" Teens watching the version in which contraception was not discussed were less likely to believe that the couple used birth control. In a second study of more than 900 eighth and ninth graders in New York, students responded favorably to anti-alcohol messages embedded into episodes of *The Cosby Show* or *Family Matters* (Borzekowski, 1996). More recently, the highly rated show *ER* has successfully incorporated several public health themes into its plot lines, including the need for emergency contraception and the risks of human papilloma virus. After an *ER* episode aired in April 1997 containing a 3-minute vignette in which a date rape victim requests information about preventing a pregnancy, viewers' awareness of emergency contraception increased 17% (see Figure 11.25) (Brodie, Foehr, et al., 2001).

Prosocial TV. Media are not intrinsically "good" or "bad." Other than the displacement effect, there is no reason why media cannot be good, healthy, and prosocial for children and adolescents (Mares & Woodard, 2001). Some researchers believe that the media could have stronger prosocial effects than negative effects because the former are more acceptable in society (Mares & Woodard, 2001; Rushton & Owen, 1979). Indeed, over 30 years of research demonstrates that watching *Sesame Street* has a positive impact on children (Fisch & Truglio, 2001). Likewise, *Barney & Friends* (J. L. Singer & D. G. Singer, 1998) and *Mister Roger's Neighborhood* (Friedrich & Stein, 1975) have been studied thoroughly. There are numerous

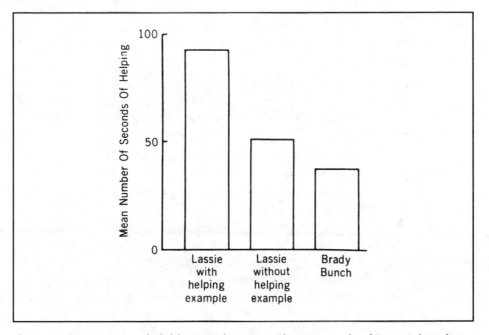

Figure 11.26. Duration of Children's Helping in a Classic Example of Prosocial Media Effects

SOURCE: Sprafkin, Liebert, and Poulos (1985). Copyright *Journal of Experimental Child Psychology.* Used with permission.

prosocial effects that have been documented in a variety of children's programming over the years:

- *Altruism and helping behavior.* In a classic experiment, 30 first graders were randomly assigned to view a prosocial episode of *Lassie* in which Jeff risked his life to save a puppy, a neutral episode of *Lassie,* or a neutral episode of *The Brady Bunch*. Afterwards, the children were all given a game to play that would earn them a prize, then were distracted by the sound of puppies in distress. To help the puppies, children had to press a button, which would then take them away from their game and earn them fewer points toward prizes. The children in the prosocial *Lassie* group pressed the button twice as long as did the children in the two other groups (see Figure 11.26) (Poulos, Rubinstein, & Liebert, 1975).

- *Helping behavior versus hurtful behavior.* In another classic experiment, researchers assigned 60 children, ages 9, 13, and 16, to view one of two versions of *The Mod Squad*. In the violent version, a police captain who is framed for bribery gets even with the villain. In the prosocial version, everything is worked out through negotiation. The children were then placed in front of a "help/hurt" machine in a mock-experimental situation. Those who had seen the prosocial version spent more time pressing the help button and less time pressing the hurt button (Collins & Getz, 1976).

• *A variety of other behaviors.* Prosocial programs can also increase children's friendliness, imagination, book buying, use of the library, racial and ethnic tolerance, and respect for elders (Hearold, 1986; Liebert & Sprafkin, 1988; Pingree, 1978).

In addition, several meta-analyses have been done. One found that positive effects of media exposure were twice as strong as negative effects (Hearold, 1986). Two more recent meta-analyses found that they are roughly equivalent (Mares & Woodard, 2001; Paik & Comstock, 1994).

So prosocial programming is, indeed, effective according to the vast majority of the research done. How exactly prosocial programming should be defined is an issue still unresolved. Clearly, most prosocial programming occurs on PBS (72% in one sample), and preschool children are the most frequent beneficiaries (Mares & Woodard, 2001). What may be more important is answering, "Do children learn prosocial messages from the mainstream programming they tend to view more often?" In one analysis (Woodard, 1999), only 4 of the top 20 Nielsen shows watched by children and teens contained social lessons: *Boy Meets World, Disney's One Saturday Morning, 7th Heaven,* and *Hey Arnold!* Of these, only 2, *Disney's One Saturday Morning* and *7th Heaven,* contained prosocial messages as narrowly defined as involving friendly interaction, aggression reduction, altruism, and stereotype reduction (Mares & Woodard, 2001, p. 185). And of those 2 shows, only the Disney program was designed explicitly for children. Therefore, perhaps the most important question is not how much prosocial content there is in children's programming but how much there is in adult programming that children are likely to watch (Mares & Woodard, 2001).

● 10. STEPPING UP MEDIA ADVOCACY

Media advocacy is the "strategic use of mass media for advancing a social or public policy initiative" (National Cancer Institute, 1988). This involves refocusing public attention and debate on health issues as a matter of public policy, not individuals' foibles. According to Wallack et al. (1993), current debates must be reframed. For example, tobacco manufacturers have deflected much attention by framing the debate about smoking as a free speech/individual freedom issue. Newer anti-smoking ads in Florida and from the "Truth" campaign, in turn, have successfully refocused the debate by showing the duplicity of the tobacco industry in not admitting that nicotine is addictive (Sly et al., 2001). Among Florida teens, rates of smoking have decreased significantly (CDC, 1999). In Massachusetts, a statewide anti-smoking campaign aggressively using TV counter-ads also resulted in a decrease in new smokers among young teens (Siegel & Biener, 2000). Calling attention to the fact that tobacco brands popular with teens are more likely to advertise in magazines with high youth readerships would represent another potentially useful media advocacy strategy (King et al., 1998).

The National Rifle Association has done likewise, despite the fact that federal courts, including the Supreme Court, have not interpreted the Second Amendment as guaranteeing everyone's right to own firearms. Simply reclassifying guns as a consumer product would have a profound public health effect, especially because there are currently more stringent regulations governing the manufacture and sale of teddy bears than of guns (Sitton, 1994).

Successful reframing involves exposing unethical industry practices rather than trying to improve individuals' behaviors by urging them to be healthy (Wallack et al., 1993). The hypothesis here is that individuals are powerless to change unhealthy behaviors unless public policy supports their changing (Brown & Steele, 1995). For example, when singer Gloria Estefan joined the federal government's anti-drug campaign and cautioned children to "Get Smart, Don't Start," media advocates publicized the fact that she later received an $18 million sponsorship from Bacardi rum for a new tour (Brown & Witherspoon, 1998; Wallack et al., 1993).

It may seem strange to raise the issue of campaign finance reform in a book about effects of media on young people, but this chapter is designed to discuss solutions. Campaign finance reform could rank as one of the most important solutions. Here, ultimately, is where media activists could make an enormous impact. As was discussed in the chapter on drugs (see Chapter 6), three major industries arguably control much of the media-related agenda in Congress—the National Rifle Association, the beer and wine manufacturers, and the tobacco manufacturers. Add a fourth, the food manufacturers and restaurant lobby, and hardly a congressman is immune from immense financial and political pressure to do what's "right" for industry and "wrong" for children (see Figure 11.27). In 1998, for example, the U.S. Senate rejected a new tobacco bill that would have tried to decrease teen smoking by increasing the tax on a pack of cigarettes to $1.10. The tobacco lobby reportedly spent millions of dollars to influence the outcome of the vote (Kaul, 1998). In the 2000 presidential campaign, business, labor, and wealthy individuals spent nearly $500 million in "soft money" contributions. Clearly, most of them were expecting something in return ("Buying Political Favors," 2001). Until Congress is freed from its dependence on these special interest groups, the federal government is unlikely to play a very large role in ameliorating the negative effects of media in the United States ("Buying Political Favors," 2001; Hitt, 1999).

Figure 11.27
SOURCE: Copyright John Branch, *San Antonio Express-News*. Used with permission.

● CONCLUSION

In 1961, Federal Communications Commission Chairman Newton Minow shocked the broadcasting industry by calling American television "a vast wasteland":

> I invite you to sit down in front of your television set when your station goes on the air and stay there . . . until the station signs off. I can assure you that you will observe a vast wasteland. You will see a procession of game shows, violence, audience participation shows, formula comedies about totally unbelievable families, blood and thunder, mayhem, violence, sadism, murder, western bad men, western good men, private eyes, gangsters, more violence and cartoons. (Barnouw, 1975, p. 300)

In over 40 years, with thousands of research studies giving ample cause for concern, how much has really changed? "Good" media messages (predominantly PBS on television; Dreamworks, Disney, and occasional other studio films) continue to be drowned out by "bad" media messages, like some perverse Gresham's Law of Media. As the public health toll continues to climb (handgun deaths, injuries and deaths from drunken driving, teen pregnancies, HIV infection), the American public will look even more to the media to become part of the solution rather than part of the problem. Thirty years after his original speech, Minow added a sad epitaph (*New York Times,* May 12, 1991):

> In 1961, I worried that my children would not benefit much from television. But in 1991, I worry that my grandchildren will actually be harmed by it.

It is a modern American tragedy that an entertainment industry that at times can be so astoundingly creative, so informative, and so provocative is allowed to continue to produce programming whose primary objective is to make as much money as possible, with so little consideration of the nation's most valuable resource, its children and adolescents.

APPENDIX A

MEDIA LITERACY SKILLS

For centuries, *literacy* has referred to the ability to read and write text. But in the past century, we have replaced text-based discourse with image-based discourse. Most Americans now get most of their information from television and, increasingly, from the Internet. Textual literacy is no longer an adequate measure of one's ability to understand and use communications media.

Media literacy—the ability to critically consume and create media—is becoming an essential skill in today's world. Media-literate individuals are better able to decipher the complex messages they receive from television, radio, newspapers, magazines, books, billboards and signs, packaging and marketing materials, video games, and the Internet. Media literacy skills can help one understand not only the surface content of media messages but the deeper and often more important meanings beneath the surface. Media literacy education seeks to give media consumers greater freedom by teaching them to analyze, access, evaluate, and produce media. What follows is a cursory treatment of basic media literacy "tools" or skills.

● GENERAL MEDIA LITERACY SKILLS OR TOOLS

1. *Media construct our culture.* Our perception of reality is shaped by the media we use to communicate with one another.

2. *Media contain ideological and value messages.* Some of these messages are intended, and some are unintended. Media messages often target specific groups, and they can be positive or negative. They can be intentionally obvious (manifest texts) or intentionally hidden (latent subtexts).

3. *Media use identifiable techniques.* TV commercials, for example, are very carefully constructed to influence our attitudes and behavior, using identifiable persuasion techniques. Flattery, repetition, fear, humor, powerful words, and sexual images are especially common and effective techniques of media persuasion.

4. *Individuals construct their own meanings from media.* Although media makers attempt to convey specific messages, people receive and interpret them differently. All meanings and interpretations should be respected.

5. *The human brain processes moving images in a different manner than text.* TV images move at 30 frames per second. The information they transmit often bypasses the analytic brain and can trigger emotions and memory in the unconscious and reactive parts of the brain. Only a small proportion surfaces in consciousness.

6. *Media are most powerful when they operate at an emotional level.* Most fiction seeks to engage our hearts as well as our minds. Advertisements take this further and seek to transfer feelings from an emotionally charged symbol to a product. Most ads tell us little that is truly useful about the product except its name and appearance.

7. *Filmic techniques and techno-effects enhance the emotional impact of media.* Camera angles, framing, reaction shots, quick cuts, lighting tricks, computer graphics, music, sound effects, and other techniques are used to reinforce the messages in the script.

8. *Most media are controlled by commercial interests.* In the United States, the marketplace largely determines what we see on television, what we hear on the radio, and what we read in newspapers or magazines. As we use media, we should always be alert to the commercial self-interest of most media makers. As global media monopolies grow and corporate interests become harder to identify, asking questions becomes even more important.

9. *Media construct fantasy worlds.* Although fantasy can be pleasurable and entertaining, it can also be harmful. Movies, TV shows, and pop songs sometimes inspire people to engage in dangerous behaviors. Advertising constructs a fantasy world where all problems can be solved with a purchase. Successful individuals are able to recognize fantasy and constructively integrate it with reality.

10. *Media messages can be decoded*. By "deconstructing" media, we can identify the techniques of persuasion being used and recognize how media makers are trying to influence us.

11. *Media-literate individuals are active consumers of media*. Many forms of media—especially television—seek to create passive, yet impulsive, consumers. Media-literate individuals attempt to consume media with a critical eye, evaluating sources, intended purposes, techniques, and deeper meanings.

● SPECIFIC TOOLS: THE LANGUAGE OF PERSUASION

Media makers—particularly advertisers—use a number of identifiable techniques to inform and persuade media consumers. We can use our understanding of these techniques as specific tools for decoding media messages and producing our own, more effective, media.

1. *Symbols* can be words, designs, places, ideas, music, and so on symbolizing tradition, nationalism, power, religion, sex, family, or any concept with emotional content. In media, people and things often symbolize some larger concept.

2. *Hyperbole* is exaggeration or "hype" (e.g., "The greatest automobile advance of the century!"). Ads often use "glittering generalities"—impressive-sounding language that is nonetheless vague and meaningless. This technique seeks to impress the target and make him or her more susceptible to the sales pitch.

3. *Fear.* Media often try to make us afraid that if we don't do or buy something, something bad could happen to us, our families and friends, or our country.

4. *Scapegoating* is a powerful technique that blames many problems on one person, group, race, religion, and so on.

5. *Humor* is a powerful tool of persuasion. If you can make people laugh, you can persuade them.

6. *The Big Lie*. Most people want to believe what they see and hear. Lies work—on cereal boxes, in ads, and on television news. According to Adolf Hitler, one of the 20th century's most dangerous propagandists, people are more suspicious of a small lie than a big one.

7. *Testimonials* use famous people or respected institutions to sell a person, idea, or product. They need have nothing in common.

8. *Repetition* drives the message home many times. Even unpleasant ads work if they are repeated enough to pound their message into our skulls.

9. *Führerprinzip* (a term coined by Nazi propaganda chief Josef Goebbels) means "leadership principle," or charisma. Be firm, bold, and strong; have dramatic confidence; and frequently combine this appeal with the "plain folks" technique. It can be very effective.

10. *Name-calling* or *ad hominem* is frequently used in media. It can be direct or delicately indirect. Audiences love it. Our violent, aggressive, sexualized media teach us from an early age to love to hear gossip. (Just tune in to daytime talk radio or TV!)

11. *Flattery* is based on the idea that if you make people feel good, they are more likely to buy your product. We like people who like us, and we tend to believe people we like. (We're sure that someone as brilliant as yourself will easily understand this technique!)

12. *Bribery* seems to give us something desirable: "Buy one, get one free." This technique plays on people's acquisitiveness and greed. Unfortunately, there is no free lunch.

13. *Diversion* seems to tackle a problem or issue but then throws in an emotional *non sequitur* or distraction.

14. *Straw man* builds up an illogical (or deliberately damaged) idea and presents it as something that one's opponent supports or represents. Knocking down the straw man reduces the opponent and builds up the attacker.

15. *Denial* is used to escape responsibility for saying something unpopular. It can be either direct or indirect. A politician who says, "I won't bring up my opponent's problems with the IRS," has just brought up the issue.

16. *Card-stacking* provides a false context, telling only part of the story, to give a misleading impression. Read the critics' quotations in any movie ad; not surprisingly, only the compliments are included.

17. *Bandwagon* insists that "everyone is doing it." It plays on feelings of loneliness and isolation. In the United States, with our incredible addiction to sports, this technique is often accompanied by the concept of "being on the winning team."

18. *Plain folks*. Many advertisers and politicians promote themselves or their products as being of humble origins, common, one of the gals or guys. Unfortunately, this technique reinforces anti-intellectualism, implying that to be "common" is unquestionably good.

19. *Nostalgia*. People tend to forget the bad parts of the past and remember the good. A nostalgic setting usually gives a product a better image.

20. *Warm and fuzzy*. Using sentimental images (especially families, kids, and animals) to sell products or ideas.

21. *Beautiful people*. Using good-looking models in ads to suggest we will look like the models if we buy the product. (How many times have you seen this one used?)

22. *Simple solutions*. Avoid complexities, unless you're talking to intellectuals. Attach many problems to one simple solution. Our sports-driven culture tends to make us forget that most problems have no simple solutions, only better questions.

23. *Scientific evidence* uses the paraphernalia of science (charts, graphs, etc.) to "prove" something that can be bogus.

24. *Maybe*. Exaggerated or outrageous claims are commonly preceded by *maybe, might,* or *could*. You could win a million dollars!

25. *Group dynamics* replaces the weakness of the individual with the strength of the group. People are often carried away by the atmosphere of live audiences, rallies, or other gatherings.

26. *Rhetorical questions* get the target to say yes to preliminary questions to build agreement and trust before the sales pitch.

27. *Timing* can be as simple as planning your sell for when your target is tired. In sophisticated propaganda, timing is the organization of multiple techniques in a pattern or "strategy" that increases the emotional impact of the sell.

APPENDIX **B**

AN ADVOCATE'S GUIDE
TO MEDIA LITERACY
RESOURCES

1. THE ECONOMY AND ECOLOGY OF MEDIA ●

- *Affluenza* (PBS): www.pbs.org/kcts/affluenza/. This PBS series deals with the social and environmental costs of materialism. A teacher's guide (many activities complement the film) and a resource section are included.

- Center for a New American Dream: www.newdream.org. Educating the public about responsible consumption and encouraging people to take action are the purpose of this organization. Their consumption puzzle includes information on topics ranging from agriculture to technology and from transportation to population.

- Center for Commercial Free Public Education: www.commercialfree.org. A national nonprofit organization that addresses commercialism in public schools. The site contains resources, including articles and activist ideas.

- The Commercialism in Education Research Unit (CERU): www.asu.edu/educ/epsl. Dr. Alex Molnar is the director of CERU. The center analyzes the amount and the types of commercialism in schools. Three reports (*Sponsored Schools and Commercialized Classrooms, The Hidden Costs of Channel One,* and *Giving Kids the Business*) can be downloaded.

• Consumers Union: www.consumersunion.org. Consumers Union, the publisher of Consumer Reports and Zillions, is a nonprofit consumer advocacy organization. The site contains much consumer information that is censored in the media, such as product safety and health care information.

• Co-Op America: www.coopamerica.org. This organization provides a directory of socially and environmentally responsible products and services. It also offers advice on how to invest, live, and clean in environmentally friendly ways.

• Getta Clue: www.dol.gov. This curriculum covers the issues connected with sweatshop labor.

• McSpotlight: www.mcspotlight.org. This site's main function is to report on anti-McDonald activities and information. It is also a great place to find information about organizations that exploit employees and the environment.

• UNITE: www.uniteunion.org. The Union of Needletrades, Industrial and Textile Employees (UNITE) maintains this Web site to provide information about sweatshops and other labor issues in the textile industry. It contains Stop Sweatshops!, a section full of activist ideas and resources for teachers and students.

● 2. MEDIA AND DEMOCRACY

• Accuracy in Media (AIM): www.aim.org/main.htm. AIM is a conservative national media watch group. Its purpose is "fairness, balance, and accuracy in media."

• Center for Media and Democracy: www.prwatch.org. Investigative reporting on the public relations industry is the purpose of this nonprofit organization.

• Center for Public Integrity: www.publicintegrity.org. This nonprofit and nonpartisan organization has published more than 40 studies, reports, and books on public service and ethics-related issues. Recent investigations have focused on issue ads and campaign finance.

• Dissect an Ad (PBS): www.pbs.org/pov/ad/.

• Democracy Project: 30 Second Candidate (PBS): www.pbs.org/30secondcandidate/index.html. These sites focus on political advertising. They allow students to watch and to create political advertising.

• Fair and Accuracy in Reporting (FAIR): www.fair.org. FAIR is a national media watch group. Through its progressive publication, *Extra!,* it examines "biased reporting, censored news, media mergers, press/state cronyism, the power of corporate owners and advertisers, and right-wing influences in the media."

- FAIR Resource List: www.fair.org/resources.html.

- Townhall: www.townhall.com/links/. This site provides contact information for progressive (FAIR) and conservative (Townhall) organizations.

- Free Speech Internet Television: www.freespeech.org. This site attempts to respond to the interests of the people whose voices are excluded or distorted in the global corporate media.

- Independent Media Center: www.indymedia.org. This collective of media producers offers noncorporate, grassroots coverage of national events, including the World Trade Organization (WTO) protests in Seattle.

- Independent Media Institute (IMI): www.mediademocracy.org. IMI, a nonprofit organization, seeks to strengthen and support independent and alternative journalism while improving the public's access to information sources.

- Media Alliance: www.media-alliance.org. For 22 years, this nonprofit organization has provided training and resources to media workers, community organizations, and political activists. Its mission is excellence, ethics, diversity, and accountability in all aspects of media for the interest of peace, social justice, and social responsibility.

- Media Channels: www.mediachannels.org. A weekly Web site devoted to featuring political and cultural coverage of the best in alternative media from around the globe, with an emphasis on media's role in covering international affairs.

- Project Vote Smart: www.vote-smart.org. Project Vote Smart is a nonpartisan organization that gathers extensive information about candidates and elected officials, including voting records and biographies. Its site contains classroom activities too.

- Propaganda Analysis: carmen.artsci.washington.edu/propaganda/home.htm. The site examines techniques of propaganda and provides examples.

- Rocky Mountain Media Watch: www.bigmedia.org. This nonprofit organization collects and analyzes the content of local news around the country in an effort to empower citizens to resist the manipulations of local news media.

- Tom Paine: www.tompaine.com. A weekly progressive Internet newsletter featuring provocative essays on contemporary political and economic life, with a continuing emphasis on journalism and other media's role in shaping our political culture.

● 3. MEDIA, STORYTELLING, AND OUR CULTURAL ENVIRONMENT

- Coalition for Quality Children's Media: www.cqcm.org. This site does something radical. It has competent, concerned, qualified people rate children's media, thousands of movies, videos, books, and so on. What a concept!

- Census Bureau: www.census.gov. At this site, you will find various statistical breakdowns of the population of the United States.

- Children and the Media: www.childrennow.org/media/media.html. Children Now researches the content of mass media, specifically focusing on the impact and the influence on children. Two reports—"A Different World: Children's Perceptions of Race" and "Class in the Media and Fall Colors: How Diverse Is the 1998 TV Season's Prime-Time Lineup?"—explore the issues surrounding stereotyping.

- Gender and Race in Media (University of Iowa—Department of Communication Studies): www.uiowa.edu/~commstud/resources/GenderMedia/. This part of the Communication Studies' Web site contains articles and extensive links regarding the issues of gender, race, and class in the media.

- Movies, Race, and Ethnicity: www.lib.berkeley.edu/MRC/EthnicImagesVid. html. Extensive videography, from the Media Resource Center at the University of California–Berkeley, attempts to give a broad sampling of films from the past century that provided ethnic and racial representations.

- National Storytelling Network: www.storynet.org. On top of getting information about storytelling conferences and festivals, this site also provides numerous links to storytelling sites (including those concerned with folklore and ethnic stories).

● 4. MEDIA AND HEALTH

- About Face: www.about-face.org. The Gallery of Shame, a showcase of the most offensive examples of degrading images of women in advertising, is one part of this Web site that combats negative and distorted images of women in the media.

- Body Icon: Fear and Loathing in the Mirror: nm-server.jrn.columbia.edu/ projects/masters/bodyimage/toc.html. This Web site examines the negative effects of advertising on body image, including eating disorders and plastic surgery.

- Florida Truth Campaign: www.thetruth.com. The Truth Campaign is one of the most successful anti-tobacco advertising programs in the country. The American Legacy Foundation is currently using similar ads across the country.

- Get Outraged: www.getoutraged.com/main_top.html. Facts, links, and activism are just a part of the information available at this anti-tobacco page.

- Girl Power! www.health.org/gpower. The Department of Health sponsors this site that contains helpful and interesting information for girls and adults. Its BodyWise handbook contains plenty of information about body image and eating disorders, including what friends and adults can do to help.

- Kaiser Family Foundation: www.kff.org. This foundation analyzes the content of entertainment media from a health standpoint. The site contains reports about violence and sex in the media.

- National Clearinghouse for Alcohol and Drug Information: www.health.org. This site is a database of information on alcohol, tobacco, and other drugs.

5. MEDIA TECHNOLOGY AND PRODUCTION ●

- Child Safety on the Information Highway: www.missingkids.com. Published by the National Center for Missing and Exploited Children, this site provides information about privacy and safety with the Internet.

- Empowerment Project: www.web.com/empower. In an attempt to democratize the mass media, this group provides facilities, training, and other support for independent producers, artists, activists, and organizations.

- Librarian's Guide to Cyberspace: www.ala.org/parentspage/greatsites/guide.html. This site contains not only guidelines for evaluating Web sites but also a suggested list of Web sites appropriate for children.

- Listen Up! (PBS) www.listenup.org. Empowering youth through media activism (including critical viewing and production) is the focus of this site. It includes more than 150 youth-produced pieces of media as well as pamphlets on how to create and distribute PSAs.

- Video Production in the Classroom: A Resource Guide: www.kqed.org/ednet/mediaeducation/mediaclassroom/videoprodclass/bibli.html. More resources (including handbooks, curriculum, textbooks, magazines, and videos) for educators.

- More worthwhile tech sites: www.childrenpartnership.org, www.getnetwise. org, www.cyberangels.com, www.familyguidebook.com, www.isafe.org, www. safekids.com.

● MISCELLANEOUS MEDIA LITERACY SITES

- Center for Media Awareness: www.media-awareness.ca. This organization offers many useful media literacy lesson plans.

- Census Bureau: www.census.gov. At this site, you will find various statistical breakdowns of the population of the United States.

- Media Channel: www.mediachannel.org. Access to hundreds of media issues organizations is provided at this site. These organizations include media watch groups, university journalism departments, anti-censorship monitors, and trade publications.

- Media Literacy On-Line Project: interact.uoregon.edu/MediaLit/HomePage. This is a comprehensive site with articles, lesson plans, and links about media education.

- TV Free America: www.tvfa.org. This organization sponsors the National TV-Turnoff Week with many useful resources.

● MAGAZINES

- *Adbusters* is not for the fainthearted. It offers priceless and unique but radical commentary, satire, and anti-ads. 1243 West 7th Avenue, Vancouver, BC, V6H 1B7 Canada; (800) 663-1243; www.adbusters.org

- *Advertising Age* is a major trade journal of the advertising industry. Get to know the way advertisers think. P.O. Box 07913, Detroit, MI 48207-9966; (888) 288-5900; adage.com

- *Brill's Content* focuses on many media issues. 521 Fifth Avenue, New York, NY 10175; (800) 829-9154; www.brillscontent.com

- *Worldwatch* follows important international media-related issues. P.O. Box 789, Oxon Hill, MD 20750-0879; (800) 555-2028; www.worldwatch.org

- *Zillions* is an online consumer awareness zine for children. Cool. P.O. Box 729, Vandalia, OH 45377; (914) 378-2000; www.zillionedcenter.org

CHILDREN'S BOOKS ●

- *Arthur's TV Trouble,* by Marc Brown (Toronto: Little, Brown, 1995). Arthur can't seem to resist the persuasive television commercials.

- *The Berenstein Bears and Too Much TV*, by Stan and Jan Berenstein (New York: Random House, 1984). Mama Bear declares a 1-week ban on television because Brother and Sister Bear are spending all their time in front of it. During this time, the family rediscovers all sorts of indoor and outdoor activities to complete together.

- *When the TV Broke*, by Harriet Ziefert (New York: Puffin, 1989). Jeffrey watches television all the time. Right after it breaks, he can't figure out what to do with his time. He soon finds much to do, realizing there's more to life than television.

- *Box-Head Boy,* by Christine Winn (Minneapolis: Fairview, 1996). This tale is about what can happen when you watch too much television.

NOVELS ●

- *Brave New World,* by Aldous Huxley (New York: Harper Perennial, 1998). Huxley's classic about a futuristic dystopian civilization is surprisingly prophetic— a provocative read for high school students or anyone who can read.

- *Fahrenheit 451,* by Ray Bradbury (New York: Ballantine, 1995). Bradbury examines issues of censorship in this science fiction classic about firemen who burn books in efforts to control the thoughts of the citizenry.

- *Snow Crash*, by Neal Stephenson (New York: Bantam, 1992). Prescient look at the coming era of corporate and Internet domination. Very accessible for kids.

- *1984*, by George Orwell (New York: Signet, 1983). Orwell's fictional account of a totalitarian state raises important questions about language, media, and power.

● ESSENTIAL NONFICTION FOR THE MEDIA LITERATE ADVOCATE

- *Age of Missing Information*, by Bill McKibben (New York: Plume, 1992). Comparing 24 hours of television watching with 24 hours spent hiking in the woods, McKibben challenges the notion that we live in the "Information Age." A well-written and lively personal meditation on our media culture.

- *Amusing Ourselves to Death*, by Neil Postman (New York: Penguin, 1985). An insightful look at how the structure of television undermines our important public conversations about politics, religion, and the news. We at NMMLP consider this book a classic.

- *Breaking the News: How the Media Undermine American Democracy*, by James Fallows (New York: Pantheon, 1996). Fallows's insider account of the news business sheds light on why the news is broken and what we can do to fix it.

- *Censored 2000*, by Peter Phillips (New York: Seven Stories Press, 2000). An annual compilation of the stories the press does not cover in any meaningful manner.

- *The Control Revolution,* by Andrew L. Shapiro (New York: Century Foundation, 1999). One of the most thoughtful books yet written on the Internet's effects on our society.

- *Corporate Media and the Threat to Democracy*, by Robert McChesney (New York: Seven Stories Press, 1997). A concise account of how corporate control of the media threatens the democratic process.

- *The Disappearance of Childhood,* by Neil Postman (New York: Vintage, 1994). A classic—even more prophetic now. How have television and other forms of electronic media undermined the notion of childhood?

- *Endangered Minds: Why Children Don't Think and What We Can Do About It*, by Jane Healy (New York: Touchstone, 1990). An engaging look at how electronic media affect childhood development. A must-read for teachers and especially parents of bright children.

- *Failure to Connect: How Computers Affect Our Children's Minds—for Better and Worse,* by Jane M. Healy (New York: Simon & Schuster, 1998). A thoughtful evaluation of computer use in the classroom, based on Healy's extensive research on computer use throughout U.S. classrooms.

- *If the Gods Had Meant for Us to Vote, They Would Have Given Us Candidates,* by Art Hightower (New York: HarperCollins, 2000). A thoroughly irreverent, humorous, and thought-provoking look at our elections, media, and "democratic" decision making.

- *Media Alert*, by Sue Lockwood-Summers (Castle Rock, CO: High Willow, 1997). One of the most useful activity guides for media literacy teachers.

- *Media Literacy: Keys to Interpreting Media Messages*, by Art Silverblatt (Westport, CT: Praeger, 2001). Concise, pragmatic, reasonable, and sufficiently complex for everyone from the middle school teacher to the university student.

- *The Media Monopoly,* by Ben Bagdikian (Boston: Beacon, 1992). Now in its fourth printing, Bagdikian's classic examines how corporations have consolidated media outlets.

- *No Logo,* by Naomi Klein (New York: Picador, 1999). A sterling description of brands, export processing zones, sweatshops, and the movement to do something about them.

- *Screen Smarts: A Family Guide to Media Literacy*, by Gloria DeGaetano and Kathleen Bander (New York: Houghton Mifflin, 1996). One of the best books ever produced for families on the subject of dealing with screens. Concise, pragmatic, and loaded with useful suggestions, exercises, and activities. Out of print, but worth a trip to the library.

- *Seducing America: How Television Charms the Modern Voter*, by Roderick Hart (New York: Oxford University Press, 1994). The best and most scholarly single book written about television's effects on our democratic process.

- *Stop Teaching Our Kids to Kill: A Call to Action Against TV, Movie, and Video Game Violence*, by Lt. Col. David Grossman and Gloria DeGaetano (New York: Crown, 1999). Succinct summary of violence research and issues.

- *Toxic Sludge Is Good For You! Lies, Damn Lies, and the Public Relations Industry,* by John Stauber and Sheldon Rampton (Monroe, ME: Common Courage, 1995). A humorous, disturbing, and well-documented look at the PR industry's new power.

- *Trust Us, We're Experts: How Industry Manipulates Science and Gambles With Your Future,* by Sheldon Rampton and John Stauber (New York: Penguin Putnam, 2001). A field guide to information age deception.

MEDIA EDUCATION VIDEOS ●

- From the Media Education Foundation: *Game Over* (video games), *Advertising & The End of the World* (advertising effects), *Dreamworlds2* (objectification and violence in music video), *Still Killing Us Softly3* (updated and wonderful classic from Jean Kilbourne), *Slim Hopes* (Jean Kilbourne on dieting), *Tough Guise* (Jackson Katz lectures on media macho), *Reviving Ophelia* (Mary Pipher on saving girls' selves), *Money for Nothing* (Big Media reducing music choices), *Behind the Scenes* (product placement and hypercommercialism in Hollywood), *The Mickey Mouse Monopoly* (is Mickey looking out for your kids interests? Disney and corporate power), *McLibel* (Global monster sues two activists for expressing their opinions about the health (?) of MickeyD's food), *Project Censored* (What Big Media news does not cover), and coming soon . . . the *Wrestling Expose!* 26 Center Street, Northampton, MA 01060; (800) 897-0089; www.igc.org/mef

• From California Newsreel: *The Ad & the Ego* (a classic, accessible tour of advertising), *Fear & Favor in the Newsroom* (what are they doing to the news?), *On Television: Teach Your Children* (slightly dated but valuable introduction to "children's" television). 149 Ninth Street, San Francisco, CA 94103; (415) 621-6196; www.newsreel.org

• From PBS: *Free Speech for Sale* (fabulous! Bill Moyers on the growth of the Big Media/corporate political power system in just the past 8 years—this should be required viewing for every voter. The oil, pharmaceutical, gambling, hog farming, and mining industries do not want you to see this video). P.O. Box 2284, South Burlington, VT 05407; (800) 336-1917; PBS.org

• From the Center for Media Literacy: *Justice for Sale* (do we have justice?), *Beyond Blame* (expensive and complex but valuable curricula helping kids surmount media violence), *Buy Me That!* (wonderful videos from HBO teaching youngsters consumerism lessons). 4727 Wilshire Boulevard, Suite 403, Los Angeles, CA 90010; (800) 226-9494; www.medialit.org

• From Face to Face Media: *Scanning Television* (many video cassettes and curricula guides teaching about media). 1818 Grant Street, Vancouver, BC, Canada V5L 2Y8; (604) 251-1800

• From the Video Data Bank: *Spin* (a marvelous look at political use of telecommunications technology). 112 South Michigan Avenue, 3rd Floor, Chicago, IL 60603; (312) 345-3550; www.vdb.org

• From California NOW: *Redefining Liberation* (provocative look at women's media issues). 926 J Street, Suite 820, Sacramento, CA 95814; (916) 442-3414; www.canow.org

• Altschul Group Corporation: *Ad-Libbing It* (wonderful treatment of smoking issues, accessible to youth). 1560 Sherman Avenue, Suite 100, Evanston, IL 60201; (800) 323-9084; www.agcmedia.com

A FEW NMMLP RESOURCES FROM WWW.NMMLP.ORG ●

- *Media Literacy for Health: A K-12 Activity Curriculum* (a health CD-ROM): 48 lessons, K-12, in six strands: nutrition, safety, alcohol and drugs, tobacco, physical activity, and relationships and sexuality. Media analysis skills and health information. Lessons can be printed and include resource sheets, activity sheets, summaries, step-by-step procedures, assessment, discussion guides with questions and answers, extensions, and more than 100 media examples. Windows and Mac.

- *Media Literacy: Reversing Addiction in Our Compulsive Culture* (CD-ROM): with five 3-hour field-tested prevention presentations or, if used in a seminar format, five prevention units; 250 examples with printable talking points. Windows and Mac.

- *Understanding Media* (CD-ROM): 221 examples (74 video) cover 33 skills and 34 issues with 400 pages of questions and answers for all ages. Windows and Mac.

- *Just Do Media Literacy: Students, Issues, Experts & Examples* (video): kids in classrooms, deconstructing ads and movies, and quotations from many experts in education and medicine, discussing central media literacy issues and skills. 55 min. Discussion guide.

A complete list of NMMLP resources can be found at www.nmmlp.org.

APPENDIX **C**

DEFINITION OF MEDIA LITERACY

Media literacy emphasizes the following elements (Silverblatt, 2001):

1. a critical thinking skill that allows audiences to develop independent judgments about media content;

2. an understanding of the process of mass communication;

3. an awareness of the impact of media on the individual and society;

4. the development of strategies with which to discuss and analyze media messages;

5. an awareness of media content as a "text" that provides insight into our contemporary culture and ourselves;

6. the cultivation of an enhanced enjoyment, understanding, and appreciation of media content; and

7. in the case of media communicators, the ability to produce effective and responsible media messages.

References

Aaron, D. J., Dearwater, S. R., Anderson, R., Olsen, T., Kriska, A. M., & LaPorte, R. E. (1995). Physical activity and the initiation of high-risk behaviors in adolescents. *Medicine and Science in Sports and Exercise, 27,* 1639-1645.

Abelson, R. P. (1976). Script processing in attitude formation and decision-making. In J. Carroll & J. Payne (Eds.), *Cognition and social behavior* (pp. 33-45). Hillsdale, NJ: Lawrence Erlbaum.

Abramson, P. R., & Mechanic, M. B. (1983). Sex and the media: Three decades of best selling books and major motion pictures. *Archives of Sexual Behavior, 12,* 185-206.

Ackerman, B. P. (1988). Reason inferences in the story comprehension of children and adults. *Child Development, 59,* 1426-1442.

Acuff, D. S. (1997). *What kids buy and why: The psychology of marketing to kids.* New York: Free Press.

Adelson, A. (1994, April 5). A campaign aimed at teenagers is at the forefront of California's $499 million battle against cancer. *New York Times,* p. C17.

Adler, J. (1999, May 10). Beyond Littleton: The truth about high school. *Newsweek,* pp. 56-58.

Adler, R. (1980). Children's television advertising: History of the issue. In E. L. Palmer & A. Dorr (Eds.), *Children and the faces of television: Teaching, violence, selling* (pp. 237-248). New York: Academic Press.

Aidman, A. (1995, December). *Advertising in the schools.* Urbana, IL: ERIC Clearinghouse on Elementary and Early Childhood Education. Retrieved from ERIC database (ERIC Document Reproduction Service No. ED 389473).

Aitken, P. P., & Eadie, D. R. (1990). Reinforcing effects of cigarette advertising on under-age smoking. *British Journal of Addiction, 85,* 399-412.

Aitken, P. P., Eadie, D. R., Leathar, D. S., McNeill, R. E. J., & Scott, A. C. (1988). Television advertisements for alcoholic drinks do reinforce under-age drinking. *British Journal of Addiction, 83,* 1399-1419.

Alan Guttmacher Institute. (1994). *Sex and America's teenagers.* New York: Author.

Alexander, A. (2001). Broadcast networks and the children's television business. In D. G. Singer & J. L. Singer (Eds.), *Handbook of children and the media* (pp. 495-505). Thousand Oaks, CA: Sage.

Alexander, A., Benjamin, L. M., Hoerrner, K., & Roe, D. (1998). "We'll be back in a moment": A content analysis of advertisements in children's television in the 1950s. *Journal of Advertising, 27*(3), 1-9.

Allen, J. C. (2001). The economic structure of the commercial electronic children's media industries. In D. G. Singer & J. L. Singer (Eds.), *Handbook of children and the media* (pp. 447-493). Thousand Oaks, CA: Sage.

Allison, D. B., Fontaine, K. R., Manson, J. E., Stevens, J., & VanItallie, T. B. (1999). Annual deaths attributable to obesity in the United States. *Journal of the American Medical Association, 282,* 1530-1538.

Alpert, B. S., & Wilson, D. K. (1992). Stress reactivity in childhood and adolescence. In J. R. Turner, A. Sherwood, & K. C. Light (Eds.), *Individual differences in cardiovascular response to stress: Perspectives on individual differences* (pp. 187-201). New York: Plenum.

Alter, J. (1994, January 17). The power to change what's "cool." *Newsweek,* p. 23.

Altman, D. G., Levine, D. W., Coeytaux, R., Slade, J., & Jaffe, R. (1996). Tobacco promotion and susceptibility to tobacco use among adolescents aged 12 through 17 years in a nationally representative sample. *American Journal of Public Health, 86,* 1590-1593.

Aluja-Fabregat, A. (2000). Personality and curiosity about TV and films violence in adolescents. *Personality and Individual Differences, 29,* 379-392.

American Academy of Pediatrics (AAP). (1995a). Alcohol use and abuse: A pediatric concern (policy statement). *Pediatrics, 95,* 439-442.

American Academy of Pediatrics (AAP). (1995b). Children, adolescents, and advertising (policy statement). *Pediatrics, 95,* 295-297.

American Academy of Pediatrics (AAP). (1996). Rock music and music lyrics (policy statement). *Pediatrics, 98,* 1219-1221.

American Academy of Pediatrics (AAP). (1999). Media literacy (policy statement). *Pediatrics, 104,* 341-343.

American Academy of Pediatrics (AAP). (2001a). Children, adolescents, and television (policy statement). *Pediatrics, 108,* 1222-1226.

American Academy of Pediatrics (AAP). (2001b). Media violence. *Pediatrics, 108,* 1222-1226.

American Academy of Pediatrics (AAP). (2001c). Sexuality, contraception, and the media. *Pediatrics, 107,* 191-194.

American Association of University Women. (1999). *Voices of a generation: Teenage girls on sex, school, and self.* Washington, DC: Author.

American Medical Association. (1996). *Physician guide to media violence.* Chicago: Author.

American Psychological Association. (1993). *Violence and youth: Psychology's response.* Washington, DC: Author.

Amos, A., Jacobson, B., & White, P. (1991). Cigarette advertising and coverage of smoking and health in British women's magazines. *Lancet, 337,* 93-96.

Andersen, R. E., Crespo, C. J., Bartlett, S. J., Cheskin, L. J., & Pratt, M. (1998). Relationship of physical activity and television watching with body weight and level of fatness among children. *Journal of the American Medical Association, 279,* 938-942.

Anderson, C. A. (1997). Effects of violent movies and trait hostility on hostile feelings and aggressive thoughts. *Aggressive Behavior, 23,* 161-178.

Anderson, C. A., Benjamin, A. J., Jr., & Bartholow, B. D. (1998). Does the gun pull the trigger? Automatic priming effects of weapon pictures and weapon names. *American Psychological Society, 9,* 308-314.

Anderson, C. A., & Bushman, B. J. (2001). Effects of violent video games on aggressive behavior, aggressive cognition, aggressive affect, physiological arousal, and prosocial behavior: A meta-analytic review of the scientific literature. *Psychological Science, 12,* 353-359.

Anderson, C. A., & Dill, K. E. (2000). Video games and aggressive thoughts, feelings, and behavior in the laboratory and in life. *Journal of Personality and Social Psychology, 78,* 772-790.

Anderson, C. A., & Morrow, M. (1995). Competitive aggression without interaction: Effects of competitive vs. cooperative instructions on aggressive behavior in video games. *Personality and Social Psychology Bulletin, 21,* 1020-1030.

Anderson, D. R., & Levin, S. R. (1976). Young children's attention to "Sesame Street." *Child Development, 47,* 806-811.

Annenberg Public Policy Center. (2000). *The Internet and the family 2000.* Philadelphia: Author.

Annest, J. L., Mercy, J. A., Gibson, D. R., & Ryan, G. W. (1995). National estimates of nonfatal firearm-related injuries: Beyond the tip of the iceberg. *Journal of the American Medical Association, 273,* 1749-1754.

Annicelli, C. (1999, June). *Monster cash; Pokemon has made a fortune; Prepare for the second wave.* Retrieved May 25, 2001, from the World Wide Web: www.findarticles.com/cf_0/m3196/6_97/55084237/p1/article.jhtml.

Ansen, D. (1999, September 13). A handful of tangos in Paris. *Newsweek,* p. 66.

Ansen, D. (2000, July 3). Gross and grosser. *Newsweek,* pp. 60-61.

Archer, D. (1994). American violence: How high and why? *Law Studies, 19,* 12-20.

Armstrong, B. K., de Klerk, N. H., Shean, R. E., Dunn, D. A., & Dolin, P. J. (1990). Influence of education and advertising on the uptake of smoking by children. *Medical Journal of Australia, 152,* 117-124.

Armstrong, C. A., Sallis, J. F., Alcaraz, J. E., Kolody, B., McKenzie, T. L., & Hovell, M. F. (1998). Children's television viewing, body fat, and physical fitness. *American Journal of Health Promotion, 12,* 363-368.

Arnett, J. (1991). Adolescents and heavy metal music: From the mouths of metalheads. *Youth & Society, 23,* 76-98.

Arnett, J. (1992a). Reckless behavior in adolescence: A developmental perspective. *Developmental Review, 12,* 339-373.

Arnett, J. (1992b). Socialization and adolescent reckless behavior: A reply to Jessor. *Developmental Review, 12,* 391-409.

Arnett, J. (1995). The soundtrack of recklessness: Musical preferences and reckless behavior among adolescents. *Journal of Adolescent Research, 7,* 313-331.

Arnett, J. (2002). The sounds of sex: Sex in teens' music and music videos. In J. D. Brown, J. R. Steele, & K. Walsh-Childers (Eds.), *Sexual teens, sexual media* (pp. 253-264). Mahwah, NJ: Lawrence Erlbaum.

Ash, P., & Kellerman, A. L. (2001). Reducing gun carrying by youth. *Archives of Pediatrics & Adolescent Medicine, 155,* 330-331.

Ashcroft blames 'culture' for school violence. (2001, March 23). Retrieved April 2, 2001, from Cable News Network on the World Wide Web: www.cnn.com/2001/ALLPOLITICS/03/23/ashcroft.shootings.reut/.

Atkin, C. K. (1976). Children's social learning from television advertising: Research evidence on observational modeling of product consumption. *Advances in Consumer Research, 3,* 513-519.

Atkin, C. K. (1978). Observation of parent-child interaction in supermarket decision-making. *Journal of Marketing, 42*(4), 41-45.

Atkin, C. K. (1980). Effects of television advertising on children. In E. L. Palmer & A. Dorr (Eds.), *Children and the faces of television: Teaching, violence, selling* (pp. 287-305). New York: Academic Press.

Atkin, C. K. (1982). Television advertising and socialization to consumer roles. In D. Pearl, L. Bouthilet, & J. Lazar (Eds.), *Television and behavior: Ten years of scientific progress and implications for the eighties* (Vol. 2, pp. 191-200). Washington, DC: Government Printing Office.

Atkin, C. K. (1983). Effects of realistic TV violence vs. fictional violence on aggression. *Journalism Quarterly, 60,* 615-621.

Atkin, C. K. (1990). Effects of televised alcohol messages on teenage drinking patterns. *Journal of Adolescent Health Care, 11,* 10-24.

Atkin, C. K. (1993a). Alcohol advertising and adolescents. *Adolescent Medicine: State of the Art Reviews, 4,* 527-542.

Atkin, C. K. (1993b, Winter). On regulating broadcast alcohol advertising. *Journal of Broadcasting & Electronic Media,* pp. 107-113.

Atkin, C. K. (1995). Survey and experimental research on effects of alcohol advertising. In S. Martin (Ed.), *The effects of the mass media and the use and abuse of alcohol* (pp. 39-68). Rockville, MD: National Institute on Alcohol Abuse and Alcoholism.

Atkin, C. K., & Block, M. (1983). Effectiveness of celebrity endorsers. *Journal of Advertising Research, 23*(1), 57-61.

Atkin, C. K., DeJong, W., & Wallack, L. (1992). *The influence of responsible drinking TV spots and automobile commercials on young drivers.* Washington, DC: AAA Foundation for Traffic Safety.

Atkin, C. K., Hocking, J., & Block, M. (1984). Teenage drinking: Does advertising make a difference? *Journal of Communications, 28,* 71-80.

Atkin, C. K., Neuendorf, K., & McDermott, S. (1983). The role of alcohol advertising in excessive and hazardous drinking. *Journal of Drug Education, 13,* 313-325.

Attie, I., & Brooks-Gunn, J. (1989). Development of eating problems in adolescent girls: A longitudinal study. *Developmental Psychology, 25,* 70-79.

Aufderheide, P. (1992). *Media literacy: A report of the national leadership conference on media literacy.* Washington, DC: Aspen Institute.

Auletta, K. (1993, May 17). Annals of communication: What won't they do? *The New Yorker, 69,* 45-53.

Austin, E. W., & Johnson, K. K. (1997). Effects of general and alcohol-specific media literacy training on children's decision making model about alcohol. *Journal of Health Communication, 2,* 17-42.

Austin, E. W., & Knaus, C. (1998, August). *Predicting future risky behavior among those "too young" to drink as the result of advertising desirability.* Paper presented at the meeting of the Association for Education in Journalism & Mass Communication, Baltimore, MD.

Austin, E. W., & Meili, H. K. (1994). Effects of interpretations of televised alcohol portrayals on children's alcohol beliefs. *Journal of Broadcasting & Electronic Media, 38,* 417-435.

Austin, E. W., & Nach-Ferguson, B. (1995). Sources and influences of young school-age children's general and brand-specific knowledge about alcohol. *Health Communication, 4,* 545-564.

Austin, E. W., Pinkleton, B. E., & Fujioka, Y. (2000). The role of interpretation processes and parental discussion in the media's effects on adolescents' use of alcohol. *Pediatrics, 105,* 343-349.

Bachen, C. M. (1998). Channel One and the education of American youths. *Annals of the American Academy of Political and Social Science, 557,* 132-147.

Badinand-Hubert, N., Bureau, M., Hirsch, E., Masnou, P., Nahum, L., Parain, D., & Naquet, R. (1998). Epilepsies and video games: Results of a multicentric study. *Electroencephalography and Clinical Neurophysiology, 107,* 422-427.

Bagdikian, B. H. (1998). The realities of media concentration and control. *Television Quarterly, 29*(3), 22-27.

Bailey, J. E., Kellermann, A. L., Somes, G. W., Banton, J. G., Rivara, F. P., & Rushforth, N. P. (1997). Risk factors for violent death of women in the home. *Archives of Internal Medicine, 157,* 777-782.

Bailey, M. (1969). The women's magazine short-story heroine in 1957 and 1967. *Journalism Quarterly, 46,* 364-366.

Ballard, M. E., & Wiest, J. R. (1996). Mortal Kombat™: The effects of violent videogame play on males' hostility and cardiovascular responding. *Journal of Applied Social Psychology, 26,* 717-730.

Ball-Rokeach, S. J. (2000, June). *The politics of studying media violence: Reflections thirty years after the violence commission.* Paper presented at the annual meeting of the International Communication Association, Acapulco, Mexico.

Bandura, A. (1965). Influence of models' reinforcement contingencies on the acquisition of imitative response. *Journal of Personality and Social Psychology, 1,* 589-595.

Bandura, A. (1977). *Social learning theory.* Englewood Cliffs, NJ: Prentice Hall.

Bandura, A. (1986). *Social foundations of thought and action: A social cognitive theory.* Englewood Cliffs, NJ: Prentice Hall.

Bandura, A. (1994). Social cognitive theory of mass communication. In J. Bryant & D. Zillmann (Eds.), *Media effects: Advances in theory and research* (pp. 61-90). Hillsdale, NJ: Lawrence Erlbaum.

Bandura, A., Ross, D., & Ross, S. A. (1961). Transmission of aggression through imitation of aggressive models. *Journal of Abnormal and Social Psychology, 63,* 575-582.

Bandura, A., Ross, D., & Ross, S. A. (1963a). Imitation of film-mediated aggressive models. *Journal of Abnormal and Social Psychology, 66,* 3-11.

Bandura, A., Ross, D., & Ross, S. A. (1963b). Various reinforcement and imitative learning. *Journal of Abnormal and Social Psychology, 67,* 601-607.

Baran, S. J. (1976a). How TV and film portrayals affect sexual satisfaction in college students. *Journalism Quarterly, 53,* 468-473.

Baran, S. J. (1976b). Sex on TV and adolescent sexual self-image. *Journal of Broadcasting, 20,* 61-68.

Barcus, F. E. (1980). The nature of television advertising to children. In E. L. Palmer & A. Dorr (Eds.), *Children and the faces of television: Teaching, violence, selling* (pp. 273-285). New York: Academic Press.

Barnett, M. A., Vitaglione, G. D., Harper, K. K. G., Quackenbush, S. W., Steadman, L. A., & Valdez, B. S. (1997). Late adolescents' experiences with and attitudes towards videogames. *Journal of Applied Social Psychology, 27,* 1316-1334.

Barnouw, E. (1975). *Tube of plenty: The evolution of American television.* New York: Oxford University Press.

Baron, J. N., & Reiss, P. C. (1985). Same time, next year: Aggregate analyses of the mass media and violent behavior. *American Sociological Review, 50,* 347-363.

Baron, R. A. (1971a). Aggression as a function of magnitude of victim's pain cues, level of prior anger arousal, and aggressor-victim similarity. *Journal of Personality and social Psychology, 18,* 48-54.

Baron, R. A. (1971b). Magnitude of victim's pain cues and level of prior anger arousal as determinants of adult aggressive behavior. *Journal of Personality and Social Psychology, 17,* 236-243.

Baron, R. A. (1978). The influence of hostile and nonhostile humor upon physical aggression. *Personality and Social Psychology Bulletin, 4,* 77-80.

Barongan, C., & Hall, G. C. N. (1995). The influence of misogynous rap music on sexual aggression against women. *Psychology of Women Quarterly, 19,* 195-207.

Barrett, R. T. (1997). Making our own meanings: A critical review of media effects research in relation to the causation of aggression and social skills difficulties in children and anorexia nervosa in young women. *Journal of Psychiatric & Mental Health Nursing, 4,* 179-183.

Bauman, K. E., LaPrelle, J., Brown, J. D., Koch, G. G., & Padgett, C. A. (1991). The influence of three mass media campaigns on variables related to adolescent cigarette smoking: Results of a field experiment. *American Journal of Public Health, 81,* 597-604.

Baxter, B. L., De Riemer, C., Landini, A., Leslie, L., & Singletary, M. W. (1985). A content analysis of music videos. *Journal of Broadcasting & Electronic Media, 29,* 333-340.

BBC bans beauty contest. (1985, June 30). *Parade Magazine.*

Becker, A. E. (1995). *Body, self and society: The view from Fiji.* Philadelphia: University of Pennsylvania Press.

Becker, A. E. (1999). *Sharp rise in eating disorders in Fiji follows arrival of TV* (press release). Boston: Harvard Medical School Office of Public Affairs.

Becker, H. J. (2000). Who's wired and who's not: Children's access to and use of computer technology. *The Future of Children, 10*(2), 44-75.

Belchak, A. M. (2000, October 25). Dinnertime is TV time for youngsters. *Reuters News Service.*

Belchak, A. M. (2001, January 16). Soap operas serve health plots, send messages. *Reuters News Service.*

Belcher, H. M. E., & Shinitzky, H. E. (1998). Substance abuse in children: Prediction, protection, and prevention. *Archives of Pediatrics & Adolescent Medicine, 152,* 952-960.

Bellisle, F., & Rolland-Cachera, M.-F. (2001). How sugar-containing drinks might increase adiposity in children. *Lancet, 357,* 490-491.

Belson, W. A. (1978). *Television violence and the adolescent boy.* Westmead, UK: Saxon House, Teakfield Ltd.

Bennett, E. M., & Kemper, K. J. (1994). Is abuse during childhood a risk factor for developing substance abuse problems as an adult? *Journal of Developmental & Behavioral Pediatrics, 15,* 426-429.

Berel, S., & Irving, L. M. (1998). Media and disturbed eating: An analysis of media influence and implications for prevention. *Journal of Primary Prevention, 18,* 415-430.

Berkowitz, L. (1970). Aggressive humor as a stimulus to aggressive responses. *Journal of Personality and Social Psychology, 2,* 359-369.

Berkowitz, L. (1973). Words and symbols as stimuli to aggressive responses. In J. F. Knutson (Ed.), *Control of aggression: Implications from basic research* (pp. 113-143). Chicago: Aldine-Atherton.

Berkowitz, L. (1984). Some effects of thoughts on anti- and prosocial influences of media events: A cognitive-neoassociation analysis. *Psychological Bulletin, 95,* 410-427.

Berkowitz, L. (1990). On the formation and regulation of anger and aggression: A cognitive neoassociationistic analysis. *American Psychologist, 45,* 494-503.

Berkowitz, L., & Geen, R. G. (1967). Stimulus qualities of the target of aggression: A further study. *Journal of Personality and Social Psychology, 5,* 364-368.

Berkowitz, L., & Powers, P. C. (1979). Effects of timing and justification of witnessed aggression on the observers' punitiveness. *Journal of Research in Personality, 13,* 71-80.

Berkowitz, L., & Rawlings, E. (1963). Effects of film violence on inhibitions against subsequent aggression. *Journal of Abnormal and Social Psychology, 66,* 405-412.

Berman, M., Gladue, B., & Taylor, S. (1993). The effects of hormones, Type A behavior pattern, and provocation on aggression in men. *Motivation and Emotion, 17,* 125-138.

Berndt, T. J. (1996). Transitions in friendship and friends' influence. In J. A. Graber, J. Brooks-Gunn, & A. C. Petersen (Eds.), *Transitions through adolescence: Interpersonal domains and context* (pp. 57-85). Mahwah, NJ: Lawrence Erlbaum.

Berry, M., Gray, T., & Donnerstein, E. (1999). Cutting film violence: Effects on perceptions, enjoyment, and arousal. *Journal of Social Psychology, 139,* 567-582.

Bever, T. G., Smith, M. L., Bengen, B., & Johnson, T. G. (1975). Young viewers' troubling response to TV ads. *Harvard Business Review, 53,* 109-120.

Bickham, D. S., Wright, J. C., & Huston, A. C. (2001). Attention, comprehension, and the educational influences of television. In D. G. Singer & J. L. Singer (Eds.), *Handbook of children and the media* (pp. 101-119). Thousand Oaks, CA: Sage.

Biener, L., & Siegel, M. (2000). Tobacco marketing and adolescent smoking: More support for a causal inference. *American Journal of Public Health, 90,* 407-411.

Bjornebekk, R. T., & Evjen, T. A. (2000). Violent pornography on the Internet. In C. Feilitzen & U. Carlsson (Eds.), *Children in the new media landscape* (pp. 185-210). Goteborg, Sweden: UNESCO.

Blanton, W. E., Moorman, G. B., Hayes, B. A., & Warner, M. L. (1997). Effects of participation in the Fifth Dimension on far transfer. *Journal of Educational Computing Research, 16,* 371-396.

Blatt, J., Spencer, L., & Ward, S. (1972). A cognitive development study of children's reactions to television advertising. In E. A. Rubinstein, G. A. Comstock, & J. P. Murray (Eds.), *Television and social behavior* (Vol. 4, pp. 452-467). Washington, DC: Government Printing Office.

Block, J., Block, J., & Keyes, S. (1988). Longitudinally foretelling drug use in adolescence: Early childhood personality and environmental precursors. *Child Development, 59,* 336-355.

Bogle, D. (2001). *Primetime blues: African Americans on network television.* New York: Farrar, Straus & Giroux.

Boihem, H., & Emmanoullides, C. (1996). *The ad and the ego.* San Francisco: California Newsreel.

Bolton, R. N. (1983). Modeling the impact of television food advertising on children's diets. *Current Issues and Research in Advertising, 6,* 173-199.

Borgman, L. (1996, December 5). Proposed TV ratings lack labels that parents can use. *Albuquerque Journal,* p. B6.

Borzekowski, D. L. G. (1996). Embedded anti-alcohol messages on commercial television: What teenagers perceive. *Journal of Adolescent Health, 19,* 345-352.

Borzekowski, D. L. G. (2001). Watching what they eat: A content analysis of televised food references reaching preschool children. Unpublished manuscript.

Borzekowski, D. L. G., & Robinson, T. N. (2001). The 30-second effect: An experiment revealing the impact of television commercials on food preferences of preschoolers. *Journal of the American Dietetic Association, 101,* 42-46.

Borzekowski, D. L. G., Robinson, T., & Killen, J. D. (2000). Does the camera add 10 pounds? Media use, perceived importance of appearance, and weight concerns among teenage girls. *Journal of Adolescent Health, 26,* 36-41.

Botta, R. A. (1999). Television images and adolescent girls' body image disturbances. *Journal of Communication, 49,* 22-41.

Boush, D. M., Friestad, M., & Rose, G. M. (1994). Adolescent skepticism toward TV advertising and knowledge of advertiser tactics. *Journal of Consumer Research, 21*(1), 165-175.

Bowles, S. (2000, September 24). USA faces fuel crisis. *USA Today,* p. 1A.

Boyatzis, J., Matillo, G. M., & Nesbitt, K. M. (1995). Effects of the "Mighty Morphin Power Rangers" on children's aggression with peers. *Child Study Journal, 25,* 45-55.

Brand, J. E., & Greenberg, B. S. (1994). Commercials in the classroom: The impact of Channel One advertising. *Journal of Advertising Research, 34*(1), 18-27.

Brasher, P. (2001a, February 7). Feds fault junk food in schools. *Associated Press,* p. A5.

Brasher, P. (2001b, February 7). USDA: Schools send mixed message [Online]. Retrieved February 7, 2001, from the World Wide Web: abcnews.com.

Brass, K. (1999, November 21). *'Pokemon' fad at a fever pitch—and what a pitch indeed.* Retrieved May 25, 2001, from the World Wide Web: www.findarticles.com/cf_0/m0VPW/47_27/58047459/p1/article.jhtml.

Braverman, P. K., & Strasburger, V. C. (1993). Adolescent sexual activity. *Clinical Pediatrics, 32,* 658-668.

Braxton, G. (1991, July 31). Producers defend violence as "honest." *Los Angeles Times,* pp. F1, F14.

Breed, W., & De Foe, J. R. (1981). The portrayal of the drinking process on prime-time television. *Journal of Communications, 31,* 58-67.

Breed, W., & De Foe, J. R. (1982). Effecting media change: The role of cooperative consultation on alcohol topics. *Journal of Communications, 32,* 88-99.

Breed, W., & De Foe, J. R. (1983). Cigarette smoking on television: 1950-1982 (letter). *New England Journal of Medicine, 309,* 617.

Breed, W., & De Foe, J. R. (1984). Drinking and smoking on television 1950-1982. *Journal of Public Health Policy, 31,* 257-270.

British Medical Association. (2000). *Eating disorders, body image & the media.* London: Author.

Broder, J. M. (1997, February 28). Broadcast industry defends TV ratings system. *New York Times,* p. A1.

Brodie, M., Foehr, U., Rideout, V., Baer, N., Miller, C., Flournoy, R., & Altman, D. (2001). Communicating health information through the entertainment media. *Health Affairs, 20,* 1-8.

Brooks, K., Schiraldi, V., & Ziedenberg, J. (2000). *School house hype: Two years later.* Washington, DC: Justice Policy Institute/Children's Law Center.

Brooks-Gunn, J., & Peterson, A. C. (Eds.). (1983). *Girls at puberty: Biological and psychosocial perspectives.* New York: Plenum.

Brown, D., & Bryant, J. (1989). Uses of pornography. In D. Zillmann & J. Bryant (Eds.), *Pornography: Research advances and policy considerations* (pp. 3-24). Hillsdale, NJ: Lawrence Erlbaum.

Brown, E. F., & Hendee, W. R. (1989). Adolescents and their music: Insights into the health of adolescents. *Journal of the American Medical Association, 262,* 1659-1663.

Brown, J. A. (2001). Media literacy and critical television viewing education. In D. G. Singer & J. L. Singer (Eds.), *Handbook of children and the media* (pp. 681-697). Thousand Oaks, CA: Sage.

Brown, J. D. (2000a). Adolescents' sexual media diets. *Journal of Adolescent Health, 27S,* 35-40.

Brown, J. D. (2000b). Can the mass media be healthy sex educators? *Family Planning Perspectives, 32,* 255-256.

Brown, J. D., Childers, K. W., & Waszak, C. S. (1990). Television and adolescent sexuality. *Journal of Adolescent Health, 11,* 62-70.

Brown, J. D., & Newcomer, S. F. (1991). Television viewing and adolescents' sexual behavior. *Journal of Homosexuality, 21,* 77-91.

Brown, J. D., & Schulze, L. (1990). The effects of race, gender, and fandom on audience interpretations of Madonna's music videos. *Journal of Communication, 40,* 88-102.

Brown, J. D., & Steele, J. R. (1995). *Sex and the mass media.* Menlo Park, CA: Kaiser Family Foundation.

Brown, J. D., Steele, J. R., & Walsh-Childers, K. (2002). *Sexual teens, sexual media.* Mahwah, NJ: Lawrence Erlbaum.

Brown, J. D., & Walsh-Childers, K. (1994). Effects of media on personal and public health. In J. Bryant & D. Zillmann (Eds.), *Media effects: Advances in theory and research* (pp. 389-415). Hillsdale, NJ: Lawrence Erlbaum.

Brown, J. D., White, A. B., & Nikopoulou, L. (1993). Disinterest, intrigue, resistance: Early adolescent girls' use of sexual media content. In B. S. Greenberg, J. D. Brown, & N. L. Buerkel-Rothfuss (Eds.), *Media, sex and the adolescent* (pp. 177-195). Cresskill, NJ: Hampton.

Brown, J. D., & Witherspoon, E. M. (1998, September). *The mass media and American adolescents' health.* Paper commissioned for Health Futures of Youth II: Pathways to Adolescent Health, U.S. Department of Health and Human Services, Annapolis, MD.

Brown, M. H., Skeen, P., & Osborn, D. K. (1979). Young children's perception of the reality of television. *Contemporary Education, 50,* 129-133.

Brown, R. T. (2000). Adolescent sexuality at the dawn of the 21st century. *Adolescent Medicine: State of the Art Reviews, 11,* 19-34.

Brown, S. J., Lieberman, D. A., Germeny, B. A., Fan, Y. C., Wilson, D. M., & Pasta, D. J. (1997). Educational video game for juvenile diabetes: Results of a controlled trial. *Medical Informatics, 22,* 77-89.

Browne, D. (1998, September 18). Devil'd ham. *Entertainment Weekly,* pp. 84-85.

Brucks, M., Armstrong, G. M., & Goldberg, M. (1988). Children's use of cognitive defenses against television advertising: A cognitive response approach. *Journal of Consumer Research, 14,* 471-482.

Bruner, J. S. (1966). On cognitive growth I & II. In J. S. Bruner, R. R. Olver, & P. M. Greenfield (Eds.), *Studies in cognitive growth* (pp. 1-67). New York: John Wiley.

Bruner, J. S., Olver, R., & Greenfield, P. (1966). *Studies in cognitive growth.* New York: John Wiley.

Brunner, R., Essex, A., Gordinier, J., Jacobs, A. J., Karger, D., Robischon, N., Snierson, D., & Svetkey, B. (1999, June 11). A special report on violence and entertainment, Part II. *Entertainment Weekly,* pp. 36-39.

Bryant, A. (2000, March 20). In tobacco's face. *Newsweek,* pp. 40-41.

Bryant, J., Carveth, R. A., & Brown, D. (1981). Television viewing and anxiety: An experimental examination. *Journal of Communication, 31*(1), 106-109.

Bryant, J., & Rockwell, S. C. (1993). Effects of massive exposure to sexually-oriented primetime television programming on adolescents' moral judgment. In D. Zillmann, J. Bryant, & A. C. Huston (Eds.), *Media, children, and the family: Social scientific, psychodynamic, and clinical perspectives* (pp. 183-195). Hillsdale, NJ: Lawrence Erlbaum.

Bryant, J., & Rockwell, S. C. (1994). Effects of massive exposure to sexually-oriented primetime television programming on adolescents' moral judgment. In D. Zillmann, J. Bryant, & A. C. Huston (Eds.), *Media, children, and the family: Social scientific, psychodynamic, and clinical perspectives* (pp. 183-195). Hillsdale, NJ: Lawrence Erlbaum.

Bryson, B. (1996). "Anything but heavy metal": Symbolic exclusion and musical dislikes. *American Sociological Review, 61,* 884-899.

Buchman, D. D., & Funk, J. B. (1996). Video and computer games in the '90s: Children's time commitment and game preference. *Children Today, 24,* 12-15, 31.

Buckingham, D. (2000). *After the death of childhood: Growing up in the age of electronic media.* Cambridge, UK: Polity.

Buerkel-Rothfuss, N. L., & Mayes, S. (1981). Soap opera viewing: The cultivation effect. *Journal of Communication, 31,* 108-115.

Buerkel-Rothfuss, N. L., Strouse, J. S., Pettey, G., & Shatzer, M. (1993). Adolescents' and young adults' exposure to sexually oriented and sexually explicit media. In B. S. Greenberg, J. D. Brown, & N. L. Buerkel-Rothfuss (Eds.), *Media, sex and the adolescent* (pp. 99-113). Cresskill, NJ: Hampton.

Buijzen, M., & Valkenburg, P. (2000). The impact of television advertising on children's Christmas wishes. *Journal of Broadcasting and Electronic Media, 44,* 456-470.

Burke, R., & Grinder, R. (1966). Personality-oriented themes and listening patterns in teenage music and their relation to certain academic and peer variables. *School Review, 74,* 196-211.

Burnett, R. (1990). From a whisper to a scream: Music video and cultural form. In K. Roe & U. Carlsson (Eds.), *Popular music research* (pp. 21-27). Goteborg, Sweden: Nordicom-Sweden.

Burr, P., & Burr, R. M. (1977). Product recognition and premium appeal. *Journal of Communication, 27,* 115-117.

Bushman, B. J., & Anderson, C. A. (2001). Media violence and the American public: Scientific facts versus media misinformation. *American Psychologist, 56,* 477-489.

Bushman, B. J., & Geen, R. G. (1990). Role of cognitive-emotional mediators and individual differences in the effects of media violence on aggression. *Journal of Personality and Social Psychology, 58,* 156-163.

Bushman, B. J., & Huesmann, L. R. (2001). Effects of televised violence on aggression. In D. G. Singer & J. L. Singer (Eds.), *Handbook of children and the media* (pp. 223-254). Thousand Oaks, CA: Sage.

Bushman, B. J., & Stack, A. D. (1996). Forbidden fruit versus tainted fruit: Effects of warning labels on attraction to television violence. *Journal of Experimental Psychology: Applied, 2,* 207-226.

Butter, E. J., Popovich, P. M., Stackhouse, R. H., & Garner, R. K. (1981). Discrimination of television programs and commercials by preschool children. *Journal of Advertising Research, 21*(2), 53-56.

Buying political favors doesn't equal free speech. (2001, March 23). *USA Today,* p. 16A.

Byrd-Bredbrenner, C., & Grasso, D. (1999). Prime-time health: An analysis of health content in television commercials broadcast during programs viewed heavily by children. *International Electronic Journal of Health Education, 2,* 159-169 [Online]. Available: www.iejhe.org. Accessed February 19, 2001.

Byrd-Bredbrenner, C., & Grasso, D. (2000a). Health, medicine, and food messages in television commercials during 1992 and 1998. *Journal of School Health, 70,* 61-65.

Byrd-Bredbrenner, C., & Grasso, D. (2000b). Trends in US prime-time television food advertising across three decades. *Nutrition & Food Sciences, 30,* 59-66.

Byrd-Bredbrenner, C., & Grasso, D. (2000c). What is television trying to make children swallow? Content analysis of the nutrition information in prime-time advertisements. Journal of Nutrition Education, 32, 187-195.

Cai, X., & Gantz, W. (2000). Online privacy issues associated with Web sites for children. *Journal of Broadcasting & Electronic Media, 44,* 197-214.

Callahan, C. M., & Rivara, F. P. (1992). Urban high school youth and handguns: A school-based survey. *Journal of the American Medical Association, 267,* 3038-3041.

Calle, E. E., Thun, M. J., Petrelli, J. M., Rodriguez, C., & Heath, C. W., Jr. (1999). Body-mass index and mortality in a prospective cohort of U.S. adults. *New England Journal of Medicine, 341,* 1097-1105.

Calvert, S. (1988). Television production feature effects on children's comprehension of time. *Journal of Applied Developmental Psychology, 9,* 263-273.

Calvert, S. (1999). *Children's journeys through the information age.* Boston: McGraw-Hill.

Calvert, S. L., & Gersh, T. L. (1987). The selective use of sound effects and visual inserts for children's story comprehension. *Journal of Applied Developmental Psychology, 8,* 363-374.

Calvert, S. L., Huston, A. C., Watkins, B. A., & Wright, J. C. (1982). The relations between selective attention to television forms and children's comprehension of content. *Child Development, 53,* 601-610.

Calvert, S. L., & Tan, S.-L. (1994). Impact of virtual reality on young adults' physiological arousal and aggressive thoughts: Interaction versus observation. *Journal of Applied Developmental Psychology, 15,* 125-139.

Campbell, T. A., Wright, J. C., & Huston, A. C. (1987). Form cues and content difficulty as determinants of children's cognitive processing of televised educational messages. *Journal of Experimental Child Psychology, 43,* 311-327.

Campos, L. A., & Barret, K. C. (1984). Toward a new understanding of emotions and their development. In C. E. Izard & R. B. Zajonc (Eds.), *Emotion, cognition, and behavior* (pp. 229-263). Cambridge, UK: Cambridge University Press.

Canonzoneri, V. (1984, January 28). TV's feminine mistake. *TV Guide,* pp. 14-15.

Cantor, J. (1994). Fright reactions to mass media. In J. Bryant & D. Zillmann (Eds.), *Media effects: Advances in theory and research* (pp. 213-245). Hillsdale, NJ: Lawrence Erlbaum.

Cantor, J. (1996). Television and children's fear. In T. M. MacBeth (Ed.), *Tuning in to young viewers* (pp. 87-115). Thousand Oaks, CA: Sage.

Cantor, J. (1998a). Children's attraction to violent television programming. In J. H. Goldstein (Ed.), *Why we watch: The attractions of violent entertainment* (pp. 116-143). New York: Oxford University Press.

Cantor, J. (1998b). *"Mommy, I'm scared": How TV and movies frighten children and what we can do to protect them.* San Diego, CA: Harcourt Brace.

Cantor, J. (1998c). Ratings for program content: The role of research findings. *Annals of the American Academy of Political and Social Science, 557,* 54-69.

Cantor, J., & Nathanson, A. I. (1996). Children's fright reactions to television news. *Journal of Communication, 46,* 139-152.

Cantor, J., & Nathanson, A. I. (1997). Predictors of children's interest in violent television programs. *Journal of Broadcasting and Electronic Media, 41,* 155-167.

Cantor, J., & Sparks, G. G. (1984). Children's fear responses to mass media: Testing some Piagetian predictions. *Journal of Communication, 34,* 90-103.

Cantor, J., & Wilson, B. J. (1984). Modifying fear responses to mass media in preschool and elementary school children. *Journal of Broadcasting, 28,* 431-443.

Cantor, J., & Wilson, B. J. (1988). Helping children cope with frightening media presentations. *Current Psychology: Research and Reviews, 7,* 58-75.

Cantor, J., Wilson, B. J., & Hoffner, C. (1986). Emotional responses to a televised nuclear holocaust film. *Communication Research, 13,* 257-277.

Carlson, M., Marcus-Newhall, A., & Miller, N. (1990). Effects of situational aggression cues: A quantitative review. *Journal of Personality and Social Psychology, 58,* 622-633.

Carmody, D. (1994, October 10). Teen-age magazines are facing a shake-out. *New York Times,* p. D5.

Carnegie Council on Adolescent Development. (1995). *Great transitions: Preparing adolescents for a new century.* New York: Carnegie Corporation.

Carveth, R., & Alexander, A. (1985). Soap opera viewing motivation and the cultivation process. *Journal of Broadcasting and Electronic Media, 29,* 259-273.

Case, R. (1995). Capacity-based explanations of working memory growth: A brief history and reevaluation. In F. Weinert & W. Schneider (Eds.), *Memory performance and competencies: Issues in growth and development* (pp. 23-44). Mahwah, NJ: Lawrence Erlbaum.

Cash, T. F., Ancis, J. R., & Strachan, M. D. (1997). Gender attitudes, feminist identity, and body images among young women. *Sex Roles, 36,* 433-447.

Cash, T. F., & Deagle, E. A., III. (1997). The nature and extent of body-image disturbances in anorexia nervosa and bulimia nervosa: A meta-analysis. *International Journal of Eating Disorders, 22,* 107-125.

Caucus for Producers, Writers, and Directors. (1983). *We've done some thinking.* Santa Monica, CA: Television Academy of Arts and Sciences.

Center for Media and Public Affairs. (1999). *The rude and the crude: Profanity in popular entertainment.* Washington, DC: Author.

Center for Media Education. (1996). *Web of deception: Threats to children from online marketing.* Washington, DC: Author. Retrieved June 1, 2001, from the World Wide Web: www.cme.org/children/marketing/deception.pdf.

Center for Media Education. (1998). *The campaign for kids' TV: Children and television.* Washington, DC: Author.

Center for Media Education. (1999). *Alcohol and tobacco on the Web: New threats to youth.* Washington, DC: Author.

Center for Media Education. (2000, October 18). *Marketing to children harmful: Experts urge candidates to lead nation in setting limits* (press release). Retrieved June 1, 2001, from the World Wide Web: www.cme.org/press/001018pr.html.

Center for Media Education. (2001). *Children's Online Privacy Protection Act: The first year.* Washington, DC: Author. Retrieved June 1, 2001, from the World Wide Web: www.cme.org/children/privacy/coppa_rept.pdf.

Center for Media Values. (1992). Media literacy. *Media & Values, 59/60,* 41-42.

Center for Science in the Public Interest. (1988, September 4). *Kids are aware of booze as presidents, survey finds* (press release). Washington, DC: Author.

Center for Science in the Public Interest. (1992). *Survey of advertising on children's TV.* Washington, DC: Author.

Center for Substance Abuse Prevention, Centers for Disease Control, and American Academy of Pediatrics. (1997). *MediaSharp: Analyzing tobacco and alcohol messages* (leader's guide). Washington, DC: Author.

Centers for Disease Control and Prevention (CDC). (1991). *Position papers from the Third National Injury Conference: Setting the National Agenda for Injury Control in the 1990s.* Washington, DC: Department of Health and Human Services.

Centers for Disease Control and Prevention (CDC). (1992a). Accessibility of cigarettes to youths aged 12-17 years—United States, 1989. *Morbidity & Mortality Weekly Report, 41,* 485-488.

Centers for Disease Control and Prevention (CDC). (1992b). Comparison of the cigarette brand preferences of adult and teenaged smokers—United States, 1989, and 10 U.S. communities, 1988 and 1990. *Morbidity & Mortality Weekly Report, 41,* 169-181.

Centers for Disease Control and Prevention (CDC). (1993). Sexual risk behaviors of STD clinic patients before and after Earvin "Magic" Johnson's HIV-infection announcement—Maryland, 1991-1992. *Morbidity & Mortality Weekly Report, 42,* 45-48.

Centers for Disease Control and Prevention (CDC). (1994a). Deaths resulting form firearm- and motor-vehicle-related injuries: United States, 1968-1991. *Morbidity & Mortality Weekly Report, 43,* 469-472.

Centers for Disease Control and Prevention (CDC). (1994b). Poll: HIV/AIDS prevention. *CDC HIV/AIDS Prevention Newsletter, 5,* 5-6.

Centers for Disease Control and Prevention (CDC). (1994c). *Preventing tobacco use among young people: A report of the Surgeon General.* Atlanta, GA: U.S. Department of Health and Human Services.

Centers for Disease Control and Prevention (CDC). (1995, January 20). Quoted in "Kids and weight." *Albuquerque Journal,* p. B1.

Centers for Disease Control (CDC). (1996). School based HIV prevention education, United States, 1994. *Morbidity & Mortality Weekly Report, 45,* 6.

Centers for Disease Control and Prevention (CDC). (1997, February 7). *Rates of homicide, suicide, and firearm-related death among Children: 26 industrialized countries, 46*(5), 101-105. Atlanta, GA: Author. Retrieved February 24, 2001, from the World Wide Web: www.cdc.gov/epo/mmwr/preview/mmwrhtml/00046149.htm.

Centers for Disease Control and Prevention (CDC). (1999). Tobacco use among middle and high school students—Florida, 1998 and 1999. *Morbidity & Mortality Weekly Report, 48,* 248-253.

Centers for Disease Control and Prevention (CDC). (2000a). Alcohol policy and sexually transmitted disease rates. *Morbidity & Mortality Weekly Reports, 49,* 346-349.

Centers for Disease Control and Prevention (CDC). (2000b). Trends in cigarette smoking among high school students—United States, 1991-1999. *Morbidity & Mortality Weekly Reports, 49,* 755-758.

Centers for Disease Control and Prevention (CDC). (2000c). Youth risk behavior surveillance—United States, 1999. *Morbidity & Mortality Weekly Reports, 49*(SS-05), 1-96.

Centerwall, B. S. (1992). Television and violence: The scale of the problem and where to go from here. *Journal of American Medicine, 267,* 22-25.

Champion, H., & Furnham, A. (1999). The effect of the media on body satisfaction in adolescent girls. *European Eating Disorders Review, 7,* 213-228.

Chassin, L. (1985). Changes in peer and parent influence during adolescence: Longitudinal versus cross-sectional perspectives on smoking initiation. *Developmental Psychology, 22,* 327-334.

Chen, M. (1994). *The smart parent's guide to kids' TV.* San Francisco: KQED Books.

Chilcoat, H. D., & Anthony, J. C. (1996). Impact of parent monitoring on initiation of drug use through late childhood. *Journal of the American Academy of Child & Adolescent Psychiatry, 35,* 91-100.

Children and the Internet: A parents' guide. (1999). *Time, 153*(18), 22-28.

Children's Advertising Review Unit (CARU). (2000). *Self regulatory guidelines for children's advertising.* Retrieved June 1, 2001, from the World Wide Web: www.bbb.org/advertising/caruguid.asp#disclosure.

Children's Television Workshop. (1996). Feeling good about visiting the doctor. *Research Roundup, 5,* 1.

Christenson, P. (1982). Children's perceptions of TV commercials and products: The effects of PSA's. *Communication Research, 9,* 491-524.

Christenson, P. (1992a). The effects of parental advisory labels on adolescent music preferences. *Journal of Communication, 42,* 106-113.

Christenson, P. (1992b). Preadolescent perceptions and interpretations of music videos. *Popular Music and Society, 16,* 63-73.

Christenson, P. G., Henriksen, L., & Roberts, D. F. (2000). *Substance use in popular prime-time television.* Washington, DC: Office of National Drug Control Policy.

Christenson, P. G., & Roberts, D. F. (1990). *Popular music in early adolescence.* Washington, DC: Carnegie Council on Adolescent Development.

Christenson, P. G., & Roberts, D. F. (1998). *It's not only rock 'n' roll: Popular music in the lives of adolescents.* Cresskill, NJ: Hampton.

Churchill, G., Jr., & Moschis, G. P. (1979). Television and interpersonal influences on adolescent consumer learning. *Journal of Consumer Research, 5*(1), 23-35.

Clay, R. A. (2000). Advertising to children: Is it ethical? *Monitor on Psychology, 31*(8). Retrieved March 8, 2001, from the World Wide Web: www.apa.org/monitor/sep00/advertising.html.

Cline, V. B. (1994). Pornography effects: Empirical and clinical evidence. In D. Zillmann, J. Bryant, & A. C. Huston (Eds.), *Media, children, and the family: Social scientific, psychodynamic, and clinical perspectives* (pp. 229-247). Hillsdale, NJ: Lawrence Erlbaum.

Cline, V. B., Croft, R. G., & Courrier, S. (1973). Desensitization of children to television violence. *Journal of Personality and Social Psychology, 35,* 450-458.

Cohall, A. T., & Cohall, R. M. (1995). "Number one with a bullet": Epidemiology and prevention of homicide among adolescents and young adults. *Adolescent Medicine: State of the Art Reviews, 6,* 183-197.

Cohen, J. (1988). *Statistical power analysis for the behavioral sciences* (2nd ed.). Hillsdale, NJ: Lawrence Erlbaum.

Cohen, J. (1999). Favorite characters of teenage viewers of Israeli serials. *Journal of Broadcasting & Electronic Media, 43,* 327-345.

Cohn, L. B. (1995). Violent video games: Aggression, arousal, and desensitization in young adolescent boys (Doctoral dissertation, University of Southern California, 1995). *Dissertation Abstracts International, 57*(2-B), 1463. (University Microfilms No. 9616947)

Colby, P. A. (1993, April). *From Hot Wheels to Teenage Mutant Ninja Turtles: The evolution of the definition of program length commercials on children's television.* Paper presented at the annual meeting of the Broadcast Education Association, Las Vegas, NV.

Cole, T. (2000, May 1). "Into evil": Death-metal fans viciously murdered two young women, and the victims' parents blame the music. *Albuquerque Journal,* pp. A1-A5.

Coles, R., & Stokes, G. (1985). *Sex and the American teenager.* New York: Harper & Row.

Collins, W. A. (1973). Effect of temporal separation between motivation, aggression, and consequences: A developmental study. *Developmental Psychology, 8,* 215-221.

Collins, W. A. (1975). The developing child as viewer. *Journal of Communication, 25*(4), 35-44.

Collins, W. A. (1983). Interpretation and inference in children's television viewing. In J. Bryant & D. R. Anderson (Eds.), *Children's understanding of television: Research on attention and comprehension* (pp. 125-150). New York: Academic Press.

Collins, W. A., Berndt, T. J., & Hess, V. L. (1974). Observational leaning of motives and consequences for television aggression: A developmental study. *Child Development, 45,* 799-802.

Collins, W. A., & Getz, S. K. (1976). Children's social responses following modeled reactions to provocation: Prosocial effects of a television drama. *Journal of Personality, 44,* 488-500.

Collins, W. A., Wellman, H., Keniston, A., & Westby, S. (1978). Age-related aspects of comprehension and inference from a televised dramatic narrative. *Child Development, 49,* 389-399.

Collins-Standley, T., Gan, S., Yu, H. J., & Zillmann, D. (1996). Choice of romantic, violent, and scary fairy-tale books by preschool girls and boys. *Child Study Journal, 26,* 279-302.

Colwell, J., Grady, C., & Rhaiti, S. (1995). Computer games, self-esteem, and gratification of needs in adolescents. *Journal of Community and Applied Psychology, 5,* 195-206.

Comerci, G. D., & Schwebel, R. (2000). Substance abuse: An overview. *Adolescent Medicine: State of the Art Reviews, 11,* 79-101.

Comings, D. E. (1997). Genetic aspects of childhood behavioral disorders. *Child Psychiatry & Human Development, 27,* 139-150.

Commonwealth Fund. (1993). *First comprehensive national health survey of American women.* New York: Author.

Comstock, G. (1991a). *Television and the American child.* San Diego, CA: Academic Press.

Comstock, G. (1991b). *Television in America* (2nd ed.). Newbury Park, CA: Sage.

Comstock, G. C., & Strasburger, V. C. (1993). Media violence: Q & A. *Adolescent Medicine: State of the Art Reviews, 4,* 495-509.

Condry, J. C., Bence, P. J., & Scheibe, C. L. (1988). Nonprogram content of children's television. *Journal of Broadcasting & Electronic Media, 32,* 255-270.

Consumer Reports. (1990, August). Selling to children. *Consumer Reports,* pp. 518-520.

Consumer Reports. (1999). *Internet blocking software.* Yonkers, NY: Consumer Union of the United States.

Consumer Reports. (2001). *Digital chaperones for kids.* Yonkers, NY: Consumer Union of the United States.

Consumers Union Education Services. (1995). *Captive kids: A report on commercial pressures on kids at school.* Yonkers, NY: Author.

Conviction urged in "wrestling" death: Youth says he was imitating moves by "The Rock." (2000, January 24). *Reuters News Service.*

Cook, D. E. (2000). *Media violence.* Testimony of the American Academy of Pediatrics before the U.S. Senate Commerce Committee. Retrieved June 15, 2001, from the World Wide Web: www.aap.org/advocacy/releases/mediaviolencetestimony.pdf.

Coon, K. A., Goldberg, J., Rogers, B. L., & Tucker, K. L. (2001). Relationships between use of television during meals and children's food consumption patterns (abstract). *Pediatrics, 107,* 167.

Cooper, B. L. (1991). *Popular music perspectives: Ideas, themes and patterns in contemporary lyrics.* Bowling Green, OH: Bowling Green University Popular Press.

Cooper, H., & Hedges, L. V. (Eds.). (1994). *The handbook of research synthesis.* New York: Russell Sage.

Cope-Farrar, K. M., & Kunkel, D. (2002). Sexual messages in teens' favorite prime-time TV programs. In J. D. Brown, J. R. Steele, & K. Walsh-Childers (Eds.), *Sexual teens, sexual media* (pp. 59-78). Hillsdale, NJ: Lawrence Erlbaum.

Corder-Bolz, C. (1981). Television and adolescents' sexual behavior. *Sex Education Coalition News, 3,* 40.

Council of Economic Advisors. (2000). *Teens and their parents in the 21st century: An examination of trends in teen behavior and the role of parental involvement* [Online]. Available: www.whitehouse.gov/media/pdf/CEAreport.pdf.

Courtright, J. A., & Baran, S. J. (1980). The acquisition of sexual information by young people. *Journalism Quarterly, 57,* 107-114.

Cowan, N., Nugent, L. D., Elliott, E. M., Ponomarev, I., & Saults, J. S. (1999). The role of attention in the development of short-term memory: Age differences in the verbal span of apprehension. *Child Development, 70,* 1082-1097.

Cowley, G., & Underwood, A. (2001, February 19). Soda pop that packs a punch: Are the new alcoholic lemonades aimed at kids? *Newsweek,* p. 45.

Crawford, D. A., Jeffery, R. W., & French, S. A. (1999). Television viewing, physical activity, and obesity. *International Journal of Obesity and Related Metabolic Disorders, 23,* 437-440.

Crespo, C. J., Smit, E., Troiano, R. P., Bartlett, S. J., Macera, C. A., & Andersen, R. E. (2001). Television watching, energy intake, and obesity in US children. *Archives of Pediatrics and Adolescent Medicine, 155,* 360-365.

Cromer, B. A., & McCarthy, M. (1999). Family planning services in adolescent pregnancy prevention: The views of key informants in four countries. *Family Planning Perspectives, 31,* 287-293.

Crouch, A., & Degelman, D. (1998). Influence of female body images in printed advertising on self-ratings of physical attractiveness by adolescent girls. *Perceptual & Motor Skills, 87,* 585-586.

Csikszentmihalyi, M., & Csikszentmihalyi, I. S. (1988). *Optimal experience: Psychological studies of flow in consciousness.* Cambridge, UK: Cambridge University Press.

Culley, J., Lazer, W., & Atkin, C. (1976). The experts look at children's television. *Journal of Broadcasting, 20,* 3-20.

Cusumano, D. L., & Thompson, J. K. (1997). Body image and body shape ideals in magazines: Exposure, awareness, and internalization. *Sex Roles, 37,* 701-721.

D'Angelo, M. D. (1999, December 17). Deflower power. *Entertainment Weekly,* pp. 88-89.

D.A.R.E. redux. (2001). *Contemporary Pediatrics, 18,* 13.

Darroch, J. E., Landry, D. J., & Singh, S. (2000). Changing emphases in sexuality education in U.S. public secondary schools, 1988-1999. *Family Planning Perspectives, 32,* 204-211.

Davidson, L. E., Rosenberg, M. L., Mercy, J. A., Franklin, J., & Simmons, J. T. (1989). An epidemiologic study of risk factors in two teenage suicide clusters. *Journal of the American Medical Association, 262,* 2687-2692.

Davidson, O. G. (1993). *Under fire: The NRA and the battle for gun control.* New York: Holt, Rinehart, & Winston.

Davis, S. (1985, Summer). Pop lyrics: A mirror and molder of society. *Et Cetra,* pp. 167-169.

Davison, K. K., & Birch, L. L. (2001). Weight status, parent reaction, and self-concept in five-year-old girls. *Pediatrics, 107,* 46-53.

Dawson, D. A. (1986). The effects of sex education on adolescent behavior. *Family Planning Perspectives, 18,* 162-170.

De Foe, J. R., & Breed, W. (1988). Youth and alcohol in television stories, with suggestions to the industry for alternative portrayals. *Adolescence, 23,* 533-550.

DeGaetano, G., & Bander, K. (1996). *Screen smarts: A family guide to media literacy.* Boston: Houghton Mifflin.

DeJong, W. (1996). When the tobacco industry controls the news: KKR, RJR Nabisco, and the Weekly Reader Corporation. *Tobacco Control, 5,* 142-148.

Dempster, F. N. (1981). Memory span: Sources of individual and developmental differences. *Psychological Bulletin, 89,* 63-100.

Denisoff, R. S., & Levine, M. H. (1971). The popular protest song: The case of "Eve of Destruction." *Public Opinion Quarterly, 35,* 119-124.

Derbaix, C., & Bree, J. (1997). The impact of children's affective reactions elicited by commercials on attitudes toward the advertisement and the brand. *International Journal of Research in Marketing, 14,* 207-229.

Desmond, R. (1987). Adolescents and music lyrics: Implications of a cognitive perspective. *Communication Quarterly, 35,* 276-284.

Diaz, T. (1999). *Making a killing: The business of guns in America.* New York: New Press.

Diener, E., & Woody, L. W. (1981). TV violence and viewer liking. *Communication Research, 8,* 281-306.

Dietz, W. H. (1993). Television, obesity, and eating disorders. *Adolescent Medicine: State of the Art Reviews, 4,* 543-549.

Dietz, W. H. (1998). Health consequences of obesity in youth: Childhood predictors of adult disease. *Pediatrics, 101*(Suppl.), 518-525.

Dietz, W. H. (2001). Overweight and precursors of type 2 diabetes mellitus in children and adolescents. *Journal of Pediatrics, 138,* 453-454.

Dietz, W. H., & Gortmaker, S. L. (1985). Do we fatten our children at the television set? Obesity and television viewing in children and adolescents. *Pediatrics, 75,* 807-812.

Dietz, W. H., & Gortmaker, S. L. (1993). TV or not TV: Fat is the question. *Pediatrics, 91,* 499-501.

DiFranza, J. R., Richards, J. W., Jr., Paulman, P. M., Fletcher, C., & Jaffe, R. D. (1992). Tobacco: Promotion and smoking (letter). *Journal of the American Medical Association, 267,* 3282-3284.

DiFranza, J. R., Richards, J. W., Jr., Paulman, P. M., Wolf-Gillespie, N., Fletcher, C., Jaffe, R. D., & Murray, D. (1991). RJR Nabisco's cartoon camel promotes Camel cigarettes to children. *Journal of the American Medical Association, 266,* 3149-3153.

DiFranza, J. R., & Tye, J. B. (1990). Who profits from tobacco sales to children? *Journal of the American Medical Association, 263,* 2784-2787.

Dill, K. E., & Dill, J. C. (1998). Video game violence: A review of the empirical literature. *Aggression and Violent Behavior, 3,* 407-428.

Dishion, T. J. (1990). The family ecology of boys' peer relations in middle childhood. *Child Development, 61,* 874-892.

Distefan, J. M., Gilpin, E. A., Sargent, J. D., & Pierce, J. P. (1999). Do movie stars encourage adolescents to start smoking? Evidence from California. *Preventive Medicine, 28,* 1-11.

Dodge, K. A., & Frame, C. L. (1982). Social cognitive biases and deficits in aggressive boys. *Child Development, 53,* 620-635.

Dominick, J. R., & Greenberg, B. S. (1972). Attitudes toward violence: The interaction of television exposure, family attitudes, and social class. In G. A. Comstock & E. A. Rubinstein (Eds.), *Television and social behavior: Vol. 3. Television and adolescent aggressiveness* (pp. 314-335). Washington, DC: Government Printing Office.

Donnerstein, E. (1984). Pornography: Its effect on violence against women. In N. M. Malamuth & E. Donnerstein (Eds.), *Pornography and sexual aggression* (pp. 53-81). Orlando, FL: Academic Press.

Donnerstein, E. (1998). What's out there in the media: The Internet. In J. Squires & T. New-lands (Eds.), *Caring for children in the media age* (pp. 142-155). Sydney, Australia: University of New South Wales.

Donnerstein, E., & Linz, D. (1994). Sexual violence in the mass media. In M. Costanzo & S. Oskamp (Eds.), *Violence and the law* (pp. 9-36). Thousand Oaks, CA: Sage.

Donnerstein, E., Linz, D., & Penrod, S. (1987). *The question of pornography: Research findings and policy implications*. New York: Free Press.

Donnerstein, E., Slaby, R., & Eron, L. (1994). The mass media and youth aggression. In L. D. Eron, J. H. Gentry, & P. Schlegel (Eds.), *Reason to hope: A psychosocial perspective on violence and youth* (pp. 219-250). Washington, DC: American Psychologial Association.

Donnerstein, E., & Smith, S. (2001). Sex in the media. In D. G. Singer & J. L. Singer (Eds.), *Handbook of children and the media* (pp. 289-307). Thousand Oaks, CA: Sage.

Donohue, T. R., Henke, L. L., & Donohue, W. A. (1980). Do kids know what TV commercials intend? *Journal of Advertising Research, 20*(5), 51-57.

Donohue, T. R., Henke, L. L., & Meyer, T. P. (1983). Learning about television commercials: The impact of instructional units on children's perceptions of motive and intent. *Journal of Broadcasting, 27,* 251-261.

Donohue, T. R., Meyer, T. P., & Henke, L. L. (1978). Black and White children's perceptions of television commercials. *Journal of Marketing, 42,* 34-40.

Dorr, A. (1980). When I was a child, I thought as a child. In S. B. Withey & P. P. Abeles (Eds.), *Television and social behavior: Beyond violence and children* (pp. 191-230). Hillsdale, NJ: Lawrence Erlbaum.

Dorr, A. (1983). No shortcuts to judging reality. In J. Bryant & D. R. Anderson (Eds.), *Children's understanding of television* (pp. 199-220). New York: Academic Press.

Dorr, A. (1986). *Television and children: A special medium for a special audience.* Thousand Oaks, CA: Sage.

Dorr, A., Graves, S. B., & Phelps, E. (1980). Television literacy for young children. *Journal of Communication, 30,* 71-83.

Dorval, M., & Pepin, M. (1986). Effect of playing a video game on a measure of spatial visualization. *Perceptual and Motor Skills, 62,* 159-162.

Downs, A. C., & Harrison, S. K. (1985). Embarrassing age spots or just plain ugly? Physical attractiveness stereotyping as an instrument of sexism on American television commercials. *Sex Roles, 13,* 9-19.

Downs, D. (1994, April). The value of media literacy. Presented at the Taos Talking Picture Festival, Taos, NM.

Doyle, R. (1996, December). Deaths due to alcohol. *Scientific American,* pp. 30-31.

Drabman, R. S., & Thomas, M. H. (1974). Does media violence increase children's toleration of real-life aggression? *Developmental Psychology, 10,* 418-421.

Dubow, J. S. (1995). Advertising recognition and recall by age—including teens. *Journal of Advertising Research, 35*(5), 55-60.

DuRant, R. (2001, April). *Viewing wrestling on television, dating violence, engaging in health-risk behaviors by adolescents.* Paper presented at the annual meeting of the Ambulatory Pediatric Association/Society for Pediatric Research, Baltimore, MD.

DuRant, R. H., Baranowski, T., Johnson, M., & Thompson, W. O. (1994). The relationship among television watching, physical activity, and body composition of young children. *Pediatrics, 94,* 449-455.

DuRant, R. H., Rich, M., Emans, S. J., Rome, E. S., Allred, E., & Woods, E. R. (1997). Violence and weapon carrying in music videos: A content analysis. *Archives of Pediatrics & Adolescent Medicine, 151,* 443-448.

DuRant, R. H., Rome, E. S., Rich, M., Allred, E., Emans, S. J., & Woods, E. R. (1997). Tobacco and alcohol use behaviors portrayed in music videos. *American Journal of Public Health, 87,* 1131-1135.

Eaton, W. O., & Enns, L. R. (1986). Sex differences in human motor activity level. *Psychological Bulletin, 100,* 19-28.

Ebert, R. (2001, February 9). A loose "Hannibal" loses power. *Albuquerque Journal,* p. 4.

Eisenberg, N., Guthrie, I. K., Murphy, B. C., Shepard, S. A., Cumberland, A., & Carlo, G. (1999). Consistency and development of prosocial dispositions: A longitudinal study. *Child Development, 70,* 1360-1372.

Elkind, D. (1967). Egocentrism in adolescence. *Child Development, 38,* 1025-1034.

Elkind, D. (1984, November/December). Teenage thinking: Implications for health care. *Pediatric Nursing,* pp. 383-385.

Elkind, D. (1985). Egocentrism redux. *Developmental Review, 5,* 218-226.

Elkind, D. (1993). *Parenting your teenager in the 90's.* Rosemont, NJ: Modern Learning Press.

Entertainers have the last laugh, pocket millions of fans' dollars. (1990, October 7). *Atlanta Journal,* p. A-3.

Entertainment Software Ratings Board. (2000). *The ESRB's guide to interactive entertainment* [Online]. Available: www.esrb.cp/parent.html.

Epstein, L. H., Paluch, R. A., Gordy, C. C., & Dorn, J. (2000). Decreasing sedentary behaviors in treating pediatric obesity. *Archives of Pediatrics & Adolescent Medicine, 154,* 220-226.

Epstein, L. H., Saelens, B., Myers, M., & Vito, D. (1997). Effects of decreasing sedentary behaviors on activity choice in obese children. *Health Psychology, 16,* 107-113.

Epstein, L. H., Valoski, A. M., Vara, L. S., & Rodefer, J. S. (1995). Effects of decreasing sedentary behavior and increasing activity on weight change in obese children. *Health Psychology, 14,* 109-115.

Erickson, S. J., Robinson, T. N., Haydel, F., & Killen, J. D. (2000). Are overweight children unhappy? Body mass index, depressive symptoms, and overweight concerns in elementary school children. *Archives of Pediatrics & Adolescent Medicine, 154,* 931-935.

Eron, L. (1995). Media violence. *Pediatric Annals, 24,* 84-87.

Eron, L., Huesmann, L. R., Brice, P., Fischer, P., & Mermelstein, R. (1983). Age trends in the development of aggression, sex typing, and related television habits. *Developmental Psychology, 19,* 71-77.

Eron, L., Huesmann, L. R., Lefkowitz, M. M., & Walder, L. O. (1972). Does television violence cause aggression? *American Psychologist, 27,* 253-263.

Escamilla, G., Cradock, A. L., & Kawachi, I. (2000). Women and smoking in Hollywood movies: A content analysis. *American Journal of Public Health, 90,* 412-414.

Ethridge, M. (1999, October 31). Kid clout. *Albuquerque Journal,* p. C1.

Evans, N., Farkas, A., Gilpin, E., Berry, C., & Pierce, J. P. (1995). Influence of tobacco marketing and exposure to smokers on adolescent susceptibility to smoking. *Journal of the National Cancer Institute, 87,* 1538-1545.

Eveland, W. P., Nathanson, A. I., Detenber, A. I., & McLeod, D. M. (1999). Rethinking the social distance corollary: Perceived likelihood of exposure and the third-person perception. *Communication Research, 26,* 275-302.

Everett, S. A., Schnuth, R. L., & Tribble, J. L. (1998). Tobacco and alcohol use in top-grossing American films. *Journal of Community Health, 23,* 317-324.

Faber, R. J., Perloff, R. M., & Hawkins, R. P. (1982). Antecedents of children's comprehension of television advertising. *Journal of Broadcasting, 26,* 575-584.

Fabes, R. A., & Strouse, J. S. (1984). Youth's perceptions of models of sexuality: Implications for sexuality education. *Journal of Sex Education and Therapy, 10,* 33-37.

Fabes, R. A., & Strouse, J. S. (1987). Perceptions of responsible and irresponsible models of sexuality: A correlational study. *Journal of Sex Research, 23,* 70-84.

Faith, M. S., Berman, N., Heo, M., Pietrobelli, A., Gallagher, D., Epstein, L. H., Eiden, M. T., & Allison, D. B. (2001). Effects of contingent television on physical activity and television viewing in obese children. *Pediatrics, 107,* 1043-1048.

Fallows, J. (1996). *Breaking the news: How the media can undermine American democracy.* New York: Pantheon.

Families sue band over sons' suicides (1990, July 16). *Albuquerque Journal,* p. C12.

Farah, M. M., Simon, H. K., & Kellermann, A. L. (1999). Firearms in the home: Parental perceptions. *Pediatrics, 104,* 1059-1063.

Farhi, P. (1999, July 23). Movie index swears "South Park" is raw. *The Washington Post.*

Federal Communications Commission (FCC). (1974). Children's television programs: Report and policy statement. *Federal Register, 39,* 39396-39409.

Federal Communications Commission (FCC). (1984, January 13). Children's television programming and advertising practices. *Federal Register, 49,* 1704-1727.

Federal Communications Commission (FCC). (1991). Report and order: Policies and rules concerning children's television programming. *Federal Communications Commission Record, 6,* 2111-2127.

Federal Trade Commission (FTC). (1978). *FTC staff report on television advertising to children.* Washington, DC: Government Printing Office.

Federal Trade Commission (FTC). (1981). *In the matter of children's advertising: FTC final staff report and recommendation.* Washington, DC: Government Printing Office.

Federal Trade Commission (FTC). (2000). *Marketing violent entertainment to children: A review of self-regulation and industry practices in the motion picture, music recording, and electronic game industries.* (Available from FTC Consumer Response Center, Room 130, 600 Pennsylvania Avenue, N.W., Washington, DC 20580)

Federal Trade Commission (FTC). (2001). *Marketing violent entertainment to children: A six-month follow-up review of industry practices in the motion picture, music recording & electronic game industries: A report to Congress.* Washington, DC: Author.

Federman, J. (1996). *Media ratings: Design, use and consequences.* Studio City, CA: Mediascope.

Federman, J. (Ed.). (1998). *National television violence study* (Vol. 3). Thousand Oaks, CA: Sage.

Federman, J., Carbone, S., Chen, H., & Munn, W. (1996). *The social effects of electronic games: An annotated bibliography.* Studio City, CA: Mediascope.

Fedler, F., Hall, J., & Tanzi, L. (1982). Popular songs emphasize sex, deemphasize romance. *Mass Communication Review, 9,* 10-15.

Fedler, F., Phillips, M., Raker, P., Schefsky, D., & Soluri, J. (1994). Network commercials promote legal drugs: Outnumber anti-drug PSAs 45-to-1. *Journal of Drug Education, 24,* 291-302.

Feldman, W., Feldman E., & Goodman, J. T. (1988). Culture versus biology: Children's attitudes towards thinness and fitness. *Pediatrics, 81,* 190-194.

Fenigstein, A. (1979). Does aggression cause a preference for viewing media violence? *Journal of Personality & Social Psychology, 37,* 2307-2317.

Feshbach, S. (1972). Reality and fantasy in filmed violence. In J. P. Murray, E. A. Rubinstein, & G. Comstock (Eds.), *Television and social behavior: Television and social learning* (Vol. 2, pp. 318-345). Washington, DC: Government Printing Office.

Feshbach, S., Feshbach, N. D., & Cohen, S. E. (1982). Enhancing children's discrimination in response to television advertising: The effects of psychoeducational training in two elementary school-age groups. *Developmental Review, 2,* 385-403.

Fessenden, F. (2000, April 9). They threaten, seethe and unhinge, then kill in quantity. *New York Times,* p. A1.

Field, A. E., Camargo, C. A., Jr., Taylor, C. B., Berkey, C. B., & Colditz, G. A. (1999). Relation of peers and media influences to the development of purging behaviors among preadolescent and adolescent girls. *Archives of Pediatrics & Adolescent Medicine, 153,* 1184-1189.

Field, A. E., Camargo, C. A., Jr., Taylor, C. B., Berkey, C. S., Roberts, S. B., & Colditz, G. A. (2001). Peer, parent, and media influences on the development of weight concerns and frequent dieting among preadolescent and adolescent girls and boys. *Pediatrics, 107,* 54-60.

Field, A. E., Cheung, L., Wolf, A. M., Herzog, D. B., Gortmaker, S. L., & Colditz, G. A. (1999). Exposure to the mass media and weight concerns among girls. *Pediatrics, 103,* e36.

Finn, P., & Bragg, B. W. (1986). Perception of risk of an accident by young and older drivers. *Accident Analysis and Prevention, 18,* 289-298.

Fisch, S. M., & Truglio, R. T. (2001). *"G" is for growing: Thirty years of research on children and Sesame Street.* Mahwah, NJ: Lawrence Erlbaum.

Fischer, P. M., Schwart, M. P., Richards, J. W., Goldstein, A. O., & Rojas, T. H. (1991). Brand logo recognition by children aged 3 to 6 years: Mickey Mouse and Old Joe the Camel. *Journal of the American Medical Association, 266,* 3145-3153.

Fisher, S. (1995). The amusement arcade as a social space for adolescents: An empirical study. *Journal of Adolescence, 18,* 71-86.

Fiske, S. T., & Taylor, S. E. (1991). *Social cognition* (2nd ed.). New York: McGraw-Hill.

Flavell, J. H., Flavell, E. R., Green, F. L., & Korfmacher, J. E. (1990). Do young children think of television images as pictures or real objects? *Journal of Broadcasting & Electronic Media, 34,* 399-417.

Flavell, J. H., Friedrichs, A. G., & Hoyt, J. (1970). Developmental changes in memorization processes. *Cognitive Psychology, 1,* 324-340.

Flavell, J. H., Miller, P. H., & Miller, S. A. (1993). *Cognitive development* (3rd ed.). Englewood Cliffs, NJ: Prentice Hall.

Fletcher-Flinn, C. M. (1995). The efficacy of computer-assisted instruction (CAI): A meta-analysis. *Journal of Educational Computing Research, 12,* 219-241.

Fling, S., Smith, L., Rodriguez, T., Thornton, D., Atkins, E., & Nixon, K. (1992). Videogames, aggression, and self-esteem: A survey. *Social Behavior and Personality, 20,* 39-46.

Flint, J., & Snierson, D. (1999, July 30). Whitewash. *Entertainment Weekly,* pp. 31-33.

Flynn, B. S., Worden, J. K., Secker-Walker, R. H., Pirie, P. L., Badger, G. J., Carpenter, J. H., & Geller, B. M. (1994). Mass media and school interventions for cigarette smoking prevention: Effects 2 years after completion. *American Journal of Public Health, 84,* 1148-1150.

Folb, K. L. (2000). "Don't touch that dial!" TV as a—what!?—positive influence. *SIECUS Report, 28,* 16-18.

Food Commission. (1997, January-March). Advertising to children: UK the worst in Europe. *Food Magazine.*

Fouts, G., & Burggraf, K. (1999). Television situation comedies: Female body images and verbal reinforcements. *Sex Roles, 40,* 473-481.

Fowles, J. (1999). *The case for television violence.* Thousand Oaks, CA: Sage.

Fox, R. F. (1996). *Harvesting minds: How TV commercials control kids.* Westport, CT: Praeger.

Frean, A. (2000, June 22). Magazines add weight to war on superwaif models. *The London Times*.

Freedman, D. S., Dietz, W. H., Srinivasan, S. R., & Berenson, G. S. (1999). The relation of overweight to cardiovascular risk factors among children and adolescents: The Bogalusa Heart Study. *Pediatrics, 103,* 1175-1182.

Freedman, J. L. (1984). Effect of television violence on aggressiveness. *Psychological Bulletin, 96,* 227-246.

Freedman, J. L. (1986). Television violence and aggression: A rejoinder. *Psychological Bulletin, 100,* 372-373.

Freuh, T., & McGhee, P. (1975). Traditional sex-role development and amount of time watching television. *Developmental Psychology, 11,* 109.

Friedman, H., Termini, S., & Washington, R. (1977). The effectiveness of advertisements utilizing four types of endorsers. *Journal of Advertising, 6,* 22-24.

Friedrich, L. K., & Stein, A. H. (1973). Aggressive and prosocial television programs and the natural behavior of preschool children. *Monographs of the Society for Research in Child Development, 38*(4, Serial No. 151), 63.

Friedrich, L. K., & Stein, A. H. (1975). Prosocial television and young children: The effects of verbal labeling and role playing on learning and behavior. *Child Development, 46,* 27-38.

Friedrich-Cofer, L., & Huston, A. C. (1986). Television violence and aggression: The debate continues. *Psychological Bulletin, 100,* 364-371.

Frith, S. (1992). The industrialization of popular music. In J. Lull (Ed.), *Popular music and communication* (2nd ed., pp. 49-71). Newbury Park, CA: Sage.

Funk, J. B. (1993). Reevaluating the impact of video games. *Clinical Pediatrics, 32,* 86-90.

Funk, J. B. (2000). Why *do* we watch? A journey through our dark side. *Contemporary Psychology, 46,* 9-11.

Funk, J. B. (2001). [Examining the appeal of violent electronic games]. Unpublished raw data.

Funk, J. B. (in press). Children and violent video games: Strategies for identifying high risk players. In D. Ravitch & J. Viteritti (Eds.), *Children and the popular culture*.

Funk, J. B., & Buchman, D. D. (1995). Video game controversies. *Pediatric Annals, 24,* 91-94.

Funk, J. B., & Buchman, D. D. (1996a). Children's perceptions of gender differences in social approval for playing electronic games. *Sex Roles, 35,* 219-231.

Funk, J. B., & Buchman, D. D. (1996b). Playing violent video and computer games and adolescent self-perception. *Journal of Communication, 46*(1), 19-32.

Funk, J. B., Buchman, D. D., & Germann, J. N. (2000). Preference for violent electronic games, self-concept and gender differences in young children. *American Journal of Orthopsychiatry, 70,* 233-241.

Funk, J. B., Buchman, D. D., Myers, M., & Jenks, J. (2000, August). *Asking the right questions in research on violent electronic games, empathy, and aggression.* Poster session presented at the annual meeting of the American Psychological Association, Washington, DC.

Funk, J. B., Buchman, D. D., Schimming, J. L., & Hagan, J. D. (1998, August). *Attitudes towards violence, empathy, and violent electronic games.* Paper presented at the annual meeting of the American Psychological Association, San Francisco.

Funk, J. B., Flores, G., Buchman, D. D., & Germann, J. N. (1999). Rating electronic games: Violence is in the eye of the beholder. *Youth & Society, 30,* 283-312.

Funk, J. B., Hagan, J. D., & Schimming, J. L. (1999). Children and electronic games: A comparison of parent and child perceptions of children's habits and preferences in a United States sample. *Psychological Reports, 85,* 883-888.

Funk, J. B., Hagan, J., Schimming, J., Bullock, W. A., Buchman, D. D., & Myers, M. *Aggression and psychopathology in adolescents with a preference for violent electronic games.* Manuscript submitted for publication.

Furstenberg, F. F., Jr., Geitz, L. M., Teitler, J. O., & Weiss, C. C. (1997). Does condom availability make a difference? An evaluation of Philadelphia's health resource centers. *Family Planning Perspectives, 29,* 123-127.

Furstenberg, F. F., Moore, K. A., & Peterson, J. L. (1985). Sex education and sexual experience among adolescents. *American Journal of Public Health, 75,* 1331-1332.

Fylan, F., Harding, G. F., Edson, A. S., & Webb, R. M. (1999). Mechanisms of video-game epilepsy. *Epilepsia, 40*(Suppl. 4), 28-30.

Gaensbauer, T., & Wamboldt, M. (2000, January 5). *Facts about gun violence.* Washington, DC: American Academy of Child and Adolescent Psychiatry. Retrieved February 19, 2001, from the World Wide Web: www.aacap.org/info_families/nationalfacts/cogunviol.htm.

Gagnon, J. H., & Simon, W. (1987). The sexual scripting of oral genital contacts. *Archives of Sexual Behavior, 16,* 1-25.

Galst, J. P. (1980). Television food commercials and pro-nutritional public service announcements as determinants of young children's snack choices. *Child Development, 51,* 935-938.

Galst, J. P., & White, M. A. (1976). The unhealthy persuader: The reinforcing value of television and children's purchase-influencing attempts at the supermarket. *Child Development, 47,* 1089-1096.

Gan, S.-L., Zillmann, D., & Mitrook, M. (1997). Stereotyping effects of black women's sexual rap on white audiences. *Basic and Applied Social Psychology, 19,* 381-399.

Gaouette, N. (1998, March 27). How Japan reforms its violent kids. *The Christian Science Monitor, International.* Retrieved June 16, 2001, from the World Wide Web: www.csmonitor.com/durable/1998/03/27/intl/intl.6.html.

Geen, R. G. (1981). Behavioral and physiological reactions to observed violence: Effects of prior exposure to aggressive stimuli. *Journal of Personality & Social Psychology, 40,* 868-875.

Geen, R. G. (1994). Television and aggression: Recent developments in research and theory. In D. Zillmann, J. Bryant, & A. C. Huston (Eds.), *Media, children, and the family: Social, scientific, psychodynamic, and clinical perspectives* (pp. 151-162). Hillsdale, NJ: Lawrence Erlbaum.

Geier, T. (2001, April 6). MTV's pain in the jackass. *Entertainment Weekly,* pp. 10-11.

Gerbner, G. (1985). Children's television: A national disgrace. *Pediatric Annals, 14,* 822-827.

Gerbner, G. (1990). Stories that hurt: Tobacco, alcohol, and other drugs in the mass media. In H. Resnik (Ed.), *Youth and drugs: Society's mixed messages* (OSAP Prevention Monograph 6, pp. 53-129). Rockville, MD: Office for Substance Abuse Prevention.

Gerbner, G. (1993, June). *Women and minorities on television: A study in casting and fate.* A report to the Screen Actors Guild and the American Federation of Radio and Television Artists, Annenberg School for Communication, Philadelphia.

Gerbner, G. (1995). Casting and fate: Women and minorities on television drama, game shows, and news. In E. Hollander, C. van der Linden, & P. Rutten (Eds.), *Communication, culture community* (pp. 172-226). Bohn: Stafleu van Loghum.

Gerbner, G. (1998, April). An invisible ministry of culture. Presented at the New Mexico Media Literacy Project, Taos, NM.

Gerbner, G., & Gross, L. (1976). Living with television: The violence profile. *Journal of Communication, 26,* 172-199.

Gerbner, G., Gross, L., Morgan, M., & Signorielli, N. (1980a). Health and medicine on television. *New England Journal of Medicine, 305,* 901-905.

Gerbner, G., Gross, L., Morgan, M., & Signorielli, N. (1980b). The "mainstreaming" of America: Violence profile no. 11. *Journal of Communication, 30*(3), 10-29.

Gerbner, G., Gross, L., Morgan, M., & Signorielli, N. (1994). Growing up with television: The cultivation perspective. In J. Bryant & D. Zillmann (Eds.), *Media effects: Advances in theory and research* (pp. 17-41). Hillsdale, NJ: Lawrence Erlbaum.

Gerbner, G., Gross, L., Signorielli, N., Morgan, M., & Jackson-Beeck, M. (1979). The demonstration of power: Violence profile no. 10. *Journal of Communication, 29*(3), 177-196.

Gerbner, G., Morgan, M., & Signorielli, N. (1982). Programming health portrayals: What viewers see, say and do. In D. Pearl, L. Bouthilet, & J. Lazar (Eds.), *Television and behavior: Ten years of scientific progress and implications for the Eighties* (Vol. 2, pp. 291-307). Rockville, MD: National Institute of Mental Health.

Gerbner, G., Morgan, M., & Signorielli, N. (1994). *Television violence profile no. 16.* Philadelphia: Annenberg School for Communication.

Gerbner, G., & Ozyegin, N. (1997). *Alcohol, tobacco, and illicit drugs in entertainment television, commercials, news, "reality shows," movies, and music channels.* New York: Robert Wood Johnson Foundation.

Gerrard, M., McCann, L., & Fortini, M. (1983). Prevention of unwanted pregnancy. *American Journal of Community Psychology, 11,* 153-167.

Gibbons, J., Anderson, D. R., Smith, R., Field, D. E., & Fischer, C. (1986). Young children's recall and reconstruction of audio and audiovisual narratives. *Child Development, 57,* 1014-1023.

Giles, J., & Fleming, C. (1993, June 28). See kids' flix make big bucks. *Newsweek,* p. 66.

Gilsky, M. L., Tataryn, D. J., Tobias, B. A., Kihlstrom, J. F., & McConkey, K. M. (1991). Absorption, openness to experience, and hypnotizability. *Journal of Personality and Social Psychology, 60,* 263-272.

Ginsberg v. New York. (1968). 290 U.S. 629 (1968).

Ginsburg, H., & Opper, S. (1979). *Piaget's theory of intellectual development* (2nd ed.). Englewood Cliffs, NJ: Prentice Hall.

Glickson, J., & Avnon, M. (1997). Explorations in virtual reality: Absorption, cognition, and altered state of consciousness. *Imagination, Cognition, and Personality, 17,* 141-151.

Glieberman, O. (1999, July 16). Virgin megascore. *Entertainment Weekly,* pp. 43-44.

Goldberg, M. (1987, November 28). TV has done more to contain AIDS than any other single factor. *TV Guide,* pp. 5-6.

Goldberg, M. (1990). A quasi-experiment assessing the effectiveness of TV advertising directed to children. *Journal of Marketing Research, 27,* 445-454.

Goldberg, M. E., & Gorn, G. J. (1978). Some unintended consequences of TV advertising to children. *Journal of Consumer Research, 5*(1), 22-29.

Goldberg, M. E., Gorn, G. J., & Gibson, W. (1978). TV messages for snack and breakfast foods: Do they influence children's preferences? *Journal of Consumer Research, 5*(2), 73-81.

Golden, D. (2001, August 28). Channel One aims to involve teachers in marketing push. *Wall Street Journal,* p. 1.

Goldman, L. K., & Glantz, S. A. (1998). Evaluation of antismoking advertising campaigns. *Journal of the American Medical Association, 279,* 772-777.

Goldstein, A. O., Fischer, P. M., Richards, J. W., Jr., & Creten, D. (1987). Relationship between high school student smoking and recognition of cigarette advertisements. *Journal of Pediatrics, 110,* 488-491.

Goldstein, A. O., Sobel, R. A., & Newman, G. R. (1999). Tobacco and alcohol use in G-rated children's animated films. *Journal of the American Medical Association, 281,* 1131-1136.

Goldstein, J. (Ed.). (1998). *Why we watch: The attractions of violent entertainment.* New York: Oxford University Press.

Goldstein, J. (1999). The attraction of violent entertainment. *Media Psychology, 1,* 271-282.

Gondoli, D. M. (1999). Adolescent development and health. In T. L. Whitman, T. V. Merluzzi, & R. D. White (Eds.), *Life-span perspectives on health and illness* (pp. 147-163). Mahwah, NJ: Lawrence Erlbaum.

Goodman, E. (1986, September 20). Commercial for teen-age pregnancy. *Washington Post.*

Goodman, E. (2000, September 25). Polluted advironment is hazardous to American youth. *Albuquerque Journal,* p. A8.

Gordinier, J. (1998, January 30). High anxiety. *Entertainment Weekly,* p. 18.

Gore, T. (1987). *Raising PG kids in an X-rated society.* Nashville, TN: Abingdon.

Gorman, S. (2000). Feminist group frowns on FOX network. Reuters News Agency, May 22, 2000 [Online]. Available: www.now.org/issues/miedia/watchout/report/.

Gorn, G. J., & Goldberg, M. E. (1977). The impact of television advertising on children from low income families. *Journal of Consumer Research, 4*(2), 86-88.

Gorn, G. J., & Goldberg, M. E. (1980). Children's responses to repetitive television commercials. *Journal of Consumer Research, 6,* 421-424.

Gorn, G. J., & Goldberg, M. E. (1982). Behavioral evidence of the effects of televised food messages on children. *Journal of Consumer Research, 9,* 200-205.

Gortmaker, S. L., Must, A., Sobol, A. M., Peterson, K., Colditz, G. A., & Dietz, W. H. (1993). Television viewing as a cause of increasing obesity among children in the United States, 1986-1990. *Archives of Pediatrics and Adolescent Medicine, 150,* 356-362.

Gostin, L. O., & Brandt, A. M. (1993). Criteria for evaluating a ban on the advertisement of cigarettes. *Journal of the American Medical Association, 269,* 904-909.

Gould, M. S., & Davidson, L. (1988). Suicide contagion among adolescents. *Advances in Adolescent Mental Health, 3,* 29-59.

Gould, M. S., Fisher, P., Parides, M., Flory, M., & Shaffer, D. (1996). Psychosocial risk factors of child and adolescent completed suicide. *Archives of General Psychiatry, 53,* 1155-1162.

Gould, M. S., & Shaffer, D. (1986). The impact of suicide in television movies. *New England Journal of Medicine, 315,* 690-694.

Gould, M. S., Shaffer, D., & Kleinman, M. (1988). The impact of suicide in television movies: Replication and commentary. *Suicide and Life Threatening Behavior, 18,* 90-99.

Gould, M. S., Wallenstein, S., Kleinman, M. H., O'Carroll, P., & Mercy, J. (1990). Suicide cluster: An examination of age-specific effects. *American Journal of Public Health, 80,* 211-212.

Gow, J. (1993). *Gender roles in popular music videos: MTV's "top 100 of all time."* Paper presented at the Popular Culture Association/American Culture Association convention, New Orleans, LA.

Graber, J. A., Brooks-Gunn, J., & Petersen, A. C. (Eds.). (1996). *Transitions through adolescence: Interpersonal domains and context.* Mahwah, NJ: Lawrence Erlbaum.

Graf, W. D., Chatrian, G. -E., Glass, S. T., & Knauss, T. A. (1994). Video game-related seizures: A report on 10 patients and a review of the literature. *Pediatrics, 93,* 551-556.

Graham, L., & Hamdan, L. (1987). *Youth trends: Capturing the $200 billion youth market.* New York: St. Martin's.

Graziano, A. B., Peterson, M., & Shaw, G. L. (1999). Enhanced learning of proportional math through music training and spatial-temporal training. *Neurological Research, 21,* 139-152.

Graziano, A. M., DeGiovanni, I. S., & Garcia, K. A. (1979). Behavioral treatment of children's fears: A review. *Psychological Bulletin, 86,* 804-830.

Greenberg, B. S. (1982). Television and role socialization: An overview. In D. Pearl, L. Bouthilet, & J. Lazar (Eds.), *Television and behavior: Ten years of scientific progress and implications for the eighties* (Vol. 2, pp. 179-190). Rockville, MD: National Institute of Mental Health.

Greenberg, B. S. (1993). Race differences in television and movie behaviors. In B. S. Greenberg, J. D. Brown, & N. L. Buerkel-Rothfuss (Eds.), *Media, sex, and the adolescent* (pp. 145-152). Cresskill, NJ: Hampton.

Greenberg, B. S. (1994). Content trends in media sex. In D. Zillmann, J. Bryant, & A. C. Huston (Eds.), *Media, children, and the family: Social scientific, psychodynamic, and clinical perspectives* (pp. 165-182). Hillsdale, NJ: Lawrence Erlbaum.

Greenberg, B. S., Abelman, R., & Neuendorf, K. (1981). Sex on the soap operas: Afternoon delight. *Journal of Communication, 31,* 83-89.

Greenberg, B. S., & Brand, J. E. (1993). Television news and advertising in schools: The "Channel One" controversy. *Journal of Communication, 43*(1), 143-151.

Greenberg, B. S., Brown, J. D., & Buerkel-Rothfuss, N. (Eds.). (1993). *Media, sex and the adolescent.* Cresskill, NJ: Hampton Press.

Greenberg, B. S., & Busselle, R. W. (1994). *Soap operas and sexual activity.* Menlo Park, CA: Kaiser Family Foundation.

Greenberg, B. S., & Busselle, R. W. (1996). Soap operas and sexual activity: A decade later. *Journal of Communication, 46*(4), 153-160.

Greenberg, B. S., & Gordon, T. F. (1972). Perceptions of violence in television programs: Critics and the public. In G. A. Comstock & E. A. Rubinstein (Eds.), *Television and social behavior: Vol. 1. Media content and control* (pp. 244-258). Washington, DC: Government Printing Office.

Greenberg, B. S., & Hofschire, L. (2000). Sex on entertainment television. In D. Zillmann & P. Vorderer (Eds.), *Media entertainment: The psychology of its appeal* (pp. 93-111). Mahwah, NJ: Lawrence Erlbaum.

Greenberg, B. S., & Linsangan, R. (1993). Gender differences in adolescents' media use, exposure to sexual content and parental mediation. In B. S. Greenberg, J. D. Brown, & N. L. Buerkel-Rothfuss (Eds.), *Media, sex and the adolescent* (pp. 134-144). Cresskill, NJ: Hampton.

Greenberg, B. S., Linsangan, R., & Soderman, A. (1993). Adolescents' reactions to television sex. In B. S. Greenberg, J. D. Brown, & N. L. Buerkel-Rothfuss (Eds.), *Media, sex and the adolescent* (pp. 196-224). Cresskill, NJ: Hampton.

Greenberg, B. S., Linsangan, R. L., Soderman, A., Heeter, C., Lin, C., Stanley, C., & Siemicki, M. (1987). *Adolescents and their exposure to television and movie sex.* Project CAST, Report No. 4, Michigan State University, Department of Telecommunications.

Greenberg, B. S., & Rampoldi, L. (1994). *Who watches daytime soap operas?* Menlo Park, CA: Kaiser Family Foundation.

Greenberg, B. S., & Rampoldi-Hnilo, L. (2001). Child and parent responses to the age-based and content-based television ratings. In D. G. Singer & J. L. Singer (Eds.), *Handbook of children and the media* (pp. 621-634). Thousand Oaks, CA: Sage.

Greenberg, B. S., Rampoldi-Hnilo, L., & Mastro, D. (2000). *The alphabet soup of television program ratings*. Cresskill, NJ: Hampton.

Greenberg, B. S., Siemicki, M., Dorfman, S., Heeter, C., Lin, C., Stanley, C., Soderman, A., & Linsangan, R. (1993). Sex content in R-rated films viewed by adolescents. In B. S. Greenberg, J. D. Brown, & N. L. Buerkel-Rothfuss (Eds.), *Media, sex, and the adolescent* (pp. 45-58). Cresskill, NJ: Hampton.

Greenberg, B. S., & Smith, S. W. (2002). Daytime talk shows: Up close and in your face. In J. D. Brown, J. R. Steele, & K. Walsh-Childers (Eds.), *Sexual teens, sexual media* (pp. 79-93). Hillsdale, NJ: Lawrence Erlbaum.

Greenberg, B. S., Smith, S., Yun, J. A., Busselle, R., Hnilo, L. R., Mitchell, M., & Sherry, J. (1995). *The content of television talk shows: Topics, guests and interactions*. Menlo Park, CA: Kaiser Family Foundation.

Greenberg, B. S., Stanley, C., Siemicki, M., Heeter, C., Soderman, A., & Linsangan, R. (1986). *Sex content on soaps and prime time television series viewed by adolescents*. Project CAST, Report No. 3, Michigan State University, Department of Telecommunications.

Greenberg, B. S., Stanley, C., Siemicki, M., Heeter, C., Soderman, A., & Linsangan, R. (1993). Sex content on soaps and prime-time television series most viewed by adolescents. In B. S. Greenberg, J. D. Brown, & N. L. Buerkel-Rothfuss (Eds.), *Media, sex and the adolescent* (pp. 29-44). Cresskill, NJ: Hampton.

Greene, J. S., & Asher, I. (1982). Electronic games. *Journal of the American Medical Association, 248,* 1308.

Greene, K., Kremar, M., Walters, L. H., Rubin, D. L., & Hale, J. (2000). Targeting adolescent risk-taking behaviors: The contributions of egocentrism and sensation-seeking. *Journal of Adolescence, 23,* 439-461.

Greenfield, P. (1984). *Mind and media: The effects of television, video games, and computers*. Cambridge, MA: Harvard University Press.

Greenfield, P., & Beagles-Roos, J. (1988). Television vs. radio: The cognitive impact on different socio-economic and ethnic groups. *Journal of Communication, 38,* 71-92.

Greenfield, P. M., Bruzzone, L., Koyamatsu, K., Satuloff, W., Nixon, K., Brodie, M., & Kingsdale, D. (1987). What is rock music doing to the minds of our youth? A first experimental look at the effects of rock music lyrics and music videos. *Journal of Early Adolescence, 7,* 315-329.

Greenfield, P. M., deWinstanley, P., Kilpatrick, H., & Kaye, D. (1996). Action video games and informal education: Effects on strategies for dividing visual attention. In P. M. Greenfield & R. R. Cocking (Eds.), *Interacting with video: Advances in applied developmental psychology* (Vol. 2, pp. 187-205). Norwood, NJ: Ablex.

Greer, D., Potts, R., Wright, J. C., & Huston, A. C. (1982). The effects of television commercial form and commercial placement on children's social behavior and attention. *Child Development, 53,* 611-619.

Greeson, L. E., & Williams, R. A. (1986). Social implications of music videos for youth: An analysis of the contents and effects of MTV. *Youth & Society, 18,* 177-189.

Griffith, J. L., Voloschin, P., Gibb, G. D., & Bailey, J. R. (1983). Differences in eye-hand coordination of video-game users and non-users. *Perceptual-Motor Skills, 57,* 155-158.

Griffiths, M. (2000). Sex on the Internet. In C. Feilitzen & U. Carlsson (Eds.), *Children in the new media landscape* (pp. 169-184). Goteborg, Sweden: UNESCO.

Griffiths, M. D., & Hunt, N. (1995). Computer game playing in adolescence: Prevalence and demographic indicators. *Journal of Community and Applied Social Psychology, 5,* 189-193.

Griffiths, M. D., & Hunt, N. (1998). Dependence on computer games by adolescents. *Psychological Reports, 82,* 475-480.

Groebel, J. (1999). Media access and media use among 12-year-olds in the world. In C. von Feilitzen & U. Carlsson (Eds.), *Children and media: Image, education, participation* (pp. 61-68). Goteborg, Sweden: UNESCO International Clearinghouse on Children and Violence on the Screen.

Grossberg, L. (1992). Rock and roll in search of an audience. In J. Lull (Ed.), *Popular music and communication* (2nd ed., pp. 152-175). Newbury Park, CA: Sage.

Grossberg, L., Wartella, E., & Whitney, D. C. (1998). *Media making: Mass media in a popular culture.* Thousand Oaks, CA: Sage.

Grossman, D. (1995). *On killing.* Boston: Little, Brown.

Grossman, D., & DeGaetano, G. (1999). *Stop teaching our kids to kill: A call to action against TV, movie and video game violence.* New York: Crown.

Grossman, D. C., Reay, D. T., & Baker, S. A. (1999). Self-inflicted and unintentional firearm injuries among children and adolescents: The source of firearms. *Archives of Pediatrics and Adolescent Medicine, 153,* 875-878.

Grossman, L. K. (1999, March/April). Making a mess of digital TV. *Columbia Journalism Review,* pp. 53-54.

Grube, J. W. (1993). Alcohol portrayals and alcohol advertising on television. *Alcohol Health & Research World, 17,* 61-66.

Grube, J. W. (1995). Television alcohol portrayals, alcohol advertising, and alcohol expectances among children and adolescents. In S. E. Martin (Ed.), *The effects of the mass media on use and abuse of alcohol* (pp. 105-121). Bethesda, MD: National Institute on Alcohol Abuse and Alcoholism.

Grube, J. W. (1999). *Alcohol advertising and alcohol consumption: A review of recent research* (NIAA 10th Special Report to Congress on Alcohol and Health). Bethesda, MD: National Institute on Alcohol Abuse and Alcoholism.

Grube, J. W., & Wallack, L. (1994). Television beer advertising and drinking knowledge, beliefs, and intentions among schoolchildren. *American Journal of Public Health, 84,* 254-259.

Gruber, E., & Grube, J. (2000). Adolescent sexuality and the media: A review of current knowledge and implications. *Western Journal of Medicine, 172,* 210-214.

Guerra, N. G., Huesmann, L. R., Tolan, P. H., VanAcker, R., & Eron, L. D. (1995). Stressful events and individual beliefs as correlates of economic disadvantage and aggression among urban children. *Consulting and Clinical Psychology, 63,* 518-528.

Guerra, N. G., Nucci, L., & Huesmann, L. R. (1994). Moral cognition and childhood aggression. In L. R. Huesmann (Ed.), *Aggressive behavior: Current perspectives* (pp. 13-33). New York: Plenum.

Guillen, E. O., & Barr, S. I. (1994). Nutrition, dieting, and fitness messages in a magazine for adolescent women. *Journal of Adolescent Health, 15,* 464-472.

Gunter, B., & Furnham, A. (1984). Perceptions of television violence: Effects of programme genre and type of violence on viewers' judgements of violent portrayals. *British Journal of Social Psychology, 23,* 155-164.

Gunter, B., & Furnham, A. (1998). *Children as consumers: A psychological analysis of young people's market.* London: Routledge Kegan Paul.

Gunther, A. C., & Thorson, E. (1992). Perceived persuasive effects of product commercials and public service announcements: Third-person effects in new domains. *Communication Research, 19*, 574-596.

Gupta, R., & Derevensky, J. L. (1996). The relationship between gambling and video-game playing behavior in children and adolescents. *Journal of Gambling Studies, 12*, 375-394.

Guttmacher, S., Lieberman, L., Ward, D., Freudenberg, N., Radosh, A., & DesJarlais, D. (1997). Condom availability in New York City public high schools: Relationships to condom use and sexual behavior. *American Journal of Public Health, 87*, 1427-1433.

Guyer, B., Hoyert, D. L., Martin, J. A., Ventura, S. J., MacDorman, M. F., & Strobino, D. M. (1999). Annual summary of vital statistics—1998. *Pediatrics, 104*, 1229-1246.

Haag, P. (1999). *Voices of a generation: Teenage girls on sex, school, and self.* Washington, DC: American Association of University Women Educational Foundation.

Haffner, D. W., & Kelly, M. (1987, March/April). Adolescent sexuality in the media. *SIECUS Report*, pp. 9-12.

Haidt, J., McCauley, C., & Rozin P. (1994). Individual differences in sensitivity to disgust: A scale sampling 7 domains of disgust elicitors. *Personality & Individual Differences, 16*, 701-713.

Hajari, N. (1993, October 22). Playing with fire. *Entertainment Weekly*, pp. 6-7.

Halebsky, M. (1987). Adolescent alcohol and substance abuse: Parent and peer effects. *Adolescence, 22*, 961-967.

Halpern, D. F. (2000). *Sex differences in cognitive abilities* (2nd ed.). Hillsdale, NJ: Lawrence Erlbaum.

Hamilton, J. T. (1998). *Channeling violence: The economic market for violent television programming.* Princeton, NJ: Princeton University Press.

Hamilton, K., & Waller, G. (1993). Media influences on body size estimation in anorexia and bulimia: An experimental study. *British Journal of Psychiatry, 162*, 837-840.

Hammond, K. M., Wyllie, A., & Casswell, S. (1999). The extent and nature of televised food advertising to New Zealand children and adolescents. *Australian and New Zealand Journal of Public Health, 23*, 49-55.

Hanratty, M. A., O'Neal, E., & Sulzer, J. L. (1972). The effect of frustration upon imitation of aggression. *Journal of Personality & Social Psychology, 21*, 30-34.

Hansen, C. H., & Hansen, R. D. (1990). The influence of sex and violence on the appeal of rock music videos. *Communication Research, 17*, 212-234.

Hansen, C. H., & Hansen, R. D. (1991a). Constructing personality and social reality through music: Individual differences among fans of punk and heavy metal music. *Journal of Broadcasting & Electronic Media, 35*, 335-350.

Hansen, C. H., & Hansen, R. D. (1991b). Rock music videos and antisocial behavior. *Basic and Applied Social Psychology, 11*, 357-369.

Hansen, C. H., & Hansen, R. D. (2000). Music and music videos. In D. Zillmann & P. Vorderer (Eds.), *Media entertainment: The psychology of its appeal* (pp. 175-196). Mahwah, NJ: Lawrence Erlbaum.

Harris, E. (2000). Violence, video games, and the First Amendment. *Free Speech* [Online]. Available: www.freedomforum.org/news/2000/04/2000-04-10-12.asp.

Harris, J. R. (1998). *The nurture assumption: Why children turn out the way they do.* New York: Free Press.

Harris, L., & Associates. (1985). *Public attitudes about sex education, family planning and abortion in the United States.* New York: Planned Parenthood Federation of America.

Harris, L., & Associates. (1986). *American teens speak: Sex, myths, TV and birth control.* New York: Planned Parenthood Federation of America.

Harris, L., & Associates. (1987). *Attitudes about television, sex and contraception advertising*. New York: Planned Parenthood Federation of America.

Harris, L., & Associates. (1988). *Sexual material on American network television during the 1987-88 season*. New York: Planned Parenthood Federation of America.

Harris, R. J. (1994a). *A cognitive psychology of mass communication* (2nd ed.). Hillsdale, NJ: Lawrence Erlbaum.

Harris, R. J. (1994b). The impact of sexually explicit media. In J. Bryant & D. Zillmann (Eds.), *Media effects: Advances in theory and research* (pp. 247-272). Hillsdale, NJ: Lawrence Erlbaum.

Harrison, K. (1998). The role of self-discrepancies in the relationship between media exposure and eating disorders. *Dissertation Abstracts International, 59,* 0648.

Harrison, K. (2000). Television viewing, fat stereotyping, body shape standards, and eating disorder symptomatology in grade school children. *Communication Research, 27,* 617-640.

Harrison, K., & Cantor, J. (1997). The relationship between media consumption and eating disorders. *Journal of Communication, 47*(1), 40-67.

Harrison, K., & Cantor, J. (1999). Tales from the screen: Enduring fright reactions to scary media. *Media Psychology, 1,* 97-116.

Hart, R. (1994). *Seducing America: How television charms the modern voter*. New York: Oxford University Press.

Hartup, W. W., & Stevens, N. (1999). Friendships and adaptation across the lifespan. *Current Directions in Psychological Science, 8*(3), 76-79.

Hawkins, K., & Hane, A. C. (2000). Adolescents' perceptions of print cigarette advertising: A case for counteradvertising. *Journal of Health Communication, 5,* 83-96.

Hawkins, R. P. (1977). The dimensional structure of children's perceptions of television reality. *Communication Research, 7,* 193-226.

Hawkins, R. P., & Pingree, S. (1980). Some processes in the cultivation effect. *Communication Research, 7,* 193-226.

Hawkins, R. P., & Pingree, S. (1981). Uniform messages and habitual viewing: Unnecessary assumptions in social reality effects. *Human Communication Research, 7,* 291-301.

Hawkins, R. P., & Pingree, S. (1982). Television's influence on social reality. In D. Pearl, L. Bouthilet, & J. Lazar (Eds.), *Television and behavior: Ten years of scientific progress and implications for the eighties* (Vol. 2, pp. 224-247). Rockville, MD: National Institute of Mental Health.

Hays, C. (2000, September 14). New report examines commercialism in U.S. schools. *New York Times*, p. A1.

Hazan, A. R., & Glantz, S. A. (1995). Current trends in tobacco use on prime-time fictional television. *American Journal of Public Health, 85,* 116-117.

Hazan, A. R., Lipton, H. L., & Glantz, S. A. (1994). Popular films do not reflect current tobacco use. *American Journal of Public Health, 84,* 998-1000.

Healy, J. (1991). *Endangered minds: Why children don't think and what we can do about it*. New York: Simon & Schuster.

Hearold, S. (1986). A synthesis of 1045 effects of television on social behavior. In F. Comstock (Ed.), *Public communication and behavior* (Vol. 1, pp. 65-133). New York: Academic Press.

Heintz-Knowles, K. E. (1996). *Sexual activity on daytime soap operas: A content analysis of five weeks of television programming*. Menlo Park, CA: Kaiser Family Foundation.

Hennes, H. (1998). A review of violence statistics among children and adolescents in the United States. *Pediatric Clinics of North America, 45,* 269-280.

Hernandez, B., Gortmaker, S. L., Colditz, G. A., Peterson, K. E., Laird, N. M., & Parra-Cabrera, S. (1999). Association of obesity with physical activity, television programs and other forms of video viewing among children in Mexico City. *International Journal of Obesity and Related Metabolic Disorders, 23,* 845 854.

Herold, E. S., & Foster, M. E. (1975). Changing sexual references in mass circulation magazines. *The Family Coordinator, 24,* 21-25.

Hershenson, K. (1999, July 23). Pushing the envelope. *Albuquerque Journal,* pp. E14-E15.

Hicks, D. J. (1965). Imitation and retention of film-mediated aggressive peer and models. *Journal of Personality & Social Psychology, 2,* 97-100.

Hill, A. J., & Pallin, V. (1998). Dieting awareness and low self-worth: Related issues in 8-year-old girls. *International Journal of Eating Disorders, 24,* 405-413.

Hill-Scott, K. (2001). Industry standards and practices: Compliance with the Children's Television Act. In D. G. Singer & J. L. Singer (Eds.), *Handbook of children and the media* (pp. 605-620). Thousand Oaks, CA: Sage.

Hind, P. A. (1995). A study of reported satisfaction with differentially aggressive computer games amongst incarcerated offenders. *Issues in Criminological and Legal Psychology* (22), 28-36.

Hingson, R. W., Heeren, T., Jamanka, A., & Howland, J. (2000). Age of drinking onset and unintentional injury involvement after drinking. *Journal of the American Medical Association, 284,* 1527-1533.

Hirsch, P. (1980). The "scary world" of the nonviewer and other anomalies: A reanalysis of Gerbner et al.'s findings of cultivation analysis: Part I. *Communication Research, 7,* 403-456.

Hirschberg, L. (1996, January 14). Does a Sugar Bear bite? *New York Times Magazine,* pp. 24-57.

Hitt, J. (1999, July 25). Real campaign-finance reform. *New York Times Magazine,* pp. 36-37.

Hochman, D. (1999, July 9). Putting the "R" in "Park." *Entertainment Weekly,* pp. 15-16.

Hockstra, S. J., Harris, R. J., & Helmick, A. L. (1999). Autobiographical memories about the experience of seeing frightening movies in childhood. *Media Psychology, 1,* 117-140.

Hoffner, C. (1996). Children's wishful identification and parasocial interaction with favorite television characters. *Journal of Broadcasting & Electronic Media, 40,* 389-402.

Hoffner, C., & Cantor, J. (1985). Developmental differences in responses to a television character's appearance and behavior. *Developmental Psychology, 21,* 1065-1074.

Hoffner, C., Cantor, J., & Badzinski, D. M. (1990). Children's understanding of adverbs denoting degree of likelihood. *Journal of Child Language, 17,* 217-231.

Hoffner, C., Cantor, J., & Thorson, E. (1989). Children's responses to conflicting auditory and visual features of a televised narrative. *Human Communication Research, 16,* 256-278.

Hofschire, L. J., & Greenberg, B. S. (2002). Media's impact on adolescents' body dissatisfaction. In J. D. Brown, J. R. Steele, & K. Walsh-Childers (Eds.), *Sexual teens, sexual media* (pp. 125-149). Mahwah, NJ: Lawrence Erlbaum.

Hogan, M. (2000). Media matters for youth health. *Journal of Adolescent Health, 27*(Suppl.), 73-76.

Hogan, M. (2001). Parents and other adults: Models and monitors of healthy media habits. In D. G. Singer & J. L. Singer (Eds.), *Handbook of children and the media* (pp. 663-680). Thousand Oaks, CA: Sage.

Holden, G., Bearison, D. J., Rode, D. C., Kapiloff, M. F., & Rosenberg, G. (2000). The effects of a computer network on pediatric pain and anxiety. *Journal of Technology in Human Services, 17,* 27-47.

Horgen, K. B., Choate, M., & Brownell, K. D. (2001). Television food advertising. In D. G. Singer & J. L. Singer (Eds.), *Handbook of children and media* (pp. 447-461). Thousand Oaks, CA: Sage.

Hough, K. J., & Erwin, P. G. (1997). Children's attitudes toward violence on television. *Journal of Psychology, 131,* 411-415.

Hoy, M. G., Young, C. E., & Mowen, J. C. (1986). Animated host-selling advertisements: Their impacts on young children's recognition, attitudes, and behavior. *Journal of Public Policy & Marketing, 5,* 171-184.

Huesmann, L. R. (1986). Psychological processes promoting the relation between exposure to media violence and aggressive behavior by the viewer. *Journal of Social Issues, 42,* 125-139.

Huesmann, L. R. (1988). An information processing model for the development of aggression. *Aggressive Behavior, 14,* 13-24.

Huesmann, L. R. (1998). The role of social information processing and cognitive schemas in the acquisition and maintenance of habitual aggressive behavior. In R. G. Geen & E. Donnerstein (Eds.), *Human aggression: Theories, research, and implications for social policy* (pp. 1120-1134). San Diego: Academic Press.

Huesmann, L. R., & Eron, L. D. (1986a). The development of aggression in American children as a consequence of television violence viewing. In L. R. Huesmann & L. D. Eron (Eds.), *Television and the aggressive child: A cross national comparison* (pp. 45-80). Hillsdale, NJ: Lawrence Erlbaum.

Huesmann, L. R., & Eron, L. D. (1986b). The development of aggression in children of different cultures: Psychological processes and exposure to violence. In L. R. Huesmann & L. D. Eron (Eds.), *Television and the aggressive child: A cross national comparison* (pp. 1-27). Hillsdale, NJ: Lawrence Erlbaum.

Huesmann, L. R., Eron, L. D., Klein, R., Brice, P., & Fischer, P. (1983). Mitigating the imitation of aggressive behaviors by changing children's attitudes about media violence. *Journal of Personality & Social Psychology, 44,* 899-910.

Huesmann, L. R., Eron, L. D., Lefkowitz, M. M., & Walder, L. O. (1984). Stability of aggression over time and generations. *Developmental Psychology, 20,* 1120-1134.

Huesmann, L. R., Lagerspetz, K., & Eron, L. D. (1984). Intervening variables in the TV violence-aggression relation: Evidence from two countries. *Developmental Psychology, 20,* 746-775.

Huesmann, L. R., & Miller, L. S. (1994). Long-term effects of repeated exposure to media violence in childhood. In L. R. Huesmann (Ed.), *Aggressive behavior: Current perspectives* (pp. 153-186). New York: Plenum.

Hughes, M. (1980). The fruits of cultivation analysis: A re-examination of television in fear of victimization, alienation, and approval of violence. *Public Opinion Quarterly, 44,* 287-302.

Hurley, J., & Schmidt, S. (1996). Hard artery cafe? *Nutrition Action Health Letter, 23,* 1.

Huston, A. C., Donnerstein, E., Fairchild, H. H., Feshbach, N. D., Katz, P. A., Murray, J. P., Rubinstein, E. A., Wilcox, B. L., & Zuckerman, D. (1992). *Big world, small screen: The role of television in American society.* Lincoln: University of Nebraska Press.

Huston, A. C., Greer, D., Wright, J. C., Welch, R., & Ross, R. (1984). Children's comprehension of televised formal features with masculine and feminine connotations. *Developmental Psychology, 20,* 707-716.

Huston, A. C., Wartella, E., & Donnerstein, E. (1998). *Measuring the effects of sexual content in the media: A report to the Kaiser Family Foundation.* Menlo Park, CA: Kaiser Family Foundation.

Huston, A. C., & Wright, J. C. (1983). Children's processing of television: The informative functions of formal features. In J. Bryant & D. R. Anderson (Eds.), *Children's understanding of television: Research on attention and comprehension* (pp. 35-68). New York: Academic Press.

Huston, A. C., Wright, J. C., Marquis, J., & Green, S. B. (1999). How young children spend their time: Television and other activities. *Developmental Psychology, 35,* 912-925.

Huxley, A. (1932). *Brave new world.* New York: HarperCollins.

Ile, M. L., & Knoll, L. A. (1990). Tobacco advertising and the First Amendment. *Journal of the American Medical Association, 264,* 1593-1594.

The impact of interactive violence on children: Hearing before the Senate Commerce, Science, and Transportation Committee, 106th Cong. (2000a, March 21) (testimony of Jeanne B. Funk).

The impact of interactive violence on children: Hearing before the Senate Commerce, Science, and Transportation Committee, 106th Cong. (2000b, March 21) (testimony of Eugene F. Provenzo).

The impact of interactive violence on children: Hearing before the Senate Commerce, Science, and Transportation Committee, 106th Cong. (2000c, March 21) (testimony of David Walsh).

Impoco, J. (1996, April 15). TV's frisky family values. *U.S. News & World Report,* pp. 58-62.

Inhelder, B., & Piaget, J. (1958). *The growth of logical thinking from childhood to adolescence.* New York: Basic Books.

Institute of Medicine. (1994). *Growing up tobacco free: Preventing nicotine addiction in children and youths.* Washington, DC: Author.

Interstate Circuit v. Dallas. (1968). 390 U.S. 676 (1968).

Irving, L. M. (1990). Mirror images: Effects of the standard of beauty on the self- and body-esteem of women exhibiting varying levels of bulimic symptoms. *Journal of Social & Clinical Psychology, 9,* 230-242.

Irving, L. M., DuPen, J., & Berel, S. (1998). A media literacy program for high school females. *Eating Disorders: The Journal of Treatment & Prevention, 6,* 119-132.

Irwin, A. R., & Gross, A. M. (1995). Cognitive tempo, violent video games, and aggressive behavior in young boys. *Journal of Family Violence, 10,* 337-350.

Irwin, H. J. (1999). Pathological and nonpathological dissociation: The relevance of childhood trauma. *Journal of Psychology, 133,* 157-164.

Ishigaki, E. H. (1991). The health and eating habits of young children in Japan. *Early Child Development & Care, 74,* 141-148.

It's a Pokemon world as Nintendo leads popular franchise into 2000; New line of video games, toys and movie sequel revealed at Toy Fair 2000. (2000, February 9). Retrieved May 25, 2001, from the World Wide Web: www.findarticles.com/cf_0/m0EIN/2000_Feb_9/59268506/p1/article.jhtml.

Ivry, B. (1998, August 28). Use of drugs is rising dramatically on the big screen. *Albuquerque Journal,* p. B4.

Iwao, S., Pool, I., & Hagiwara, S. (1981). Japanese and U.S. media: Some cross-cultural insights into TV violence. *Journal of Communication, 31*(2), 29-36.

Jackass imitation stunt: Boy recovering after imitating MTV show stunt. (2001, January 29). *Albuquerque Journal.*

Jackson, D. Z. (1998, November 30). Big tobacco's chump change. *Liberal Opinion Week,* p. 23.

Jackson, D. Z. (2001, March 26). Bush tax cut pitched to our gluttony. *Liberal Opinion Week,* p. 9.

Jackson, G. A., Farrah, M. M., Kellermann, A. L., & Simon, S. (2001). Seeing is believing: What do boys do when they find a real gun? *Pediatrics, 107,* 1247-1250.

Jackson, W. (1999, April 12). Viewer's call. *Variety,* pp. 37, 46.

Jacobs, A. J. (1999, August 6). The XXX files. *Entertainment Weekly,* pp. 21-25.

Jacobs, A. J., & Shaw, J. (1999, April 2). Virgin spring. *Entertainment Weekly,* pp. 10-11.

Jacobson, M. (1999). Diet & disease: Time to act. *Nutrition Action Health Letter, 26,* 2.

Jacobson, M. (2000). Tax junk foods. *Nutrition Action Health Letter, 27,* 2.

Jacobson, M. F., & Collins, R. (1985, March 10). There's too much harm to let beer, wine ads continue. *Los Angeles Times,* p. V3

Jaglom, L. M., & Gardner, H. (1981). The preschool television viewer as anthropologist. In H. Kelly & H. Gardner (Eds.), *New directions for child development: Viewing children through television* (pp. 9-30). San Francisco: Jossey-Bass.

Jahns, L., Siega-Riz, A. M., & Popkin, B. M. (2001). The increasing prevalence of snacking among US children from 1977 to 1996. *Journal of Pediatrics, 138,* 493-498.

Jain, A., & Tirodkar, M. (2001, April). *Food, obesity, and advertising and the African-American audience.* Paper presented at the annual meeting of the Ambulatory Pediatric Association/Society for Pediatric Research, Baltimore, MD.

James, A., Allison, J., Jenks, C., & Prout, A. (1998). *Theorizing childhood.* New York: Teachers College Press.

Jeffery, R. W., & French, S. A. (1998). Epidemic obesity in the United States: Are fast foods and television viewing contributing? *American Journal of Public Health, 88,* 277-280.

Jeffrey, D. B., McLellarn, R. W., & Fox, D. T. (1983). The development of children's eating habits: The role of television commercials. *Health Education Quarterly, 9,* 78-93.

Jemmott, J. B., III, Jemmott, L. S., & Fong, G. T. (1998). Abstinence and safer sex HIV risk-reduction interventions for African American adolescents. *Journal of the American Medical Association, 279,* 1529-1536.

Jessor, R. (1992). Risk behavior in adolescence: A psychosocial framework for understanding and action. *Developmental Review, 12,* 374-390.

Jessor, R., & Jessor, S. L. (1977). *Problem behavior and psychological development: A longitudinal study of youth.* New York: Academic Press.

Jhally, S. (1995). *Dreamworlds II.* Northhampton, MA: Media Education Foundation.

Jo, E., & Berkowitz, L. (1994). A priming effect analysis of media influences: An update. In J. Bryant & D. Zillmann (Eds.), *Media effects: Advances in theory and research* (pp. 43-60). Hillsdale, NJ: Lawrence Erlbaum.

Jobes, D. A., Berman, A. L., O'Carroll, P. W., Eastgard, S., & Knickmeyer, S. (1996). The Kurt Cobain suicide crisis: Perspectives from research, public health, and the news media. *Suicide and Life Threatening Behavior, 26,* 260-269.

John, D. R. (1999). Through the eyes of a child: Children's knowledge and understanding of advertising. In M. C. Macklin & L. Carlson (Eds.), *Advertising to children: Concepts and controversies* (pp. 3-26). Thousand Oaks, CA: Sage.

Johnson, J. D., Adams, M. S., Ashburn, L., & Reed, W. (1995). Differential gender effects of exposure to rap music in African American adolescents' acceptance of teen dating violence. *Sex Roles, 33,* 597-606.

Johnson, J. D., Jackson, L. A., & Gatto, L. (1995). Violent attitudes and deferred academic aspirations: Deleterious effects of exposure to rap music. *Basic & Applied Social Psychology, 16,* 27-41.

Johnson, S. (2001, March 24). The new MTV: Be very afraid. *Albuquerque Journal,* p. E27.

Johnston, C. (2001). Commercialism in classrooms. *Pediatrics, 107,* e44.

Johnston, D. D. (1995). Adolescents' motivations for viewing graphic horror. *Human Communication Research, 21*, 522-552.

Johnston, J., & Brzezinski, E. (1992). *Taking the measure of Channel One: The first year.* Ann Arbor: University of Michigan, Institute for Social Research.

Johnston, L. D., Bachman, J. G., & O'Malley, P. M. (1994). *National survey results on drug use from the Monitoring the Future Study, 1975-1993.* Washington, DC: National Institute on Drug Abuse.

Johnston, L. D., O'Malley, P. M., & Bachman, J. G. (2001). *Monitoring the Future: National results on adolescent drug use: Overview of key findings, 2001* (Press release). Ann Arbor: University of Michigan.

Jones, D. (1988, April 13). We rely on TV for AIDS information. *USA Today.*

Jones, E. F., Forrest, J. D., Goldman, N., Henshaw, S. K., Lincoln, R., Rosoff, J. I., Westoff, C. F., & Wulf, D. (1985). Teenage pregnancy in developed countries: Determinants and policy implications. *Family Planning Perspectives, 17*, 53-63.

Jones, E. F., Forrest, J. D., Henshaw, S. K., Silverman, J., & Torres, A. (1988). Unintended pregnancy, contraceptive practice and family planning services in developed countries. *Family Planning Perspectives, 20,* 53-67.

Jones, K. (1997). Are rap videos more violent? Style differences and the prevalence of sex and violence in the age of MTV. *Howard Journal of Communications, 8,* 343-356.

Jones, M. G. (1999). *What can we learn from computer games? Strategies for learner involvement.* Paper presented at the National Convention of the Association for Educational Communications and Technology, Houston, TX.

Jones, R. (2000). *Kids are target of Pokemon's shrewd marketing effort.* Retrieved May 25, 2001, from the World Wide Web: abcnews.go.com/sections/business/thestreet/pokemon_991117.html.

Jordan, A. (1998). *The 1998 state of children's television report: Programming for children over broadcast and cable television.* Philadelphia: Annenberg Public Policy Center.

Jordan, A. (2000). *Is the three-hour rule living up to its potential? An analysis of educational television for children in the 1999/2000 broadcast season.* Philadelphia: Annenberg Public Policy Center.

Jordan, A. (2001). Public policy and private practice. In D. G. Singer & J. L. Singer (Eds.), *Handbook of children and the media* (pp. 651-662). Thousand Oaks, CA: Sage.

Jordan, A. B., & Woodard, E. H., IV. (1998). Growing pains: Children's television in the new regulatory environment. *Annals of the American Academy of Political and Social Science, 557,* 83-95.

Jose, P. E., & Brewer, W. F. (1984). Development of story liking: Character identification, suspense, and outcome resolution. *Developmental Psychology, 20,* 911-924.

Josephson, W. L. (1987). Television violence and children's aggression: Testing the priming, social script, and disinhibition predictions. *Journal of Personality and Social Psychology, 53,* 882-890.

Journal Wire Reports. (2001, March 15). Advertising rose after tobacco suits. *Albuquerque Journal,* p. A4.

Kagan, J. (1997). Temperament and the reactions to unfamiliarity. *Child Development, 68,* 139-143.

Kail, R. (1990). *The development of memory in children* (3rd ed.). New York: W. H. Freeman.

Kail, R. (1991). Developmental changes in speed of processing during childhood and adolescence. *Psychological Bulletin, 109,* 490-501.

Kaiser Family Foundation. (1996). *The Kaiser Family Foundation survey on teens and sex: What they say teens today need to know, and who they listen to.* Menlo Park, CA: Author.

Kaiser Family Foundation. (1998). *Kaiser Family Foundation and YM Magazine national survey of teens: Teens talk about dating, intimacy, and their sexual experiences*. Menlo Park, CA: Author.

Kaiser Family Foundation. (1999a). *Kids and media at the new millennium*. Menlo Park, CA: Author.

Kaiser Family Foundation. (1999b). *National survey of public secondary school principals: The politics of sex education*. Menlo Park, CA: Author.

Kaiser Family Foundation. (2000a). *Teen sexual activity* (fact sheet). Menlo Park, CA: Author.

Kaiser Family Foundation. (2000b). *Teens and sex: The role of popular television* (fact sheet). Menlo Park, CA: Author.

Kaiser Family Foundation/Children Now. (1996). *The family hour focus groups: Children's responses to sexual content on TV and their parents' reactions*. Menlo Park, CA: Author.

Kaiser Family Foundation/Children Now. (1999). *Talking with kids about tough issues: A national survey of parents and kids*. Menlo Park, CA: Author.

Kalb, C. (2001, February 26). DARE checks into rehab. *Newsweek,* p. 56.

Kalichman, S. C., & Hunter, T. L. (1992). The disclosure of celebrity HIV infection: Its effects on public attitudes. *American Journal of Public Health, 82,* 1374-1376.

Kandakai, T. L., Price, J. H., Telljohann, S. K., & Wilson, C. A. (1999). Mothers' perceptions of factors influencing violence in schools. *Journal of School Health, 69,* 189-195.

Kappes, B. M., & Thompson, D. L. (1985). Biofeedback vs. video games: Effects on impulsivity, locus of control and self-concept with incarcerated individuals. *Journal of Clinical Psychology, 41,* 698-706.

Kasteleijn-Nolst Trenite, D. G. A. (1994). Video-game epilepsy. *The Lancet, 344,* 1102-1103.

Kasteleijn-Nolst Trenite, D. G. A., da Silva, A. M., Ricci, S., Binnie, C. D., Rubboli, G., Tassinari, C. A., & Segers, J. P. (1999). Video-game epilepsy: A European study. *Epilepsia, 40*(Suppl. 4), 70-74.

Kaufman, L. (1980). Prime-time nutrition. *Journal of Communication, 30,* 37-45.

Kaufmann, R. B., Spitz, A. M., Strauss, L. T., Morris, L., Santelli, J. S., Koonin, L. M., & Marks, J. S. (1998). The decline in US teen pregnancy rates, 1990-1995. *Pediatrics, 102,* 1141-1147.

Kaul, D. (1998, June 29). GOP called to task by one of its own. *Liberal Opinion Week,* p. 1.

Kegeles, S. M., Adler, N. E., & Irwin, C. E. (1988). Sexually active adolescents and condoms: Changes over one year in knowledge, attitude and use. *American Journal of Public Health, 78,* 460-461.

Keith, R. (2000, May 9). 2 retailers halt sale of violent video games. *Chicago Tribune,* p. A1.

Kelder, S. H., Maibach, E., Worden, J. K., Biglan, A., & Levitt, A. (2000). Planning and initiation of the ONDCP National Youth Anti-Drug Media Campaign. *Journal of Public Health Management and Practice, 6,* 14-26.

Kellerman, A. L., & Reay, D. T. (1986). Protection or peril? An analysis of firearm-related deaths in the home. *New England Journal of Medicine, 314,* 1557-1560.

Kellermann, A. L., Rivara, F. P., Rushforth, N. B., Banton, J. G., Reay, D. T., Francisco, J. T., Locci, A. B., Prodzinski, J., Hackman, B. B., & Somes, G. (1993). Gun ownership as a risk factor for homicide in the home. *New England Journal of Medicine, 329,* 1084-1091.

Kellermann, A. L., Somes, G., Rivara, F. P., Lee, R. K., & Banton, J. G. (1998). Injuries and deaths due to firearms in the home. *Journal of Trauma, Injury Infection and Critical Care, 45,* 263-267.

Kelly, M. A., & McGee, M. (1999). Report from a study tour: Teen sexuality education in the Netherlands, France, and Germany. *SIECUS Report, 27,* 11-14.

Kenrick, D. T., & Guttieres, S. E. (1980). Contrast effects and judgements of physical attractiveness: When beauty becomes a social problem. *Journal of Personality & Social Psychology, 38,* 131-140.

Kessler, D. (2001). *A question of intent: A great American battle with a deadly industry.* New York: PublicAffairs.

Kessler, D. A., Wilkenfeld, J. P., & Thompson, L. J. (1997). The Food and Drug Administration's rule on tobacco: Blending science and law. *Pediatrics, 99,* 884-887.

Kessler, L. (1989). Women's magazines coverage of smoking related health hazards. *Journalism Quarterly, 66,* 316-323.

Key, W. B. (1989). *The age of manipulation: The con in consciousness.* Lanham, MD: Madison.

Kilbourne, J. (1993). Killing us softly: Gender roles in advertising. *Adolescent Medicine: State of the Art Reviews, 4,* 635-649.

Kilbourne, J. (1999). *Deadly persuasion: Why women and girls must fight the addictive power of advertising.* New York: Free Press.

Kilbourne, J. E., Painton, S., & Ridley, D. (1985). The effect of sexual embedding on responses to magazine advertisements. *Journal of Advertising, 14,* 48-56.

King, C., III, Siegel, M., Celebucki, C., & Connolly, G. N. (1998). Adolescent exposure to cigarette advertising in magazines. *Journal of the American Medical Association, 279,* 516-520.

King, N., Touyz, S., & Charles, M. (2000). The effect of body dissatisfaction on women's perceptions of female celebrities. *International Journal of Eating Disorders, 27,* 341-347.

King, P. (1988). Heavy metal music and drug abuse in adolescents. *Postgraduate Medicine, 83,* 295-302.

Kirby, D. (1997). *No easy answers: Research findings on programs to reduce teen pregnancy.* Washington, DC: National Campaign to Prevent Teen Pregnancy.

Kirby, D., Brener, N. D., Brown, N. L., Peterfreund, N., Hillard, P., & Harrist, R. (1999). The impact of condom distribution in Seattle schools on sexual behavior and condom use. *American Journal of Public Health, 89,* 182-187.

Kirsh, S. J. (1998). Seeing the world through Mortal Kombat-colored glasses: Violent video games and the development of a short-term hostile attribution bias. *Childhood, 5,* 177-184.

Klein, J. D., Brown, J. D., Childers, K. W., Oliveri, J., Porter, C., & Dykers, C. (1993). Adolescents' risky behavior and mass media use. *Pediatrics, 92,* 24-31.

Klesges, R. C., Shelton, M. L., & Klesges, L. M. (1993). Effects of television on metabolic rate: Potential implications for childhood obesity. *Pediatrics, 91,* 281-286.

Kline, S. (1993). *Out of the garden: Toys, TV, and children's culture in the age of marketing.* New York: Verso.

Klitzner, M., Gruenewald, P. J., & Bamberger, E. (1991). Cigarette advertising and adolescent experimentation with smoking. *British Journal of Addiction, 86,* 287-298.

Knupfer, N., & Hayes, P. (1994). The effects of the Channel One broadcast on students' knowledge of current events. In A. DeVaney (Ed.), *Watching Channel One* (pp. 42-60). Albany, NY: SUNY.

Kohl, H. W., III, & Hobbs, K. E. (1998). Development of physical activity behaviors among children and adolescents. *Pediatrics, 101*(Suppl.), 549-554.

Kohn, P. M., & Smart, R. G. (1984). The impact of television advertising on alcohol consumption: An experiment. *Journal of Studies on Alcohol, 45,* 295-301.

Kohn, P. M., & Smart, R. G. (1987). Wine, women, suspiciousness and advertising. *Journal of Studies on Alcohol, 48,* 161-166.

Kopel, D. B. (1993). Japanese gun control. *Asia Pacific Law Review, 2*(2), 26-52. Retrieved June 16, 2001, from the World Wide Web: www.2ndlawlib.com/journals/dkjgc.html.

Koplan, J. P., & Dietz, W. H. (1999). Caloric imbalance and public health policy. *Journal of the American Medical Association, 282,* 1579-1581.

Kosterman, R., Hawkins, J. D., Guo, J., Catalano, R. F., & Abbott, R. D. (2000). The dynamics of alcohol and marijuana initiation: Patterns and predictors of first use in adolescence. *American Journal of Public Health, 90,* 360-366.

Kostinsky, S., Bixler, E. O., & Kettl, P. A. (2001). Threats of school violence in Pennsylvania after media coverage of the Columbine High School massacre. *Archives of Pediatrics and Adolescent Medicine, 155,* 994-1001.

Kotz, K., & Story, M. (1994). Food advertisements during children's Saturday morning television programming: Are they consistent with dietary recommendations? *Journal of the American Dietetic Association, 94,* 1296-1300.

Krayeske, K. (1999). Branded! Americans are losing their identities to marketing mania. *Hartford Advocate* [Online]. Available: www.hartfordadvocate.com/articles/branded.html.

Krcmar, M., & Greene, K. (1999). Predicting exposure to and uses of television violence. *Journal of Communication, 49,* 24-45.

Krichevets, A. N., Sirotkina, E. B., Yevsevicheva, I. V., & Zeldin, L. M. (1995). Computer games as a means of movement rehabilitation. *Disability and Rehabilitation, 17,* 100-105.

Krowchuk, D. P., Kreiter, S. R., Woods, C. R., Sinal, S. H., & DuRant, R. H. (1998). Problem dieting behaviors among young adolescents. *Archives of Pediatrics & Adolescent Medicine, 152,* 884-888.

Krugman, D. M., Cameron, G. T., & White, C. M. (1995). Visual attention to programming and commercials: The use of in-home observations. *Journal of Advertising, 24*(1), 1-12.

Ku, L., Sonenstein, F. L., & Pleck, J. H. (1993). Young men's risk behaviors for HIV infection and sexually transmitted diseases, 1988 through 1991. *American Journal of Public Health, 83,* 1609-1615.

Kubey, R. (1996). Television dependence, diagnosis, and prevention. In T. M. Macbeth (Ed.), *Tuning in to young viewers: Social science perspectives* (pp. 221-260). Thousand Oaks, CA: Sage.

Kubey, R., & Baker, F. (1999). Has media literacy found a curricular foothold? *Education Week, 19,* 38, 56.

Kubey, R., & Csikszentmihalyi, M. (1990). *Television and the quality of life.* Hillsdale, NJ: Lawrence Erlbaum.

Kunkel, D. (1988). Children and host-selling television commercials. *Communication Research, 15,* 71-92.

Kunkel, D. (1998). Policy battles over defining children's educational television. *Annals of the American Academy of Political and Social Science, 557,* 39-53.

Kunkel, D. (2001). Children and television advertising. In D. G. Singer & J. L. Singer (Eds.), *Handbook of children and the media* (pp. 375-393). Thousand Oaks, CA: Sage.

Kunkel, D., Cope, K. M., & Biely, E. (1999). Sexual messages on television: Comparing findings from three studies. *Journal of Sex Research, 36,* 230-236.

Kunkel, D., Cope, K. M., & Colvin, C. (1996). *Sexual messages on family hour television: Content and context.* Menlo Park, CA: Kaiser Family Foundation.

Kunkel, D., Cope, K. M., Farinola, W. J. M., Biely, E., Rollin, E., & Donnerstein, E. (1999). *Sex on TV: A biennial report to the Kaiser Family Foundation.* Santa Barbara: University of California, Santa Barbara.

Kunkel, D., Cope-Farrar, K. M., Biely, E., Farinola, W. J. M., & Donnerstein, E. (2001). *Sex on TV: A biennial report to the Kaiser Family Foundation*. Santa Barbara: University of California, Santa Barbara.

Kunkel, D., Farinola, W. J. M., Cope, K. M., Donnerstein, E., Biely, E., & Zwarun, L. (1998). *Rating the TV ratings: One year out*. Menlo Park, CA: Kaiser Family Foundation.

Kunkel, D., & Gantz, W. (1991). *Television advertising to children: Message content in 1990*. Report to the Children's Advertising Review Unit of the National Advertising Division, Council of Better Business Bureaus, Indiana University, Bloomington.

Kunkel, D., & Gantz, W. (1992). Children's television advertising in the multichannel environment. *Journal of Communication, 42*(3), 134-152.

Kunkel, D., & Gantz, W. (1993). Assessing compliance with industry self-regulation of television advertising to children. *Journal of Applied Communication Research, 21,* 148-162.

Kunkel, D., & Roberts, D. (1991). Young minds and marketplace values: Issues in children's advertising. *Journal of Social Issues, 47,* 57 72.

Kunkel, D., & Watkins, B. (1987). Evolution of children's television regulatory policy. *Journal of Broadcasting & Electronic Media, 31,* 367-389.

Kunkel, D., & Wilcox, B. (2001). Children and media policy. In D. G. Singer & J. L. Singer (Eds.), *Handbook of children and the media* (pp. 589-604). Thousand Oaks, CA: Sage.

Kurtz, M. E., Kurtz, J. C., Johnson, S. M., & Cooper, W. (2001). Sources of information on the health effects of environmental tobacco smoke among African-American children and adolescents. *Journal of Adolescent Health, 28,* 458-464.

Lacayo, R. (1995, June 12). Violent reaction. *Time, 145,* 24-28.

Lacey, M. (2000, January 16). Federal script approval. *New York Times,* p. A1.

Landry, D. J., Kaeser, L., & Richards, C. L. (1999). Abstinence promotion and the provision of information about contraception in public school strict sexuality education policies. *Family Planning Perspectives, 31,* 280-286.

Lang, A. (2000). The limited capacity model of mediated message processing. *Journal of Communication, 50*(1), 46-70.

Larson, M. S. (1996). Sex roles and soap operas: What adolescents learn about single motherhood. *Sex Roles, 35,* 97-110.

Larson, M. S. (2001). Interactions, activities and gender in children's television commercials: A content analysis. *Journal of Broadcasting & Electronic Media, 45,* 41-56.

Larson, R., & Kubey, R. (1983). Television and music: Contrasting media in adolescent life. *Youth & Society, 15,* 13-31.

Larson, R., Kubey, R., & Colletti, J. (1989). Changing channels: Early adolescent media choices and shifting investments in family and friends. *Journal of Youth and Adolescence, 18,* 583-599.

Larson, R., Richards, M. H., Moneta, G., Holmbeck, G., & Duckett, E. (1996). Changes in adolescents' daily interactions with their families from ages 10 to 18: Disengagement and transformation. *Developmental Psychology, 32,* 744-754.

Laugesen, M., & Meads, C. (1991). Tobacco advertising restrictions, price, income and tobacco consumption in OECD countries, 1960-1986. *British Journal of Addiction, 86,* 1343-1354.

Laumann, E. O., Paik, A., & Rosen, R. C. (1999). Sexual dysfunction in the United States. *Journal of the American Medical Association, 281,* 537-544.

Lauro, P. W. (1999, November 1). Coaxing the smile that sells; Baby wranglers in demand in marketing for children. *New York Times,* p. C1.

Lavine, H., Sweeney, D., & Wagner, S. H. (1999). Depicting women as sex objects in television advertising: Effects on body dissatisfaction. *Personality & Social Psychology Bulletin, 25,* 1049-1058.

LaVoie, J., & Collins, B. (1975). Effects of youth culture music on high school students' academic performance. *Journal of Youth and Adolescence, 4,* 57-65.

Lazarus, R. S., & Alfert, E. (1964). Short-circuiting of threat by experimentally altering cognitive appraisal. *Journal of Abnormal & Social Psychology, 69,* 195-205.

LeDuc, D. (2001, February 21). Legislators urge ban on ads in Md. schools. *Washington Post,* p. B1.

Lee, E. B., & Browne, L. A. (1995). Effects of television advertising on African American teenagers. *Journal of Black Studies, 25,* 523-536.

Lefkowitz, M. M., Eron, L. D., Walder, L. O., & Huesmann, L. R. (1972). Television violence and child aggression: A follow-up study. In G. A. Comstock & E. A. Rubinstein (Eds.), *Television and social behavior: Vol. 3. Television and adolescent aggressiveness* (pp. 33-135). Washington, DC: Government Printing Office.

Leiber, L. (1996). *Commercial and character slogan recall by children aged 9 to 11 years: Budweiser frogs versus Bugs Bunny.* Berkeley, CA: Center on Alcohol Advertising.

Leiss, W., Kline, S., & Jhally, S. (1990). *Social communication in advertising.* Scarborough, Ontario: Routledge Kegan Paul.

Leland, J. (1992, June 29). Rap and rage. *Newsweek,* pp. 46-52.

Leland, J. (1993, November 29). Criminal records: Gangsta rap and the culture of violence. *Newsweek,* pp. 60-64.

Leming, J. (1987). Rock music and the socialization of moral values in early adolescence. *Youth & Society, 18,* 363-383.

Lemish, D. (1987). Viewers in diapers: The early development of television viewing. In T. R. Lindlof (Ed.), *Natural audiences: Qualitative research of media uses and effects* (pp. 33-57). Norwood, NJ: Ablex.

Leo, J. (1993, October 20). '90s advertisements portray women with "attitude." *Albuquerque Journal,* p. A11.

Leo, J. (1998, February 2). Raging hormones on TV. *U.S. News & World Report,* p. 9.

Levin, S. R., Petros, T. V., & Petrella, F. W. (1982). Preschoolers' awareness of television advertising. *Child Development, 53,* 933-937.

Levine, M. P. (2000). Mass media and body image: A brief review of the research. *Health Weight Journal, 14,* 84-85, 95.

Levine, M. P., Piran, N., & Stoddard, C. (1999). Mission more probable: Media literacy, activism, and advocacy as primary prevention. In N. Piran, M. P. Levine, & C. Steiner-Adair (Eds.), *Preventing eating disorders: A handbook of interventions and special challenges* (pp. 3-25). Philadelphia: Brunner/Mazel.

Levine, M. P., & Smolak, L. (1996). Media as a context for the development of disordered eating. In L. Smolak, M. P. Levine, & R. Striegel-Moore (Eds.), *The developmental psychopathology of eating disorders* (pp. 235-257). Mahwah, NJ: Lawrence Erlbaum.

Levine, M. P., & Smolak, L. (1998). The mass media and disordered eating: Implications for primary prevention. In W. Vandereycken & G. Noordenbos (Eds.), *The prevention of eating disorders* (pp. 23-56). London: Athlone.

Levine, M. P., & Smolak, L. (2001). Primary prevention of body image disturbances and disordered eating in childhood and early adolescence. In J. K. Thompson & L. Smolak (Eds.), *Body image, eating disorders, and obesity in childhood and adolescence* (pp. 237-260). Washington, DC: American Psychological Association.

Levine, M. P., Smolak, L., & Hayden, H. (1994). The relation of sociocultural factors to eating attitudes and behaviors among middle school girls. *Journal of Early Adolescence, 14,* 471-490.

Levine, M. P., Smolak, L., Moodey, A. F., Shuman, M. D., & Hessen, L. D. (1994). Normative developmental challenges and dieting and eating disturbances in middle school girls. *International Journal of Eating Disorders, 15,* 11-20.

Lewis, M. K., & Hill, A. J. (1998). Food advertising on British children's television: A content analysis and experimental study with nine-year-olds. *International Journal of Obesity and Related Metabolic Disorders, 22,* 206-214.

LH Research, Inc. (1993). *A survey of experiences, perceptions, and apprehensions about guns among young people in America.* Report of the Harvard School of Public Health under a grant from the Joyce Foundation.

Liebert, D. E., Sprafkin, J. N., Liebert, R. M., & Rubinstein, E. A. (1977). Effects of television commercial disclaimers on the product expectations of children. *Journal of Communication, 27*(1), 118-124.

Liebert, R. M., & Sprafkin, J. (1988). *The early window: Effects of television on children and youth* (3rd ed.). New York: Pergamon.

Lies, E. (2001, June 8). *Random violence on the rise in Japan.* Retrieved June 16, 2001, from CBS News on the World Wide Web: cbsnews.com/now/story/0%2c1597%2c295560-412%2c00.html.

Linz, D., & Donnerstein E. (1988). The methods and merits of pornography research. *Journal of Communication, 38,* 180-184.

Linz, D., Donnerstein, E., & Penrod, S. (1984). The effects of multiple exposures to filmed violence against women. *Journal of Communication, 34,* 130-147.

Linz, D., Donnerstein, E., & Penrod, S. (1988). Effects of long-term exposure to violent and sexually degrading depictions of women. *Journal of Personality & Social Psychology, 55,* 758-768.

Linz, D., & Malamuth, N. (1993). *Pornography.* Newbury Park, CA: Sage.

Lipman, J. (1991, August 21). Alcohol firms put off public. *Wall Street Journal,* p. B1.

Liss, M. B., Reinhardt, L. C., & Fredriksen, S. (1983). TV heroes: The impact of rhetoric and deeds. *Journal of Applied Developmental Psychology, 4,* 175-187.

Livingstone, S., Holden, K. J., & Bovill, M. (1999). Children's changing media environment: Overview of a European comparative study. In C. von Feilitzen & U. Carlsson (Eds.), *Children and media: Image, education, participation* (pp. 39-59). Goteborg, Sweden: UNESCO International Clearinghouse on Children and Violence on the Screen.

Livni, E. (2000). *Selling teens on truth* [Online]. Retrieved October 23, 2000, from the World Wide Web: abcnews.com.

Locard, E., Mamelle, N., Billette, A., Miginiac, M., Munoz, F., & Rey, S. (1992). Risk factors of obesity in a five-year-old population: Parental versus environmental factors. *International Journal of Obesity and Related Metabolic Disorders, 16,* 721-729.

Loewenson, P. R., & Blum, R. W. (2001). The resilient adolescent: Implications for the pediatrician. *Pediatric Annals, 30,* 76-80.

Logan, M. (2000, March 4). Daycamp. *TV Guide,* pp. 35-37.

Lorch, E. P., Bellack, D. R., & Augsbach, L. H. (1987). Young children's memory for televised stories: Effects of importance. *Child Development, 58,* 453-463.

Lovaas, O. I. (1961). Effect of exposure to symbolic aggression on aggressive behavior. *Child Development, 32,* 37-44.

Lovett, S. B., & Flavell, J. H. (1990). Understanding and remembering: Children's knowledge about the differential effects of strategy and task variables on comprehension and memorization. *Child Development, 61,* 1842-1858.

Lowe, P., & Durkin, K. (1999). The effect of flashback on children's understanding of television on crime content. *Journal of Broadcasting & Electronic Media, 43,* 83-97.

Lowery, S. A. (1980). Soap and booze in the afternoon: An analysis of the portrayal of alcohol use in daytime serials. *Journal of Studies on Alcohol, 41,* 829-838.

Lowry, B. (1997, September 21). The times poll: TV on decline, but few back U.S. regulation. *Los Angeles Times,* p. A1.

Lowry, D. T., Love, G., & Kirby, M. (1987). Sex on the soap operas: Patterns of intimacy. *Journal of Communication, 31,* 90-96.

Lowry, D. T., & Shidler, J. A. (1993). Prime time TV portrayals of sex, "safe sex" and AIDS: A longitudinal analysis. *Journalism Quarterly, 70,* 628-637.

Lowry, D. T., & Towles, D. E. (1989). Soap opera portrayals of sex, contraception, and sexually transmitted diseases. *Journal of Communication, 39*(2), 76-83.

Ludwig, D. S., Peterson, K. E., & Gortmaker, S. L. (2001). Relation between consumption of sugar-sweetened drinks and childhood obesity: A prospective, observational analysis. *Lancet, 357,* 505-508.

Lull, J. (1987). Listeners' communicative uses of popular music. In J. Lull (Ed.), *Popular music and communication* (pp. 140-174). Newbury Park, CA: Sage.

Lyons, J. S., Anderson, R. L., & Larson, D. B. (1994). A systematic review of the effects of aggressive and nonaggressive pornography. In D. Zillmann, J. Bryant, & A. C. Huston (Eds.), *Media, children, and the family: Social scientific, psychodynamic, and clinical perspectives* (pp. 271-310). Hillsdale, NJ: Lawrence Erlbaum.

Mackay, J. (1999). International aspects of US government tobacco bills. *Journal of the American Medical Association, 281,* 1849-1850.

MacKenzie, R. G. (1993). Influence of drug use on adolescent sexual activity. *Adolescent Medicine: State of the Art Reviews, 4,* 417-422.

MacKenzie, T. D., Bartecchi, C. E., & Schrier, R. W. (1994). The human costs of tobacco use: Part 2. *New England Journal of Medicine, 30,* 975-980.

Macklin, M. C. (1985). Do young children understand the selling intent of commercials? *Journal of Consumer Affairs, 19,* 293-304.

Macklin, M. C. (1987). Preschoolers' understanding of the informational function of television advertising. *Journal of Consumer Research, 14,* 229-239.

Macklin, M. C., & Carlson, L. (Eds.). (1999). *Advertising to children: Concepts and controversies.* Thousand Oaks, CA: Sage.

MacNeil, R. (1983). Is television shortening our attention span? *New York University Education Quarterly, 14,* 2.

Madden, P. A., & Grube, J. W. (1994). The frequency and nature of alcohol and tobacco advertising in televised sports, 1990 through 1992. *American Journal of Public Health, 84,* 297-299.

Maeda, Y., Kurokawa, T., Sakamoto, K., Kitamoto, I., Ueda, K., & Tashima, S. (1990). Electroclinical study of video-game epilepsy. *Developmental Medicine and Child Neurology, 32,* 493-500.

Malamuth, N. (1993). Pornography's impact on male adolescents. *Adolescent Medicine: State of the Art Reviews, 4,* 563-576.

Malamuth, N., & Impett, E. A. (2001). Research on sex in the media. In D. G. Singer & J. L. Singer (Eds.), *Handbook of children and the media* (pp. 269-287). Thousand Oaks, CA: Sage.

Males, M. (1999). *Smoked: Why big tobacco is still smiling*. Monroe, ME: Common Courage Press.

Maloney, M. J., McGuire, J., Daniels, S. R., & Specker, B. (1989). Dieting behavior and eating attitudes in children. *Pediatrics, 84,* 482-489.

Mander, G. (1978). *Four arguments for the elimination of television*. New York: Quill.

Mandler, J. M. (1998). Representation. In D. Kuhn & R. S. Siegler (Eds.), *Handbook of child psychology: Vol. 2. Cognition, perception, and language* (5th ed., pp. 255-308). New York: John Wiley.

Mangleburg, T. F., & Bristol, T. (1999). Socialization and adolescents' skepticism toward advertising. In M. C. Macklin & L. Carlson (Eds.), *Advertising to children: Concepts and controversies* (pp. 27-48). Thousand Oaks, CA: Sage.

Manning, S. (1999). Students for sale: How corporations are buying their way into America's classrooms. *The Nation, 269,* 11-18.

Mares, M., & Woodard, E. H. (2001). Prosocial effects on children's social interactions. In D. G. Singer & J. L. Singer (Eds.), *Handbook of children and the media* (pp. 183-205). Thousand Oaks, CA: Sage.

MarketResearch.com. (2001). *Internet advertising skyrockets*. Retrieved June 1, 2001, from the World Wide Web: preview.marketresearch.com/info/com.marketresearh_reports_275889.html.

Marsh, D. (1993). *Louie Louie*. New York: Hyperion.

Marshall, E. (1991). Sullivan overrules NIH on sex survey. *Science, 253,* 502.

Marsiglio, W., & Mott, F. L. (1986). The impact of sex education on sexual activity, contraceptive use and premarital pregnancy among American teenagers. *Family Planning Perspectives, 18,* 151-161.

Martin, J. R., Sklar, D. P., & McFeeley, P. (1991). Accidental firearm fatalities among New Mexico children. *Annals of Emergency Medicine, 20,* 58-61.

Martin, M. C. (1997). Children's understanding of the intent of advertising: A meta-analysis. *Journal of Public Policy & Marketing, 16,* 205-216.

Martin, M. C., & Gentry, J. W. (1997). Stuck in the model trap: The effects of beautiful models in ads on female pre-adolescents and adolescents. *Journal of Advertising, 26,* 19-33.

Martin, M. C., & Kennedy, P. F. (1993). Advertising and social comparison: Consequences for female pre-adolescents and adolescents. *Psychology & Marketing, 10,* 513-530.

Martin, M. C., & Kennedy, P. F. (1994). Social comparison and the beauty of advertising models: The role of motives for comparison. *Advances in Consumer Research, 21,* 365-371.

Massing, M. (1998, March 22). Why beer won't go up in smoke. *New York Times Magazine,* pp. 36-41, 48, 58, 72-73.

Mathios, A., Avery, R., Bisogni, C., & Shanahan, J. (1998). Alcohol portrayal on prime-time television: Manifest and latent messages. *Journal of Studies on Alcohol, 59,* 305-310.

McCall, R. B., Parke, R. D., & Kavanaugh, R. D. (1977). Imitation of live and televised models by children one to three years of age. *Monographs of the Society for Research in Child Development, 42,* 94.

McCannon, B. (1996). *Just do media literacy: Students, experts, issues, and examples*. Albuquerque: New Mexico Media Literacy Project. [Video]

McCannon, B. (1998). *Understanding media*. Albuquerque: New Mexico Media Literacy Project.

McCannon, B., & Hizel, E. (1995). *Media literacy: Introductory concepts, resources and activities*. Albuquerque: New Mexico Media Literacy Project.

McCannon, B., & Williams, R. (1997). *Media literacy: The language of persuasion*. Albuquerque: New Mexico Media Literacy Project.

McChesney, R. W. (1994). *Telecommunications, mass media, and democracy: The battle for the control of U.S. broadcasting, 1928-1935*. New York: Oxford University Press.

McChesney, R. W. (1997). *Corporate media and the threat to democracy*. New York: Seven Stories Press.

McChesney, R. W. (1999). *Rich media, poor democracy*. Urbana: University of Illinois Press.

McGinnis, J. M. (1992). The public health burden of a sedentary lifestyle. *Medical Science and Sports Exercise, 24,* S196-S200.

McIntosh, W. D., Bazzini, D. G., Smith, S. M., & Wayne, S. M. (1998). Who smokes in Hollywood? Characteristics of smokers in popular films from 1940 to 1989. *Addictive Behavior, 23,* 395-398.

McIntyre, J. J., & Teevan, J. J., Jr. (1972). Television violence and deviant behavior. In G. A. Comstock & E. A. Rubinstein (Eds.), *Television and social behavior: Vol. 3. Television and adolescent aggressiveness* (pp. 383-435). Washington, DC: Government Printing Office.

McKeganey, N., Forsyth, A., Barnard, M., & Hay, G. (1996). Designer drinks and drunkenness amongst a sample of Scottish schoolchildren. *British Medical Journal, 313,* 401.

McKibben, B. (1992). *The age of missing information*. New York: Plume.

McLeod, J. M., Atkin, C. K., & Chaffee, S. H. (1972a). Adolescents, parents, and television use: Adolescent self-report measures from Maryland and Wisconsin samples. In G. A. Comstock & E. A. Rubinstein (Eds.), *Television and social behavior: Vol. 3. Television and adolescent aggressiveness* (pp. 173-238). Washington, DC: Government Printing Office.

McLeod, J. M., Atkin, C. K., & Chaffee, S. H. (1972b). Self-report and other-report measures from the Wisconsin sample. In G. A. Comstock & E. A. Rubinstein (Eds.), *Television and social behavior: Vol. 3. Television and adolescent aggressiveness* (pp. 239-313). Washington, DC: Government Printing Office.

McMahon, R. L. (1994). Diagnosis, assessment and treatment of externalizing problems in children: The role of longitudinal data. *Journal of Consulting & Clinical Psychology, 62,* 901-917.

McNeal, J. U. (1998). Tapping the three kids' markets. *American Demographics, 20*(4), 36-41.

McNeal, J. U. (1999). *The kids' market: Myths and realities*. Ithaca, NY: Paramount Market.

Meadowcroft, J. M., & Reeves, B. (1989). Influence of story scheme development on children's attention to television. *Communication Research, 16,* 352-374.

Mediascope. (2000a). *Violence, women, and the media*. Studio City, CA: Author.

Mediascope. (2000b). *Youth and violent music*. Studio City, CA: Author.

Medved, M. (1992). *Hollywood vs. America: Popular culture and the war on traditional values*. New York: HarperCollins.

Medved, M. (1995). *Protecting our children from a plague of pessimism*. Hillsdale, NY: Imprimis.

Melkman, R., Tversky, B., & Baratz, D. (1981). Developmental trends in the use of perceptual and conceptual attributes in grouping, clustering, and retrieval. *Journal of Experimental Child Development, 31,* 470-486.

Meltzoff, A. N. (1988). Imitation of televised models by infants. *Child Development, 59,* 1221-1229.

Merckelbach, H., Muris, P., & Rassin, E. (1999). Fantasy proneness and cognitive failures as correlates of dissociative experiences. *Personality and Individual Differences, 26,* 961-967.

Merzenich, M. M., Jenkins, W. M., Johnston, P., Schreiner, C., Miller, S. L., & Tallal, P. (1996). Temporal processing deficits of language-learning impaired children ameliorated by training. *Science, 271,* 77-81.

Metcalfe, J., & Shimamura, A. P. (Eds.). (1994). *Metacognition: Knowing about knowing.* Cambridge: MIT Press.

Meyer, M., & Tsiantar, D. (1994, August 8). Ninja turtles, eat our dust. *Newsweek,* pp. 34-35.

Meyrowitz, J. (1985). *No sense of place: The impact of electronic media on social behavior.* New York: Oxford University Press.

Milavsky, J. R., Kessler, R., Stipp, H. H., & Rubens, W. S. (1982). *Television and aggression: A panel study.* New York: Academic Press.

Miles, D. R., & Carey, G. (1997). Genetic and environmental architecture on human aggression. *Journal of Personality & Social Psychology, 72,* 207-217.

Miller, F. C. (2000). Impact of adolescent pregnancy as we approach the new millenium. *Journal of Pediatric and Adolescent Gynecology, 13,* 5-8.

Miller, J. H., & Busch, P. (1979). Host selling vs. premium TV commercials: An experimental evaluation of their influence on children. *Journal of Marketing Research, 16,* 323-332.

Miller, M. C. (1988). *Boxed in: The culture of TV.* Evanston, IL: Northwestern University Press.

Miller, P., & Plant, M. (1996). Drinking, smoking and illicit drug use among 15 and 16 year olds in the United Kingdom. *British Medical Journal, 313,* 394-397.

Millett, C. J., Fish, D. R., & Thompson, P. J. (1997). A survey of epilepsy-patient perceptions of video-game material/electronic screens and other factors as seizure precipitants. *Seizure, 6,* 457-459.

Millett, C. J., Fish, D. R., Thompson, P. J., & Johnson, A. (1999). Seizures during video-game play and other common leisure pursuits in known epilepsy patients without visual sensitivity. *Epilepsia, 40*(Suppl. 4), 59-64.

Minow, N. N. (1995). *Abandoned in the wasteland: Children, television and the First Amendment.* New York: Hill & Wang.

Mokdad, A. H., Serdula, M. K., Dietz, W. H., Bowman, B. A., Marks, J. S., & Koplan, J. P. (1999). The spread of the obesity epidemic in the United States, 1991-1998. *Journal of the American Medical Association, 282,* 1519-1522.

Molitor, F., & Hirsch, K. W. (1994). Children's toleration of real-life aggression after exposure to media violence: A replication of the Drabman and Thomas studies. *Child Study Journal, 24,* 191-207.

Molnar, A. (1996). *Giving kids the business: The commercialization of America's schools.* Boulder, CO: Westview.

Molnar, A., & Morales, J. (2000). *Commercialism@schools.com: The third annual report on trends in schoolhouse commercialism* [Online]. Available: www.uwm.edu/ Dept/CACE/ documents/cace02-execsum.htm. Accessed January 6, 2001.

Mom says MTV's "Beavis" led son to start fatal fire. (1993, October 17). *Albuquerque Journal.*

Moneta, G. B., & Csikszentmihalyi, M. (1996). The effect of perceived challenges and skills on the quality of subjective experience. *Journal of Personality, 64,* 275-310.

Moneta, G. B., & Csikszentmihalyi, M. (1999). Models of concentration in natural environments: A comparative approach based on streams of experiential data. *Social Behavior and Personality, 27,* 603-638.

Montgomery, K. C. (2000). Children's media culture. In Packard Foundation (Ed.), *The future of children: Children and computer technology* (pp. 145-167). Los Altos, CA: Packard Foundation.

Moog, C. (1991). The selling of addiction to women. *Media & Values, 54/55,* 20-22.

Moore, R. L., & Stephens, L. F. (1975). Some communication and demographic determinants of adolescent consumer learning. *Journal of Communication, 29,* 197-201.

Moran, T. (1985, August 12-19). Sounds of sex. *The New Republic,* pp. 14-16.

Moreno, L. A., Fleta, J., & Mur, L. (1998). Television watching and fatness in children (letter). *Journal of the American Medical Association, 280,* 1230-1231.

Morgan, M. (1987). Television, sex role attitudes, and sex role behavior. *Journal of Early Adolescence, 7,* 269-282.

Morgan, M., & Shanahan, J. (1996). Two decades of cultivation research: An appraisal and meta-analysis. In B. R. Burleson (Ed.), *Communication yearbook* (Vol. 20, pp. 1-45). Newbury Park, CA: Sage.

Morrison, P., Kelly, H., & Gardner, H. (1981). Reasoning about the realities of television: A developmental study. *Journal of Broadcasting, 25,* 229-242.

Moschis, G. P. (1978). Teenagers' responses to retailing stimuli. *Journal of Retailing, 54,* 80-93.

Moschis, G. P., & Churchill, G. A. (1978). Consumer socialization: A theoretical and empirical analysis. *Journal of Marketing Research, 15,* 599-609.

Moschis, G. P., & Moore, R. L. (1979). Decision making among the young: A socialization perspective. *Journal of Consumer Research, 6,* 101-112.

Moschis, G. P., & Moore, R. L. (1982). A longitudinal study of television advertising effects. *Journal of Consumer Research, 9,* 279-286.

Moses, N., Banilivy, M. M., & Lifshitz, F. (1989). Fear of obesity among adolescent girls. *Pediatrics, 83,* 393-398.

Mozes, A. (2001, June 19). US TV viewers find condom ads acceptable. *Reuters Health* [Online]. Retrieved June 20, 2001, from the World Wide Web: www.reutershealth.com.

Muehling, D. D., & Kolbe, R. H. (1999). A comparison of children's and prime-time fine-print advertising disclosure practices. In M. C. Macklin & L. Carlson (Eds.), *Advertising to children: Concepts and controversies* (pp. 143-164). Thousand Oaks, CA: Sage.

Mullen, B. (1989). *Advanced basic meta analysis.* Hillsdale, NJ: Lawrence Erlbaum.

Mullin, C. R., & Linz, D. (1995). Desensitization and resensitization to violence against women: Effects of exposure to sexually violent films on judgments of domestic violence victims. *Journal of Personality & Social Psychology, 69,* 449-459.

Mulvey, L. (1975). Visual pleasure and narrative cinema. *Screen, 16,* 198-209.

Munoz, K. A., Krebs-Smith, S. M., Ballard-Barbash, R., & Cleveland, G. E. (1997). Food intakes of U.S. children and adolescents compared with recommendations. *Pediatrics, 100,* 323-329.

Murchek, P. (1994, January 6). Dear Abby: Reduce abortion need. *Albuquerque Journal,* p. B2.

Murphy, B. C., Eisenberg, N., Fabes, R. A., Shepard, S., & Guthrie, I. K. (1999). Consistency and change in children's emotionality and regulation: A longitudinal study. *Merrill-Palmer Quarterly, 45,* 413-444.

Murphy, J., Stoney, C. M., Alpert, B. S., & Walker, S. S. (1995). Gender and ethnicity in children's cardiovascular reactivity: Seven years of study. *Health Psychology, 14,* 48-55.

Murphy, J., & Tucker, K. (1996). *Stay tuned!* New York: Doubleday.

Murray, S. H., Touyz, S. W., & Beumont, P. J. V. (1996). Awareness and perceived influence of body ideals in the media: A comparison of eating disorder patients and the general community. *Eating Disorders: The Journal of Treatment and Prevention, 4,* 33-46.

Murrow, E. R. (1958, November 13). A broadcaster talks to his colleagues. *The Reporter,* p. 12.

Musante, L., Turner, R., Treiber, F. A., Davis, H., & Strong, W. B. (1996). Moderators of ethnic differences in vasoconstrictive reactivity in youth. *Ethnicity and Disease, 6,* 224-234.

Must, A., Spadano, J., Coakley, E. H., Field, A. E., Colditz, G., & Dietz, W. H. (1999). The disease burden associated with overweight and obesity. *Journal of the American Medical Association, 282,* 1523-1529.

Myers, L., Strikmiller, P. K., Webber, L. S., & Berenson, G. S. (1996). Physical and sedentary activity in school children Grades 5-8: The Bogalusa Heart Study. *Medicine and Science in Sports and Exercise, 28,* 852-859.

Myers, P. N., & Biocca, F. A. (1992). The elastic body image: The effect of television advertising programming on body image distortions in young women. *Journal of Communication, 42*(3), 108-133.

Nader, R. (2000, June). *Green Party presidential nomination acceptance speech* [Online]. Available: votenader.com/press/000625acceptance_speech.html.

Nagourney, A. (2000, September 27). Mrs. Clinton proposes ban on ads for young children. *New York Times,* p. B5.

Naisbitt, J., Naisbitt, N., & Philips, D. (1999). *High tech, high touch: Technology and our search for meaning.* New York: Broadway.

Nansel, T. R., Overpeck, M., Pilla, R. S., Ruan, W. J., Simons-Morton, B., & Scheidt, P. (2001). Bullying behaviors among US youth: Prevalence and association with psychosocial adjustment. *Journal of the American Medical Association, 285,* 2094-2100.

Nashawaty, C. (1999, July 16). Pie in your face. *Entertainment Weekly,* pp. 26-28.

National Association of Broadcasters (NAB). (2000). *The broadband revolution: How superfast Internet access changes media habits in American households.* Washington, DC: National Association of Broadcasters.

National Cancer Institute. (1988). *Media strategies for smoking control* (NIH Pub. No. 89-3013). Washington, DC: Government Printing Office.

National Center for Chronic Disease Prevention and Health Promotion. (2000). *Targeting tobacco use: The nation's leading cause of death* [Online]. Available: www.cdc.gov/tobacco/overview/oshaag.htm.

National Center for Injury Prevention and Control. (2000a). *Fact book for the year 2000: Working to prevent and control injury in the United States.* Atlanta, GA: Author. Retrieved February 24, 2001, from the World Wide Web: www.cdc.gov/ncipc/pub-res/FactBook/youthviolence.htm.

National Center for Injury Prevention and Control. (2000b). *Youth violence in the United States.* Atlanta, GA: Author. Retrieved January 23, 2001, from the World Wide Web: www.cdc.gov/ncipc/factsheets/yvfacts.htm.

National Institute on Child Health and Development (NICHD). (2000, December). Workshop on Sex & the Media, Bethesda, MD.

National Institute on Drug Abuse (NIDA). (1995). *Drug use among racial/ethnic minorities 1995* (NIH Pub. No. 95-3888). Rockville, MD: Author.

National Institute on Drug Abuse (NIDA). (1997). *Preventing drug use among children and adolescents: A research-based guide* (NIH Pub. No. 97-4212). Rockville, MD: Author.

National Science Foundation. (1977). *Research on the effects of television advertising on children: A review of the literature and recommendations for future research.* Washington, DC: Author.

Nationline. (1997, October 3). Teen accused in killings wrote note, officials say. *USA Today,* p. 3A.

Neergaard, L. (1999, April 19). Bicycle-powered TV set may take weight off children. *Albuquerque Journal,* p. A4.

Nelson, K. (1986). *Event knowledge: Structure and function in development.* Hillsdale, NJ: Lawrence Erlbaum.

Nemeroff, C. J., Stein, R. I., Diehl, N. S., & Smilack, K. M. (1994). From the Cleavers to the Clintons: Role choices and body orientation as reflected in magazine article content. *International Journal of Eating Disorders, 16,* 167-176.

Newman, A. (2001, February 4). Rotten teeth and dead babies. *New York Times Magazine,* p. 16.

Nichter, M., & Nichter, M. (1991). Hype and weight. *Medical Anthropology, 13,* 249-284.

Nielsen Media Research. (2000). *2000 report on television.* New York: Author.

Nielsen Media Research. (2001). *2001 report on television.* New York: Author.

Noam, E. M., & Freeman, R. N. (1997). The media monopoly and other myths. *Television Quarterly, 29*(1), 18-23.

Noble, G. (1975). *Children in front of the small screen.* Beverly Hills, CA: Sage.

Obarzanek, E., Schreiber, G. B., Crawford, P. B., Goldman, S. R., Barrier, P. M., Frederick, M. M., & Lakatos, E. (1994). Energy intake and physical activity in relation to indexes of body fat: The National Heart, Lung, and Blood Institute Growth and Health Study. *American Journal of Clinical Nutrition, 60,* 15-22.

O'Bryan, K. G., & Boersma, F. J. (1971). Eye movements, perceptual activity, and conservation development. *Journal of Experimental Child Psychology, 12,* 157-169.

O'Bryant, S. L., & Corder-Bolz, C. R. (1978). The effects of television on children's stereotyping of women's work roles. *Journal of Vocational Behavior, 12,* 233-244.

O'Dea, J. A., & Abraham, S. (2000). Improving the body image, eating attitudes, and behaviors of young male and female adolescents: A new educational approach that focuses on self-esteem. *International Journal of Eating Disorders, 28,* 43-57.

Office of Film and Literature Classification. (1999). *Computer games and Australians today.* Sydney, Australia: Author.

Office of the Surgeon General. (2001, January 17). *Archived Webcast of news conference to release of Youth violence: A report of the Surgeon General.* Retrieved February 23, 2001, from the World Wide Web: www.surgeongeneral.gov/library/youthviolence/youvioreport.htm.

Ogles, R. M., & Hoffner, C. (1987). Film violence and perceptions of crime: The cultivation effect. In M. L. Mclaughlin (Ed.), *Communication yearbook* (Vol. 10, pp. 384-394). Newbury Park, CA: Sage.

Ogletree, S. M., Williams, S. W., Raffeld, P., & Mason, B. (1990). Female attractiveness and eating disorders: Do children's television commercials play a role? *Sex Roles, 22,* 791-797.

Oleck, J. (1994, July 20). Go ahead, make my lunch: Restaurant chains vying for school media market. *Restaurant Business Magazine,* p. 54.

Oliver, M. B. (2000). The respondent gender gap. In D. Zillmann & P. Vorderer (Eds.), *Media entertainment: The psychology of its appeal* (pp. 215-234). Mahwah, NJ: Lawrence Erlbaum.

O'Malley, P. M., & Johnston, L. D. (1999). Drinking and driving among U.S. high school seniors, 1984-1997. *American Journal of Public Health, 89,* 678-684.

Orlandi, M. A., Lieberman, L. R., & Schinke, S. P. (1989). The effects of alcohol and tobacco advertising on adolescents. In M. A. Orlandi, L. R. Lieberman, & S. P. Schinke (Eds.), *Perspectives on adolescent drug use* (pp. 77-97). Binghamton, NY: Haworth.

Packard Foundation. (2000). *The future of children: Children and computer technology.* Los Altos, CA: Author.

Paik, H. (2001). The history of children's use of electronic media. In D. G. Singer & J. L. Singer (Eds.), *Handbook of children and the media* (pp. 7-27). Thousand Oaks, CA: Sage.

Paik, H. J., & Comstock, G. (1994). The effects of television violence on antisocial behavior: A meta-analysis. *Communication Research, 21,* 516-546.

Painter, K. (1994, January 5). AIDS ads get less "timid." *USA Today,* p. 1A.

Palmer, E. L. (1988). *Television and America's children.* New York: Oxford University Press.

Palmer, E. L., & McDowell, C. N. (1979). Program/commercial separators in children's television programming. *Journal of Communication, 29,* 197-201.

Palmer, E. L., & McDowell, C. N. (1981). Children's understanding of nutritional information presented in breakfast cereal commercials. *Journal of Broadcasting, 25,* 295-301.

Palmerton, P. R., & Judas, J. (1994, July). *Selling violence: Television commercials targeted to children.* Paper presented at the annual meeting of the International Communication Association, Sydney, New South Wales, Australia.

Pardun, C. J. (2002). Romancing the script: Identifying the romantic agenda in top-grossing movies. In J. D. Brown, J. R. Steele, & K. Walsh-Childers (Eds.), *Sexual teens, sexual media* (pp. 211-225). Hillsdale, NJ: Lawrence Erlbaum.

Pareles, J. (1990, June 17). Rap: Slick, violent, nasty, and, maybe, hopeful. *New York Times,* p. 19.

Parents Music Resource Center. (1985). *PMRC, PTA, and RIAA agree on record lyrics identification* (press release). Arlington, VA: Author.

Parke, R. D., & Slaby, R. G. (1983). The development of aggression. In E. M. Hetherinton (Ed.), *Handbook of child psychology: Vol. 4. Socialization, personality, and social development* (pp. 567-641). New York: John Wiley.

Partnership for a Drug-Free America. (2000). *Anti-drug media campaign making inroads* (press release). New York: Author.

Pate, R. R., & Ross, J. G. (1987). The national children and youth fitness study II: Factors associated with health-related fitness. *Journal of Physical Education, Recreation, and Dance, 58,* 93-95.

Pazos, B., Fullwood, E. U., Allan, M. J., Graff, C. A., Wilson, K. M., Laneri, H., & Klein, J. D. (2001, March). *Media use and sexual behaviors among Monroe County adolescents.* Paper presented at the annual meeting of the Society for Adolescent Medicine, San Diego.

Pearl, D., Bouthilet, L., & Lazar, J. (Eds.). (1982). *Television and behavior: Ten years of scientific progress and implications for the eighties* (Vol. 1, DHHS Pub. No. ADM 82-1195). Washington, DC: Government Printing Office.

Pearson, L., & Lewis, K. E. (1988). Preventive intervention to improve children's discrimination of the persuasive tactics in television advertising. *Journal of Pediatric Psychology, 13,* 163-170.

Pecora, N. O. (1998). *The business of children's entertainment.* New York: Guilford.

Peirce, K. (1993). Socialization of teenage girls through teen-magazine fiction: The making of a new woman or an old lady? *Sex Roles, 29,* 59-68.

Pelletier, A. R., Quinlan, K. P., Sacks, J. J., Van Gilder, T. J., Gulchrist, J., & Ahluwalia, H. K. (1999). Firearm use in G- and PG-rated movies. *Journal of the American Medical Association, 282,* 428.

Perloff, R. M. (1993). Third-person effect research 1983-1992: A review and synthesis. *International Journal of Public Opinion Research, 5,* 167-184.

Perry, I. (1995). It's my thang and i'll swing it the way that i feel! In J. G. Dines & J. M. Humez (Eds.), *Gender, race and class in media: A test reader* (pp. 524-530). Thousand Oaks, CA: Sage.

Perse, E. M. (1990). Cultivation and involvement with local television news. In N. Signorielli & M. Morgan (Eds.), *Cultivation analysis: New directions in media effects research* (pp. 51-69). Newbury Park, CA: Sage.

Petersen, A. C. (1988). Adolescent development. *Annual Reviews in Psychology, 39,* 583-607.

Petersen, A. C., & Taylor, B. (1980). The biological approach to adolescence: Biological change and psychological adaptation. In J. Adelson (Ed.), *Handbook of adolescent psychology* (pp. 117-155). New York: John Wiley.

Peterson, D. L., & Pfost, K. S. (1989). Influence of rock videos on attitudes of violence against women. *Psychological Reports, 64,* 319-322.

Peterson, J. L., Moore, K. A., & Furstenberg, F. F., Jr. (1991). Television viewing and early initiation of sexual intercourse: Is there a link? *Journal of Homosexuality, 21,* 93-118.

Peterson, L., & Lewis, K. E. (1988). Preventive intervention to improve children's discriminating of the persuasive tactics in televised advertising. *Journal of Pediatric Psychology, 3,* 163-170.

Peterson, R. A., & Kahn, J. R. (1984, August). *Media preferences of sexually active teens.* Paper presented at the meeting of the American Psychological Association, Toronto, Canada.

Peto, R., Lopez, A. D., Boreham, J., Thun, M., & Heath, C., Jr. (1992). Mortality from tobacco in developed countries: Indirect estimation from national vital statistics. *Lancet, 339,* 1268-1278.

Pew Foundation. (2001). *The Pew Internet & American Life Project: The growth of the Internet population in America in the last half of 2000.* Philadelphia: Pew Charitable Trusts.

Phillips, C. A., Rolls, S., Rouse, A., & Griffiths, M. D. (1995). Home video game playing in schoolchildren: A study of incidence and patterns of play. *Journal of Adolescence, 18,* 687-691.

Phillips, D. P., & Carstensen, L. L. (1986). Clustering of teenage suicides after television news stories about suicide. *New England Journal of Medicine, 315,* 685-689.

Phillips, D. P., Carstensen, L. L., & Paight, D. J. (1989). Effects of mass media news stories on suicide, with new evidence on the old of story content. In C. R. Pfeffer (Ed.), *Suicide among youth: Perspectives on risk and prevention* (pp. 101-116). Washington, DC: American Psychiatric Press.

Phillips, D. P., & Paight, D. J. (1987). The impact of televised movies about suicide: A replicative study. *New England Journal of Medicine, 317,* 809-811.

Piaget, J. (1930). *The child's conception of the world.* New York: Harcourt, Brace & World.

Piaget, J. (1950). *The psychology of intelligence.* New York: International Universities Press.

Piaget, J. (1952). *The origins of intelligence in children.* New York: International Universities Press.

Piaget, J. (1972). Intellectual evolution from adolescence to adulthood. *Human Development, 15,* 1-12.

Piaget, J., & Inhelder, B. (1975). *The origin of the idea of chance in children.* New York: Norton.

Pierce, J. P., Choi, W. S., Gilpin, E. A., Farkas, A. J., & Berry, C. (1998). Industry promotion of cigarettes and adolescent smoking. *Journal of the American Medical Association, 279,* 511-515.

Pierce, J. P., Gilpin, E., Burns, D. M., Whalen, E., Rosbrook, B., Shopland, D., & Johnson, M. (1991). Does tobacco advertising target young people to start smoking? *Journal of the American Medical Association, 266,* 3154-3158.

Pierce, J. P., Lee, L., & Gilpin, E. A. (1994). Smoking initiation by adolescent girls, 1944 through 1988: An association with targeted advertising. *Journal of the American Medical Association, 271,* 608-611.

Pingree, S. (1978). The effects of nonsexist television commercials and perceptions of reality on children's attitudes about women. *Psychology of Women Quarterly, 2,* 262-277.

Pinhas, L., Toner, B. B., Ali, A., Garfinkel, P. E., & Stuckless, N. (1999). The effects of the ideal of female beauty on mood and body satisfaction. *International Journal of Eating Disorders, 25,* 223-226.

Pinhas-Hamiel, O., & Zeitler, P. (2001). Type 2 diabetes: Not just for grownups anymore. *Contemporary Pediatrics, 18,* 102-125.

Pipher, M. (1997, February 1). Bland, beautiful, and boy-crazy. *TV Guide,* pp. 22-25.

Plagens, P., Miller, M., Foote, D., & Yoffe, E. (1991, April 1). Violence in our culture. *Newsweek, 117,* 46-52.

Pollack, W. (1999, October 30). Boy trouble. *TV Guide,* pp. 29-32.

Pollay, R. W., Siddarth, S., Siegel, M., Haddix, A., Merritt, R. K., Giovino, G. A., & Eriksen, M. P. (1996). The last straw? Cigarette advertising and realized market shares among youth and adults, 1979-1993. *Journal of Marketing, 50,* 1-7.

Polskin, H. (1991, August 3). MTV at 10. *TV Guide,* pp. 4-8.

Pool, B. (1991, November 3). Screen violence would stop if it didn't sell tickets, filmmakers say. *Los Angeles Times,* pp. B1, B6.

Pope, H. (1999, Summer). Toy muscles linked to harmful image of male body. *Harvard Medical Alumni Bulletin,* p. 13.

Posavac, H. D. (1998). Reducing the impact of exposure to idealized media images of feminine attractiveness on college-age women with psychoeducational interventions. *Dissertation Abstracts International, 58,* 4466.

Postman, N. (1985). *Amusing ourselves to death: Public discourse in the age of show business.* New York: Penguin.

Postman, N., Nystrom, C., Strate, L., & Weingartner, C. (1988). *Myths, men, & beer: An analysis of beer commercials on broadcast television, 1987.* Washington, DC: AAA Foundation for Traffic Safety.

Potter, W. J. (1986). Perceived reality and the cultivation hypothesis. *Journal of Broadcasting and Electronic Media, 30,* 159-174.

Potter, W. J. (1993). Cultivation theory and research: A conceptual critique. *Human Communication Research, 19,* 564-601.

Potter, W. J. (1998). *Media literacy.* Thousand Oaks, CA: Sage.

Potter, W. J. (1999). *On media violence.* Thousand Oaks, CA: Sage.

Potter, W. J. (2001). *Media literacy* (2nd ed.). Thousand Oaks, CA: Sage.

Poulos, R. W., Rubinstein, E. A., & Liebert, R. M. (1975). Positive social learning. *Journal of Communication, 25,* 90-97.

Prasad, V. K., Rao, T. R., & Sheikh, A. A. (1978). Mother vs. commercial. *Journal of Communication, 28*(4), 91-96.

Preston, J. (1998). From mediated environments to the development of consciousness. In J. Gackenbach (Ed.), *Psychology and the Internet* (pp. 255-291). San Diego: Academic Press.

Prinsky, L. E., & Rosenbaum, J. L. (1987). "Leer-ics" or lyrics: Teenage impressions of rock 'n' roll. *Youth & Society 18,* 384-397.

Provenzo, E. F. (1991). *Video kids: Making sense of Nintendo.* Cambridge, MA: Harvard University Press.

Public Agenda. (1999). *Kids these days '99: What Americans really think about the next generation* [Online]. Available: www.publicagenda.org/aboutpa/aboutpa3u.htm.7.

Public Health Association of Australia. (1999). *Television food advertising during children's viewing times* [Online]. Retrieved January 6, 2001, from the World Wide Web: www.phaa.net.au/policy/TVadv.HTM.

Puig, C. (1995, August 31). Teaching children to watch TV. *Los Angeles Times,* p. A1.

Purugganan, O. H., Stein, R. E. K., Silver, E. J., & Benenson, B. S. (2000). Exposure to violence among urban school-aged children: Is it only on television? *Pediatrics, 106,* 949-953.

Putnam, F. W. (1993). Dissociative disorders in children: Behavioral profiles and problems. *Child Abuse & Neglect, 17,* 39-45.

Qian, J., Preston, J., & House, M. (1999, August). *Personality trait absorption and reality status evaluations of narrative mediated messages.* Paper presented at the annual meeting of the American Psychological Association, Boston.

Quigley, E. V. (1987, October 30). ABC, CBS, and NBC refuse to air "pill" commercials. *Los Angeles Times.*

Rabak-Wagener, J., Eickhoff-Shemek, J., & Kelly-Vance, L. (1998). The effect of media analysis on attitudes and behaviors regarding body image among college students. *Journal of American College Health, 47,* 29-35.

Rajecki, D. W., McTavish, D. G., Rasmussen, J. L., Schreuders, M., Byers, D. C., & Jessup, K. S. (1994). Violence, conflict, trickery, and other story themes in TV ads for food for children. *Journal of Applied Social Psychology, 24,* 1685-1700.

The ratings wars. (1996, December 15). *New York Times,* p. E12.

Rauzi, R. (1998, June 9). The teen factor: Today's media-savvy youths influence what others are seeing and hearing. *Los Angeles Times,* p. F1

Ray, J. W., & Klesges, R. C. (1993). Influences on the eating behavior of children. *Annals of the New York Academy of Sciences, 699,* 57-69.

Reece, B. B., Rifon, N. J., & Rodriguez, K. (1999). Selling food to children: Is fun part of a balanced breakfast? In M. C. Macklin & L. Carlson (Eds.), *Advertising to children: Concepts and controversies* (pp. 189-208). Thousand Oaks, CA: Sage.

Rehman, S. N., & Reilly, S. S. (1985). Music videos: A new dimension of televised violence. *The Pennsylvania Speech Communication Annual, 41,* 61-64.

Reichelt, P. A. (1978). Changes in sexual behavior among unmarried teenage women utilizing oral contraception. *Journal of Population Behavior, 1,* 59-68.

Reid, P., & Finchilescu, G. (1995). The disempowering effects of media violence against women on college women. *Psychology of Women Quarterly, 19,* 397-411.

Reilly, J. J., & Dorosty, A. R. (1999). Epidemic of obesity in U.K. children. *Lancet, 354,* 1874-1875.

Reis, E. C., Duggan, A. K., Adger, H., & DeAngelis, C. (1992). The impact of anti-drug advertising on youth substance abuse (abstract). *American Journal of Diseases of Children, 146,* 519.

Reiss, A., & Roth, J. (Eds.). (1993). *Understanding and preventing violence.* Washington, DC: National Academy Press.

Rekers, G. A. (1992). Development of problems of puberty and sex roles in adolescence. In C. E. Walker & M. C. Roberts (Eds.), *Handbook of clinical child psychology* (pp. 607-622). New York: John Wiley.

Resnick, M. D., Bearman, P. S., Blum, R. W., Bauman, K. E., Harris, K. M., Jones, J., Tabor, J., Beuhring, T., Sieving, R. E., Shew, M., Ireland, M., Bearinger, L. H., & Udry, J. R. (1997). Protecting adolescents from harm: Findings from the national longitudinal study on adolescent health. *Journal of American Medical Association, 278,* 823-832.

Resnicow, K., & Robinson, T. N. (1997). School-based cardiovascular disease prevention studies: Review and synthesis. *Annals of Epidemiology, 7*(Suppl.), 14-31.

Resnik, A., & Stern, B. L. (1977). Children's television advertising and brand choice: A laboratory experiment. *Journal of Advertising, 6*(3), 11-17.

Ricci, S., & Vigevano, F. (1999). The effect of video-game software in video-game epilepsy. *Epilepsia, 40,* 31-37.

Rice, L. (2000, April 14). Ready to swear. *Entertainment Weekly,* pp. 20-21.

Rich, M. (2001). For a child, every moment is a teachable moment. *Pediatrics, 108,* 179-180.

Rich, M., & Bar-on, M. (2001). Child health in the information age: Media education of pediatricians. *Pediatrics, 107,* 156-162.

Rich, M., Woods, E. R., Goodman, E., Emans, E. J., & DuRant, R. H. (1998). Aggressors or victims: Gender and race in music video violence. *Pediatrics, 101,* 669-674.

Richards, J. I., Wartella, E. A., Morton, C., & Thompson, L. (1998). The growing commercialization of schools: Issues and practices. *Annals of the American Academy of Political and Social Science, 557,* 148-163.

Richardson, J. L., Dwyer, K., McGuigan, K., Hansen, W. B., Dent, C., Johnson, C. A., Sussman, S. Y., Brannon, B., & Flay, B. (1989). Substance use among eighth grade students who take care of themselves after school. *Pediatrics, 84,* 556-566.

Richins, M. L. (1991). Social comparison and the idealized images of advertising. *Journal of Consumer Research, 18,* 71-83.

Ritzer, G. (1993). *The McDonaldisation of society.* Thousand Oaks, CA: Pine Forge.

Riva, G. (2000). Virtual reality in rehabilitation of spinal cord injuries: A case report. *Rehabilitation Psychology, 45,* 81-88.

Roberts, D. F. (1982). Children and commercials: Issues, evidence, interventions. *Prevention in Human Services, 2*(1-2), 19-35.

Roberts, D. F., & Christenson, P. G. (2000). *"Here's looking at you, kid": Alcohol, drugs and tobacco in entertainment media.* Menlo Park, CA: Kaiser Family Foundation.

Roberts, D. F., & Christenson, P. G. (2001). Popular music in childhood and adolescence. In D. G. Singer & J. L. Singer (Eds.), *Handbook of children and the media* (pp. 395-413). Thousand Oaks, CA: Sage.

Roberts, D. F., Christenson, P., Gibson, W. A., Mooser, L., & Goldberg, M. E. (1980). Developing discriminating consumers. *Journal of Communication, 30*(3), 94-105.

Roberts, D. F., Foehr, U. G., Rideout, V. J., & Brodie, M. (1999). *Kids and media at the new millenium: A Kaiser Family Foundation Report.* Menlo Park, CA: Henry J. Kaiser Family Foundation.

Roberts, D. F., Henriksen, L., & Christenson, P. G. (1999). *Substance use in popular movies and music.* Washington, DC: Office of National Drug Control Policy, 1999.

Roberts, E. (1982). Television and sexual learning in childhood. In D. Pearl, L. Bouthilet, & J. Lazar (Eds.), *Television and behavior: Ten years of scientific progress and implications for the Eighties* (Vol. 2, pp. 209-223). Rockville, MD: National Institute of Mental Health.

Roberts, E. (1983). Teens, sexuality and sex: Our mixed messages. *Television & Children, 6,* 9-12.

Roberts, K. R., Dimsdale, J., East, P., & Friedman, L. (1998). Adolescent emotional response to music and its relationship to risk-taking behavior. *Journal of Adolescent Health, 23,* 49-54.

Robertson, T. S., & Rossiter, J. R. (1974). Children and commercial persuasion: An attribution theory analysis. *Journal of Consumer Research, 1,* 13-20.

Robertson, T. S., & Rossiter, J. R. (1977). Children's responsiveness to commercials. *Journal of Communication, 27,* 101-106.

Robertson, T. S., Ward, S., Gatignon, H., & Klees, D. M. (1989). Advertising and children: A cross-cultural study. *Communication Research, 16,* 459-485.

Robin, S. S., & Johnson, E. O. (1996). Attitude and peer cross pressure: Adolescent drug and alcohol use. *Journal of Drug Education, 26,* 69-99.

Robinson, J. P., & Bachman, J. G. (1972). Television viewing habits and aggression. In G. A. Comstock & E. A. Rubinstein (Eds.), *Television and social behavior: Vol. 3. Television and adolescent aggressiveness* (pp. 173-238). Washington, DC: Government Printing Office.

Robinson, T. N. (1998). Does television cause childhood obesity? *Journal of the American Medical Association, 279,* 959-960.

Robinson, T. N. (1999). Reducing children's television viewing to prevent obesity: A randomized controlled trial. *Journal of the American Medical Association, 282,* 1561-1567.

Robinson, T. N. (2000). Can a school-based intervention to reduce television use decrease adiposity in children in Grades 3 and 4? *Western Journal of Medicine, 173,* 40.

Robinson, T. N., Chen, H. L., & Killen, J. D. (1998). Television and music video exposure and risk of adolescent alcohol use. *Pediatrics, 102,* e54.

Robinson, T. N., Hammer, L. D., Killen, J. D., Kraemer, H. C., Wilson, D. M., Hayward, C., & Taylor, C. B. (1993). Does television viewing increase obesity and reduce physical activity? Cross-sectional and longitudinal analyses among adolescent girls. *Pediatrics, 91,* 273-280.

Robinson, T. N., & Killen, J. D. (1995). Ethnic and gender differences in the relationships between television viewing and obesity, physical activity and dietary fat intake. *Journal of Health Education, 26*(Suppl.), 91-98.

Robinson, T. N., Saphir, M. N., Kraemer, H. C., Varady, A., & Haydel, K. F. (2001). Effects of reducing television viewing on children's requests for toys: A randomized controlled trial. *Journal of Developmental and Behavioral Pediatrics, 22,* 179-184.

Robinson, T. N., Wilde, M. L., Navracruz, L. C., Haydel, K. F., & Varady, A. (2000). Effects of reducing children's television and video game use on aggressive behavior. *Archives of Pediatrics & Adolescent Medicine, 156,* 17-23.

Robischon, N. (2001, April 20). Back in bleecch! *Entertainment Weekly,* pp. 24-29.

Robischon, N., Snierson, D., & Svetkey, B. (1999, June 11). A special report on violence and entertainment, part II. *Entertainment Weekly,* pp. 36-39.

Roche, S. M., & McConkey, K. M. (1990). Absorption: Nature, assessment, and correlates. *Journal of Personality and Social Psychology, 59,* 91-101.

Roe, K. (1984). *Youth and music in Sweden: Results from a longitudinal study of teenagers' media use* (Media Panel Reports No. 32). Lund, Sweden: Sociologiska Institutionen.

Roe, K. (1990). Adolescent music use: A structural-cultural approach. In K. Roe & U. Carlsson (Eds.), *Popular music research* (pp. 41-52). Goteborg, Sweden: Nordicom-Sweden.

Roe, K. (1995). Adolescents' use of socially disvalued media: Towards a theory of media delinquency. *Journal of Youth and Adolescence, 24,* 617-631.

Roe, K., & Muijs, D. (1998). Children and computer games: A profile of the heavy user. *European Journal of Communication, 13,* 181-200.

Romelsjo, A. (1987). Decline in alcohol-related problems in Sweden greatest among young people. *British Journal of Addiction, 82,* 1111-1124.

Roper Starch Worldwise, Inc. (1994). *Teens talk about sex: Adolescent sexuality in the 90's.* New York: Sex Information & Education Council of the U.S. (SIECUS).

Roschelle, J., Pea, R., Hoaddley, C., Gordin, D., & Means, B. (2000). Changing how and what children learn in school with computer-based technologies. In Packard Foundation (Ed.), *The future of children: Children and computer technology* (pp. 145-167). Los Altos, CA: Packard Foundation.

Rosenberg, J. M. (1992, February 18). Toymaker upbeat about coming year. *Santa Barbara News Press,* p. C4.

Rosenberg, M. L., Mercy, J. A., & Houk, V. N. (1991). Guns and adolescent suicides. *Journal of the American Medical Association, 266,* 3030.

Ross, C. A., Joshi, S., & Currie, R. (1990). Dissociative experiences in the general population. *American Journal of Psychiatry, 147,* 1547-1552.

Ross, R. P., Campbell, T. A., Wright, J. C., Huston, A. C., Rice, M. L., & Turk, P. (1984). When celebrities talk, children listen: An experimental analysis of children's responses to TV ads with celebrity endorsement. *Journal of Applied Developmental Psychology, 5*(3), 185-202.

Roth, J., & Brooks-Gunn, J. (2000). What do adolescents need for healthy development? Implications for youth policy. *Social Policy Report, 14,* 3-19.

Rothenberg, G. (1988, August 31). TV industry plans fight against drunken driving. *New York Times.*

Rothenberg, M. B. (1975). Effect of television violence on children and youth. *Journal of the American Medical Association, 234,* 1043-1046.

Roush, M. (2001, February 10). The Roush review: Isle of the dead; A sorry molehill. *TV Guide,* p. 12.

Rubinstein, S., & Caballero, B. (2000). Is Miss America an under-nourished role model? *Journal of the American Medical Association, 283,* 1569.

Ruble, D. N., Balaban, T., & Cooper, J. (1981). Gender constancy and the effects of sex-typed television toy commercials. *Child Development, 52,* 667-673.

Rudman, W. J., & Verdi, P. (1993). Exploitation: Comparing sexual and violent imagery of females and males in advertising. *Women & Health, 20,* 1-14.

Rushton, J. P., & Owen, D. (1979). Immediate and delayed effects of TV modeling and preaching on children's generosity. *British Journal of Social and Clinical Psychology, 14,* 309-310.

Saffer, H. (1997). Alcohol advertising and motor vehicle fatalitics. *Review of Economics and Statistics, 79,* 431-442.

Sagan, C. (1995, June 4). What TV could do for America. *Parade Magazine,* p. 15.

Sakamoto, A. (1994). Video game use and the development of sociocognitive abilities in children: Three surveys of elementary school children. *Journal of Applied Social Psychology, 24,* 21-42.

Salamon, J. (2000, December 10). Sex at 8: The Partridges don't live here anymore. *New York Times,* p. 6WK.

Salamon, J. (2001, March 13). When it comes to TV, coveted adolescents prove to be unpredictable. *New York Times,* p. E1.

Salomon, G. (1983). Television watching and mental effort: A social psychological view. In J. Bryant & D. R. Anderson (Eds.), *Children's understanding of television: Research on attention and comprehension* (pp. 181-198). New York: Academic Press.

Salomon, G., & Leigh, T. (1984). Predispositions about learning from print and television. *Journal of Communication, 34*(2), 119-135.

Samuels, A., Croal, N., & Gates, D. (2000, October 9). The rap on rap. *Newsweek,* pp. 58-65.

Samuelson, R. J. (1991, August 19). The end of advertising? *Newsweek,* p. 40.

Santelli, J. (1997). Human subjects protection and parental permission in adolescent health research. *Journal of Adolescent Health, 21,* 384-387.

Sapolsky, B. S., & Tabarlet, J. O. (1991). Sex in primetime television: 1979 versus 1989. *Journal of Broadcasting and Electronic Media, 35,* 505-516.

Sargent, J. D., Dalton, M., & Beach, M. (2000). Exposure to cigarette promotions and smoking uptake in adolescents: Evidence of a dose-response relation. *Tobacco Control, 9,* 163-168.

Sargent, J. D., Dalton, M. A., Beach, M., Bernhardt, A., Pullin, D., & Stevens, M. (1997). Cigarette promotional items in public schools. *Archives of Pediatrics & Adolescent Medicine, 151,* 1189-1196.

Sargent, J. D., Tickle, J. J., Beach, M. L., Dalton, M. A., Ahrens, M. B., & Heatherton, T. F. (2001). Brand appearances in contemporary cinema films and contribution to global marketing of cigarettes. *Lancet, 357,* 29-32.

Savan, L. (1994). *The sponsored life: Ads, TV and American culture.* Philadelphia: Temple University Press.

Savitsky, J. C., Rogers, R. W., Izard, C. E., & Liebert, R. M. (1971). Role of frustration and anger in the imitation of filmed aggression against a human victim. *Psychological Reports, 29,* 807-810.

Scammon, D. L., & Christopher, C. L. (1981). Nutrition education with children via television: A review. *Journal of Advertising, 6,* 131-133.

Scarr, S. (1992). Developmental theories for the 1990s: Development and individual differences. *Child Development, 63,* 1-19.

Schaefer, S. (1999, June 28). Natural born scapegoats? Hollywood takes it on the chops in wake of high school shootings. *The Boston Herald,* p. 37.

Schechter, D. (1997). *The more you watch, the less you know.* New York: Seven Stories Press.

Scheel, K. R., & Westefeld, J. S. (1999). Heavy metal music and adolescent suicidality: An empirical investigation. *Adolescence, 34,* 253-273.

Schemo, D. J. (2000, December 28). Sex education with just one lesson: No sex. *New York Times,* p. A1.

Schinke, S. P., & Botvin, G. J. (1999). Life skills training: A prevention program that works. *Contemporary Pediatrics, 16,* 108-117.

Schlosser, E. (2001). *Fast food nation.* Boston: Houghton Mifflin.

Schmitt, K. L. (2000). *Public policy, family rules and children's media use in the home.* Philadelphia: Annenberg Public Policy Center.

Schmitt, K. L., Anderson, D. R., & Collins, P. A. (1999). Form and content: Looking at visual features of television. *Developmental Psychology, 35,* 1156-1167.

Scholz, R. W., & Waller, M. (1983). Conceptual and theoretical issues in developmental research on the acquisition of the probability concept. In R. W. Scholz (Ed.), *Decision making under uncertainty* (pp. 291-311). New York: North Holland.

Schooler, C., Feighery, E., & Flora, J. A. (1996). Seventh graders' self-reported exposure to cigarette marketing and its relationship to their smoking behavior. *American Journal of Public Health, 86,* 1216-1221.

Schur, E. A., Sanders, M., & Steiner, H. (2000). Body dissatisfaction and dieting in young children. *International Journal of Eating Disorders, 27,* 74-82.

Schuster, M. A., Bell, R. M., Berry, S. H., & Kanouse, D. E. (1998). Impact of a high school condom availability program on sexual attitudes and behaviors. *Family Planning Perspectives, 30,* 67-72.

Schuster, M. A., Franke, T. M., Bastian, A. M., Sor, S., & Halfon, N. (2000). Firearm storage patterns in US homes with children. *American Journal of Public Health, 90,* 588-594.

Schwartz, J. (2001, June 20). Studies detail solicitation of children for sex online. *New York Times,* p. A20.

Schwarzbaum, L. (2000, August 11). Lewd awakening. *Entertainment Weekly,* pp. 20-26.

Schydlower, M., & Rogers, P. D. (Eds.). (1993). Adolescent substance abuse and addictions. *Adolescent Medicine: State of the Art Reviews, 4,* 227-477.

Scott, D. (1995). The effect of video games on feelings of aggression. *Journal of Psychology, 129,* 121-132.

Scott, J. E. (1986). An updated longitudinal content analysis of sex references in mass circulation magazines. *Journal of Sex Research, 22,* 385-392.

Segal, K. R., & Dietz, W. H. (1991). Physiologic responses to playing a video game. *American Journal of Diseases of Children, 145,* 1034-1036.

Seiter, E. (1993). *Sold separately: Children and parents in consumer culture.* New Brunswick, NJ: Rutgers University Press.

Selverstone, R. (1992). Sexuality education for adolescents. *Adolescent Medicine: State of the Art Reviews, 3,* 195-205.

Servin, A., Bohlin, G., & Berlin, L. (1999). Sex differences in 1-, 3-, and 5-year-olds' toy-choice in a structured play-session. *Scandinavian Journal of Psychology, 40,* 43-48.

Sexuality Information and Education Council of the U.S. (SIECUS). (1999). *Public support for sexuality education reaches highest level* (press release). New York: Author.

Sexuality Information and Education Council of the U.S. (SIECUS). (2000). Public support for sexuality education reaches highest level. *Siecus Developments, 8,* pp. 1, 4.

Shaker, E. (Ed.). (2000, July). *In the corporate interest: The YNN experience in Canadian schools.* Retrieved June 20, 2001, from Canadian Centre for Policy Alternatives on the World Wide Web: www.policyalternatives.ca/publications/ynnexperience.pdf.

Shales, T. (1993, December 19). Sunday night sleaze parade on Fox. *Albuquerque Journal,* p. C1.

Shannon, B., Peacock, J., & Brown, M. J. (1991). Body fatness, television viewing and calorie intake of a sample of Pennsylvania sixth grade children. *Journal of Nutritional Education, 23,* 262-268.

Shaw, J. (1995). Effects of fashion magazines on body dissatisfaction and eating psychopathology in adolescent and adult females. *European Eating Disorders Review, 3,* 15-23.

Shaw, J., & Waller, G. (1995). The media's impact on body image: Implications for prevention and treatment. *Eating Disorders: The Journal of Treatment & Prevention, 3,* 115-123.

Sheikh, A. A., & Moleski, L. M. (1977). Conflict in the family over commercials. *Journal of Communication, 27,* 152-157.

Shepard, P. (2000, July 4). Hispanic TV roles sought. *Albuquerque Journal,* p. A11.

Sherer, M. (1998). The effect of computerized simulation games on the moral development of junior and senior high-school students. *Computers in Human Behavior, 14,* 375-386.

Sherman, B. L., & Dominick, J. R. (1986). Violence and sex in music videos: TV and rock 'n' roll. *Journal of Communication, 36*(1), 79-93.

Shields, D. L., Carol, J., Balbach, E. D., & McGee, S. (1999). Hollywood on tobacco: How the entertainment industry understands tobacco portrayal. *Tobacco Control, 8,* 378-386.

Shiffrin, S. H. (1991). How free is commercial speech? *Media & Values, 54/55,* 8-9.

Shiffrin, S. H. (1993). Alcohol and cigarette advertising: A legal primer. *Adolescent Medicine: State of the Art Reviews, 4,* 623-634.

Shrum, L. J. (2001). Processing strategy moderates the cultivation effect. *Human Communication Research, 27,* 94-120.

Siegel, M., & Biener, L. (2000). The impact of an antismoking media campaign on progression to established smoking: Results of a longitudinal youth study. *American Journal of Public Health, 90,* 380-386.

Siegler, R. S. (1991). *Children's thinking* (2nd ed.). Englewood Cliffs, NJ: Prentice Hall.

Signorielli, N. (1990). Television and health: Images and impact. In C. Atkin & L. Wallack (Eds.), *Mass communication and public health: Complexities and conflicts* (pp. 96-113). Newbury Park, CA: Sage.

Signorielli, N. (1993). Sex roles and stereotyping on television. *Adolescent Medicine: State of the Art Reviews, 4,* 551-561.

Signorielli, N. (1997). *A content analysis: Reflections of girls in the media.* Menlo Park, CA: Kaiser Family Foundation.

Signorielli, N. (2001). Television's gender role images and contribution to stereotyping. In D. G. Singer & J. L. Singer (Eds.), *Handbook of children and the media* (pp. 341-358). Thousand Oaks, CA: Sage.

Signorielli, N., & Lears, M. (1992). Television and children's conceptions of nutrition: Unhealthy messages. *Health Communication, 4,* 245-257.

Signorielli, N., McLeod, D., & Healy, E. (1994). Gender stereotypes in MTV commercials: The beat goes on. *Journal of Broadcasting & Electronic Media, 38,* 91-101.

Signorielli, N., & Morgan, M. (Eds.). (1990). *Cultivation analysis: New directions in media effects research.* Newbury Park, CA: Sage.

Signorielli, N., & Staples, J. (1997). Television and children's conception of nutrition. *Health Communication, 9,* 289-301.

Silverblatt, A. (2001). *Media literacy: Keys to interpreting media messages.* Westport, CT: Praeger.

Silverman-Watkins, L. T. (1983). Sex in the contemporary media. In J. Q. Maddock, G. Neubeck, & M. B. Sussman (Eds.), *Human sexuality and the family* (pp. 125-140). New York: Haworth.

Silverman-Watkins, L. T., & Sprafkin, J. N. (1983). Adolescents' comprehension of televised sexual innuendoes. *Journal of Applied Developmental Psychology, 4,* 359-369.

Silverstein, B., Perdue, L., Peterson, B., & Kelly, E. (1986). The role of mass media in promoting a thin standard of bodily attractiveness for women. *Sex Roles, 14,* 519-532.

Silverstein, B., & Perlick, D. (1995). *The cost of competence: Why inequality causes depression, eating disorders, and illness in women.* New York: Oxford University Press.

Singer, D. G., & Singer, J. L. (1994). Evaluating the classroom viewing of a television series, "Degrassi Junior High." In D. Zillmann, J. Bryant, & A. C. Huston (Eds.), *Media, children, and the family: Social scientific, psychodynamic, and clinical perspectives* (pp. 97-115). Hillsdale, NJ: Lawrence Erlbaum.

Singer, D. G., & Singer, J. L. (1998). Developing critical viewing skills and media literacy in children. *Annals of the American Academy of Political and Social Science, 557,* 164-179.

Singer, J. L., & Singer, D. G. (1986). Family experiences and television viewing as predictors of children's imagination, restlessness, and aggression. *Journal of Social Issues, 42,* 107-124.

Singer, J. L., & Singer, D. G. (1998). Barney & Friends as entertainment and education. In J. K. Asamen & G. Berry (Eds.), *Research paradigms, television, and social behavior* (pp. 305-367). Thousand Oaks, CA: Sage.

Singer, J. L., Singer, D. G., & Rapaczynski, W. (1984). Family patterns and television viewing as predictors of children's beliefs and aggression. *Journal of Communication, 34*(2), 73-89.

Singer, D. G., Zuckerman, D. M., & Singer, J. L. (1980). Helping elementary school children learn about TV. *Journal of Communication, 30,* 84-93.

Singer, M. I., Miller, D. B., Guo, S., Flannery, D. J., Frierson, T., & Slovak, K. (1999). Contributors to violent behavior among elementary and middle school children. *Pediatrics, 104,* 878-884.

Singh, S., & Darroch, J. E. (2000). Adolescent pregnancy and childbearing: Levels and trends in developed countries. *Family Planning Perspectives, 32,* 14-23.

Sitton, L. (1994, May 15). Labeling gun a consumer product stirs safety debate. *Albuquerque Journal,* p. B5.

Skelton, R. (1998, February 7). Japan desperately seeks response to the surge in teenage violence. *The Age, Melbourne Online.* Retrieved June 16, 2001, from the World Wide Web: www.theage.com.au/daily/980207/news/news16.html.

Sly, D. F., Hopkins, R. S., Trapido, E., & Ray, S. (2001). Influence of a counteradvertising media campaign on initiation of smoking: The Florida "truth" campaign. *American Journal of Public Health, 91,* 233-238.

Smith, G. (1989). The effects of tobacco advertising on children. *British Journal of Addiction, 84,* 1275-1277.

Smith, R., Anderson, D. R., & Fischer, C. (1985). Young children's of montage. *Child Development, 56,* 962-971.

Smith, R. D., Fosarelli, P. D., Palumbo, F., Loening, V., & Melmed, R. (1986). The impact of television on children: Current pediatric training practices. *American Journal of Diseases of Children, 140,* 78-79.

Smith, S. L., & Boyson, A. R. (in press). Violence in music videos: Examining the prevalence and context of physical aggression. *Journal of Communication.*

Smith, S. L., Boyson, A. R., Pieper, K. M., & Wilson, B. J. (2001, May). *Brandishing guns on American television: How often do such weapons appear and in what context?* Paper presented at the annual meeting of the International Communication Association, Washington, DC.

Smith, S. L., & Donnerstein, E. (1998). Harmful effects of exposure to media violence: Learning of aggression, emotional desensitization, and fear. In R. G. Geen & E. Donnerstein (Eds.), *Human aggression: Theories, research, and implications for social policy* (pp. 167-202). San Diego: Academic Press.

Smith, S. L., & Wilson, B. J. (2002). Children's comprehension of and fright reactions to television news. *Media Psychology, 4,* 1-26.

Smith, S. L., Wilson, B. J., Kunkel, D., Linz, D., Potter, W. J., Colvin, C., & Donnerstein, E. (1998). Violence in television programming overall: University of California, Santa Barbara study. In *National television violence study* (Vol. 3, pp. 5-220). Newbury Park, CA: Sage.

Smolkin, R. (1999, March 30). Tuning out Channel One: Commercials, educational value questioned. *Washington Times,* p. A4.

Snyder, H. N., & Sickmund, M. (1999). *Juvenile offenders and victims: 1999 national report* (NCJ 178257). Washington, DC: U.S. Department of Justice, Office of Juvenile Justice and Delinquency Prevention.

Society for Adolescent Medicine. (2000). Media and contraception (policy statement). *Journal of Adolescent Health, 27,* 290-291.

Sokol, R. J. (2000). The chronic disease of childhood obesity: The sleeping giant has awakened. *Journal of Pediatrics, 136,* 711-713.

Sommers-Flanagan, R., Sommers-Flanagan, J., & Davis, B. (1993). What's happening on music television? A gender role content analysis. *Sex Roles, 28,* 745-753.

Southern Poverty Law Center. (1999). *Hate group Web sites on the rise.* Montgomery, AL: Author.

Span, P. (1999, June 27). Marketers hang on affluent teen-agers' every wish. *Albuquerque Journal,* p. C3.

Sparks, G. G. (1986). Developmental differences in children's reports of fear induced by the mass media. *Child Study Journal, 16,* 55-66.

Speaking out: The legacy of Columbine. (2000, April 20). *The Washington Post,* p. C4.

Speisman, J. C., Lazarus, R. S., Davidson, L., & Mordkoff, A. M. (1964). Experimental analysis of a film used as a threatening stimulus. *Journal of Consulting Psychology, 28,* 23-33.

Spencer, T. (2001, January 25). Wrestling death case deliberated. Retrieved on January 25, 2001, from the *Los Angeles Times* on the World Wide Web: www.latimes.com/wires/20010125/tCB00V0225.html.

Sports Illustrated for Kids. (1996, January). Quaker Oats (back inside cover).

Sprafkin, J., Liebert, R. M., & Poulos, R. W. (1985). Effects of a prosocial televised example on children's helping. *Journal of Experimental Child Psychology, 20,* 117-126.

Sprafkin, J., & Silverman, L. T. (1982). Sex on prime-time. In M. Schwartz (Ed.), *TV and teens* (pp. 130-135). Reading, MA: Addison-Wesley.

Springen, K., Figueroa, A., & Joseph-Goteiner, N. (1999, October 18). The truth about tweens. *Newsweek, 134,* 62-72.

Springer, E. A., Winzelberg, A. J., Perkins, R., & Taylor, C. B. (1999). Effects of a body image curriculum for college students on improved body image. *International Journal of Eating Disorders, 26,* 13-20.

Stack, S., Gundlach, J., & Reeves, J. L. (1994). The heavy metal subculture and suicide. *Suicide and Life-Threatening Behavior, 24,* 15-23.

Staffieri, J. R. (1967). A study of social stereotype of body image in children. *Journal of Personality and Social Psychology, 7,* 101-104.

Stanger, J. D. (1997). *Television in the home: The 1997 survey of parents and children.* Philadelphia: Annenberg Public Policy Center.

Stanger, J. D. (1998). *Television in the home 1998: The Third Annual National Survey of Parents and Children.* Philadelphia: Annenberg Public Policy Center.

Stangor, C., & Ruble, D. N. (1989). Differential influences of gender schemata and gender constancy on children's information processing and behavior. *Social Cognition, 7,* 353-372.

Starker, S. (1989). *Evil influences: Crusades against the mass media.* Brunswick, NJ: Transaction Publishers.

Stauber, J., & Rampton, S. (1995). *Toxic sludge is good for you! Lies, damn lies, and the public relations industry.* Monroe, ME: Common Courage.

Steele, J. R. (1999). Teenage sexuality and media practice: Factoring in the influences of family, friends, and school. *Journal of Sex Research, 36,* 331-341.

Steele, J. R. (2002). Teens and movies: Something to do, plenty to learn. In J. D. Brown, J. R. Steele, & K. Walsh-Childers (Eds.), *Sexual teens, sexual media* (pp. 227-251). Mahwah, NJ: Lawrence Erlbaum.

Steenland, S. (1988). *Growing up in prime time: An analysis of adolescent girls on television*. Washington, DC: National Commission on Working Women of Wider Opportunities for Women.

Steinberger, J., Moran, A., Hong, C.-P., Jacobs, D. R., & Sinaiko, A. R. (2001). Adiposity in childhood predicts obesity and insulin resistance in young adulthood. *Journal of Pediatrics, 138,* 469-473.

Stern, B. L., & Resnik, A. J. (1978). Children's understanding of a televised commercial disclaimer. In S. C. Jain (Ed.), *Research frontiers in marketing: Dialogues and directions* (pp. 332-336). Chicago: American Marketing Association.

Steuer, F. B., Applefield, J. M., & Smith, R. (1971). Televised aggression and interpersonal aggression of preschool children. *Journal of Experimental Child Psychology, 11,* 442-447.

Stice, E. (1998). Modeling of eating pathology and social reinforcement of the thin-ideal predict onset of bulimic symptoms. *Behaviour Research and Therapy, 36,* 931-944.

Stice, E., Schupak-Neuberg, E., Shaw, H. E., & Stein, R. I. (1994). Relation of media exposure to eating disorder symptomatology: An examination of mediating mechanisms. *Journal of Abnormal Psychology, 103,* 836-840.

Stice, E., & Shaw, H. E. (1994). Adverse effects of the media portrayed thin-ideal on women and linkages to bulimic symptomatology. *Journal of Social and Clinical Psychology, 13,* 288-308.

St. Lawrence, J. S., & Joyner, D. J. (1991). The effects of sexually violent rock music on males' acceptance of violence against women. *Psychology of Women Quarterly, 15,* 49-63.

Stockwell, T. F., & Glantz, S. A. (1997). Tobacco use is increasing in popular films. *Tobacco Control, 6,* 282-284.

Stoneman, Z., & Brody, G. H. (1981). The indirect impact of child-oriented advertisement on mother-child interactions. *Journal of Applied Developmental Psychology, 2,* 369-376.

Stormshak, E. A., Bierman, K. L., McMahon, R. J., Lengua, L. J., & Conduct Problems Prevention Research Group. (2000). Parenting practices and child disruptive behavior problems in early elementary school. *Journal of Clinical Child Psychology, 29,* 17-29.

Story, M., & Faulkner, P. (1990). The prime time diet: A content analysis of eating behavior and food messages in television program content and commercials. *American Journal of Public Health, 80,* 738-740.

Story, M., & Neumark-Sztainer, D. (1991). Promoting health eating and physical activity in adolescents. *Adolescent Medicine: State of the Art Reviews, 10,* 109-123.

Strasburger, V. C. (1988, July 31). Children need national TV network. *Hartford Courant,* p. B1.

Strasburger, V. C. (1989). Adolescent sexuality and the media. *Pediatric Clinics of North America, 36,* 747-774.

Strasburger, V. C. (1992). Children, adolescents, and television. *Pediatrics in Review, 13,* 144-151.

Strasburger, V. C. (1993). Adolescents and the media: Five crucial issues. *Adolescent Medicine: State of the Art Reviews, 1,* 161-194.

Strasburger, V. C. (1995). *Adolescents and the media: Medical and psychological impact.* Thousand Oaks, CA: Sage.

Strasburger, V. C. (1997a). "Make love, not war": Violence and weapon carrying in music videos. *Archives of Pediatrics & Adolescent Medicine, 151,* 441-442.

Strasburger, V. C. (1997b, May 19). My turn: Tuning in to teenagers. *Newsweek,* pp. 18-19.

Strasburger, V. C. (1997c). "Sex, drugs, rock 'n' roll," and the media: Are the media responsible for adolescent behavior? *Adolescent Medicine: State of the Art Reviews, 8,* 403-414.

Strasburger, V. C. (1998a). Adolescents, drugs, and the media (letter). *Archives of Pediatrics & Adolescent Medicine, 153,* 313.

Strasburger, V. C. (1998b). Parental permission in adolescent health research (letter). *Journal of Adolescent Health, 22,* 362.

Strasburger, V. C. (1999). Duck and take cover. *Clinical Pediatrics, 38,* 41-43.

Strasburger, V. C. (2001a). Children, adolescents, drugs, and the media. In D. G. Singer & J. L. Singer (Eds.), *Handbook of children and the media* (pp. 415-445). Thousand Oaks, CA: Sage.

Strasburger, V. C. (2001b). Children and TV advertising: Nowhere to run, nowhere to hide. *Journal of Developmental and Behavioral Pediatrics, 22,* 185-187.

Strasburger, V. C., & Brown, R. T. (1998). *Adolescent medicine: A practical guide.* Philadelphia: Lippincott/Williams & Wilkins.

Strasburger, V. C., & Donnerstein, E. (1999). Children, adolescents, and the media: Issues and solutions. *Pediatrics, 103,* 129-139.

Strasburger, V. C., & Donnerstein, E. (2000). Adolescents and the media in the 21st century. *Adolescent Medicine: State of the Art Reviews, 11,* 51-68.

Strasburger, V. C., & Furno-Lamude, D. (1997). *The effects of media consumption on adolescents' sexual attitudes and practices: Results of a pilot study.* Unpublished manuscript.

Strasburger, V. C., & Grossman, D. (2001). How many more Columbines? What can pediatricians do about school and media violence? *Pediatric Annals, 30,* 87-94.

Strasburger, V. C., & Hendren, R. O. (1995). Rock music and music videos. *Pediatric Annals, 24,* 97-103.

Strauss, R. S. (1999). Self-reported weight status and dieting in a cross-sectional sample of young adolescents. *Archives of Pediatrics & Adolescent Medicine, 153,* 741-747.

Strauss, R. S. (2000). Childhood obesity and self-esteem (abstract). *Pediatrics, 105,* 111.

Strouse, J. S., & Buerkel-Rothfuss, N. (1987). Self-reported media exposure and sexual attitudes and behaviors of college students. *Journal of Sex Education and Therapy, 13,* 43-51.

Strouse, J. S., Buerkel-Rothfuss, N., & Long, E. C. (1995). Gender and family as moderators of the relationship between music video exposure and adolescent sexual permissiveness. *Adolescence, 30,* 505-521.

Strouse, J. S., Goodwin, M. P., & Roscoe, B. (1994). Correlates of attitudes toward sexual harassment among early adolescents. *Sex Roles, 31,* 559-577.

Stutts, M. A., & Hunnicutt, G. G. (1987). Can young children understand disclaimers in television commercials? *Journal of Advertising, 16,* 41-46.

Stutts, M. A., Vance, D., & Hudleson, S. (1981). Program-commercial separators in children's television: Do they help a child tell the difference between Bugs Bunny and the Quik Rabbit? *Journal of Advertising, 10*(2), 16-25.

Subrahmanyam, K., & Greenfield, P. M. (1994). Effect of video game practice on spatial skills in girls and boys. *Journal of Applied Developmental Psychology, 15,* 13-32.

Subrahmanyam, K., Greenfield, P., Kraut, R., & Gross, E. (2001). The impact of computer use on children's and adolescents' development. *Journal of Applied Developmental Psychology, 22,* 7-30.

Subrahmanyam, K., Kraut, R., Greenfield, P., & Gross, E. (2000). The impact of home computer use on children's activities and development. In Packard Foundation (Ed.), *The future of children: Children and computer technology* (pp. 123-144). Los Altos, CA: Author.

Subrahmanyam, K., Kraut, R., Greenfield, P., & Gross, E. (2001). New forms of electronic media. In D. Singer & J. Singer (Eds.), *Handbook of children and the media* (pp. 73-99). Thousand Oaks, CA: Sage.

Su-Lin, G., Zillmann, D., & Mitrook, M. (1997). Stereotyping effect of Black women's sexual rap on White audiences. *Basic and Applied Social Psychology, 19,* 381-399.

Sun, S.-W., & Lull, J. (1986). The adolescent audience for music videos and why they watch. *Journal of Communication, 36*(1) 115-125.

Surgeon General's Scientific Advisory Committee on Television and Social Behavior. (1972). *Television and growing up: The impact of televised violence: Report to the Surgeon General, United States Public Health Service.* Washington, DC: Government Printing Office.

Sutton, M. J., Brown, J. D., Wilson, K. M., & Klein, J. D. (2002). Shaking the tree of knowledge for forbidden fruit: Where adolescents learn about sexuality and contraception. In J. D. Brown, J. R. Steele, & K. Walsh-Childers (Eds.), *Sexual teens, sexual media* (pp. 25-55). Mahwah, NJ: Lawrence Erlbaum.

Svetkey, B. (1994, March 18). Here's the beef. *Entertainment Weekly,* pp. 26-28.

Sylvester, G. P., Williams, J., & Achterberg, C. (1993). Food and nutrition messages in film: A preliminary content analysis. *Annals of the New York Academy of Science, 699,* 295-297.

Tallal, P., Miller, S. L., Bedi, G., Byma, G., Wang, X., Nagarajan, S. S., Schreiner, C., Jenkins, W. M., & Merzenich, M. M. (1996). Language comprehension in language-learning impaired children improved with acoustically modified speech. *Science, 271,* 81-84.

Tamborini, R., & Stiff, J. (1987). Predictors of horror film attendance and appeal: An analysis of the audience for frightening films. *Communication Research, 14,* 415-436.

Tan, A. S. (1979). TV beauty ads and role expectations of adolescent female viewers. *Journalism Quarterly, 56,* 283-288.

Tanner, J. (1981). Pop music and peer groups: A study of Canadian high school students' responses to pop music. *Canadian Review of Sociology and Anthropology, 18,* 1-13.

Tanner, L. (1998, September 30). Many teens think designated drivers still can drink. *Albuquerque Journal,* p. A3.

Tapert, S. F., Aarons, G. A., Sedlar, G. R., & Brown, S. A. (2001). Adolescent substance abuse and sexual risk-taking behavior. *Journal of Adolescent Health, 28,* 181-189.

Tapper, J., Thorson, E., & Black, D. (1994). Variations in music videos as a function of their musical genre. *Journal of Broadcasting & Electronic Media, 38,* 103-113.

Tapscott, D. (1998). *Growing up digital: The rise of the net generation.* New York: McGraw-Hill.

Taras, H. L., & Gage, M. (1995). Advertised foods on children's television. *Archives of Pediatrics and Adolescent Medicine, 149,* 649-652.

Taras, H. L., Sallis, J. F., Patterson, T. L., Nader, P. R., & Nelson, J. A. (1989). Television's influence on children's diet and physical activity. *Developmental and Behavioral Pediatrics, 10,* 176-180.

Tarpley, T. (2001). Children, the Internet, and other new technologies. In D. Singer & J. Singer (Eds.), *Handbook of children and the media* (pp. 547-556). Thousand Oaks, CA: Sage.

Taylor, C. B., Sharpe, T., Shisslak, C., Bryson, S., Estes, L. S., Gray, N., McKnight, K. M., Crago, M., Kraemer, H. C., & Killen, J. D. (1998). Factors associated with weight concerns in adolescent girls. *International Journal of Eating Disorders, 24,* 31-42.

Tazawa, Y., Soukalo, A. V., Okada, K., & Takada, G. (1997). Excessive playing of home computer games by children presenting unexplained symptoms. *Journal of Pediatrics, 130,* 1010-1011.

Tellegen, A., & Atkinson, G. (1974). Openness to absorbing and self-altering experiences ("absorption"), a trait related to hypnotic susceptibility. *Journal of Abnormal Psychology, 83,* 268-277.

Terry, E., & Manlove, J. (2000). *Trends in sexual activity and contraceptive use among teens.* Washington, DC: National Campaign to Prevent Teen Pregnancy.

Thomas, H. (2001, March 26). Supreme Court should rule on the Second Amendment. *Liberal Opinion Week,* p. 7.

Thomas, K. (1996, November 7). Lighting up: Tobacco has a role in most movies. *USA Today,* p. D1.

Thomas, M. H., & Drabman, R. S. (1975). Toleration of real life aggression as a function of exposure to televised violence and age of subject. *Merrill-Palmer Quarterly, 21,* 227-232.

Thomas, M. H., Horton, R. W., Lippincott, E. C., & Drabman, R. S. (1977). Desensitization to portrayals of real-life aggression as a function of exposure to television violence. *Journal of Personality & Social Psychology, 35,* 450-458.

Thomas, M. H., & Tell, P. M. (1974). Effects of viewing real versus fantasy violence upon interpersonal aggression. *Journal of Research in Personality, 8,* 153-160.

Thomas, R., Cahill, J., & Santilli, L. (1997). Using an interactive computer game to increase skill and self-efficacy regarding safer sex negotiation: Field test results. *Health Education & Behavior, 24,* 71-86.

Thompson, J. G., & Myers, N. A. (1985). Inferences and recall at ages four and seven. *Child Development, 56,* 1134-1144.

Thompson, J. K., Heinberg, L. J., Altabe, M., & Tantleff-Dunn, S. (1999). *Exacting beauty: Theory, assessment, and treatment of body image disturbance.* Washington, DC: American Psychological Association.

Thompson, J. K., & Smolak, L. (Eds.). (2001). *Body image, eating disorders, and obesity in childhood and adolescence.* Washington, DC: American Psychological Association.

Thompson, K. M., & Yokota, F. (2001). Depiction of alcohol, tobacco, and other substances in G-rated animated films. *Pediatrics, 107,* 1369-1374.

Thompson, P. M., Giedd, J. N., Woods, R. P., MacDonald, D., Evans, A. C., & Toga, A. W. (2000). Growth patterns in the developing brain detected by using continuum mechanical tensor maps. *Nature, 404,* 190-192.

Thornburg, H. (1981). Adolescent sources of information on sex. *Journal of School Health, 51,* 274-277.

Thorne, B. (1993). *Gender play: Girls and boys in school.* New Brunswick, NJ: Rutgers University Press.

Thurow, L. (1996). *The future of capitalism: How today's economic forces shape tomorrow's world.* New York: Penguin.

Tickle, J. J., Sargent, J. D., Dalton, M. A., Beach, M. L., & Heatherton, T. F. (2001). Favorite movie stars, their tobacco use in contemporary movies and its association with adolescent smoking. *Tobacco Control, 10,* 16-22.

Tiggemann, M., & Pickering, A. S. (1996). Role of television in adolescent women's body dissatisfaction and drive for thinness. *International Journal of Eating Disorders, 20,* 199-203.

Tobacco's toll. (1992). *Lancet, 339,* 1267.

Torney-Purta, J. (1990). Youth in relation to social thinking. In S. S. Feldman & G. R. Elliott (Eds.), *At the threshold: The developing adolescent* (pp 431-519). Cambridge, MA: Harvard University Press.

Treise, D., & Gotthoffer, A. (2001). Stuff you couldn't ask your parents about: Teens talking about using magazines for sex information. In J. D. Brown, J. R. Steele, & K. Walsh-Childers (Eds.), *Sexual teens, sexual media* (pp. 173-189). Mahwah, NJ: Lawrence Erlbaum.

Troiano, R. P., & Flegal, K. M. (1998). Overweight children and adolescents: Description, epidemiology, and demographics. *Pediatrics, 101,* 497-504.

Truglio, R. T. (1992). *Adolescents' use of prime-time TV for sexual information: What are the risks?* Paper presented at the Society for Research on Adolescence, Washington, DC.

Tsao, J. C. (1997). Informational and symbolic content of over-the-counter drug advertising on television. *Journal of Drug Education, 27,* 173-197.

Tucker, K. (1999, December 17). Kids these days. *Entertainment Weekly,* pp. 62-63.

Tucker, L. A. (1986). The relationship of television viewing to physical fitness and obesity. *Adolescence, 21,* 797-806.

Tucker, M. E. (2000, April). Teen sex. *Pediatric News,* p. 5.

Tulving, E., & Thomson, D. M. (1973). Encoding specificity and retrieval processes in episodic memory. *Psychological Review, 80,* 359-380.

Turner, S. L., Hamilton, H., Jacobs, M., Angood, L. M., & Dwyer, D. H. (1997). The influence of fashion magazines on the body image satisfaction of college women: An exploratory analysis. *Adolescence, 32,* 603-610.

Turow, J. (2001). *Privacy policies on children's Websites: Do they play by the rule?* Washington, DC: Annenberg Public Policy Center of the University of Pennsylvania.

Turow, J., & Nir, L. (2000). *The Internet and the family 2000: The view from parents, the view from kids.* Washington, DC: Annenberg Public Policy Center of the University of Pennsylvania.

TV parental guidelines. (n.d.). Washington, DC: TV Parental Guidelines Monitoring Board. Retrieved February 21, 2001, from the World Wide Web: www.tvguidelines.org/guidelin.htm.

Tversky, B. (1985). Development of taxonomic organization of named and pictured categories. *Developmental Psychology, 21,* 1111-1119.

University of California at Santa Barbara, University of North Carolina, University of Texas, & University of Wisconsin. (1996). *The national television violence study.* Los Angeles: Mediascope.

Unnikrishnan, N., & Bajpai, S. (1996). *The impact of television advertising on children.* Thousand Oaks, CA: Sage.

Ursin, H., & Eriksen, H. R. (2001). Sensitization, subjective health complaints, and sustained arousal. *Annals of the New York Academy of Sciences, 933,* 119-129.

U.S. Department of Health and Human Services. (1994). *Preventing tobacco use among young people: Report of the Surgeon General.* Washington, DC: Government Printing Office.

U.S. Department of Justice. (1996). *National Crime Victimization Survey.* Washington, DC: Bureau of Justice Statistics.

U.S. Department of Justice. (1998). *Source book of criminal justice statistics 1997.* Washington, DC: Government Printing Office.

Vaidya, S. G., Naik, U. D., & Vaidya, J. S. (1996). Effects of sports sponsorship by tobacco companies on children's experimentation with tobacco. *British Medical Journal, 313,* 400-416.

Valerio, M., Amodio, P., Dal Zio, M., Vianello, A., & Zacchello, G. (1997). The use of television in 2- to 8-year-old children and the attitude of parents about such use. *Archives of Pediatrics & Adolescent Medicine, 151,* 22-26.

Valkenburg, P. M. (2000). Media and youth consumerism. *Journal of Adolescent Health, 27*(Suppl.), 52-56.

Valkenburg, P. M., & Cantor, J. (2000). Children's likes and dislikes of entertainment programs. In D. Zillmann & P. Vorderer (Eds.), *Media entertainment: The psychology of its appeal* (pp. 135-152). Mahwah, NJ: Lawrence Erlbaum.

Valkenburg, P. M., & Cantor, J. (2001). The development of a child into a consumer. *Journal of Applied Developmental Psychology, 22*(1), 61-72.

van den Broek, P., Lorch, E. P., & Thurlow, R. (1996). Children's and adults' memory for television stories: The role of causal factors, story-grammar categories, and hierarchical level. *Child Development, 67,* 3010-3028.

van Schie, E. G. M., & Wiegman, O. (1997). Children and videogames: Leisure activities, aggression, social integration, and school performance. *Journal of Applied Social Psychology, 27,* 1175-1194.

Verri, A. P., Verticale, M. S., Vallero, E., Bellone, S., & Nespoli, L. (1997). Television and eating disorders: Study of adolescent eating behavior. *Minerva Pediatrica, 49,* 235-243.

Vickers, A. (1992). Why cigarette advertising should be banned. *British Medical Journal, 304,* 1195-1196.

Vidmar, N., & Rokeach, M. (1974). Archie Bunker's bigotry: A study in selective perception and exposure. *Journal of Communication, 24*(1), 36-47.

Villani, S. (2001). Impact of media on children and adolescents: A 10-year review of the research. *Journal of the American Academy of Child & Adolescent Psychiatry, 40,* 392-401.

Vincent, R. C., Davis, D. K., & Bronszkowski, L. A. (1987). Sexism in MTV: The portrayal of women in rock videos. *Journalism Quarterly, 64,* 750-755.

Waite, B. M., Hillbrand, M., & Foster, H. G. (1992). Reduction of aggressive behavior after removal of Music Television. *Hospital and Community Psychiatry, 43,* 173-175.

Wakefield, D. (1987, November 7). Teen sex and TV: How the medium has grown up. *TV Guide,* pp. 4-6.

Wallack, L., Cassady, D., & Grube, J. (1990). *TV beer commercials and children: Exposure, attention, beliefs, and expectations about drinking as an adult.* Washington, DC: AAA Foundation for Traffic Safety.

Wallack, L., & Dorfman, L. (1992). Health messages on television commercials. *American Journal of Health Promotion, 6,* 190-196.

Wallack, L., Dorfman, L., Jernigan, D., & Themba, M. (1993). *Media advocacy and public health.* Newbury Park, CA: Sage.

Wallack, L., Grube, J. W., Madden, P. A., & Breed, W. (1990). Portrayals of alcohol on primetime television. *Journal of Studies on Alcohol, 51,* 428-437.

Waller, G., Hamilton, K., & Shaw, J. (1992). Media influences on body size estimation in eating disordered and comparison subjects. *British Review of Bulimia & Anorexia Nervosa, 6,* 81-87.

Waller, G., Shaw, J., Hamilton, K., & Baldwin, G. (1994). Beauty is in the eye of the beholder: Media influences on the psychopathology of eating problems. *Appetite, 23,* 287.

Walsh, D. (1994). *Selling out America's children.* Minneapolis, MN: Fairview.

Walsh, D. A. (2000). The challenge of the evolving media environment. *Journal of Adolescent Health, 27*(Suppl.), 69-72.

Walsh, D. A., & Gentile, D. A. (2001). A validity test of movie, television, and video game ratings. *Pediatrics, 107*(6), 1302-1308.

Walsh-Childers, K. (1991, May). *Adolescents' interpretations of the birth control behavior of a soap opera couple.* Paper presented at the annual meeting of the International Communication Association, Chicago.

Walsh-Childers, K. (1997). *A content analysis: Sexual health coverage in women's, men's, teen and other specialty magazines.* Menlo Park, CA: Kaiser Family Foundation.

Walsh-Childers, K., & Brown, J. D. (1993). Adolescents' acceptance of sex-role stereotypes and television viewing. In B. S. Greenberg, J. D. Brown, & N. L. Buerkel-Rothfuss (Eds.), *Media, sex and the adolescent* (pp. 117-133). Cresskill, NJ: Hampton.

Walsh-Childers, K., Gotthoffer, A., & Lepre, C. R. (2002). From "just the facts" to "downright salacious": Teens' and women's magazines' coverage of sex and sexual health. In J. D. Brown, J. R. Steele, & K. Walsh-Childers (Eds.), *Sexual teens, sexual media* (pp. 153-171). Hillsdale, NJ: Lawrence Erlbaum.

Walters, R. H., & Parke, R. D. (1964). Influence of response consequences to a social model on resistance to deviation. *Journal of Experimental Child Psychology, 1,* 269-280.

Ward, C. L. (2000, September 14). New report examines commercialism in U.S. schools. *New York Times,* p. D1.

Ward, E., Stokes, G., & Tucker, K. (1986). *Rock of ages: The Rolling Stone history of rock and roll.* New York: Rolling Stone Books.

Ward, L. M. (1995). Talking about sex: Common themes about sexuality in the prime time television programs children and adolescents view most. *Journal of Youth and Adolescence, 24,* 595-615.

Ward, L. M., Gorvine, B., & Cytron, A. (2002). Would that really happen? Adolescents' perceptions of sexual relationships according to prime-time television. In J. D. Brown, J. R. Steele, & K. Walsh-Childers (Eds.), *Sexual teens, sexual media* (pp. 95-123). Hillsdale, NJ: Lawrence Erlbaum.

Ward, L. M., & Rivadeneyra, R. (1999). Contributions of entertainment television to adolescents' sexual attitudes and expectations: The role of viewing amount versus viewer involvement. *Journal of Sex Research, 36,* 237-249.

Ward, S., Levison, D., & Wackman, D. (1972). Children's attention to advertising. In E. A. Rubinstein, G. A. Comstock, & J. P. Murray (Eds.), *Television and social behavior* (Vol. 4, pp. 491-515). Washington, DC: Government Printing Office.

Ward, S., Reale, S., & Levinson, D. (1972). Children's perceptions, explanations, and judgments of television advertising: A further explanation. In E. A. Rubinstein, G. A. Comstock, & J. P. Murray (Eds.), *Television and social behavior* (Vol. 4, pp. 468-490). Washington, DC: Government Printing Office.

Ward, S., & Wackman, D. (1972). Family and media influences on adolescent consumer learning. In E. A. Rubinstein, G. A. Comstock, & J. P. Murray (Eds.), *Television and social behavior* (Vol. 4, pp. 554-565). Washington, DC: Government Printing Office.

Ward, S., & Wackman, D. (1973). Children's information processing of television advertising. In P. Clarke (Ed.), *New models for mass communication research* (pp. 119-146). Beverly Hills, CA: Sage.

Ward, S., Wackman, D. B., & Wartella, E. (1977). *How children learn to buy: The development of consumer information-processing skills.* Beverly Hills, CA: Sage.

Warner, K. E., Goldenhar, L. M., & McLaughlin, C. G. (1992). Cigarette advertising and magazine coverage of the hazards of smoking. *New England Journal of Medicine, 326,* 305-309.

Wartella, E. (1980). Individual differences in children's responses to television advertising. In E. L. Palmer & A. Dorr (Eds.), *Children and the faces of television: Teaching, violence, selling* (pp. 307-322). New York: Academic Press.

Wartella, E., & Ettema, J. S. (1974). A cognitive developmental study of children's attention to television commercials. *Communication Research, 1,* 69-88.

Wartella, E., & Jennings, N. (2000). Children and computers. In Packard Foundation (Ed.), *The future of children: Children and computer technology* (pp. 31-43). Los Altos, CA: Author.

Wartella, E., & Jennings, N. (2001). Hazards and possibilities of commercial TV in the schools. In D. G. Singer & J. L. Singer (Eds.), *Handbook of children and the media* (pp. 557-570). Thousand Oaks, CA: Sage.

Wartella, E., Olivarez, A., & Jennings, N. (1998). Children and television violence in the United States. In U. Carlsson & C. von Feilitzen (Eds.), *Children and media violence* (pp. 55-62). Goteborg, Sweden: UNESCO International Clearinghouse on Children and Violence on the Screen.

Wartella, E., & Reeves, B. (1985). Historical trends in research on children and the media: 1900-1960. *Journal of Communication, 35*(2), 118-132.

Wass, H., Raup, J. L., Cerullo, K., Martel, L. G., Mingione, L. A., & Sperring, A. M. (1988). Adolescents' interest in and views of destructive themes in rock music. *Omega, 19,* 177-186.

Waters, H. F., & Beachy, L. (1993, March 1). Next year, 500 channels. *Newsweek,* pp. 75-76.

Waters, H. F., & Uehling, M. D. (1985, May 13). Toying with kids' TV. *Newsweek, 105,* 85.

Wattleton, F. (1987). American teens: Sexually active, sexually illiterate. *Journal of School Health, 57,* 379-380.

Waxman, S. (2001a, April 8). Rated S, for secret. *Washington Post,* p. G1.

Waxman, S. (2001b, May 31). Rating enforcement changes Hollywood's picture. *Washington Post,* p. C1.

Way, W. L. (1983). Food-related behaviors on prime-time television. *Journal of Nutritional Education, 15,* 105-109.

Weaver, J., III. (1994). Pornography and sexual callousness: The perceptual and behavioral consequences of exposure to pornography. In D. Zillmann, J. Bryant, & A. C. Huston (Eds.), *Media, children, and the family: Social scientific, psychodynamic, and clinical perspectives* (pp. 215-228). Hillsdale, NJ: Lawrence Erlbaum.

Weaver, J., Masland, J. L., & Zillmann, D. (1984). Effect of erotica on young men's aesthetic perception of their female sexual partners. *Perceptual and Motor Skills, 58,* 929-930.

Weaver, J., & Wakshlag, J. (1986). Perceived vulnerability to crime: Criminal victimization experience, and television viewing. *Journal of Broadcasting & Electronic Media, 30,* 141-158.

Wechsler, H., Rigotti, N. A., Gledhill-Hoyt, J., & Lee, H. (1998). Increased levels of cigarette use among college students. *Journal of the American Medical Association, 280,* 1673-1678.

Weidinger, C. K., & Demi, A. S. (1991). Music listening preferences and preadmission dysfunctional psychosocial behaviors of adolescents hospitalized on an in-patient psychiatric unit. *Journal of Child and Adolescent Psychiatric Mental Health Nursing, 4,* 3-8.

Weinstein, H. (1998, January 15). Papers: RJR went for teens. *Los Angeles Times,* p. A1.

Weiss, A. J., & Wilson, B. J. (1998). Children's cognitive and emotional responses to the portrayal of negative emotions in family-formatted situation comedies. *Human Communication Research, 24,* 584-609.

Welch, R. L., Huston-Stein, A., Wright, J. C., & Plehal, R. (1979). Subtle sex-role cues in children's commercials. *Journal of Communication, 29,* 202-209.

Wertheim, E. H., Paxton, S. J., Schutz, H. K., & Muir, S. L. (1997). Why do adolescent girls watch their weight? An interview study examining pressures to be thin. *Journal of Psychosomatic Research, 42*, 345-355.

While, D., Kelly, S., Huang, W., & Charlton, A. (1996). Cigarette advertising and onset of smoking in children: Questionnaire survey. *British Medical Journal, 313*, 398-399.

Whitbeck, L., Yoder, K. A., Hoyt, D. R., & Conger, R. D. (1999). Early adolescent sexual activity: A developmental study. *Journal of Marriage & the Family, 61*, 934-946.

Wiecha, J. L., Sobol, A. M., Peterson, K. E., & Gortmaker, S. L. (2001). Household television access: Associations with screen time, reading and homework among youth. *Ambulatory Pediatrics, 1*, 244-251.

Wiegman, O., & van Schie, E. G. M. (1998). Video game playing and its relations with aggressive and prosocial behavior. *British Journal of Social Psychology, 37*, 367-378.

Wiencke, J. K., Thurston, S. W., Kelsey, K. T., Varkonyi, A., Wain, J. C., Mark, E. J., & Christiani, D. C. (1999). Early age at smoking initiation and tobacco carcinogen DNA damage in the lung. *Journal of the National Cancer Institute, 91*, 614-619.

Wilcox, B. L., & Kunkel, D. (1996). Taking television seriously: Children and television policy. In E. F. Zigler & S. L. Kagan (Eds.), *Children, families, and government: Preparing for the twenty-first century* (pp. 333-352). New York: Cambridge University Press.

Wilke, J., Therrien, L., Dunkin, A., & Vamos, M. N. (1985, March 25). Are the programs your kids watch simply commercials? *Business Week*, p. 53.

Will, G. (2001, May 6). Consumer cadets. *Washington Post*, p. A-18.

Williams, J. O., Achterberg, C., & Sylvester, G. P. (1993). Targeting marketing of food products to ethnic minority youths. *Annals of the New York Academy of Sciences, 699*, 107-114.

Williams, M. (2001, January 15). The soda subsidy. *Liberal Opinion Week*, p. 6.

Williams, M. E., & Hall, E. R. (1994). Creating educational television programs that are relevant to the lives of children. *Youth & Society, 26*, 243-255.

Williams, T. B. (Ed.). (1986). *The impact of television: A natural experiment in three communities*. New York: Academic Press.

Willis, E., McCoy, B., & Berman, M. (1990). The effect of a weight management program on self esteem and body image in obese youth (abstract). *American Journal of Diseases of Children, 144*, 417.

Willis, E., & Strasburger, V. C. (1998). Media violence *Pediatric Clinics of North America, 45*, 319-331.

Willman, C. (2001, January 19). Midlife crisis? *Entertainment Weekly*, pp. 82-83.

Wilson, B. J. (1991). Children's reactions to dreams conveyed in mass media programming. *Communication Research, 18*, 283-305.

Wilson, B. J., Colvin, C. M., & Smith, S. L. (in press). Engaging in violence on American television: A comparison of child, teen, and adult perpetrators. *Journal of Communication*.

Wilson, B. J., Hoffner, C., & Cantor, J. (1987). Children's perceptions of the effectiveness of techniques to reduce fear from mass media. *Journal of Applied Developmental Psychology, 8*, 39-52.

Wilson, B. J., Kunkel, D., Linz, D., Potter, W. J., Donnerstein, E., Smith, S. L., Blumenthal, E., & Berry, M. (1998). Violence in television programming overall: University of California, Santa Barbara study. In *National television violence study* (Vol. 2, pp. 3-204). Thousand Oaks, CA: Sage.

Wilson, B. J., Kunkel, D., Linz, D., Potter, W. J., Donnerstein, E., Smith, S. L., Blumenthal, E., Berry, M., & Federman, J. (1999). The nature and context of violence on American television. In U. Carlsson & C. von Feilitzen (Eds.), *Children and media violence* (pp. 63-79).

Goteborg, Sweden: UNESCO International Clearinghouse on Children and Violence on the Screen.

Wilson, B. J., Kunkel, D., Linz, D., Potter, W. J., Donnerstein, E., Smith, S. L., Blumenthal, E., & Gray, T. (1997). Violence in television programming overall: University of California, Santa Barbara study. In *National television violence study* (Vol. 1, pp. 3-268). Thousand Oaks, CA: Sage.

Wilson, B. J., Linz, D., Donnerstein, E., & Stipp, H. (1992). The impact of social issue television programming on attitudes toward rape. *Human Communication Research, 19,* 179-208.

Wilson, B. J., Linz, D., Federman, J., Smith, S., Paul, B., Nathanson, A., Donnerstein, E., & Lingsweiler, R. (1999). *The choices and consequences evaluation: A study of court TV's anti-violence curriculum.* Santa Barbara: Center for Communication and Social Policy, University of California.

Wilson, B. J., & Smith, S. L. (1995, May). *Children's comprehension of and emotional reactions to TV news.* Paper presented at the annual conference of the International Communication Association, Albuquerque, NM.

Wilson, B. J., & Smith, S. L. (1998). Children's responses to emotional portrayals on television. In P. Anderson & L. Guerrero (Eds.), *Handbook of communication and emotion: Research, theory, applications, and contexts* (pp. 533-569). New York: Academic Press.

Wilson, B. J., Smith, S. L., Potter, W. J., Kunkel, D., Linz, D., Colvin, C., & Donnerstein, E. I. (in press). Violence in children's television programming: Assessing the risks. *Journal of Communication.*

Wilson, B. J., & Weiss, A. J. (1992). Developmental differences in children's reactions to a toy advertisement linked to a toy-based cartoon. *Journal of Broadcasting & Electronic Media, 36,* 371-394.

Wilson, B. J., & Weiss, A. J. (1995, May). *Children's reactions to a toy-based cartoon: Entertainment or commercial message?* Paper presented to the International Communication Association, Albuquerque, NM.

Wilson, D. K., Holmes, S. D., Arheart, K., & Alpert, B. S. (1995). Cardiovascular reactivity in Black and White siblings versus matched controls. *Annals of Behavioral Medicine, 17,* 202-212.

Wilson, N., Quigley, R., & Mansoor, O. (1999). Food ads on TV: A health hazard for children? *Australia and New Zealand Journal of Public Health, 23,* 647-650.

Wilson, P. N., Foreman, N., & Stanton, D. (1997). Virtual reality, disability and rehabilitation. *Disability and Rehabilitation: An International Multidisciplinary Journal, 19,* 213-220.

Wilson, S. N. (2000). Sexuality education: Our current status, and an agenda for 2010. *Family Planning Perspectives, 32,* 252-254.

Wingood, G. M., & DiClemente, R. J. (1998, November). *Viewing sexually explicit and violent television and its impact on pregnancy and sexual risk taking among female adolescents.* Paper presented at the annual meeting of the American Public Health Association, Washington, DC.

Wingood, G. M., DiClemente, R. J., Bernhardt, J. M., Harrington, K., Robillard, A., Davies, S. L., Hook, E. W., & Oh, M. K. (2001). *A longitudinal study of exposure to rap music videos and adolescent health.* Unpublished manuscript.

Wingood, G. M., DiClemente, R. J., Harrington, K., Davies, S., Hook, E. W., & Oh, M. K. (2001). Exposure to X-rated movies and adolescents' sexual and contraceptive-related attitudes and behavior. *Pediatrics, 107,* 1116-1119.

Winn, M. (1985). *The plug-in drug: Television, children, and the family.* New York: Penguin.

Wiseman, C. V., Gray, J. J., Mosimann, J. E., & Ahrens, A. H. (1992). Cultural expectations of thinness in women: An update. *International Journal of Eating Disorders, 11,* 85-89.

Wiseman, C. V., Gunning, F. M., & Gray, J. J. (1993). Increasing pressure to be thin: 19 years of diet products in television commercials. *Eating Disorders, 1,* 52-61.

Witt, S. D. (1997). Parental influence on children's socialization to gender roles. *Adolescence, 32,* 253-259.

Woloshin, S., Schwartz, L. M., Tremmel, H., & Welch, H. G. (2001). Direct-to-consumer advertisements for prescription drugs: What are Americans being sold? *Lancet, 358,* 1141-1146.

Wong, N. D., Hei, T. K., Qaqundah, P. Y., Davidson, D. M., Bassin, S. L., & Gold, K. V. (1992). Television viewing and pediatric hypercholesterolemia. *Pediatrics, 90,* 75-79.

Wood, W., Wong, F., & Chachere, J. G. (1991). Effects of media violence on viewers' aggression in unconstrained social interaction. *Psychological Bulletin, 109,* 371-383.

Woodard, E. H. (1999). *The 1999 state of children's television report: Programming for children over broadcast and cable television.* Philadelphia: Annenberg Public Policy Center.

Woodard, E. H., & Gridina, N. (2000). *Media in the home 2000: The fifth annual survey of parents and children.* Washington, DC: Annenberg Public Policy Center of the University of Pennsylvania.

World Health Organization (WHO). (1998). *Obesity: Preventing and managing the global epidemic.* Geneva, Switzerland: Author.

Wotring, C. E., & Greenberg, B. S. (1973). Experiments in televised violence and verbal aggression: Two exploratory studies. *Journal of Communication, 23,* 446-460.

Wray, J., & Steele, J. (2002). Girls in print: Figuring out what it means to be a girl. In J. D. Brown, J. R. Steele, & K. Walsh-Childers (Eds.), *Sexual teens, sexual media* (pp. 191-208). Hillsdale, NJ: Lawrence Erlbaum.

Wright, J. C., Huston, A. C., Reitz, A. L., & Piemyat, S. (1994). Young children's perceptions of television reality: Determinants and developmental differences. *Developmental Psychology, 30,* 229-239.

Wright, J. C., Huston, A. C., Ross, R. P., Calvert, S. L., Rolandelli, D., Weeks, L. A., Raessi, P., & Potts, R. (1984). Pace and continuity of television programs: Effects on children's attention and comprehension. *Developmental Psychology, 20,* 653-666.

Wright, J. C., Huston, A. C., Vandewater, E., Bickham, D. S., Scantlin, R. M., Kotler, J. A., Caplovitz, A. G., & Lee, J. (2001). American children's use of electronic media in 1997: A national survey. *Journal of Applied Developmental Psychology, 22,* 31-48.

Wyllie, A., Zhang, J. F., & Casswell, S. (1998). Positive responses to televised beer advertisements associated with drinking and problems reported by 18 to 29-year-olds. *Addiction, 93,* 749-760.

Wyshak, G. (2000). Teenaged girls, carbonated beverage consumption, and bone fractures. *Archives of Pediatrics & Adolescent Medicine, 154,* 610-613.

Yanovski, J. A., & Yanovski, S. Z. (1999). Recent advances in basic obesity research. *Journal of the American Medical Association, 282,* 1504-1506.

Yokota, F., & Thompson, K. M. (2000). Violence in G-rated animated films. *Journal of the American Medical Association, 283,* 2716-2720.

Young, B. M. (1990). *Television advertising and children.* New York: Oxford University Press.

Young, T. L., & Zimmerman, R. (1998). Clueless: Parental knowledge of risk behaviors of middle school students. *Archives of Pediatrics & Adolescent Medicine, 152,* 1137-1139.

Youth Risk Behavior Surveillance System. (1999). *Youth risk behavior surveillance—United States, 1999.* Retrieved February 23, 2001, from the World Wide Web: www.cdc.gov/mmwr/preview/mmwrhtml/ss4905a1.htm.

Youth violence: A report of the Surgeon General. (2001, January). Washington, DC: U.S. Department of Health and Human Services. Retrieved January 25, 2001, from the World Wide Web: www.surgeongeneral.gov/library/youthviolence/default.htm.

Yuji, H. (1996). Computer games and information-processing skills. *Perceptual and Motor Skills, 83,* 643-647.

Zabin, L. S., Hirsch, M. B., Smith, E. A., & Hardy, J. B. (1984). Adolescent sexual attitudes and behavior: Are they consistent? *Family Planning Perspectives, 16,* 181-185.

Zabin, L. S., Kantner, J. F., & Zelnik, M. (1979). The risk of adolescent pregnancy in the first months of intercourse. *Family Planning Perspectives, 11,* 215-222.

Zelnik, M., & Kim, Y. J. (1982). Sex education and its association with teenage sexual activity, pregnancy, and contraceptive use. *Family Planning Perspectives, 14,* 117-126.

Zillmann, D. (1971). Excitation transfer in communication-mediated aggressive behavior. *Journal of Experimental Social Psychology, 7,* 419-434.

Zillmann, D. (1991). Television viewing and physiological arousal. In J. Bryant & D. Zillmann (Eds.), *Responding to the screen: Reception and reaction processes* (pp. 103-133). Hillsdale, NJ: Lawrence Erlbaum.

Zillmann, D. (1994). Erotica and family values. In D. Zillmann, J. Bryant, & A. C. Huston (Eds.), *Media, children, and the family: Social scientific, psychodynamic, and clinical perspectives* (pp. 199-213). Hillsdale, NJ: Lawrence Erlbaum.

Zillmann, D. (1998). The psychology of the appeal of portrayals of violence. In J. H. Goldstein (Ed.), *Why we watch: The attractions of violent entertainment* (pp. 179-211). New York: Oxford University Press.

Zillmann, D., & Bryant, J. (1982). Pornography, sexual callousness and the trivialization of rape. *Journal of Communication, 32,* 10-21.

Zillmann, D., & Bryant, J. (1988). Pornography's impact on sexual satisfaction. *Journal of Applied Social Psychology, 18,* 438-453.

Zillmann, D., & Mundorf, N. (1987). Image effects in the appreciation of video rock. *Communication Research, 14,* 316-334.

Zillmann, D., & Wakshlag, J. (1985). Fear of victimization and the appeal of crime drama. In D. Zillmann & J. Bryant (Eds.), *Selective exposure to communication* (pp. 141-156). Hillsdale, NJ: Lawrence Erlbaum.

Zollo, P. (1995). *Wise up to teens: Insights into marketing and advertising to teens.* Ithaca, NY: New Strategist.

Zuckerman, M. (1979). *Sensation-seeking: Beyond the optimal level of arousal.* Hillsdale, NJ: Lawrence Erlbaum.

Zuckerman, M. (1994). *Behavioral expressions and biosocial bases of sensation seeking.* New York: Cambridge University Press.

Zuckerman, M., & Litle, P. (1986). Personality and curiosity about morbid and sexual events. *Personality and Individual Differences, 7,* 49-56.

Zuckerman, P., Ziegler, M., & Stevenson, H. W. (1978). Children's viewing of television and recognition memory of commercials. *Child Development, 49,* 96-104.

Name Index

Subject Index

About the Authors

Edward Donnerstein is Professor of Communication and Psychology, Director of the Center for Communication and Social Policy, and Dean of Social Sciences at the University of California, Santa Barbara. A social psychologist, he received his Ph.D. in psychology in 1972. Prior to his position at the University of California, in 1986 he taught at the University of Wisconsin, as well as visiting positions at the University of Lethbridge and Beijing University, China. His major research interests are in mass media violence, as well as mass media policy. He has published more than 180 scientific articles in these general areas and serves on the editorial boards of a number of academic journals in both psychology and communication. He was a member of the American Psychological Association's Commission on Violence and Youth and the APA Task Force on Television and Society. He currently serves on the Advisory Council of the American Medical Association Alliance's violence prevention program and is president of the International Society for Research on Aggression. In addition, he was primary research site director for the National Cable Television Association's $3.5 million project on TV violence. He has testified at numerous governmental hearings both in the United States and abroad regarding the effects and policy implications surrounding mass media violence and pornography, including testimony before the U.S. Senate on TV violence. He has served as a member of the U.S. Surgeon General's Panel on Pornography and the National Academy of Sciences Subpanel on Child Pornography and Child Abuse.

Jeanne B. Funk is a clinical child psychologist. She is Professor and Director of Clinical Training in the Department of Psychology, University of Toledo. She has been conducting research on topics in clinical child psychology for more than 20 years. She currently directs a research team investigating aspects of children's preference for violent electronic games, including their experience of game playing and the relationship between a preference for violent games, empathy, and attitudes toward violence.

Bob McCannon is the Executive Director of the New Mexico Media Literacy Project, the most successful independent media literacy project in the United States and the only major media project to emphasize grassroots activism. With an undergraduate degree in psychology and 20th-century German history and a graduate degree in cognition, he has taught propaganda, history, advertising, and media education in middle school, high school, and graduate school. He does more than a hundred presentations, workshops, and keynotes per year, nationally and internationally, and over 700 volunteers have taken his intensive 4-day workshops, becoming "Catalysts" who train others. He teaches skills to successfully approach media issues such as addictions, violence, technology, parenting, reading, self-esteem, body image, racism, sexism, democracy, compulsivity, debt, and stereotyping. He has also developed nationally recognized media literacy curricula and resources, including the video *Just Do Media Literacy* and the CD-ROMs *Understanding Media, Reversing Addiction,* and *Media Literacy for Health: A K-12 Curriculum*.

Dorothy G. Singer, Ed.D., is a Research Scientist in the Department of Psychology at Yale University. She is also Codirector of the Yale University Family Television Research and Consultation Center and a Fellow of Morse College. In addition, she is a Research Associate at the Yale Child Study Center. Formerly, she was the William Benton Professor of Psychology, University of Bridgeport. She is also a Fellow of the American Psychology Association.

Victor C. Strasburger is currently Chief of the Division of Adolescent Medicine, Professor of Pediatrics, and Professor of Family and Community Medicine at the University of New Mexico. He graduated from Yale College (*summa cum laude* and Phi Beta Kappa), where he studied fiction writing with Robert Penn Warren, and from Harvard Medical School. He trained at the Children's Hospital in Seattle, St. Mary's Hospital Medical School in London, and the Boston Children's Hospital. He has authored more than 120 articles and papers and 8 books on the subject of adolescent medicine and the effects of television on children and adolescents, including *Getting Your Kids to Say No in the 1990's When You Said Yes in the 1960's* (1993), which has sold more than 15,000 copies to date; *Adolescent Medicine: A Practical Guide* (1991, 1998 [2nd ed.]); and *Adolescents and the Media* (1995). In the year 2000, he was named the recipient of the American Academy of Pediatrics' Adele Delenbaugh Hofmann Award for outstanding lifetime achievement in Adolescent Medicine and the Holroyd-Sherry Award for outstanding achievement in public health and the media. He is a consultant to the American Academy of Pediatrics' Committee on Communications, has served as a consultant to the National PTA and the American Medical Association on the subject of children and television, and lectures frequently throughout the country.

Barbara J. Wilson is a Professor in the Department of Speech Communication at the University of Illinois at Urbana-Champaign. She received her Ph.D. from the University of Wisconsin–Madison. Before joining the University of Illinois, she was on the faculty at the University of California, Santa Barbara for 12 years. Her research focuses on the social and psychological effects of mass media on youth. She is coauthor of three book volumes of the *National Television Violence Study* (1997-1998). In addition, she has published more than 50 scientific articles and chapters on media effects and their implications for public policy. Recent projects include children's emotional reactions to television news and adolescents' interpretations of sexual messages in the media. Professor Wilson has served as a consultant for Nickelodeon, the National Association of Television Program Executives, and Discovery Channel Pictures. She is Associate Editor of the *Journal of Communication* and serves on the editorial boards of several other academic journals (*Communication Monographs, Communication Reports, Human Communication Research,* and *Media Psychology*).